Database Design, Application Development, and Administration

Michael V. Mannino
University of Colorado, Denver

www.mmannino.com

DATABASE DESIGN, APPLICATION DEVELOPMENT, AND ADMINISTRATION

ISBN 978-061523104-4

Brief Contents

Contents

Preface

Motivating Example

Paul Hong, the owner of International Industrial Adhesives, Inc., is elated about the recent performance of his business but cautious about future prospects. Revenue and profit growth exceeded forecasts while expenses remained below the general level of inflation. He attributes the success to the introduction of new adhesive products, increased global demand, usage of outsourcing to focus resources, and strategic deployment of information technology. His elation about recent performance is tempered by future prospects. The success of his business has attracted new competitors focusing on his most profitable customers and products. The credit crunch and economic slowdown may trim revenues while the rising price of raw materials especially petroleum may squeeze profit margins. The payback from costly new industry initiatives for electronic commerce is uncertain. As a newly formed public corporation, government regulations will significantly increase reporting and compliance costs. Despite the recent success of his business, he remains cautious about new directions to ensure continued growth of his business.

Paul Hong needs to evaluate information technology investments to stay ahead of competitors and control costs of industry and government mandates. To match competitors, he needs more detailed and timely data about industry trends, competitors' actions, and distributor transactions. He wants to find a cost-effective solution to support an industry initiative for electronic commerce. To function as a public company, he must conduct information technology audits and fulfill other government reporting requirements for public companies. For all of these concerns, he is unsure about proprietary versus open technologies and standards.

These concerns involve significant usage of database technology as part of a growing enterprise computing infrastructure. Transaction processing features in enterprise DBMSs provide a foundation to ensure reliability of online order processing to support industry initiatives for increased electronic commerce. Data warehouse features in enterprise DBMSs provide the foundation to support large data warehouses and capture source data in a timelier manner. Parallel database technology can improve performance and reliability of both transaction processing and data warehouse queries through incremental addition of computing capacity. Object database features provide the ability to manage large collections of XML documents generated by industry initiatives for electronic commerce.

However, the solutions to Paul Hong's concerns are found not just in technology. Utilization of the appropriate level of technology involves a vision for an organization's future, a deep understanding of technology, and traditional management skills to manage risk. Paul Hong realizes that his largest challenge is to blend these skills so that effective solutions can be developed for International Industrial Adhesives, Inc.

Introduction

This textbook provides a foundation to understand database technology supporting enterprise computing concerns such as those faced by Paul Hong. As a new student of database management, you first need to understand the fundamental concepts of database management and the relational data model. Then you need to master skills in database design and database application development. This textbook provides tools to help you understand relational databases and acquire skills to solve basic and advanced problems in query formulation, data modeling, normalization, application data requirements, and customization of database applications.

After establishing these skills, you are ready to study the role of database specialists and the processing environments in which databases are used. This textbook presents the fundamental database technologies in each processing environment and relates these technologies to new advances in electronic commerce and enterprise computing. You will learn the vocabulary, architectures, and design issues of database technology that provide a background for advanced study of individual database management systems, electronic commerce applications, and enterprise computing.

What's New in the Fourth Edition

The fourth edition makes significant revisions to the third edition while preserving the proven pedagogy developed in the first three editions. Experience gained from my own instruction of undergraduate and graduate students along with feedback from adopters of the earlier editions have led to the development of new material and refinements to existing material. The most significant changes in the fourth edition are in advanced application development and database administration: (Chapters 8, 11, 14, 15, and 17, 18): new material on Oracle storage concepts, expanded presentation of access plan choices in query optimization, triggers to maintain generalization hierarchies, database security policies, a mini case study for transaction design, additional coverage of Oracle database links, and new coverage of XML database concepts. In addition, refinements and updates to most chapters have improved the presentation and currency of the material. The new and revised material strengthens the proven approach of the third edition that provided business rules in data modeling, guidelines for analyzing business information needs, expanded coverage of design errors in data modeling, expanded coverage of functional dependency identification, and new coverage of query optimization tips.

For database application development, the fourth edition features SQL:2006, an evolutionary change to SQL:1999 and SQL:2003. The fourth edition explains the scope of SQL:2006, the difficulty of conformance with the standard, and new elements of the standard. Numerous refinements of database application development coverage extend the proven coverage of the first three editions: query formulation guidelines, advanced matching problems, query formulation tips for hierarchal forms and reports, and triggers for soft constraints.

For database administration and processing environments, the fourth edition provides expanded coverage of new technology in SQL:2006 and Oracle 11g. The most significant new topics are Oracle storage concepts, triggers to support generalization hierarchies, security policies, and XML support. Significantly revised coverage is provided for deadlock control, database recovery checkpointing, user interaction time in transaction design, Web services in client-server database processing, and commercial acceptance of object database architectures.

In addition to new material and refinements to existing material, the fourth edition extends the chapter supplements. The fourth edition contains new end-of-chapter questions and problems. New material in the textbook's website includes case studies, assignments in first and second database courses, and sample exams.

The fourth edition uses the same finer chapter organization originally introduced in the third edition. Part 1 covers introductory material about database management and database development to provide a conceptual foundation for detailed knowledge and skills in subsequent chapters. Part 2 covers the essential elements of the relational data model for database creation and query formulation. Database development is split between data modeling in Part 3 and logical and physical table design in Part 4. Advanced application development covering advanced matching problems, database views, and stored procedures and triggers is covered in Part 5. Part 6 covers advanced database development with view integration and a comprehensive case study. Part 7 covers database administration and processing environments for DBMSs.

Competitive Advantages

This textbook provides outstanding features unmatched in competing textbooks. The unique features include detailed SQL coverage for both Access and Oracle, problem-solving guidelines to aid acquisition of key skills, carefully designed sample databases and examples, a comprehensive case study, advanced topic coverage, and integrated lab material. These features provide a complete package for an introductory database course. Each of these features is described in more detail in the list below whereas Table P-1 summarizes the competitive advantages by chapter.

SQL Coverage: The breadth and depth of the SQL coverage in this text is unmatched by competing textbooks. Table P-2 summarizes SQL coverage by chapter. Parts 2 and 5 provide a thorough coverage of the CREATE TABLE, SELECT, UPDATE, INSERT, DELETE, CREATE VIEW, and CREATE TRIGGER statements. Numerous examples of basic, intermediate, and advanced problems are presented. The chapters in Part 7 cover statements useful for database administrators as well as statements used in specific processing environments.

Access and Oracle Coverage: The chapters in Parts 2 and 5 provide detailed coverage of both Access and Oracle SQL. Each example for the SELECT, INSERT, UPDATE, DELETE, and CREATE VIEW statements are shown for both database management systems. Significant coverage of new Oracle 11g SQL features appears in Chapters 8, 9, 11, 15, 16, and 18. In addition, the chapters in Parts 2 and 5 cover SQL:2006 syntax to support instruction with other prominent database management systems.

Problem-Solving Guidelines: Students need more than explanations of concepts and examples to solve problems. Students need guidelines to help structure their thinking process to tackle problems in a systematic manner. The guidelines provide mental models to help students apply the concepts to solve basic and advanced problems. Table P-3 summarizes the unique problem-solving guidelines by chapter.

Sample Databases and Examples: Two sample databases are used throughout the chapters of Parts 2 and 5 to provide consistency and continuity. The University database is used in the chapter examples, while the Order Entry database is used in the end-of-chapter problems. Numerous examples and problems with these databases depict the fundamental skills of query formulation and application data requirements. Revised versions of the databases provide separation between basic and advanced examples. The website contains CREATE TABLE statements, sample data, data manipulation statements, and Access database files for both databases.

Chapters in Parts 3, 4, and 7 use additional databases to broaden exposure to more diverse business situations. Students need exposure to a variety of business situations to acquire database design skills and understand concepts important to database specialists. Other databases covering water utility operations, patient visits, academic paper reviews, personal financial tracking, airline reservations, placement office operations, automobile insurance, store sales tracking, and real estate sales supplement the University and Order Entry databases in the chapter examples and end-of-chapter problems.

Comprehensive Case Study: The Student Loan Limited Case is found at the end of Part 6. The case description along with its solution integrates the concepts students learned in the preceding 12 chapters on application development and database design. The follow-up problems at the end of the chapter provide additional opportunities for students to apply their knowledge on a realistic case.

Optional Integrated Labs: Database management is best taught when concepts are closely linked to the practice of designing and implementing databases using a commercial DBMS. To help students apply the concepts described in the textbook, optional supplementary lab materials are available on the text's website. The website contains labs for two Microsoft Access versions (2003 and 2007) as well as practice databases and practice exercises. The Microsoft Access labs integrate a detailed coverage of Access with the application development concepts covered in Parts 2 and 5.

Current and Cutting-Edge Topics: This book covers some topics that are missing from competing textbooks: advanced query formulation, updatable views, development and management of stored procedures and triggers, data requirements for data entry forms and reports, view integration, management of the refresh process for data warehouses, the data warehouse maturity model, parallel database architectures, object database architectures, data warehouse features in SQL:2006 and Oracle 10g, object-relational features in SQL:2006 and Oracle 11g, and transaction design principles. These topics enable motivated students to obtain a deeper understanding of database management.

Complete Package for Course: Depending on the course criteria, some students may need to purchase as many as four books for an introductory database course: a textbook covering principles, laboratory books covering details of a DBMS and a CASE tool, a supplemental SQL book, and a casebook with realistic practice problems. This textbook and supplemental material provide one complete, integrated, and less expensive source for the student.

Table P-1: Summary of Competitive Advantages by Chapter

Chapter	Unique Features
2	Unique chapter providing a conceptual introduction to the database development process
3	Visual representation of relational algebra operators
4	Query formulation guidelines; Oracle, Access, and SQL:2006 SQL coverage
5	Emphasis on ERD notation, business rules, and diagram rules
6	Strategies for analyzing business information needs, data modeling transformations, and detection of common design errors
7	Normalization guidelines and procedures
8	Index selection rules; SQL tuning guidelines, integrated coverage of query optimization, file structures, and index selection
9	Query formulation guidelines; Oracle 11g, Access, and SQL:2006 coverage; advanced topic coverage of nested queries, division problems, and null value handling
10	Rules for updatable views, data requirement guidelines for forms and reports
11	Unique chapter covering concepts and practices of database programming languages, stored procedures, and triggers
12	Unique chapter covering concepts and practices of view integration and design
13	Unique chapter providing a comprehensive case study on student loan processing
14	Guidelines for important processes used by database administrators
15	Transaction design guidelines and advanced topic coverage
16	Data warehouse maturity model for evaluating technology impact on organizations; advanced topic coverage of relational database features for data warehouse processing and the data warehouse refresh process; extensive Oracle 11g data warehouse coverage
17	Integrated coverage of client-server processing, parallel database processing, and distributed databases
18	Advanced topic coverage of object-relational features in SQL:2006 and Oracle 11g

Table P-2: SQL Statement Coverage by Chapter

Chapter	SQL Statement Coverage
3	CREATE TABLE
4	SELECT, INSERT, UPDATE, DELETE
9	SELECT (nested queries, outer joins, null value handling); Access, Oracle 11g, and SQL:2006 coverage
10	CREATE VIEW; queries and manipulation statements using views
11	CREATE PROCEDURE (Oracle), CREATE TRIGGER (Oracle and SQL:2006)
14	GRANT, REVOKE, CREATE ROLE, CREATE ASSERTION, CHECK clause of the CREATE TABLE statement, CREATE DOMAIN
15	COMMIT, ROLLBACK, SET TRANSACTION, SET CONSTRAINTS, SAVEPOINT
16	CREATE MATERIALIZED VIEW (Oracle), GROUP BY clause extensions (Oracle and SQL:2006), CREATE DIMENSION (Oracle)
18	CREATE TYPE, CREATE TABLE (typed tables and subtables), SELECT (object identifiers, path expressions, dereference operator); SQL:2006 and Oracle 11g coverage

Table P-3: Problem Solving Guidelines by Chapter

Chapter	Problem-Solving Guidelines
3	Visual representation of relationships and relational algebra operators
4	Conceptual evaluation process; query formulation questions
5	Diagram rules
6	Guidelines for analyzing business information needs; design transformations; identification of common design errors; conversion rules
7	Guidelines for identifying functional dependencies; usage of sample data to eliminate functional dependencies; simple synthesis procedure
8	Index selection rules; SQL tuning guidelines
9	Difference problem formulation guidelines; nested query evaluation; count method for division problems
10	Rules for updatable join queries; steps for analyzing data requirements in forms and reports
11	Trigger execution procedure
12	Form analysis steps; view integration strategies
14	Guidelines to manage stored procedures and triggers; data planning process; DBMS selection process
15	Transaction timeline; transaction design guidelines
16	Guidelines for relational database representations of multidimensional data; guidelines for time representation in dimension tables, trade-offs for refreshing a data warehouse
17	Progression of transparency levels for distributed databases
18	Object database architectures; comparison between relational and object-relational representations

Text Audience

This book is intended for a first undergraduate or graduate course in database management. At the undergraduate level, students should have a concentration (major or minor) or active interest in information systems. For two-year institutions, the instructor may want to skip the advanced topics and place more emphasis on the optional Access lab book. Undergraduate students should have a first course covering general information systems concepts, spreadsheets, word processing, and possibly a brief introduction to databases. Except for Chapter 11, a previous course in computer programming can be useful background but is not mandatory. The other chapters reference some computer programming concepts, but writing code is not covered. For a complete understanding of Chapter 11, a computer programming background is essential. However, the basic concepts in Chapter 11 can be covered even if students do not have a computer programming background.

At the graduate level, this book is suitable in either MBA or Master of Science (in information systems) programs. The advanced material in this book should be especially suitable for Master of Science students.

Organization

As the title suggests, *Database Design, Application Development, and Administration* emphasizes three sets of skills. Before acquiring these skills, students need a foundation about basic concepts. Part 1 provides conceptual background for subsequent detailed study of database design, database application development, and database administration. The chapters in Part 1 present the principles of database management and a conceptual overview of the database development process.

Part 2 provides foundational knowledge about the relational data model. Chapter 3 covers table definition, integrity rules, and operators to retrieve useful information from relational databases. Chapter 4 presents guidelines for query formulation and numerous examples of SQL SELECT statements.

Parts 3 and 4 emphasize practical skills and design guidelines for the database development process. Students desiring a career as a database specialist should be able to perform each step of the database development process. Students should learn skills of data modeling, schema conversion, normalization, and physical database design. The Part 3 chapters (Chapters 5 and 6) cover data modeling using the Entity Relationship Model. Chapter 5 covers the structure of entity relationship diagrams, while Chapter 6 presents usage of entity relationship diagrams to analyze business information needs. The Part 4 chapters (Chapters 7 and 8) cover table design principles and practice for logical and physical design. Chapter 7 covers the motivation, functional dependencies, normal forms, and practical considerations of data normalization. Chapter 8 contains broad coverage of physical database design including the objectives, inputs, file structure and query optimization background, and important design choices.

Part 5 provides a foundation for building database applications by helping students acquire skills in advanced query formulation, specification of data requirements for data entry forms and reports, and coding triggers and stored procedures. Chapter 9 presents additional examples of intermediate and advanced SQL, along with corresponding query formulation skills. Chapter 10 describes the motivation, definition, and usage of relational views along with specification of view definitions for data entry forms and reports. Chapter 11 presents concepts and coding practices of database programming languages, stored procedures, and triggers for customization of database applications.

Part 6 covers advanced topics of database development. Chapter 12 describes view design and view integration, which are data modeling concepts for large database development efforts. Chapter 13 provides a comprehensive case study that enables students to gain insights about the difficulties of applying database design and application development skills to a realistic business database.

Beyond the database design and application development skills, this textbook prepares students for careers as database specialists. Students need to understand the responsibilities, tools, and processes employed by data administrators and database administrators as well as the various environments in which databases operate.

The chapters in Part 7 emphasize the role of database specialists and the details of managing databases in various operating environments. Chapter 14 provides a context for the other chapters through coverage of the responsibilities, tools, and processes used by database administrators and data administrators. The other chapters in Part 4 provide a foundation for managing databases in important environments: Chapter 15 on transaction processing, Chapter 16 on data warehouses, Chapter 17 on distributed processing and data, and Chapter 18 on object database management. These chapters emphasize concepts, architectures, and design choices important for database specialists.

Text Approach and Theme

To support acquisition of the necessary skills for learning and understanding application development, database design, and managing databases, this book adheres to three guiding principles:

Combine concepts and practice. Database management is more easily learned when concepts are closely linked to the practice of designing and implementing databases using a commercial DBMS. The textbook and the accompanying supplements have been designed to provide close integration between concepts and practice through the following features:
SQL examples for both Access and Oracle as well as SQL: 2006 coverage
Emphasis of the relationship between application development and query formulation
Usage of a data modeling notation supported by professional CASE tools
Supplemental laboratory practice chapters that combine textbook concepts with details of commercial DBMSs

Emphasize problem-solving skills. This book features problem-solving guidelines to help students master the fundamental skills of data modeling, normalization, query formulation, and application development. The textbook and associated supplements provide a wealth of questions, problems, case studies, and laboratory practices in which students can apply their skills. With mastery of the fundamental skills, students will be poised for future learning about databases and change the way they think about computing in general.

Provide introductory and advanced material. Business students who use this book may have a variety of backgrounds. This book provides enough depth to satisfy the most eager students. However, the advanced parts are placed so that they can be skipped by the less inclined.

Pedagogical Features

This book contains the following pedagogical features to help students navigate through chapter content in a systematic fashion:

Learning Objectives focus on the knowledge and skills students will acquire from studying the chapter.

Overviews provide a snapshot or preview of chapter contents.

Key Terms are highlighted and defined in the boxed areas as they appear in the chapter.

Examples are clearly separated from the rest of the chapter material for easier review and studying purposes.

Running Database Examples — University and Order Entry with icons in margins to draw student attention to examples.

Closing Thoughts summarize chapter content in relation to the learning objectives.

Review Concepts are the important conceptual highlights from the chapter, not just a list of terminology.

Questions are provided to review the chapter concepts.

Problems help students practice and implement the detailed skills presented in the chapter.

References for Further Study point students to additional sources on chapter content.

Chapter Appendixes provide additional details and convenient summaries of certain principles or practices.

Glossary: Provides a complete list of terms and definitions used throughout the text.

Bibliography: A list of helpful industry, academic, and other printed material for further research or study.

Microsoft Access Labs

Lab books for both Microsoft Access 2003 and 2007 are available on the textbook's website. The lab books provide detailed coverage of features important to beginning database students as well as many advanced features. The lab chapters provide a mixture of guided practice and reference material organized into the following chapters:

An Introduction to Microsoft Access
Database Creation Lab
Query Lab
Single Table Form Lab
Hierarchical Form Lab
Report Lab
Pivot Tables
User Interface Lab

Each lab chapter follows the pedagogy of the textbook with Learning Objectives, Overview, Closing Thoughts, Additional Practice exercises, and Appendixes of helpful tips. Most lab chapters reference concepts from the textbook for close integration with corresponding textbook chapters. Each lab book also includes a glossary of terms and an index.

Instructor Resources

A comprehensive set of supplements for the text and lab manuals is available to adopters.

- Powerpoint slides for each chapter
- Solutions to end of chapter problems for each chapter
- Solutions to end of chapter questions for each chapter
- Access databases for the university and order entry textbook databases
- Oracle SQL statements to create and populate the university and order entry textbook databases
- Files containing SQL statements used in the textbook chapters
- Case studies along with case study solutions
- Assignments used in a first database course. The assignments involve database creation, query formulation, application development with forms, data modeling, and normalization. In addition, a project assignment integrates material about database development and application development.
- Assignments used in a second database course. The assignments involve database creation, triggers, data warehouse usage, and object relational databases. In addition, projects about Oracle advanced features, benchmark development, and management practices involve integrative skills for database specialists.
- Sample exams for a first course in database management
- Sample exams for an advanced course in database management
- Access databases for each lab chapter
- Access databases for end of chapter problems in each lab chapter

Teaching Paths

The textbook can be covered in several orders in a one- or a two-semester sequence. The author has taught a one-semester course with the ordering of relational database basics, query formulation, application development, database development, and database processing environments. This ordering has the advantage of covering the more concrete material (query formulation and application development) before the more abstract material (database development). Lab chapters and assignments are used for practice beyond the textbook chapters. To fit into one semester, advanced topics are skipped in Chapters 8 and 11 to 18.

A second ordering is to cover database development before application development. For this ordering, the author recommends following the textbook chapter ordering: 1, 2, 5, 6, 3, 7, 4, 9, and 10. The material on schema conversion in Chapter 6 should be covered after Chapter 3. This ordering supports a more thorough coverage of database development while not neglecting application development. To fit into one semester, advanced topics are skipped in Chapters 8 and 11 to 18.

A third possible ordering is to use the textbook in a two-course sequence. The first course covers database management fundamentals from Parts 1 and 2, data modeling and normalization from Parts 3 and 4, and advanced query formulation, application development with views, and view integration from Parts 5 and 6. The second course emphasizes database administration skills with physical database design from Part 4, triggers and stored procedures from Part 5, and the processing environments from Part 7 along with additional material on managing enterprise databases. A comprehensive project can be used in the second course to integrate application development, database development, and database administration.

Acknowledgments

The fourth edition is the culmination of many years of work. Before beginning the first edition, I wrote tutorials, laboratory practices, and case studies. This material was first used to supplement other textbooks. After encouragement from students, this material was used without a textbook. This material, revised many times through student comments, was the foundation for the first edition. During the development of the first edition, the material was classroom tested for three years with hundreds of undergraduate and graduate students, along with careful review through four drafts by many outside reviewers. The second edition was developed through classroom usage of the first edition for three years, along with teaching an advanced database course for several years. The third edition was developed through three years experience with the second edition in basic and advanced database courses. The fourth edition was developed through three years of instruction with the third edition in beginning and advanced database courses.

I wish to acknowledge the excellent support that I have received in completing this project. I thank my many database students, especially those in ISMG6080, ISMG6480, and ISMG4500 at the University of Colorado Denver. Your comments and reaction to the textbook have been invaluable to its improvement.

About the Author

Michael V. Mannino has been involved in the database field since 1980. He has taught database management since 1983 at several major universities (University of Florida, University of Texas at Austin, University of Washington, and University of Colorado Denver). His audiences have included undergraduate MIS students, graduate MIS students, MBA students, and doctoral students as well as corporate employees in retraining programs. He has also been active in database research as evidenced by publications in major journals of the IEEE (*Transactions on Knowledge and Data Engineering* and *Transactions on Software Engineering*), ACM (*Communications* and *Computing Surveys*), and INFORMS (*Informs Journal on Computing* and *Information Systems Research*). His research includes several popular survey and tutorial articlesas well as many papers describing original research. Practical results of his research on a form-driven approach to database design are incorporated into Chapter 12.

Dedication

I dedicate this book to my daughters, Julia and Aimee. Your smiles and affection inspire me every day.

1

Introduction to Database Management

Learning Objectives

This chapter provides an introduction to database technology and the impact of this technology on organizations. After this chapter the student should have acquired the following knowledge and skills:

- Describe the characteristics of business databases and the features of database management systems
- Understand the importance of nonprocedural access for software productivity
- Appreciate the advances in database technology and the contributions of database technology to modern society
- Understand the impact of database management system architectures on distributed processing and software maintenance
- Perceive career opportunities related to database application development and database administration

Overview

You may not be aware of it, but your life is dramatically affected by database technology. Computerized databases are vital to the functioning of modern organizations. You come into contact with databases on a daily basis through activities such as shopping at a supermarket, withdrawing cash using an automated teller machine, making an airline reservation, ordering a book online, and registering for classes. The convenience of your daily life is partly due to proliferation of computerized databases and supporting database technology.

Database technology is not only improving the daily operations of organizations but also the quality of decisions that affect our lives. Databases contain a flood of data about many aspects of our lives: consumer preferences, telecommunications usage, credit history, television viewing habits, and so on. Database technology helps to summarize this mass of data into useful information for decision making. Management uses information gleaned from databases to make long-range decisions such as investing in plants and equipment, locating stores, adding new items to inventory, and entering new businesses.

This first chapter provides a starting point for your exploration of database technology. It surveys database characteristics, database management system features, system architectures, and human roles in managing and using databases. The other chapter in Part 1 (Chapter 2) provides a conceptual overview of the database development process. This chapter provides a broad picture of database technology and shares the excitement about the journey ahead.

1.1 Database Characteristics

Every day, businesses collect mountains of facts about persons, things, and events such as credit card numbers, bank balances, and purchase amounts. Databases contain these sorts of simple facts as well as nonconventional facts such as medical images, fingerprints, product photos, and maps. With the proliferation of the Internet and the means to capture data in computerized form, a vast amount of data is available at the click of a mouse button. Organizing these data for ease of retrieval and maintenance is paramount. Thus, managing databases has become a vital task in most organizations.

Database: a collection of <u>persistent</u> data that can be <u>shared</u> and <u>interrelated</u>.

Before learning about managing databases, you must first understand some important properties of databases, as discussed in the following list:

Persistent means that data reside on stable storage such as a magnetic disk. For example, organizations need to retain data about customers, suppliers, and inventory on stable storage because these data are repetitively used. A variable in a computer program is not persistent because it resides in main memory and disappears after the program terminates. Persistency does not mean that data lasts forever. When data are no longer relevant (such as a supplier going out of business), they are removed or archived.

Persistency depends on relevance of intended usage. For example, the mileage you drive for work is important to maintain if you are self-employed. Likewise, the amount of your medical expenses is important if you can itemize your deductions or you have a health savings account. Because storing and maintaining data is costly, only data likely to be relevant to decisions should be stored.

Shared means that a database can have multiple uses and users. A database provides a common memory for multiple functions in an organization. For example, a personnel database can support payroll calculations, performance evaluations, government reporting requirements, and so on. Many users can access a database at the same time. For example, many customers can simultaneously make airline reservations. Unless two users are trying to change the same part of the database at the same time, they can proceed without waiting on each other.

Interrelated means that data stored as separate units can be connected to provide a whole picture. For example, a customer database relates customer data (name, address, ...) to order data (order number, order date, ...) to facilitate order processing. Databases contain both entities and relationships among entities. An entity is a cluster of data usually about a single subject that can be accessed together. An entity can denote a person, place, thing, or event. For example, a personnel database contains entities such as employees, departments, and skills as well as relationships showing employee assignments to departments, skills possessed by employees, and salary history of employees. A typical business database may have hundreds of entities and relationships.

To depict these characteristics, let us consider a number of databases. We begin with a simple university database (Figure 1.1) since you have some familiarity with the workings of a university. A simplified university database contains data about students, faculty, courses, course offerings, and enrollments. The database supports procedures such as registering for classes, assigning faculty to course offerings, recording grades, and scheduling course offerings. Relationships in the university database support answers to questions such as

What offerings are available for a course in a given academic period?
Who is the instructor for an offering of a course?
What students are enrolled in an offering of a course?

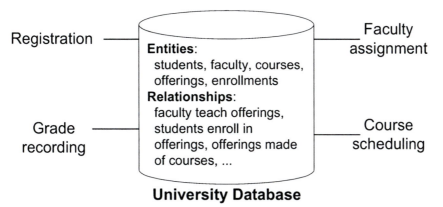

University Database

Figure 1.1: Depiction of a Simplified University Database
Note: Words surrounding the database denote procedures that use the database.

Next, let us consider a water utility database as depicted in Figure 1.2. The primary function of a water utility database is billing customers for water usage. Periodically, a customer's water consumption is measured from a meter and a bill is prepared. Many aspects can influence the preparation of a bill such as a customer's payment history, meter characteristics, type of customer (low income, renter, homeowner, small business, large business, etc.), and billing cycle. Relationships in the water utility database support answers to questions such as

What is the date of the last bill sent to a customer?

How much water usage was recorded when a customer's meter was last read?

When did a customer make his/her last payment?

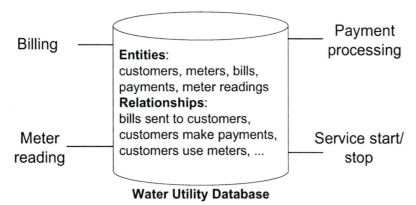

Water Utility Database

Figure 1.2: Depiction of a Simplified Water Utility Database

Finally, let us consider a hospital database as depicted in Figure 1.3. The hospital database supports treatment of patients by physicians. Many different health providers read and contribute to a patient's medical record. Physicians make diagnoses and prescribe treatments based on symptoms. Nurses are responsible for monitoring symptoms and providing medication. Food staff prepare meals according to a dietary plan. Relationships in the database support answers to questions such as

What are the most recent symptoms of a patient?

Who prescribed a given treatment of a patient?

What diagnosis did a doctor make for a patient?

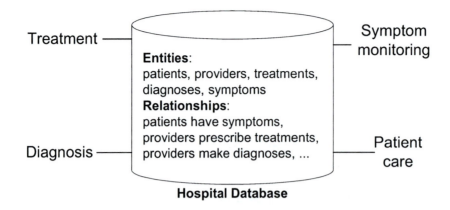

Hospital Database

Figure 1.3: Depiction of a Simplified Hospital Database

These simplified databases lack many kinds of data found in real databases. For example, the simplified university database does not contain data about course prerequisites and classroom capacities and locations. Real versions of these databases would have many more entities, relationships, and additional uses. Nevertheless, these simple databases have the essential characteristics of business databases: persistent data, multiple users and uses, and multiple entities connected by relationships.

1.2 Features of Database Management Systems

A <u>database management system</u> (DBMS) is a collection of components that supports the creation, use, and maintenance of databases. Initially, DBMSs provided efficient storage and retrieval of data. Due to marketplace demands and product innovation, DBMSs have evolved to provide a broad range of features for data acquisition, storage, dissemination, maintenance, retrieval, and formatting. The evolution of these features has made DBMSs rather complex. It can take years of study and use to master a particular DBMS. Because DBMSs continue to evolve, you must continually update your knowledge.

Database Management System (DBMS): a collection of components that support data acquisition, dissemination, maintenance, retrieval, and formatting.

To provide insight about features that you will encounter in commercial DBMSs, Table 1-1 summarizes a common set of features. The remainder of this section presents examples of these features. Some examples are drawn from Microsoft Access, a popular desktop DBMS. Later chapters expand upon the introduction provided here.

Table 1-1: Summary of Common Features of DBMSs

Feature	Description
Database definition	Language and graphical tools to define entities, relationships, integrity constraints, and authorization rights
Nonprocedural access	Language and graphical tools to access data without complicated coding
Application development	Graphical tools to develop menus, data entry forms, and reports; data requirements for forms and reports are specified using nonprocedural access.
Procedural language interface	Language that combines nonprocedural access with full capabilities of a programming language
Transaction processing	Control mechanisms to prevent interference from simultaneous users and recover lost data after a failure
Database tuning	Tools to monitor and improve database performance

1.2.1 Database Definition

To define a database, the entities and relationships must be specified. In most commercial DBMSs, <u>tables</u> store collections of entities. A table (Figure 1.4) has a heading row (first row) showing the column names and a body (other rows) showing the contents of the table. Relationships indicate connections among tables. For example, the relationship connecting the student table to the enrollment table shows the course offerings taken by each student.

> **Table**: a named, two-dimensional arrangement of data. A table consists of a heading part and a body part.

StdFirstName	StdLastName	StdCity	StdState	StdZip	StdMajor	StdClass	StdGPA
HOMER	WELLS	SEATTLE	WA	98121-1111	IS	FR	3.00
BOB	NORBERT	BOTHELL	WA	98011-2121	FIN	JR	2.70
CANDY	KENDALL	TACOMA	WA	99042-3321	ACCT	JR	3.50
WALLY	KENDALL	SEATTLE	WA	98123-1141	IS	SR	2.80
JOE	ESTRADA	SEATTLE	WA	98121-2333	FIN	SR	3.20
MARIAH	DODGE	SEATTLE	WA	98114-0021	IS	JR	3.60
TESS	DODGE	REDMOND	WA	98116-2344	ACCT	SO	3.30

Figure 1.4: Display of Student Table in Microsoft Access

Most DBMSs provide several tools to define databases. The Structured Query Language (SQL) is an industry standard language supported by most DBMSs. SQL can be used to define tables, relationships among tables, integrity constraints (rules that define allowable data), and authorization rights (rules that restrict access to data). Chapter 3 describes SQL statements to define tables and relationships.

> **SQL**: an industry standard database language that includes statements for database definition, database manipulation, and database control.

In addition to SQL, many DBMSs provide graphical, window-oriented tools. Figures 1.5 and 1.6 depict graphical tools for defining tables and relationships. Using the Table Definition window in Figure 1.5, a user can define properties of columns such as the data type and field size. Using the Relationship Definition window in Figure 1.6, relationships among tables can be defined. After defining the structure, a database can be populated. The data in Figure 1.4 should be added after the Table Definition window and Relationship Definition window are complete.

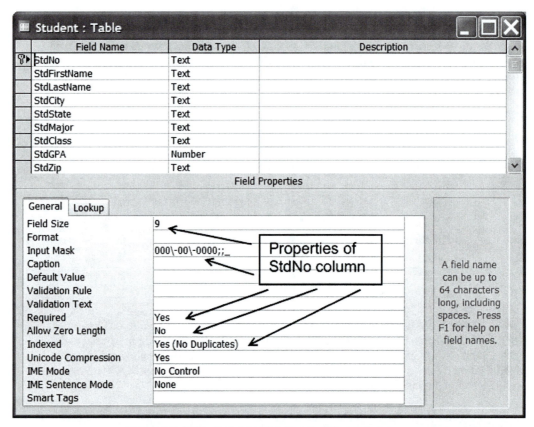

Figure 1.5: Table Definition Window in Microsoft Access

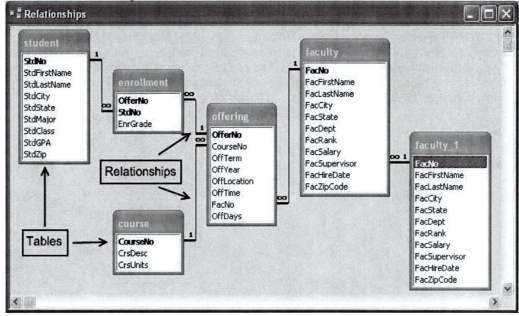

Figure 1.6: Relationship Definition Window in Microsoft Access

1.2.2 Nonprocedural Access

The most important feature of a DBMS is the ability to answer queries. A query is a request for data to answer a question. For example, the user may want to know customers having large balances or products with strong sales in a particular region. <u>Nonprocedural</u> access allows users with limited computing skills to submit queries. The user specifies the parts of a database to retrieve, not implementation details of how retrieval occurs. Implementation details involve coding complex procedures with loops. Nonprocedural languages do not have looping statements (for, while, and so on) because only the parts of a database to retrieve are specified.

> **Nonprocedural Database Language**: a language such as SQL that allows you to specify the parts of a database to access rather than to code a complex procedure. Nonprocedural languages do not include looping statements.

Nonprocedural access can reduce the number of lines of code by a factor of 100 as compared to procedural access. Because a large part of business software involves data access, nonprocedural access can provide a dramatic improvement in software productivity.

To appreciate the significance of nonprocedural access, consider an analogy to planning a vacation. You specify your destination, travel budget, length of stay, and departure date. These facts indicate the "what" of your trip. To specify the "how" of your trip, you need to indicate many more details such as the best route to your destination, the most desirable hotel, ground transportation, and so on. Your planning process is much easier if you have a professional to help with these additional details. Like a planning professional, a DBMS performs the detailed planning process to answer queries expressed in a nonprocedural language.

Most DBMSs provide more than one tool for nonprocedural access. The SELECT statement of SQL, described in Chapter 4, provides a nonprocedural way to access a database. Most DBMSs also provide graphical tools to access databases. Figure 1.7 depicts a graphical tool available in Microsoft Access. To pose a query to the database, a user only has to indicate the required tables, relationships, and columns. Access is responsible for generating the plan to retrieve the requested data. Figure 1.8 shows the result of executing the query in Figure 1.7.

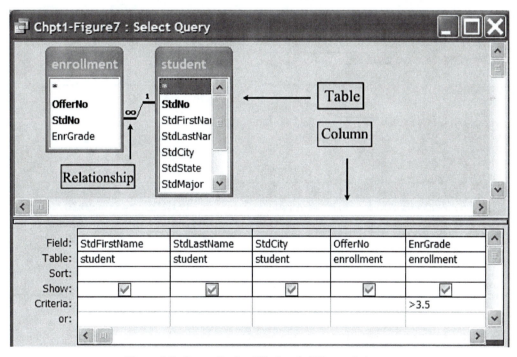

Figure 1.7: Query Design Window in Microsoft Access

StdFirstName	StdLastName	StdCity	OfferNo	EnrGrade
MARIAH	DODGE	SEATTLE	1234	3.8
BOB	NORBERT	BOTHELL	5679	3.7
ROBERTO	MORALES	SEATTLE	5679	3.8
MARIAH	DODGE	SEATTLE	6666	3.6
LUKE	BRAZZI	SEATTLE	7777	3.7
WILLIAM	PILGRIM	BOTHELL	9876	4

Figure 1.8: Result of Executing Query in Figure 1.7

1.2.3 Application Development and Procedural Language Interface

Most DBMSs go well beyond simply accessing data. Graphical tools are provided for building complete applications using forms and reports. Data entry forms provide a convenient tool to enter and edit data, while reports enhance the appearance of data that is displayed or printed. The form in Figure 1.9 can be used to add new course assignments for a professor and to change existing assignments. The report in Figure 1.10 uses indentation to show courses taught by faculty in various departments. The indentation style can be easier to view than the tabular style shown in Figure 1.8. Many forms and reports can be developed with a graphical tool without detailed coding. For example, Figures 1.9 and 1.10 were developed without coding. Chapter 10 describes concepts underlying form and report development.

Nonprocedural access makes form and report creation possible without extensive coding. As part of creating a form or report, the user indicates the data requirements using a nonprocedural language (SQL) or graphical tool. To complete a form or report definition, the user indicates formatting of data, user interaction, and other details.

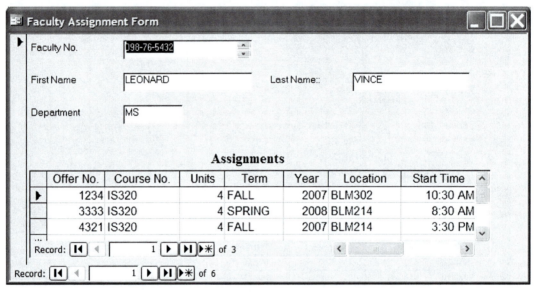

Figure 1.9: Microsoft Access Form for Assigning Courses to Faculty

Faculty Work Load Report for the 2007-2008 Academic Year

Department Name	Term	Offer Number	Units	Limit	Enrollment	Percent Full	Low Enrollment
FIN							
JULIA MILLS							
	WINTER	5678	4	20	1	5.00%	✔

Summary for 'term' = WINTER (1 detail record)

Sum			4		1		
Avg						5.00%	

Summary for JULIA MILLS

Sum			4		1		
Avg						5.00%	

Summary for 'department' = FIN (1 detail record)

Figure 1.10: Microsoft Access Report of Faculty Workload

In addition to application development tools, a <u>procedural language interface</u> adds the full capabilities of a computer programming language. Nonprocedural access and application development tools, though convenient and powerful, are sometimes not efficient enough or do not provide the level of control necessary for application development. When these tools are not adequate, DBMSs provide the full capabilities of a programming language. Most commercial DBMSs have a procedural language interface. For example, Oracle has the language PL/SQL and Microsoft SQL Server has the language Transact-SQL. Chapter 11 describes procedural language interfaces and the PL/SQL language.

> **Procedural Language Interface**: a method to combine a nonprocedural language such as SQL with a programming language such as Java or Visual Basic.

1.2.4 Features to Support Database Operations

Transaction processing enables a DBMS to process large volumes of repetitive work. A <u>transaction</u> is a unit of work that should be processed reliably without interference from other users and without loss of data due to failures. Examples of transactions are withdrawing cash at an ATM, making an airline reservation, and registering for a course. A DBMS ensures that transactions are free of interference from other users, parts of a transaction are not lost due to a failure, and transactions do not make the database inconsistent. Transaction processing is largely an unseen, back-office affair. The user does not know the details about transaction processing other than the assurances about reliability.

> **Transaction Processing**: reliable and efficient processing of large volumes of repetitive work. DBMSs ensure that simultaneous users do not interfere with each other and that failures do not cause lost work.

Database tuning includes a number of monitors and utility programs to improve performance. Some DBMSs can monitor how a database is used, the distribution of various parts of a database, and the growth of the database. Utility programs can be provided to reorganize a database, select physical structures for better performance, and repair damaged parts of a database.

Transaction processing and database tuning are most prominent on DBMSs that support large databases with many simultaneous users. These DBMSs are known as enterprise DBMSs because the databases they support databases are often critical to the functioning of an organization. Enterprise DBMSs usually run on powerful servers and have a high cost. In contrast, desktop DBMSs running on personal computers and small servers support limited transaction processing features but have a much lower cost. Desktop DBMSs support databases used by work teams and small businesses. Embedded DBMSs are an emerging category of database software. As its name implies, an embedded DBMS resides in a larger system, either an application or a device such as a personal digital assistant (PDA) or a smart card. Embedded DBMSs provide limited transaction processing features but have low memory, processing, and storage requirements.

1.2.5 Third-Party Features

In addition to features provided directly by vendors of DBMSs, third-party software is also available for many DBMSs. In most cases, third-party software extends the features available with the database software. For example, many third-party vendors provide advanced database design tools that extend the database definition and tuning capabilities provided by DBMSs. Figure 1.11 shows a database diagram (an entity relationship diagram) created with Visio Professional, a tool for database design. The ERD in Figure 1.11 can be converted into the tables supported by most commercial DBMSs. In some cases, third-party software competes directly with the database product. For example, third-party vendors provide application development tools that can be used in place of the ones provided with the database product.

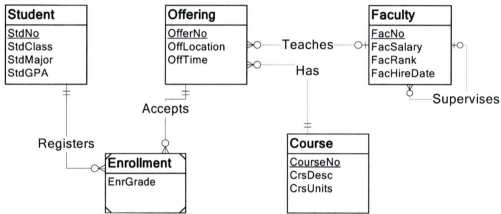

Figure 1.11: Entity Relationship Diagram (ERD) for the University Database

1.3 Development of Database Technology and Market Structure

The previous section provided a quick tour of the features found in typical DBMSs. The features in today's products are a significant improvement over just a few years ago. Database management, like many other areas of computing, has undergone tremendous technological growth. To provide a context to appreciate today's DBMSs, this section reviews past changes in technology and suggests future trends. After this review, the current market for database software is presented.

1.3.1 Evolution of Database Technology

Table 1-2 depicts a brief history of database technology through four generations[1] of systems. The first generation supported sequential and random searching, but the user was required to write a computer program to obtain access. For example, a program could be written to retrieve all customer records or to just find the customer record with a specified customer number. Because first-generation systems did not offer much support for relating data, they are usually regarded as file processing systems rather than DBMSs. File processing systems can manage only one entity rather than many entities and relationships managed by a DBMS.

Table 1-2: Brief Evolution of Database Technology

Era	Generation	Orientation	Major Features
1960s	1st generation	File	File structures and proprietary program interfaces
1970s	2nd generation	Network navigation	Networks and hierarchies of related records, standard program interfaces
1980s	3rd generation	Relational	Nonprocedural languages, optimization, transaction processing
1990s to 2000s	4th generation	Object	Multi-media, active, distributed processing, more powerful operators, data warehouse processing, XML enabled

The second-generation products were the first true DBMSs as they could manage multiple entity types and relationships. However, to obtain access to data, a computer program still had to be written. Second-generation systems are referred to as "navigational" because the programmer had to write code to navigate among a network of linked records. Some of the second-generation products adhered to a standard database definition and manipulation language developed by the Committee on Data Systems Languages (CODASYL), a standards organization. The CODASYL standard had only limited market acceptance partly because IBM, the dominant computer company during this time, ignored the standard. IBM supported a different approach known as the hierarchical data model.

Rather than focusing on the second-generation standard, research labs at IBM and academic institutions developed the foundations for a new generation of DBMSs. The most important development involved nonprocedural languages for database access. Third-generation systems are known as relational DBMSs because of the foundation based on mathematical relations and associated operators. Optimization technology was developed so that access using nonprocedural languages would be efficient. Because nonprocedural access provided such an improvement over navigational access, third-generation systems supplanted the second generation. Since the technology was so different, most of the new systems were founded by start-up companies rather than by vendors of previous generation products. IBM was the major exception. It was IBM's weight that led to the adoption of SQL as a widely accepted standard.

Fourth-generation DBMSs are extending the boundaries of database technology to unconventional data, new kinds of distributed processing, and data warehouse processing. Fourth-generation systems can store and manipulate unconventional data types such as images, videos, maps, sounds, animations, and Web data. Most DBMSs now feature convenient ways to publish static and dynamic Web data using the eXtensible Markup Language (XML) as a publishing

---

[1] The generations of DBMSs should not be confused with the generations of programming languages. In particular, fourth-generation language refers to programming language features, not DBMS features.

standard. Because these DBMSs view any kind of data as an object to manage, fourth-generation systems are sometimes called "object-relational." Chapter 18 presents details about object features in DBMSs. In addition to the emphasis on objects, DBMSs have developed new forms of distributed processing. Chapter 17 presents details about parallel and distributed database technology to support increased performance, improved reliability, and local control of data.

A recent development in fourth-generation DBMSs is support for data warehouse processing. A data warehouse is a database that supports mid-range and long-range decision making in organizations. The retrieval of summarized data dominate data warehouse processing, whereas a mixture of updating and retrieving data occur for databases that support the daily operations of an organization. Chapter 16 presents details about DBMS features to support data warehouse processing.

The market for fourth generation systems is a battle between vendors of third-generation systems who are upgrading their products against a new group of systems developed as open-source software. The existing companies seem to have the upper hand, but the open source DBMS products have gained important commercial usage.

1.3.2 Current Market for Database Software

According to the International Data Corporation (IDC), sales (license and maintenance) of enterprise relational DBMS software reached $14.6 billion in 2005, a 9.4 % increase since 2004. Enterprise DBMSs use mainframe servers running IBM's MVS operating system and mid-range servers running Unix (Linux, Solaris, AIX, and other variations) and Microsoft Windows Server operating systems. Three products dominate the market for enterprise database software as shown in Table 1-3. According to 2005 report by the Gartner Group, sales of Microsoft SQL Server are growing faster than the other products.

Table 1-3: 2003 Market Shares[2] by Revenue of Enterprise Database Software

Product	Total Market Share	Comments
Oracle 10g, 11g	44.6%	Dominates the Unix environment; strong performance in the Windows market also
IBM DB2, Informix	21.4%	Dominates the MVS and AS/400 environments; acquired Informix in 2001; 25% share of the Unix market
Microsoft SQL Server	16.8%	Strong position in the Windows market; no presence in other environments
Sybase	3.5%	Popular among financial services firms on Unix platforms
Teradata	2.9%	Usage as a data warehouse platform
Other	10.8%	Includes Progress Software, MySQL, PostgreSQL, open source Ingres, Firebird, and others

Open source DBMS products have begun to challenge the commercial DBMS products at the low end of the enterprise DBMS market. Although source code for open source DBMS products is available without charge, most organizations purchase support contracts so the open source products are not free. Still, many organizations have reported lower cost of ownership

---

[2] Market shares according to a 2005 study by the International Data Corporation.

using open source DBMS products. MySQL, first introduced in 1995, is the leader in the open source DBMS market. According to MySQL.com in January 2008, "more than 100 million copies of MySQL's high-performance open source database software have been downloaded and distributed and an additional 50,000 copies are downloaded daily." Besides, MySQL, PostgreSQL and open source Ingres are mature open source DBMS products. Firebird is a newer open source product that is gaining usage.

In the market for desktop database software, Microsoft Access dominates at least in part because of the dominance of Microsoft Office. Desktop database software is primarily sold as part of office productivity software. With Microsoft Office holding about 90% of the office productivity market, Access holds a comparable share of the desktop database software market. Other significant products in the desktop database software market are Paradox, Approach, FoxPro, and FileMaker Pro.

To provide coverage of both enterprise and desktop database software, this book provides significant coverage of Oracle and Microsoft Access. In addition, the emphasis on the SQL standard in Parts 2 and 5 provides database language coverage for the other major products.

Because of the potential growth of personal computing devices, most major DBMS vendors have now entered the embedded DBMS market. Embedded DBMS software is sold primarily by value-added software resellers as part of an application, such as an accounting package. According to an IDC 2007 report, Oracle is the market leader with 23.2% of the embedded market in 2006 following by Progress Software with 14.1% and IBM with 10.2%.

1.4 Architectures of Database Management Systems

To provide insight about the internal organization of DBMSs, this section describes two architectures or organizing frameworks. The first architecture describes an organization of database definitions to reduce the cost of software maintenance. The second architecture describes an organization of data and software to support remote access. These architectures promote a conceptual understanding rather than indicate actual DBMS implementation.

1.4.1 Data Independence and the Three Schema Architecture

In early DBMSs, there was a close connection between a database and computer programs that accessed the database. Essentially, the DBMS was considered part of a programming language. As a result, the database definition was part of the computer programs that accessed the database. In addition, the conceptual meaning of a database was not separate from its physical implementation on magnetic disk. The definitions about the structure of a database and its physical implementation were mixed inside computer programs.

The close association between a database and related programs led to problems in software maintenance. Software maintenance encompassing requirement changes, corrections, and enhancements can consume a large fraction of software development budgets. In early DBMSs, most changes to the database definition caused changes to computer programs. In many cases, changes to computer programs involved detailed inspection of the code, a labor-intensive process. This code inspection work is similar to year 2000 compliance in which date formats were changed to four digits. Performance tuning of a database was difficult because sometimes hundreds of computer programs had to be recompiled for every change. Because database definition changes are common, a large fraction of software maintenance resources were devoted to database changes. Some studies have estimated the percentage as high as 50% of software maintenance resources.

The concept of data independence emerged to alleviate problems with program maintenance. Data independence means that a database should have an identity separate from the applications (computer programs, forms, and reports) that use it. The separate identity allows the database definition to be changed without affecting related applications. For example, if a new column is added to a table, applications not using the new column should not be affected. Likewise if a new table is added, only applications that need the new table should be affected. This separation should be even more pronounced if a change only affects physical implementation of a database. Database specialists should be free to experiment with performance tuning without concern about computer program changes.

> **Data Independence**: a database should have an identity separate from the applications (computer programs, forms, and reports) that use it. The separate identity allows the database definition to be changed without affecting related applications.

In the mid-1970s, the concept of data independence led to the proposal of the Three Schema Architecture depicted in Figure 1.12. The word <u>schema</u> as applied to databases means database description. The Three Schema Architecture includes three levels of database description. The <u>external</u> level is the user level. Each group of users can have a separate external view (or view for short) of a database tailored to the group's specific needs.

> **Three Schema Architecture**: an architecture for compartmentalizing database descriptions. The Three Schema Architecture was proposed as a way to achieve data independence.

In contrast, the conceptual and internal schemas represent the entire database. The <u>conceptual schema</u> defines the entities and relationships. For a business database, the conceptual schema can be quite large, perhaps hundreds of entity types and relationships. Like the conceptual schema, the internal schema represents the entire database. However, the <u>internal schema</u> represents the storage view of the database whereas the conceptual schema represents the logical meaning of the database. The internal schema defines files, collections of data on a storage device such as a hard disk. A file can store one or more entity types described in the conceptual schema.

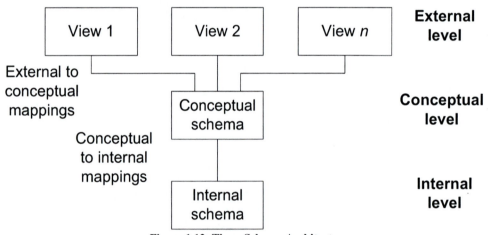

Figure 1.12: Three Schema Architecture

To make the three schema levels clearer, Table 1-4 shows differences among database definition at the three schema levels using examples from the features described in Section 1.2. Even in a simplified university database, the differences among the schema levels are clear. With a more complex database, the differences would be even more pronounced with many more views, a much larger conceptual schema, and a more complex internal schema.

Table 1-4: University Database Example Depicting Differences among Schema Levels

Schema Level	Description
External	HighGPAView: data required for the query in Figure 1.7
	FacultyAssignmentFormView: data required for the form in Figure 1.9
	FacultyWorkLoadReportView: data required for the report in Figure 1.10
Conceptual	Student, Enrollment, Course, Faculty, and Enrollment tables and relationships (Figure 1.6)
Internal	Files needed to store the tables; extra files (indexed property in Figure 1.5) to improve performance

The schema mappings describe how a schema at a higher level is derived from a schema at a lower level. For example, the external views in Table 1-4 are derived from the tables in the conceptual schema. The mapping provides the knowledge to convert a request using an external view (for example, HighGPAView) into a request using the tables in the conceptual schema. The mapping between conceptual and internal levels shows how entities are stored in files.

DBMSs, using schemas and mappings, ensure data independence. Typically, applications access a database using a view. The DBMS converts an application's request into a request using the conceptual schema rather than the view. The DBMS then transforms the conceptual schema request into a request using the internal schema. Most changes to the conceptual or internal schema do not affect applications because applications do not use the lower schema levels. The DBMS, not the user, is responsible for using the mappings to make the transformations. For more details about mappings and transformations, Chapter 10 describes views and transformations between the external and conceptual levels. Chapter 8 describes query optimization, the process of converting a conceptual level query into an internal level representation.

The Three Schema Architecture is an official standard of the American National Standards Institute (ANSI). However, the specific details of the standard were never widely adopted. Rather, the standard serves as a guideline about data independence. The spirit of the Three Schema Architecture is widely implemented in third- and fourth-generation DBMSs.

1.4.2 Parallel and Distributed Database Processing

With the growing importance of computer networks and electronic commerce, distributed processing is becoming a crucial function of DBMSs. Distributed processing allows geographically dispersed computers to cooperate when providing data access. A large part of electronic commerce on the Web involves accessing and updating remote databases. Many databases in retail, banking, and security trading are now available through the Web. DBMSs use available network capacity and local processing capabilities to provide efficient remote database access.

Distributed processing can be applied to databases to distribute tasks among servers, divide a task among processing resources, and distribute data among network sites. To distribute tasks among servers, many DBMSs use the client-server architecture. A client is a program that submits requests to a server. A server processes requests on behalf of a client. For example, a client may request a server to retrieve product data. The server locates the data and sends them back to the client. The client may perform additional processing on the data before displaying the results to the user. DBMSs may employ one or more levels of servers to distribute different kinds of database processing. In Figure 1.13(a), the database server and database are located on a remote computer. In Figure 1.13(b), an additional middleware server is added to efficiently process messages from a large number of clients.

15

Client-Server Architecture: an arrangement of components (clients and servers) among computers connected by a network. The client-server architecture supports efficient processing of messages (requests for service) between clients and servers.

a) Client-server processing with database server

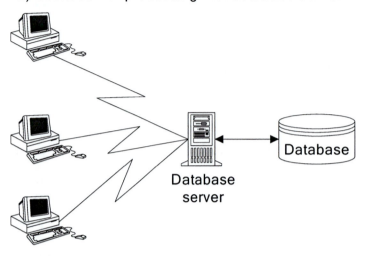

b) Client-server processing with middleware and database servers

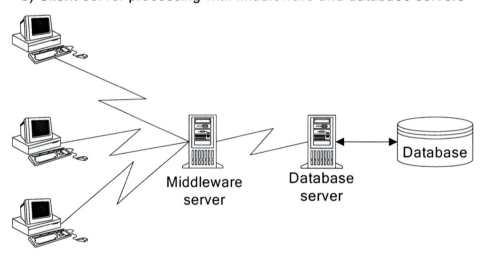

Figure 1.13: Typical Client-Server Architectures

In the last decade, parallel database technology has gained commercial acceptance for large organizations. Most enterprise DBMS vendors and some open source DBMSs support parallel database technology to meet market demand. Organizations are utilizing these products to realize the benefits of improved performance and availability. Parallel database processing can improve performance through speedup (performing a task faster) and scaleup (performing more work in the same time). Parallel database processing can increase availability because a DBMS can dynamically adjust to the level of available resources. Figure 1.14 depicts two common parallel database architectures that can provide improved performance and availability. In Figure 1.14(a) known as the shared disk architecture, each processor has its own memory but the processors share the disks. In Figure 1.14(b) known as shared nothing architecture, each processor has its own memory and disks.

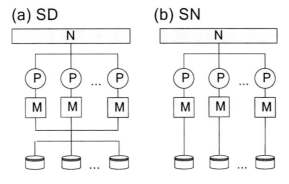

Legend
P: processor
M: memory
N: high-speed network
SD: shared disk
SN: shared nothing

Figure 1.14: Basic Parallel Database Architectures

Parallel DBMS: a DBMS capable of utilizing tightly-coupled computing resources (processors, disks, and memory). Tight coupling is achieved by networks with data exchange time comparable to the time of the data exchange with a disk. Parallel database technology promises performance improvements and high availability.

Distributed data provides local control and reduced communication costs. Distributing a database allows the location of data to match an organization's structure. Decisions about sharing and maintaining data can be set locally to provide control closer to the data usage. Data should be located so that 80 percent of the requests are local. Local requests incur little or no communication costs and delays compared to remote requests. Figure 1.15 depicts a distributed database with three sites in Denver, London, and Tokyo. Each site can control access to its local data and cooperate to provide data sharing for tasks needing data from more than one site.

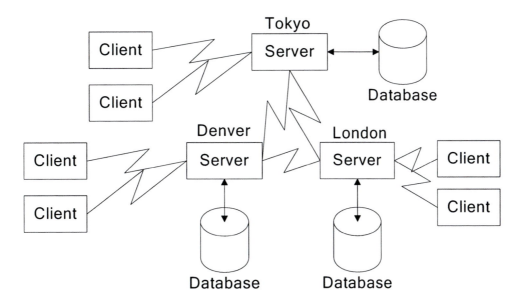

Figure 1.15: Distributed Database with Three Sites

> **Distributed Database**: a database in which parts are located at different network sites. Distributed database technology supports local control of data, data sharing for requests involving data from more than one site, and reduced communication overhead.

Client-server architectures, parallel database processing, and distributed databases provide flexible ways for DBMSs to interact with computer networks. The distribution of data and processing among clients and servers and the possible choices to locate data and software are much more complex than described here. You will learn more details about these architectures in Chapter 17.

1.5 Organizational Impacts of Database Technology

This section completes your introduction to database technology by discussing the effects of database technology on organizations. The first section describes possible interactions that you may have with a database in an organization. The second section describes information resource management, an effort to control the data produced and used by an organization. Special attention is given to management roles that you can play as part of an effort to control information resources. Chapter 14 provides more detail about the tools and processes used in these management roles.

1.5.1 Interacting with Databases

Because databases are pervasive, there are a variety of ways in which you may interact with databases. The classification in Figure 1.16 distinguishes between functional users who interact with databases as part of their work and information systems professionals who participate in designing and implementing databases. Each box in the hierarchy represents a role that you may play. You may simultaneously play more than one role. For example, a functional user in a job such as a financial analyst may play all three roles in different databases. In some organizations, the distinction between functional users and information systems professionals is blurred. In these organizations, functional users may participate in designing and using databases.

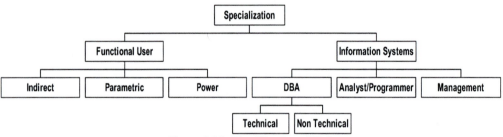

Figure 1.16: Classification of Roles

Functional users can play a passive or an active role when interacting with databases. Indirect usage of a database is a passive role. An <u>indirect</u> user is given a report or some data extracted from a database. A parametric user is more active than an indirect user. A <u>parametric</u> user requests existing forms or reports using parameters, input values that change from usage to usage. For example, a parameter may indicate a date range, sales territory, or department name. The <u>power</u> user is the most active. Because decision-making needs can be difficult to predict, ad hoc or unplanned usage of a database is important. A power user is skilled enough to build a form or report when needed. Power users should have a good understanding of nonprocedural access, a skill described in parts 2 and 5 of this book.

Information systems professionals interact with databases as part of developing an information system. <u>Analyst/programmers</u> are responsible for collecting requirements, designing applications, and implementing information systems. They create and use external views to develop forms, reports, and other parts of an information system. Management has an oversight role in the development of databases and information systems. Information systems professionals in analyst/programmer roles should have a good knowledge of database development and application development in parts 3 to 5 of this book.

Database administrators assist both information systems professionals and functional users. Database administrators have a variety of both technical and non-technical responsibilities (Table 1-5). Technical skills are more detail-oriented; non-technical responsibilities are more people-oriented. The primary technical responsibility is database design. On the non-technical side, the database administrator's time is split among a number of activities. Database administrators can also have responsibilities in planning databases and evaluating DBMSs. Chapter 14 provides more details about responsibilities and tools of database administrators.

> **Database Administrator**: a support position that specializes in managing individual databases and DBMSs.

Table 1-5: Responsibilities of the Database Administrator

Technical	Non-technical
Designing conceptual schemas	Setting database standards
Designing internal schemas	Devising training materials
Monitoring database performance	Promoting benefits of databases
Selecting and evaluating database software	Consulting with users
Managing security for database usage	Planning new databases
Troubleshooting database problems	

1.5.2 Information Resource Management

Information resource management is a response to the challenge of effectively utilizing information technology. The goal of information resource management is to use information technology as a tool for processing, distributing, and integrating information throughout an organization. Management of information resources has many similarities with managing physical resources such as inventory. Inventory management involves activities such as safeguarding inventory from theft and deterioration, storing it for efficient usage, choosing suppliers, handling waste, coordinating movement, and reducing holding costs. Information resource management involves similar activities: planning databases, acquiring data, protecting data from unauthorized access, ensuring reliability, coordinating flow among information systems, and eliminating duplication.

As part of controlling information resources, new management responsibilities have arisen. The data administrator is a management role with many of these responsibilities; the major responsibility being planning the development of new databases. The data administrator maintains an enterprise data architecture that describes existing databases and new databases and also evaluates new information technologies and determines standards for managing databases.

> **Data Administrator**: a management position that performs planning and policy setting for the information resources of an entire organization.

The data administrator typically has broader responsibilities than the database administrator. The data administrator has primarily a planning role, while the database administrator has a more technical role focused on individual databases and DBMSs. The data administrator also views the information resource in a broader context and considers all kinds of data, both computerized and noncomputerized. A major effort in many organizations is to computerize nontraditional data such as video, training materials, images, and correspondence. The data administrator develops long-range plans for nontraditional data, while the database administrator implements the plans using appropriate database technology.

Because of broader responsibilities, the data administrator typically is higher in an organization chart. Figure 1.17 depicts two possible placements of data administrators and database administrators. In a small organization, both roles may be combined in systems administration.

a) Data administrator under MIS director

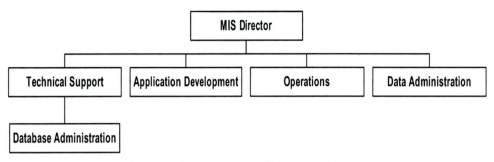

b) Data administrator parallel to MIS director

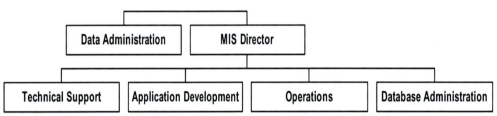

Figure 1.17: Organizational Placement of Data and Database Administration

Closing Thoughts

Chapter 1 has provided a broad introduction to DBMSs. You should use this background as a context for the skills you will acquire in subsequent chapters. You learned that databases contain interrelated data that can be shared across multiple parts of an organization. DBMSs support transformation of data for decision making. To support this transformation, database technology has evolved from simple file access to powerful systems that support database definition, nonprocedural access, application development, transaction processing, and performance tuning. Nonprocedural access is the most vital element because it allows access without detailed coding. You learned about two architectures that provide organizing principles for DBMSs. The Three Schema Architecture supports data independence, an important concept for reducing the cost of software maintenance. Client-server architectures, parallel database processing, and distributed databases allow databases to be accessed over computer networks, a feature vital in today's networked world.

The skills emphasized in later chapters should enable you to work as an active functional user or analyst. Both kinds of users need to understand the skills taught in the second part of this book. The fifth part of the book provides skills for analysts/programmers. This book also provides the foundation of skills to obtain a specialist position as a database or data administrator. The skills in the third, fourth, sixth, and seventh parts of this book are most useful for a position as a database administrator. However, you will probably need to take additional courses, learn details of popular DBMSs, and acquire management experience before obtaining a specialist role. A position as a database specialist can be an exciting and lucrative career opportunity that you should consider.

Review Concepts

- Database characteristics: persistent, interrelated, and shared
- Features of database management systems (DBMSs)
- Nonprocedural access: a key to software productivity
- Transaction: a unit of work that should be processed reliably
- Application development using nonprocedural access to specify the data requirements of forms and reports
- Procedural language interface for combining nonprocedural access with a programming language such as Java or Visual Basic
- Evolution of database software over four generations of technological improvement
- Current emphasis on database software for multimedia support, distributed processing, more powerful operators, and data warehouses
- Types of DBMSs: enterprise, desktop, embedded
- Data independence to alleviate problems with maintenance of computer programs
- Three Schema Architecture for reducing the impact of database definition changes
- Client-server processing, parallel database processing, and distributed database processing for using databases over computer networks
- Database specialist roles: database administrator and data administrator
- Information resource management for utilizing information technology

Questions

1. Describe a database that you have used on a job or as a consumer. List the entities and relationships that the database contains. If you are not sure, imagine the entities and relationships that are contained in the database.
2. For the database in question (1), list different user groups that can use the database.
3. For one of the groups in question (2), describe an application (form or report) that the group uses.
4. Explain the persistent property for databases.
5. Explain the interrelated property for databases.
6. Explain the shared property for databases.
7. What is a DBMS?
8. What is SQL?
9. Describe the difference between a procedural and a nonprocedural language. What statements belong in a procedural language but not in a nonprocedural language?
10. Why is nonprocedural access an important feature of DBMSs?
11. What is the connection between nonprocedural access and application (form or report) development? Can nonprocedural access be used in application development?
12. What is the difference between a form and a report?
13. What is a procedural language interface?
14. What is a transaction?
15. What features does a DBMS provide to support transaction processing?
16. For the database in question (1), describe a transaction that uses the database. How often do you think that the transaction is submitted to the database? How many users submit transactions at the same time? Make guesses for the last two parts if you are unsure.
17. What is an enterprise DBMS?
18. What is a desktop DBMS?
19. What is an embedded DBMS?
20. What were the prominent features of first-generation DBMSs?
21. What were the prominent features of second-generation DBMSs?
22. What were the prominent features of third-generation DBMSs?
23. What are the prominent features of fourth-generation DBMSs?
24. For the database you described in question (1), make a table to depict differences among schema levels. Use Table 1-4 as a guide.

25. What is the purpose of the mappings in the Three Schema Architecture? Is the user or DBMS responsible for using the mappings?
26. Explain the ways that the Three Schema Architecture supports data independence.
27. In a client-server architecture, why are processing capabilities divided between a client and server? In other words, why not have the server do all the processing?
28. What benefits can be provided by parallel database processing?
29. What benefits can be provided by distributing parts of a database among different network sites?
30. For the database in question (1), describe how functional users may interact with the database. Try to identify indirect, parametric, and power uses of the database.
31. Explain the differences in responsibilities between an active functional user of a database and an analyst. What schema level is used by both kinds of users?
32. Which role, database administrator or data administrator, is more appealing to you as a long-term career goal? Briefly explain your preference.
33. What market niche is occupied by open source DBMS products?

Problems

Because of the introductory nature of this chapter, there are no problems in this chapter. Problems appear at the end of most other chapters.

References for Further Study

The DBAZine (www.dbazine.com), the *Intelligent Enterprise* (www.intelligententerprise.com), and the *Advisor.com* (www.advisor.com) websites provide detailed technical information about commercial DBMSs, database design, and database application development. To learn more about the role of database specialists and information resource management, you should consult Mullin (2002).

Introduction to Database Development

Learning Objectives

This chapter provides an overview of the database development process. After this chapter, the student should have acquired the following knowledge and skills:

- List the steps in the information systems life cycle
- Describe the role of databases in an information system
- Explain the goals of database development
- Understand the relationships among phases in the database development process
- List features typically provided by CASE tools for database development

Overview

Chapter 1 provided a broad introduction to database usage in organizations and database technology. You learned about the characteristics of business databases, essential features of database managements systems (DBMSs), architectures for deploying databases, and organizational roles interacting with databases. This chapter continues your introduction to database management with a broad focus on database development. You will learn about the context, goals, phases, and tools of database development to facilitate the acquisition of specific knowledge and skills in Parts 3 and 4.

Before you can learn specific skills, you need to understand the broad context for database development. This chapter discusses a context for databases as part of an information system. You will learn about components of information systems, the life cycle of information systems, and the role of database development as part of information systems development. This information systems context provides a background for database development. You will learn the phases of database development, the kind of skills used in database development, and software tools that can help you develop databases.

2.1 Information Systems

Databases exist as part of an information system. Before you can understand database development, you must understand the larger environment that surrounds a database. This section describes the components of an information system and several methodologies to develop information systems.

2.1.1 Components of Information Systems

A <u>system</u> is a set of related components that work together to accomplish some objectives. Objectives are accomplished by interacting with the environment and performing functions. For example, the human circulatory system, consisting of blood, blood vessels, and the heart, makes blood flow to various parts of the body. The circulatory system interacts with other systems of the body to ensure that the right quantity and composition of blood arrives in a timely manner to various body parts.

An information system is similar to a physical system (such as the circulatory system) except that an information system manipulates data rather than a physical object like blood. An <u>information system</u> accepts data from its environment, processes data, and produces output data for decision making. For example, an information system for processing student loans (Figure 2.1) helps a service provider track loans for lending institutions. The environment of this system consists of lenders, students, and government agencies. Lenders send approved loan applications and students receive cash for school expenses. After graduation, students receive monthly statements and remit payments to retire their loans. If a student defaults, a government agency receives a delinquency notice.

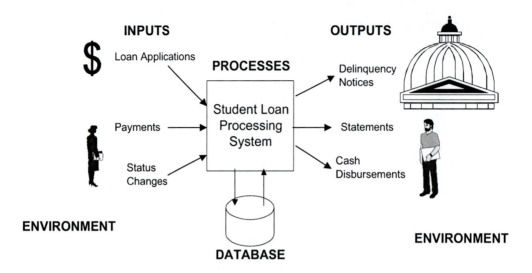

Figure 2.1: Overview of Student Loan Processing System

Databases are essential components of many information systems. The role of a database is to provide long-term memory for an information system. The long-term memory contains entities and relationships. For example, the database in Figure 2.1 contains data about students, loans, and payments so that the statements, cash disbursements, and delinquency notices can be generated. Information systems without permanent memory or with only a few variables in permanent memory are typically embedded in a device to provide a limited range of functions rather than an open range of functions as business information systems provide.

Databases are not the only components of information systems. Information systems also contain people, procedures, input data, output data, software, and hardware. Thus, developing an information system involves more than developing a database, as discussed in the next subsection.

2.1.2 Information Systems Development Process

Figure 2.2 shows the phases of the traditional systems development life cycle. The particular phases of the life cycle are not standard. Different authors and organizations have proposed from 3 to 20 phases. The traditional life cycle is often known as the waterfall model or methodology because the result of each phase flows to the next phase. The traditional life cycle is mostly a reference framework. For most systems, the boundary between phases is blurred and there is considerable backtracking between phases. But the traditional life cycle is still useful because it describes the kind of activities and shows addition of detail until an operational system emerges. The following items describe the activities in each phase:

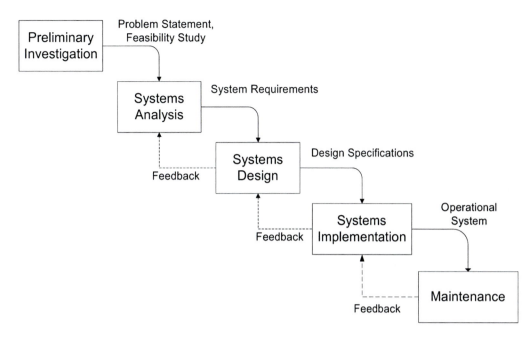

Figure 2.2: Traditional Systems Development Life Cycle

Preliminary Investigation Phase: Produces a problem statement and feasibility study. The problem statement includes the objectives, constraints, and scope of the system. The feasibility study identifies the costs and benefits of the system. If the system is feasible, approval is given to begin systems analysis.

Systems Analysis Phase: Produces requirements describing processes, data, and environment interactions. Diagramming techniques are used to document processes, data, and environment interactions. To produce the requirements, the current system is studied and users of the proposed system are interviewed.

Systems Design Phase: Produces a plan to efficiently implement the requirements. Design specifications are created for processes, data, and environment interaction. The design specifications focus on choices to optimize resources given constraints.

Systems Implementation Phase: Produces executable code, databases, and user documentation. To implement the system, the design specifications are coded and tested. Before making the new system operational, a transition plan from the old system to the new system is devised. To gain confidence and experience with the new system, an organization may run the old system in parallel to the new system for a period of time.

Maintenance Phase: Produces corrections, changes, and enhancements to an operating information system. The maintenance phase commences when an information system becomes operational. The maintenance phase is fundamentally different from other phases because it comprises activities from all of the other phases. The maintenance phase ends when a replacement system is deployed and the current system is retired. Due to the high fixed costs of developing new systems, the maintenance phase can last decades.

The traditional life cycle has been criticized for several reasons. First, an operating system is not produced until late in the process. By the time a system is operational, the requirements may have already changed. Second, there is often a rush to begin implementation so that a product is visible. In this rush, appropriate time may not be devoted to analysis and design.

A number of alternative methodologies have been proposed to alleviate these difficulties. In spiral development methodologies, the life cycle phases are performed for subsets of a system, progressively producing a larger system until the complete system emerges. Rapid application development methodologies delay producing design documents until requirements are clear. Scaled-down versions of a system, known as prototypes, are used to clarify requirements. Prototypes can be implemented rapidly using graphical development tools for generating menus, forms, reports, and other code. Implementing a prototype allows users to provide meaningful feedback to developers. Often, users may not understand the requirements unless they can experience a prototype. Thus, prototyping can reduce the risk of developing an information system because it allows earlier and more direct feedback about the system.

In all development methodologies, graphical models of the data, processes, and environment interactions should be produced. The data model describes the kinds of data and relationships. The process model describes relationships among processes. A process can provide input data used by other processes and use the output data of other processes. The environment interaction model describes relationships between events and processes. An event such as the passage of time or an action from the environment can trigger a process to start or stop. The systems analysis phase produces an initial version of these models. The systems design phase adds more details so that the models can be efficiently implemented.

Even though models of data, processes, and environment interactions are necessary to develop an information system, this book emphasizes data models only. In many information systems development efforts, the data model is the most important. For business information systems, the process and environment interaction models are usually produced after the data model. Rather than present notation for the process and environment interaction models, this book emphasizes form and report development to depict connections among data, processes, and the environment. For more details about process and environment interaction models, please consult several references at the end of the chapter.

2.2 Goals of Database Development

Broadly, the goal of database development is to create a database that provides an important resource for an organization. To fulfill this broad goal, the database should serve a large community of users, support organizational policies, contain high quality data, and provide efficient access. The remainder of this section describes the goals of database development in more detail.

2.2.1 Develop a Common Vocabulary

A database provides a common vocabulary for an organization. Before a common database is implemented, different parts of an organization may have different terminology. For example, there may be multiple formats for addresses, multiple ways to identify customers, and different ways to calculate interest rates. After a database is implemented, communication can improve among different parts of an organization. Thus, a database can unify an organization by establishing a common vocabulary.

Achieving a common vocabulary is not easy. Developing a database requires compromise to satisfy a large community of users. In some sense, a good database designer shares some characteristics with a good politician. A good politician often finds solutions with which everyone finds something to agree or disagree. In establishing a common vocabulary, a good database designer also finds similar imperfect solutions. Forging compromises can be difficult, but the results can improve productivity, customer satisfaction, and other measures of organizational performance.

2.2.2 Define the Meaning of Data

A database contains business rules to support organizational policies. Defining business rules is the essence of defining the semantics or meaning of a database. For example, in an order entry system, an important rule is that an order must precede a shipment. The database can contain an integrity constraint to support this rule. Defining business rules enables the database to actively support organizational policies. This active role contrasts with the more passive role that databases have in establishing a common vocabulary.

In establishing the meaning of data, a database designer must choose appropriate constraint levels. Selecting appropriate constraint levels may require compromise to balance the needs of different groups. Constraints that are too strict may force work-around solutions to handle exceptions. In contrast, constraints that are too loose may allow incorrect data in a database. For example, in a university database, a designer must decide if a course offering can be stored without knowing the instructor. Some user groups may want the instructor to be entered initially to ensure that course commitments can be met. Other user groups may want more flexibility because course catalogs are typically printed well in advance of the beginning of the academic period. Forcing the instructor to be entered at the time a course offering is stored may be too strict. If the database contains this constraint, users may be forced to circumvent it by using a default value such as TBA (to be announced). The appropriate constraint (forcing entry of the instructor or allowing later entry) depends on the importance of the needs of the user groups to the goals of the organization.

2.2.3 Ensure Data Quality

The importance of data quality is analogous to the importance of product quality in manufacturing. Poor product quality can lead to loss of sales, lawsuits, and customer dissatisfaction. Because data are the product of an information system, data quality is equally important. Poor data quality can lead to poor decision making about communicating with customers, identifying repeat customers, tracking sales, and resolving customer problems. For example, communicating with customers can be difficult if addresses are outdated or customer names are inconsistently spelled on different orders.

Data quality has many dimensions or characteristics, as depicted in Table 2-1. The importance of data quality characteristics can depend on the part of the database in which they are applied. For example, in the product part of a retail grocery database, important characteristics of data quality may be the timeliness and consistency of prices. For other parts of the database, other characteristics may be more important.

Table 2-1: Common Characteristics of Data Quality

Characteristic	Meaning
Completeness	Database represents all important parts of the information system
Lack of ambiguity	Each part of the database has only one meaning
Correctness	Database contains values perceived by the user
Timeliness	Business changes are posted to the database without excessive delays
Reliability	Failures or interference do not corrupt database
Consistency	Different parts of the database do not conflict

A database design should help achieve adequate data quality. When evaluating alternatives, a database designer should consider data quality characteristics. For example, in a customer database, a database designer should consider the possibility that some customers may not have U.S. addresses. Therefore, the database design may be incomplete if it fails to support non-U.S. addresses.

Achieving adequate data quality may require a cost-benefit trade-off. For example, in a grocery store database, the benefits of timely price updates are reduced consumer complaints and less loss in fines from government agencies. Achieving data quality can be costly both in preventative and monitoring activities. For example, to improve the timeliness and accuracy of price updates, automated data entry may be used (preventative activity) as well as sampling the accuracy of the prices charged to consumers (monitoring activity).

The cost-benefit trade-off for data quality should consider long-term as well as short-term costs and benefits. Often the benefits of data quality are long-term, especially data quality issues that cross individual databases. For example, consistency of customer identification across databases can be a crucial issue for strategic decision making. The issue may not be important for individual databases. Chapter 16 on data warehouses addresses issues of data quality related to strategic decision making.

2.2.4 Find an Efficient Implementation

Even if the other design goals are met, a slow-performing database will not be used. Thus, finding an efficient implementation is paramount. However, an efficient implementation should respect the other goals as much as possible. An efficient implementation that compromises the meaning of the database or database quality may be rejected by database users.

Finding an efficient implementation is an optimization problem with an objective and constraints. Informally, the objective is to maximize performance subject to constraints about resource usage, data quality, and data meaning. Finding an efficient implementation can be difficult because of the number of choices available, the interaction among choices, and the difficulty of describing inputs. In addition, finding an efficient implementation is a continuing effort. Performance should be monitored and design changes should be made if warranted.

2.3 Database Development Process

This section describes the phases of the database development process and discusses relationships to the information systems development process. The chapters in Parts 3 and 4 elaborate on the framework provided here.

2.3.1 Phases of Database Development

The goal of the database development process is to produce an operational database for an information system. To produce an operational database, you need to define the three schemas (external, conceptual, and internal) and populate (supply with data) the database. To create these schemas, you can follow the process depicted in Figure 2.3. The first two phases are concerned with the information content of the database while the last two phases are concerned with efficient implementation. These phases are described in more detail in the remainder of this section.

Conceptual Data Modeling

The conceptual data modeling phase uses data requirements and produces entity relationship diagrams (ERDs) for the conceptual schema and for each external schema. Data requirements can have many formats such as interviews with users, documentation of existing systems, and proposed forms and reports. The conceptual schema should represent all the requirements and formats. In contrast, the external schemas (or views) represent the requirements of a particular usage of the database such as a form or report rather than all requirements. Thus, external schemas are generally much smaller than the conceptual schema.

The conceptual and external schemas follow the rules of the Entity Relationship Model, a graphical representation that depicts things of interest (entities) and relationships among entities. Figure 2.4 depicts an entity relationship diagram (ERD) for part of a student loan system. The rectangles (*Student* and *Loan*) represent entity types and labeled lines (*Receives*) represent relationships. Attributes or properties of entities are listed inside the rectangle. The underlined attribute, known as the primary key, provides unique identification for the entity type. Chapter 3 provides a precise definition of primary keys. Chapters 5 and 6 present more details about the Entity Relationship Model. Because the Entity Relationship Model is not fully supported by any DBMS, the conceptual schema is not biased toward any specific DBMS.

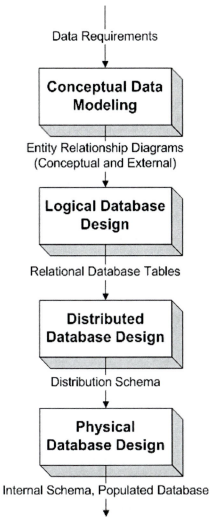

Data Requirements

Conceptual Data Modeling

Entity Relationship Diagrams
(Conceptual and External)

Logical Database Design

Relational Database Tables

Distributed Database Design

Distribution Schema

Physical Database Design

Internal Schema, Populated Database

Figure 2.3: Phases of Database Development

Figure 2.4: Partial ERD for the Student Loan System

Logical Database Design

The logical database design phase transforms the conceptual data model into a format understandable by a commercial DBMS. The logical design phase is not concerned with efficient implementation. Rather, the logical design phase is concerned with refinements to the conceptual data model. The refinements preserve the information content of the conceptual data model while enabling implementation on a commercial DBMS. Because most business databases are implemented on relational DBMSs, the logical design phase usually produces a table design.

The logical database design phase consists of two refinement activities: conversion and normalization. The conversion activity transforms ERDs into table designs using conversion rules. As you will learn in Chapter 3, a table design includes tables, columns, primary keys, foreign keys (links to other related tables), and other constraints. For example, the ERD in Figure 2.4 is converted into two tables as depicted in Figure 2.5. The normalization activity removes redundancies in a table design using constraints or dependencies among columns. Chapter 6 presents conversion rules while Chapter 7 presents normalization techniques.

```
CREATE TABLE Student
(  StdNo     INTEGER      NOT NULL,
   StdName   CHAR(50),
   ...
PRIMARY KEY (StdNo)      )
CREATE TABLE Loan
( LoanNo     INTEGER      NOT NULL,
  LoanAmt    DECIMAL(10,2),
  StdNo      INTEGER      NOT NULL,
  ...
PRIMARY KEY (LoanNo),
FOREIGN KEY (StdNo) REFERENCES Student   )
```

Figure 2.5: Conversion of Figure 2.4

Distributed Database Design

The distributed database design phase marks a departure from the first two phases. The distributed database design and physical database design phases are both concerned with an efficient implementation. In contrast, the first two phases (conceptual data modeling and logical database design) are concerned with the information content of the database.

Distributed database design involves choices about the location of data and processes to improve performance and provide local control of data. Performance can be measured in many ways such as reduced response time, improved availability of data, and improved control. For data location decisions, the database can be split in many ways to distribute it among computer sites. For example, a loan table can be distributed according to the location of the bank granting the loan. Another technique to improve performance is to replicate or make copies of parts of the database. Replication improves availability of the database but makes updating more difficult because multiple copies must be kept consistent.

Data location decisions should respect data ownership. An organization that controls some part of a database should control access to its data. For example, a franchise store should have control over access to its locally generated data. Distributed database technology presented in Chapter 17 enables an organization to align data location with data control.

For process location decisions, some of the work is typically performed on a server and some of the work is performed by a client. For example, the server often retrieves data and sends them to the client. The client displays the results in an appealing manner. There are many other options about the location of data and processing that are explored in Chapter 17.

Physical Database Design

The physical database design phase, like the distributed database design phase, is concerned with an efficient implementation. Unlike distributed database design, physical database design is concerned with performance at one computer location only. If a database is distributed, physical design decisions are necessary for each location. An efficient implementation minimizes response time without using too many resources such as disk space and main memory. Because response time is difficult to directly measure, other measures such as the amount of disk input-output activity is often used as a substitute.

In the physical database design phase, two important choices are about indexes and data placement. An index is an auxiliary file that can improve performance. For each column of a table, the designer decides whether an index can improve performance. An index can improve performance on retrievals but reduce performance on updates. For example, indexes on the primary keys (*StdNo* and *LoanNo* in Figure 2.5) can usually improve performance. For data placement, the designer decides how data should be clustered or located close together on a disk. For example, performance might improve by placing student rows near the rows of associated loans. Chapter 8 describes details of physical database design including index selection and data placement.

Splitting Conceptual Design for Large Projects

The database development process shown in Figure 2.3 works well for moderate-size databases. For large databases, the conceptual modeling phase is usually modified. Designing large databases is a time-consuming and labor-intensive process often involving a team of designers. The development effort can involve requirements from many different groups of users. To manage complexity, a divide and conquer strategy is used in many areas of computing. Dividing a large problem into smaller problems allows the smaller problems to be solved independently. The solutions to the smaller problems are then combined into a solution for the entire problem.

View design and integration (Figure 2.6) is an approach to managing the complexity of large database development efforts. In view design, an ERD is constructed for each group of users. A view is typically small enough for a single person to design. Multiple designers can work on views covering different parts of the database. The view integration process merges the views into a complete and consistent conceptual schema. Integration involves recognizing and resolving conflicts. To resolve conflicts, it is sometimes necessary to revise the conflicting views. Compromise is an important part of conflict resolution in the view integration process. Chapter 12 provides details about the view design and view integration processes.

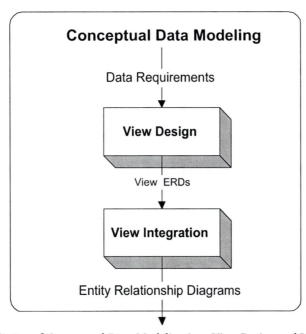

Figure 2.6: Splitting of Conceptual Data Modeling into View Design and View Integration

Cross-Checking with Application Development

The database development process does not exist in isolation. Database development is conducted along with activities in the systems analysis, systems design, and systems implementation phases.

The conceptual data modeling phase is performed as part of the systems analysis phase. The logical database design phase is performed during systems design. The distributed database design and physical database design phases are usually divided between systems design and systems implementation. Most of the preliminary decisions for the last two phases can be made in systems design. However, many physical design and distributed design decisions must be tested on a populated database. Thus, some activities in the last two phases occur in systems implementation.

To fulfill the goals of database development, the database development process must be tightly integrated with other parts of information systems development. To produce data, process, and interaction models that are consistent and complete, cross-checking can be performed, as depicted in Figure 2.7. The information systems development process can be split between database development and applications development. The database development process produces ERDs, table designs, and so on as described in this section. The applications development process produces process models, interaction models, and prototypes. Prototypes are especially important for cross-checking. A database has no value unless it supports intended applications such as forms and reports. Prototypes can help reveal mismatches between the database and applications using the database.

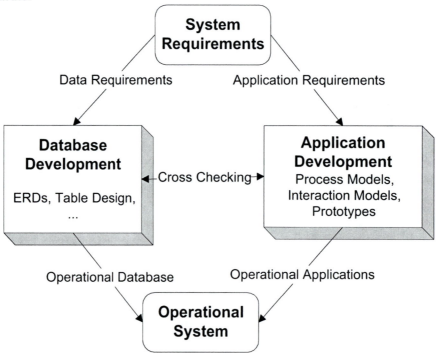

Figure 2.7: Interaction between Database and Application Development

2.3.2 Skills in Database Development

As a database designer, you need two different kinds of skills as depicted in Figure 2.8. The conceptual data modeling and logical database design phases involve mostly soft skills. Soft skills are qualitative, subjective, and people-oriented. Qualitative skills emphasize the generation of feasible alternatives rather than the best alternatives. As a database designer, you want to generate a range of feasible alternatives. The choice among feasible alternatives can be subjective. You should note the assumptions in which each feasible alternative is preferred. The alternative chosen is often subjective based on the designer's assessment of the most reasonable assumptions. Conceptual data modeling is especially people-oriented. In the performing data modeling, you need to obtain requirements from diverse groups of users. Compromise and effective listening are essential skills in data modeling.

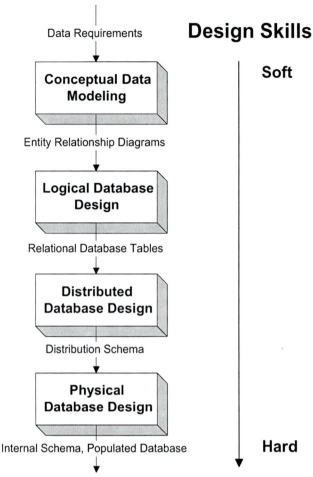

Design Skills

Data Requirements

Soft

Conceptual Data Modeling

Entity Relationship Diagrams

Logical Database Design

Relational Database Tables

Distributed Database Design

Distribution Schema

Physical Database Design

Internal Schema, Populated Database

Hard

Figure 2.8: Design Skills Used in Database Development

Distributed database design and physical database design involve mostly <u>hard</u> skills. Hard skills are quantitative, objective, and data intensive. A background in quantitative disciplines such as statistics and operations management can be useful to understand mathematical models used in these phases. Many of the decisions in these phases can be modeled mathematically using an objective function and constraints. For example, the objective function for index selection is to minimize disk reads and writes with constraints about the amount of disk space and response time limitations. Many decisions cannot be based on objective criteria alone because of uncertainty about database usage. To resolve uncertainty, intensive data analysis can be useful. The database designer should collect and analyze data to understand patterns of database usage and database performance.

Because of the diverse skills and background knowledge required in different phases of database development, role specialization can occur. In large organizations, database design roles are divided between data modelers and database performance experts. Data modelers are mostly involved in the conceptual data modeling and logical database design phases. Database performance experts are mostly involved in the distributed and physical database design phases. Because the skills are different in these roles, the same person will not perform both roles in large organizations. In small organizations, the same person may fulfill both roles.

2.4 Tools of Database Development

To improve productivity in developing information systems, computer-aided software engineering (CASE) tools have been created. CASE tools can help improve the productivity of information systems professionals working on large projects as well as end users working on small projects. A number of studies have provided evidence that CASE tools facilitate improvements in the early phases of systems development leading to lower cost, higher quality, and faster implementations.

Most CASE tools support the database development process. Some CASE tools support database development as a part of information systems development. Other CASE tools target various phases of database development without supporting other aspects of information systems development.

CASE tools often are classified as front-end and back-end tools. Front-end CASE tools can help designers diagram, analyze, and document models used in the database development process. Back-end CASE tools create prototypes and generate code that can be used to cross-check a database with other components of an information system. This section discusses the functions of CASE tools in more detail and demonstrates a commercial CASE tool, Microsoft Office Visio Professional 2003.

2.4.1 Diagramming

Diagramming is the most important and widely used function in CASE tools. Most CASE tools provide predefined shapes and connections among the shapes. The connection tools typically allow shapes to be moved while remaining connected as though glued. This glue feature provides important flexibility because symbols on a diagram typically are rearranged many times.

For large drawings, CASE tools provide several features. Most CASE tools allow diagrams to span multiple pages. Multiple-page drawings can be printed so that the pages can be pasted together to make a wall display. Layout can be difficult for large drawings. Some CASE tools try to improve the visual appeal of a diagram by performing automatic layout. The automatic layout feature may minimize the number of crossing connections in a diagram. Although automated layout is not typically sufficient by itself, a designer can use it as a first step to improve the visual appearance of a large diagram.

2.4.2 Documentation

Documentation is one of the oldest and most valuable functions of CASE tools. CASE tools can store various properties of a data model and link the properties to symbols on the diagram. Example properties stored in a CASE tool include alias names, integrity rules, data types, and owners. In addition to properties, CASE tools can store text describing assumptions, alternatives, and notes. Both the properties and text are stored in the data dictionary, the database of the CASE tool. The data dictionary is also known as the repository or encyclopedia.

To support system evolution, many CASE tools can document versions. A version is a group of changes and enhancements to a system that is released together. Because of the volume of changes, groups of changes rather than individual changes are typically released together. In the life of an information system, many versions can be made. To aid in understanding relationships between versions, many CASE tools support documentation for individual changes and entire versions.

2.4.3 Analysis

CASE tools can provide active assistance to database designers through analysis functions. In documentation and diagramming, CASE tools help designers become more proficient. In analysis functions, CASE tools can perform the work of a database designer. An analysis function is any form of reasoning applied to specifications produced in the database development process. For example, an important analysis function is to convert between an ERD and a table design. Converting from an ERD to a table design is known as forward engineering and converting in the reverse direction is known as reverse engineering.

Analysis functions can be provided in each phase of database development. In the conceptual data modeling phase, analysis functions can reveal conflicts in an ERD. In the logical database design phase, conversion and normalization are common analysis functions. Conversion produces a table design from an ERD. Normalization removes redundancy in a table design. In the distributed database design and physical database design phases, analysis functions can suggest decisions about data location and index selection. In addition, analysis functions for version control can cross database development phases. Analysis functions can convert between versions and show a list of differences between versions.

Because analysis functions are advanced features in CASE tools, availability of analysis functions varies widely. Some CASE tools support little or no analysis functions while others support extensive analysis functions. Because analysis functions can be useful in each phase of database development, no single CASE tool provides a complete range of analysis functions. CASE tools tend to specialize by the phases supported. CASE tools independent of a DBMS typically specialize in analysis functions in the conceptual data modeling phase. In contrast, CASE tools offered by a DBMS vendor often specialize in the distributed database design and physical database design phases.

2.4.4 Prototyping Tools

Prototyping tools provide a link between database development and application development. Prototyping tools can be used to create forms and reports that use a database. Because prototyping tools may generate code (SQL statements and programming language code), they are sometimes known as code generation tools. Prototyping tools are often provided as part of a DBMS. The prototyping tools may provide wizards to aid a developer in quickly creating applications that can be tested by users. Prototyping tools can also create an initial database design by retrieving existing designs from a library of designs. This kind of prototyping tool can be very useful to end users and novice database designers.

2.4.5 Commercial CASE Tools

As shown in Table 2-2, there are a number of CASE tools that provide extensive functionality for database development. Each product in Table 2-2 supports the full life cycle of information systems development although the quality, depth, and breadth of the features may vary across products. In addition, most of the products in Table 2-2 have several different versions that vary in price and features. All of the products are relatively neutral to a particular DBMS even though four products are offered by organizations with major DBMS products. Besides the full featured products listed in Table 2-2, other companies offer CASE tools that specialize in a subset of database development phases.

To provide a flavor for some features of commercial CASE tools, a brief depiction is given of Microsoft Office Visio 2003 Professional, an entry-level version of Visual Studio .Net Enterprise Architect 2003. Visio Professional provides excellent drawing capabilities and a number of useful analysis tools. This section depicts Visio Professional because it is an easy-to-use and powerful tool for introductory database courses.

For database development, Visio Professional features several templates (collections of shapes) and data dictionary support. As shown in Figure 2.9, Visio provides templates for several data modeling notations (Database Model Diagram, Express-G, and Object Role Modeling (ORM) notations) as well as the Unified Modeling Language (available in the software folder). Figure 2.10 depicts the Entity Relationship template (on the left) and the drawing window (on the right). If a symbol is moved, it stays connected to other symbols because of a feature known as "glue." For example, if the Product rectangle is moved, it stays connected to the OrdLine rectangle through the PurchasedIn line. Visio Professional can automatically lay out the entire diagram if requested.

Table 2-2: Prominent CASE Tools for Database Development

Tool	Vendor	Innovative Features
PowerDesigner 12	Sybase	Forward and reverse engineering for relational databases and many programming languages; model management support for comparing and merging models; application code generation; UML support; business process modeling; XML code generation; version control; data warehouse modeling support
Oracle Designer 10g	Oracle	Forward and reverse engineering for relational databases; reverse engineering of forms; application code generation; version control; dependency analysis; business process modeling; cross reference analysis
Visual Studio Team System 2008 Database Edition	Microsoft	Forward and reverse engineering for relational databases and the Unified Modeling Language; code generation for XML Web Services; generation of data models from natural language descriptions; T-SQL static code analysis; schema comparison; test data generation
CA ERWin Data Modeler 7	Computer Associates	Forward and reverse engineering for relational databases; application code generation; data warehouse data modeling support; model reuse tools; bi-directional compare facility for synchronizing use cases
ER/Studio, Schema Examiner, DB Artisan	Embarcadero Technologies	Forward and reverse engineering for relational databases; Java and other language code generation; model management support for comparing and merging models; UML support; version control; administration support for multiple DBMSs; diagnosis of schema problems
Visible Analyst 2008	Visible Systems Corporation	Forward and reverse engineering for relational databases; model management support for comparing and merging models; version control; methodology and rules checking support; strategic planning support

Visio provides a data dictionary to accompany the Entity Relationship template. For entity types (rectangle symbols), Visio supports the name, data type, required (Req'd), primary key (PK), and notes properties as shown in the Columns category of Figure 2.11 as well as many other properties in the nonselected categories. For relationships (connecting line symbols), Visio supports properties about the definition, name, cardinality, and referential action as shown in Figure 2.12. For additional data dictionary support, custom properties and properties specific to a DBMS can be added.

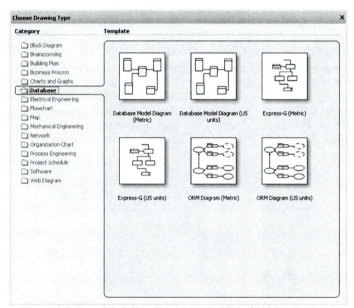

Figure 2.9: Data Modeling Templates in Visio 2003 Professional

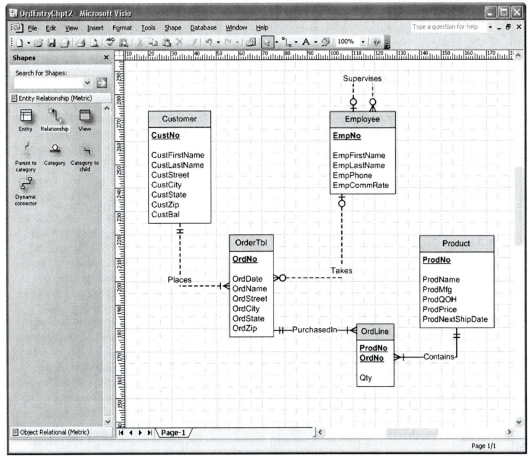

Figure 2.10: Template and Canvas Windows in Visio Professional

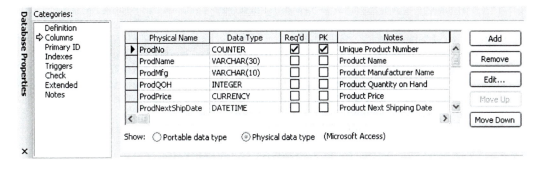

Figure 2.11: Database Properties Window in Visio Professional for the *Product* Entity Type

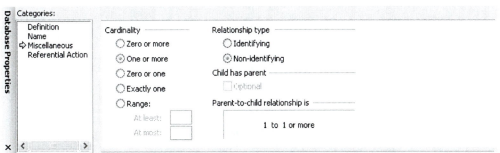

Figure 2.12: Database Properties Window in Visio Professional for the *Places* Relationship

37

Visio provides several analysis and prototyping tools beyond its template and data dictionary features. The analysis tools primarily support the schema conversion task in the logical database design phase. The Refresh Model Wizard detects and resolves differences between a Visio database diagram and an existing relational database. The Reverse Engineer Wizard performs the reverse task of converting a relational database definition into a Visio database diagram. Visio also supports various error checks to ensure consistent database diagrams. For prototyping, Visio can store shapes in relational databases. This feature can be particularly useful for providing a visual interface for hierarchical data such as organization charts and bill of material data. For more powerful prototyping, Visio supports the Visual Basic with Applications (VBA) language, an event-driven language integrated with Microsoft Office.

Closing Thoughts

This chapter initially described the role of databases in information systems and the nature of the database development process. Information systems are collections of related components that produce data for decision making. Databases provide the permanent memory for information systems. Development of an information system involves a repetitive process of analysis, design, and implementation. Database development occurs in all phases of systems development. Because a database is often a crucial part of an information system, database development can be the dominant part of information systems development. Development of the processing and environment interaction components are often performed after the database development. Cross-checking between the database and applications is the link that connects the database development process to the information systems development process.

After presenting the role of databases and the nature of database development, this chapter described the goals, phases, and tools of database development. The goals emphasize both the information content of the database as well as efficient implementation. The phases of database development first establish the information content of the database and then find an efficient implementation. The conceptual data modeling and logical database design phases involve the information content of the database. The distributed database design and physical database design phases involve efficient implementation. Because developing databases can be a challenging process, computer-aided software engineering (CASE) tools have been created to improve productivity. CASE tools can be essential in helping the database designer to draw, document, and prototype the database. In addition, some CASE tools provide active assistance with analyzing a database design.

This chapter provides a context for the chapters in Parts 3 and 4. You might want to reread this chapter after completing the chapters in Parts 3 and 4. The chapters in Parts 3 and 4 provide details about the phases of database development. Chapters 5 and 6 present details of the Entity Relationship Model, data modeling practice using the Entity Relationship Model, and conversion from the Entity Relationship Model to the Relational Model. Chapter 7 presents normalization techniques for relational tables. Chapter 8 presents physical database design techniques.

Review Concepts

- System: related components that work together to accomplish objectives
- Information system: system that accepts, processes, and produces data
- Waterfall model of information systems development: reference framework for activities in the information systems development process
- Spiral development methodologies and rapid application development methodologies to alleviate the problems in the traditional waterfall development approach
- Role of databases in information systems: provide permanent memory
- Define a common vocabulary to unify an organization
- Define business rules to support organizational processes
- Ensure data quality to improve the quality of decision making
- Evaluate investment in data quality using a cost-benefit approach

- Find an efficient implementation to ensure adequate performance while not compromising other design goals
- Conceptual data modeling to represent the information content independent of a target DBMS
- View design and view integration to manage the complexity of large data modeling efforts
- Logical database design to refine a conceptual data model to a target DBMS
- Distributed database design to determine locations of data and processing to achieve an efficient and reliable implementation
- Physical database design to achieve efficient implementations on each computer site
- Develop prototype forms and reports to cross check among the database and applications using the database
- Soft skills for conceptual data modeling: qualitative, subjective, and people-oriented
- Hard skills for finding an efficient implementation: quantitative, objective, and data intensive
- Computer-aided software engineering (CASE) tools to improve productivity in the database development process
- Fundamental assistance of CASE tools: drawing and documenting
- Active assistance of CASE tools: analysis and prototyping

Questions

1. What is the relationship between a system and an information system?
2. Provide an example of a system that is not an information system.
3. For an information system of which you are aware, describe some of the components (input data, output data, people, software, hardware, and procedures).
4. Briefly describe some of the kinds of data in the database for the information system in question 3.
5. Describe the phases of the waterfall model.
6. Why is the waterfall model considered only a reference framework?
7. What are the shortcomings in the waterfall model?
8. What alternative methodologies have been proposed to alleviate the difficulties of the waterfall model?
9. What is the relationship of the database development process to the information systems development process?
10. What is a data model? Process model? Environment interaction model?
11. What is the purpose of prototyping in the information systems development process?
12. How is a database designer like a politician in establishing a common vocabulary?
13. Why should a database designer establish the meaning of data?
14. What factors should a database designer consider when choosing database constraints?
15. Why is data quality important?
16. Provide examples of data quality problems according to two characteristics mentioned in Section 2.2.3.
17. How does a database designer decide on the appropriate level of data quality?
18. Why is it important to find an efficient implementation?
19. What are the inputs and the outputs of the conceptual data modeling phase?
20. What are the inputs and the outputs of the logical database design phase?
21. What are the inputs and the outputs of the distributed database design phase?
22. What are the inputs and the outputs of the physical database design phase?
23. What does it mean to say that the conceptual data modeling phase and the logical database design phase are concerned with the information content of the database?

24. Why are there two phases (conceptual data modeling and logical database design) that involve the information content of the database?
25. What is the relationship of view design and view integration to conceptual data modeling?
26. What is a soft skill?
27. What phases of database development primarily involve soft skills?
28. What is a hard skill?
29. What phases of database development primarily involve hard skills?
30. What kind of background is appropriate for hard skills?
31. Why do large organizations sometimes have different people performing design phases dealing with information content and efficient implementation?
32. Why are CASE tools useful in the database development process?
33. What is the difference between front-end and back-end CASE tools?
34. What kinds of support can a CASE tool provide for drawing a database diagram?
35. What kinds of support can a CASE tool provide for documenting a database design?
36. What kinds of support can a CASE tool provide for analyzing a database design?
37. What kinds of support can a CASE tool provide for prototyping?
38. Should you expect to find one software vendor providing a full range of functions (drawing, documenting, analyzing, and prototyping) for the database development process? Why or why not?

Problems

Because of the introductory nature of this chapter, there are no problems in this chapter. Problems appear at the end of chapters in Parts 3 and 4.

References for Further Study

For a more detailed description of the database development process, you can consult specialized books on database design such as Batini, Ceri, and Navathe (1992) and Teorey (1999). For more details on the systems development process, you can consult books on systems analysis and design such as Whitten and Bentley (2001). For more details about data quality, consult specialized books about data quality including Olson (2002) and Redman (2001) along with the International Conference on Information Quality (mitiq.mit.edu/iciq).

3

The Relational Data Model

Learning Objectives

This chapter provides the foundation for using relational databases. After this chapter the student should have acquired the following knowledge and skills:

- Recognize relational database terminology
- Understand the meaning of the integrity rules for relational databases
- Understand the impact of referenced rows on maintaining relational databases
- Understand the meaning of each relational algebra operator
- List tables that must be combined to obtain desired results for simple retrieval requests

Overview

The chapters in Part 1 provided a starting point for your exploration of database technology and your understanding of the database development process. You broadly learned about database characteristics, DBMS features, the goals of database development, and the phases of the database development process. This chapter narrows your focus to the relational data model. Relational DBMSs dominate the market for business DBMSs. You will undoubtedly use relational DBMSs throughout your career as an information systems professional. This chapter provides background so that you may become proficient in designing databases and developing applications for relational databases in later chapters.

To effectively use a relational database, you need two kinds of knowledge. First, you need to understand the structure and contents of the database tables. Understanding the connections among tables is especially critical because many database retrievals involve multiple tables. To help you understand relational databases, this chapter presents the basic terminology, the integrity rules, and a notation to visualize connections among tables. Second, you need to understand the operators of relational algebra as they are the building blocks of most commercial query languages. Understanding the operators will improve your knowledge of query languages such as SQL. To help you understand the meaning of each operator, this chapter provides a visual representation of each operator and several convenient summaries.

3.1 Basic Elements

Relational database systems were originally developed because of familiarity and simplicity. Because tables are used to communicate ideas in many fields, the terminology of tables, rows, and columns is not intimidating to most users. During the early years of relational databases (1970s), the simplicity and familiarity of relational databases had strong appeal especially as compared to the procedural orientation of other data models that existed at the time. Despite the familiarity and simplicity of relational databases, there is a strong mathematical basis also. The mathematics of relational databases involves conceptualizing tables as sets. The combination of familiarity and simplicity with a mathematical foundation is so powerful that relational DBMSs are commercially dominant.

This section presents the basic terminology of relational databases and introduces the CREATE TABLE statement of the Structured Query Language (SQL). Sections 3.2 through 3.4 provide more detail on the elements defined in this section.

3.1.1 Tables

A relational database consists of a collection of tables. Each table has a heading or definition part and a body or content part. The <u>heading</u> part consists of the table name and the column names. For example, a student table may have columns for student number, name, street address, city, state, zip, class (freshman, sophomore, etc.), major, and cumulative grade point average (GPA). The <u>body</u> shows the rows of the table. Each row in a student table represents a student enrolled at a university. A student table for a major university may have more than 30,000 rows, too many to view at one time.

> **Table**: a two dimensional arrangement of data. A table consists of a heading defining the table name and column names and a body containing rows of data.

To understand a table, it is also useful to view some of its rows. A table listing or datasheet shows the column names in the first row and the body in the other rows. Table 3-1 shows a table listing for the *Student* table. Three sample rows representing university students are displayed. In this book, the naming convention for column names uses a table abbreviation (Std) followed by a descriptive name. Because column names are often used without identifying the associated tables, the abbreviation supports easy table association. Mixed case highlights the different parts of a column name.

Table 3-1: Sample Table Listing of the

StdNo	StdFirstNam	StdLastName	StdCity	StdState	StdZip	StdMajo	StdClass	StdGP
123-45-6789	HOMER	WELLS	SEATTLE	WA	98121-1111	IS	FR	3.00
124-56-7890	BOB	NORBERT	BOTHELL	WA	98011-2121	FIN	JR	2.70
234-56-7890	CANDY	KENDALL	TACOMA	WA	99042-3321	ACCT	JR	3.50

A CREATE TABLE statement can be used to define the heading part of a table. CREATE TABLE is a statement in the Structured Query Language (SQL). Because SQL is an industry standard language, the CREATE TABLE statement can be used to create tables in most DBMSs. The CREATE TABLE statement that follows[1] creates the *Student* table. For each column, the column name and data type are specified. Data types indicate the kind of data (character, numeric, Yes/No, etc.) and permissible operations (numeric operations, string operations etc.) for the column. Each data type has a name (for example, CHAR for character) and usually a length specification. Table 3-2 lists common data types[2] used in relational DBMSs.

> **Data Type**: defines a set of values and permissible operations on the values. Each column of a table is associated with a data type.

```
CREATE TABLE Student
(       StdNo           CHAR(11),
        StdFirstName    VARCHAR(50),
        StdLastName     VARCHAR(50),
        StdCity         VARCHAR(50),
        StdState        CHAR(2),
        StdZip          CHAR(10),
        StdMajor        CHAR(6),
        StdClass        CHAR(6),
        StdGPA          DECIMAL(3,2)
```

---

[1] The CREATE TABLE statements in this chapter conform to the standard SQL syntax. There are slight syntax differences for most commercial DBMSs.

[2] Data types are not standard across relational DBMSs. The data types used in this chapter are specified in the latest SQL standard. Most DBMSs support these data types although the data type names may differ.

Table 3-2: Brief Description of Common SQL Data Types

Data Type	Description
CHAR(L)	For fixed length text entries such as state abbreviations and fixed length zip codes. Each column value using CHAR contains the maximum number of characters (L) even if the actual length is shorter. Most DBMSs have an upper limit on the length (L) such as 255.
VARCHAR(L)	For variable length text such as names and street addresses. Column values using VARCHAR contain only the actual number of characters, not the maximum length for CHAR columns. Most DBMSs have an upper limit on the length such as 255.
FLOAT(P)	For columns containing numeric data with a floating precision such as interest rate calculations and scientific calculations. The precision parameter P indicates the number of significant digits. Most DBMSs have an upper limit on P such as 38. Some DBMSs have two data types, REAL and DOUBLE PRECISION, for low- and high-precision floating point numbers instead of the variable precision with the FLOAT data type.
DATE/TIME	For columns containing dates and times such as an order date. These data types are not standard across DBMSs. Some systems support three data types (DATE, TIME, and TIMESTAMP) while other systems support a combined data type (DATE) storing both the date and time.
DECIMAL(W,R)	For columns containing numeric data with a fixed precision such as monetary amounts. The W value indicates the total number of digits and the R value indicates the number of digits to the right of the decimal point. This data type is also called NUMERIC in some systems.
INTEGER	For columns containing whole numbers (i.e., numbers without a decimal point). Some DBMSs have the SMALLINT data type for very small whole numbers and the LONG data type for very large integers.
BOOLEAN	For columns containing data with two values such as true/false or yes/no.

3.1.2 Connections among Tables

It is not enough to understand each table individually. To understand a relational database, connections or <u>relationships</u> among tables also must be understood. The rows in a table are usually related to rows in other tables. Matching (identical) values indicate relationships between tables. Consider the sample *Enrollment* table (Table 3-3) in which each row represents a student enrolled in an offering of a course. The values in the *StdNo* column of the *Enrollment* table match the *StdNo* values in the sample *Student* table (Table 3-1). For example, the first and third rows of the *Enrollment* table have the same *StdNo* value (123-45-6789) as the first row of the *Student* table. Likewise, the values in the *OfferNo* column of the *Enrollment* table match the *OfferNo* column in the *Offering* table (Table 3-4). Figure 3.1 shows a graphical depiction of the matching values.

> **Relationship**: connection between rows in two tables. Relationships are shown by column values in one table that match column values in another table.

Table 3-3: Sample Enrollment Table

OfferNo	StdNo	EnrGrade
1234	123-45-6789	3.3
1234	234-56-7890	3.5
4321	123-45-6789	3.5
4321	124-56-7890	3.2

Table 3-4: Sample Offering Table

OfferNo	CourseN	OffTerm	OffYear	OffLocation	OffTime	FacNo	OffDays
1111	is320	summer	2008	BLM302	10:30 AM		MW
1234	is320	fall	2007	BLM302	10:30 AM	098-76-5432	MW
2222	is460	summer	2007	BLM412	1:30 PM		TTH
3333	is320	spring	2008	BLM214	8:30 AM	098-76-5432	MW
4321	is320	fall	2007	BLM214	3:30 PM	098-76-5432	TTH
4444	is320	spring	2008	BLM302	3:30 PM	543-21-0987	TTH
5678	is480	spring	2008	BLM302	10:30 AM	987-65-4321	MW
5679	is480	spring	2008	BLM412	3:30 PM	876-54-3210	TTH
9876	is460	spring	2008	BLM307	1:30 PM	654-32-1098	TTH

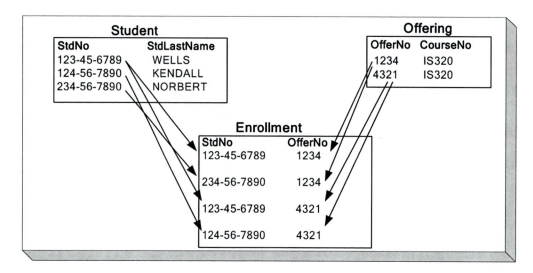

Figure 3.1: Matching Values among the Enrollment, Offering, and Student Tables

The concept of matching values is crucial in relational databases. As you will see, relational databases typically contain many tables. Even a modest-size database can have 10 to 15 tables. Large databases can have hundreds of tables. To extract meaningful information, it is often necessary to combine multiple tables using matching values. By matching on *Student.StdNo* and *Enrollment.StdNo*, you could combine the *Student* and *Enrollment* tables[5]. Similarly, by matching on *Enrollment.OfferNo* and *Offering.OfferNo*, you could combine the *Enrollment* and *Offering* tables. As you will see later in this chapter, the operation of combining tables on matching values is known as a join. Understanding the connections between tables (or ways that tables can be combined) is crucial for extracting useful data.

3.1.3 Alternative Terminology

You should be aware that other terminology is used besides table, row, and column. Table 3-5 shows three roughly equivalent terminologies. The divergence in terminology is due to the different groups that use databases. The table-oriented terminology appeals to end users; the set-oriented terminology appeals to academic researchers; and the record-oriented terminology appeals to information systems professionals. In practice, these terms may be mixed. For

---

[5] When columns have identical names in two tables, it is customary to precede the column name with the table name and a period as *Student.StdNo* and *Enrollment.StdNo*.

example, in the same sentence you might hear both "tables" and "fields." You should expect to see a mix of terminology in your career.

Table 3-5: Alternative Terminology for Relational Databases

Table-Oriented	Set-Oriented	Record-Oriented
Table	Relation	Record type, file
Row	Tuple	Record
Column	Attribute	Field

3.2 Integrity Rules

In the previous section, you learned that a relational database consists of a collection of interrelated tables. To ensure that a database provides meaningful information, integrity rules are necessary. This section describes two important integrity rules (entity integrity and referential integrity), examples of their usage, and a notation to visualize referential integrity.

3.2.1 Definition of the Integrity Rules

Entity integrity[6] means that each table must have a column or combination of columns with unique values. Unique means that no two rows of a table have the same value. For example, *StdNo* in *Student* is unique and the combination of *StdNo* and *OfferNo* is unique in *Enrollment*. Entity integrity ensures that entities (people, things, and events) are uniquely identified in a database. For auditing, security, and communication reasons, it is important that business entities be easily traceable.

Referential integrity means that the column values in one table must match column values in a related table. For example, the value of *StdNo* in each row of the *Enrollment* table must match the value of *StdNo* in some row of the *Student* table. Referential integrity ensures that a database contains valid connections. For example, it is critical that each row of the *Enrollment* table contains a student number of a valid student. Otherwise, some enrollments can be meaningless, possibly resulting in students denied enrollment because non existing students took their places.

For more precise definitions of entity integrity and referential integrity, some other definitions are necessary. These prerequisite definitions and the more precise definitions follow.

Definitions

Superkey: a column or combination of columns containing unique values for each row. The combination of every column in a table is always a superkey because rows in a table must be unique[7].

Candidate key: a minimal superkey. A superkey is minimal if removing any column makes it no longer unique.

Null value: a special value that represents the absence of an actual value. A null value can mean that the actual value is unknown or does not apply to the given row.

Primary key: a specially designated candidate key. The primary key for a table cannot contain null values.

Foreign key: a column or combination of columns in which the values must match those of a candidate key. A foreign key must have the same data type as its associated candidate key. In the

[6] Entity integrity is also known as uniqueness integrity.

[7] The uniqueness of rows is a feature of the relational model that SQL does not require.

CREATE TABLE statement of SQL, a foreign key must be associated with a primary key rather than merely a candidate key.

Integrity Rules

Entity integrity rule: No two rows of a table can contain the same value for the primary key. In addition, no row can contain a null value for any column of a primary key.
Referential integrity rule: Only two kinds of values can be stored in a foreign key:
a value matching a candidate key value in some row of the table containing the associated candidate key or a null value.

3.2.2 Application of the Integrity Rules

To extend your understanding, let us apply the integrity rules to several tables in the university database. The primary key of *Student* is *StdNo*. A primary key can be designated as part of the CREATE TABLE statement. To designate *StdNo* as the primary key of *Student*, you use a CONSTRAINT clause for the primary key at the end of the CREATE TABLE statement. The constraint name (PKStudent) following the CONSTRAINT keyword facilitates identification of the constraint if a violation occurs when a row is inserted or updated.

```
CREATE TABLE Student
(       StdNo           CHAR(11),
        StdFirstName    VARCHAR(50),
        StdLastName     VARCHAR(50),
        StdCity         VARCHAR(50),
        StdState        CHAR(2),
        StdZip          CHAR(10),
        StdMajor        CHAR(6),
        StdClass        CHAR(2),
        StdGPA          DECIMAL(3,2),
CONSTRAINT PKStudent PRIMARY KEY (StdNo)    )
```

Many organizations including universities used to use Social Security numbers as unique identifiers. Because of the increase in identity theft, most organizations have eliminated the usage of Social Security numbers. Instead, organizations have generated unique identifiers specific to the organization. For example, customer numbers, product numbers, and employee numbers are typically assigned by the organization controlling the underlying database. In these cases, automatic generation of unique values is required. Some DBMSs support automatic generation of unique values as explained in Appendix 3.C.

Entity Integrity Variations

Candidate keys that are not primary keys are declared with the UNIQUE keyword. The *Course* table (see Table 3-6) contains two candidate keys: *CourseNo* (primary key) and *CrsDesc* (course description). The *CourseNo* column is the primary key because it is more stable than the *CrsDesc* column. Course descriptions may change over time, but course numbers remain the same.

Table 3-6: Sample Course Table

CourseNo	CrsDesc	CrsUnits
is320	fundamentals of business programming	4
is460	systems analysis	4
is470	business data communications	4
is480	fundamentals of database management	4

```
CREATE TABLE Course
(     CourseNo           CHAR(6),
      CrsDesc            VARCHAR(250),
      CrsUnits           SMALLINT,
CONSTRAINT PKCourse PRIMARY KEY(CourseNo),
CONSTRAINT UniqueCrsDesc UNIQUE (CrsDesc)   )
```

Some tables need more than one column in the primary key. In the *Enrollment* table, the combination of *StdNo* and *OfferNo* is the only candidate key and thus the primary key. Both columns are needed to identify a row. A primary key consisting of more than one column is known as a composite or a combined primary key.

```
CREATE TABLE Enrollment
(     OfferNo            INTEGER,
      StdNo              CHAR(11),
      EnrGrade           DECIMAL(3,2),
CONSTRAINT PKEnrollment PRIMARY KEY(OfferNo, StdNo)  )
```

Superkeys that are not candidate keys are not important. Recall that a candidate key is a minimal superkey. Nonminimal superkeys are not important because they are common and contain columns that do not contribute to the uniqueness property. For example, the combination of *StdNo* and *StdLastName* is unique. However, if *StdLastName* is removed, *StdNo* is still unique.

Referential Integrity

For referential integrity, the columns *StdNo* and *OfferNo* are foreign keys in the *Enrollment* table. The *StdNo* column refers to the *Student* table and the *OfferNo* column refers to the *Offering* table (Table 3-4). An *Offering* row represents a course given in an academic period (summer, winter, etc.), year, time, location, and days of the week. The primary key of *Offering* is *OfferNo*. A course such as IS480 will have different offer numbers each time it is taught.

Referential integrity constraints can be defined similarly to the way of defining primary keys. For example, to define the foreign keys in *Enrollment*, you should use CONSTRAINT clauses for foreign keys at the end of the CREATE TABLE statement as shown in the revised CREATE TABLE statement for the *Enrollment* table.

```
CREATE TABLE Enrollment
(     OfferNo            INTEGER,
      StdNo              CHAR(11),
      EnrGrade           DECIMAL(3,2),
CONSTRAINT PKEnrollment PRIMARY KEY(OfferNo, StdNo),
CONSTRAINT FKOfferNo FOREIGN KEY (OfferNo) REFERENCES Offering,
CONSTRAINT FKStdNo FOREIGN KEY (StdNo) REFERENCES Student  )
```

Although referential integrity permits foreign keys to have null values, it is not common for foreign keys to have null values. When a foreign key is part of a primary key, null values are not permitted because of the entity integrity rule. For example, null values are not permitted for either *Enrollment.StdNo* or *Enrollment.OfferNo* because each column is part of the primary key.

When a foreign key is not part of a primary key, usage dictates whether null values should be permitted. For example, *Offering.CourseNo*, a foreign key referring to *Course* (Table 3-4), is not part of a primary key yet null values are not permitted. In most universities, a course cannot be offered before it is approved. Thus, an offering should not be inserted without a related course.

The NOT NULL keywords indicate that a column cannot have null values as shown in the CREATE TABLE statement for the *Offering* table. The NOT NULL constraints are inline constraints associated with a specific column. In contrast, the primary and foreign key constraints in the CREATE TABLE statement for the *Offering* table are table constraints in which the associated columns must be specified in the constraint. Constraint names should be used with both table and inline constraints to facilitate identification when a violation occurs.

In contrast, *Offering.FacNo* referring to the faculty member teaching the offering may be null. The *Faculty* table (Table 3-7) stores data about instructors of courses. A null value for *Offering.FacNo* means that a faculty member is not yet assigned to teach the offering. For example, an instructor is not assigned in the first and third rows of Table 3-4. Because offerings must be scheduled perhaps a year in advance, it is likely that instructors for some offerings will not be known until after the offering row is initially stored. Therefore, permitting null values in the *Offering* table is prudent.

```
CREATE TABLE Offering
(     OfferNo          INTEGER,
      CourseNo         CHAR(6)
                       CONSTRAINT OffCourseNoRequired NOT NULL,
      OffLocation      VARCHAR(50),
      OffDays          CHAR(6),
      OffTerm          CHAR(6)
                       CONSTRAINT OffTermRequired NOT NULL,
      OffYear          INTEGER
                       CONSTRAINT OffYearRequired NOT NULL,
      FacNo            CHAR(11),
      OffTime          DATE,
CONSTRAINT PKOffering PRIMARY KEY (OfferNo),
CONSTRAINT FKCourseNo FOREIGN KEY(CourseNo) REFERENCES Course,
CONSTRAINT FKFacNo    FOREIGN KEY(FacNo) REFERENCES Faculty )
```

Table 3-7a: Sample Faculty Table (Part 1)

FacNo	FacFirstName	FacLastName	FacCity	FacState	FacZipCode
098-76-5432	LEONARD	VINCE	SEATTLE	WA	98111-9921
543-21-0987	VICTORIA	EMMANUEL	BOTHELL	WA	98011-2242
654-32-1098	LEONARD	FIBON	SEATTLE	WA	98121-0094
765-43-2109	NICKI	MACON	BELLEVUE	WA	98015-9945
876-54-3210	CRISTOPHER	COLAN	SEATTLE	WA	98114-1332
987-65-4321	JULIA	MILLS	SEATTLE	WA	98114-9954

Table 3-7b: Sample Faculty Table (Part 2)

FacNo	FacDept	FacRank	FacSalary	FacSupervisor	FacHireDate
098-76-5432	MS	ASST	$35,000	654-32-1098	10-Apr-1997
543-21-0987	MS	PROF	$120,000		15-Apr-1998
654-32-1098	MS	ASSC	$70,000	543-21-0987	01-May-1996
765-43-2109	FIN	PROF	$65,000		11-Apr-1999
876-54-3210	MS	ASST	$40,000	654-32-1098	01-Mar-2001
987-65-4321	FIN	ASSC	$75,000	765-43-2109	15-Mar-2002

Referential Integrity for Self-Referencing (Unary) Relationships

A referential integrity constraint involving a single table is known as a <u>self-referencing</u> relationship or unary relationship. Self-referencing relationships are not common, but they are important when they occur. In the university database, a faculty member can supervise other faculty members and be supervised by a faculty member. For example, Victoria Emmanuel (second row) supervises Leonard Fibon (third row). The *FacSupervisor* column shows this relationship: the *FacSupervisor* value in the third row (543-21-0987) matches the *FacNo* value in the second row. A referential integrity constraint involving the *FacSupervisor* column represents the self-referencing relationship. In the CREATE TABLE statement, the referential integrity constraint for a self-referencing relationship can be written the same way as other referential integrity constraints.

> **Self-Referencing Relationship**: a relationship in which a foreign key refers to the same table. Self-referencing relationships represent associations among members of the same set.

```
CREATE TABLE Faculty
( FacNo        CHAR(11),
  FacFirstName  VARCHAR(50)
                CONSTRAINT FacFirstNameRequired NOT NULL,
  FacLastName   VARCHAR(50)
                CONSTRAINT FacLastNameRequired NOT NULL,
  FacCity       VARCHAR(50) CONSTRAINT FacCityRequired NOT NULL,
  FacState      CHAR(2)  CONSTRAINT FacStateRequired NOT NULL,
  FacZipCode    CHAR(10) CONSTRAINT FacZipRequired NOT NULL,
  FacHireDate   DATE,
  FacDept       CHAR(6),
  FacRank       CHAR(4),
  FacSalary     DECIMAL(10,2),
  FacSupervisor CHAR(11),
CONSTRAINT PKFaculty PRIMARY KEY (FacNo),
CONSTRAINT FKFacSupervisor
          FOREIGN KEY (FacSupervisor) REFERENCES Faculty )
```

3.2.3 Graphical Representation of Referential Integrity

In recent years, commercial DBMSs have provided graphical representations for referential integrity constraints. The graphical representation makes referential integrity easier to define and understand than the text representation in the CREATE TABLE statement. In addition, a graphical representation supports nonprocedural data access.

To depict a graphical representation, let us study the Relationship window in Microsoft Access. Access provides the Relationship window to visually define and display referential integrity constraints. Figure 3.2 shows the Relationship window for the tables of the university database. Each line represents a referential integrity constraint or relationship. In a relationship, the primary key table is known as the parent or "1" table (for example, *Student*) and the foreign key table (for example, *Enrollment*) is known as the child or "M" (many) table.

The relationship from *Student* to *Enrollment* is called "1-M" (one-to-many) because a student can be related to many enrollments but an enrollment can be related to only one student. Similarly, the relationship from the *Offering* table to the *Enrollment* table means that an offering can be related to many enrollments but an enrollment can be related to only one offering. You should practice by writing similar sentences for the other relationships in Figure 3.2.

> **1-M Relationship**: a connection between two tables in which one row of a parent table can be referenced by many rows of a child table. 1-M relationships are the most common kind of relationship.

M-N (many-to-many) relationships are not directly represented in the Relational Model. An M-N relationship means that rows from each table can be related to many rows of the other table. For example, a student enrolls in many course offerings and a course offering contains many students. In the Relational Model, a pair of 1-M relationships and a linking or associative table represents an M-N relationship. In Figure 3.2, the linking table *Enrollment* and its relationships with *Offering* and *Student* represent an M-N relationship between the *Student* and *Offering* tables.

> **M-N Relationship:** a connection between two tables in which rows of each table can be related to many rows of the other table. M-N relationships cannot be directly represented in the Relational Model. Two 1-M relationships and a linking or associative table represent an M-N relationship.

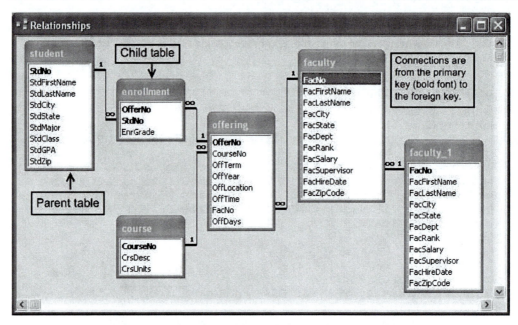

Figure 3.2: Relationship Window for the University Database

Self-referencing relationships are represented indirectly in the Relationship window. The self-referencing relationship involving *Faculty* is represented as a relationship between the *Faculty* and *Faculty_1* tables. *Faculty_1* is not a real table as it is created only inside the Access Relationship window. Access can only indirectly show self-referencing relationships.

A graphical representation such as the Relationship window makes it easy to identify tables that should be combined to answer a retrieval request. For example, assume that you want to find instructors who teach courses with "database" in the course description. Clearly, you need the *Course* table to find "database" courses. You also need the *Faculty* table to display instructor data. Figure 3.2 shows that you also need the *Offering* table because *Course* and *Faculty* are not directly connected. Rather, *Course* and *Faculty* are connected through *Offering*. Thus, visualizing relationships helps to identify tables needed to fulfill retrieval requests. Before attempting the retrieval problems in later chapters, you should carefully study a graphical representation of the relationships. You should construct your own diagram if one is not available.

3.3 Delete and Update Actions for Referenced Rows

For each referential integrity constraint, you should carefully consider actions on <u>referenced</u> rows in parent tables of 1-M relationships. A parent row is referenced if there are rows in a child table with foreign key values identical to the primary key value of the parent table row. For example, the first row of the *Course* table (Table 3-6) with *CourseNo* "IS320" is referenced by the first row of the *Offering* table (Table 3-4). It is natural to consider what happens to related *Offering* rows when the referenced *Course* row is deleted or the *CourseNo* is updated. More generally, these concerns can be stated as actions on referenced rows are important when changing the rows of a database. When developing data entry forms (discussed in Chapter 10), actions on referenced rows can be especially important. For example, if a data entry form permits deletion of rows in the *Course* table, actions on related rows in the *Offering* table must be carefully planned. Otherwise, the database can become inconsistent or difficult to use.

Possible Actions

There are several possible actions in response to the deletion of a referenced row or the update of the primary key of a referenced row. The appropriate action depends on the tables involved. The following list describes the actions and provides examples of usage.

Restrict[1]: Do not allow the action on the referenced row. For example, do not permit a *Student* row to be deleted if there are any related *Enrollment* rows. Similarly, do not allow *Student.StdNo* to be changed if there are related *Enrollment* rows.

Cascade: Perform the same action (cascade the action) to related rows. For example, if a *Student* is deleted, then delete the related *Enrollment* rows. Likewise, if *Student.StdNo* is changed in some row, update *StdNo* in the related *Enrollment* rows.

Nullify: Set the foreign key of related rows to null. For example, if a *Faculty* row is deleted, then set *FacNo* to NULL in related *Offering* rows. Likewise, if *Faculty.FacNo* is updated, then set *FacNo* to NULL in related *Offering* rows. The nullify action is not permitted if the foreign key does not allow null values. For example, the nullify option is not valid when deleting rows of the *Student* table because *Enrollment.StdNo* is part of the primary key.

Default: Set the foreign key of related rows to its default value. For example, if a *Faculty* row is deleted, then set *FacNo* to a default faculty in related *Offering* rows. The default faculty might have an interpretation such as "to be announced". Likewise, if *Faculty.FacNo* is updated, then set *FacNo* to its default value in related *Offering* rows. The default action is an alternative to the nullify action as the default action avoids null values.

The delete and update actions can be specified in SQL using the ON DELETE and ON UPDATE clauses. These clauses are part of foreign key constraints. For example, the revised CREATE TABLE statement for the *Enrollment* table shows ON UPDATE clauses for the *Enrollment* table. The ON DELETE clause is not used because the default is to restrict deletions with referenced rows[2]. The keywords CASCADE, SET NULL, and SET DEFAULT can be used to specify the second through fourth options, respectively.

```
CREATE TABLE Enrollment
(      OfferNo          INTEGER,
       StdNo            CHAR(11),
       EnrGrade         DECIMAL(3,2),
CONSTRAINT PKEnrollment PRIMARY KEY(OfferNo, StdNo),
CONSTRAINT FKOfferNo FOREIGN KEY (OfferNo) REFERENCES Offering
  ON UPDATE CASCADE,
CONSTRAINT FKStdNo FOREIGN KEY (StdNo) REFERENCES Student
  ON UPDATE CASCADE )
```

Before finishing this section, you should understand the impact of referenced rows on insert operations. A referenced row must be inserted before its related rows. For example, before inserting a row in the *Enrollment* table, the referenced rows in the *Student* and *Offering* tables must exist. Referential integrity places an ordering on insertion of rows from different tables.

---

[1] There is a related action designated by the keywords NO ACTION. The difference between RESTRICT and NO ACTION involves the concept of deferred integrity constraints, discussed in Chapter 15.
[2] Note that the RESTRICT keyword is not valid syntax in Oracle. No specification for the referenced row action must be used in Oracle for the restrict action.

When designing data entry forms, you should carefully consider the impact of referential integrity on the order that users complete forms.

3.4 Operators of Relational Algebra

In previous sections of this chapter, you have studied the terminology and integrity rules of relational databases with the goal of understanding existing relational databases. In particular, understanding connections among tables was emphasized as a prerequisite to retrieving useful information. This section describes some fundamental operators that can be used to retrieve useful information from a relational database.

You can think of relational algebra similarly to the algebra of numbers except that the objects are different: algebra applies to numbers and relational algebra applies to tables. In algebra, each operator transforms one or more numbers into another number. Similarly, each operator of relational algebra transforms a table (or two tables) into a new table.

This section emphasizes the study of each relational algebra operator in isolation. For each operator, you should understand its purpose and inputs. While it is possible to combine operators to make complicated formulas, this level of understanding is not important for developing query formulation skills. Using relational algebra by itself to write queries can be awkward because of details such as ordering of operations and parentheses. Therefore, you should seek only to understand the meaning of each operator, not how to combine operators to write expressions. You will use the SELECT statement of SQL to perform retrievals that would involve complex combinations of relational algebra operators.

The coverage of relational algebra groups the operators into three categories. The most widely used operators (restrict, project, and join) are presented first. The extended cross product operator is also presented to provide background for the join operator. Knowledge of these operators will help you to formulate a large percentage of queries. More specialized operators are covered in latter parts of the section. The more specialized operators include the traditional set operators (union, intersection, and difference) and advanced operators (summarize and divide). Knowledge of these operators will help you formulate more difficult queries.

3.4.1 Restrict (Select) and Project Operators

The restrict[1] (also known as select) and project operators produce subsets of a table. Because users often want to see a subset rather than an entire table, these operators are widely used. These operators are also popular because they are easy to understand.

The restrict and project operators produce an output table that is a subset of an input table (Figure 3.3). Restrict produces a subset of the rows, while project produces a subset of the columns. Restrict uses a condition or logical expression to indicate the rows to retain in the output. Project uses a list of column names to indicate the columns to retain in the output. Restrict and project are often used together because tables can have many rows and columns. It is rare that a user wants to see all rows and columns.

> **Restrict:** an operator that retrieves a subset of the rows of the input table that satisfy a given condition.

> **Project:** an operator that retrieves a specified subset of the columns of the input table.

The logical expression used in the restrict operator can include comparisons involving columns and constants. Complex logical expressions can be formed using the logical operators AND, OR,

---

[1] In this book, the operator name restrict is used to avoid confusion with the SQL SELECT statement. The operator is more widely known as select.

and NOT. For example, Table 3-8 shows the result of a restrict operation on Table 3-4 where the logical expression is: OffDays = 'MW' AND OffTerm = 'SPRING' AND OffYear = 2008.

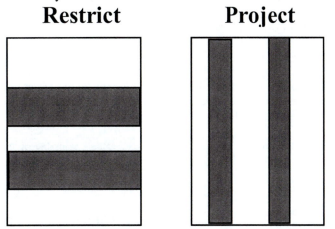

Figure 3.3: Graphical Representation of Restrict and Project Operators

Table 3-8: Result of Restrict Operation on the Sample Offering Table (Table 3-4)

OfferN	CourseN	OffTer	OffYear	OffLocation	OffTime	FacNo	OffDays
3333	is320	spring	2008	BLM214	8:30 AM	098-76-5432	MW
5678	is480	spring	2008	BLM302	10:30 AM	987-65-4321	MW

A project operation can have a side effect. Sometimes after a subset of columns is retrieved, there are duplicate rows. When this occurs, the project operator removes the duplicate rows. For example, if *Offering.CourseNo* is the only column used in a project operation, only

three rows are in the result (Table 3-9) even though the *Offering* table (Table 3-4) has nine rows. The column *Offering.CourseNo* contains only three unique values in Table 3-4. Note that if the primary key or a candidate key is included in the list of columns, the resulting table has no duplicates. For example, if *OfferNo* was included in the list of columns, the result table would have nine rows with no duplicate removal necessary.

Table 3-9: Result of a Project Operation on *Offering.CourseNo*

CourseNo
is320
is460
is480

This side effect is due to the mathematical nature of relational algebra. In relational algebra, tables are considered sets. Because sets do not have duplicates, duplicate removal is a possible side effect of the project operator. Commercial languages such as SQL usually take a more pragmatic view. Because duplicate removal can be computationally expensive, duplicates are not removed unless the user specifically requests it.

3.4.2 Extended Cross Product Operator

The extended cross product operator can combine any two tables. Other table combining operators have conditions about the tables to combine. Because of its unrestricted nature, the extended cross product operator can produce tables with excessive data. The extended cross product operator is important because it is a building block for the join operator. When you initially learn the join operator, knowledge of the extended cross product operator can be useful. After you gain experience with the join operator, you will not need to rely on the extended cross product operator.

The extended cross product[1] (product for short) operator shows everything possible from two tables. The product of two tables is a new table consisting of all possible combinations of rows from the two input tables. Figure 3.4 depicts a product of two single column tables. Each result row consists of the columns of the *Faculty* table (only *FacNo*) and the columns of the *Student* table (only *StdNo*). The name of the operator (product) derives from the number of rows in the result. The number of rows in the resulting table is the product of the number of rows of the two input tables. In contrast, the number of result columns is the sum of the columns of the two input tables. In Figure 3.4, the result table has nine rows and two columns.

Extended Cross Product: an operator that builds a table consisting of all combinations of rows from each of the two input tables.

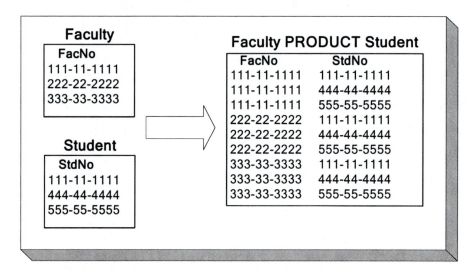

Figure 3.4: Cross Product Example

As another example, consider the product of the sample *Student* (Table 3-10) and *Enrollment* (Table 3-11) tables. The resulting table (Table 3-12) has 9 rows (3 × 3) and 7 columns (4 + 3). Note that most rows in the result are not meaningful as only three rows have the same value for *StdNo*.

Table 3-10: Sample *Student* Table

StdNo	StdLastName	StdMajor	StdClass
123-45-6789	WELLS	IS	FR
124-56-7890	NORBERT	FIN	JR
234-56-7890	KENDALL	ACCT	JR

Table 3-11: Sample *Enrollment* Table

OfferNo	StdNo	EnrGrade
1234	123-45-6789	3.3
1234	234-56-7890	3.5
4321	124-56-7890	3.2

---

[1] The extended cross product operator is also known as the Cartesian product after the French mathematician René Descartes.

Table 3-12: *Student* PRODUCT *Enrollment*

Student.StdNo	StdLastName	StdMajor	StdClass	OfferNo	Enrollment.StdNo	EnrGrade
123-45-6789	Wells	IS	FR	1234	123-45-6789	3.3
123-45-6789	Wells	IS	FR	1234	234-56-7890	3.5
123-45-6789	Wells	IS	FR	4321	124-56-7890	3.2
124-56-7890	Norbert	FIN	JR	1234	123-45-6789	3.3
124-56-7890	Norbert	FIN	JR	1234	234-56-7890	3.5
124-56-7890	Norbert	FIN	JR	4321	124-56-7890	3.2
234-56-7890	Kendall	ACCT	JR	1234	123-45-6789	3.3
234-56-7890	Kendall	ACCT	JR	1234	234-56-7890	3.5
234-56-7890	Kendall	ACCT	JR	4321	124-56-7890	3.2

As these examples show, the extended cross product operator often generates excessive data. Excessive data are as bad as lack of data. For example, the product of a student table of 30,000 rows and an enrollment table of 300,000 rows is a table of nine billion rows! Most of these rows would be meaningless combinations. So it is rare that a cross product operation by itself is needed. Rather, the importance of the cross product operator is as a building block for other operators such as the join operator.

3.4.3 Join Operator

Join is the most widely used operator for combining tables. Because most databases have many tables, combining tables is important. Join differs from cross product because join requires a matching condition on rows of two tables. Most tables are combined in this way. To a large extent, your skill in retrieving useful data will depend on your ability to use the join operator.

The join operator builds a new table by combining rows from two tables that match on a join condition. Typically, the join condition specifies that two rows have an identical value in one or more columns. When the join condition involves equality, the join is known as an equi-join, for equality join. Figure 3.5 shows a join of sample *Faculty* and *Offering* tables where the join condition is that the *FacNo* columns are equal. Note that only a few columns are shown to simplify the illustration. The arrows indicate the manner that rows from the input tables combine to form rows in the result table. For example, the first row of the *Faculty* table combines with the first and third rows of the *Offering* table to yield two rows in the result table.

> **Join:** an operator that produces a table containing rows that match on a condition involving a column from each input table.

The natural join operator is the most common join operation. In a natural join operation, the join condition is equality (equi-join), one of the join columns is removed, and the join columns have the same unqualified[1] name. In Figure 3.5, the result table contains only three columns because the natural join removes one of the *FacNo* columns. The particular column (*Faculty.FacNo* or *Offering.FacNo*) removed does not matter.

> **Natural Join:** a commonly used join operator where the matching condition is equality (equi-join), one of the matching columns is discarded in the result table, and the join columns have the same unqualified names.

---

[1] An unqualified name is the column name without the table name. The full name of a column includes the table name. Thus, the full names of the join columns in Figure 3.5 are *Faculty.FacNo* and *Offering.FacNo*.

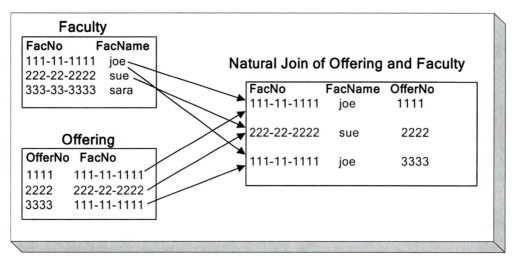

Figure 3.5: Sample Natural Join Operation

As another example, consider the natural join of *Student* (Table 3-13) and *Enrollment* (Table 3-14) shown in Table 3-15. In each row of the result, *Student.StdNo* matches *Enrollment.StdNo*. Only one of the join columns is included in the result. Arbitrarily, *Student.StdNo* is shown although *Enrollment.StdNo* could be included without changing the result.

Table 3-13: Sample Student Table

StdNo	StdLastName	StdMajor	StdClass
123-45-6789	WELLS	IS	FR
124-56-7890	NORBERT	FIN	JR
234-56-7890	KENDALL	ACCT	JR

Table 3-14: Sample Enrollment Table

OfferNo	StdNo	EnrGrade
1234	123-45-6789	3.3
1234	234-56-7890	3.5
4321	124-56-7890	3.2

Table 3-15: Natural Join of *Student* and *Enrollment*

Student.StdNo	StdLastName	StdMajor	StdClass	OfferNo	EnrGrade
123-45-6789	Wells	IS	FR	1234	3.3
124-56-7890	Norbert	FIN	JR	4321	3.2
234-56-7890	Kendall	ACCT	JR	1234	3.5

Derivation of the Natural Join

The natural join operator is not primitive because it can be derived from other operators. The natural join operator consists of three steps:

1. A product operation to combine the rows.
2. A restrict operation to remove rows not satisfying the join condition.
3. A project operation to remove one of the join columns.

To depict these steps, the first step to produce the natural join in Table 3-15 is the product result shown in Table 3-12. The second step is to retain only the matching rows (rows 1, 6, and 8 of Table 3-12). A restrict operation is used with Student.StdNo = Enrollment.StdNo as the restriction condition. The final step is to eliminate one of the join columns (*Enrollment.StdNo*). The project operation includes all columns except for *Enrollment.StdNo*.

Although the join operator is not primitive, it can be conceptualized directly without its primitive operations. When you are initially learning the join operator, it can be helpful to derive the results using the underlying operations. As an exercise, you are encouraged to derive the result in Figure 3.5. After learning the join operator, you should not need to use the underlying operations.

Visual Formulation of Join Operations

As a query formulation aid, many DBMSs provide a visual way to formulate joins. Microsoft Access provides a visual representation of the join operator using the Query Design window. Figure 3.6 depicts a join between *Student* and *Enrollment* on *StdNo* using the Query Design window. To form this join, you need only to select the tables. Access determines that you should join over the *StdNo* column. Access assumes that most joins involve a primary key and foreign key combination. If Access chooses the join condition incorrectly, you can choose other join columns.

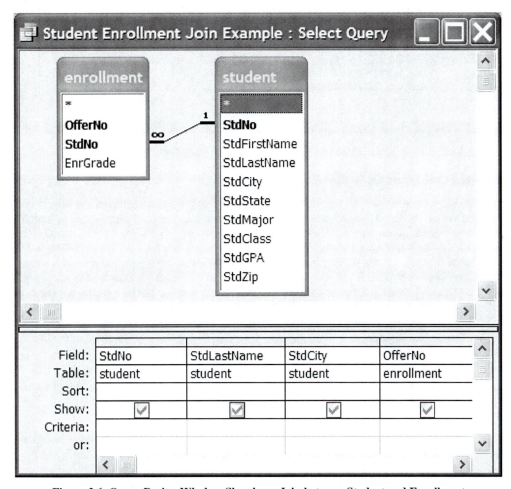

Figure 3.6: Query Design Window Showing a Join between Student and Enrollment

3.4.4 Outer Join Operator

The result of a join operation includes the rows matching on the join condition. Sometimes it is useful to include both matching and nonmatching rows. For example, you may want to know offerings that have an assigned instructor as well as offerings without an assigned instructor. In these situations, the outer join operator is useful.

The <u>outer join</u> operator provides the ability to preserve <u>nonmatching rows</u> in the result as well as to include the matching rows. Figure 3.7 depicts an outer join between sample *Faculty* and *Offering* tables. Note that each table has one row that does not match any row in the other table. The third row of *Faculty* and the fourth row of *Offering* do not have matching rows in the other table. For nonmatching rows, null values are used to complete the column values in the other table. In Figure 3.7, blanks (no values) represent null values. The fourth result row is the nonmatched row of *Faculty* with a null value for the *OfferNo* column. Likewise, the fifth result row contains a null value for the first two columns because it is a nonmatched row of *Offering*.

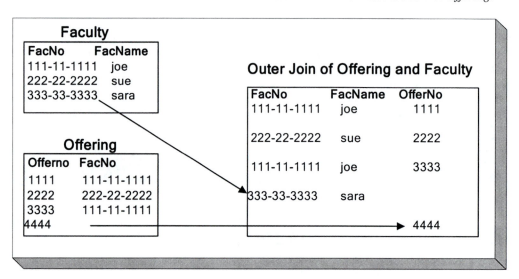

Figure 3.7: Sample Outer Join Operation

Full versus One-Sided Outer Join Operators

The outer join operator has two variations. The <u>full outer join</u> preserves nonmatching rows from both input tables. Figure 3.7 shows a full outer join because the nonmatching rows from both tables are preserved in the result. Because it is sometimes useful to preserve the nonmatching rows from just one input table, the <u>one-sided</u> outer join operator has been devised. In Figure 3.7, only the first four rows of the result would appear for a one-sided outer join that preserves the rows of the *Faculty* table. The last row would not appear in the result because it is an unmatched row of the *Offering* table. Similarly, only the first three rows and the last row would appear in the result for a one-sided outer join that preserves the rows of the *Offering* table.

> **Full Outer Join:** an operator that produces the matching rows (the join part) as well as the non-matching rows from both input tables.

> **One-Sided Outer Join:** an operator that produces the matching rows (the join part) as well as the non-matching rows from the designated input table.

The outer join is useful in two situations. A full outer join can be used to combine two tables with some common columns and some unique columns. For example, to combine the *Student* and *Faculty* tables on *FacNo* and *StdNo*, a full outer join can be used to show all columns about all university people. In Table 3-18, the first two rows are only from the sample *Student* table (Table 3-16), while the last two rows are only from the sample *Faculty* table (Table 3-17). Note the use of null values for the columns from the other table. The third row in Table 3-18 is the row common to the sample *Faculty* and *Student* tables.

Table 3-16: Sample *Student* Table

StdNo	StdLastName	StdMajor	StdClass
123-45-6789	WELLS	IS	FR
124-56-7890	NORBERT	FIN	JR
876-54-3210	COLAN	MS	SR

Table 3-17: Sample *Faculty* Table

FacNo	FacLastName	FacDep	FacRank
098-76-5432	VINCE	MS	ASST
543-21-0987	EMMANUEL	MS	PROF
876-54-3210	COLAN	MS	ASST

Table 3-18: Result of Full Outer Join on Faculty.FacNo = Student.StdNo

StdNo	StdLastName	StdMajor	StdClass	FacNo	FacLastName	FacDept	FacRank
123-45-6789	WELLS	IS	FR				
124-56-7890	NORBERT	FIN	JR				
876-54-3210	COLAN	MS	SR	876-54-3210	COLAN	MS	ASST
				098-76-5432	VINCE	MS	ASST
				543-21-0987	EMMANUEL	MS	PROF

A one-sided outer join can be useful when a table has null values in a foreign key. For example, the *Offering* table (Table 3-19) can have null values in the *FacNo* column representing course offerings without an assigned professor. A one-sided outer join between *Offering* and *Faculty* preserves the rows of *Offering* that do not have an assigned *Faculty* as shown in Table 3-20. With a natural join, the first and third rows of Table 3-20 would not appear. As you will see in Chapter 10, one-sided joins can be useful in data entry forms.

Table 3-19: Sample *Offering* Table

OfferNo	CourseNo	OffTerm	FacNo
1111	is320	summer	
1234	is320	fall	098-76-5432
2222	is460	summer	
3333	is320	spring	098-76-5432
4444	is320	spring	543-21-0987

Table 3-20: Result of a One-Sided Outer Join between *Offering* (Table 3-19) and *Faculty* (Table 3-17)

OfferNo	CourseNo	OffTerm	Offering.FacNo	Faculty.FacNo	FacLastName	FacDept	FacRank
1111	is320	summer					
1234	is320	fall	098-76-5432	098-76-5432	VINCE	MS	Asst
2222	is460	summer					
3333	is320	spring	098-76-5432	098-76-5432	VINCE	MS	Asst
4444	is320	spring	543-21-0987	543-21-0987	EMMANUEL	MS	Prof

Visual Formulation of Outer Join Operations

As a query formulation aid, many DBMSs provide a visual way to formulate outer joins. Microsoft Access provides a visual representation of the one-sided join operator in the Query Design window. Figure 3.8 depicts a one-sided outer join that preserves the rows of the *Offering*. The arrow from *Offering* to *Faculty* means that the nonmatched rows of *Offering* are preserved in the result. When combining the *Faculty* and *Offering* tables, Microsoft Access provides three choices: (1) show only the matched rows (a join); (2) show matched rows and nonmatched rows of

Faculty; and (3) show matched rows and nonmatched rows of *Offering*. Choice (3) is shown in Figure 3.8. Choice (1) would appear similar to Figure 3.6. Choice (2) would have the arrow from *Faculty* to *Offering*.

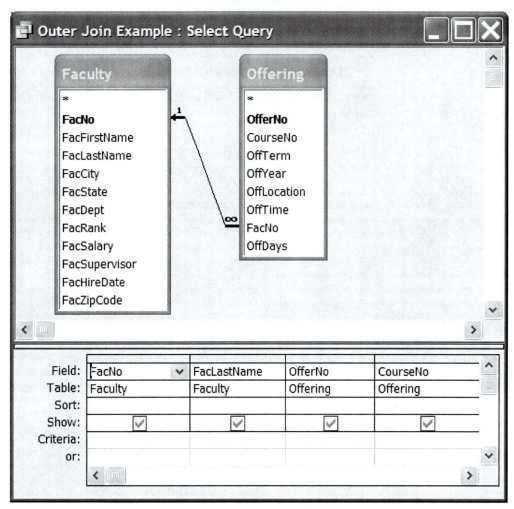

Figure 3.8: Query Design Window Showing a One-Sided Outer Join Preserving the Offering Table

3.4.5 Union, Intersection, and Difference Operators

The union, intersection, and difference table operators are similar to the traditional set operators. The traditional set operators are used to determine all members of two sets (union), common members of two sets (intersection), and members unique to only one set (difference), as depicted in Figure 3.9.

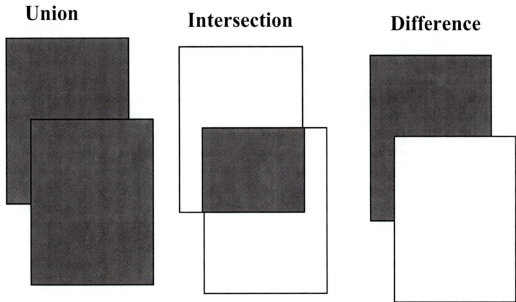

Figure 3.9: Venn Diagrams for Traditional Set Operators

The union, intersection, and difference operators for tables apply to rows of a table but otherwise operate in the same way as the traditional set operators. A <u>union</u> operation retrieves all the rows in either table. For example, a union operator applied to two student tables at different universities can find all student rows. An <u>intersection</u> operation retrieves just the common rows. For example, an intersection operation can determine the students attending both universities. A <u>difference</u> operation retrieves the rows in the first table but not in the second table. For example, a difference operation can determine the students attending only one university.

> **Traditional Set Operators**: the union operator produces a table containing rows in either input table. The intersection operator produces a table containing rows common to both input tables. The difference operator produces a table containing rows in the first input table but not in the second input table.

Union Compatibility

Compatibility is a new concept for the table operators as compared to the traditional set operators. With the table operators, both tables must be union compatible because all columns are compared. <u>Union compatibility</u> means that each table must have the same number of columns and each corresponding column must have a compatible data type. Union compatibility can be confusing because it involves <u>positional</u> correspondence of the columns. That is, the first columns of the two tables must have compatible data types, the second columns must have compatible data types, and so on.

> **Union Compatibility**: a requirement on the input tables for the traditional set operators. Each table must have the same number of columns and each corresponding column must have a compatible data type.

To depict the union, intersection, and difference operators, let us apply them to the *Student1* and *Student2* tables (Tables 3-21 and 3-22). These tables are union compatible because they have identical columns listed in the same order. The results of union, intersection, and difference operators are shown in Tables 3-23 through 3-25, respectively. Even though we can determine that two rows are identical from looking only at *StdNo*, all columns are compared due to the way that the operators are designed.

Note that the result of *Student1* DIFFERENCE *Student2* would not be the same as *Student2* DIFFERENCE *Student1*. The result of the latter (*Student2* DIFFERENCE *Student1*) is the second and third rows of *Student2* (rows in *Student2* but not in *Student1*).

Table 3-21: *Student1* Table

StdNo	StdLastName	StdCity	StdState	StdMajor	StdClass	StdGPA
123-45-6789	WELLS	SEATTLE	WA	IS	FR	3.00
124-56-7890	NORBERT	BOTHELL	WA	FIN	JR	2.70
234-56-7890	KENDALL	TACOMA	WA	ACCT	JR	3.50

Table 3-22: *Student2* Table

StdNo	StdLastName	StdCity	StdState	StdMajor	StdClass	StdGPA
123-45-6789	WELLS	SEATTLE	WA	IS	FR	3.00
995-56-3490	BAGGINS	AUSTIN	TX	FIN	JR	2.90
111-56-4490	WILLIAMS	SEATTLE	WA	ACCT	JR	3.40

Table 3-23: *Student1* UNION *Student2*

StdNo	StdLastName	StdCity	StdState	StdMajor	StdClass	StdGPA
123-45-6789	WELLS	SEATTLE	WA	IS	FR	3.00
124-56-7890	NORBERT	BOTHELL	WA	FIN	JR	2.70
234-56-7890	KENDALL	TACOMA	WA	ACCT	JR	3.50
995-56-3490	BAGGINS	AUSTIN	TX	FIN	JR	2.90
111-56-4490	WILLIAMS	SEATTLE	WA	ACCT	JR	3.40

Table 3-24: *Student1* INTERSECT *Student2*

StdNo	StdLastName	StdCity	StdState	StdMajor	StdClass	StdGPA
123-45-6789	WELLS	SEATTLE	WA	IS	FR	3.00

Table 3-25: *Student1* DIFFERENCE *Student2*

StdNo	StdLastName	StdCity	StdState	StdMajor	StdClass	StdGPA
124-56-7890	NORBERT	BOTHELL	WA	FIN	JR	2.70
234-56-7890	KENDALL	TACOMA	WA	ACCT	JR	3.50

Because of the union compatibility requirement, the union, intersection, and difference operators are not as widely used as other operators. However, these operators have some important, specialized uses. One use is to combine tables distributed over multiple locations. For example, suppose there is a student table at Big State University (*BSUStudent*) and a student table at University of Big State (*UBSStudent*). Because these tables have identical columns, the traditional set operators are applicable. To find students attending either university, you should use *UBSStudent* UNION *BSUStudent*. To find students only attending Big State, you should use *BSUStudent* DIFFERENCE *UBSStudent*. To find students attending both universities, you should use *UBSStudent* INTERSECT *BSUStudent*. Note that the resulting table in each operation has the same number of columns as the two input tables.

The traditional operators are also useful if there are tables that are similar but not union compatible. For example, the *Student* and *Faculty* tables have some compatible columns (*StdNo* with *FacNo*, *StdLastName* with *FacLastName*, and *StdCity* with *FacCity*), but other columns are different. The union compatible operators can be used if the *Student* and *Faculty* tables are first made union compatible using the project operator presented in Section 3.4.1.

3.4.6 Summarize Operator

Summarize is a powerful operator for decision making. Because tables can contain many rows, it is often useful to see statistics about groups of rows rather than individual rows. The <u>summarize</u> operator allows groups of rows to be compressed or summarized by a calculated value. Almost any kind of statistical function can be used to summarize groups of rows. Because this is not a statistics book, we will use only simple functions such as count, min, max, average, and sum.

The summarize operator compresses a table by replacing groups of rows with individual rows containing calculated values. A statistical or <u>aggregate function</u> is used for the calculated values. Figure 3.10 depicts a summarize operation for a sample enrollment table. The input table is grouped on the *StdNo* column. Each group of rows is replaced by the average of the grade column.

> **Summarize:** an operator that produces a table with rows that summarize the rows of the input table. Aggregate functions are used to summarize the rows of the input table.

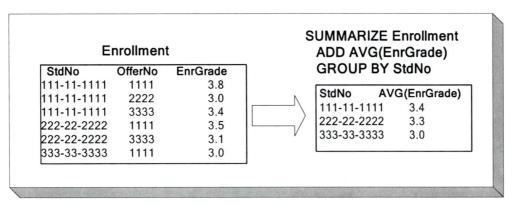

Figure 3.10: Sample Summarize Operation

As another example, Table 3-27 shows the result of a summarize operation on the sample *Faculty* table in Table 3-26. Note that the result contains one row per value of the grouping column, *FacDept*.

Table 3-26: Sample *Faculty* Table

FacNo	FacLastName	FacDep	FacRank	FacSalary	FacSupervisor	FacHireDat
098-76-5432	VINCE	MS	ASST	$35,000	654-32-1098	01-Apr-1997
543-21-0987	EMMANUEL	MS	PROF	$120,000		01-Apr-1998
654-32-1098	FIBON	MS	ASSC	$70,000	543-21-0987	01-Apr-1996
765-43-2109	MACON	FIN	PROF	$65,000		01-Apr-1999
876-54-3210	COLAN	MS	ASST	$40,000	654-32-1098	01-Apr-2001
987-65-4321	MILLS	FIN	ASSC	$75,000	765-43-2109	01-Apr-2002

Table 3-27: Result Table for SUMMARIZE *Faculty* ADD AVG(*FacSalary*) GROUP BY *FacDept*

FacDept	FacSalary
MS	$66,250
FIN	$70,000

The summarize operator can include additional calculated values (also showing the minimum salary, for example) and additional grouping columns (also grouping on *FacRank*, for example). When grouping on multiple columns, each result row shows one combination of values for the grouping columns.

3.4.7 Divide Operator

The *divide* operator is a more specialized and difficult operator than join because the matching requirement in divide is more stringent than join. For example, a join operator is used to retrieve offerings taken by <u>any</u> student. A divide operator is required to retrieve offerings taken by <u>all</u> (or every) students. Because divide has more stringent matching conditions, it is not as widely used as join, and it is more difficult to understand. When appropriate, the divide operator provides a powerful way to combine tables.

The divide operator for tables is somewhat analogous to the divide operator for numbers. In numerical division, the objective is to find the number of times one number contains another number. In table division, the objective is to find values of one column that contain <u>every</u> value in another column. Stated another way, the divide operator finds values of one column that are associated with <u>every</u> value in another column.

> **Divide**: an operator that produces a table in which the values of a column from one input table are associated with all the values from a column of a second input table.

To understand more concretely how the divide operator works, consider an example with sample *Part* and *SuppPart* (supplier-part) tables as depicted in Figure 3.11. The divide operator uses two input tables. The first table (*SuppPart*) has two columns (a binary table) and the second table (*Part*) has one column[1] (a unary table). The result table has one column where the values come from the first column of the binary table. The result table in Figure 3.11 shows the suppliers who supply every part. The value s3 appears in the output because it is associated with <u>every</u> value in the *Part* table. Stated another way, the set of values associated with s3 contains the set of values in the *Part* table.

To understand the divide operator in another way, rewrite the *SuppPart* table as three rows using the angle brackets <> to surround a row: <s3, {p1, p2, p3}>, <s0, {p1}>, <s1, {p2}>. Rewrite the *Part* table as a set: {p1, p2, p3}. The value s3 is in the result table because its set of second column values {p1, p2, p3} contains the values in the second table {p1, p2, p3}. The other *SuppNo* values (s0 and s1) are not in the result because they are not associated with all values in the *Part* table.

---

[1] The divide by operator can be generalized to work with input tables containing more columns. However, the details are not important in this book.

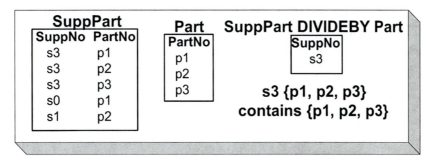

Figure 3.11: Sample Divide Operation

As an example using the university database tables, Table 3-30 shows the result of a divide operation involving the sample *Enrollment* (Table 3-28) and *Student* tables (Table 3-29). The result shows offerings in which every student is enrolled. Only *OfferNo* 4235 has all three students enrolled.

Table 3-28: Sample *Enrollment* Table

OfferNo	StdNo
1234	123-45-6789
1234	234-56-7890
4235	123-45-6789
4235	234-56-7890
4235	124-56-7890
6321	124-56-7890

Table 3-29: Sample *Student* Table

StdNo
123-45-6789
124-56-7890
234-56-7890

Table 3-30: Result of *Enrollment* DIVIDEBY *Student*

OfferNo
4235

3.4.8 Summary of Operators

To help you recall the relational algebra operators, Tables 3-31 and 3-32 provide a convenient summary of the meaning and usage of each operator. You might want to refer to these tables when studying query formulation in later chapters.

Table 3-31: Summary of Meanings of the Relational Algebra Operators

Operator	Meaning
Restrict (Select)	Extracts rows that satisfy a specified condition.
Project	Extracts specified columns.
Product	Builds a table from two tables consisting of all possible combinations of rows, one from each of the two tables.
Union	Builds a table consisting of all rows appearing in either of two tables.
Intersect	Builds a table consisting of all rows appearing in both of two specified tables.
Difference	Builds a table consisting of all rows appearing in the first table but not in the second table.
Join	Extracts rows from a product of two tables such that two input rows contributing to any output row satisfy some specified condition.
Outer Join	Extracts the matching rows (the join part) of two tables and the unmatched rows from one or both tables.
Divide	Builds a table consisting of all values of one column of a binary (two-column) table that match (in the other column) all values in a unary (one-column) table.
Summarize	Organizes a table on specified grouping columns. Specified aggregate computations are made on each value of the grouping columns.

Table 3-32: Summary of Usage of the Relational Algebra Operators

Operator	Notes
Union	Input tables must be union compatible.
Difference	Input tables must be union compatible.
Intersection	Input tables must be union compatible.
Product	Conceptually underlies join operator.
Restrict (Select)	Uses a logical expression.
Project	Eliminates duplicate rows if necessary.
Join	Only matched rows are in the result. Natural join eliminates one join column.
Outer Join	Retains both matched and unmatched rows in the result. Uses null values for some columns of the unmatched rows.
Divide	Stronger operator than join, but less frequently used.
Summarize	Specify grouping column(s) if any and aggregate function(s).

Closing Thoughts

Chapter 3 has introduced the Relational Data Model as a prelude to developing queries, forms, and reports with relational databases. As a first step to work with relational databases, you should understand the basic terminology and integrity rules. You should be able to read table definitions in SQL and other proprietary formats. To effectively query a relational database, you must understand the connections among tables. Most queries involve multiple tables using relationships defined by referential integrity constraints. A graphical representation such as the Relationship window in Microsoft Access provides a powerful tool to conceptualize referential integrity constraints. When developing applications that can change a database, it is important to respect the action rules for referenced rows.

The final part of this chapter described the operators of relational algebra. At this point, you should understand the purpose of each operator, the number of input tables, and other inputs used. You do not need to write complicated formulas that combine operators. Eventually, you should be comfortable understanding statements such as "write an SQL SELECT statement to join three tables." The SELECT statement will be presented in Chapters 4 and 9, but the basic idea of a join is important to learn now. As you learn to extract data using the SQL SELECT statement in Chapter 4, you may want to review this chapter again. To help you remember the major points about the operators, the last section of this chapter presented several convenient summaries.

Understanding the operators will improve your knowledge of SQL and your query formulation skills. The meaning of SQL queries can be understood as relational algebra operations. Chapter 4 provides a flowchart demonstrating this correspondence. For this reason, relational algebra provides a yardstick to measure commercial languages: the commercial languages should provide at least the same retrieval ability as the operators of relational algebra.

Review Concepts

- Tables: heading and body
- Primary keys and entity integrity rule
- Foreign keys, referential integrity rule, and matching values
- Visualizing referential integrity constraints
- Relational Model representation of 1-M relationships, M-N relationships, and self-referencing relationships
- Actions on referenced rows: cascade, nullify, restrict, default
- Subset operators: restrict (select) and project
- Join operator for combining two tables using a matching condition to compare join columns
- Natural join using equality for the matching operator, join columns with the same unqualified name, and elimination of one join column
- Most widely used operator for combining tables: natural join
- Less widely used operators for combining tables: full outer join, one-sided outer join, divide
- Outer join operator extending the join operator by preserving nonmatching rows
- One-sided outer join preserving the nonmatching rows of one input table
- Full outer join preserving the nonmatching rows of both input tables
- Traditional set operators: union, intersection, difference, extended cross product
- Union compatibility for comparing rows for the union, intersection, and difference operators
- Complex matching operator: divide operator for matching on a subset of rows
- Summarize operator that replaces groups of rows with summary rows

Questions

1. How is creating a table similar to writing a chapter of a book?
2. With what terminology for relational databases are you most comfortable? Why?
3. What is the difference between a primary key and a candidate key?
4. What is the difference between a candidate key and a superkey?
5. What is a null value?
6. What is the motivation for the entity integrity rule?
7. What is the motivation for the referential integrity rule?
8. What is the relationship between the referential integrity rule and foreign keys?
9. How are candidate keys that are not primary keys indicated in the CREATE TABLE statement?
10. What is the advantage of using constraint names when defining primary key, candidate key, and referential integrity constraints in CREATE TABLE statements?
11. When is it not permissible for foreign keys to store null values?
12. What is the purpose of a database diagram such as the Access Relationship window?
13. How is a 1-M relationship represented in the Relational Model?
14. How is an M-N relationship represented in the Relational Model?
15. What is a self-referencing relationship?
16. How is a self-referencing relationship represented in the Relational Model?

17. What is a referenced row?
18. What two actions on referenced rows can affect related rows in a child table?
19. What are the possible actions on related rows after a referenced row is deleted or its primary key is updated?
20. Why is the restrict action for referenced rows more common than the cascade action?
21. When is the nullify action not allowed?
22. Why study the operators of relational algebra?
23. Why are the restrict and the project operators widely used?
24. Explain how the union, intersection, and difference operators for tables differ from the traditional operators for sets.
25. Why is the join operator so important for retrieving useful information?
26. What is the relationship between the join and the extended cross product operators?
27. Why is the extended cross product operator used sparingly?
28. What happens to unmatched rows with the join operator?
29. What happens to unmatched rows with the full outer join operator?
30. What is the difference between the full outer join and the one-sided outer join?
31. Define a decision-making situation that might require the summarize operator.
32. What is an aggregate function?
33. How are grouping columns used in the summarize operator?
34. Why is the divide operator not as widely used as the join operator?
35. What are the requirements of union compatibility?
36. What are the requirements of the natural join operator?
37. Why is the natural join operator widely used for combining tables?
38. How do visual tools such as the Microsoft Access Query Design tool facilitate the formulation of join operations?

Problems

The problems use the *Customer*, *OrderTbl*, and *Employee* tables of the simplified Order Entry database. Chapters 4 and 10 extend the database to increase its usefulness. The *Customer* table records clients who have placed orders. The *OrderTbl* contains the basic facts about customer orders. The *Employee* table contains facts about employees who take orders. The primary keys of the tables are *CustNo* for *Customer*, *EmpNo* for *Employee*, and *OrdNo* for *OrderTbl*.

Customer

CustNo	CustFirstName	CustLastName	CustCity	CustState	CustZip	CustBal
C0954327	Sheri	Gordon	Littleton	CO	80129-5543	$230.00
C1010398	Jim	Glussman	Denver	CO	80111-0033	$200.00
C2388597	Beth	Taylor	Seattle	WA	98103-1121	$500.00
C3340959	Betty	Wise	Seattle	WA	98178-3311	$200.00
C3499503	Bob	Mann	Monroe	WA	98013-1095	$0.00
C8543321	Ron	Thompson	Renton	WA	98666-1289	$85.00

Employee

EmpNo	EmpFirstName	EmpLastName	EmpPhone	EmpEmail
E1329594	Landi	Santos	(303) 789-1234	LSantos@bigco.com
E8544399	Joe	Jenkins	(303) 221-9875	JJenkins@bigco.com
E8843211	Amy	Tang	(303) 556-4321	ATang@bigco.com
E9345771	Colin	White	(303) 221-4453	CWhite@bigco.com
E9884325	Thomas	Johnson	(303) 556-9987	TJohnson@bigco.com
E9954302	Mary	Hill	(303) 556-9871	MHill@bigco.com

OrderTbl

OrdNo	OrdDate	CustNo	EmpNo
01116324	01/23/2008	C0954327	E8544399
02334661	01/14/2008	C0954327	E1329594
03331222	01/13/2008	C1010398	
02233457	01/12/2008	C2388597	E9884325
04714645	01/11/2008	C2388597	E1329594
05511365	01/22/2008	C3340959	E9884325
07989497	01/16/2008	C3499503	E9345771
01656777	02/11/2008	C8543321	
07959898	02/19/2008	C8543321	E8544399

1. Write a CREATE TABLE statement for the *Customer* table. Choose data types appropriate for the DBMS used in your course. Note that the *CustBal* column contains numeric data. The currency symbols are not stored in the database. The *CustFirstName* and *CustLastName* columns are required (not null).

2. Write a CREATE TABLE statement for the *Employee* table. Choose data types appropriate for the DBMS used in your course. The *EmpFirstName*, *EmpLastName*, and *EmpEMail* columns are required (not null).

3. Write a CREATE TABLE statement for the *OrderTbl* table. Choose data types appropriate for the DBMS used in your course. The *OrdDate* column is required (not null).

4. Identify the foreign keys and draw a relationship diagram for the simplified Order Entry database. The *CustNo* column references the *Customer* table and the *EmpNo* column references the *Employee* table. For each relationship, identify the parent table and the child table.

5. Extend your CREATE TABLE statement from problem (3) with referential integrity constraints. Updates and deletes on related rows are restricted.

6. From examination of the sample data and your common understanding of order entry businesses, are null values allowed for the foreign keys in the *OrderTbl* table? Why or why not? 7. Extend the CREATE TABLE statement in problem (5) to enforce the null value restrictions if any.

7. Extend your CREATE TABLE statement for the *Employee* table (problem 2) with a unique constraint for *EmpEMail*. Use a named constraint clause for the unique constraint.

8. Show the result of a restrict operation that lists the orders in February 2008.

9. Show the result of a restrict operation that lists the customers residing in Seattle, WA.

10. Show the result of a project operation that lists the *CustNo*, *CustFirstName*, and *CustLastName* columns of the *Customer* table.

11. Show the result of a project operation that lists the *CustCity* and *CustState* columns of the *Customer* table.

12. Show the result of a natural join that combines the *Customer* and *OrderTbl* tables.

13. Show the steps to derive the natural join for problem (10). How many rows and columns are in the extended cross product step?

14. Show the result of a natural join of the *Employee* and *OrderTbl* tables.

15. Show the result of a one-sided outer join between the *Employee* and *OrderTbl* tables. Preserve the rows of the *OrderTbl* table in the result.

16. Show the result of a full outer join between the *Employee* and *OrderTbl* tables.

17. Show the result of the restrict operation on *Customer* where the condition is *CustCity* equals "Denver" or "Seattle" followed by a project operation to retain the *CustNo*, *CustFirstName*, *CustLastName*, and *CustCity* columns.

18. Show the result of a natural join that combines the *Customer* and *OrderTbl* tables followed by a restrict operation to retain only the Colorado customers (CustState = "CO").

19. Show the result of a summarize operation on *Customer*. The grouping column is *CustState* and the aggregate calculation is COUNT. COUNT shows the number of rows with the same value for the grouping column.

20. Show the result of a summarize operation on *Customer*. The grouping column is *CustState* and the aggregate calculations are the minimum and maximum *CustBal* values.

21. What tables are required to show the *CustLastName*, *EmpLastName*, and *OrdNo* columns in the result table?

22. Extend your relationship diagram from problem (4) by adding two tables (*OrdLine* and *Product*). Partial CREATE TABLE statements for the primary keys and referential integrity constraints are shown below:

```
CREATE TABLE Product … PRIMARY KEY (ProdNo)
CREATE TABLE OrdLine … PRIMARY KEY (OrdNo, ProdNo)
  FOREIGN KEY (OrdNo) REFERENCES Order
  FOREIGN KEY (ProdNo) REFERENCES Product
```

23. Extend your relationship diagram from problem (22) by adding a foreign key in the *Employee* table. The foreign key *SupEmpNo* is the employee number of the supervising employee. Thus, the *SupEmpNo* column references the *Employee* table.

24. What relational algebra operator do you use to find products contained in <u>every</u> order? What relational algebra operator do you use to find products contained in <u>any</u> order?

25. Are the *Customer* and *Employee* tables union compatible? Why or why not?

26. Using the database after problem (23), what tables must be combined to list the product names on order number O1116324?

27. Using the database after problem (23), what tables must be combined to list the product names ordered by customer number C0954327?

28. Using the database after problem (23), what tables must be combined to list the product names ordered by the customer named Sheri Gordon?

29. Using the database after problem (23), what tables must be combined to list the number of orders submitted by customers residing in Colorado?

30. Using the database after problem (23), what tables must be combined to list the product names appearing on an order taken by an employee named Landi Santos?

References for Further Study

Codd defined the Relational Model in a seminal paper in 1970. His paper inspired research projects at the IBM research laboratories and the University of California at Berkeley that led to commercial relational DBMSs. Date (2003) provides a syntax for the relational algebra. Elmasri and Navathe (2007) provide a more theoretical treatment of the Relational Model, especially the relational algebra.

Appendix 3.A: CREATE TABLE Statements for the University Database Tables

The following are the CREATE TABLE statements for the university database tables (Tables 3-1, 3-3, 3-4, 3-6, and 3-7) using the SQL data types and syntax. Data names vary by DBMS. For example, Microsoft Access SQL supports the TEXT data type instead of CHAR and VARCHAR. In Oracle, you should use VARCHAR2 instead of VARCHAR. In addition, certain syntax such as the rules for referenced rows follow the SQL standard, not Oracle syntax.

```
CREATE TABLE Student
(       StdNo               CHAR(11),
        StdFirstName        VARCHAR(50)
                            CONSTRAINT StdFirstNameRequired NOT NULL,
        StdLastName         VARCHAR(50)
                            CONSTRAINT StdLastNameRequired NOT NULL,
        StdCity             VARCHAR(50)
                            CONSTRAINT StdCityRequired NOT NULL,
        StdState            CHAR(2)
                            CONSTRAINT StdStateRequired NOT NULL,
        StdZip              CHAR(10)
                            CONSTRAINT StdZipRequired NOT NULL,
        StdMajor            CHAR(6),
        StdClass            CHAR(2),
        StdGPA              DECIMAL(3,2),
        CONSTRAINT PKStudent PRIMARY KEY (StdNo) )

CREATE TABLE Course
(       CourseNo            CHAR(6),
        CrsDesc             VARCHAR(250)
                            CONSTRAINT CrsDescRequired NOT NULL,
        CrsUnits            INTEGER,
        CONSTRAINT PKCourse PRIMARY KEY (CourseNo),
        CONSTRAINT UniqueCrsDesc UNIQUE (CrsDesc)  )

CREATE TABLE Faculty
(       FacNo               CHAR(11),
        FacFirstName        VARCHAR(50)
                            CONSTRAINT FacFirstNameRequired NOT NULL,
        FacLastName         VARCHAR(50)
                            CONSTRAINT FacLastNameRequired NOT NULL,
        FacCity             VARCHAR(50)
                            CONSTRAINT FacCityRequired NOT NULL,
        FacState            CHAR(2)
                            CONSTRAINT FacStateRequired NOT NULL,
        FacZipCode          CHAR(10)
                            CONSTRAINT FacZipRequired NOT NULL,
        FacHireDate         DATE,
        FacDept             CHAR(6),
        FacRank             CHAR(4),
        FacSalary           DECIMAL(10,2),
        FacSupervisor       CHAR(11),
        CONSTRAINT PKFaculty PRIMARY KEY (FacNo),
        CONSTRAINT FKFacSupervisor
                    FOREIGN KEY (FacSupervisor) REFERENCES Faculty
                    ON DELETE SET NULL ON UPDATE CASCADE )
```

```
CREATE TABLE Offering
(       OfferNo             INTEGER,
        CourseNo            CHAR(6)
                            CONSTRAINT OffCourseNoRequired NOT NULL,
        OffLocation         VARCHAR(50),
        OffDays             CHAR(6),
        OffTerm             CHAR(6)
                            CONSTRAINT OffTermRequired NOT NULL,
        OffYear             INTEGER
                            CONSTRAINT OffYearRequired NOT NULL,
        FacNo               CHAR(11),
        OffTime             DATE,
CONSTRAINT PKOffering PRIMARY KEY (OfferNo),
CONSTRAINT FKCourseNo FOREIGN KEY (CourseNo) REFERENCES Course
        ON DELETE RESTRICT
        ON UPDATE RESTRICT,
CONSTRAINT FKFacNo FOREIGN KEY (FacNo) REFERENCES Faculty
        ON DELETE SET NULL
        ON UPDATE CASCADE                               )


CREATE TABLE Enrollment
(       OfferNo             INTEGER,
        StdNo               CHAR(11),
        EnrGrade            DECIMAL(3,2),
CONSTRAINT PKEnrollment PRIMARY KEY (OfferNo, StdNo),
CONSTRAINT FKOfferNo FOREIGN KEY (OfferNo) REFERENCES Offering
        ON DELETE CASCADE
        ON UPDATE CASCADE,
CONSTRAINT FKStdNo FOREIGN KEY (StdNo) REFERENCES Student
        ON DELETE CASCADE
        ON UPDATE CASCADE                               )
```

Appendix 3.B: SQL:2006 Syntax Summary

This appendix provides a convenient summary of the SQL:2006 syntax for the CREATE TABLE statement along with several related statements. For brevity, only the syntax of the most common parts of the statements is described. SQL:2006 is the current version of the SQL standard. The syntax in SQL:2006 for the statements described in this appendix is identical to the syntax in the previous SQL standards, SQL:2003, SQL:1999 and SQL-92. For the complete syntax, refer to a SQL:2006 or a SQL-92 reference book such as Groff and Weinberg (2002). The conventions used in the syntax notation are listed before the statement syntax:

Uppercase words denote reserved words.

Mixed-case words without hyphens denote names that the user substitutes.

The asterisk * after a syntax element indicates that a comma-separated list can be used.

The plus symbol + after a syntax element indicates that a list can be used. No commas appear in the list.

Names enclosed in angle brackets <> denote definitions defined later in the syntax. The definitions occur on a new line with the element and colon followed by the syntax.

Square brackets [] enclose optional elements.

Curly brackets {} enclose choice elements. One element must be chosen among the elements separated by the vertical bars |.

The parentheses () denote themselves.

Double hyphens — denote comments that are not part of the syntax.

CREATE TABLE[14] Syntax

```
CREATE TABLE   TableName
  ( <Column-Definition>*  [ ,  <Table-Constraint>*  ]  )

<Column-Definition>: ColumnName DataType
[ DEFAULT { DefaultValue | USER | NULL } ]
[ <Embedded-Column-Constraint>+ ]

<Embedded-Column-Constraint>:
  { [ CONSTRAINT ConstraintName ] NOT NULL     |
    [ CONSTRAINT ConstraintName ] UNIQUE       |
    [ CONSTRAINT ConstraintName ] PRIMARY KEY  |
    [ CONSTRAINT ConstraintName ] FOREIGN KEY
        REFERENCES TableName [ ( ColumnName ) ]
        [ ON DELETE   <Action-Specification> ]
        [ ON UPDATE   <Action-Specification> ] }

<Table-Constraint>: [ CONSTRAINT ConstraintName ]
    { <Primary-Key-Constraint>  |
      <Foreign-Key-Constraint>  |
      <Uniqueness-Constraint>  }

<Primary-Key-Constraint>: PRIMARY KEY ( ColumnName* )
```

---

[14] The CHECK constraint, an important kind of table constraint, is described in Chapter 14.

```
<Foreign-Key-Constraint>: FOREIGN KEY ( ColumnName* )
    REFERENCES TableName [( ColumnName* )]
    [ ON DELETE  <Action-Specification> ]
    [ ON UPDATE  <Action-Specification> ]

<Action-Specification>: { CASCADE | SET NULL |
    SET DEFAULT | RESTRICT }

<Uniqueness-Constraint>: UNIQUE ( ColumnName* )
```

Other related statements

The ALTER TABLE and DROP TABLE statements support modification of a table definition and deleting a table definition. The ALTER TABLE statement is particularly useful because table definitions often change over time. In both statements, the keyword RESTRICT means that the statement cannot be performed if related tables exist. The keyword CASCADE means that the same action will be performed on related tables.

```
ALTER TABLE   TableName
  { ADD { <Column-Definition> |  <Table-Constraint> } |
     ALTER ColumnName { SET DEFAULT DefaultValue  |
          DROP DEFAULT } |
     DROP ColumnName { CASCADE | RESTRICT }  |
     DROP CONSTRAINT ConstraintName {CASCADE | RESTRICT }
  }

DROP TABLE  TableName { CASCADE | RESTRICT }
```

Notes on Oracle Syntax

The CREATE TABLE statement in Oracle 11g SQL conforms closely to the SQL:2006 standard. Here is a list of the most significant syntax differences:
Oracle SQL does not support the ON UPDATE clause for referential integrity constraints.
Oracle SQL only supports CASCADE and SET NULL as the action specifications of the ON DELETE clause. If an ON DELETE clause is not specified, the deletion is not allowed (restricted) if related rows exist.
Oracle SQL does not support dropping columns in the ALTER statement.
Oracle SQL supports the MODIFY keyword in place of the ALTER keyword in the ALTER TABLE statement (use MODIFY ColumnName instead of ALTER ColumnName).
Oracle SQL supports data type changes using the MODIFY keyword in the ALTER TABLE statement.

Appendix 3.C: Generation of Unique Values for Primary Keys

The SQL:2006 standard provides the GENERATED clause to support the generation of unique values for selected columns, typically primary keys. The GENERATED clause is used in place of a default value as shown in the following syntax specification. Typically a whole number data type such as INTEGER should be used for columns with a GENERATED clause. The START BY and INCREMENT BY keywords can be used to indicate the initial value and the increment value. The ALWAYS keyword indicates that the value is always automatically generated. The BY DEFAULT clause allows a user to specify a value, overriding the automatic value generation.

```
<Column-Definition>: ColumnName DataType
[ <Default-Specification> ]
[ <Embedded-Column-Constraint>+ ]

<Default-Specification>:
  { DEFAULT { DefaultValue | USER | NULL } |
    GENERATED {ALWAYS | BY DEFAULT } AS IDENTITY
      START WITH NumericConstant
  [ INCREMENT BY NumericConstant ] }
```

Conformance to the SQL:2006 syntax for the GENERATED clause varies among DBMSs. IBM DB2 conforms closely to the syntax. Microsoft SQL Server uses slightly different syntax and only supports the ALWAYS option unless a SET IDENTITY statement is also used. Microsoft Access provides the AutoNumber data type to generate unique values. Oracle uses sequence objects in place of the GENERATED clause. Oracle sequences have similar features except that users must maintain the association between a sequence and a column, a burden not necessary with the SQL:2006 standard.

The following examples contrast the SQL:2006 and Oracle approaches for automatic value generation. Note that the primary key constraint is not required for columns with generated values although generated values are mostly used for primary keys. The Oracle example contains two statements: one for the sequence creation and another for the table creation. Because sequences are not associated with columns, Oracle provides functions that should be used when inserting a row into a table. In contrast, the usage of extra functions is not necessary in SQL:2006.

SQL:2006 GENERATED Clause Example

```
CREATE TABLE Customer
( CustNo INTEGER GENERATED ALWAYS AS IDENTITY
        START WITH 1 INCREMENT BY 1,
...,
CONSTRAINT PKCustomer PRIMARY KEY (CustNo)   )
```

Oracle Sequence Example

```
CREATE SEQUENCE CustNoSeq START WITH 1 INCREMENT BY 1;

CREATE TABLE Customer
( CustNo INTEGER,
...,
CONSTRAINT PKCustomer PRIMARY KEY (CustNo)   );
```

4

Learning Objectives

This chapter provides the foundation for query formulation using the industry standard Structured Query Language (SQL). Query formulation is the process of converting a request for data into a statement of a database language such as SQL. After this chapter the student should have acquired the following knowledge and skills:

- Write SQL SELECT statements for queries involving the restrict, project, and join operators
- Use the critical questions to transform a problem statement into a database representation
- Write SELECT statements for difficult joins involving three or more tables, self joins, and multiple joins between tables
- Understand the meaning of the GROUP BY clause using the conceptual evaluation process
- Write English descriptions to document SQL statements
- Write INSERT, UPDATE, and DELETE statements to change the rows of a table

Overview

Chapter 3 provided a foundation for using relational databases. Most importantly, you learned about connections among tables and fundamental operators to extract useful data. This chapter shows you how to apply this knowledge in using the data manipulation statements of SQL.

Much of your skill with SQL or other computer languages is derived from imitating examples. This chapter provides many examples to facilitate your learning process. Initially you are presented with relatively simple examples so that you become comfortable with the basics of the SQL SELECT statement. To prepare you for more difficult examples, two problem-solving guidelines (conceptual evaluation process and critical questions) are presented. The conceptual evaluation process explains the meaning of the SELECT statement through the sequence of operations and intermediate tables that produce the result. The critical questions help you transform a problem statement into a relational database representation in a language such as SQL. These guidelines are used to help formulate and explain the advanced problems presented in the last part of this chapter.

4.1 Background

Before using SQL, it is informative to understand its history and scope. The history reveals the origin of the name and the efforts to standardize the language. The scope puts the various parts of SQL into perspective. You have already seen the CREATE TABLE statement in Chapter 3. The SELECT, UPDATE, DELETE, and INSERT statements are the subject of this chapter and Chapter 9. To broaden your understanding, you should be aware of other parts of SQL and different usage contexts.

4.1.1 Brief History of SQL

The Structured Query Language (SQL) has a colorful history. Table 4-1 depicts the highlights of SQL's development. SQL began life as the SQUARE language in IBM's System R project. The System R project was a response to the interest in relational databases sparked by Dr. Ted Codd, an IBM fellow who wrote a famous paper in 1970 about relational databases. The SQUARE language was somewhat mathematical in nature. After conducting human factors experiments, the IBM research team revised the language and renamed it SEQUEL (a follow-up to SQUARE). After another revision, the language was dubbed SEQUEL 2. Its current name, SQL, resulted from legal issues surrounding the name SEQUEL. Because of this naming history, a number of database professionals, particularly those working during the 1970s, pronounce the name as "sequel" rather than SQL.

Table 4-1: SQL Timeline

Year	Event
1972	System R project at IBM Research Labs
1974	SQUARE language developed
1975	Language revision and name change to SEQUEL
1976	Language revision and name change to SEQUEL 2
1977	Name change to SQL
1978	First commercial implementation by Oracle Corporation
1981	IBM product SQL/DS featuring SQL
1986	SQL-86 (SQL1) standard approved
1989	SQL-89 standard approved (revision to SQL-86)
1992	SQL-92 (SQL2) standard approved
1999	SQL:1999 (SQL3) standard approved
2003	SQL:2003 approved
2006	SQL:2006 approved

SQL is now an international standard[15] although it was not always so. With the force of IBM behind SQL, many imitators used some variant of SQL. Such was the old order of the computer industry when IBM was dominant. It may seem surprising, but IBM was not the first company to commercialize SQL. Until a standards effort developed in the 1980s, SQL was in a state of confusion. Many vendors implemented different subsets of SQL with unique extensions. The standards efforts by the American National Standards Institute (ANSI), the International Organization for Standards (ISO), and the International Electrotechnical Commission (IEC) have restored some order. Although SQL was not initially the best database language developed, the standards efforts have improved the language as well as standardized its specification.

The size and scope of the SQL standard has increased significantly since the first standard was adopted. The original standard (SQL-86) contained about 150 pages, while the SQL-92 standard contained more than 600 pages. In contrast, the most recent standards (SQL:1999 through SQL:2006) contained more than 2,000 pages. The early standards (SQL-86 and SQL-89) had two levels (entry and full). SQL-92 added a third level (entry, intermediate, and full). The SQL:1999 through SQL:2006 standards contain a single level called Core SQL along with additional parts and packages for noncore features. SQL:2006 contains three core parts, six optional parts, and seven optional packages.

The weakness of the SQL standards is the lack of conformance testing. Until 1996, the U.S. Department of Commerce's National Institute of Standards and Technology conducted conformance tests to provide assurance that government software can be ported among conforming DBMSs. Since 1996, however, DBMS vendor claims have substituted for independent conformance testing. Even for Core SQL, the major vendors lack support for some features and provide proprietary support for other features. With the optional parts and packages, conformance has much greater variance. Writing portable SQL code requires careful study for Core SQL but is not possible for advanced parts of SQL.

The presentation in this chapter is limited to a subset of Core SQL:2006. Most features presented in this chapter were part of SQL-92 as well as Core SQL:2006. Other chapters present other parts of Core SQL as well as important features from selected SQL:2006 packages.

---

[15] Dr. Michael Stonebraker, an early database pioneer, has even referred to SQL as "intergalactic data speak."

4.1.2 Scope of SQL

SQL was designed as a language for database definition, manipulation, and control. Table 4-2 shows a quick summary of important SQL statements. Only database administrators use most of the database definition and database control statements. You have already seen the CREATE TABLE statement in Chapter 3. This chapter and Chapter 9 cover the database manipulation statements. Power users and analysts use the database manipulation statements. Chapter 10 covers the CREATE VIEW statement. The CREATE VIEW statement can be used by either database administrators or analysts. Chapter 11 covers the CREATE TRIGGER statement used by both database administrators and analysts. Chapter 14 covers the GRANT, REVOKE, and CREATE ASSERTION statements used primarily by database administrators. The transaction control statements (COMMIT and ROLLBACK) presented in Chapter 15 are used by analysts.

Table 4-2: Selected SQL Statements

Statement Type	Statements	Purpose
Database definition	CREATE SCHEMA, TABLE, VIEW	Define a new database, table, and view
	ALTER TABLE	Modify table definition
Database manipulation	SELECT	Retrieve contents of tables
	UPDATE, DELETE, INSERT	Modify, remove, and add rows
Database control	COMMIT, ROLLBACK	Complete, undo transaction
	GRANT, REVOKE	Add and remove access rights
	CREATE ASSERTION	Define integrity constraint
	CREATE TRIGGER	Define database rule

SQL can be used in two contexts: stand-alone and embedded. In the stand-alone context, the user submits SQL statements with the use of a specialized editor. The editor alerts the user to syntax errors and sends the statements to the DBMS. The presentation in this chapter assumes stand-alone usage. In the embedded context, an executing program submits SQL statements, and the DBMS sends results back to the program. The program includes SQL statements along with statements of the host programming language such as Java or Visual Basic. Additional statements allow SQL statements (such as SELECT) to be used inside a computer program. Chapter 11 covers embedded SQL.

> **SQL Usage Contexts**: SQL statements can be used stand-alone with a specialized editor, or embedded inside a computer program.

4.2 Getting Started with the SELECT Statement

The SELECT statement supports data retrieval from one or more tables. This section describes a simplified format of the SELECT statement. More complex formats are presented in Chapter 9. The SELECT statement described here has the following format:

```
SELECT <list of columns and expressions usually involving
columns>
    FROM <list of tables and join operations>
    WHERE <list of row conditions connected by AND, OR, NOT>
    GROUP BY <list of grouping columns>
    HAVING <list of group conditions connected by AND, OR, NOT >
    ORDER BY <list of sorting specifications>
```

In the preceding format, the uppercase words are keywords. You replace the angle brackets <> with information to make a meaningful statement. For example, after the keyword SELECT, type the list of columns that should appear in the result, but do not type the angle brackets. The result list can include columns such as *StdFirstName* or expressions involving constants, column names, and functions. Example expressions are Price * Qty and 1.1 *

`FacSalary`. To make meaningful names for computed columns, you can rename a column in the result table using the AS keyword. For example, SELECT Price * Qty AS Amount renames the expression `Price * Qty` to `Amount` in the result table.

> **Expression**: a combination of constants, column names, functions, and operators that produces a value. In conditions and result columns, expressions can be used in any place that column names can appear.

To depict this SELECT format and show the meaning of statements, this chapter shows numerous examples. Examples are provided for both Microsoft Access, a popular desktop DBMS, and Oracle, a prominent enterprise DBMS. Most examples execute on both systems. Unless noted, the examples run on the 1997 through 2003 versions of Access and the 8i through 11g versions of Oracle. Examples that only execute on one product are marked. In addition to the examples, Appendix 4.B summarizes syntax differences among major DBMSs.

The examples use the university database tables introduced in Chapter 3. Tables 4-3 through 4-7 list the contents of the tables. CREATE TABLE statements are listed in Appendix 3.A. For your reference, the relationship diagram showing the primary and foreign keys is repeated in Figure 4.1. Recall that the *Faculty1* table with relationship to the *Faculty* table represents a self-referencing relationship with *FacSupervisor* as the foreign key.

Table 4-3a: Sample *Student* Table (part 1)

StdNo	StdFirstName	StdLastName	StdCity	StdState	StdZip
123-45-6789	HOMER	WELLS	SEATTLE	WA	98121-1111
124-56-7890	BOB	NORBERT	BOTHELL	WA	98011-2121
234-56-7890	CANDY	KENDALL	TACOMA	WA	99042-3321
345-67-8901	WALLY	KENDALL	SEATTLE	WA	98123-1141
456-78-9012	JOE	ESTRADA	SEATTLE	WA	98121-2333
567-89-0123	MARIAH	DODGE	SEATTLE	WA	98114-0021
678-90-1234	TESS	DODGE	REDMOND	WA	98116-2344
789-01-2345	ROBERTO	MORALES	SEATTLE	WA	98121-2212
876-54-3210	CRISTOPHER	COLAN	SEATTLE	WA	98114-1332
890-12-3456	LUKE	BRAZZI	SEATTLE	WA	98116-0021
901-23-4567	WILLIAM	PILGRIM	BOTHELL	WA	98113-1885

Table 4-3b: Sample *Student* Table (part 2)

StdNo	StdMajor	StdClass	StdGPA
123-45-6789	IS	FR	3.00
124-56-7890	FIN	JR	2.70
234-56-7890	ACCT	JR	3.50
345-67-8901	IS	SR	2.80
456-78-9012	FIN	SR	3.20
567-89-0123	IS	JR	3.60
678-90-1234	ACCT	SO	3.30
789-01-2345	FIN	JR	2.50
876-54-3210	IS	SR	4.00
890-12-3456	IS	SR	2.20
901-23-4567	IS	SO	3.80

Table 4-4a: Sample *Faculty* Table (part 1)

FacNo	FacFirstName	FacLastName	FacCity	FacState	FacZipCode
098-76-5432	LEONARD	VINCE	SEATTLE	WA	98111-9921
543-21-0987	VICTORIA	EMMANUEL	BOTHELL	WA	98011-2242
654-32-1098	LEONARD	FIBON	SEATTLE	WA	98121-0094
765-43-2109	NICKI	MACON	BELLEVUE	WA	98015-9945
876-54-3210	CRISTOPHER	COLAN	SEATTLE	WA	98114-1332
987-65-4321	JULIA	MILLS	SEATTLE	WA	98114-9954

Table 4-4b: Sample *Faculty* Table (part 2)

FacNo	FacSupervisor	FacHireDate	FacDept	FacRank	FacSalary
098-76-5432	654-32-1098	10-Apr-1997	MS	ASST	$35,000
543-21-0987		15-Apr-1998	MS	PROF	$120,000
654-32-1098	543-21-0987	01-May-1996	MS	ASSC	$70,000
765-43-2109		11-Apr-1999	FIN	PROF	$65,000
876-54-3210	654-32-1098	01-Mar-2001	MS	ASST	$40,000
987-65-4321	765-43-2109	15-Mar-2002	FIN	ASSC	$75,000

Table 4-5: Sample *Offering* Table

OfferNo	CourseNo	OffTerm	OffYear	OffLocation	OffTime	FacNo	OffDays
1111	IS320	SUMMER	2008	BLM302	10:30 AM		MW
1234	IS320	FALL	2007	BLM302	10:30 AM	098-76-5432	MW
2222	IS460	SUMMER	2007	BLM412	1:30 PM		TTH
3333	IS320	SPRING	2008	BLM214	8:30 AM	098-76-5432	MW
4321	IS320	FALL	2007	BLM214	3:30 PM	098-76-5432	TTH
4444	IS320	WINTER	2008	BLM302	3:30 PM	543-21-0987	TTH
5555	FIN300	WINTER	2008	BLM207	8:30 AM	765-43-2109	MW
5678	IS480	WINTER	2008	BLM302	10:30 AM	987-65-4321	MW
5679	IS480	SPRING	2008	BLM412	3:30 PM	876-54-3210	TTH
6666	FIN450	WINTER	2008	BLM212	10:30 AM	987-65-4321	TTH
7777	FIN480	SPRING	2008	BLM305	1:30 PM	765-43-2109	MW
8888	IS320	SUMMER	2008	BLM405	1:30 PM	654-32-1098	MW
9876	IS460	SPRING	2008	BLM307	1:30 PM	654-32-1098	TTH

Table 4-6: Sample *Course* Table

CourseNo	CrsDesc	CrsUnits
FIN300	FUNDAMENTALS OF FINANCE	4
FIN450	PRINCIPLES OF INVESTMENTS	4
FIN480	CORPORATE FINANCE	4
IS320	FUNDAMENTALS OF BUSINESS PROGRAMMING	4
IS460	SYSTEMS ANALYSIS	4
IS470	BUSINESS DATA COMMUNICATIONS	4
IS480	FUNDAMENTALS OF DATABASE MANAGEMENT	4

Table 4-7: Sample *Enrollment* Table

OfferNo	StdNo	EnrGrade
1234	123-45-6789	3.3
1234	234-56-7890	3.5
1234	345-67-8901	3.2
1234	456-78-9012	3.1
1234	567-89-0123	3.8
1234	678-90-1234	3.4
4321	123-45-6789	3.5
4321	124-56-7890	3.2
4321	789-01-2345	3.5
4321	876-54-3210	3.1
4321	890-12-3456	3.4
4321	901-23-4567	3.1
5555	123-45-6789	3.2
5555	124-56-7890	2.7
5678	123-45-6789	3.2
5678	234-56-7890	2.8
5678	345-67-8901	3.3
5678	456-78-9012	3.4
5678	567-89-0123	2.6
5679	123-45-6789	2
5679	124-56-7890	3.7
5679	678-90-1234	3.3
5679	789-01-2345	3.8
5679	890-12-3456	2.9
5679	901-23-4567	3.1
6666	234-56-7890	3.1
6666	567-89-0123	3.6
7777	876-54-3210	3.4
7777	890-12-3456	3.7
7777	901-23-4567	3.4
9876	124-56-7890	3.5
9876	234-56-7890	3.2
9876	345-67-8901	3.2
9876	456-78-9012	3.4
9876	567-89-0123	2.6
9876	678-90-1234	3.3
9876	901-23-4567	4

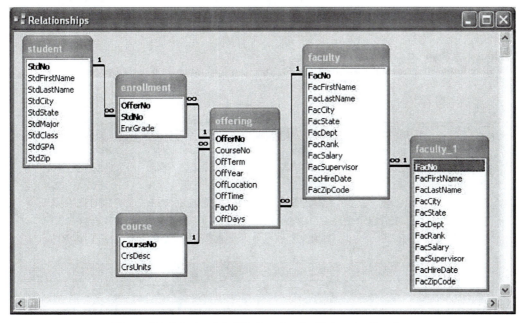

Figure 4.1: Relationship Window for the University Database

4.2.1 Single Table Problems

Let us begin with the simple SELECT statement in Example 4.1. In all the examples, keywords appear in uppercase while information specific to the query appears in mixed case. In Example 4.1, only the *Student* table is listed in the FROM clause because the conditions in the WHERE clause and columns after the SELECT keyword involve only the *Student* table. In Oracle, a semicolon or / (on a separate line) terminates a statement.

Example 4.1: Testing Rows Using the WHERE Clause
Retrieve the name, city, and grade point average (GPA) of students with a high GPA (greater than or equal to 3.7). The result follows the SELECT statement.

```
SELECT StdFirstName, StdLastName, StdCity, StdGPA
  FROM Student
  WHERE StdGPA >= 3.7
```

StdFirstName	StdLastName	StdCity	StdGPA
CRISTOPHER	COLAN	SEATTLE	4.00
WILLIAM	PILGRIM	BOTHELL	3.80

Table 4-8 depicts the standard comparison operators. Note that the symbol for some operators depends on the DBMS.

Table 4-8: Standard Comparison Operators

Comparison Operator	Meaning
=	equal to
<	less than
>	greater than
<=	less than or equal to
>=	greater than or equal to
<> or !=	not equal (check your DBMS)

Example 4.2 is even simpler than Example 4.1. The result is identical to the original *Faculty* table in Table 4-4. Example 4.2 uses a shortcut to list all columns. The asterisk * in the

column list indicates that all columns of the tables in the FROM clause appear in the result. The asterisk serves as a wildcard character matching all column names.

Example 4.2: Show all Columns
List all columns and rows of the *Faculty* table. The resulting table is shown in two parts.

```
SELECT * FROM Faculty
```

FacNo	FacFirstName	FacLastName	FacCity	FacState	FacZipCode
098-76-	LEONARD	VINCE	SEATTLE	WA	98111-9921
543-21-	VICTORIA	EMMANUEL	BOTHELL	WA	98011-2242
654-32-	LEONARD	FIBON	SEATTLE	WA	98121-0094
765-43-	NICKI	MACON	BELLEVUE	WA	98015-9945
876-54-	CRISTOPHER	COLAN	SEATTLE	WA	98114-1332
987-65-	JULIA	MILLS	SEATTLE	WA	98114-9954

FacNo	FacSupervisor	FacHireDate	FacDept	FacRank	FacSalary
098-76-	654-32-1098	10-Apr-1997	MS	ASST	$35,000
543-21-		15-Apr-1998	MS	PROF	$120,000
654-32-	543-21-0987	01-May-1996	MS	ASSC	$70,000
765-43-		11-Apr-1999	FIN	PROF	$65,000
876-54-	654-32-1098	01-Mar-2001	MS	ASST	$40,000
987-65-	765-43-2109	15-Mar-2002	FIN	ASSC	$75,000

Example 4.3 depicts expressions in the SELECT and WHERE clauses. The expression in the SELECT clause increases the salary by 10 percent. The AS keyword is used to rename the computed column. Without renaming, most DBMSs will generate a meaningless name such as Expr001. The expression in the WHERE clause extracts the year from the hiring date. Because functions for the date data type are not standard, Access and Oracle formulations are provided. To become proficient with SQL on a particular DBMS, you will need to study the available functions especially with date columns.

Example 4.3 (Access): Expressions in SELECT and WHERE Clauses
List the name, city, and increased salary of faculty hired after 1996. The **year** function extracts the year part of a column with a date data type.

```
SELECT FacFirstName, FacLastName, FacCity,
       FacSalary*1.1 AS IncreasedSalary, FacHireDate
  FROM Faculty
 WHERE year(FacHireDate) > 1998
```

FacFirstName	FacLastName	FacCity	IncreasedSalary	FacHireDate
NICKI	MACON	BELLEVUE	71500	11-Apr-1999
CRISTOPHER	COLAN	SEATTLE	44000	01-Mar-2001
JULIA	MILLS	SEATTLE	82500	15-Mar-2002

Example 4.3 (Oracle): Expressions in SELECT and WHERE Clauses

The **to_char** function extracts the four-digit year from the *FacHireDate* column and the **to_number** function converts the character representation of the year into a number.

```
SELECT FacFirstName, FacLastName, FacCity,
       FacSalary*1.1 AS IncreasedSalary, FacHireDate
FROM Faculty
WHERE to_number(to_char(FacHireDate, 'YYYY' ) ) > 1998
```

Inexact matching supports conditions that match some pattern rather than matching an identical string. One of the most common types of inexact matching is to find values having a common prefix such as "IS4" (400 level IS Courses). Example 4.4 uses the LIKE operator along with a pattern-matching character * to perform prefix matching[16]. The string constant `'IS4*'` means match strings beginning with "IS4" and ending with anything. The wildcard character * matches any string. The Oracle formulation of Example 4.4 uses the percent symbol %, the SQL:2006 standard for the wildcard character. Note that string constants must be enclosed in quotation marks[17].

Example 4.4 (Access): Inexact Matching with the LIKE Operator

List the senior-level IS courses.

```
SELECT *
FROM Course
WHERE CourseNo LIKE 'IS4*'
```

CourseNo	CrsDesc	CrsUnits
IS460	SYSTEMS ANALYSIS	4
IS470	BUSINESS DATA COMMUNICATIONS	4
IS480	FUNDAMENTALS OF DATABASE MANAGEMENT	4

Example 4.4 (Oracle): Inexact Matching with the LIKE Operator

List the senior-level IS courses.

```
SELECT *
FROM Course
WHERE CourseNo LIKE 'IS4%'
```

Another common type of inexact matching is to match strings containing a substring. To perform this kind of matching, a wildcard character should be used before and after the substring. For example, to find courses containing the word DATABASE anywhere in the course description, write the condition: `CrsDesc LIKE '*DATABASE*'` in Access or `CrsDesc LIKE '%DATABASE%'` in Oracle.

---

[16] Beginning with Access 2002, the standard SQL pattern-matching characters can be used by specifying ANSI 92 query mode in the Options window. Since earlier Access versions do not support this option and this option is not default in Access 2002, the textbook uses the * and ? pattern-matching characters for Access SQL statements.

[17] Most DBMSs require single quotes, the SQL:2006 standard. Microsoft Access allows either single or double quotes for string constants.

The wildcard character is not the only pattern-matching character. SQL:2006 specifies the underscore character _ to match any single character. Some DBMSs such as Access use the question mark ? to match any single character. In addition, most DBMSs have pattern-matching characters for matching a range of characters (for example, the digits 0 to 9) and any character from a list of characters. The symbols used for these other pattern-matching characters are not standard. To become proficient at writing inexact matching conditions, you should study the pattern-matching characters available with your DBMS.

In addition to performing pattern matching with strings, you can use exact matching with the equality = comparison operator. For example, the condition, CourseNo = 'IS480', matches a single row in the *Course* table. For both exact and inexact matching, case sensitivity is an important issue. Some DBMSs such as Microsoft Access are not case sensitive. In Access SQL, the previous condition matches "is480", "Is480", and "iS480" in addition to "IS480". Other DBMSs such as Oracle are case sensitive. In Oracle SQL, the previous condition matches only "IS480", not "is480", "Is480", or "iS480". To alleviate confusion, you can use the Oracle **upper** or **lower** functions to convert strings to upper or lowercase, respectively.

Example 4.5 depicts range matching on a column with the date data type. In Access SQL, pound symbols enclose date constants, while in Oracle SQL, single quotation marks enclose date constants. Date columns can be compared just like numbers with the usual comparison operators (=, <, etc.). The BETWEEN-AND operator defines a closed interval (includes end points). In Access Example 4.5, the BETWEEN-AND condition is a shortcut for FacHireDate >= #1/1/2001# AND FacHireDate <= #12/31/2002#.

> **BETWEEN-AND Operator**: a shortcut operator to test a numeric or date column against a range of values. The BETWEEN-AND operator returns true if the column is greater than or equal to the first value and less than or equal to the second value.

Example 4.5 (Access): Conditions on Date Columns
List the name and hiring date of faculty hired in 2001 or 2002.

```
SELECT FacFirstName, FacLastName, FacHireDate
 FROM  Faculty
 WHERE FacHireDate BETWEEN #1/1/2001# AND #12/31/2002#
```

FacFirstName	FacLastName	FacHireDate
CRISTOPHER	COLAN	01-Mar-2001
JULIA	MILLS	15-Mar-2002

Example 4.5 (Oracle): Conditions on Date Columns
In Oracle SQL, the standard format for dates is DD-Mon-YYYY where DD is the day number, Mon is the month abbreviation, and YYYY is the four-digit year.

```
SELECT FacFirstName, FacLastName, FacHireDate
 FROM Faculty
 WHERE FacHireDate BETWEEN '1-Jan-2001' AND '31-Dec-2002'
```

Besides testing columns for specified values, you sometimes need to test for the lack of a value. Null values are used when there is no normal value for a column. A null can mean that the value is unknown or the value is not applicable to the row. For the *Offering* table, a null value for *FacNo* means that the instructor is not yet assigned. Testing for null values is done with the IS NULL comparison operator as shown in Example 4.6. You can also test for a normal value using IS NOT NULL.

Example 4.6: Testing for Nulls
List the offering number and course number of summer 2006 offerings without an assigned instructor.

```
SELECT OfferNo, CourseNo
 FROM Offering
 WHERE FacNo IS NULL AND OffTerm = 'SUMMER'
   AND OffYear = 2008
```

OfferNo	CourseNo
1111	IS320

Example 4.7 depicts a complex logical expression involving both logical operators AND and OR. When mixing AND and OR in a logical expression, it is a good idea to use parentheses. Otherwise, the reader of the SELECT statement may not understand how the AND and OR conditions are grouped. Without parentheses, you must depend on the default way that AND and OR conditions are grouped.

Mixing AND and OR: always use parentheses to make the grouping of conditions explicit.

Example 4.7: Complex Logical Expression
List the offer number, course number, and faculty Social Security number for course offerings scheduled in fall 2007 or winter 2008.

```
SELECT OfferNo, CourseNo, FacNo
 FROM Offering
 WHERE (OffTerm = 'FALL' AND OffYear = 2007)
    OR (OffTerm = 'WINTER' AND OffYear = 2008)
```

OfferNo	CourseNo	FacNo
1234	IS320	098-76-5432
4321	IS320	098-76-5432
4444	IS320	543-21-0987
5555	FIN300	765-43-2109
5678	IS480	987-65-4321
6666	FIN450	987-65-4321

4.2.2 Joining Tables

Example 4.8 demonstrates a join of the *Course* and *Offering* tables. The join condition `Course.CourseNo = Offering.CourseNo` is specified in the WHERE clause.

Example 4.8 (Access): Join Tables but Show Columns from One Table Only
List the offering number, course number, days, and time of offerings containing the words *database* or *programming* in the course description and taught in spring 2008. The Oracle version of this example uses the % instead of the * as the wildcard character.

```
SELECT OfferNo, Offering.CourseNo, OffDays, OffTime
 FROM Offering, Course
 WHERE OffTerm = 'SPRING' AND OffYear = 2008
   AND (CrsDesc LIKE '*DATABASE*'
    OR CrsDesc LIKE '*PROGRAMMING*')
   AND Course.CourseNo = Offering.CourseNo
```

OfferNo	CourseNo	OffDays	OffTime
3333	IS320	MW	8:30 AM
5679	IS480	TTH	3:30 PM

There are two additional points of interest about Example 4.8. First, the *CourseNo* column names must be <u>qualified</u> (prefixed) with a table name (*Course* or *Offering*). Otherwise, the SELECT statement is ambiguous because *CourseNo* can refer to a column in either the *Course* or *Offering* tables. Second, both tables must be listed in the FROM clause even though the result columns come from only the *Offering* table. The *Course* table is needed in the FROM clause because conditions in the WHERE clause reference *CrsDesc*, a column of the *Course* table.

Example 4.9 demonstrates another join, but this time the result columns come from both tables. There are conditions on each table in addition to the join conditions. The Oracle formulation uses the % instead of the * as the wildcard character.

Example 4.9 (Access): Join Tables and Show Columns from Both Tables
List the offer number, course number, and name of the instructor of IS course offerings scheduled in fall 2007 taught by assistant professors.

```
SELECT OfferNo, CourseNo, FacFirstName, FacLastName
 FROM Offering, Faculty
 WHERE OffTerm = 'FALL' AND OffYear = 2007
   AND FacRank = 'ASST' AND CourseNo LIKE 'IS*'
   AND Faculty.FacNo = Offering.FacNo
```

OfferNo	CourseNo	FacFirstName	FacLastName
1234	IS320	LEONARD	VINCE
4321	IS320	LEONARD	VINCE

Example 4.9 (Oracle): Join Tables and Show Columns from Both Tables
List the offer number, course number, and name of the instructor of IS course offerings scheduled in fall 2007 taught by assistant professors.

```
SELECT OfferNo, CourseNo, FacFirstName, FacLastName
 FROM Offering, Faculty
 WHERE OffTerm = 'FALL' AND OffYear = 2007
   AND FacRank = 'ASST' AND CourseNo LIKE 'IS%'
   AND Faculty.FacNo = Offering.FacNo
```

In the SQL:2006 standard, a join operation can be expressed directly in the FROM clause rather than being expressed in both the FROM and WHERE clauses as shown in Examples 4.8 and 4.9. Note that Oracle beginning with version 9i supports join operations in the FROM clause, but previous versions do not support join operations in the FROM clause. To make a join operation in the FROM clause, use the keywords INNER JOIN as shown in Example 4.10. The join conditions are indicated by the ON keyword inside the FROM clause. Notice that the join condition no longer appears in the WHERE clause.

Example 4.10 (Access): Join Tables Using a Join Operation in the FROM Clause
List the offer number, course number, and name of the instructor of IS course offerings scheduled in fall 2007 that are taught by assistant professors (result is identical to Example 4.9). In Oracle, you should use the % instead of *.

```
SELECT OfferNo, CourseNo, FacFirstName, FacLastName
  FROM Offering INNER JOIN Faculty
    ON Faculty.FacNo = Offering.FacNo
  WHERE OffTerm = 'FALL' AND OffYear = 2007
    AND FacRank = 'ASST' AND CourseNo LIKE 'IS*'
```

4.2.3 Summarizing Tables with GROUP BY and HAVING

So far, the results of all examples in this section relate to individual rows. Even Example 4.9 relates to a combination of columns from individual *Offering* and *Faculty* rows. As mentioned in Chapter 3, it is sometimes important to show summaries of rows. The GROUP BY and HAVING clauses are used to show results about groups of rows rather than individual rows.

Example 4.11 depicts the GROUP BY clause to summarize groups of rows. Each result row contains a value of the grouping column (*StdMajor*) along with the aggregate calculation summarizing rows with the same value for the grouping column. The GROUP BY clause must contain every column in the SELECT clause except for aggregate expressions. For example, adding the *StdClass* column in the SELECT clause would make Example 4.11 invalid unless *StdClass* was also added to the GROUP BY clause.

Example 4.11: Grouping on a Single Column
Summarize the averageGPA of students by major.

```
SELECT StdMajor, AVG(StdGPA) AS AvgGPA
  FROM Student
  GROUP BY StdMajor
```

StdMajor	AvgGPA
ACCT	3.39999997615814
FIN	2.80000003178914
IS	3.23333330949148

GROUP BY Reminder: the columns in the SELECT clause must either be in the GROUP BY clause or be part of a summary calculation with an aggregate function.

Table 4-9 shows the standard aggregate functions. If you have a statistical calculation that cannot be performed with these functions, check your DBMS. Most DBMSs feature many functions beyond these standard ones.

Table 4-9: Standard Aggregate Functions

Aggregate Function	Meaning and Comments
COUNT(*)	Computes the number of rows.
COUNT(column)	Counts the non-null values in column; DISTINCT can be used to count the unique column values.
AVG	Computes the average of a numeric column or expression excluding null values; DISTINCT can be used to compute the average of unique column values.
SUM	Computes the sum of a numeric column or expression excluding null values; DISTINCT can be used to compute the average of unique column values.
MIN	Computes the smallest value. For string columns, the collating sequence is used to compare strings.
MAX	Computes the largest value. For string columns, the collating sequence is used to compare strings.

The COUNT, AVG, and SUM functions support the DISTINCT keyword to restrict the computation to unique column values. Example 4.12 demonstrates the DISTINCT keyword for the COUNT function. This example retrieves the number of offerings in a year as well as the number of distinct courses taught. Some DBMSs such as Microsoft Access do not support the DISTINCT keyword inside of aggregate functions. Chapter 9 presents an alternative formulation in Access SQL to compensate for the inability to use the DISTINCT keyword inside the COUNT function.

> **COUNT Function Usage**: COUNT(*) and COUNT(column) produce identical results except when "column" contains null values. See Chapter 9 for more details about the effect of null values on aggregate functions.

Example 4.12 (Oracle): Counting Rows and Unique Column Values
Summarize the number of offerings and unique courses by year.

```
SELECT OffYear, COUNT(*) AS NumOfferings,
       COUNT(DISTINCT CourseNo) AS NumCourses
  FROM Offering
  GROUP BY OffYear
```

OffYear	NumOfferings	NumCourses
2007	3	2
2008	10	6

Examples 4.13 and 4.14 contrast the WHERE and HAVING clauses. In Example 4.13, the WHERE clause selects upper-division students (juniors or seniors) before grouping on major. Because the WHERE clause eliminates students before grouping occurs, only upper-division students are grouped. In Example 4.14, a HAVING condition retains groups with an average GPA greater than 3.1. The HAVING clause applies to groups of rows, whereas the WHERE clause applies to individual rows. To use a HAVING clause, there must be a GROUP BY clause.

> **WHERE vs. HAVING**: use the WHERE clause for conditions that can be tested on individual rows. Use the HAVING clause for conditions that can be tested only on groups. Conditions in the HAVING clause should involve aggregate functions, whereas conditions in the WHERE clause cannot involve aggregate functions.

Example 4.13: Grouping with Row Conditions
Summarize the average GPA of upper division (junior or senior) students by major.

```
SELECT StdMajor, AVG(StdGPA) AS AvgGpa
  FROM Student
  WHERE StdClass = 'JR' OR StdClass = 'SR'
  GROUP BY StdMajor
```

StdMajor	AvgGPA
ACCT	3.5
FIN	2.8000000317891
IS	3.1499999761581

Example 4.14: Grouping with Row and Group Conditions

Summarize the average GPA of upper-division (junior or senior) students by major. Only list the majors with average GPA greater than 3.1.

```
SELECT StdMajor, AVG(StdGPA) AS AvgGpa
 FROM Student
 WHERE StdClass IN ('JR', 'SR')
 GROUP BY StdMajor
 HAVING AVG(StdGPA) > 3.1
```

StdMajor	AvgGPA
ACCT	3.5
IS	3.14999997615814

HAVING Reminder: the HAVING clause must be preceded by the GROUP BY clause.

One other point about Examples 4.13 and 4.14 is the use of the OR operator as compared to the IN operator (set element of operator). The WHERE condition in Examples 4.13 and 4.14 retains the same rows. The IN condition is true if *StdClass* matches any value in the parenthesized list. Chapter 9 provides additional explanation about the IN operator for nested queries.

To summarize all rows, aggregate functions can be used in SELECT without a GROUP BY clause as demonstrated in Example 4.15. The result is always a single row containing just the aggregate calculations.

Example 4.15: Grouping all Rows

List the number of upper-division students and their average GPA.

```
SELECT COUNT(*) AS StdCnt, AVG(StdGPA) AS AvgGPA
 FROM Student
 WHERE StdClass = 'JR' OR StdClass = 'SR'
```

StdCnt	AvgGPA
8	3.0625

Sometimes it is useful to group on more than one column as demonstrated by Example 4.16. The result shows one row for each combination of *StdMajor* and *StdClass*. Some rows have the same value for both aggregate calculations because there is only one associated row in the *Student* table. For example, there is only one row for the combination ('ACCT', 'JR').

Example 4.16: Grouping on Two Columns

Summarize the minimum and maximum GPA of students by major and class.

```
SELECT StdMajor, StdClass, MIN(StdGPA) AS MinGPA,
       MAX(StdGPA) AS MaxGPA
 FROM Student
 GROUP BY StdMajor, StdClass
```

StdMajor	StdClass	MinGPA	MaxGPA
ACCT	JR	3.5	3.5
ACCT	SO	3.3	3.3
FIN	JR	2.5	2.7
FIN	SR	3.2	3.2
IS	FR	3	3
IS	JR	3.6	3.6
IS	SO	3.8	3.8
IS	SR	2.2	4

A powerful combination is to use grouping with joins. There is no reason to restrict grouping to just one table. Often, more useful information is obtained by summarizing rows that result from a join. Example 4.17 demonstrates grouping applied to a join between *Course* and *Offering*. It is important to note that the join is performed before the grouping occurs. For example, after the join, there are six rows for BUSINESS PROGRAMMING. Because queries combining joins and grouping can be difficult to understand, Section 4.3 provides a more detailed explanation.

Example 4.17 (Access): Combining Grouping and Joins
Summarize the number of IS course offerings by course description.

```
SELECT CrsDesc, COUNT(*) AS OfferCount
  FROM Course, Offering
  WHERE Course.CourseNo = Offering.CourseNo
    AND Course.CourseNo LIKE 'IS*'
  GROUP BY CrsDesc
```

CrsDesc	OfferCount
FUNDAMENTALS OF BUSINESS PROGRAMMING	6
FUNDAMENTALS OF DATABASE MANAGEMENT	2
SYSTEMS ANALYSIS	2

Example 4.17 (Oracle): Combining Grouping and Joins
Summarize the number of IS course offerings by course description.

```
SELECT CrsDesc, COUNT(*) AS OfferCount
  FROM Course, Offering
  WHERE Course.CourseNo = Offering.CourseNo
    AND Course.CourseNo LIKE 'IS%'
  GROUP BY CrsDesc
```

4.2.4 Improving the Appearance of Results

We finish this section with two parts of the SELECT statement that can improve the appearance of results. Examples 4.18 and 4.19 demonstrate sorting using the ORDER BY clause. The sort sequence depends on the date type of the sorted field (numeric for numeric data types, ASCII collating sequence for string fields, and calendar sequence for data fields). By default, sorting occurs in ascending order. The keyword DESC can be used after a column name to sort in descending order as demonstrated in Example 4.19.

Example 4.18: Sorting on a Single Column
List the GPA, name, city, and state of juniors. Order the result by GPA in ascending order.

```
SELECT StdGPA, StdFirstName, StdLastName, StdCity,
       StdState
FROM Student
WHERE StdClass = 'JR'
ORDER BY StdGPA
```

StdGPA	StdFirstName	StdLastName	StdCity	StdState
2.50	ROBERTO	MORALES	SEATTLE	WA
2.70	BOB	NORBERT	BOTHELL	WA
3.50	CANDY	KENDALL	TACOMA	WA
3.60	MARIAH	DODGE	SEATTLE	WA

Example 4.19: Sorting on Two Columns with Descending Order
List the rank, salary, name, and department of faculty. Order the result by ascending (alphabetic) rank and descending salary.

```
SELECT FacRank, FacSalary, FacFirstName, FacLastName,
       FacDept
FROM Faculty
ORDER BY FacRank, FacSalary DESC
```

FacRank	FacSalary	FacFirstName	FacLastName	FacDept
ASSC	75000.00	JULIA	MILLS	FIN
ASSC	70000.00	LEONARD	FIBON	MS
ASST	40000.00	CRISTOPHER	COLAN	MS
ASST	35000.00	LEONARD	VINCE	MS
PROF	120000.00	VICTORIA	EMMANUEL	MS
PROF	65000.00	NICKI	MACON	FIN

Some students confuse ORDER BY and GROUP BY. In most systems, GROUP BY has the side effect of sorting by the grouping columns. You should not depend on this side effect. If you just want to sort, use ORDER BY rather than GROUP BY. If you want to sort and group, use both ORDER BY and GROUP BY.

Another way to improve the appearance of the result is to remove duplicate rows. By default, SQL does not remove duplicate rows. Duplicate rows are not possible when the primary keys of the result tables are included. There are a number of situations in which the primary key does not appear in the result. Example 4.21 demonstrates the DISTINCT keyword to remove duplicates that appear in the result of Example 4.20.

ORDER BY vs. DISTINCT: use the ORDER BY clause to sort a result table on one or more columns. Use the DISTINCT keyword to remove duplicates in the result.

Example 4.20: Result with Duplicates
List the city and state of faculty members.

```
SELECT FacCity, FacState
FROM Faculty
```

FacCity	FacState
SEATTLE	WA
BOTHELL	WA
SEATTLE	WA
BELLEVUE	WA
SEATTLE	WA
SEATTLE	WA

Example 4.21: Eliminating Duplicates with DISTINCT
List the unique city and state combinations in the *Faculty* table.

```
SELECT DISTINCT FacCity, FacState
  FROM Faculty
```

FacCity	FacState
BELLEVUE	WA
BOTHELL	WA
SEATTLE	WA

4.3 Conceptual Evaluation Process for SELECT Statements

To develop a clearer understanding of the SELECT statement, it is useful to understand the conceptual evaluation process or sequence of steps to produce the desired result. The conceptual evaluation process describes operations (mostly relational algebra operations) that produce intermediate tables leading to the result table. You may find it useful to refer to the conceptual evaluation process when first learning to write SELECT statements. After you gain initial competence with the SELECT statement, you should not need to refer to the conceptual evaluation process except to gain insight about difficult problems.

> **Conceptual Evaluation Process**: the sequence of operations and intermediate tables used to derive the result of a SELECT statement. The conceptual evaluation process may help you gain an initial understanding of the SELECT statement as well as help you to understand more difficult problems.

To demonstrate the conceptual evaluation process, consider Example 4.22 which involves many parts of the SELECT statement. It involves multiple tables (*Enrollment* and *Offering* in the FROM clause), row conditions (following WHERE), aggregate functions (COUNT and AVG) over groups of rows (GROUP BY), a group condition (following HAVING), and sorting of the final result (ORDER BY).

Example 4.22 (Access): Depict Many Parts of the SELECT Statement
List the course number, offer number, and average grade of students enrolled in fall 2005, IS course offerings in which more than one student is enrolled. Sort the result by course number in ascending order and average grade in descending order. The Oracle version of Example 4.22 is identical except for the % instead of the * as the wildcard character.

```
SELECT CourseNo, Offering.OfferNo,
       AVG(EnrGrade) AS AvgGrade
  FROM Enrollment, Offering
  WHERE CourseNo LIKE 'IS*' AND OffYear = 2007
    AND OffTerm = 'FALL'
    AND Enrollment.OfferNo = Offering.OfferNo
  GROUP BY CourseNo, Offering.OfferNo
  HAVING  COUNT(*) > 1
  ORDER BY CourseNo, 3 DESC
```

In the ORDER BY clause, note the number 3 as the second column to sort. The number 3 means sort by the third column (*AvgGrade*) in SELECT. Some DBMSs do not allow aggregate expressions or alias names (*AvgGrade*) in the ORDER BY clause.

Tables 4-10 to 4-12 show the input tables and the result. Only small input and result tables have been used so that you can understand more clearly the process to derive the result. It does not take large tables to depict the conceptual evaluation process well.

Table 4-10: Sample *Offering* Table

OfferNo	CourseNo	OffYear	OffTerm
1111	is480	2007	Fall
2222	is480	2007	Fall
3333	is320	2007	Fall
5555	is480	2008	Winter
6666	is320	2008	Spring

Table 4-11: Sample *Enrollment* Table

StdNo	OfferNo	EnrGrade
111-11-1111	1111	3.1
111-11-1111	2222	3.5
111-11-1111	3333	3.3
111-11-1111	5555	3.8
222-22-2222	1111	3.2
222-22-2222	2222	3.3
333-33-3333	1111	3.6

Table 4-12: Example 4.22 Result

CourseNo	OfferNo	AvgGrade
IS480	2222	3.4
IS480	1111	3.3

The conceptual evaluation process is a sequence of operations as indicated in Figure 4.2. This process is conceptual rather than actual because most SQL compilers can produce the same output using many shortcuts. Because the shortcuts are system specific, rather mathematical, and performance oriented, we will not review them. The conceptual evaluation process provides a foundation for understanding the meaning of SQL statements that is independent of system and performance issues. The remainder of this section applies the conceptual evaluation process to Example 4.22.

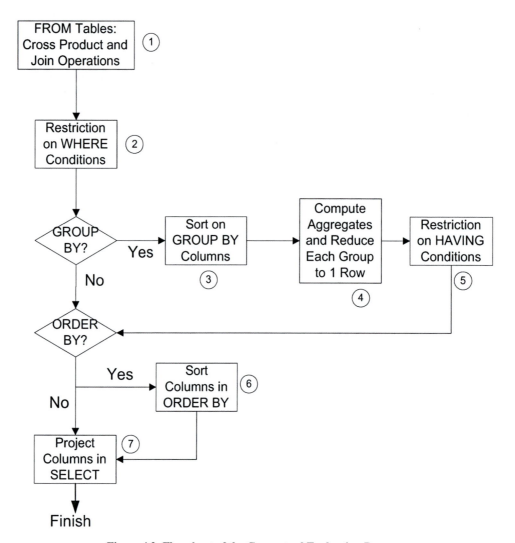

Figure 4.2: Flowchart of the Conceptual Evaluation Process

1 - The first step in the conceptual process combines the tables in the FROM clause with the cross product and join operators. In Example 4.22, a cross product operation is necessary because two tables are listed. A join operation is not necessary because the INNER JOIN keyword does not appear in the FROM statement. Recall that the cross product operator shows all possible rows by combining two tables. The resulting table contains the product of the number of rows and the sum of the columns. In this case, the cross product contains 35 rows (5 × 7) and 7 columns (3+4). Table 4-13 shows a partial result. As an exercise, you are encouraged to derive the entire result. As a notational shortcut here, the table name (abbreviated as E and O) is prefixed before the column name for OfferNo.

Table 4-13: Partial Result of Step 1 for First Two *Offering* Rows (1111 and 2222)

O.OfferNo	CourseNo	OffYear	OffTerm	StdNo	E.OfferNo	EnrGrade
1111	IS480	2007	FALL	111-11-1111	1111	3.1
1111	IS480	2007	FALL	111-11-1111	2222	3.5
1111	IS480	2007	FALL	111-11-1111	3333	3.3
1111	IS480	2007	FALL	111-11-1111	5555	3.8
1111	IS480	2007	FALL	222-22-2222	1111	3.2
1111	IS480	2007	FALL	222-22-2222	2222	3.3
1111	IS480	2007	FALL	333-33-3333	1111	3.6
2222	IS480	2007	FALL	111-11-1111	1111	3.1
2222	IS480	2007	FALL	111-11-1111	2222	3.5
2222	IS480	2007	FALL	111-11-1111	3333	3.3
2222	IS480	2007	FALL	111-11-1111	5555	3.8
2222	IS480	2007	FALL	222-22-2222	1111	3.2
2222	IS480	2007	FALL	222-22-2222	2222	3.3
2222	IS480	2007	FALL	333-33-3333	1111	3.6

2 - The second step uses a restriction operation to retrieve rows that satisfy the conditions in the WHERE clause from the result of step 1. We have four conditions: a join condition on *OfferNo*, a condition on *CourseNo*, a condition on *OffYear*, and a condition on *OffTerm*. Note that the condition on *CourseNo* includes the wildcard character (*). Any course numbers beginning with IS match this condition. Table 4-14 shows that the result of the cross product (35 rows) is reduced to six rows.

Table 4-14: Result of Step 2

O.OfferNo	CourseNo	OffYear	OffTerm	StdNo	E.OfferNo	EnrGrade
1111	IS480	2007	FALL	111-11-1111	1111	3.1
2222	IS480	2007	FALL	111-11-1111	2222	3.5
1111	IS480	2007	FALL	222-22-2222	1111	3.2
2222	IS480	2007	FALL	222-22-2222	2222	3.3
1111	IS480	2007	FALL	333-33-3333	1111	3.6
3333	IS320	2007	FALL	111-11-1111	3333	3.3

3 - The third step sorts the result of step 2 by the columns specified in the GROUP BY clause. The GROUP BY clause indicates that the output should relate to groups of rows rather than individual rows. If the output relates to individual rows rather than groups of rows, the GROUP BY clause is omitted. When using the GROUP BY clause, you must include <u>every</u> column from the SELECT clause except for expressions that involve an aggregate function[18]. Table 4-15 shows the result of step 2 sorted by *CourseNo* and *O.OfferNo*. Note that the columns have been rearranged to make the result easier to read.

---

[18] In other words, when using the GROUP BY clause, every column in the SELECT clause should either be in the GROUP BY clause or be part of an expression with an aggregate function.

Table 4-15: Result of Step 3

CourseNo	O.OfferNo	OffYear	OffTerm	StdNo	E.OfferNo	EnrGrade
IS320	3333	2007	FALL	111-11-1111	3333	3.3
IS480	1111	2007	FALL	111-11-1111	1111	3.1
IS480	1111	2007	FALL	222-22-2222	1111	3.2
IS480	1111	2007	FALL	333-33-3333	1111	3.6
IS480	2222	2007	FALL	111-11-1111	2222	3.5
IS480	2222	2007	FALL	222-22-2222	2222	3.3

4 - The fourth step is only necessary if there is a GROUP BY clause. The fourth step computes aggregate function(s) for each group of rows and reduces each group to a single row. All rows in a group have the same values for the GROUP BY columns. In Table 4-16, there are three groups {<IS320,3333>, <IS480, 1111>, <IS480,2222>}. Computed columns are added for aggregate functions in the SELECT and HAVING clauses. Table 4-16 shows two new columns for the AVG function in the SELECT clause and the COUNT function in the HAVING clause. Note that remaining columns are eliminated at this point because they are not needed in the remaining steps.

Table 4-16: Result of Step 4

CourseNo	O.OfferNo	AvgGrade	Count(*)
IS320	3333	3.3	1
IS480	1111	3.3	3
IS480	2222	3.4	2

5 - The fifth step eliminates rows that do not satisfy the HAVING condition. Table 4-17 shows that the first row in Table 4-16 is removed because it fails the HAVING condition. Note that the HAVING clause specifies a restriction operation for groups of rows. The HAVING clause cannot be present without a preceding GROUP BY clause. The conditions in the HAVING clause always relate to groups of rows, not to individual rows. Typically, conditions in the HAVING clause involve aggregate functions.

Table 4-17: Result of Step 5

CourseNo	O.OfferNo	AvgGrade	Count(*)
IS480	1111	3.3	3
IS480	2222	3.4	2

6 - The sixth step sorts the results according to the ORDER BY clause. Note that the ORDER BY clause is optional. Table 4-18 shows the result table after sorting.

Table 4-18: Result of Step 6

CourseNo	O.OfferNo	AvgGrade	Count(*)
IS480	2222	3.4	3
IS480	1111	3.3	2

7 - The seventh step performs a final projection. Columns appearing in the result of step 6 are eliminated if they do not appear in the SELECT clause. Table 4-19 (identical to Table 4-12) shows the result after the projection of step 6. The Count(*) column is eliminated because it does not appear in the SELECT list. The seventh step (projection) occurs after the sixth step (sorting) because the ORDER BY clause can contain columns that do not appear in the SELECT list.

Table 4-19: Result of Step 7

CourseNo	O.OfferNo	AvgGrade
IS480	2222	3.4
IS480	1111	3.3

This section finishes by discussing three major lessons about the conceptual evaluation process. These lessons are more important to remember than the specific details about the conceptual process.

GROUP BY conceptually occurs after WHERE. If you have an error in a SELECT statement involving WHERE or GROUP BY, the problem is most likely in the WHERE clause. You can check the intermediate results after the WHERE clause by submitting a SELECT statement without the GROUP BY clause.

Grouping occurs only one time in the evaluation process. If your problem involves more than one independent aggregate calculation, you may need more than one SELECT statement.

Using sample tables can help you analyze difficult problems. It is often not necessary to go through the entire evaluation process. Rather, use sample tables to understand only the difficult part. Section 4.5 and Chapter 9 depict the use of sample tables to help analyze difficult problems.

4.4 Critical Questions for Query Formulation

The conceptual evaluation process depicted in Figure 4.2 should help you understand the meaning of most SELECT statements, but it will probably not help you to formulate queries. Query formulation involves a conversion from a problem statement into a statement of a database language such as SQL as shown in Figure 4.3. In between the problem statement and the database language statement, you convert the problem statement into a database representation. Typically, the difficult part is to convert the problem statement into a database representation. This conversion involves a detailed knowledge of the tables and relationships and careful attention to possible ambiguities in the problem statement. The critical questions presented in this section provide a structured process to convert a problem statement into a database representation.

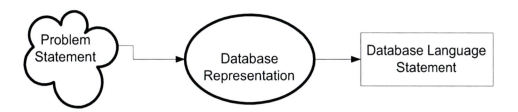

Figure 4.3: Query Formulation Process

Critical Questions for Query Formulation: provide a checklist to convert a problem statement into a database representation consisting of tables, columns, table connection operations, and row grouping requirements.

In converting from the problem statement into a database representation, you should answer three critical questions. Table 4-20 summarizes the analysis for the critical questions.

What tables are needed? For the first question, you should match data requirements to columns and tables. You should identify columns that are needed for output and conditions as well as intermediate tables needed to connect other tables. For example, if you want to join the *Student* and *Offering* tables, the *Enrollment* table should be included because it provides a connection to these tables. The *Student* and *Offering* tables cannot be combined directly. All tables needed in the query should be listed in the FROM clause.

How are the tables combined? For the second question, most tables are combined by a join operation. In Chapter 9, you will use the outer join, difference, and division operators to combine tables. For now, just concentrate on combining tables with joins. You need to identify the matching columns for each join. In most joins, the primary key of a parent table is matched with a foreign key of a related child table. Occasionally, the primary key of the parent table contains multiple columns. In this case, you need to match on both columns. In some situations, the matching columns do not involve a primary key/foreign key combination. You can perform a join as long as the matching columns have compatible data types. For example, when joining customer tables from different databases, there may not be a common primary key. Joining on other columns such as name, address, and so on may be necessary.

Does the output involve individual rows or groups of rows? For the third question, look for computations involving aggregate functions in the problem statement. For example, the problem "list the name and average grade of students" contains an aggregate computation. Problems referencing an aggregate function indicate that the output relates to groups of rows. Hence the SELECT statement requires a GROUP BY clause. If the problem contains conditions with aggregate functions, a HAVING clause should accompany the GROUP BY clause. For example, the problem "list the offer number of course offerings with more than 30 students" needs a HAVING clause with a condition involving the COUNT function.

Table 4-20: Summary of Critical Questions for Query Formulation

Question	Analysis Tips
What tables are needed?	Match columns to output data requirements and conditions to test. If tables are not directly related, identify intermediate tables to provide a join path between tables.
How are the tables combined?	Most tables are combined using a primary key from a parent table to a foreign key of a child table. More difficult problems may involve other join conditions as well as other combining operators (outer join, difference, or division).
Does the output involve individual rows or groups of rows?	Identify aggregate functions used in output data requirements and conditions to test. A SELECT statement requires a GROUP BY clause if aggregate functions are needed. A HAVING clause is needed if conditions use aggregate functions.

After answering these questions, you are ready to convert the database representation into a database language statement. To help in this process, you should develop a collection of statements for each kind of relational algebra operator using a database that you understand well. For example, you should have statements for problems that involve join operations, joins with grouping, and joins with grouping conditions. As you increase your understanding of SQL, this conversion will become easy for most problems. For difficult problems such as those discussed in Section 4.5 and Chapter 9, relying on similar problems may be necessary because difficult problems are not common.

4.5 Refining Query Formulation Skills with Examples

Let's apply your query formulation skills and knowledge of the SELECT statement to more difficult problems. All problems in this section involve the parts of SELECT discussed in Sections 4.2 and 4.3. The problems involve more difficult aspects such as joining more than two tables, grouping after joins of several tables, joining a table to itself, and traditional set operators.

4.5.1 Joining Multiple Tables with the Cross Product Style

We begin with a number of join problems that are formulated using cross product operations in the FROM clause. This way to formulate joins is known as the cross product style because of the implied cross product operations. Query language compilers recognize the join conditions in the WHERE clause so cross product operations are not actually performed. The next subsection uses join operations in the FROM clause to contrast the ways that joins can be expressed.

> **Cross Product Style**: lists tables in the FROM clause and join conditions in the WHERE clause. The cross product style is easy to read but does not support outer join operations.

In Example 4.23, some student rows appear more than once in the result. For example, Roberto Morales appears twice. Because of the 1-M relationship between the *Student* and *Enrollment* tables, a *Student* row can match multiple *Enrollment* rows.

Example 4.23: Joining Two Tables

List the student name, offering number, and grade of students who have a grade ≥ 3.5 in a course offering.

```
SELECT StdFirstName, StdLastName, OfferNo, EnrGrade
  FROM Student, Enrollment
  WHERE EnrGrade >= 3.5
    AND Student.StdNo = Enrollment.StdNo
```

StdFirstName	StdLastName	OfferNo	EnrGrade
CANDY	KENDALL	1234	3.5
MARIAH	DODGE	1234	3.8
HOMER	WELLS	4321	3.5
ROBERTO	MORALES	4321	3.5
BOB	NORBERT	5679	3.7
ROBERTO	MORALES	5679	3.8
MARIAH	DODGE	6666	3.6
LUKE	BRAZZI	7777	3.7
BOB	NORBERT	9876	3.5
WILLIAM	PILGRIM	9876	4

Examples 4.24 and 4.25 depict duplicate elimination after a join. In Example 4.24, some students appear more than once as in Example 4.23. Because only columns from the *Student* table are used in the output, duplicate rows appear. When you join a parent table to a child table and show only columns from the parent table in the result, duplicate rows can appear in the result. To eliminate duplicate rows, you can use the DISTINCT keyword as shown in Example 4.25.

Example 4.24: Join with Duplicates

List the names of students who have a grade ≥ 3.5 in a course offering.

```
SELECT StdFirstName, StdLastName
  FROM Student, Enrollment
  WHERE EnrGrade >= 3.5
    AND Student.StdNo = Enrollment.StdNo
```

StdFirstName	StdLastName
CANDY	KENDALL
MARIAH	DODGE
HOMER	WELLS
ROBERTO	MORALES
BOB	NORBERT
ROBERTO	MORALES
MARIAH	DODGE
LUKE	BRAZZI
BOB	NORBERT
WILLIAM	PILGRIM

Example 4.25: Join with Duplicates Removed

List the student names (without duplicates) that have a grade ≥ 3.5 in a course offering.

```
SELECT DISTINCT StdFirstName, StdLastName
 FROM Student, Enrollment
 WHERE EnrGrade >= 3.5
   AND Student.StdNo = Enrollment.StdNo
```

StdFirstName	StdLastName
BOB	NORBERT
CANDY	KENDALL
HOMER	WELLS
LUKE	BRAZZI
MARIAH	DODGE
ROBERTO	MORALES
WILLIAM	PILGRIM

Examples 4.26 through 4.29 depict problems involving more than two tables. In these problems, it is important to identify the tables in the FROM clause. Make sure that you examine conditions to test as well as columns in the result. In Example 4.28, the *Enrollment* table is needed even though it does not supply columns in the result or conditions to test. The *Enrollment* table is needed to connect the *Student* table with the *Offering* table. Example 4.29 extends Example 4.28 with details from the *Course* table. All five tables are needed to supply outputs, to test conditions, or to connect other tables.

Example 4.26: Joining Three Tables with Columns from Only Two Tables

List the student name and the offering number in which the grade is greater than 3.7 and the offering is given in fall 2007.

```
SELECT StdFirstName, StdLastName, Enrollment.OfferNo
 FROM Student, Enrollment, Offering
 WHERE Student.StdNo = Enrollment.StdNo
   AND Offering.OfferNo = Enrollment.OfferNo
   AND OffYear = 2007 AND OffTerm = 'FALL'
   AND EnrGrade >= 3.7
```

StdFirstName	StdLastName	OfferNo
MARIAH	DODGE	1234

Example 4.27: Joining Three Tables with Columns from Only Two Tables

List Leonard Vince's teaching schedule in fall 2007. For each course, list the offering number, course number, number of units, days, location, and time.

```
SELECT OfferNo, Offering.CourseNo, CrsUnits, OffDays,
       OffLocation, OffTime
 FROM Faculty, Course, Offering
 WHERE Faculty.FacNo = Offering.FacNo
   AND Offering.CourseNo = Course.CourseNo
   AND OffYear = 2007 AND OffTerm = 'FALL'
   AND FacFirstName = 'LEONARD'
   AND FacLastName = 'VINCE'
```

OfferNo	CourseNo	CrsUnits	OffDays	OffLocation	OffTime
1234	IS320	4	MW	BLM302	10:30 AM
4321	IS320	4	TTH	BLM214	3:30 PM

Example 4.28: Joining Four Tables

List Bob Norbert's course schedule in spring 2008. For each course, list the offering number, course number, days, location, time, and faculty name.

```
SELECT Offering.OfferNo, Offering.CourseNo, OffDays,
       OffLocation, OffTime, FacFirstName, FacLastName
 FROM Faculty, Offering, Enrollment, Student
 WHERE Offering.OfferNo = Enrollment.OfferNo
   AND Student.StdNo = Enrollment.StdNo
   AND Faculty.FacNo = Offering.FacNo
   AND OffYear = 2008 AND OffTerm = 'SPRING'
   AND StdFirstName = 'BOB'
   AND StdLastName = 'NORBERT'
```

OfferNo	CourseNo	OffDays	OffLocation	OffTime	FacFirstName	FacLastName
5679	IS480	TTH	BLM412	3:30 PM	CRISTOPHER	COLAN
9876	IS460	TTH	BLM307	1:30 PM	LEONARD	FIBON

Example 4.29: Joining Five Tables

List Bob Norbert's course schedule in spring 2008. For each course, list the offering number, course number, days, location, time, course units, and faculty name.

```
SELECT Offering.OfferNo, Offering.CourseNo, OffDays,
       OffLocation, OffTime, CrsUnits, FacFirstName,
       FacLastName
 FROM Faculty, Offering, Enrollment, Student, Course
 WHERE Faculty.FacNo = Offering.FacNo
   AND Offering.OfferNo = Enrollment.OfferNo
   AND Student.StdNo = Enrollment.StdNo
   AND Offering.CourseNo = Course.CourseNo
   AND OffYear = 2008 AND OffTerm = 'SPRING'
   AND StdFirstName = 'BOB'
   AND StdLastName = 'NORBERT'
```

OfferNo	CourseNo	OffDays	OffLocation	OffTime	CrsUnits	FacFirstName	FacLastName
5679	IS480	TTH	BLM412	3:30 PM	4	CRISTOPHER	COLAN
9876	IS460	TTH	BLM307	1:30 PM	4	LEONARD	FIBON

Example 4.30 demonstrates another way to combine the *Student* and *Faculty* tables. In Example 4.28, you saw it was necessary to combine the *Student*, *Enrollment*, *Offering*, and *Faculty* tables to find faculty teaching a specified student. To find students who are on the faculty (perhaps teaching assistants), the tables can be joined directly. Combining the *Student* and *Faculty* tables in this way is similar to an intersection operation. However, intersection cannot actually be performed here because the *Student* and *Faculty* tables are not union compatible.

Example 4.30: Joining Two Tables without Matching on a Primary and Foreign Key
List students who are on the faculty. Include all student columns in the result.

```
SELECT Student.*
  FROM Student, Faculty
  WHERE StdNo = FacNo
```

StdNo	StdFirstName	StdLastName	StdCity	StdState	StdMajor	StdClass	StdGPA	StdZip
876-54-3210	CRISTOPHER	COLAN	SEATTLE	WA	IS	SR	4.00	98114-1332

A minor point about Example 4.30 is the use of the * after the SELECT keyword. Prefixing the * with a table name and period indicates all columns of the specified table are in the result. Using an * without a table name prefix indicates that all columns from all FROM tables are in the result.

4.5.2 Joining Multiple Tables with the Join Operator Style

As demonstrated in Section 4.2, join operations can be expressed directly in the FROM clause using the INNER JOIN and ON keywords. This <u>join operator style</u> can be used to combine any number of tables. To ensure that you are comfortable using this style, this subsection presents examples of multiple table joins beginning with a two-table join in Example 4.31. Note that these examples do not execute in Oracle versions before 9i.

> **Join Operator Style**: lists join operations in the FROM clause using the INNER JOIN and ON keywords. The join operator style can be somewhat difficult to read for many join operations, but it supports outer join operations as shown in Chapter 9.

Example 4.31 (Access and Oracle): Join Two Tables Using the Join Operator Style
Retrieve the name, city, and grade of students who have a high grade (greater than or equal to 3.5) in a course offering.

```
SELECT StdFirstName, StdLastName, StdCity, EnrGrade
  FROM Student INNER JOIN Enrollment
    ON Student.StdNo = Enrollment.StdNo
  WHERE EnrGrade >= 3.5
```

StdFirstName	StdLastName	StdCity	EnrGrade
CANDY	KENDALL	TACOMA	3.5
MARIAH	DODGE	SEATTLE	3.8
HOMER	WELLS	SEATTLE	3.5
ROBERTO	MORALES	SEATTLE	3.5
BOB	NORBERT	BOTHELL	3.7
ROBERTO	MORALES	SEATTLE	3.8
MARIAH	DODGE	SEATTLE	3.6
LUKE	BRAZZI	SEATTLE	3.7
BOB	NORBERT	BOTHELL	3.5
WILLIAM	PILGRIM	BOTHELL	4

The join operator style can be extended to handle any number of tables. Think of the join operator style as writing a complicated formula with lots of parentheses. To add another part to the formula, you need to add the arguments, operator, and another level of parentheses. For example, with the formula $(X + Y) * Z$, you can add another operation as $((X + Y) * Z) / W$. This same principle can be applied with the join operator style. Examples 4.32 and 4.33 extend Example 4.31 with additional conditions that need other tables. In both examples, another INNER JOIN is added to the end of the previous INNER JOIN operations. The INNER JOIN could also have been added at the beginning or middle if desired. The ordering of INNER JOIN operations is not important.

Example 4.32 (Access and Oracle): Join Three Tables using the Join Operator Style
Retrieve the name, city, and grade of students who have a high grade (greater than or equal 3.5) in a course offered in fall 2007.

```
SELECT StdFirstName, StdLastName, StdCity, EnrGrade
 FROM ( Student INNER JOIN Enrollment
     ON Student.StdNo = Enrollment.StdNo )
   INNER JOIN Offering
     ON Offering.OfferNo = Enrollment.OfferNo
 WHERE EnrGrade >= 3.5 AND OffTerm = 'FALL'
   AND OffYear = 2007
```

StdFirstName	StdLastName	StdCity	EnrGrade
CANDY	KENDALL	TACOMA	3.5
MARIAH	DODGE	SEATTLE	3.8
HOMER	WELLS	SEATTLE	3.5
ROBERTO	MORALES	SEATTLE	3.5

Example 4.33 (Access and Oracle): Join Four tables Using the Join Operator Style
Retrieve the name, city, and grade of students who have a high grade (greater than or equal to 3.5) in a course offered in fall 2007 taught by Leonard Vince.

```
SELECT StdFirstName, StdLastName, StdCity, EnrGrade
 FROM ( (Student INNER JOIN Enrollment
       ON Student.StdNo = Enrollment.StdNo )
   INNER JOIN Offering
     ON Offering.OfferNo = Enrollment.OfferNo )
   INNER JOIN Faculty ON Faculty.FacNo = Offering.FacNo
 WHERE EnrGrade >= 3.5 AND OffTerm = 'FALL'
   AND OffYear = 2007 AND FacFirstName = 'LEONARD'
   AND FacLastName = 'VINCE'
```

StdFirstName	StdLastName	StdCity	EnrGrade
CANDY	KENDALL	TACOMA	3.5
MARIAH	DODGE	SEATTLE	3.8
HOMER	WELLS	SEATTLE	3.5
ROBERTO	MORALES	SEATTLE	3.5

The cross product and join operator styles can be mixed as demonstrated in Example 4.34. In most cases, it is preferable to use one style or the other, however.

Example 4.34 (Access and Oracle): Combine the Cross Product and Join Operator Styles
Retrieve the name, city, and grade of students who have a high grade (greater than or equal to 3.5) in a course offered in fall 2007 taught by Leonard Vince (same result as Example 4.33).

```
SELECT StdFirstName, StdLastName, StdCity, EnrGrade
  FROM ( (Student INNER JOIN Enrollment
    ON Student.StdNo = Enrollment.StdNo )
    INNER JOIN Offering
    ON Offering.OfferNo = Enrollment.OfferNo ),
    Faculty
 WHERE EnrGrade >= 3.5 AND OffTerm = 'FALL'
   AND OffYear = 2007 AND FacFirstName = 'LEONARD'
   AND FacLastName = 'VINCE'
   AND Faculty.FacNo = Offering.FacNo
```

The choice between the cross product and the join operator styles is largely a matter of preference. In the cross product style, it is easy to see the tables in the SQL statement. The cross product style has been criticized because users sometimes forget a join condition in the WHERE clause leading to a disk intensive cross product operation. For multiple joins, the join operator style can be difficult to read because of nested parentheses. The primary advantage of the join operator style is that you can formulate queries involving outer joins as described in Chapter 9.

You should be comfortable reading both join styles even if you only write SQL statements using one style. You may need to maintain statements written with both styles. In addition, some visual query languages generate code in one of the styles. For example, Query Design, the visual query language of Microsoft Access, generates code in the join operator style.

4.5.3 Self-Joins and Multiple Joins between Two Tables

Example 4.35 demonstrates a <u>self-join</u>, a join involving a table with itself. A self-join is necessary to find relationships among rows of the same table. The foreign key, *FacSupervisor*, shows relationships among *Faculty* rows. To find the supervisor name of a faculty member, match on the *FacSupervisor* column with the *FacNo* column. The trick is to imagine that you are working with two copies of the *Faculty* table. One copy plays the role of the subordinate, while the other copy plays the role of the superior. In SQL, a self-join requires alias names (*Subr* and *Supr*) in the FROM clause to distinguish between the two roles or copies.

> **Self-Join**: a join between a table and itself (two copies of the same table). Self-joins are useful for finding relationships among rows of the same table.

Example 4.35: Self-join

List faculty members who have a higher salary than their supervisor. List the Social Security number, name, and salary of the faculty and supervisor.

```
SELECT Subr.FacNo, Subr.FacLastName, Subr.FacSalary,
       Supr.FacNo, Supr.FacLastName, Supr.FacSalary
  FROM Faculty Subr, Faculty Supr
  WHERE Subr.FacSupervisor = Supr.FacNo
    AND Subr.FacSalary > Supr.FacSalary
```

Subr.FacNo	Subr.FacLastName	Subr.FacSalary	Supr.FacNo	Supr.FacLastName	Supr.FacSalary
987-65-4321	MILLS	75000.00	765-43-2109	MACON	65000.00

Problems involving self-joins can be difficult to understand. If you are having trouble understanding Example 4.35, use the conceptual evaluation process to help. Start with a small *Faculty* table. Copy this table and use the names *Subr* and *Supr* to distinguish between the two copies. Join the two tables over *Subr.FacSupervisor* and *Supr.FacNo*. If you need, derive the join using a cross product operation. You should be able to see that each result row in the join shows a subordinate and supervisor pair.

Problems involving self-referencing (unary) relationships are part of tree-structured queries. In tree-structured queries, a table can be visualized as a structure such as a tree or hierarchy. For example, the *Faculty* table has a structure showing an organization hierarchy. At the top, the college dean resides. At the bottom, faculty members without subordinates reside. Similar structures apply to the chart of accounts in accounting systems, part structures in manufacturing systems, and route networks in transportation systems.

A more difficult problem than a self-join is to find all subordinates (direct or indirect) in an organization hierarchy. This problem can be solved in SQL if the number of subordinate levels is known. One join for each subordinate level is needed. Without knowing the number of subordinate levels, this problem cannot be done in SQL-92 although it can be solved in SQL:2006 using the WITH RECURSIVE clause and in proprietary SQL extensions. In SQL-92, tree-structured queries can be solved by using SQL inside a programming language.

Example 4.36 shows another difficult join problem. This problem involves two joins between the same two tables (*Offering* and *Faculty*). Alias table names (*O1* and *O2*) are needed to distinguish between the two copies of the *Offering* table used in the statement.

Example 4.36: More Than One Join between Tables using Alias Table Names

List the names of faculty members and the course number for which the faculty member teaches the same course number as his or her supervisor in 2008.

```
SELECT FacFirstName, FacLastName, O1.CourseNo
  FROM Faculty, Offering O1, Offering O2
  WHERE Faculty.FacNo = O1.FacNo
    AND Faculty.FacSupervisor = O2.FacNo
    AND O1.OffYear = 2008 AND O2.OffYear = 2008
    AND O1.CourseNo = O2.CourseNo
```

FacFirstName	FacLastName	CourseNo
LEONARD	VINCE	IS320
LEONARD	FIBON	IS320

If this problem is too difficult, use the conceptual evaluation process (Figure 4.2) with sample tables to gain insight. Perform a join between the sample *Faculty* and *Offering* tables, then join this result to another copy of *Offering* (*O2*) matching *FacSupervisor* with *O2.FacNo*. In the resulting table, select the rows that have matching course numbers and year equal to 2006.

4.5.4 Combining Joins and Grouping

Example 4.37 demonstrates why it is sometimes necessary to group on multiple columns. After studying Example 4.37, you might be confused about the necessity to group on both *OfferNo* and *CourseNo*. One simple explanation is that any columns appearing in a SELECT list must be either a grouping column or an aggregrate expression. However, this explanation does not quite tell the entire story. Grouping on *OfferNo* alone produces the same values for the computed column (*NumStudents*) because *OfferNo* is the primary key. Including nonunique columns such as *CourseNo* adds information to each result row but does not change the aggregate calculations. If you do not understand this point, use sample tables to demonstrate it. When evaluating your sample tables, remember that joins occur before grouping as indicated in the conceptual evaluation process.

Example 4.37: Join with Grouping on Multiple Columns

List the course number, the offering number, and the number of students enrolled. Only include courses offered in spring 2008.

```
SELECT CourseNo, Enrollment.OfferNo,
       Count(*) AS NumStudents
 FROM Offering, Enrollment
 WHERE Offering.OfferNo = Enrollment.OfferNo
   AND OffYear = 2008 AND OffTerm = 'SPRING'
 GROUP BY Enrollment.OfferNo, CourseNo
```

CourseNo	OfferNo	NumStudents
FIN480	7777	3
IS460	9876	7
IS480	5679	6

Example 4.38 demonstrates another problem involving joins and grouping. An important part of this problem is the need for the *Student* table and the HAVING condition. They are needed because the problem statement refers to an aggregate function involving the *Student* table.

Example 4.38: Joins, grouping, and group conditions

List the course number, the offering number, and the average GPA of students enrolled. Only include courses offered in fall 2007 in which the average GPA of enrolled students is greater than 3.0.

```
SELECT CourseNo, Enrollment.OfferNo, Avg(StdGPA) AS
AvgGPA
 FROM Student, Offering, Enrollment
 WHERE Offering.OfferNo = Enrollment.OfferNo
   AND Enrollment.StdNo = Student.StdNo
   AND OffYear = 2007 AND OffTerm = 'FALL'
 GROUP BY CourseNo, Enrollment.OfferNo
 HAVING Avg(StdGPA) > 3.0
```

CourseNo	OfferNo	AvgGPA
IS320	1234	3.23
IS320	4321	3.03

4.5.5 Traditional Set Operators in SQL

In SQL, you can directly use the traditional set operators with the UNION, INTERSECT, and EXCEPT keywords. Some DBMSs including Microsoft Access do not support the INTERSECT and EXCEPT keywords. As with relational algebra, the problem is always to make sure that the tables are union compatible. In SQL, you can use a SELECT statement to make tables compatible by listing only compatible columns. Examples 4.39 through 4.41 demonstrate set operations on column subsets of the *Faculty* and *Student* tables. The columns have been renamed to avoid confusion.

Example 4.39: UNION Query
Show all faculty and students. Only show the common columns in the result.

```
SELECT FacNo AS PerNo, FacFirstName AS FirstName,
       FacLastName AS LastName, FacCity AS City,
       FacState AS State
  FROM Faculty
     UNION
SELECT StdNo AS PerNo, StdFirstName AS FirstName,
       StdLastName AS LastName, StdCity AS City,
       StdState AS State
  FROM Student
```

PerNo	FirstName	LastName	City	State
098765432	LEONARD	VINCE	SEATTLE	WA
123456789	HOMER	WELLS	SEATTLE	WA
124567890	BOB	NORBERT	BOTHELL	WA
234567890	CANDY	KENDALL	TACOMA	WA
345678901	WALLY	KENDALL	SEATTLE	WA
456789012	JOE	ESTRADA	SEATTLE	WA
543210987	VICTORIA	EMMANUEL	BOTHELL	WA
567890123	MARIAH	DODGE	SEATTLE	WA
654321098	LEONARD	FIBON	SEATTLE	WA
678901234	TESS	DODGE	REDMOND	WA
765432109	NICKI	MACON	BELLEVUE	WA
789012345	ROBERTO	MORALES	SEATTLE	WA
876543210	CRISTOPHER	COLAN	SEATTLE	WA
890123456	LUKE	BRAZZI	SEATTLE	WA
901234567	WILLIAM	PILGRIM	BOTHELL	WA
987654321	JULIA	MILLS	SEATTLE	WA

Example 4.40 (Oracle only): INTERSECT Query
Show teaching assistants, faculty who are students. Only show the common columns in the result.

```
SELECT FacNo AS PerNo, FacFirstName AS FirstName,
       FacLastName AS LastName, FacCity AS City,
       FacState AS State
  FROM Faculty
     INTERSECT
SELECT StdNo AS PerNo, StdFirstName AS FirstName,
       StdLastName AS LastName, StdCity AS City,
       StdState AS State
  FROM Student
```

PerNo	FirstName	LastName	City	State
876543210	CRISTOPHER	COLAN	SEATTLE	WA

Example 4.41 (Oracle only): Difference Query

Show faculty who are <u>not</u> students (pure faculty). Only show the common columns in the result. Oracle uses the MINUS keyword instead of the EXCEPT keyword used in SQL:2006.

```
SELECT FacNo AS PerNo, FacFirstName AS FirstName,
       FacLastName AS LastName, FacCity AS City,
       FacState AS State
  FROM Faculty
     MINUS
SELECT StdNo AS PerNo, StdFirstName AS FirstName,
       StdLastName AS LastName, StdCity AS City,
       StdState AS State
  FROM Student
```

PerNo	FirstName	LastName	City	State
098765432	LEONARD	VINCE	SEATTLE	WA
543210987	VICTORIA	EMMANUEL	BOTHELL	WA
654321098	LEONARD	FIBON	SEATTLE	WA
765432109	NICKI	MACON	BELLEVUE	WA
987654321	JULIA	MILLS	SEATTLE	WA

By default, duplicate rows are removed in the results of SQL statements with the UNION, INTERSECT, and EXCEPT (MINUS) keywords. If you want to retain duplicate rows, use the ALL keyword after the operator. For example, the UNION ALL keyword performs a union operation but does not remove duplicate rows.

4.6 SQL Modification Statements

The modification statements support entering new rows (INSERT), changing columns in one or more rows (UPDATE), and deleting one or more rows (DELETE). Although well designed and powerful, they are not as widely used as the SELECT statement because data entry forms are easier to use for end users.

The INSERT statement has two formats as demonstrated in Examples 4.42 and 4.43. In the first format, one row at a time can be added. You specify values for each column with the VALUES clause. You must format the constant values appropriately for each column. Refer to the documentation of your DBMS for details about specifying constants, especially string and date constants. Specifying a null value for a column is also not standard across DBMSs. In some systems, you simply omit the column name and the value. In other systems, you use a particular symbol for a null value. Of course, you must be careful that the table definition permits null values for the column of interest. Otherwise, the INSERT statement will be rejected.

Example 4.42: Single Row Insert

Insert a row into the *Student* table supplying values for all columns.

```
INSERT INTO Student
  (StdNo, StdFirstName, StdLastName,
   StdCity, StdState, StdZip, StdClass, StdMajor, StdGPA)
  VALUES ('999999999', 'JOE', 'STUDENT', 'SEATAC',
          'WA', '98042-1121', 'FR', 'IS', 0.0)
```

The second format of the INSERT statement supports addition of a set of records as shown in Example 4.43. Using the SELECT statement inside the INSERT statement, you can specify any derived set of rows. You can use the second format when you want to create temporary tables for specialized processing.

Example 4.43: Multiple Row Insert

Assume a new table *ISStudent* has been previously created. *ISStudent* has the same columns as *Student*. This INSERT statement adds rows from *Student* into *ISStudent*.

```
INSERT INTO ISStudent
  SELECT * FROM Student WHERE StdMajor = 'IS'
```

The UPDATE statement allows one or more rows to be changed, as shown in Examples 4.44 and 4.45. Any number of columns can be changed, although typically only one column at a time is changed. When changing the primary key, update rules on referenced rows may not allow the operation.

Example 4.44: Single Column Update

Give faculty members in the MS department a 10 percent raise. Four rows are updated.

```
UPDATE Faculty
  SET FacSalary = FacSalary * 1.1
  WHERE FacDept = 'MS'
```

Example 4.45: Update Multiple Columns

Change the major and class of Homer Wells. One row is updated.

```
UPDATE Student
  SET StdMajor = 'ACCT', StdClass = 'SO'
  WHERE StdFirstName = 'HOMER'
    AND StdLastName = 'WELLS'
```

The DELETE statement allows one or more rows to be removed, as shown in Examples 4.46 and 4.47. DELETE is subject to the rules on referenced rows. For example, a *Student* row cannot be deleted if related *Enrollment* rows exist and the deletion action is restrict.

Example 4.46: Delete Selected Rows

Delete all IS majors who are seniors. Three rows are deleted.

```
DELETE FROM Student
  WHERE StdMajor = 'IS' AND StdClass = 'SR'
```

Example 4.47: Delete All Rows in a Table.

Delete all rows in the *ISStudent* table. This example assumes that the *ISStudent* table has been previously created.

```
DELETE FROM ISStudent
```

Sometimes it is useful for the condition inside the WHERE clause of the DELETE statement to reference rows from other tables. Microsoft Access supports the join operator style to combine tables as shown in Example 4.48. You cannot use the cross product style inside a DELETE statement. Chapter 9 shows another way to reference other tables in a DELETE statement that most DBMSs (including Access and Oracle) support.

Example 4.48 (Access): DELETE Statement Using the Join Operator Style

Delete offerings taught by Leonard Vince. Three Offering rows are deleted. In addition, this statement deletes related rows in the Enrollment table because the ON DELETE clause is set to CASCADE.

```
DELETE Offering.*
  FROM Offering INNER JOIN Faculty
    ON Offering.FacNo = Faculty.FacNo
  WHERE FacFirstName = 'LEONARD'
    AND FacLastName = 'VINCE'
```

Closing Thoughts

Chapter 4 has introduced the fundamental statements of the industry standard Structured Query Language (SQL). SQL has a wide scope covering database definition, manipulation, and control. As a result of careful analysis and compromise, standards groups have produced a well designed language. SQL has become the common glue that binds the database industry even though strict conformance to the standard is sometimes lacking. You will no doubt continually encounter SQL throughout your career.

This chapter has focused on the most widely used parts of the SELECT statement from the core part of the SQL:2006 standard. Numerous examples were shown to demonstrate conditions on different data types, complex logical expressions, multiple table joins, summarization of tables with GROUP BY and HAVING, sorting of tables, and the traditional set operators. To facilitate hands-on usage of SQL, examples were shown for both Oracle and Access with special attention to deviations from the SQL:2006 standard. This chapter also briefly described the modification statements INSERT, UPDATE, and DELETE. These statements are not as complex and widely used as SELECT.

This chapter has emphasized two problem-solving guidelines to help you formulate queries. The conceptual evaluation process was presented to demonstrate derivation of result rows for SELECT statements involving joins and grouping. You may find this evaluation process helps in your initial learning of the SELECT statement as well as provides insight on more challenging problems. To help formulate queries, three questions were provided to guide you. You should explicitly or implicitly answer these questions before writing a SELECT statement to solve a problem. An understanding of both the critical questions and the conceptual evaluation process will provide you a solid foundation for using relational databases. Even with these formulation aids, you need to work many problems to learn query formulation and the SELECT statement.

This chapter covered an important subset of the SELECT statement. Other parts of the SELECT statement not covered in this chapter are outer joins, nested queries, and division problems. Chapter 9 covers advanced query formulation and additional parts of the SELECT statement so that you can hone your skills.

Review Concepts

- SQL consists of statements for database definition (CREATE TABLE, ALTER TABLE, etc.), database manipulation (SELECT, INSERT, UPDATE, and DELETE), and database control (GRANT, REVOKE, etc.).
- The most recent SQL standard is known as SQL:2006. Major DBMS vendors support most features in the core part of this standard although the lack of independent conformance testing hinders strict conformance with the standard.

- SELECT is a complex statement. Chapter 4 covered SELECT statements with the format:

  ```
  SELECT <list of column and column expressions>
      FROM <list of tables and join operations>
      WHERE <list of row conditions connected by AND, OR, and NOT>
      GROUP BY <list of columns>
      HAVING <list of group conditions connected by AND, OR, and NOT>
      ORDER BY <list of sorting specifications>
  ```

- Use the standard comparison operators to select rows:

  ```
  SELECT StdFirstName, StdLastName, StdCity, StdGPA
      FROM Student
      WHERE StdGPA >= 3.7
  ```

- Inexact matching is done with the LIKE operator and pattern-matching characters:
- Oracle and SQL:2006

  ```
  SELECT CourseNo, CrsDesc
      FROM Course
      WHERE CourseNo LIKE 'IS4%'
  ```

- Access

  ```
  SELECT CourseNo, CrsDesc
      FROM Course
      WHERE CourseNo LIKE 'IS4*'
  ```

- Use BETWEEN … AND to compare dates:
- Oracle

  ```
  SELECT FacFirstName, FacLastName, FacHireDate
          FROM Faculty
          WHERE FacHireDate BETWEEN '1-Jan-2001'
                                  AND '31-Dec-2002'
  ```

- Access:

  ```
  SELECT FacFirstName, FacLastName, FacHireDate
          FROM Faculty
          WHERE FacHireDate BETWEEN #1/1/2001# AND #12/31/2002#
  ```

- Use expressions in the SELECT column list and WHERE clause:
- Oracle

  ```
  SELECT FacFirstName, FacLastName, FacCity,
              FacSalary*1.1 AS InflatedSalary, FacHireDate
          FROM Faculty
          WHERE to_number(to_char(FacHireDate, 'YYYY' ) ) > 2001
  ```

- Access

  ```
  SELECT FacFirstName, FacLastName, FacCity,
              FacSalary*1.1 AS InflatedSalary, FacHireDate
          FROM Faculty
          WHERE year(FacHireDate) > 2001
  ```

- Test for null values:

  ```
  SELECT OfferNo, CourseNo
          FROM Offering
          WHERE FacNo IS NULL AND OffTerm = 'SUMMER'
          AND OffYear = 2008
  ```

- Create complex logical expressions with AND and OR:

  ```
  SELECT OfferNo, CourseNo, FacNo
          FROM Offering
          WHERE (OffTerm = 'FALL' AND OffYear = 2007)
          OR (OffTerm = 'WINTER' AND OffYear = 2008)
  ```

- Sort results with the ORDER BY clause:

  ```
  SELECT StdGPA, StdFirstName, StdLastName, StdCity,
              StdState
          FROM Student
          WHERE StdClass = 'JR'
          ORDER BY StdGPA
  ```

- Eliminate duplicates with the DISTINCT keyword:

```
SELECT DISTINCT FacCity, FacState
        FROM Faculty
```

- Qualify column names in join queries:

```
SELECT Course.CourseNo, CrsDesc
       FROM Offering, Course
       WHERE OffTerm = 'SPRING' AND OffYear = 2008
       AND Course.CourseNo = Offering.CourseNo
```

- Use the GROUP BY clause to summarize rows:

```
SELECT StdMajor, AVG(StdGPA) AS AvgGpa
       FROM Student
       GROUP BY StdMajor
```

- GROUP BY must precede HAVING:

```
SELECT StdMajor, AVG(StdGPA) AS AvgGpa
       FROM Student
       GROUP BY StdMajor
       HAVING AVG(StdGPA) > 3.1
```

- Use WHERE to test row conditions and HAVING to test group conditions:

```
SELECT StdMajor, AVG(StdGPA) AS AvgGpa
       FROM Student
       WHERE StdClass IN ('JR', 'SR')
       GROUP BY StdMajor
       HAVING AVG(StdGPA) > 3.1
```

- Difference between COUNT(*) and COUNT(DISTINCT column) - not supported by Access:

```
SELECT OffYear, COUNT(*) AS NumOfferings,
       COUNT(DISTINCT CourseNo) AS NumCourses
       FROM Offering
       GROUP BY OffYear
```

- Conceptual evaluation process lessons: use small sample tables, GROUP BY occurs after WHERE, only one grouping per SELECT statement.
- Query formulation questions: what tables?, how combined?, and row or group output?
- Joining more than two tables with the cross product and join operator styles (not supported by Oracle versions before 9i):

```
SELECT OfferNo, Offering.CourseNo, CrsUnits, OffDays,
       OffLocation, OffTime
       FROM Faculty, Course, Offering
       WHERE Faculty.FacNo = Offering.FacNo
       AND Offering.CourseNo = Course.CourseNo
       AND OffYear = 2007 AND OffTerm = 'FALL'
       AND FacFirstName = 'LEONARD'
       AND FacLastName = 'VINCE'
SELECT OfferNo, Offering.CourseNo, CrsUnits, OffDays,
       OffLocation, OffTime
       FROM ( Faculty INNER JOIN Offering
       ON Faculty.FacNo = Offering.FacNo )
       INNER JOIN Course
       ON Offering.CourseNo = Course.CourseNo
       WHERE OffYear = 2007 AND OffTerm = 'FALL'
       AND FacFirstName = 'LEONARD'
       AND FacLastName = 'VINCE'
```

- Self-joins:

```
SELECT Subr.FacNo, Subr.FacLastName, Subr.FacSalary,
       Supr.FacNo, Supr.FacLastName, Supr.FacSalary
       FROM Faculty Subr, Faculty Supr
       WHERE Subr.FacSupervisor = Supr.FacNo
       AND Subr.FacSalary > Supr.FacSalary
```

- Combine joins and grouping:
```
SELECT CourseNo, Enrollment.OfferNo,
       COUNT(*) AS NumStudents
    FROM Offering, Enrollment
    WHERE Offering.OfferNo = Enrollment.OfferNo
    AND OffYear = 2006 AND OffTerm = 'SPRING'
    GROUP BY Enrollment.OfferNo, CourseNo
```
- Traditional set operators and union compatibility:
```
SELECT FacNo AS PerNo, FacLastName AS LastName
       FacCity AS City, FacState AS State
    FROM Faculty
    UNION
SELECT StdNo AS PerNo, StdLastName AS LastName,
       StdCity AS City, StdState AS State
    FROM Student
```
- Use the INSERT statement to add one or more rows:
```
INSERT INTO Student
    (StdNo, StdFirstName, StdLastName, StdCity, StdState,
    StdClass, StdMajor, StdGPA)
    VALUES ('999999999', 'JOE', 'STUDENT', 'SEATAC', 'WA',
       'FR', 'IS', 0.0)
```
- Use the UPDATE statement to change columns in one or more rows:
```
UPDATE Faculty
    SET FacSalary = FacSalary * 1.1
    WHERE FacDept = 'MS'
```
- Use the DELETE statement to remove one or more rows:
```
DELETE FROM Student
    WHERE StdMajor = 'IS' AND StdClass = 'SR'
```
- Use a join operation inside a DELETE statement (Access only):
```
DELETE Offering.*
    FROM Offering INNER JOIN Faculty
    ON Offering.FacNo = Faculty.FacNo
    WHERE FacFirstName = 'LEONARD' AND FacLastName =
    'VINCE'
```

Questions

1. Why do some people pronounce SQL as "sequel"?
2. Why are the manipulation statements of SQL more widely used than the definition and control statements?
3. How many levels do the SQL-92, SQL:1999, SQL:2003, and SQL:2006 standards have?
4. Why is conformance testing important for the SQL standard?
5. In general, what is the state of conformance among major DBMS vendors for the SQL:2006 standard?
6. What is stand-alone SQL?
7. What is embedded SQL?
8. What is an expression in the context of database languages?
9. From the examples and the discussion in Chapter 4, what parts of the SELECT statement are not supported by all DBMSs?
10. Recite the rule about the GROUP BY and HAVING clauses.
11. Recite the rule about columns in SELECT when a GROUP BY clause is used.
12. How does a row condition differ from a group condition?
13. Why should row conditions be placed in the WHERE clause rather than the HAVING clause?
14. Why are most DBMSs not case sensitive when matching on string conditions?
15. Explain how working with sample tables can provide insight about difficult problems.
16. When working with date columns, why is it necessary to refer to documentation of your DBMS?
17. How do exact and inexact matching differ in SQL?

18. How do you know when the output of a query relates to groups of rows as opposed to individual rows?
19. What tables belong in the FROM statement?
20. Explain the cross product style for join operations.
21. Explain the join operator style for join operations.
22. Discuss the pros and cons of the cross product versus the join operator styles. Do you need to know both the cross product and the join operator styles?
23. What is a self-join? When is a self-join useful?
24. Provide a SELECT statement example in which a table is needed even though the table does not provide conditions to test or columns to show in the result.
25. What is the requirement when using the traditional set operators in a SELECT statement?
26. When combining joins and grouping, what conceptually occurs first, joins or grouping?
27. How many times does grouping occur in a SELECT statement?
28. Why is the SELECT statement more widely used than the modification statements INSERT, UPDATE, and DELETE?
29. Provide an example of an INSERT statement that can insert multiple rows.
30. What is the relationship between the DELETE statement and the rules about deleting referenced rows?
31. What is the relationship between the UPDATE statement and the rules about updating the primary key of referenced rows?
32. How does COUNT(*) differ from COUNT(ColumnName)?
33. How does COUNT(DISTINCT ColumnName) differ from COUNT(ColumnName)?
34. When mixing AND and OR in a logical expression, why is it a good idea to use parentheses?
35. What are the most important lessons about the conceptual evaluation process?
36. What are the mental steps involved in query formulation?
37. What kind of join queries often have duplicates in the result?
38. What mental steps in the query formulation process are addressed by the conceptual evaluation process and critical questions?

Problems

The problems use the tables of the Order Entry database, an extension of the order entry tables used in the problems of Chapter 3. Table 4-P1 lists the meaning of each table and Figure 4.P1 shows the Access Relationship window. After the relationship diagram, row listings and Oracle CREATE TABLE statements are shown for each table. In addition to the other documentation, here are some notes about the Order Entry Database:

The primary key of the *OrdLine* table is a combination of *OrdNo* and *ProdNo*.

The *Employee* table has a self-referencing (unary) relationship to itself through the foreign key, *SupEmpNo*, the employee number of the supervising employee. In the relationship diagram, the table *Employee_1* is a representation of the self-referencing relationship, not a real table.

The relationship from *OrderTbl* to *OrdLine* cascades deletions and primary key updates of referenced rows. All other relationships restrict deletions and primary key updates of referenced rows if related rows exist.

Table 4-P1: Tables of the Order Entry Database

Table Name	Description
Customer	List of customers who have placed orders
OrderTbl	Contains the heading part of an order; Internet orders do not have an employee
Employee	List of employees who can take orders
OrdLine	Contains the detail part of an order
Product	List of products that may be ordered

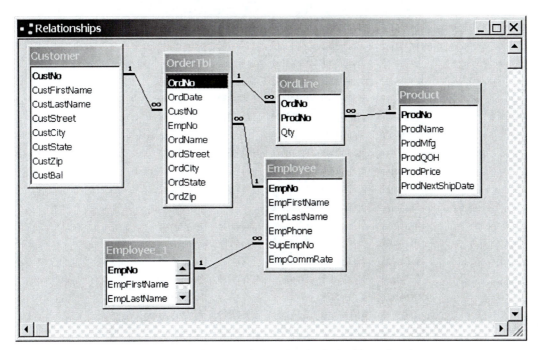

Figure 4.P1: Relationship Window for the Order Entry Database

117

Customer

CustNo	CustFirstName	CustLastName	CustStreet	CustCity	CustState	CustZip	CustBal
C0954327	Sheri	Gordon	336 Hill St.	Littleton	CO	80129-5543	$230.00
C1010398	Jim	Glussman	1432 E. Ravenna	Denver	CO	80111-0033	$200.00
C2388597	Beth	Taylor	2396 Rafter Rd	Seattle	WA	98103-1121	$500.00
C3340959	Betty	Wise	4334 153rd NW	Seattle	WA	98178-3311	$200.00
C3499503	Bob	Mann	1190 Lorraine Cir.	Monroe	WA	98013-1095	$0.00
C8543321	Ron	Thompson	789 122nd St.	Renton	WA	98666-1289	$85.00
C8574932	Wally	Jones	411 Webber Ave.	Seattle	WA	98105-1093	$1,500.00
C8654390	Candy	Kendall	456 Pine St.	Seattle	WA	98105-3345	$50.00
C9128574	Jerry	Wyatt	16212 123rd Ct.	Denver	CO	80222-0022	$100.00
C9403348	Mike	Boren	642 Crest Ave.	Englewood	CO	80113-5431	$0.00
C9432910	Larry	Styles	9825 S. Crest Lane	Bellevue	WA	98104-2211	$250.00
C9543029	Sharon	Johnson	1223 Meyer Way	Fife	WA	98222-1123	$856.00
C9549302	Todd	Hayes	1400 NW 88th	Lynnwood	WA	98036-2244	$0.00
C9857432	Homer	Wells	123 Main St.	Seattle	WA	98105-4322	$500.00
C9865874	Mary	Hill	206 McCaffrey	Littleton	CO	80129-5543	$150.00
C9943201	Harry	Sanders	1280 S. Hill Rd.	Fife	WA	98222-2258	$1,000.00

OrderTbl (Part 1)

OrdNo	OrdDate	CustNo	EmpNo	OrdName
O1116324	01/23/2008	C0954327	E8544399	Sheri Gordon
O1231231	01/23/2008	C9432910	E9954302	Larry Styles
O1241518	02/10/2008	C9549302		Todd Hayes
O1455122	01/09/2008	C8574932	E9345771	Wally Jones
O1579999	01/05/2008	C9543029	E8544399	Tom Johnson
O1615141	01/23/2008	C8654390	E8544399	Candy Kendall
O1656777	02/11/2008	C8543321		Ron Thompson
O2233457	01/12/2008	C2388597	E9884325	Beth Taylor
O2334661	01/14/2008	C0954327	E1329594	Mrs. Ruth Gordon
O3252629	01/23/2008	C9403348	E9954302	Mike Boren
O3331222	01/13/2008	C1010398		Jim Glussman
O3377543	01/15/2008	C9128574	E8843211	Jerry Wyatt
O4714645	01/11/2008	C2388597	E1329594	Beth Taylor
O5511365	01/22/2008	C3340959	E9884325	Betty White
O6565656	01/20/2008	C9865874	E8843211	Mr. Jack Sibley
O7847172	01/23/2008	C9943201		Harry Sanders
O7959898	02/19/2008	C8543321	E8544399	Ron Thompson
O7989497	01/16/2008	C3499503	E9345771	Bob Mann
O8979495	01/23/2008	C9865874		Helen Sibley
O9919699	02/11/2008	C9857432	E9954302	Homer Wells

OrderTbl (Part 2)

OrdNo	OrdStreet	OrdCity	OrdState	OrdZip
01116324	336 Hill St.	Littleton	CO	80129-5543
01231231	9825 S. Crest Lane	Bellevue	WA	98104-2211
01241518	1400 NW 88th	Lynnwood	WA	98036-2244
01455122	411 Webber Ave.	Seattle	WA	98105-1093
01579999	1632 Ocean Dr.	Des Moines	WA	98222-1123
01615141	456 Pine St.	Seattle	WA	98105-3345
01656777	789 122nd St.	Renton	WA	98666-1289
02233457	2396 Rafter Rd	Seattle	WA	98103-1121
02334661	233 S. 166th	Seattle	WA	98011
03252629	642 Crest Ave.	Englewood	CO	80113-5431
03331222	1432 E. Ravenna	Denver	CO	80111-0033
03377543	16212 123rd Ct.	Denver	CO	80222-0022
04714645	2396 Rafter Rd	Seattle	WA	98103-1121
05511365	4334 153rd NW	Seattle	WA	98178-3311
06565656	166 E. 344th	Renton	WA	98006-5543
07847172	1280 S. Hill Rd.	Fife	WA	98222-2258
07959898	789 122nd St.	Renton	WA	98666-1289
07989497	1190 Lorraine Cir.	Monroe	WA	98013-1095
08979495	206 McCaffrey	Renton	WA	98006-5543
09919699	123 Main St.	Seattle	WA	98105-4322

Employee

EmpNo	EmpFirstName	EmpLastName	EmpPhone	EmpEMail	SupEmpNo	EmpCommRate
E1329594	Landi	Santos	(303) 789-1234	LSantos@bigco.com	E8843211	0.02
E8544399	Joe	Jenkins	(303) 221-9875	JJenkins@bigco.com	E8843211	0.02
E8843211	Amy	Tang	(303) 556-4321	ATang@bigco.com	E9884325	0.04
E9345771	Colin	White	(303) 221-4453	CWhite@bigco.com	E9884325	0.04
E9884325	Thomas	Johnson	(303) 556-9987	TJohnson@bigco.com		0.05
E9954302	Mary	Hill	(303) 556-9871	MHill@bigco.com	E8843211	0.02
E9973110	Theresa	Beck	(720) 320-2234	TBeck@bigco.com	E9884325	

Product

ProdNo	ProdName	ProdMfg	ProdQOH	ProdPrice	ProdNextShipDate
P0036566	17 inch Color Monitor	ColorMeg, Inc.	12	$169.00	2/20/2008
P0036577	19 inch Color Monitor	ColorMeg, Inc.	10	$319.00	2/20/2008
P1114590	R3000 Color Laser Printer	Connex	5	$699.00	1/22/2008
P1412138	10 Foot Printer Cable	Ethlite	100	$12.00	
P1445671	8-Outlet Surge Protector	Intersafe	33	$14.99	
P1556678	CVP Ink Jet Color Printer	Connex	8	$99.00	1/22/2008
P3455443	Color Ink Jet Cartridge	Connex	24	$38.00	1/22/2008
P4200344	36-Bit Color Scanner	UV Components	16	$199.99	1/29/2008
P6677900	Black Ink Jet Cartridge	Connex	44	$25.69	
P9995676	Battery Back-up System	Cybercx	12	$89.00	2/1/2008

OrdLine

OrdNo	ProdNo	Qty
01116324	P1445671	1
01231231	P0036566	1
01231231	P1445671	1
01241518	P0036577	1
01455122	P4200344	1
01579999	P1556678	1
01579999	P6677900	1
01579999	P9995676	1
01615141	P0036566	1
01615141	P1445671	1
01615141	P4200344	1
01656777	P1445671	1
01656777	P1556678	1
02233457	P0036577	1
02233457	P1445671	1
02334661	P0036566	1
02334661	P1412138	1
02334661	P1556678	1
03252629	P4200344	1
03252629	P9995676	1
03331222	P1412138	1
03331222	P1556678	1
03331222	P3455443	1
03377543	P1445671	1
03377543	P9995676	1
04714645	P0036566	1
04714645	P9995676	1
05511365	P1412138	1
05511365	P1445671	1
05511365	P1556678	1
05511365	P3455443	1
05511365	P6677900	1
06565656	P0036566	10
07847172	P1556678	1
07847172	P6677900	1
07959898	P1412138	5
07959898	P1556678	5
07959898	P3455443	5
07959898	P6677900	5
07989497	P1114590	2
07989497	P1412138	2
07989497	P1445671	3
08979495	P1114590	1
08979495	P1412138	1
08979495	P1445671	1
09919699	P0036577	1
09919699	P1114590	1
09919699	P4200344	1

```
CREATE TABLE Customer
( CustNo             CHAR(8),
  CustFirstName      VARCHAR2(20)
                     CONSTRAINT CustFirstNameRequired NOT NULL,
  CustLastName       VARCHAR2(30)
                     CONSTRAINT CustLastNameRequired NOT NULL,
  CustStreet         VARCHAR2(50),
  CustCity           VARCHAR2(30),
  CustState          CHAR(2),
  CustZip            CHAR(10),
  CustBal            DECIMAL(12,2) DEFAULT 0,
  CONSTRAINT PKCustomer PRIMARY KEY (CustNo)   )
```

```
CREATE TABLE OrderTbl
( OrdNo     CHAR(8),
  OrdDate   DATE      CONSTRAINT OrdDateRequired NOT NULL,
  CustNo    CHAR(8) CONSTRAINT CustNoRequired NOT NULL,
  EmpNo     CHAR(8),
  OrdName   VARCHAR2(50),
  OrdStreet VARCHAR2(50),
  OrdCity   VARCHAR2(30),
  OrdState  CHAR(2),
  OrdZip    CHAR(10),
CONSTRAINT PKOrderTbl PRIMARY KEY (OrdNo) ,
CONSTRAINT FKCustNo FOREIGN KEY (CustNo) REFERENCES Customer,
CONSTRAINT FKEmpNo FOREIGN KEY (EmpNo) REFERENCES Employee   )
```

```
CREATE TABLE OrdLine
( OrdNo     CHAR(8),
  ProdNo    CHAR(8),
    Qty     INTEGER DEFAULT 1,
CONSTRAINT PKOrdLine PRIMARY KEY (OrdNo, ProdNo),
CONSTRAINT FKOrdNo FOREIGN KEY (OrdNo) REFERENCES OrderTbl
    ON DELETE CASCADE,
CONSTRAINT FKProdNo FOREIGN KEY (ProdNo) REFERENCES Product )
```

```
CREATE TABLE Employee
(     EmpNo          CHAR(8),
      EmpFirstName   VARCHAR2(20)
                     CONSTRAINT EmpFirstNameRequired NOT NULL,
      EmpLastName    VARCHAR2(30)
                     CONSTRAINT EmpLastNameRequired NOT NULL,
      EmpPhone       CHAR(15),
      EmpEMail       VARCHAR(50)
                     CONSTRAINT EmpEMailRequired NOT NULL,
      SupEmpNo       CHAR(8),
      EmpCommRate    DECIMAL(3,3),
CONSTRAINT PKEmployee PRIMARY KEY (EmpNo),
CONSTRAINT UNIQUEEMail UNIQUE(EmpEMail),
CONSTRAINT FKSupEmpNo FOREIGN KEY (SupEmpNo) REFERENCES Employee
)
```

```
CREATE TABLE Product
(       ProdNo              CHAR(8),
        ProdName            VARCHAR2(50)
                            CONSTRAINT ProdNameRequired NOT NULL,
        ProdMfg             VARCHAR2(20)
                            CONSTRAINT ProdMfgRequired NOT NULL,
        ProdQOH             INTEGER DEFAULT 0,
        ProdPrice           DECIMAL(12,2) DEFAULT 0,
        ProdNextShipDate    DATE,
 CONSTRAINT PKProduct PRIMARY KEY (ProdNo)    )
```

Part 1: SELECT

1. List the customer number, the name (first and last), and the balance of customers.
2. List the customer number, the name (first and last), and the balance of customers who reside in Colorado (CustState is CO).
3. List all columns of the *Product* table for products costing more than $50. Order the result by product manufacturer (*ProdMfg*) and product name.
4. List the order number, order date, and shipping name (*OrdName*) of orders sent to addresses in Denver or Englewood.
5. List the customer number, the name (first and last), the city, and the balance of customers who reside in Denver with a balance greater than $150 or who reside in Seattle with a balance greater than $300.
6. List the cities and states where orders have been placed. Remove duplicates from the result.
7. List all columns of the *OrderTbl* table for Internet orders placed in January 2008. An Internet order does not have an associated employee.
8. List all columns of the *OrderTbl* table for phone orders placed in February 2008. A phone order has an associated employee.
9. List all columns of the *Product* table that contain the words Ink Jet in the product name.
10. List the order number, order date, and customer number of orders placed after January 23, 2008, shipped to Washington recipients.
11. List the order number, order date, customer number, and customer name (first and last) of orders placed in January 2008 sent to Colorado recipients.
12. List the order number, order date, customer number, and customer name (first and last) of orders placed in January 2008 placed by Colorado customers (*CustState*) but sent to Washington recipients (*OrdState*).
13. List the customer number, name (first and last), and balance of Washington customers who have placed one or more orders in February 2008. Remove duplicate rows from the result.
14. List the order number, order date, customer number, customer name (first and last), employee number, and employee name (first and last) of January 2008 orders placed by Colorado customers.
15. List the employee number, name (first and last), and phone of employees who have taken orders in January 2008 from customers with balances greater than $300. Remove duplicate rows in the result.
16. List the product number, name, and price of products ordered by customer number C0954327 in January 2008. Remove duplicate products in the result.
17. List the customer number, name (first and last), order number, order date, employee number, employee name (first and last), product number, product name, and order cost (OrdLine.Qty * ProdPrice) for products ordered on January 23, 2008, in which the order cost exceeds $150.
18. List the average balance of customers by city. Include only customers residing in Washington state (WA).
19. List the average balance of customers by city and short zip code (the first five digits of the zip code). Include only customers residing in Washington State (WA). In Microsoft Access, the expression left(CustZip, 5) returns the first five digits of the zip code. In Oracle, the expression substr(CustZip, 1, 5) returns the first five digits.

20. List the average balance and number of customers by city. Only include customers residing in Washington State (WA). Eliminate cities in the result with less than two customers.

21. List the number of unique short zip codes and average customer balance by city. Only include customers residing in Washington State (WA). Eliminate cities in the result in which the average balance is less than $100. In Microsoft Access, the expression left(CustZip, 5) returns the first five digits of the zip code. In Oracle, the expression substr(CustZip, 1, 5) returns the first five digits. (Note: this problem requires two SELECT statements in Access SQL or a nested query in the FROM clause, see Chapter 9).

22. List the order number and total amount for orders placed on January 23, 2008. The total amount of an order is the sum of the quantity times the product price of each product on the order.

23. List the order number, order date, customer name (first and last), and total amount for orders placed on January 23, 2008. The total amount of an order is the sum of the quantity times the product price of each product on the order.

24. List the customer number, customer name (first and last), the sum of the quantity of products ordered, and the total order amount (sum of the product price times the quantity) for orders placed in January 2008. Only include products in which the product name contains the string Ink Jet or Laser. Only include customers who have ordered more than two Ink Jet or Laser products in January 2008.

25. List the product number, product name, sum of the quantity of products ordered, and total order amount (sum of the product price times the quantity) for orders placed in January 2008. Only include products that have more than five products ordered in January 2008. Sort the result in descending order of the total amount.

26. List the order number, the order date, the customer number, the customer name (first and last), the customer state, and the shipping state (*OrdState*) in which the customer state differs from the shipping state.

27. List the employee number, the employee name (first and last), the commission rate, the supervising employee name (first and last), and the commission rate of the supervisor.

28. List the employee number, the employee name (first and last), and total amount of commissions on orders taken in January 2008. The amount of a commission is the sum of the dollar amount of products ordered times the commission rate of the employee.

29. List the union of customers and order recipients. Include the name, street, city, state, and zip in the result. You need to use the concatenation function to combine the first and last names so that they can be compared to the order recipient name. In Access SQL, the & symbol is the concatenation function. In Oracle SQL, the ‖ symbol is the concatenation function.

30. List the first and last name of customers who have the same name (first and last) as an employee.

31. List the employee number and the name (first and last) of second-level subordinates (subordinates of subordinates) of the employee named Thomas Johnson.

32. List the employee number and the name (first and last) of the first- and second-level subordinates of the employee named Thomas Johnson. To distinguish the level of subordinates, include a computed column with the subordinate level (1 or 2).

33. Using a mix of the join operator and the cross product styles, list the names (first and last) of customers who have placed orders taken by Amy Tang. Remove duplicate rows in the result. Note that the join operator style is supported only in Oracle versions 9i and beyond.

34. Using the join operator style, list the product name and the price of all products ordered by Beth Taylor in January 2008. Remove duplicate rows from the result.

35. For Colorado customers, compute the number of orders placed in January 2008. The result should include the customer number, last name, and number of orders placed in January 2008.

36. For Colorado customers, compute the number of orders placed in January 2008 in which the orders contain products made by Connex. The result should include the customer number, last name, and number of orders placed in January 2008.

37. For each employee with a commission rate of less than 0.04, compute the number of orders taken in January 2008. The result should include the employee number, employee last name, and number of orders taken.
38. For each employee with a commission rate greater than 0.03, compute the total commission earned from orders taken in January 2008. The total commission earned is the total order amount times the commission rate. The result should include the employee number, employee last name, and total commission earned.
39. List the total amount of all orders by month in 2008. The result should include the month and the total amount of all orders in each month. The total amount of an individual order is the sum of the quantity times the product price of each product in the order. In Access, the month number can be extracted by the **Month** function with a date as the argument. You can display the month name using the **MonthName** function applied to a month number. In Oracle, the function `to_char(OrdDate, 'MON')` extracts the three-digit month abbreviation from *OrdDate*.
40. List the total commission earned by each employee in each month of 2008. The result should include the month, employee number, employee last name, and the total commission amount earned in that month. The amount of a commission for an individual employee is the sum of the dollar amount of products ordered times the commission rate of the employee. Sort the result by the month in ascending month number and the total commission amount in descending order. In Access, the month number can be extracted by the **Month** function with a date as the argument. You can display the month name using the **MonthName** function applied to a month number. In Oracle, the function `to_char(OrdDate, 'MON')` extracts the three-digit month abbreviation from *OrdDate*.

Part 2: INSERT, UPDATE, and DELETE statements

1. Insert yourself as a new row in the *Customer* table.
2. Insert your roommate, best friend, or significant other as a new row in the *Employee* table.
3. Insert a new *OrderTbl* row with you as the customer, the person from problem 2 (Part 2) as the employee, and your choice of values for the other columns of the *OrderTbl* table.
4. Insert two rows in the *OrdLine* table corresponding to the *OrderTbl* row inserted in problem 3 (Part 2).
5. Increase the price by 10 percent of products containing the words Ink Jet.
6. Change the address (street, city, and zip) of the new row inserted in problem 1 (Part 2).
7. Identify an order that respects the rules about deleting referenced rows to delete the rows inserted in problems 1 to 4 (part 2).
8. Delete the new row(s) of the table listed first in the order for problem 7 (Part 2).
9. Delete the new row(s) of the table listed second in the order for problem 7 (Part 2).
10. Delete the new row(s) of the remaining tables listed in the order for problem 7 (Part 2).

References for Further Study

There are many SQL books varying by emphasis on basic coverage, advanced coverage, and product specific coverage. A good summary of SQL books can be found at www.ocelot.ca/books.htm. The DBAZine site (www.dbazine.com) and the DevX.com Database Zone (www.devx.com) have plenty of practical advice about query formulation and SQL. For product-specific SQL advice, the DataBased Advisor site (my.advisor.com/pub/DataBasedAdvisor) features forums and articles about a number of DBMSs including Microsoft SQL Server and Microsoft Access. Oracle documentation can be found at the Oracle Technet site (www.oracle.com/technology).

Appendix 4.A: SQL:2006 Syntax Summary

This appendix summarizes SQL:2006 syntax for the SELECT, INSERT, UPDATE, and DELETE statements presented in this chapter. The syntax is limited to the simplified statement structure presented in this chapter. More complex syntax is introduced in Part 5 of this textbook. The conventions used in the syntax notation are identical to those used at the end of Chapter 3.

Simplified SELECT Syntax

```
<Select-Statement>: { <Simple-Select> | <Set-Select> }
   [ ORDER BY <Sort-Specification>* ]

<Simple-Select>:
   SELECT  [ DISTINCT ] <Column-Specification>*
     FROM <Table-Specification>*
     [ WHERE <Row-Condition> ]
     [ GROUP BY ColumnName* ]
     [ HAVING <Group-Condition> ]

<Column-Specification>: { <Column-List> | <Column-Item> }

<Column-List>: { * | TableName.* }
   -- * is a literal here not a syntax symbol

<Column-Item>: <Column-Expression> [ AS ColumnName ]

<Column-Expression>:
  { <Scalar-Expression> | <Aggregate-Expression> }

<Scalar-Expression>:
  { <Scalar-Item> |
    <Scalar-Item> <Arith-Operator> <Scalar-Item> }

<Scalar-Item>:
  { [ TableName.]ColumnName  |
     Constant      |
     FunctionName [ (Argument*) ] |
     <Scalar-Expression>  |
     ( <Scalar-Expression> ) }

<Arith-Operator>:  { + | - | * | / }
   -- * and + are literals here not syntax symbols

<Aggregate-Expression>:
 { SUM ( {<Scalar-Expression> | DISTINCT ColumnName } )
 |
                                          AVG (
{<Scalar-Expression> | DISTINCT ColumnName } )  |
                                          MIN (
<Scalar-Expression> )  |
                                          MAX (
<Scalar-Expression> )  |
                                          COUNT ( [
DISTINCT ] ColumnName ) |
                                          COUNT ( * )
} -- * is a literal symbol here, not a special syntax
symbol

<Table-Specification>: { <Simple-Table>  |
                         <Join-Operation> }
```

```
<Simple-Table>: TableName [ [ AS ] AliasName ]

<Join-Operation>:
  { <Simple-Table> [INNER] JOIN <Simple-Table>
    ON <Join-Condition>  |
      { <Simple-Table> | <Join-Operation> } [INNER] JOIN
        { <Simple-Table> | <Join-Operation> }
        ON <Join-Condition>  |
      ( <Join-Operation> )  }

<Join-Condition>: { <Simple-Join-Condition> |
                    <Compound-Join-Condition> }

<Simple-Join-Condition>:
  <Scalar-Expression> <Comparison-Operator>
  <Scalar-Expression>

<Compound-Join-Condition>:
   { NOT <Join-Condition>  |
     <Join-Condition> AND <Join-Condition>  |
     <Join-Condition> OR <Join-Condition>  |
     ( <Join-Condition> )

<Comparison-Operator>: { = | < | > | <= | >= | <> }

<Row-Condition>:
 { <Simple-Condition> | <Compound-Condition> }

<Simple-Condition>:
{ <Scalar-Expression> <Comparison-Operator>
      <Scalar-Experssion>  |
  <Scalar-Expression> [ NOT ] IN ( Constant* )  |
  <Scalar-Expression> BETWEEN <Scalar-Expression> AND
      <Scalar-Expression> |
  <Scalar-Expression> IS [NOT] NULL  |
  ColumnName [ NOT ] LIKE StringPattern  }

<Compound-Condition>:
                                        { NOT <Row-
Condition>  |
                                          <Row-
Condition> AND <Row-Condition>  |
                                          <Row-
Condition> OR <Row-Condition>  |
                                          ( <Row-
Condition> )  }

<Group-Condition>:
 { <Simple-Group-Condition> | <Compound-Group-Condition>
}

<Simple-Group-Condition>:-- permits both scalar and
aggregate expressions
{ <Column-Expression> ComparisonOperator
      < Column-Experssion>  |
  <Column-Expression> [ NOT ] IN ( Constant* )  |
  <Column-Expression> BETWEEN <Column-Expression> AND
      <Column-Expression> |
  <Column-Expression> IS [NOT] NULL  |
  ColumnName [ NOT ] LIKE StringPattern  }
```

```
<Compound-Group-Condition>:
                                                    { NOT
<Group-Condition>   |
                                                        <Group-
Condition> AND <Group-Condition>   |
                                                        <Group-
Condition> OR <Group-Condition>   |
                                                    ( <Group-
Condition> )   }

<Sort-Specification>:
 { ColumnName | ColumnNumber } [ { ASC | DESC } ]

<Set-Select>:
 { <Simple-Select> | <Set-Select> } <Set-Operator>
 { <Simple-Select> | <Set-Select> }

<Set-Operator>: { UNION | INTERSECT | EXCEPT } [ ALL ]
```

INSERT Syntax

```
INSERT INTO TableName ( ColumnName* )
   VALUES ( Constant* )

INSERT INTO TableName [ ( ColumnName* ) ]
   <Simple-Select>
```

UPDATE Syntax

```
UPDATE TableName
  SET <Column-Assignment>*
  [ WHERE <Row-Condition> ]

<Column-Assignment>: ColumnName = <Scalar-Expression>
```

DELETE Syntax

```
DELETE FROM TableName
   [ WHERE  <Row-Condition> ]
```

Appendix 4.B: Syntax Differences among Major DBMS Products

Table 4B-1 summarizes syntax differences among Microsoft Access (1997 to 2003 versions), Oracle 8i to 11g, Microsoft SQL Server, and IBM's DB2. The differences involve the parts of the SELECT statement presented in the chapter.

Table 4B-1: SELECT Syntax Differences among Major DBMS Products

Element\Product	Oracle 8i, 9i, 10g, 11g	Access 97/2000/2003/2007	MS SQL Server 2000	DB2
Pattern-matching characters	%, _	*, ? although the % and _ characters can be used in the 2002/2003 versions by setting the query mode	%, _	%, _
Case sensitivity in string matching	Yes	No	Yes	Yes
Date constants	Surround in single quotation marks	Surround in # symbols	Surround in single quotation marks	Surround in single quotation marks
Inequality symbol	< >	< >	!=	< >
Join operator style	No in 8i, Yes in 9i and later versions	Yes	Yes	Yes
Difference operations	MINUS keyword	Not supported	Not supported	EXCEPT keyword

5

Understanding Entity Relationship Diagrams

Learning Objectives

This chapter explains the notation of entity relationship diagrams as a prerequisite to using entity relationship diagrams in the database development process. After this chapter, the student should have acquired the following knowledge and skills:

- Know the symbols and vocabulary of the Crow's Foot notation for entity relationship diagrams
- Use the cardinality symbols to represent 1-1, 1-M, and M-N relationships
- Compare the Crow's Foot notation to the representation of relational tables
- Understand important relationship patterns
- Use generalization hierarchies to represent similar entity types
- Detect notational errors in an entity relationship diagram
- Understand the representation of business rules in an entity relationship diagram
- Appreciate the diversity of notation for entity relationship diagrams

Overview

Chapter 2 provided a broad presentation about the database development process. You learned about the relationship between database development and information systems development, the phases of database development, and the kinds of skills you need to master. This chapter presents the notation of entity relationship diagrams to provide a foundation for using entity relationship diagrams in the database development process. To extend your database design skills, Chapter 6 describes the process of using entity relationship diagrams to develop data models for business databases.

To become a good data modeler, you need to understand the notation in entity relationship diagrams and apply the notation on problems of increasing complexity. To help you master the notation, this chapter presents the symbols used in entity relationship diagrams and compares entity relationship diagrams to relational database diagrams that you have seen in previous chapters. This chapter then probes deeper into relationships, the most distinguishing part of entity relationship diagrams. You will learn about identification dependency, relationship patterns, and equivalence between two kinds of relationships. Finally, you will learn how to represent similarities among entities using generalization hierarchies.

The next part of the chapter presents business rule representation and diagram rules to deepen your understanding of the Crow's Foot notation. To provide an organizational focus, this chapter presents formal and informal representation of business rules in an entity relationship diagram. To help you avoid common notation errors, this chapter presents consistency and completeness rules.

Because of the plethora of entity relationship notations, you may not have the opportunity to use the Crow's Foot notation exactly as shown in Chapters 5 and 6. To prepare you for understanding other notations, the chapter concludes with a presentation of diagram variations including the Class Diagram notation of the Unified Modeling Notation, one of the popular alternatives to the Entity Relationship Model.

This chapter provides the basic skills of data modeling to enable you to understand the notation of entity relationship diagrams. To apply data modeling as part of the database development process, you should study Chapter 6 on developing data models for business databases. Chapter 6 emphasizes the problem-solving skills of generating alternative designs, mapping a problem statement to an entity relationship diagram, and justifying design decisions. With the background provided in both chapters, you will be prepared to perform data modeling on case studies and databases for moderate-size organizations.

5.1 Introduction to Entity Relationship Diagrams

Gaining an initial understanding of entity relationship diagrams (ERDs) requires careful study. This section introduces the Crow's Foot notation for ERDs, a popular notation supported by many

CASE tools. To get started, this section begins with the basic symbols of entity types, relationships, and attributes. This section then explains cardinalities and their appearance in the Crow's Foot notation. This section concludes by comparing the Crow's Foot notation to relational database diagrams. If you are covering data modeling before relational databases, you may want to skip the last part of this section.

5.1.1 Basic Symbols

ERDs have three basic elements: entity types, relationships, and attributes. Entity types are collections of things of interest (entities) in an application. Entity types represent collections of physical things such as books, people, and places, as well as events such as payments. An entity is a member or instance of an entity type. Entities are uniquely identified to allow tracking across business processes. For example, customers have a unique identification to support order processing, shipment, and product warranty processes. In the Crow's Foot notation as well as most other notations, rectangles denote entity types. In Figure 5.1, the *Course* entity type represents the set of courses in the database.

> **Entity Type**: a collection of entities (persons, places, events, or things) of interest represented by a rectangle in an entity relationship diagram.

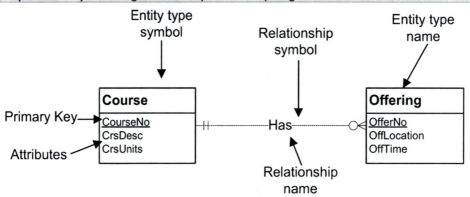

Figure 5.1: Entity Relationship Diagram Illustrating Basic Symbols

Attributes are properties of entity types or relationships. An entity type should have a primary key as well as other descriptive attributes. Attributes are shown inside an entity type rectangle. If there are many attributes, the attributes can be suppressed and listed on a separate page. Some ERD drawing tools show attributes in a zoomed view, separate from the rest of the diagram. Underlining indicates that the attribute(s) serves as the primary key of the entity type.

> **Attribute**: a property of an entity type or relationship. Each attribute has a data type that defines the kind of values and permissible operations on the attribute.

Relationships are named associations among entity types. In the Crow's Foot notation, relationship names appear on the line connecting the entity types involved in the relationship. In Figure 5.1, the *Has* relationship shows that the *Course* and *Offering* entity types are directly related. Relationships store associations in both directions. For example, the *Has* relationship shows the offerings for a given course and the associated course for a given offering. The *Has* relationship is binary because it involves two entity types. Section 5.2 presents examples of more complex relationships involving only one distinct entity type (unary relationships) and more than two entity types (M-way relationships).

> **Relationship**: a named association among entity types. A relationship represents a two-way or bidirectional association among entities. Most relationships involve two distinct entity types.

In a loose sense, ERDs have a natural language correspondence. Entity types can correspond to nouns and relationships to verbs or prepositional phrases connecting nouns. In this sense, one can read an entity relationship diagram as a collection of sentences. For example, the ERD in Figure 5.1 can be read as "course has offerings." Note that there is an implied direction in each relationship. In the other direction, one could write, "offering is given for a course." If practical, it is a good idea to use active rather than passive verbs for relationships. Therefore, *Has* is preferred as the relationship name. You should use the natural language correspondence as a guide rather than as a strict rule. For large ERDs, you will not always find a good natural language correspondence for all parts of the diagrams.

5.1.2 Relationship Cardinality

<u>Cardinalities</u> constrain the number of objects that participate in a relationship. To depict the meaning of cardinalities, an instance diagram is useful. Figure 5.2 shows a set of courses ({Course1, Course2, Course3}), a set of offerings ({Offering1, Offering2, Offering3, Offering4}), and connections between the two sets. In Figure 5.2, Course1 is related to Offering1, Offering2, and Offering3, Course2 is related to Offering4, and Course3 is not related to any *Offering* entities. Likewise, Offering1 is related to Course1, Offering2 is related to Course1, Offering3 is related to Course1, and Offering4 is related to Course2. From this instance diagram, we might conclude that each offering is related to exactly one course. In the other direction, each course is related to 0 or more offerings.

> **Cardinality**: a constraint on the number of entities that participate in a relationship. In an ERD, the minimum and maximum cardinalities are specified for both directions of a relationship.

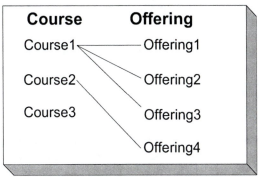

Figure 5.2: Instance Diagram for the *Has* Relationship

Crow's Foot Representation of Cardinalities

The Crow's Foot notation uses three symbols to represent cardinalities. The Crow's Foot symbol (two angled lines and one straight line) denotes many (zero or more) related entities. In Figure 5.3, the Crow's Foot symbol near the *Offering* entity type means that a course can be related to many offerings. The circle means a cardinality of zero, while a line perpendicular to the relationship line means a cardinality of one.

131

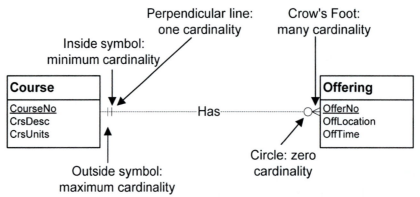

Figure 5.3: Entity Relationship Diagram with Cardinalities Noted

To depict minimum and maximum cardinalities, the cardinality symbols are placed adjacent to each entity type in a relationship. The minimum cardinality symbol appears toward the relationship name while the maximum cardinality symbol appears toward the entity type. In Figure 5.3, a course is related to a minimum of zero offerings (circle in the inside position) and a maximum of many offerings (Crow's Foot in the outside position). Similarly, an offering is related to exactly one (one and only one) course as shown by the single vertical lines in both inside and outside positions.

Classification of Cardinalities

Cardinalities are classified by common values for minimum and maximum cardinality. Table 5-1 shows two classifications for minimum cardinalities. A minimum cardinality of one or more indicates a <u>mandatory relationship</u>. For example, participation in the *Has* relationship is mandatory for each *Offering* entity due to the minimum cardinality of one. A mandatory relationship makes the entity type <u>existence dependent</u> on the relationship. The *Offering* entity type depends on the *Has* relationship because an *Offering* entity cannot be stored without a related *Course* entity. In contrast, a minimum cardinality of zero indicates an <u>optional relationship</u>. For example, the *Has* relationship is optional to the *Course* entity type because a *Course* entity can be stored without being related to an *Offering* entity. Figure 5.4 shows that the *Teaches* relationship is optional for both entity types.

> **Existence Dependency**: an entity that cannot exist unless another related entity exists. A mandatory relationship creates an existence dependency.

Table 5-1: Summary of Cardinality Classifications

Classification	Cardinality Restrictions
Mandatory	Minimum cardinality ≥ 1
Optional	Minimum cardinality $= 0$
Functional or single-valued	Maximum cardinality $= 1$
1-M	Maximum cardinality $= 1$ in one direction and maximum cardinality > 1 in the other direction.
M-N	Maximum cardinality is > 1 in both directions.
1-1	Maximum cardinality $= 1$ in both directions.

Figure 5.4: Optional Relationship for Both Entity Types

Table 5-1 also shows several classifications for maximum cardinalities. A maximum cardinality of one means the relationship is single-valued or functional. For example, the *Has* and *Teaches* relationships are functional for *Offering* because an *Offering* entity can be related to a maximum of one *Course* and one *Faculty* entity. The word function comes from mathematics where a function gives one value. A relationship that has a maximum cardinality of one in one direction and more than one (many) in the other direction is called a 1-M (read one-to-many) relationship. Both the *Has* and *Teaches* relationships are 1-M.

Similarly, a relationship that has a maximum cardinality of more than one in both directions is known as an M-N (many-to-many) relationship. In Figure 5.5, the *TeamTeaches* relationship allows multiple professors to jointly teach the same offering, as shown in the instance diagram of Figure 5.6. M-N relationships are common in business databases to represent the connection between parts and suppliers, authors and books, and skills and employees. For example, a part can be supplied by many suppliers and a supplier can supply many parts.

Less common are 1-1 relationships in which the maximum cardinality equals one in both directions. For example, the *WorksIn* relationship in Figure 5.5 allows a faculty to be assigned to one office and an office to be occupied by at most one faculty.

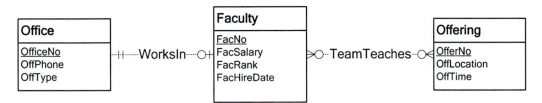

Figure 5.5: M-N and 1-1 Relationship Examples

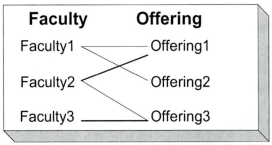

Figure 5.6: Instance Diagram for the M-N *TeamTeaches* Relationship

5.1.3 Comparison to Relational Database Diagrams

To finish this section, let us compare the notation in Figure 5.3 with the relational database diagrams (from Microsoft Access) which you seen in previous chapters. It is easy to become confused between the two notations. Some of the major differences are listed below[19]. To help you visualize these differences, Figure 5.7 shows a relational database diagram for the *Course-Offering* example.

Relational database diagrams do not use names for relationships. Instead foreign keys represent relationships. The ERD notation does not use foreign keys. For example, *Offering.CourseNo* is a column in Figure 5.7 but not an attribute in Figure 5.3. Relational database diagrams show only maximum cardinalities.

Some ERD notations (including the Crow's Foot notation) allow both entity types and relationships to have attributes. Relational database diagrams only allow tables to have columns.

---

[19] Chapter 6 presents conversion rules that describe the differences more precisely.

Relational database diagrams allow a relationship between two tables. Some ERD notations (although not the Crow's Foot notation) allow M-way relationships involving more than two entity types. The next section shows how to represent M-way relationships in the Crow's Foot notation. In some ERD notations (although not the Crow's Foot notation), the position of the cardinalities is reversed.

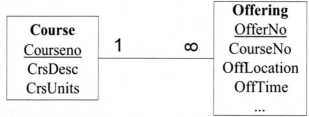

Figure 5.7: Relational Database Diagram for the Course-Offering Example

5.2 Understanding Relationships

This section explores the entity relationship notation in more depth by examining important aspects of relationships. The first subsection describes identification dependency, a specialized kind of existence dependency. The second subsection describes three important relationship patterns: (1) relationships with attributes, (2) self-referencing relationships, and (3) associative entity types representing multiway (M-way) relationships. The final subsection describes an important equivalence between M-N and 1-M relationships.

5.2.1 Identification Dependency (Weak Entities and Identifying Relationships)

In an ERD, some entity types may not have their own primary key. Entity types without their own primary key must borrow part (or all) of their primary key from other entity types. Entity types that borrow part or their entire primary key are known as <u>weak entities</u>. A relationship that provides a component of the primary key is known as an <u>identifying relationship</u>. Thus, an identification dependency involves a weak entity and one or more identifying relationships.

> **Weak Entity**: an entity type that borrows all or part of its primary key from another entity type. Identifying relationships indicate the entity types that supply components of the borrowed primary key.

Identification dependency occurs because some entities are closely associated with other entities. For example, a room does not have a separate identity from its building because a room is physically contained in a building. You can reference a room only by providing its associated building identifier. In the ERD for buildings and rooms (Figure 5.8), the *Room* entity type is identification dependent on the *Building* entity type in the *Contains* relationship. A solid relationship line indicates an identifying relationship. For weak entities, the underlined attribute (if present) is part of the primary key, but not the entire primary key. Thus, the primary key of *Room* is a combination of *BldgID* and *RoomNo*. As another example, Figure 5.9 depicts an identification dependency involving the weak entity *State* and the identifying relationship *Holds*.

Identification dependency symbols:
- Solid relationship line for identifying relationships
- Diagonal lines in the corners of rectangles for weak entities

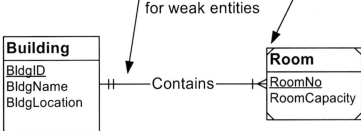

Figure 5.8: Identification Dependency Example

Note: The weak entity's cardinality is always (1,1) in each identifying relationship.

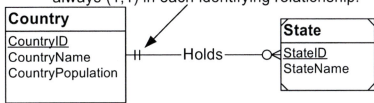

Figure 5.9: Another Identification Dependency Example

Identification dependency is a specialized kind of existence dependency. Recall that an existent-dependent entity type has a mandatory relationship (minimum cardinality of one). Weak entities are existent dependent on the identifying relationships. In addition to the existence dependency, a weak entity borrows at least part of its entire primary key. Because of the existence dependency and the primary key borrowing, the minimum and maximum cardinalities of a weak entity are always 1.

The next section shows several additional examples of identification dependency in the discussion of associative entity types and M-way relationships. The use of identification dependency is necessary for associative entity types.

5.2.2 Relationship Patterns

This section discusses three patterns for relationships that you may encounter in database development efforts: (1) M-N relationships with attributes, (2) self-referencing (unary) relationships, and (3) associative entity types representing M-way relationships. Although these relationship patterns are not common, they are important when they occur. You need to study these patterns carefully to apply them correctly in database development efforts.

M-N Relationships with Attributes

As briefly mentioned in Section 5.1, relationships can have attributes. This situation typically occurs with M-N relationships. In an M-N relationship, attributes are associated with the combination of entity types, not just one of the entity types. If an attribute is associated with only one entity type, then it should be part of that entity type, not the relationship. Figures 5.10 and 5.11 depict M-N relationships with attributes. In Figure 5.10, the attribute *EnrGrade* is associated with the combination of a student and offering, not either one alone. For example, the *EnrollsIn* relationship records the fact that the student with *StdNo* 123-77-9993 has a grade of 3.5 in the offering with offer number 1256. In Figure 5.11(a), the attribute *Qty* represents the quantity of a part supplied by a given supplier. In Figure 5.11(b), the attribute *AuthOrder* represents the order in which the author's name appears in the title of a book. To reduce clutter on a large diagram, relationship attributes may not be shown.

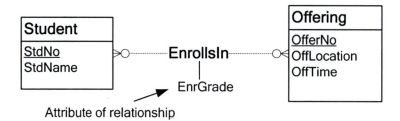

Attribute of relationship

Figure 5.10: M-N Relationship with an Attribute

a) *Provides* relationship

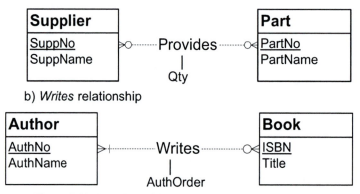

b) *Writes* relationship

Figure 5.11: Additional M-N Relationships with Attributes

       1-M relationships also can have attributes, but 1-M relationships with attributes are much less common than M-N relationships with attributes. In Figure 5.12, the *Commission* attribute is associated with the *Lists* relationship, not with either the *Agent* or the *Home* entity type. A home will only have a commission if an agent lists it. Typically, 1-M relationships with attributes are optional for the child entity type. The *Lists* relationship is optional for the *Home* entity type.

Figure 5.12: 1-M Relationship with an Attribute

Self-Referencing (Unary) Relationships

A <u>self referencing relationship</u> involves connections among members of the same set. Self-referencing relationships are sometimes called reflexive relationships because they are like a reflection in a mirror. Figure 5.13 displays two self-referencing relationships involving the *Faculty* and *Course* entity types. Both relationships involve two entity types that are the same (*Faculty* for *Supervises* and *Course* for *PreReqTo*). These relationships depict important concepts in a university database. The *Supervises* relationship depicts an organizational chart, while the *PreReqTo* relationship depicts course dependencies that can affect a student's course planning.

> **Self-Referencing Relationship**: a relationship involving the same entity type. Self-referencing relationships represent associations among members of the same set.

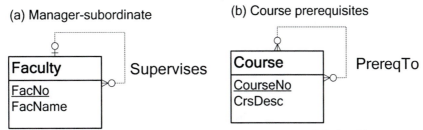

(a) Manager-subordinate   (b) Course prerequisites

Figure 5.13: Examples of Self-Referencing (Unary) Relationships

For self-referencing relationships, it is important to distinguish between 1-M and M-N relationships. An instance diagram can help you understand the difference. Figure 5.14(a) shows an instance diagram for the *Supervises* relationship. Notice that each faculty can have at most one superior. For example, Faculty2 and Faculty3 have Faculty1 as a superior. Therefore, *Supervises* is a 1-M relationship because each faculty can have at most one supervisor. In contrast, there is no such restriction in the instance diagram for the *PreReqTo* relationship (Figure 5.14(b)). For example, IS461 has two prerequisites (IS480 and IS460), while IS320 is a prerequisite to both IS480 and IS460. Therefore, *PreReqTo* is an M-N relationship because a course can be a prerequisite to many courses, and a course can have many prerequisites.

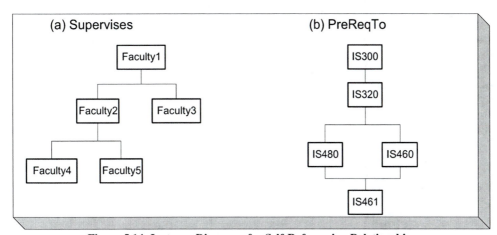

Figure 5.14: Instance Diagrams for Self-Referencing Relationships

Self-referencing relationships occur in a variety of business situations. Any data that can be visualized like Figure 5.14 can be represented as a self-referencing relationship. Typical examples include hierarchical charts of accounts, genealogical charts, part designs, and transportation routes. In these examples, self-referencing relationships are an important part of the database.

There is one other noteworthy aspect of self-referencing relationships. Sometimes a self-referencing relationship is not needed. For example, if you only want to know whether an employee is a supervisor, a self-referencing relationship is not needed. Rather, an attribute can be used to indicate whether an employee is a supervisor.

Associative Entity Types Representing Multi-Way (M-Way) Relationships

Some ERD notations support relationships involving more than two entity types known as <u>M-way (multiway) relationships</u> where the *M* means more than two. For example, the Chen[20] ERD

---

[20] The Chen notation is named after Dr. Peter Chen, who published the paper defining the Entity Relationship Model in 1976.

notation (with diamonds for relationships) allows relationships to connect more than two entity types, as depicted in Figure 5.15. The *Uses* relationship lists suppliers and parts used on projects. For example, a relationship instance involving Supplier1, Part1, and Project1 indicates that Supplier1 Supplies Part1 on Project1. An M-way relationship involving three entity types is called a <u>ternary relationship</u>.

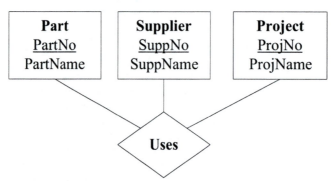

Figure 5.15: M-Way (Ternary) Relationship Using the Chen Notation

Although you cannot directly represent M-way relationships in the Crow's Foot notation, you should understand how to indirectly represent them. You use an <u>associative entity type</u> and a collection of identifying 1-M relationships to represent an M-way relationship. In Figure 5.16, three 1-M relationships link the associative entity type, *Uses*, to the *Part*, the *Supplier*, and the *Project* entity types. The *Uses* entity type is associative because its role is to connect other entity types. Because associative entity types provide a connecting role, they are sometimes given names using active verbs. In addition, associative entity types are always weak as they must borrow the entire primary key. For example, the *Uses* entity type obtains its primary key through the three identifying relationships.

> **Associative Entity Type**: a weak entity that depends on two or more entity types for its primary key. An associative entity type with more than two identifying relationships is known as an M-way associative entity type.

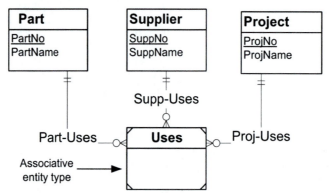

Figure 5.16: Associative Entity Type to Represent a Ternary Relationship

As another example, Figure 5.17 shows the associative entity type *Provides* that connects the *Employee*, *Skill*, and *Project* entity types. An example instance of the *Provides* entity type contains Employee1 providing Skill1 on Project1.

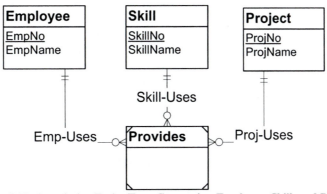

Figure 5.17: Associative Entity Type Connecting Employee, Skill, and Project

The issue of when to use an M-way associative entity type (i.e., an associative entity type representing an M-way relationship) can be difficult to understand. If a database only needs to record pairs of facts, an M-way associative entity type is not needed. For example, if a database only needs to record who supplies a part and what projects use a part, then an M-way associative entity type should not be used. In this case, there should be binary relationships between *Supplier* and *Part* and between *Project* and *Part*. You should use an M-way associative entity type when the database should record combinations of three (or more) entities rather than just combinations of two entities. For example, if a database needs to record which supplier provides parts on specific projects, an M-way associative entity type is needed. Because of the complexity of M-way relationships, Chapter 7 provides a way to reason about them using constraints, while Chapter 12 provides a way to reason about them using data entry forms.

5.2.3 Equivalence between 1-M and M-N Relationships

To improve your understanding of M-N relationships, you should know an important equivalence for M-N relationships. An M-N relationship can be replaced by an associative entity type and two identifying 1-M relationships. Figure 5.18 shows the *EnrollsIn* (Figure 5.10) relationship converted to this 1-M style. In Figure 5.18, two identifying relationships and an associative entity type replace the *EnrollsIn* relationship. The relationship name (*EnrollsIn*) has been changed to a noun (*Enrollment*) to follow the convention of nouns for entity type names. The 1-M style is similar to the representation in a relational database diagram. If you feel more comfortable with the 1-M style, then use it. In terms of the ERD, the M-N and 1-M styles have the same meaning.

> **Relationship Equivalence**: a M-N relationship can be replaced by an associative entity type and two identifying 1-M relationships. In most cases the choice between a M-N relationship and the associative entity type is personal preference.

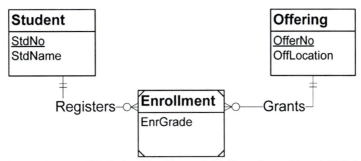

Figure 5.18: *EnrollsIn* **M-N Relationship (Figure 5.10) Transformed into 1-M Relationships**

The transformation of an M-N relationship into 1-M relationships is similar to representing an M-way relationship using 1-M relationships. Whenever an M-N relationship is represented as an associative entity type and two 1-M relationships, the new entity type is identification dependent on both 1-M relationships, as shown in Figure 5.18. Similarly, when representing M-way relationships, the associative entity type is identification dependent on all 1-M relationships as shown in Figures 5.16 and 5.17.

There is one situation when the 1-M style is preferred to the M-N style. When an M-N relationship must be related to other entity types in relationships, you should use the 1-M style. For example, assume that in addition to enrollment in a course offering, attendance in each class session should be recorded. In this situation, the 1-M style is preferred because it is necessary to link an enrollment with attendance records. Figure 5.19 shows the *Attendance* entity type added to the ERD of Figure 5.18. Note that an M-N relationship between the *Student* and *Offering* entity types would not have allowed another relationship with *Attendance*.

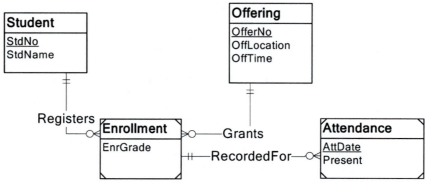

Figure 5.19: Attendance Entity Type Added to the ERD of Figure 18

Figure 5.19 provides other examples of identification dependencies. *Attendance* is identification dependent on *Enrollment* in the *RecordedFor* relationship. The primary key of *Attendance* consists of *AttDate* along with the primary key of *Enrollment*. Similarly, *Enrollment* is identification dependent on both *Student* and *Offering*. The primary key of *Enrollment* is a combination of *StdNo* and *OfferNo*.

5.3 Classification in the Entity Relationship Model

People classify entities to better understand their environment. For example, animals are classified into mammals, reptiles, and other categories to understand the similarities and differences among different species. In business, classification is also pervasive. Classification can be applied to investments, employees, customers, loans, parts, and so on. For example, when applying for a home mortgage, an important distinction is between fixed- and adjustable-rate mortgages. Within each kind of mortgage, there are many variations distinguished by features such as the repayment period, the prepayment penalties, and the loan amount.

This section describes ERD notation to support classification. You will learn to use generalization hierarchies, specify cardinality constraints for generalization hierarchies, and use multiple-level generalization hierarchies for complex classifications.

5.3.1 Generalization Hierarchies

Generalization hierarchies allow entity types to be related by the level of specialization. Figure 5.20 depicts a generalization hierarchy to classify employees as salaried versus hourly. Both salaried and hourly employees are specialized kinds of employees. The *Employee* entity type is known as the supertype (or parent). The entity types *SalaryEmp* and *HourlyEmp* are known as the subtypes (or children). Because each subtype entity *is a* supertype entity, the relationship between a subtype and supertype is known as ISA. For example, a salaried employee is an employee. Because the relationship name (ISA) is always the same, it is not shown on the diagram.

> **Generalization Hierarchy**: a collection of entity types arranged in a hierarchical structure to show similarity in attributes. Each subtype or child entity type contains a subset of entities of its supertype or parent entity type.

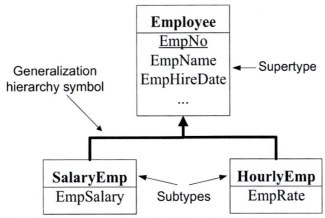

Figure 5.20: Generalization Hierarchy for Employees

Inheritance supports sharing between a supertype and its subtypes. Because every subtype entity is also a supertype entity, the attributes of the supertype also apply to all subtypes. For example, every entity of *SalaryEmp* has an employee number, name, and hiring date because it is also an entity of *Employee*. Inheritance means that the attributes of a supertype are automatically part of its subtypes. That is, each subtype inherits the attributes of its supertype. For example, the attributes of the *SalaryEmp* entity type are its direct attribute (*EmpSalary*) and its inherited attributes from *Employee* (*EmpNo*, *EmpName*, *EmpHireDate*, etc.). Inherited attributes are not shown in an ERD. Whenever you have a subtype, assume that it inherits the attributes from its supertype.

> **Inheritance**: a data modeling feature that supports sharing of attributes between a supertype and a subtype. Subtypes inherit attributes from their supertypes.

Disjointness and Completeness Constraints

Generalization hierarchies do not show cardinalities because they are always the same. Rather disjointness and completeness constraints can be shown. Disjointness means that subtypes in a generalization hierarchy do not have any entities in common. In Figure 5.21, the generalization hierarchy is disjoint because a security cannot be both a stock and a bond. In contrast, the generalization hierarchy in Figure 5.22 is not disjoint because teaching assistants can be considered both students and faculty. Thus, the set of students overlaps with the set of faculty. C

Completeness means that every entity of a supertype must be an entity in one of the subtypes in the generalization hierarchy. The completeness constraint in Figure 5.21 means that every security must be either a stock or a bond.

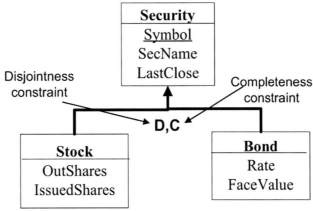

Figure 5.21: Generalization Hierarchy for Securities

141

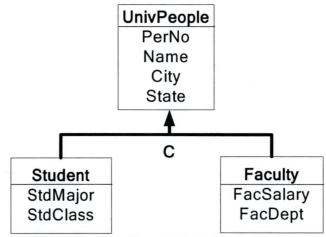

Figure 5.22: Generalization Hierarchy for University People

Some generalization hierarchies lack both disjointness and completeness constraints. In Figure 5.20, the lack of a disjointness constraint means that some employees can be both salaried and hourly. The lack of a completeness constraint indicates that some employees are not paid by salary or the hour (perhaps by commission).

5.3.3 Multiple Levels of Generalization

Generalization hierarchies can be extended to more than one level. This practice can be useful in disciplines such as investments where knowledge is highly structured. In Figure 5.23, there are two levels of subtypes beneath securities. Inheritance extends to all subtypes, direct and indirect. Thus, both the *Common* and *Preferred* entity types inherit the attributes of *Stock* (the immediate parent) and *Security* (the indirect parent). Note that disjointness and completeness constraints can be made for each group of subtypes.

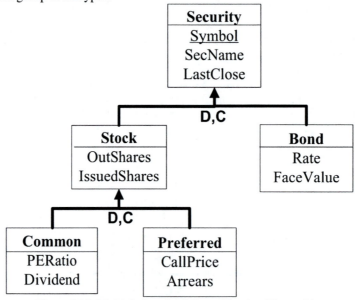

Figure 5.23: Multiple Levels of Generalization Hierarchies

5.4 Notation Summary and Diagram Rules

You have seen a lot of ERD notation in the previous sections of this chapter. So that you do not become overwhelmed, this section provides a convenient summary as well as rules to help you avoid common diagramming errors.

5.4.1 Notation Summary

To help you recall the notation introduced in previous sections, Table 5-2 presents a summary while Figure 5.24 demonstrates the notation for the university database of Chapter 4. Figure 5.24 differs in some ways from the university database in Chapter 4 to depict most of the Crow's Foot notation. Figure 5.24 contains a generalization hierarchy to depict the similarities among students and faculty. You should note that the primary key of the *Student* and the *Faculty* entity types is *PerNo*, an attribute inherited from the *UnivPerson* entity type. The *Enrollment* entity type (associative) and the identifying relationships (*Registers* and *Grants*) could appear as an M-N relationship as previously shown in Figure 5.10. In addition to these issues, Figure 5.24 omits some attributes for brevity.

Table 5-2: Summary of Crow's Foot Notation

Symbol	Meaning
Student StdNo StdName ...	Entity type with attributes (primary key underlined)
Enrolls_In---O< EnrGrade	M-N relationship with attributes: attributes are shown if room permits; otherwise attributes are listed separately.
Contains ---O<	Identification dependency: identifying relationship(s) (solid relationship lines) and weak entity (diagonal lines in the corners of the rectangle). Associative entity types also are weak because they are (by definition) identification dependent.
D,C	Generalization hierarchy with disjointness and completeness constraints
Contains----++--	Existence dependent cardinality (minimum cardinality of 1): inner symbol is a line perpendicular to the relationship line.
Teaches ----O+	Optional cardinality (minimum cardinality of 0): inner symbol is a circle.
Has ---------++--	Single-valued cardinality (maximum cardinality of 1): outer symbol is a perpendicular line.

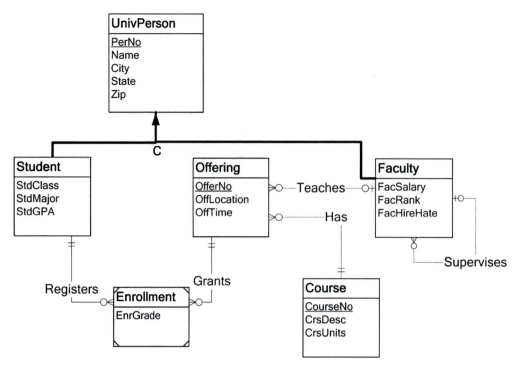

Figure 5.24: ERD for the University Database

Representation of Business Rules in an ERD

As you develop an ERD, you should remember that an ERD contains business rules that enforce organizational policies and promote efficient communication among business stakeholders. An ERD contains important business rules represented as primary keys, relationships, cardinalities, and generalization hierarchies. Primary keys support entity identification, an important requirement in business communication. Identification dependency involves an entity that depends on other entities for identification, a requirement in some business communication. Relationships indicate direct connections among units of business communication. Cardinalities restrict the number of related entities in relationships supporting organizational policies and consistent business communication. Generalization hierarchies with disjointness and completeness constraints support classification of business entities and organizational policies. Thus, the elements of an ERD are crucial for enforcement of organizational policies and efficient business communication.

For additional kinds of business constraints, an ERD can be enhanced with informal documentation or a formal rules language. Since SQL:2006 supports a formal rules language (see Chapters 11 and 14), a language is not proposed here. In the absence of a formal rules language, business rules can be stored as informal documentation associated with entity types, attributes, and relationships. Typical kinds of business rules to specify as informal documentation are candidate key constraints, attribute comparison constraints, null value constraints, and default values. Candidate keys provide alternative ways to identify business entities. Attribute comparison constraints restrict the values of attributes either to a fixed collection of values or to values of other attributes. Null value constraints and default values support policies about completeness of data collection activities. Table 5-3 summarizes the common kinds of business rules that can be specified either formally or informally in an ERD.

Table 5-3: Summary of Business Rules in an ERD

Business Rule	ERD Representation
Entity identification	Primary keys for entity types, identification dependency (weak entities and identifying relationships), informal documentation about other unique attributes
Connections among business entities	Relationships
Number of related entities	Minimum and maximum cardinalities
Inclusion among entity sets	Generalization hierarchies
Reasonable values	Informal documentation about attribute constraints (comparison to constant values or other attributes)
Data collection completeness	Informal documentation about null values and default values

5.4.2 Diagram Rules

To provide guidance about correct usage of the notation, Table 5-4 presents completeness and consistency rules. You should apply these rules when completing an ERD to ensure that there are no notation errors in your ERD. Thus, the diagram rules serve a purpose similar to syntax rules for a computer language. The absence of syntax errors does not mean that a computer program performs its tasks correctly. Likewise, the absence of notation errors does not mean that an ERD provides an adequate data representation. The diagram rules do not ensure that you have considered multiple alternatives, correctly represented user requirements, and properly documented your design. Chapter 6 discusses these issues to enhance your data modeling skills.

Table 5-4: Completeness and Consistency Rules

Type of Rule	Description
Completeness	Primary key rule: All entity types have a primary key (direct, borrowed, or inherited).
	Naming rule: All entity types, relationships, and attributes are named.
	Cardinality rule: Cardinality is given for both entity types in a relationship.
	Entity participation rule: All entity types except those in a generalization hierarchy participate in at least one relationship.
	Generalization hierarchy participation rule: Each generalization hierarchy participates in at least one relationship with an entity type not in the generalization hierarchy.
Consistency	Entity name rule: Entity type names are unique.
	Attribute name rule: Attribute names are unique within entity types and relationships.
	Inherited attribute name rule: Attribute names in a subtype do not match inherited (direct or indirect) attribute names.
	Relationship/entity type connection rule: All relationships connect two entity types (not necessarily distinct).
	Relationship/relationship connection rule: Relationships are not connected to other relationships.
	Weak entity rule: Weak entities have at least one identifying relationship.
	Identifying relationship rule: For each identifying relationship, at least one participating entity type must be weak.
	Identification dependency cardinality rule: For each identifying relationship, the minimum and maximum cardinality must be 1 in the direction from the child (weak entity) to the parent entity type.
	Redundant foreign key rule: Redundant foreign keys are not used.

Most of the rules in Table 5-4 do not require much elaboration. The first three completeness rules and the first five consistency rules are simple to understand. Even though the rules are simple, you should still check your ERDs for compliance as it is easy to overlook a violation in a moderate-size ERD.

The consistency rules do not require unique relationship names because participating entity types provide a context for relationship names. However, it is good practice to use unique relationship names as much as possible to make relationships easy to distinguish. In addition, two or more relationships involving the same entity types should be unique because the entity types no longer provide a context to distinguish the relationships. Since it is uncommon to have more than one relationship between the same entity types, the consistency rules do not include this provision.

Completeness rules 4 (entity participation rule) and 5 (generalization hierarchy participation rule) require elaboration. Violating these rules is a warning, not necessarily an error. In most ERDs, all entity types not in a generalization hierarchy and all generalization hierarchies are connected to at least one other entity type. In rare situations, an ERD contains an unconnected entity type just to store a list of entities. Rule 5 applies to an entire generalization hierarchy, not to each entity type in a generalization hierarchy. In other words, at least one entity type in a generalization hierarchy should be connected to at least one entity type not in the generalization hierarchy. In many generalization hierarchies, multiple entity types participate in relationships. Generalization hierarchies permit subtypes to participate in relationships thus constraining relationship participation. For example in Figure 5.24, *Student* and *Faculty* participate in relationships.

Consistency rules 6 through 9 involve common errors in the ERDs of novice data modelers. Novice data modelers violate consistency rules 6 to 8 because of the complexity of identification dependency. Identification dependency involving a weak entity and identifying relationships provides more sources of errors than other parts of the Crow's Foot notation. In addition, each identifying relationship also requires a minimum and maximum cardinality of 1 in the direction from the child (weak entity) to the parent entity type. Novice data modelers violate consistency rule 9 (redundant foreign key rule) because of confusion between an ERD and the relational data model. The conversion process transforms 1-M relationships into foreign keys.

Example of Rule Violations and Resolutions

Because the identification dependency rules and the redundant foreign key rule are a frequent source of errors to novice designers, this section provides an example to depict rule violations and resolutions. Figure 5.25 demonstrates violations of the identification dependency rules (consistency rules 6 to 9) and the redundant foreign key rule (consistency rule 9) for the university database ERD. The following list explains the violations:

- Consistency rule 6 (weak entity rule) violation: *Faculty* cannot be a weak entity without at least one identifying relationship.
- Consistency rule 7 (identifying relationship rule) violation: The *Has* relationship is identifying but neither *Offering* nor *Course* is a weak entity.
- Consistency rule 8 (identification dependency cardinality rule) violation: The cardinality of the *Registers* relationship from *Enrollment* to *Student* should be (1, 1) not (0, Many).
- Consistency rule 9 (redundant foreign key rule) violation: The *CourseNo* attribute in the *Offering* entity type is redundant with the *Has* relationship. Because *CourseNo* is the primary key of *Course*, it should not be an attribute of *Offering* to link an *Offering* to a *Course*. The *Has* relationship provides the linkage to *Course*.

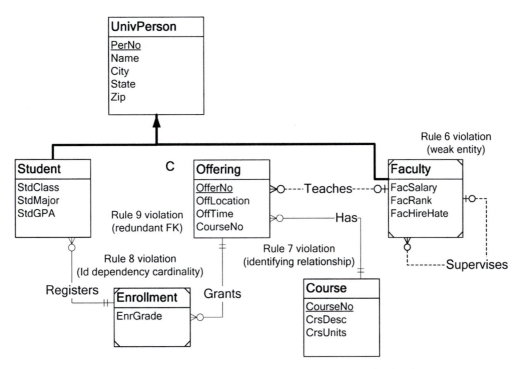

Figure 5.25: ERD with Violations of Consistency Rules 6 to 9

For most rules, resolving violations is easy. The major task is recognition of the violation. For the identification dependency rules, resolution can depend on the problem details. The following list suggests possible corrective actions for diagram errors:

- Consistency rule 6 (weak entity rule) resolution: The problem can be resolved by either adding one or more identifying relationships or by changing the weak entity into a regular entity. In Figure 5.25, the problem is resolved by making *Faculty* a regular entity. The more common resolution is to add one or more identifying relationships.
- Consistency rule 7 (identifying relationship rule) resolution: The problem can be resolved by adding a weak entity or making the relationship non-identifying. In Figure 5.25, the problem is resolved by making the *Has* relationship non-identifying. If there is more than one identifying relationship involving the same entity type, the typical resolution involves designating the common entity type as a weak entity.
- Consistency rule 8 (identification dependency cardinality rule) resolution: The problem can be resolved by changing the weak entity's cardinality to (1,1). Typically, the cardinality of the identifying relationship is reversed. In Figure 5.25, the cardinality of the *Registers* relationship should be reversed ((1,1) near *Student* and (0, Many) near *Enrollment*).
- Consistency rule 9 (redundant foreign key rule) resolution: Normally the problem can be resolved by removing the redundant foreign key. In Figure 5.25, *CourseNo* should be removed as an attribute of *Offering*. In some cases, the attribute may not represent a foreign key. If the attribute does not represent a foreign key, it should be renamed instead of removed.

Alternative Organization of Rules

The organization of rules in Table 5-4 may be difficult to remember. Table 5-5 provides an alternative grouping by rule purpose. If you find this organization more intuitive, you should use it. However you choose to remember the rules, the important point is to apply them after you have completed an ERD.

Support in CASE Tools

To help you apply diagram rules, most CASE tools perform checks specific to the notations supported by the tools. A CASE tool can support consistency rules 4 and 5 through its diagramming tools. Relationships must be connected to two entity types (not necessarily distinct) prohibiting violations of consistency rules 4 and 5. For the other completeness and consistency rules, a CASE tool can provide a diagram check feature to generate a report of rule violations. Because the diagram check feature may be used when an ERD is not complete, a CASE tool may not require fixing rule violations found in an ERD. Before completing an ERD, you should address each violation noted a CASE tool.

For the redundant foreign key rule (consistency rule 9), a CASE tool can use a simple implementation to determine if an ERD contains a redundant foreign key. A CASE tool can check the child entity type (entity type on the many side of the relationship) for an attribute with the same name and data type as the primary key in the parent entity type (entity type on the one side of the relationship). If a CASE tool finds an attribute with the same name and data type, a violation is listed in a consistency report.

Table 5-5: Alternative Rule Organization

Category	Rules
Names	All entity types, relationships, and attributes are named. (Completeness rule 2)
	Entity type names are unique. (Consistency rule 1)
	Attribute names are unique within entity types and relationships. (Consistency rule 2)
	Attribute names in a subtype do not match inherited (direct or indirect) attribute names. (Consistency rule 3)
Content	All entity types have a primary key (direct, borrowed, or inherited). (Completeness rule 1)
	Cardinality is given for both entity types in a relationship. (Completeness rule 3)
Connection	All entity types except those in a generalization hierarchy participate in at least one relationship. (Completeness rule 4)
	Each generalization hierarchy participates in at least one relationship with an entity type not in the generalization hierarchy. (Completeness rule 5)
	All relationships connect two entity types. (Consistency rule 4)
	Relationships are not connected to other relationships. (Consistency rule 5)
	Redundant foreign keys are not used. (Consistency rule 9)
Identification Dependency	Weak entities have at least one identifying relationship. (Consistency rule 6)
	For each identifying relationship, at least one participating entity type must be weak. (Consistency rule 7)
	For each weak entity, the minimum and maximum cardinality must equal 1 for each identifying relationship. (Consistency rule 8)

5.5 Comparison to Other Notations

The ERD notation presented in this chapter is similar to but not identical to what you may encounter later. There is no standard notation for ERDs. There are perhaps six reasonably popular ERD notations, each having its own small variations that appear in practice. The notation in this chapter comes from the Crow's Foot stencil in Visio Professional 5 with the addition of the generalization notation. The notations that you encounter in practice will depend on factors such as the data modeling tool (if any) used in your organization and the industry. One thing is certain: you should be prepared to adapt to the notation in use. This section describes ERD variations that you may encounter as well as the Class Diagram notation of the Unified Modeling Language (UML), an emerging standard for data modeling.

5.5.1 ERD Variations

Because there is no widely accepted ERD standard, different symbols can be used to represent the same concept. Relationship cardinalities are a source of wide variation. You should pay attention to the placement of the cardinality symbols. The notation in this chapter places the symbols close to the "far" entity type, while other notations place the cardinality symbols close to the "near" entity type. The notation in this chapter uses a visual representation of cardinalities with the minimum and maximum cardinalities given by three symbols. Other notations use a text representation with letters and integers instead of symbols. For example, Figure 5.26 shows a Chen ERD with the position of cardinalities reversed, cardinalities depicted with text, and relationships denoted by diamonds.

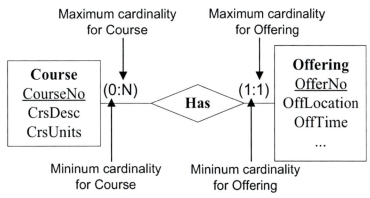

Figure 5.26: Chen Notation for the Course-Offering ERD

Other symbol variations are visual representations for certain kinds of entity types. In some notations, weak entities and M-N relationships have special representations. Weak entities are sometimes enclosed in double rectangles. Identifying relationships are sometimes enclosed in double diamonds. M-N relationships with attributes are sometimes shown as a rectangle with a diamond inside denoting the dual qualities (both relationship and entity type).

In addition to symbol variations, there are also rule variations, as shown in the following list. For each restriction, there is a remedy. For example, if only binary relationships are supported, M-way relationships must be represented as an associative entity type with 1-M relationships.

Some notations do not support M-way relationships.
Some notations do not support M-N relationships.
Some notations do not support relationships with attributes.
Some notations do not support self-referencing (unary) relationships.
Some notations permit relationships to be connected to other relationships.
Some notations show foreign keys as attributes.
Some notations allow attributes to have more than one value (multivalued attributes).

Restrictions in an ERD notation do not necessarily make the notation less expressive than other notations without the restrictions. Additional symbols in a diagram may be necessary, but the same concepts can still be represented. For example, the Crow's Foot notation does not support M-way relationships. However, M-way relationships can be represented using M-way associative entity types. M-way associative entity types require additional symbols than M-way relationships, but the same concepts are represented.

5.5.2 Class Diagram Notation of the Unified Modeling Language

The Unified Modeling Language has become the standard notation for object-oriented modeling. Object-oriented modeling emphasizes objects rather than processes, as emphasized in traditional systems development approaches. In object-oriented modeling, one defines the objects first, followed by the features (attributes and operations) of the objects, and then the dynamic interaction among objects. The UML contains class diagrams, interface diagrams, and interaction diagrams to support object-oriented modeling. The class diagram notation provides an alternative to the ERD notations presented in this chapter.

Class diagrams contain classes (collections of objects), associations (binary relationships) among classes, and object features (attributes and operations). Figure 5.27 shows a simple class diagram containing the *Offering* and *Faculty* classes. The association in Figure 5.27 represents a 1-M relationship. The UML supports role names and cardinalities (minimum and maximum) for each direction in an association. The 0..1 cardinality means that an offering object can be related to a minimum of zero faculty objects and a maximum of one faculty object. Operations are listed below the attributes. Each operation contains a parenthesized list of parameters along with the data type returned by the operation.

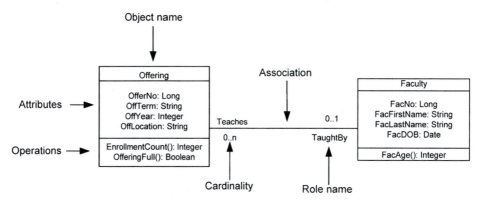

Figure 5.27: Simple Class Diagram

Associations in the UML are similar to relationships in the Crow's Foot notation. Associations can represent binary or unary relationships. To represent an M-way relationship, a class and a collection of associations are required. To represent an M-N relationship with attributes, the UML provides the association class to allow associations to have attributes and operations. Figure 5.28 shows an association class that represents an M-N relationship between the *Student* and the *Offering* classes. The association class contains the relationship attributes.

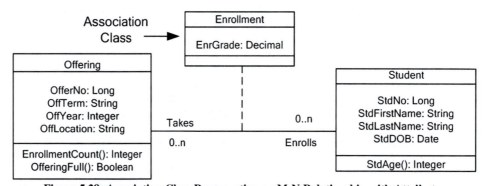

Figure 5.28: Association Class Representing an M-N Relationship with Attributes

Unlike most ERD notations, support for generalization was built into the UML from its inception. In most ERD notations, generalization was added as an additional feature after a notation was well established. In Figure 5.29, the large empty arrow denotes a classification of the *Student* class into *Undergraduate* and *Graduate* classes. The UML supports generalization names and constraints. In Figure 5.29, the *Status* generalization is complete, meaning that every student must be an undergraduate or a graduate student.

150

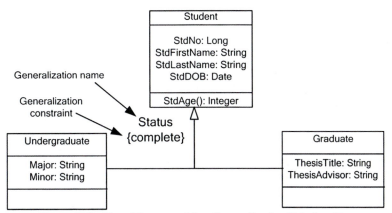

Figure 5.29: Class Diagram with a Generalization Relationship

The UML also provides a special symbol for composition relationships, similar to identification dependencies in ERD notations. In a composition relationship, the objects in a child class belong only to objects in the parent class. In Figure 5.30, each *OrdLine* object belongs to one *Order* object. Deletion of a parent object causes deletion of the related child objects. As a consequence, the child objects usually borrow part of their primary key from the parent object. However, the UML does not require this identification dependency.

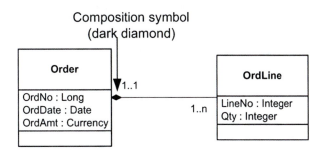

Figure 5.30: Class Diagram with a Composition Relationship

UML class diagrams provide many other features not presented in this brief overview. The UML supports different kinds of classes to integrate programming language concerns with data modeling concerns. Other kinds of classes include value classes, stereotype classes, parameterized classes, and abstract classes. For generalization, the UML supports additional constraints such as static and dynamic classification and different interpretations of generalization relationships (subtype and subclass). For data integrity, the UML supports the specification of constraints in a class diagram.

You should note that class diagrams are just one part of the UML. To some extent, class diagrams must be understood in the context of object-oriented modeling and the entire UML. You should expect to devote an entire academic term to understanding object-oriented modeling and the UML.

Closing Thoughts

This chapter has explained the notation of entity relationship diagrams as a prerequisite to applying entity relationship diagrams in the database development process. Using the Crow's Foot notation, this chapter described the symbols, important relationship patterns, and generalization hierarchies. The basic symbols are entity types, relationships, attributes, and cardinalities to depict the number of entities participating in a relationship. Four important relationship patterns were described: many-to-many (M-N) relationships with attributes, associative entity types representing M-way relationships, identifying relationships providing primary keys to weak entities, and self-referencing (unary) relationships. Generalization hierarchies allow classification of entity types to depict similarities among entity types.

To help improve your usage of the Crow's Foot notation, business rule representations, diagram rules, and comparisons to other notations were presented. This chapter presented formal and informal representation of business rules in an entity relationship diagram to provide an organizational context for entity relationship diagrams. The diagram rules involve completeness and consistency requirements. The diagram rules ensure that an ERD does not contain obvious errors. To help you apply the rules, some CASE tools provide features to check the rules on completed ERDs. To broaden your background of ERD notations, this chapter presented common variations that you may encounter as well as the Class Diagram notation of the Unified Modeling Language, the standard notation for object-oriented modeling.

This chapter emphasized the notation of ERDs to provide a solid foundation for the more difficult study of applying the notation on business problems. To master data modeling, you need to understand the ERD notation and obtain ample practice building ERDs. Chapter 6 emphasizes the practice of building ERDs for business problems. Applying the notation involves consistent and complete representation of user requirements, generation of alternative designs, and documentation of design decisions. In addition to these skills, Chapter 6 presents rules to convert an ERD into a table design. With careful study, Chapters 5 and 6 provide a solid foundation to perform data modeling on business databases.

Review Concepts

- Basic concepts: entity types, relationships, and attributes
- Minimum and maximum cardinalities to constrain relationship participation
- Classification of cardinalities as optional, mandatory, and functional
- Existence dependency for entities that cannot be stored without storage of related entities
- Identification dependency involving weak entities and identifying relationships to support entity types that borrow at least part of their primary keys
- M-N relationships with attributes: attributes are associated with the combination of entity types, not just with one of the entity types
- Equivalence between an M-N relationship and an associative entity type with identifying 1-M relationships
- M-way associative entity types to represent M-way relationships among more than two entity types
- Self-referencing (unary) relationships to represent associations among entities of the same entity type
- Instance diagrams to help distinguish between 1-M and M-N self-referencing relationships
- Generalization hierarchies to show similarities among entity types
- Representation of business rules in an ERD: entity identification, connections among business entities, number of related entities, inclusion among entity sets, reasonable values, and data collection completeness
- Diagram rules to prevent obvious data modeling errors
- Common sources of diagram errors: identification dependency and redundant foreign keys
- Support for the diagram rules in CASE tools
- ERD variations: symbols and diagram rules
- Class Diagram notation of the Unified Modeling Language as an alternative to the Entity Relationship Model

Questions

1. What is an entity type?
2. What is an attribute?
3. What is a relationship?
4. What is the natural language correspondence for entity types and relationships?
5. What is the difference between an ERD and an instance diagram?
6. What symbols are the ERD counterparts of foreign keys in the Relational Model?

7. What cardinalities indicate functional, optional, and mandatory relationships?
8. When is it important to convert an M-N relationship into 1-M relationships?
9. How can an instance diagram help to determine whether a self-referencing relationship is a 1-M or an M-N relationship?
10. When should an ERD contain weak entities?
11. What is the difference between an existence-dependent and a weak entity type?
12. Why is classification important in business?
13. What is inheritance in generalization hierarchies?
14. What is the purpose of disjointness and completeness constraints for a generalization hierarchy?
15. What symbols are used for cardinality in the Crow's Foot notation?
16. What are the two components of identification dependency?
17. How are M-way relationships represented in the Crow's Foot notation?
18. What is an associative entity type?
19. What is the equivalence between an M-N relationship and 1-M relationships?
20. What does it mean to say that part of a primary key is borrowed?
21. What is the purpose of the diagram rules?
22. What are the limitations of the diagram rules?
23. What consistency rules are commonly violated by novice data modelers?
24. Why do novice data modelers violate the identification dependency rules (consistency rules 6 through 8)?
25. Why do novice data modelers violate consistency rule 9 about redundant foreign keys?
26. Why should a CASE tool support diagram rules?
27. How can a CASE tool support consistency rules 4 and 5?
28. How can a CASE tool support all rules except consistency rules 4 and 5?
29. Why should a CASE tool not require resolution of all diagram errors found in an ERD?
30. How can a CASE tool implement consistency rule 9 about redundant foreign keys?
31. List some symbol differences in ERD notation that you may experience in your career.
32. List some diagram rule differences in ERD notation that you may experience in your career.
33. What is the Unified Modeling Language (UML)?
34. What are the modeling elements in a UML class diagram?
35. What kinds of business rules are formally represented in the Crow's Foot ERD notation?
36. What kinds of business rules are defined through informal documentation in the absence of a rules language for an ERD?
37. How are M-way relationships represented in the Crow's Foot notation?
38. What is a self-referencing relationship?
39. What tool can be useful to distinguish between a 1-M and M-N self-referencing relationship?
40. Please explain the importance of specialized modeling elements including M-way relationships and self-referencing relationships.
41. What is the difference between a weak entity type and an associative entity type?

Problems

The problems emphasize correct usage of the Crow's Foot notation and application of the diagram rules. This emphasis is consistent with the pedagogy of the chapter. The more challenging problems in Chapter 6 emphasize user requirements, diagram transformations, design documentation, and schema conversion. To develop a good understanding of data modeling, you should complete the problems in both chapters.

1. Draw an ERD containing the *Order* and *Customer* entity types connected by a 1-M relationship from *Customer* to *Order*. Choose an appropriate relationship name using your common knowledge of interactions between customers and orders. Define minimum cardinalities so that an order is optional for a customer and a customer is mandatory for an order. For the *Customer* entity type, add attributes *CustNo* (primary key), *CustFirstName*, *CustLastName*, *CustStreet*, *CustCity*, *CustState*, *CustZip*, and *CustBal* (balance). For the *Order* entity type, add attributes for the *OrdNo* (primary key), *OrdDate*, *OrdName*, *OrdStreet*, *OrdCity*, *OrdState*, and *OrdZip*. If you are using the ER

Assistant or another drawing tool that supports data type specification, choose appropriate data types for the attributes based on your common knowledge.

2. Extend the ERD from problem 1 with the *Employee* entity type and a 1-M relationship from *Employee* to *Order*. Choose an appropriate relationship name using your common knowledge of interactions between employees and orders. Define minimum cardinalities so that an employee is optional to an order and an order is optional to an employee. For the *Employee* entity type, add attributes *EmpNo* (primary key), *EmpFirstName*, *EmpLastName*, *EmpPhone*, *EmpEmail*, *EmpCommRate* (commission rate), and *EmpDeptName*. If you are using the ER Assistant or another drawing tool that supports data type specification, choose appropriate data types for the attributes based on your common knowledge.

3. Extend the ERD from problem 2 with a self-referencing 1-M relationship involving the *Employee* entity type. Choose an appropriate relationship name using your common knowledge of organizational relationships among employees. Define minimum cardinalities so that the relationship is optional in both directions.

4. Extend the ERD from problem 3 with the *Product* entity type and an M-N relationship between *Product* and *Order*. Choose an appropriate relationship name using your common knowledge of connections between products and orders. Define minimum cardinalities so that an order is optional to a product, and a product is mandatory to an order. For the *Product* entity type, add attributes *ProdNo* (primary key), *ProdName*, *ProdQOH*, *ProdPrice*, and *ProdNextShipDate*. For the M-N relationship, add an attribute for the order quantity. If you are using the ER Assistant or another drawing tool that supports data type specification, choose appropriate data types for the attributes based on your common knowledge.

5. Revise the ERD from problem 4 by transforming the M-N relationship into an associative entity type and two identifying, 1-M relationships.

6. Check your ERDs from problems 4 and 5 for violations of the diagram rules. If you followed the problem directions, your diagrams should not have any errors. Perform the check without using a CASE tool such as the ER Assistant. Then, if you are using the ER Assistant, you can use the Check Diagram feature after checking the rules yourself.

7. Using your corrected ERD from problem 6, add violations of consistency rules 6 to 9. If available, you can use the Check Diagram feature of the ER Assistant to identify the errors.

8. Design an ERD for the *Task* entity type and an M-N self-referencing relationship. For the *Task* entity type, add attributes *TaskNo* (primary key), *TaskDesc*, *TaskEstDuration*, *TaskStatus*, *TaskStartTime*, and *TaskEndTime*. Choose an appropriate relationship name using your common knowledge of precedence connections among tasks. Define minimum cardinalities so that the relationship is optional in both directions.

9. Revise the ERD from problem 8 by transforming the M-N relationship into an associative entity type and two identifying, 1-M relationships.

10. Define a generalization hierarchy containing the *Student* entity type, the *UndStudent* entity type, and the *GradStudent* entity type. The *Student* entity type is the supertype and *UndStudent* and *GradStudent* are subtypes. The *Student* entity type has attributes *StdNo* (primary key), *StdName*, *StdGender*, *StdDOB* (date of birth), *StdEmail*, and *StdAdmitDate*. The *UndStudent* entity type has attributes *UndMajor*, *UndMinor*, and *UndClass*. The *GradStudent* entity type has attributes *GradAdvisor*, *GradThesisTitle*, and *GradAsstStatus* (assistantship status). The generalization hierarchy should be complete and disjoint.

11. Define a generalization hierarchy containing the *Employee* entity type, the *Faculty* entity type, and the *Administrator* entity type. The *Employee* entity type is the supertype and *Faculty* and *Administrator* are subtypes. The *Employee* entity type has attributes *EmpNo* (primary key), *EmpName*, *EmpGender*, *EmpDOB* (date of birth), *EmpPhone*, *EmpEmail*, and *EmpHireDate*. The *Faculty* entity type has attributes *FacRank*, *FacPayPeriods*, and *FacTenure*. The *Administrator* entity type has attributes *AdmTitle*, *AdmContractLength*, and *AdmAppointmentDate*. The generalization hierarchy should be complete and overlapping.

12. Combine the generalization hierarchies from problems 10 and 11. The root of the generalization hierarchy is the *UnivPerson* entity type. The primary key of *UnivPerson* is

UnvPerNo. The other attributes in the *UnivPerson* entity type should be the attributes common to *Employee* and *Student*. You should rename the attributes to be consistent with inclusion in the *UnivPerson* entity type. The generalization hierarchy should be complete and disjoint.

13. Draw an ERD containing the *Patient*, *Physician*, and *Visit* entity types connected by 1-M relationships from *Patient* to *Visit* and *Physician* to *Visit*. Choose appropriate names for the relationships. Define minimum cardinalities so that patients and physicians are mandatory for a visit, but visits are optional for patients and physicians. For the *Patient* entity type, add attributes *PatNo* (primary key), *PatFirstName*, *PatLastName*, *PatStreet*, *PatCity*, *PatState*, *PatZip*, and *PatHealthPlan*. For the *Physician* entity type, add attributes *PhyNo* (primary key), *PhyFirstName*, *PhyLastName*, *PhySpecialty*, *PhyPhone*, *PhyEmail*, *PhyHospital*, and *PhyCertification*. For the *Visit* entity type, add attributes for the *VisitNo* (primary key), *VisitDate*, *VisitPayMethod* (cash, check, or credit card), and *VisitCharge*. If you are using the ER Assistant or another drawing tool that supports data type specification, choose appropriate data types for the attributes based on your common knowledge.

14. Extend the ERD in problem 13 with the *Nurse*, the *Item*, and the *VisitDetail* entity types connected by 1-M relationships from *Visit* to *VisitDetail*, *Nurse* to *VisitDetail*, and *Item* to *VisitDetail*. *VisitDetail* is a weak entity with the 1-M relationship from *Visit* to *VisitDetail* an identifying relationship. Choose appropriate names for the relationships. Define minimum cardinalities so that a nurse is optional for a visit detail, an item is mandatory for a visit detail, and visit details are optional for nurses and items. For the *Item* entity type, add attributes *ItemNo* (primary key), *ItemDesc*, *ItemPrice*, and *ItemType*. For the *Nurse* entity type, add attributes *NurseNo* (primary key), *NurseFirstName*, *NurseLastName*, *NurseTitle*, *NursePhone*, *NurseSpecialty*, and *NursePayGrade*. For the *VisitDetail* entity type, add attributes for the *DetailNo* (part of the primary key) and *DetailCharge*. If you are using the ER Assistant or another drawing tool that supports data type specification, choose appropriate data types for the attributes based on your common knowledge.

15. Refine the ERD from problem 14 with a generalization hierarchy consisting of *Provider*, *Physician*, and *Nurse*. The root of the generalization hierarchy is the *Provider* entity type. The primary key of *Provider* is *ProvNo* replacing the attributes *PhyNo* and *NurseNo*. The other attributes in the *Provider* entity type should be the attributes common to *Nurse* and *Physician*. You should rename the attributes to be consistent with inclusion in the *Provider* entity type. The generalization hierarchy should be complete and disjoint.

16. Check your ERD from problem 15 for violations of the diagram rules. If you followed the problem directions, your diagram should not have any errors. Apply the consistency and completeness rules to ensure that your diagram does not have errors. If you are using the ER Assistant, you can use the Check Diagram feature after checking the rules yourself.

17. Using your corrected ERD from problem 16, add violations of consistency rules 3 and 6 to 9. If you are using the ER Assistant, you can use the Check Diagram feature after checking the rules yourself.

18. For each consistency error in Figure 5.P1, identify the consistency rule violated and suggest possible resolutions of the error. The ERD has generic names so that you will concentrate on finding diagram errors rather than focusing on the meaning of the diagram. If you are using the ER Assistant, you can compare your solution to the result using the Check Diagram feature.

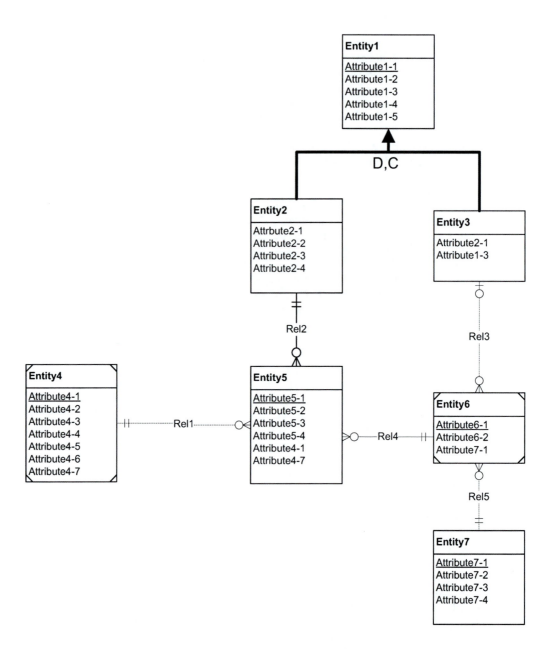

Figure 5.P1: ERD for Problem 18

19. For each consistency error in Figure 5.P2, identify the consistency rule violated and suggest possible resolutions of the error. The ERD has generic names so that you will concentrate on finding diagram errors rather than focusing on the meaning of the diagram. If you are using the ER Assistant, you can compare your solution to the result using the Check Diagram feature.

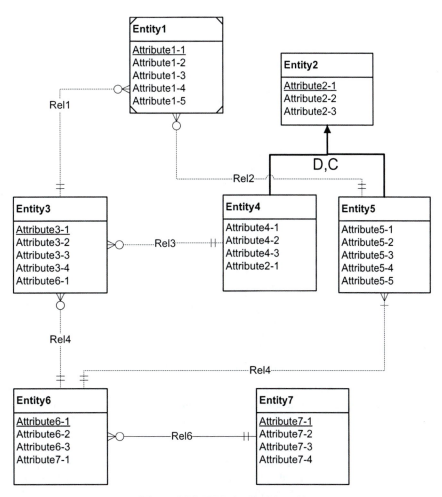

Figure 5.P2: ERD for Problem 19

20. For each consistency error in Figure 5.P3, identify the consistency rule violated and suggest possible resolutions of the error. The ERD has generic names so that you will concentrate on finding diagram errors rather than focusing on the meaning of the diagram. If you are using the ER Assistant, you can compare your solution to the result using the Check Diagram feature.

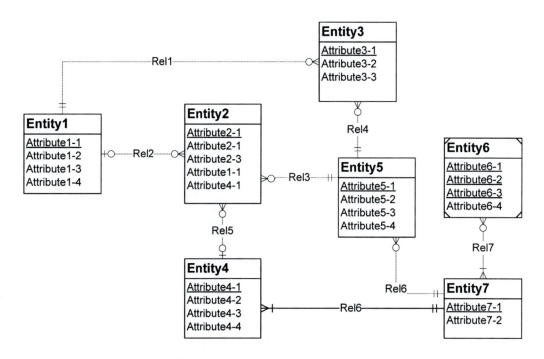

Figure 5.P3: ERD for Problem 20

21. Draw an ERD containing the *Employee* and *Appointment* entity types connected by an M-N relationship. Choose an appropriate relationship name using your common knowledge of interactions between employees and appointments. Define minimum cardinalities so that an appointment is optional for an employee and an employee is mandatory for an appointment. For the *Employee* entity type, add attributes *EmpNo* (primary key), *EmpFirstName*, *EmpLastName*, *EmpPosition*, *EmpPhone*, and *EmpEmail*. For the *Appointment* entity type, add attributes for *AppNo* (primary key), *AppSubject*, *AppStartTime*, *AppEndTime*, and *AppNotes*. For the M-N relationship, add an attribute *Attendance* indicating whether the employee attended the appointment. If you are using the ER Assistant or another drawing tool that supports data type specification, choose appropriate data types for the attributes based on your common knowledge.

22. Extend the ERD from problem 21 with the *Location* entity type and a 1-M relationship from *Location* to *Appointment*. Choose an appropriate relationship name using your common knowledge of interactions between locations and appointments. Define minimum cardinalities so that a location is optional for an appointment and an appointment is optional for a location. For the *Location* entity type, add attributes *LocNo* (primary key), *LocBuilding*, *LocRoomNo*, and *LocCapacity*. If you are using the ER Assistant or another drawing tool that supports data type specification, choose appropriate data types for the attributes based on your common knowledge.

23. Extend the ERD in problem 22 with the *Calendar* entity type and an M-N relationship from *Appointment* to *Calendar*. Choose an appropriate relationship name using your common knowledge of interactions between appointments and calendars. Define minimum cardinalities so that an appointment is optional for a calendar and a calendar is mandatory for an appointment. For the *Calendar* entity type, add attributes *CalNo* (primary key), *CalDate*, and *CalHour*. If you are using the ER Assistant or another drawing tool that supports data type specification, choose appropriate data types for the attributes based on your common knowledge.

24. Revise the ERD from problem 23 by transforming the M-N relationship between *Employee* and *Appointment* into an associative entity type along with two identifying 1-M relationships.

25. Draw an ERD containing *Student* and *Paper* entity types connected by 1-M relationships. The Student entity type should have attributes for *StdNo* (primary key), *StdFirstName*, *StdLastName*, *StdAdmitSemester*, *StdAdmitYear*, and *StdEnrollStatus* (full or part-time).

The Paper entity type should have attributes for *PaperNo* (primary key), *PaperTitle*, *PaperSubmitDate*, *PaperAccepted* (yes or no), and *PaperType* (first, second, proposal, or dissertation). Add a 1-M relationship from *Student* to *Paper*.

26. Extend the ERD with an *Evaluator* entity type and an M-N relationship between *Paper* and *Evaluator*. The Evaluator entity type should have attributes for *EvalNo* (primary key), *EvalFirstName*, *EvalLastName*, *EvalEmail*, and *EvalOffice*. The M-N relationship should have attributes for *EvalDate*, *EvalLitReview* (1 to 5 rating), *EvalProbId* (1 to 5 rating), *EvalTechWriting* (1 to 5 rating), *EvalModelDev* (1 to 5 rating), *EvalOverall* (1 to 5 rating), and *EvalComments*.

27. Transform the M-N relationship from problem 26 into an associative entity type and identifying relationships.

28. Transform the M-N relationship from problem 26 into three 1-M relationships from Evaluator to Paper. Each paper can have up to three evaluations. Each relationship should be optional to both evaluators and papers. The five evaluation attributes should be associated with each 1-M relationship.

References for Further Study

Four specialized books on database design are Batini, Ceri, and Navathe (1992); Nijssen and Halpin (1989); Teorey (1999); and Carlis and Maguire (2001). The DBAZine site (www.dbazine.com) and the DevX Database Zone (www.devx.com) have plenty of practical advice about database development and data modeling. If you would like more details about the UML, consult the UML Resources Center (umlcenter.visual-paradigm.com/index.html) for tutorials and other resources.

Developing Data Models for Business Databases

Learning Objectives

This chapter extends your knowledge of data modeling from the notation of entity relationship diagrams (ERDs) to the development of data models for business databases along with rules to convert entity relationship diagrams to relational tables. After this chapter, the student should have acquired the following knowledge and skills:

- Develop ERDs that are consistent with narrative problems
- Use transformations to generate alternative ERDs
- Document design decisions implicit in an ERD
- Analyze an ERD for common design errors
- Convert an ERD to a table design using conversion rules

Overview

Chapter 5 explained the Crow's Foot notation for entity relationship diagrams. You learned about diagram symbols, relationship patterns, generalization hierarchies, and rules for consistency and completeness. Understanding the notation is a prerequisite for applying it to represent business databases. This chapter explains the development of data models for business databases using the Crow's Foot notation and rules to convert ERDs to table designs.

To become a good data modeler, you need to understand the notation in entity relationship diagrams and get plenty of practice building diagrams. This chapter provides practice with applying the notation. You will learn to analyze a narrative problem, refine a design through transformations, document important design decisions, and analyze a data model for common design errors. After finalizing an ERD, the diagram should be converted to relational tables so that it can be implemented with a commercial DBMS. This chapter presents rules to convert an entity relationship diagram to a table design. You will learn about the basic rules to convert common parts of a diagram along with specialized rules for less common parts of a diagram.

With this background, you are ready to build ERDs for moderate-size business situations. You should have confidence in your knowledge of the Crow's Foot notation, applying the notation to narrative problems, and converting diagrams to table designs.

6.1 Analyzing Business Data Modeling Problems

After studying the Crow's Foot notation, you are now ready to apply your knowledge. This section presents guidelines to analyze information needs of business environments. The guidelines involve analysis of narrative problem descriptions as well as the challenges of determining information requirements in unstructured business situations. After presenting the guidelines, they are applied to develop an ERD for an example business data modeling problem.

6.1.1 Guidelines for Analyzing Business Information Needs

Data modeling involves the collection and analysis of business requirements resulting in an ERD to represent the requirements. Business requirements are rarely well structured. Rather, as an analyst you will often face an ill-defined business situation in which you need to add structure. You will need to interact with a variety of stakeholders who sometimes provide competing statements about the database requirements. In collecting the requirements, you will conduct interviews, review documents and system documentation, and examine existing data. To determine the scope of the database, you will need to eliminate irrelevant details and add missing details. On large projects, you may to work on a subset of the requirements and then collaborate with a team of designers to determine the complete data model.

These challenges make data modeling a stimulating and rewarding intellectual activity. A data model provides an essential element to standardize organizational vocabulary, enforce business rules, and ensure adequate data quality. Many users will experience the results of your efforts as they use a database on a daily basis. Because electronic data has become a vital corporate resource, your data modeling efforts can make a significant contribution to an organization's future success.

A textbook cannot provide the experience of designing real databases. The more difficult chapter problems and associated case studies on the course website can provide insights into the difficulties of designing real databases but will not provide you with practice with the actual experience. To acquire this experience, you must interact with organizations through class projects, internships, and job experience. Thus, this chapter emphasizes the more limited goal of analyzing narrative problems as a step to developing data modeling skills for real business situations. Analyzing narrative problems will help you gain confidence in translating a problem statement into an ERD and identifying ambiguous and incomplete parts of problem statements.

The main goal when analyzing narrative problem statements is to create an ERD that is consistent with the narrative. The ERD should not contradict the implied ERD elements in the problem narrative. For example, if the problem statement indicates that concepts are related by words indicating more than one, the ERD should have a cardinality of many to match that part of the problem statement. The remainder of this section and Section 6.3.2 provide more details about achieving a consistent ERD.

In addition to the goal of consistency, you should have a bias toward simpler rather than more complex designs. For example, an ERD with one entity type is less complex than an entity type with two entity types and a relationship. In general, when a choice exists between two ERDs, you should choose the simpler design especially in the initial stages of the design process. As the design process progresses, you can add details and refinements to the original design. Section 6.2 provides a list of transformations that can help you to consider alternative designs.

> **Goals of Narrative Problem Analysis**: strive for a simple design that is consistent with the narrative. Be prepared to follow up with additional requirements collection and consideration of alternative designs.

Identifying Entity Types

In a narrative, you should look for nouns involving people, things, places, and events as potential entity types. The nouns may appear as subjects or objects in sentences. For example, the sentence "Students take courses at the university," indicates that student and course may be entity types. You also should look for nouns that have additional sentences describing their properties. The properties often indicate attributes of entity types. For example, the sentence "Students choose their major and minor in their first year," indicates that major and minor may be attributes of student. The sentence "Courses have a course number, semester, year, and room listed in the catalog," indicates that course number, semester, year, and room are attributes of the course entity type.

The simplicity principle should be applied during the search for entity types in the initial ERD, especially involving choices between attributes and entity types. Unless the problem description contains additional sentences or details about a noun, you should consider it initially as an attribute. For example, if courses have an instructor name listed in the catalog, you should consider instructor name as an attribute of the course entity type rather than as an entity type unless additional details are provided about instructors in the problem statement. If there is confusion between considering a concept as an attribute or entity type, you should follow-up with more requirements collection later.

Determining Primary Keys

Identification of primary keys is an important part of entity type identification. Ideally, primary keys should be stable and single purpose. *Stable* means that a primary key should never change after it has been assigned to an entity. For example, phone numbers, email addresses, and names are not good choices for primary keys because they are not stable. *Single purpose* means that a primary key should have no purpose other than entity identification. For example, phone numbers and bank routing numbers are not good choices because they contain location information. Typically, good choices for primary keys are integer values automatically generated by a DBMS. For example, Access has the AutoNumber data type for primary keys and Oracle has the Sequence object for primary keys.

If the requirements indicate the primary key for an entity type, you should ensure that the proposed primary key is stable and single purpose. If the proposed primary key does not meet either criterion, you should probably reject it as a primary key. If the proposed primary key only meets one criterion, you should explore other attributes for the primary key. Sometimes, industry or organizational practices dictate the choice of a primary key even if the choice is not ideal. For example, email addresses and phone numbers, although not ideal, are sometimes used as primary keys because customers can provide them.

Besides primary keys, you should also identify other unique attributes (candidate keys). For example, an employee's email address is often unique. The integrity of candidate keys may be important for searching and integration with external databases. Depending on the features of the ERD drawing tool that you are using, you should note that an attribute is unique either in the attribute specification or in free-format documentation. Uniqueness constraints can be enforced after an ERD is converted to a table design.

Adding Relationships

Relationships often appear as verbs connecting nouns previously identified as entity types. For example, the sentence, "Students enroll in courses each semester," indicates a relationship between students and courses. For relationship cardinality, you should look at the number (singular or plural) of nouns along with other words that indicate cardinality. For example, the sentence, "A course offering is taught by an instructor," indicates that there is one instructor per course offering. You should also look for words such as "collection" and "set" that indicate a maximum cardinality of more than one. For example, the sentence, "An order contains a collection of items," indicates that an order is related to multiple items. Minimum cardinality can be indicated by words such as "optional" and "required." In the absence of indication of minimum cardinality, the default should be mandatory. Additional requirements collection should be conducted to confirm default choices.

You should be aware that indications of relationships in problem statements may lead to direct or indirect connections in an ERD. A direct connection involves a relationship between the entity types. An indirect connection involves a connection through other entity types and relationships. For example, the sentence, "An advisor counsels students about the choice of a major," may indicate direct or indirect relationships between advisor, student, and major.

To help with difficult choices between direct and indirect connections, you should look for entity types that are involved in multiple relationships. These entity types can reduce the number of relationships in an ERD by being placed in the center as a hub connected directly to other entity types as spokes of a wheel. Entity types derived from important documents (orders, registrations, purchase orders, etc.) are often hubs in an ERD. For example, an order entity type can be directly related to customer, employee, and product removing the need for direct connections among all entity types. These choices will be highlighted in the analysis of the water utility information requirements in the following section.

Summary of Analysis Guidelines

When analyzing a narrative problem statement, you should develop an ERD that consistently represents the complete narrative. Given a choice among consistent ERDs, you should favor simpler rather than more complex designs. You also should note the ambiguities and incompleteness in the problem statement. The guidelines discussed in this section can help in your initial analysis of data modeling problems. Sections 6.2 and 6.3 present additional analysis methods to revise and finalize ERDs. To help you recall the guidelines discussed in this section, Table 6-1 presents a summary.

Table 6-1: Summary of Analysis Guidelines for Narrative Problems

Diagram Element	Analysis Guidelines	ERD Effect
Entity type identification	Look for nouns used as subjects or objects along with additional details in other sentences.	Add entity types to ERD. If noun does not have supporting details, consider it as an attribute.
Primary key determination	Strive for stable and single-purpose attributes for primary keys. Narrative should indicate uniqueness.	Specify primary and candidate keys.
Relationship (direct or indirect) detection	Look for verbs that connect nouns identified as entity types.	Add a direct relationship between entity types or note that an indirect connection must exist between entity types.
Cardinality determination (maximum)	Look for singular or plural designation of nouns in sentences indicating relationships.	Specify cardinalities of 1 and M (many).
Cardinality determination (minimum)	Look for optional or required language in sentences. Set required as the default if problem statement does not indicate minimum cardinality.	Specify cardinalities of 0 (optional) and 1 (mandatory).
Relationship simplification	Look for hub entity types as nouns used in multiple sentences linked to other nouns identified as entity types.	Entity type hub has direct relationships with other entity types. Eliminate other relationships if a direct connection exists through a hub entity type.

6.1.2 Information Requirements for the Water Utility Database

This section presents requirements for a customer database for a municipal water utility. You can assume that this description is the result of an initial investigation with appropriate personnel at the water utility. After the description, the guidelines presented in Section 6.1.1 are used to analyze the narrative description and develop an ERD.

Information Requirements

The water utility database should support the recording of water usage and billing for water usage. To support these functions, the database should contain data about customers, rates, water usage, and bills. Other functions such as payment processing and customer service are omitted from this description for brevity. The following list describes the data requirements in more detail.

- Customer data include a unique customer number, a name, a billing address, a type (commercial or residential), an applicable rate, and a collection (one or more) of meters.
- Meter data include a unique meter number, an address, a size, and a model. The meter number is engraved on the meter before it is placed in service. A meter is associated with one customer at a time.
- An employee periodically reads each meter on a scheduled date. When a meter is read, a meter-reading document is created containing a unique meter reading number, an employee number, a meter number, a timestamp (includes date and time), and a consumption level. When a meter is first placed in service, there are no associated readings for it.
- A rate includes a unique rate number, a description, a fixed dollar amount, a consumption threshold, and a variable amount (dollars per cubic foot). Consumption up to the threshold is billed at the fixed amount. Consumption greater than the threshold is billed at the variable amount.

- Customers are assigned rates using a number of factors such as customer type, address, and adjustment factors. Many customers can be assigned the same rate. Rates are typically proposed months before approved and associated with customers.
- Water utility bills are based on customers' most recent meter readings and applicable rates. A bill consists of a heading part and a list of detail lines. The heading part contains a unique bill number, a customer number, a preparation date, a payment due date, and a date range for the consumption period. Each detail line contains a meter number, a water consumption level, and an amount. The water consumption level is computed by subtracting the consumption levels in the two most recent meter readings. The amount is computed by multiplying the consumption level by the customer's rate.

Identifying Entity Types and Primary Keys

Prominent nouns in the narrative are customer, meter, bill, reading (for meter reading), and rate. For each of these nouns, the narrative describes associated attributes. Figure 6.1 shows a preliminary ERD with entity types for nouns and associated attributes. Note that collections of things are not attributes. For example, the fact that a customer has a collection of meters will be shown as a relationship, rather than as an attribute of the *Customer* entity type. In addition, references between these entity types will be shown as relationships rather than as attributes. For example, the fact that a reading contains a meter number will be recorded as a relationship.

The narrative specifically mentions uniqueness of customer number, meter number, reading number, bill number, and rate number. The bill number, reading number, and meter number seem to be stable and single purpose as they are imprinted on physical objects. Additional investigation should be conducted to determine if customer number and rate number are stable and single purpose. Since the narrative does not describe additional uses of these attributes, the initial assumption in the ERD is that these attributes are suitable as primary keys.

Customer	Meter	Reading
CustNo	MeterNo	ReadNo
CustName	MtrAddr	ReadTime
CustAddr	MtrSize	ReadLevel
CustType	MtrModel	EmpNo

Bill	Rate
BillNo	RateNo
BillDate	RateDesc
BillStartDate	RateFixedAmt
BillEndDate	RateThresh
BillDueDate	RateVarAmt

Figure 6.1: Preliminary Entity Types and Attributes in the Water Utility Database

Adding Relationships

After identifying entity types and attributes, let us continue by connecting entity types with relationships as shown in Figure 6.2. To reduce the size of the ERD, only the primary keys are shown in Figure 6.2. The following list explains the derivation of relationships with a focus on parts of the narrative that indicate relationships among entity types.

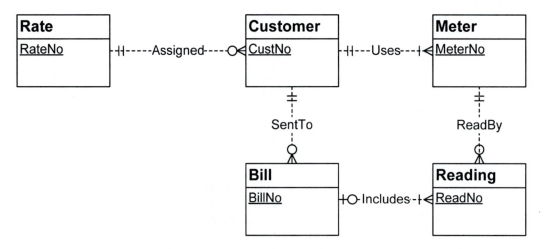

Figure 6.2: Entity Types Connected by Relationships

- For the *Assigned* relationship, the narrative states that a customer has a rate, and many customers can be assigned the same rate. These two statements indicate a 1-M relationship from *Rate* to *Customer*. For the minimum cardinalities, the narrative indicates that a rate is required for a customer, and that rates are proposed before being associated with customers.
- For the *Uses* relationship, the narrative states that a customer includes a collection of meters and a meter is associated with one customer at a time. These two statements indicate a 1-M relationship from *Customer* to *Meter*. For the minimum cardinalities, the narrative indicates that a customer must have at least one meter. The narrative does not indicate the minimum cardinality for a meter so either 0 or 1 can be chosen. The documentation should note this incompleteness in the specifications.
- For the *ReadBy* relationship, the narrative states that a meter reading contains a meter number, and meters are periodically read. These two statements indicate a 1-M relationship from *Meter* to *Reading*. For the minimum cardinalities, the narrative indicates that a meter is required for a reading, and a new meter does not have any associated readings.
- For the *SentTo* relationship, the narrative indicates that the heading part of a bill contains a customer number and bills are periodically sent to customers. These two statements indicate a 1-M relationship from *Customer* to *Bill*. For the minimum cardinalities, the narrative indicates that a customer is required for a bill, and a customer does not have an associated bill until the customer's meters are read.

The *Includes* relationship between the *Bill* and the *Reading* entity types is subtle. The *Includes* relationship is 1-M because a bill may involve a collection of readings (one on each detail line), and a reading relates to one bill. The consumption level and the amount on a detail line are calculated values. The *Includes* relationship connects a bill to its most recent meter readings, thus supporting the consumption and the amount calculations. These values can be stored if it is more efficient to store them rather than compute them when needed. If the values are stored, attributes can be added to the *Includes* relationship or the *Reading* entity type.

6.2 Refinements to an ERD

Data modeling is usually an iterative or repetitive process. You construct a preliminary data model and then refine it many times. In refining a data model, you should generate feasible alternatives and evaluate them according to user requirements. You typically need to gather additional information from users to evaluate alternatives. This process of refinement and evaluation may continue many times for large databases. To depict the iterative nature of data modeling, this section describes some refinements to the initial ERD design of Figure 6.2.

6.2.1 Transforming Attributes into Entity Types

A common refinement is to transform an <u>attribute into an entity type</u>. When the database should contain more than just the identifier of an entity, this transformation is useful. This transformation involves the addition of an entity type and a 1-M relationship. In the water utility ERD, the *Reading* entity type contains the *EmpNo* attribute. If other data about an employee are needed, *EmpNo* can be expanded into an entity type and 1-M relationship as shown in Figure 6.3.

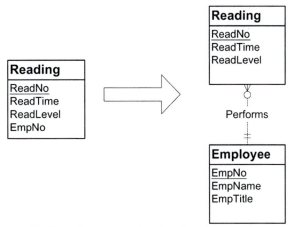

Figure 6.3: Transformation of an Attribute into an Entity Type

6.2.2 Splitting Compound Attributes

Another common refinement is to split <u>compound attributes into smaller attributes</u>. A compound attribute contains multiple kinds of data. For example, the *Customer* entity type has an address attribute containing data about a customer's street, city, state, and postal code. Splitting compound attributes can facilitate search of the embedded data. Splitting the address attribute as shown in Figure 6.4 supports searches by street, city, state, and postal code.

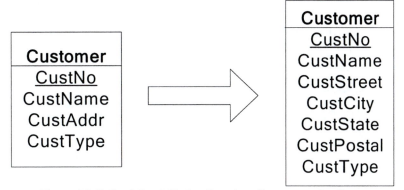

Figure 6.4: Split of *CustAddr* Attribute into Component Attributes

6.2.3 Expanding Entity Types

A third transformation is to make an <u>entity type into two entity types and a relationship</u>. This transformation can be useful to record a finer level of detail about an entity. For example, rates in the water utility database apply to all levels of consumption beyond a fixed level. It can be useful to have a more complex rate structure in which the variable amount depends on the consumption level. Figure 6.5 shows a transformation to the *Rate* entity type to support a more complex rate structure. The *RateSet* entity type represents a set of rates approved by the utility's governing commission. The primary key of the *Rate* entity type borrows from the *RateSet* entity type.

Identification dependency is not required when transforming an entity type into two entity types and a relationship. In this situation, identification dependency is useful, but in other situations, it may not be appropriate.

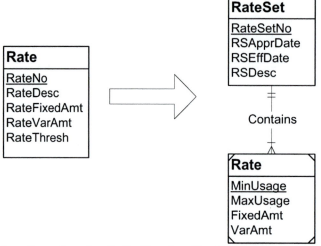

Figure 6.5: Transformation of an Entity Type into Two Entity Types and a Relationship

6.2.4 Transforming a Weak Entity into a Strong Entity

A fourth transformation is to make a <u>weak entity into a strong entity and change the associated identifying relationships into nonidentifying relationships</u>. This transformation can make it easier to reference an entity type after conversion to a table design. After conversion, a reference to a weak entity will involve a combined foreign key with more than one column. This transformation is most useful for associative entity types, especially associative entity types representing M-way relationships.

Figure 6.6 depicts the transformation of the weak entity *Rate* to a strong entity. The transformation involves changing the weak entity to a strong entity and changing each identifying relationship to a nonidentifying relationship. In addition, it may be necessary to add a new attribute to serve as the primary key. In Figure 6.6, the new attribute *RateNo* is the primary key as *MinUsage* does not uniquely identify rates. The designer should note that the combination of *RateSetNo* and *MinUsage* is unique in design documentation so that a candidate key constraint can be specified after conversion to a table design.

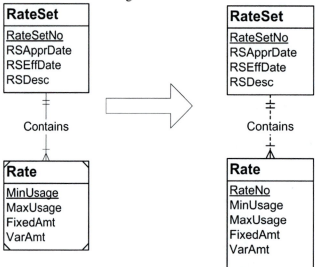

Figure 6.6: Transformation of a Weak Entity into a Strong Entity

6.2.5 Adding History

A fifth transformation is to add historical details to a data model. Historical details may be necessary for legal requirements as well as strategic reporting requirements. This transformation can be applied to attributes and relationships. When applied to attributes, the transformation is similar to the attribute to entity type transformation. For example, to maintain a history of employee titles, the *EmpTitle* attribute is replaced with an entity type and a 1-M relationship. The new entity type typically contains a version number as part of its primary key and borrows from the original entity type for the remaining part of its primary key, as shown in Figure 6.7. The beginning and ending dates indicate the effective dates for the change.

When applied to a relationship, this transformation typically involves changing a 1-M relationship into an associative entity type and a pair of identifying 1-M relationships. Figure 6.8 depicts the transformation of the 1-M *Uses* relationship into an associative entity type with attributes for the version number and effective dates. The associative entity type is necessary because the combination of customer and meter may not be unique without a version number.

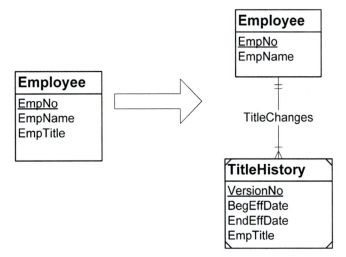

Figure 6.7: Adding History to the *EmpTitle* Attribute

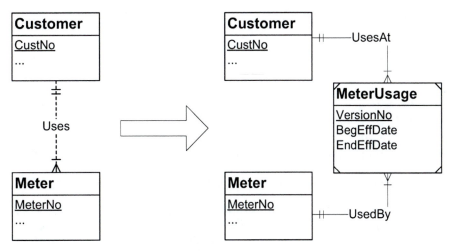

Figure 6.8: Adding History to a 1-M Relationship

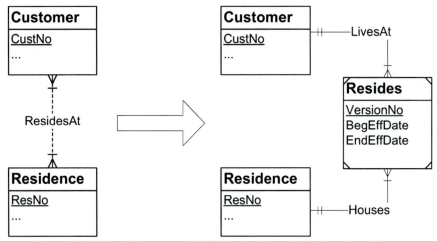

Figure 6.9: Adding History to a M-N Relationship with Independent Change

When applied to an M-N relationship, this transformation can be more complex. The appropriate transformation depends on the ability of the associated entities to change independently. In Figure 6.9, the transformation allows the entities to change independently connected by the effective date attributes. For example, if customer C1 resides at residence R1 from 2007 to 2008 and C2 resides at R1 from 2008 to 2009, there will be two *MeterUsage* entities with different version numbers but overlap among the effective date attributes for the two entities. In Figure 6.10, the transformation does not allow the entities to change independently. The *ResidesPeriod* entity type connects all customers that share a residence during the same time period using the *LivesAt* M-N relationship. The transformation in Figure 6.9 is appropriate for roommates in which roommates can change independently. The transformation in Figure 6.10 is appropriate for home ownership in which home owners change as a unit.

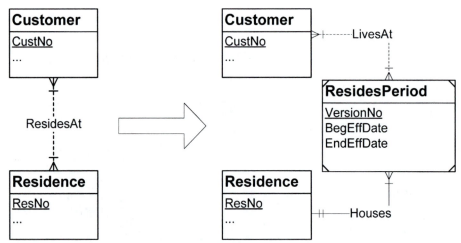

Figure 6.10: Adding History to a M-N Relationship with Connections among Associated Entities

The transformations in Figures 6.7 to 6.10 support an unlimited history. For a limited history, a fixed number of attributes can be added to the same entity type. For example, to maintain a history of the current and the last employee titles, two attributes (*EmpCurrTitle* and *EmpPrevTitle*) can be used as depicted in Figure 6.11. To record the change dates for employee titles, two effective date attributes per title attribute can be added.

Employee

EmpNo
EmpName
EmpCurrTitle
EmpCurrTitleBegEffDate
EmpCurrTitleEndEffDate
EmpPrevTitle
EmpPrevTitleBegEffDate
EmpPrevTitleEndEffDate

Figure 6.11: Adding Limited History to the *Employee* Entity Type

6.2.6 Adding Generalization Hierarchies

A sixth transformation is to make an <u>entity type into a generalization hierarchy</u>. This transformation should be used sparingly because the generalization hierarchy is a specialized modeling tool. If there are multiple attributes that do not apply to all entities and there is an accepted classification of entities, a generalization hierarchy may be useful. For example, water utility customers can be classified as commercial or residential. The attributes specific to commercial customers (*TaxPayerID* and *EnterpriseZone*) do not apply to residential customers and vice-versa. In Figure 6.12, the attributes specific to commercial and residential customers have been moved to the subtypes. An additional benefit of this transformation is the avoidance of null values. For example, entities in the *Commercial* and the *Residential* entity types will not have null values. In the original *Customer* entity type, residential customers would have had null values for *TaxPayerID* and *EnterpriseZone*, while commercial customers would have had null values for *Subsidized* and *DwellingType*.

This transformation also can be applied to a collection of entity types. In this situation, the transformation involves the addition of a supertype and a generalization hierarchy. In addition, the common attributes in the collection of entity types are moved to the supertype.

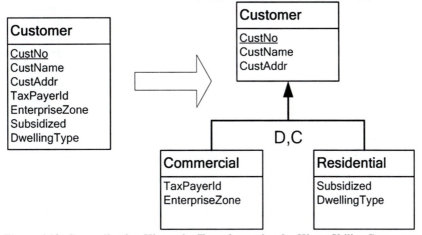

Figure 6.12: Generalization Hierarchy Transformation for Water Utility Customers

6.2.7 Summary of Transformations

When designing a database, you should carefully explore alternative designs. The transformations discussed in this section can help you consider alternative designs. The possible transformations are not limited to those discussed in this section. You can reverse most of these transformations. For example, you can eliminate a generalization hierarchy if the subtypes do not have unique attributes. For additional transformations, you should check the references at the end of this chapter for specialized books on database design. To help you recall the transformations shown in this section, Table 6-2 presents a summary.

Table 6-2: Summary of Transformations

Transformation	Details	When to Use
Attribute to entity type	Replace an attribute with an entity type and a 1-M relationship.	Additional details about an attribute are needed.
Split a compound attribute	Replace an attribute with a collection of attributes.	Standardize the data in an attribute.
Expand entity type	Add a new entity type and a 1-M relationship.	Add a finer level of detail about an entity.
Weak entity to strong entity	Remove identification dependency symbols and possibly add a primary key.	Remove combined foreign keys after conversion to tables.
Add history	For attribute history, replace an attribute with a weak entity type and an identifying 1-M relationship. For relationship history, change the relationship into an associative entity type. For a limited history, you should add attributes to the entity type.	Add detail for legal requirements or strategic reporting.
Add generalization hierarchy	Starting from a supertype: add subtypes, a generalization hierarchy, and redistribute attributes to subtypes. Starting from subtypes: add a supertype, a generalization hierarchy, and redistribute common attributes and relationships to the supertype.	Accepted classification of entities; specialized attributes and relationships for the subtypes.

6.3 Finalizing an ERD

After iteratively evaluating alternative ERDs using the transformations presented in Section 6.2, you are ready to finalize your data model. Your data model is not complete without adequate design documentation and careful consideration of design errors. You should strive to write documentation and perform design error checking throughout the design process. Even with due diligence during the design process, you will still need to conduct final reviews to ensure adequate design documentation and lack of design errors. Often these reviews are conducted with a team of designers to ensure completeness. This section presents guidelines to aid you when writing design documentation and checking design errors.

6.3.1 Documenting an ERD

Chapter 5 (Section 5.4.1) prescribed informal documentation for business rules involving uniqueness of attributes, attribute value restrictions, null values, and default values. It is important to document these kinds of business rules because they can be converted to a formal specification in SQL as described in Chapters 11 and 14. You should use informal documentation associated with entity types, attributes, and relationships to record these kinds of business rules.

Resolving Specification Problems

Beyond informal representation of business rules, documentation plays an important role in resolving questions about a specification and in communicating the design to others. In the process of revising an ERD, you should carefully document inconsistency and incompleteness in a specification. A large specification typically contains many points of inconsistency and incompleteness. Recording each point allows systematic resolution through additional requirements-gathering activities.

As an example of inconsistency, the water utility requirements would be inconsistent if one part indicated that a meter is associated with one customer, but another part stated that a meter can be associated with multiple customers. In resolving an inconsistency, a user can indicate that the inconsistency is an exception. In this example, a user may indicate the circumstances in which a meter can be associated with multiple customers. The designer must decide on the resolution in the ERD such as permitting multiple customers for a meter, allowing a second responsible customer, or prohibiting more than one customer. The designer should carefully document the resolution of each inconsistency, including a justification for the chosen solution.

As an incompleteness example, the narrative does not specify the minimum cardinality for a meter in the *Uses* relationship of Figure 6.2. The designer should gather additional requirements to resolve the incomplete specification. Incomplete parts of a specification are common for relationships as complete specification involves two sets of cardinalities. It is easy to omit a relationship cardinality in an initial specification.

Improving Communication

Besides identifying problems in a specification, documentation should be used to communicate a design to others. Databases can have a long lifetime owing to the economics of information systems. An information system can undergo a long cycle of repair and enhancement before there is sufficient justification to redesign the system. Good documentation enhances an ERD by communicating the justification for important design decisions. Your documentation should not repeat the constraints in an ERD. For example, you do not need to document that a customer can use many meters as the ERD contains this information.

You should document decisions in which there is more than one feasible choice. For example, you should carefully document alternative designs for rates (a single consumption level versus multiple consumption levels) as depicted in Figure 6.5. You should document your decision by recording the recommender and justification for the alternative. Although all transformations presented in the previous section can lead to feasible choices, you should focus on the transformations most relevant to the specification.

You also should document decisions that might be unclear to others even if there are no feasible alternatives. For example, the minimum cardinality of 0 from the *Reading* entity type to the *Bill* entity type might be unclear. You should document the need for this cardinality because of the time difference between the creation of a bill and its associated readings. A meter may be read days before an associated bill is created.

> **Design Documentation**: include justification for design decisions involving multiple feasible choices and explanations of subtle design choices. Do not use documentation just to repeat the information already contained in an ERD. You also should provide a description for each attribute especially where an attribute's name does not indicate its purpose. As an ERD is developed, you should document incompleteness and inconsistency in the requirements.

Example Design Documentation

Design documentation should be incorporated into your ERD. If you are using a drawing tool that has a data dictionary, you should include design justifications in the data dictionary. For example, the ER Assistant supports design justifications as well as comments associated with each item on a diagram. You can use the comments to describe the meaning of attributes. If you are not using a tool that supports documentation, you can list the justifications on a separate page and annotate your ERD as shown in Figure 6.13. The circled numbers in Figure 6.13 refer to explanations in Table 6-3. Note that some of the refinements shown previously were not used in the revised ERD.

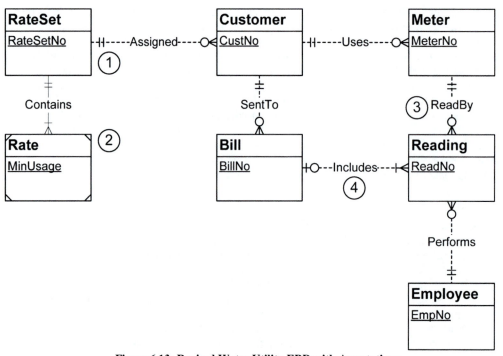

Figure 6.13: Revised Water Utility ERD with Annotations

Table 6-3: List of Design Justifications for the Revised ERD

1. A rate set is a collection of rates approved by the governing commission of the utility.

2. Rates are similar to lines on a tax table. An individual rate is identified by the rate set identifier along with the minimum consumption level of the rate.

3. The minimum cardinality indicates that a meter must always be associated with a customer. For new property, the developer is initially responsible for the meter. If a customer forecloses on a property, the financial institution holding the deed will be responsible.

4. A reading is not associated with a bill until the bill is prepared. A reading may be created several days before the associated bill.

6.3.2 Detecting Common Design Errors

As indicated in Chapter 5, you should use the diagram rules to ensure that there are no obvious errors in your ERD. You also should use the guidelines in this section to check for design errors. Design errors are more difficult to detect and resolve than diagram errors because design errors involve the meaning of elements on a diagram, not just a diagram's structure. The following subsections explain common design problems, while Table 6-4 summarizes them.

Misplaced and Missing Relationships

In a large ERD, it is easy to connect the wrong entity types or omit a necessary relationship. You can connect the wrong entity types if you do not consider all of the queries that a database should support. For example in Figure 6.13, if *Customer* is connected directly to *Reading* instead of being connected to *Meter*, the control of a meter cannot be established unless the meter has been read for the customer. Queries that involve meter control cannot be answered except through consideration of meter readings.

If the requirements do not directly indicate a relationship, you should consider indirect implications to detect whether a relationship is required. For example, the requirements for the water utility database do not directly indicate the need for a relationship from *Bill* to *Reading*.

However, careful consideration of the consumption calculation reveals the need for a relationship. The *Includes* relationship connects a bill to its most recent meter readings, thus supporting the consumption calculation.

Incorrect Cardinalities

The typical error involves the usage of a 1-M relationship instead of an M-N relationship. This error can be caused by an omission in the requirements. For example, if the requirements just indicate that work assignments involve a collection of employees, you should not assume that an employee can be related to just one work assignment. You should gather additional requirements to determine if an employee can be associated with multiple work assignments.

Other incorrect cardinality errors that you should consider are reversed cardinalities (1-M relationship should be in the opposite direction) and errors on a minimum cardinality. The error of reversed cardinality is typically an oversight. The incorrect cardinalities indicated in the relationship specification are not noticed after the ERD is displayed. You should carefully check all relationships after specification to ensure consistency with your intent. Errors on minimum cardinality are typically the result of overlooking key words in problem narratives such as "optional" and "required."

Overuse of Specialized Data Modeling Constructs

Generalization hierarchies and M-way associative entity types are specialized data modeling constructs. A typical novice mistake is to use them inappropriately. You should not use generalization hierarchies just because an entity can exist in multiple states. For example, the requirement that a project task can be started, in process, or complete does not indicate the need for a generalization hierarchy. If there is an established classification and specialized attributes and relationships for subtypes, a generalization hierarchy is an appropriate tool.

An M-way associative entity type (an associative entity type representing an M-way relationship) should be used when the database is to record combinations of three (or more) objects rather than just combinations of two objects. In most cases, only combinations of two objects should be recorded. For example, if a database needs to record the skills provided by an employee and the skills required by a project, binary relationships should be used. If a database needs to record the skills provided by employees for specific projects, an M-way associative entity type is needed. Note that the former situation with binary relationships is much more common than the latter situation represented by an M-way associative entity type.

Redundant Relationships

Cycles in an ERD may indicate redundant relationships. A cycle involves a collection of relationships arranged in a loop starting and ending with the same entity type. For example in Figure 6.13, there is a cycle of relationships connecting *Customer*, *Bill*, *Reading*, and *Meter*. In a cycle, a relationship is redundant if it can be derived from other relationships. For the *SentTo* relationship, the bills associated with a customer can be derived from the relationships *Uses*, *ReadBy*, and *Includes*. In the opposite direction, the customer associated with a bill can be derived from the *Includes*, *ReadBy*, and *Uses* relationships. Although a bill can be associated with a collection of readings, each associated reading must be associated with the same customer. Because the *SentTo* relationship can be derived, it is removed in the final ERD (see Figure 6.14).

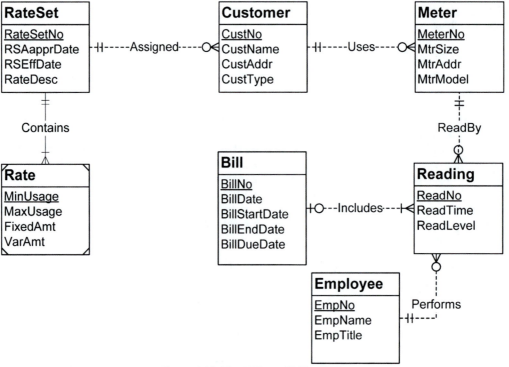

Figure 6.14: Final Water Utility ERD

Another example of a redundant relationship would be a relationship between *Meter* and *Bill*. The meters associated with a bill can be derived using the *Includes* and the *ReadBy* relationships. Note that using clusters of entity types such as *Reading* in the center connected to *Meter*, *Employee*, and *Bill* avoids redundant relationships.

You should take care when removing redundant relationships, as removing a necessary relationship is a more serious error than retaining a redundant relationship. When in doubt, you should retain the relationship.

Table 6-4: Summary of Design Errors

Design Error	Description	Resolution
Misplaced relationship	Wrong entity types connected.	Consider all queries that the database should support.
Missing relationship	Entity types should be connected directly.	Examine implications of requirements.
Incorrect cardinality	Typically using a 1-M relationship instead of an M-N relationship.	Incomplete requirements: inferences beyond the requirements.
Overuse of generalization hierarchies	Generalization hierarchies are not common. A typical novice mistake is to use them inappropriately.	Ensure that subtypes have specialized attributes and relationships.
Overuse of M-way associative entity types	M-way relationships are not common. A typical novice mistake is to use them inappropriately.	Ensure that the database records combinations of three or more entities.
Redundant relationship	Relationship derived from other relationships.	Examine each relationship cycle to see if a relationship can be derived from other relationships.

6.4 Converting an ERD to Relational Tables

Conversion from the ERD notation to relational tables is important because of industry practice. Computer-aided software engineering (CASE) tools support varying notations for ERDs. It is common practice to use a CASE tool as an aid in developing an ERD. Because most commercial DBMSs use the Relational Model, you must convert an ERD to relational tables to implement your database design.

Even if you use a CASE tool to perform conversion, you should still have a basic understanding of the conversion process. Understanding the conversion rules improves your understanding of the ER model, particularly the difference between the Entity Relationship Model and the Relational Model. Some typical errors by novice data modelers are due to confusion between the models. For example, usage of foreign keys in an ERD is due to confusion about relationship representation in the two models.

This section describes the conversion process in two parts. First, the basic rules to convert entity types, relationships, and attributes are described. Second, specialized rules to convert optional 1-M relationships, generalization hierarchies, and 1-1 relationships are shown. The CREATE TABLE statements in this section conform to the SQL:2006 syntax.

6.4.1 Basic Conversion Rules

The basic rules convert everything on an ERD except generalization hierarchies. You should apply these rules until everything in your ERD is converted except for generalization hierarchies. You should use the first two rules before the other rules. As you apply these rules, you can use a check mark to indicate the converted parts of an ERD.

1. **Entity Type Rule**: Each entity type (except a subtype) becomes a table. The primary key of the entity type (if not weak) becomes the primary key of the table. The attributes of the entity type become columns in the table. This rule should be used first before the relationship rules.
2. **1-M Relationship Rule**: Each 1-M relationship becomes a foreign key in the table corresponding to the child entity type (the entity type near the Crow's Foot symbol). If the minimum cardinality on the parent side of the relationship is one, the foreign key cannot accept null values.
3. **M-N Relationship Rule**: Each M-N relationship becomes a separate table. The primary key of the table is a combined key consisting of the primary keys of the entity types participating in the M-N relationship.
4. **Identification Dependency Rule**: Each identifying relationship (denoted by a solid relationship line) adds a component to a primary key. The primary key of the table corresponding to the weak entity consists of (i) the underlined local key (if any) in the weak entity and (ii) the primary key(s) of the entity type(s) connected by identifying relationship(s).

To understand these rules, you can apply them to some of the ERDs used in Chapter 5. Using Rules 1 and 2, you can convert Figure 6.15 into the CREATE TABLE statements shown in Figure 6.16. Rule 1 is applied to convert the *Course* and *Offering* entity types to tables. Then, Rule 2 is applied to convert the *Has* relationship to a foreign key (*Offering.CourseNo*). The *Offering* table contains the foreign key because the *Offering* entity type is the child entity type in the *Has* relationship.

Figure 6.15: ERD with 1-M Relationship

```
CREATE TABLE Course
(   CourseNo CHAR(6),
    CrsDesc  VARCHAR(30),
    CrsUnits SMALLINT,
CONSTRAINT PKCourse PRIMARY KEY (CourseNo)   )

CREATE TABLE Offering
( OfferNo                INTEGER,
  OffLocation            CHAR(20),
  CourseNo               CHAR(6)                          NOT NULL,
  OffTime                TIMESTAMP,
  ...
CONSTRAINT PKOffering PRIMARY KEY (OfferNo),
CONSTRAINT FKCourseNo FOREIGN KEY (CourseNo) REFERENCES Course   )
```

Figure 6.16: Conversion of Figure 6.15 (SQL:2006 Syntax)

Next, you can apply the M-N relationship rule (Rule 3) to convert the ERD in Figure 6.17. Following this rule leads to the *Enrolls_In* table in Figure 6.18. The primary key of *Enrolls_In* is a combination of the primary keys of the *Student* and *Offering* entity types.

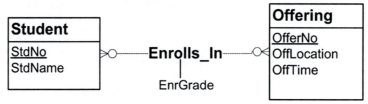

Figure 6.17: M-N Relationship with an Attribute

```
CREATE TABLE Student
(       StdNo               CHAR(11),
        StdName             VARCHAR(30),
    ...
CONSTRAINT PKStudent PRIMARY KEY (StdNo)                 )

CREATE TABLE Offering
(       OfferNo             INTEGER,
        OffLocation         VARCHAR(30),
        OffTime             TIMESTAMP,
    ...
CONSTRAINT PKOffering PRIMARY KEY (OfferNo) )

CREATE TABLE Enrolls_In
(       OfferNo             INTEGER,
        StdNo               CHAR(11),
        EnrGrade            DECIMAL(2,1),
CONSTRAINT PKEnrolls_In PRIMARY KEY (OfferNo, StdNo),
CONSTRAINT FKOfferNo FOREIGN KEY (OfferNo) REFERENCES Offering,
CONSTRAINT FKStdNo FOREIGN KEY (StdNo) REFERENCES Student )
```

Figure 6.18: Conversion of Figure 6.17 (SQL:2006 Syntax)

To gain practice with the identification dependency rule (Rule 4), you can use it to convert the ERD in Figure 6.19. The result of converting Figure 6.19 is identical to Figure 6.18 except that the *Enrolls_In* table is renamed *Enrollment*. The ERD in Figure 6.19 requires two applications of the identification dependency rule. Each application of the identification dependency rule adds a component to the primary key of the *Enrollment* table.

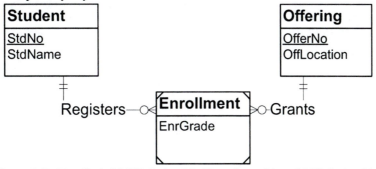

Figure 6.19: *Enrolls_in* **M-N Relationship Transformed into 1-M Relationships**

You can also apply the rules to convert self-referencing relationships. For example, you can apply the 1-M and M-N relationship rules to convert the self-referencing relationships in Figure 6.20. Using the 1-M relationship rule, the *Supervises* relationship converts to a foreign key in the *Faculty* table, as shown in Figure 6.21. Using the M-N relationship rule, the *Prereq_To* relationship converts to the *Prereq_To* table with a combined primary key of the course number of the prerequisite course and the course number of the dependent course.

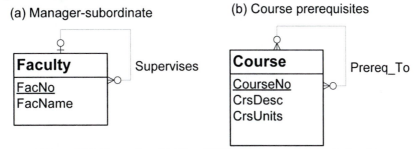

Figure 6.20: Examples of 1-M and M-N Self-Referencing Relationships

```
CREATE TABLE Faculty
(     FacNo            CHAR(11),
      FacName          VARCHAR(30),
      FacSupervisor    CHAR(11),
      ...
CONSTRAINT PKFaculty PRIMARY KEY (FacNo),
CONSTRAINT FKSupervisor FOREIGN KEY (FacSupervisor)
   REFERENCES Faculty  )

CREATE TABLE Course
(     Courseno         CHAR(6),
      CrsDesc          VARCHAR(30),
      CrsUnits         SMALLINT,
CONSTRAINT PKCourse PRIMARY KEY (CourseNo) )

CREATE TABLE Prereq_To
(     PrereqCNo        CHAR(6),
      DependCNo        CHAR(6),
CONSTRAINT PKPrereq_To PRIMARY KEY (PrereqCNo, DependCNo),
CONSTRAINT FKPrereqCNo FOREIGN KEY (PrereqCNo) REFERENCES Course,
CONSTRAINT FKDependCNo FOREIGN KEY (DependCNo) REFERENCES Course
)
```

Figure 6.21: Conversion of Figure 6.20 (SQL:2006 Syntax)

You also can apply conversion rules to more complex identification dependencies as depicted in Figure 6.22. The first part of the conversion is identical to the conversion of Figure 6.19. Application of the 1-M rule makes the combination of *StdNo* and *OfferNo* foreign keys in the *Attendance* table (Figure 6.23). Note that the foreign keys in *Attendance* refer to *Enrollment*, not to *Student* and *Offering*. Finally, one application of the identification dependency rule makes the combination of *StdNo*, *OfferNo*, and *AttDate* the primary key of the *Attendance* table.

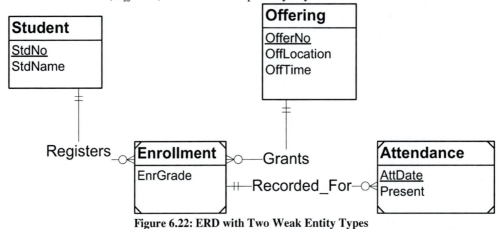

Figure 6.22: ERD with Two Weak Entity Types

```
CREATE TABLE Attendance
(     OfferNo         INTEGER,
      StdNo           CHAR(11),
      AttDate         DATE,
      Present         BOOLEAN,
CONSTRAINT PKAttendance PRIMARY KEY (OfferNo, StdNo, AttDate),
CONSTRAINT FKOfferNoStdNo FOREIGN KEY (OfferNo, StdNo)
  REFERENCES Enrollment   )
```

Figure 6.23: Conversion of the Attendance Entity Type in Figure 6.22 (SQL:2006 Syntax)

The conversion in Figure 6.23 depicts a situation in which the transformation of a weak to a strong entity may apply (Section 6.2.3). In the conversion, the *Attendance* table contains a combined foreign key (*OfferNo*, *StdSSN*). Changing *Enrollment* into a strong entity will eliminate the combined foreign key in the *Attendance* table.

6.4.2 Converting Optional 1-M Relationships

When you use the 1-M relationship rule for optional relationships, the resulting foreign key contains null values. Recall that a relationship with a minimum cardinality of 0 is optional. For example, the *Teaches* relationship (Figure 6.24) is optional to *Offering* because an *Offering* entity can be stored without being related to a *Faculty* entity. Converting Figure 6.24 results in two tables (*Faculty* and *Offering*) as well as a foreign key (*FacNo*) in the *Offering* table. The foreign key should allow null values because the minimum cardinality of the *Offering* entity type in the relationship is optional (0). However, null values can lead to complications in evaluating the query results.

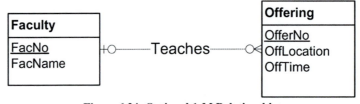

Figure 6.24: Optional 1-M Relationship

To avoid null values when converting an optional 1-M relationship, you can apply Rule 5 to convert an optional 1-M relationship into a table instead of a foreign key. Figure 6.25 shows an application of Rule 5 to the ERD in Figure 6.24. The *Teaches* table contains the foreign keys *OfferNo* and *FacNo* with null values not allowed for both columns. In addition, the *Offering* table no longer has a foreign key referring to the *Faculty* table. Figures 6.26 and 6.27 depict an example of converting an optional 1-M relationship with an attribute. Note that the *Lists* table contains the *Commission* column.

Optional 1-M Relationship Rule: Each 1-M relationship with 0 for the minimum cardinality on the parent side becomes a new table. The primary key of the new table is the primary key of the entity type on the child (many) side of the relationship. The new table contains foreign keys for the primary keys of both entity types participating in the relationship. Both foreign keys in the new table do not permit null values. The new table also contains the attributes of the optional 1-M relationship.

```
CREATE TABLE Faculty
(     FacNo             CHAR(11),
      FacName           VARCHAR(30),

      ...
CONSTRAINT PKFaculty PRIMARY KEY (FacSSN)                    )

CREATE TABLE Offering
(     OfferNo           INTEGER,
      OffLocation       VARCHAR(30),
      OffTime           TIMESTAMP,

      ...
CONSTRAINT PKOffering PRIMARY KEY (OfferNo)   )

CREATE TABLE Teaches
(     OfferNo           INTEGER,
      FacNo             CHAR(11)    NOT NULL,
CONSTRAINT PKTeaches PRIMARY KEY (OfferNo),
CONSTRAINT FKFacNo FOREIGN KEY (FacNo) REFERENCES Faculty,
CONSTRAINT FKOfferNo FOREIGN KEY (OfferNo) REFERENCES Offer )
```

Figure 6.25: Conversion of Figure 6.24 (SQL:2006 Syntax)

Figure 6.26: Optional 1-M Relationship with an Attribute

```
CREATE TABLE Agent
(       AgentId              CHAR(10),
        AgentName            VARCHAR(30),
        ...
CONSTRAINT PKAgent PRIMARY KEY (AgentId)                          )

CREATE TABLE Home
(       HomeNo               INTEGER,
        HomeAddress          VARCHAR(50),
        ...
CONSTRAINT PKHome PRIMARY KEY (HomeNo)   )

CREATE TABLE Lists
(       HomeNo               INTEGER,
        AgentId              CHAR(10)      NOT NULL,
        Commission           DECIMAL(10,2),
CONSTRAINT PKLists PRIMARY KEY (HomeNo),
CONSTRAINT FKAgentId FOREIGN KEY (AgentId) REFERENCES Agent,
CONSTRAINT FKHomeNo FOREIGN KEY (HomeNo) REFERENCES Home )
```

Figure 6.27: Conversion of Figure 6.26 (SQL:2006 Syntax)

Rule 5 is controversial. Using Rule 5 in place of Rule 2 (1-M Relationship Rule) avoids null values in foreign keys. However, the use of Rule 5 results in more tables. Query formulation can be more difficult with additional tables. In addition, query execution can be slower due to extra joins. The choice of using Rule 5 in place of Rule 2 depends on the importance of avoiding null values versus avoiding extra tables. In many situations, avoiding extra tables may be more important than avoiding null values.

6.4.3 Converting Generalization Hierarchies

The approach to convert generalization hierarchies mimics the entity relationship notation as much as possible. Rule 6 converts each entity type of a generalization hierarchy into a table. The only columns that are different from attributes in the associated ERD are the inherited primary key attributes. In Figure 6.28, *EmpNo* is a column in the *SalaryEmp* and *HourlyEmp* tables because it is the primary key of the parent entity type (*Employee*). In addition, the *SalaryEmp* and *HourlyEmp* tables have a foreign key constraint referring to the *Employee* table. The CASCADE delete option is set in both foreign key constraints (see Figure 6.29).

Generalization Hierarchy Rule: Each entity type of a generalization hierarchy becomes a table. The columns of a table are the attributes of the corresponding entity type plus the primary key of the parent entity type. For each table representing a subtype, define a foreign key constraint that references the table corresponding to the parent entity type. Use the CASCADE option for deletions of referenced rows.

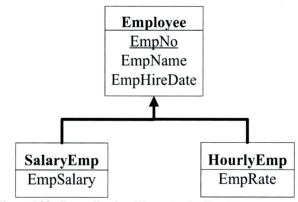

Figure 6.28: Generalization Hierarchy for Employees

```
CREATE TABLE Employee
(      EmpNo             INTEGER,
       EmpName           VARCHAR(30),
       EmpHireDate       DATE,
CONSTRAINT PKEmployee PRIMARY KEY (EmpNo)                    )


CREATE TABLE SalaryEmp
(      EmpNo             INTEGER,
       EmpSalary         DECIMAL(10,2),
CONSTRAINT PKSalaryEmp PRIMARY KEY (EmpNo),
CONSTRAINT FKSalaryEmp FOREIGN KEY (EmpNo)   REFERENCES Employee
    ON DELETE CASCADE   )


CREATE TABLE HourlyEmp
(      EmpNo             INTEGER,
       EmpRate           DECIMAL(10,2),
CONSTRAINT PKHourlyEmp PRIMARY KEY (EmpNo),
CONSTRAINT FKHourlyEmp FOREIGN KEY (EmpNo)   REFERENCES Employee
    ON DELETE CASCADE   )
```

Figure 6.29: Conversion of the Generalization Hierarchy in Figure 6.28 (SQL:2006 Syntax)

Rule 6 also applies to generalization hierarchies of more than one level. To convert the generalization hierarchy of Figure 6.30, five tables are produced (see Figure 6.31). In each table, the primary key of the parent (*Security*) is included. In addition, foreign key constraints are added in each table corresponding to a subtype.

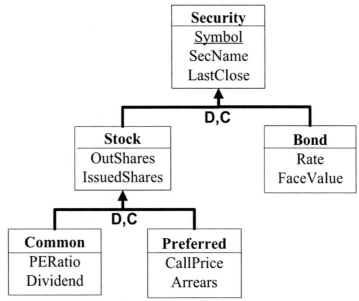

Figure 6.30: Multiple Levels of Generalization Hierarchies

```
CREATE TABLE Security
(     Symbol            CHAR(6),
      SecName           VARCHAR(30),
      LastClose         DECIMAL(10,2),
CONSTRAINT PKSecurity PRIMARY KEY (Symbol)   )


CREATE TABLE Stock
(     Symbol            CHAR(6),
      OutShares         INTEGER,
      IssuedShares      INTEGER,
CONSTRAINT PKStock PRIMARY KEY (Symbol),
CONSTRAINT FKStock FOREIGN KEY (Symbol)   REFERENCES Security
   ON DELETE CASCADE   )


CREATE TABLE Bond
(     Symbol            CHAR(6),
      Rate              DECIMAL(12,4),
      FaceValue         DECIMAL(10,2),
CONSTRAINT PKBond PRIMARY KEY (Symbol),
CONSTRAINT FKBond FOREIGN KEY (Symbol) REFERENCES Security
   ON DELETE CASCADE   )


CREATE TABLE Common
(     Symbol            CHAR(6),
      PERatio           DECIMAL(12,4),
      Dividend          DECIMAL(10,2),
CONSTRAINT PKCommon PRIMARY KEY (Symbol),
CONSTRAINT FKCommon FOREIGN KEY (Symbol) REFERENCES Stock
   ON DELETE CASCADE )


CREATE TABLE Preferred
(     Symbol            CHAR(6),
      CallPrice         DECIMAL(12,2),
      Arrears           DECIMAL(10,2),
CONSTRAINT PKPreferred PRIMARY KEY (Symbol),
CONSTRAINT FKPreferred FOREIGN KEY (Symbol) REFERENCES Stock
   ON DELETE CASCADE   )
```

Figure 6.31: Conversion of the Generalization Hierarchy in Figure 6.30 (SQL:2006 Syntax)

Because the Relational Model does not directly support generalization hierarchies, there are several other ways to convert generalization hierarchies. The other approaches vary depending on the number of tables and the placement of inherited columns. Rule 6 may result in extra joins to gather all data about an entity, but there are no null values and only small amounts of duplicate data. For example, to collect all data about a common stock, you should join the *Common*, *Stock*, and *Security* tables. Other conversion approaches may require fewer joins, but result in more redundant data and null values. The references at the end of this chapter discuss the pros and cons of several approaches to convert generalization hierarchies.

You should note that generalization hierarchies for tables are directly supported in SQL:2006, the standard for object relational databases presented in Chapter 18. In the SQL:2006 standard, subtable families provide a direct conversion from generalization hierarchies avoiding the loss of semantic information when converting to the traditional Relational Model. However, few commercial DBMS products fully support the object relational features in SQL:2006. Thus, usage of the generalization hierarchy conversion rule will likely be necessary.

To support usage of the Generalization Hierarchy Rule, Chapter 11 presents triggers to support operations on tables in a generalization hierarchy. The triggers support propagation among tables when inserting and updating rows in a generalization hierarchy as well as enforcement of generalization hierarchy constraints.

6.4.4 Converting 1-1 Relationships

Outside of generalization hierarchies, 1-1 relationships are not common. They can occur when entities with separate identifiers are closely related. For example, Figure 6.32 shows the *Employee* and *Office* entity types connected by a 1-1 relationship. Separate entity types seem intuitive, but a 1-1 relationship connects the entity types. Rule 7 converts 1-1 relationships into two foreign keys unless many null values will result. In Figure 6.32, most employees will not manage offices. Thus, the conversion in Figure 6.33 eliminates the foreign key (*OfficeNo*) in the employee table.

Relationship Rule: Each 1-1 relationship is converted into two foreign keys. If the relationship is optional with respect to one of the entity types, the corresponding foreign key may be dropped to eliminate null values.

Figure 6.32: 1-1 Relationship

```
CREATE TABLE Employee
(       EmpNo                INTEGER,
        EmpName              VARCHAR(30),
CONSTRAINT PKEmployee PRIMARY KEY (EmpNo)   )


CREATE TABLE Office
(       OfficeNo             INTEGER,
        OffAddress           VARCHAR(30),
        OffPhone             CHAR(10),
        EmpNo                INTEGER,
CONSTRAINT PKOffice PRIMARY KEY (OfficeNo),
CONSTRAINT FKEmpNo FOREIGN KEY (EmpNo) REFERENCES Employee,
CONSTRAINT EmpNoUnique UNIQUE (EmpNo)  )
```

Figure 6.33: Conversion of the 1-1 Relationship in Figure 6.32 (SQL:2006 Syntax)

6.4.5 Comprehensive Conversion Example

This section presents a larger example to integrate your knowledge of the conversion rules. Figure 6.34 shows an ERD similar to the final ERD for the water utility problem discussed in Section 6.1. For brevity, some attributes have been omitted. Figure 6.35 shows the relational tables derived through the conversion rules. Table 6-5 lists the conversion rules used along with brief explanations.

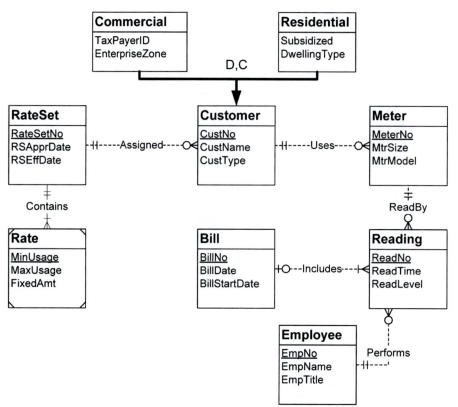

Figure 6.34: Water Utility ERD with a Generalization Hierarchy

```
CREATE TABLE Customer
(      CustNo            INTEGER,
       CustName          VARCHAR(30),
       CustType          CHAR(6),
       RateSetNo         INTEGER          NOT NULL,
CONSTRAINT PKCustomer PRIMARY KEY (CustNo),
CONSTRAINT FKRateSetNo FOREIGN KEY (RateSetNo) REFERENCES RateSet
)
CREATE TABLE Commercial
(      CustNo            INTEGER,
       TaxPayerID        CHAR(20)         NOT NULL,
       EnterpiseZone     BOOLEAN,
CONSTRAINT PKCommercial PRIMARY KEY (CustNo),
CONSTRAINT FKCommercial FOREIGN KEY (CustNo) REFERENCES Customer
ON DELETE CASCADE   )

CREATE TABLE Residential
(      CustNo            INTEGER,
       Subsidized        BOOLEAN,
       DwellingType      CHAR(6),
CONSTRAINT PKResidential PRIMARY KEY (CustNo),
CONSTRAINT FKResidential FOREIGN KEY (CustNo) REFERENCES Customer
   ON DELETE CASCADE     )

CREATE TABLE RateSet
(      RateSetNo         INTEGER,
       RSApprDate        DATE,
       RSEffDate         DATE,
CONSTRAINT PKRateSet PRIMARY KEY (RateSetNo)   )
CREATE TABLE Rate
(      RateSetNo         INTEGER,
```

```
        MinUsage            INTEGER,
        MaxUsage            INTEGER,
        FixedAmt            DECIMAL(10,2),
CONSTRAINT PKRate PRIMARY KEY (RateSetNo, MinUsage),
CONSTRAINT FKRateSetNo2 FOREIGN KEY(RateSetNo) REFERENCES RateSet
)
CREATE TABLE Meter
(       MeterNo             INTEGER,
        MtrSize             INTEGER,
        MtrModel            CHAR(6),
        CustNo              INTEGER         NOT NULL,
CONSTRAINT PKMeter PRIMARY KEY (MeterNo),
CONSTRAINT FKCustNo FOREIGN KEY (CustNo) REFERENCES Customer  )
CREATE TABLE Reading
(       ReadNo              INTEGER,
        ReadTime            TIMESTAMP,
        ReadLevel           INTEGER,
        MeterNo             INTEGER         NOT NULL,
        EmpNo               INTEGER         NOT NULL,
        BillNo              INTEGER,
CONSTRAINT PKReading PRIMARY KEY (ReadNo),
CONSTRAINT FKEmpNo FOREIGN KEY (EmpNo) REFERENCES Employee,
CONSTRAINT FKMeterNo FOREIGN KEY (MeterNo) REFERENCES Meter,
CONSTRAINT FKBillNo FOREIGN KEY (BillNo) RERERENCES Bill  )


CREATE TABLE Bill
(       BillNo              INTEGER,
        BillDate            DATE,
        BillStartDate       DATE,
CONSTRAINT PKBill PRIMARY KEY (BillNo) )


CREATE TABLE Employee
(       EmpNo               INTEGER,
        EmpName             VARCHAR(50),
        EmpTitle            VARCHAR(20),
CONSTRAINT PKEmployee PRIMARY KEY (EmpNo) )
```

Figure 6.35: Conversion of the ERD in Figure 6.34 (SQL:2006 Syntax)
Table 6-5: Conversion Rules Used for Figure 6.34

Rule	Usage
1	All entity types except subtypes converted to tables with primary keys.
2	1-M relationships converted to foreign keys: *Contains* relationship to *Rate.RateSetNo*; *Uses* relationship to *Meter.CustNo*; *ReadBy* relationship to *Reading.MeterNo*; *Includes* relationship to *Reading.BillNo*; *Performs* relationship to *Reading.EmpNo*; *Assigned* relationship to *Customer.RateSetNo*
3	Not used because there are no M-N relationships.
4	Primary key of *Rate* table is a combination of *RateSetNo* and *MinUsage*.
5	Not used although it could have been used for the *Includes* relationship.
6	Subtypes (*Commercial* and *Residential*) converted to tables. Primary key of *Customer* is added to the *Commercial* and *Residential* tables. Foreign key constraints with CASCADE DELETE options added to tables corresponding to the subtypes.

Closing Thoughts

This chapter has described the practice of data modeling, building on your understanding of the Crow's Foot notation presented in Chapter 5. To master data modeling, you need to understand the notation used in entity relationship diagrams (ERDs) and get plenty of practice building ERDs. This chapter described techniques to derive an initial ERD from a narrative problem, refine the ERD through transformations, document important design decisions, and check the ERD for design errors. To apply these techniques, a practice problem for a water utility database was presented. You are encouraged to apply these techniques using the problems at the end of the chapter.

The remainder of this chapter presented rules to convert an ERD into relational tables and alternative ERD notations. The rules will help you convert modest-size ERDs into tables. For large problems, you should use a good CASE tool. Even if you use a CASE tool, understanding the conversion rules provides insight into the differences between the Entity Relationship Model and the Relational Model.

This chapter emphasized the data modeling skills for constructing ERDs using narrative problems, refining ERDs, and converting ERDs into relational tables. The next chapter presents normalization, a technique to remove redundancy from relational tables. Together, data modeling and normalization are fundamental skills for database development.

After you master these database development skills, you are ready to apply them to database design projects. An additional challenge of applying your skills is requirements definition. It is a lot of work to collect requirements from users with diverse interests and backgrounds. You may spend as much time gathering requirements as performing data modeling and normalization. With careful study and practice, you will find database development to be a challenging and highly rewarding activity.

Review Concepts

- Identifying entity types and attributes in a narrative
- Criteria for primary keys: stable and single purpose
- Identifying relationships in a narrative
- Transformations to add detail to an ERD: attribute to entity type, expanding an entity type, adding history
- Splitting an attribute to standardize information content
- Changing a weak entity to a strong entity to remove combined foreign keys after conversion
- Adding a generalization hierarchy to avoid null values
- Documentation practices for important design decisions: justification for design decisions involving multiple feasible choices and explanations of subtle design choices.
- Poor documentation practices: repeating the information already contained in an ERD
- Common design errors: misplaced relationships, missing relationships, incorrect cardinalities, overuse of generalization hierarchies, overuse of associative entity types representing M-way relationships, and redundant relationships
- Basic rules to convert entity types and relationships
- Specialized conversion rules to convert optional 1-M relationships, generalization hierarchies, and 1-1 relationships

Questions

1. What does it mean to say that constructing an ERD is an iterative process?
2. Why decompose a compound attribute into smaller attributes?
3. When is it appropriate to transform an attribute into an entity type?
4. Why transform an entity type into two entity types and a relationship?
5. Why transform a weak entity to a strong entity?
6. Why transform an entity type into a generalization hierarchy?
7. Why add history to an attribute or relationship?

8. What changes to an ERD are necessary when transforming an attribute to an entity type?
9. What changes to an ERD are necessary when splitting a compound attribute?
10. What changes to an ERD are necessary when expanding an entity type?
11. What changes to an ERD are necessary when transforming a weak entity to a strong entity?
12. What changes to an ERD are necessary when adding unlimited history to an attribute or a relationship?
13. What changes to an ERD are necessary when adding a generalization hierarchy?
14. What should you document about an ERD?
15. What should you omit in ERD documentation?
16. Why are design errors more difficult to detect and resolve than diagram errors?
17. What is a misplaced relationship and how is it resolved?
18. What is an incorrect cardinality and how is it resolved?
19. What is a missing relationship and how is it resolved?
20. What is overuse of a generalization hierarchy and how is it resolved?
21. What is a relationship cycle?
22. What is a redundant relationship and how is it resolved?
23. How is an M-N relationship converted to the Relational Model?
24. How is a 1-M relationship converted to the Relational Model?
25. What is the difference between the 1-M relationship rule and the optional 1-M relationship rule?
26. How is a weak entity type converted to the Relational Model?
27. How is a generalization hierarchy converted to the Relational Model?
28. How is a 1-1 relationship converted to the Relational Model?
29. What are the criteria for choosing a primary key?
30. What should you do if a proposed primary key does not meet the criteria?
31. Why should you understand the conversion process even if you use a CASE tool to perform the conversion?
32. What are the goals of narrative problem analysis?
33. What are some difficulties with collecting information requirements to develop a business data model?
34. How are entity types identified in a problem narrative?
35. How should the simplicity principle be applied during the search for entity types in a problem narrative?
36. How are relationships and cardinalities identified in a problem narrative?
37. How can you reduce the number of relationships in an initial ERD?
38. What changes to an ERD are necessary when adding limited history to an attribute?
39. How can design documentation help in resolving specification problems?
40. How can design documentation help in improving communication?

Problems

The problems are divided between data modeling problems and conversion problems. Additional conversion problems are found in Chapter 7, where conversion is followed by normalization. In addition to the problems presented here, the case study in Chapter 13 provides practice on a larger problem.

Data Modeling Problems

1. Define an ERD for the following narrative. The database should track homes and owners. A home has a unique home identifier, a street address, a city, a state, a zip, a number of bedrooms, a number of bathrooms, and square feet. A home is either owner occupied or rented. An owner has a Social Security number, a name, an optional spouse name, a profession, and an optional spouse profession. An owner can possess one or more homes. Each home has only one owner.
2. Refine the ERD from problem 1 by adding an agent entity type. Agents represent owners in the sale of a home. An agent can list many homes, but only one agent can list a home. An agent has a unique agent identifier, a name, an office identifier, and a phone number.

When an owner agrees to list a home with an agent, a commission (percentage of the sales price) and a selling price are determined.

3. In the ERD from problem 2, transform the attribute, office identifier, into an entity type. Data about an office include the phone number, the manager name, and the address.
4. In the ERD from problem 3, add a buyer entity type. A buyer entity type has a Social Security number, a name, a phone, preferences for the number of bedrooms and bathrooms, and a price range. An agent can work with many buyers, but a buyer works with only one agent.
5. Refine the ERD from problem 4 with a generalization hierarchy to depict similarities between buyers and owners.
6. Revise the ERD from problem 5 by adding an offer entity type. A buyer makes an offer on a home for a specified sales price. The offer starts on the submission date and time and expires on the specified date and time. A unique offer number identifies an offer. A buyer can submit multiple offers for the same home.
7. Construct an ERD to represent accounts in a database for personal financial software. The software supports checking accounts, credit cards, and two kinds of investments (mutual funds and stocks). No other kinds of accounts are supported, and every account must fall into one of these account types. For each kind of account, the software provides a separate data entry screen. The following list describes the fields on the data entry screens for each kind of account:
    a. For all accounts, the software requires the unique account identifier, the account name, date established, and the balance.
    b. For checking accounts, the software supports attributes for the bank name, the bank address, the checking account number, and the routing number.
    c. For credit cards, the software supports attributes for the credit card number, the expiration date, and the credit card limit.
    d. For stocks, the software supports attributes for the stock symbol, the stock type (common or preferred), the last dividend amount, the last dividend date, the exchange, the last closing price, and the number of shares (a whole number).
    e. For mutual funds, the software supports attributes for the mutual fund symbol, the share balance (a real number), the fund type (stock, bond, or mixed), the last closing price, the region (domestic, international, or global), and the tax-exempt status (yes or no).
8. Construct an ERD to represent categories in a database for personal financial software. A category has a unique category identifier, a name, a type (expense, asset, liability, or revenue), and a balance. Categories are organized hierarchically so that a category can have a parent category and one or more subcategories. For example, the category "household" can have subcategories for "cleaning" and "maintenance." A category can have any number of levels of subcategories. Make an instance diagram to depict the relationships among categories.
9. Design an ERD for parts and relationships among parts. A part has a unique identifier, a name, and a color. A part can have multiple subparts and multiple parts that use it. The quantity of each subpart should be recorded. Make an instance diagram to depict relationships among parts.
10. Design an ERD to represent a credit card statement. The statement has two parts: a heading containing the unique statement number, the account number of the credit card holder, and the statement date; and a detail section containing a list of zero or more transactions for which the balance is due. Each detail line contains a line number, a transaction date, a merchant name, and the amount of the transaction. The line number is unique within a statement.
11. Modify your ERD from problem 10. Everything is the same except that each detail line contains a unique transaction number in place of the line number. Transaction numbers are unique across statements.
12. Using the ERD in Figure 6.P1, transform the *ProvNo* attribute into an entity type (*Provider*) and a 1-M relationship (*Treats*). A provider has a unique provider number, a first name, a last name, a phone, a specialty, a hospital name in which the provider practices, an e-mail address, a certification, a pay grade, and a title. A provider is required for a visit. New providers do not have associated visits.

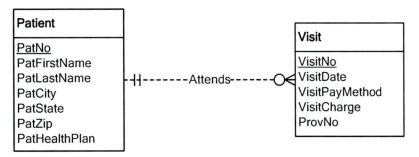

Figure 6.P1: ERD for Problem 12

13. In the result for problem 12, expand the *Visit* entity type to record details about a visit. A visit detail includes a detail number, a detail charge, an optional provider number, and an associated item. The combination of the visit number and visit detail number is unique for a visit detail. An item includes a unique item number, an item description, an item price, and an item type. An item can be related to multiple visit details. New items may not be related to any visit details. A provider can be related to multiple visit details. Some providers may not be associated to any visit details. In addition, a provider can be related to multiple visits as indicated in problem 12. The provider for a visit detail (usually a nurse or a lab technician) is typically different than the provider for the visit (usually a physician).

14. In the result for problem 13, add a generalization hierarchy to distinguish between nurse and physician providers. A nurse has a pay grade and a title. A physician has a residence hospital, e-mail address, and a certification. The other attributes of provider apply to both physicians and nurses. A visit involves a physician provider while a visit detail may involve a nurse provider.

15. In the result for problem 14, transform *VisitDetail* into a strong entity with *VisitDetailNo* as the primary key.

16. In the result for problem 15, add a history of item prices. Your solution should support the current price along with the two most recent prices. Include change dates for each item price.

17. In the result for problem 15, add a history of item prices. Your solution should support an unlimited number of prices and change dates.

18. Design an ERD with entity types for projects, specialties, and contractors. Add relationships and/or entity types as indicated in the following description. Each contractor has exactly one specialty, but many contractors can provide the same specialty. A contractor can provide the same specialty on multiple projects. A project can use many specialties, and a specialty can be used on many projects. Each combination of project and specialty should have at least two contractors.

19. For the following problem, define an ERD for the initial requirements and then revise the ERD for the new requirements. Your solution should have an initial ERD, a revised ERD, and a list of design decisions for each ERD. In performing your analysis, you may want to follow the approach presented in Section 6.1. The database supports the placement office of a leading graduate school of business. The primary purpose of the database is to schedule interviews and facilitate searches by students and companies. Consider the following requirements in your initial ERD:

   a. Student data include a unique student identifier, a name, a phone number, an e-mail address, a web address, a major, a minor, and a GPA.

   b. The placement office maintains a standard list of positions based on the Labor Department's list of occupations. Position data include a unique position identifier and a position description.

   c. Company data include a unique company identifier, a company name, and a list of positions and interviewers. Each company must map its positions into the position list maintained by the placement office. For each available position, the company lists the cities in which positions are available.

191

a. Interviewer data include a unique interviewer identifier, a name, a phone, an e-mail address, and a web address. Each interviewer works for one company and conducts interviews at the placement office.

b. An interview includes a unique interview identifier, a date, a time, a location (building and room), an interviewer, and a student. A student may have multiple interviews.

c. After reviewing your initial design, the placement office decides to revise the requirements. Make a separate ERD to show your refinements. Refine your original ERD to support the following new requirements:

d. Allow companies to use their own language to describe positions. The placement office will not maintain a list of standard positions.

e. Allow companies to indicate availability dates and number of openings for positions.

f. Allow companies to reserve blocks of interview time. The interview blocks will not specify times for individual interviews. Rather a company will request a block of X hours during a specified week. Companies reserve interview blocks before the placement office schedules individual interviews. Thus, the placement office needs to store interviews as well as interview blocks.

Allow students to submit bids for interview blocks. Students receive a set amount of bid dollars that they can allocate among bids. The bid mechanism is a pseudo-market approach to allocating interviews, a scarce resource. A bid contains a unique bid identifier, a bid amount, and a company. A student can submit many bids and an interview block can receive many bids.

20. For the following problem, define an ERD for the initial requirements and then revise the ERD for the new requirements. Your solution should have an initial ERD, a revised ERD, and a list of design decisions for each ERD. In performing your analysis, you may want to follow the approach presented in Section 6.1. Design a database for managing the task assignments on a work order. A work order records the set of tasks requested by a customer at a specified location.

a. A customer has a unique customer identifier, a name, a billing address (street, city, state, and zip), and a collection of submitted work orders.

b. A work order has a unique work order number, a creation date, a date required, a completion date, an optional supervising employee, a work address (street, city, state, zip), and a set of tasks.

c. Each task has a unique task identifier, a task name, an hourly rate, and estimated hours. Tasks are standardized across work orders so that the same task can be performed on many work orders.

d. Each task on a work order has a status (not started, in progress, or completed), actual hours, and a completion date. The completion date is not entered until the status changes to complete.

After reviewing your initial design, the company decides to revise the requirements. Make a separate ERD to show your refinements. Refine your original ERD to support the following new requirements:

e. The company wants to maintain a list of materials. The data about materials include a unique material identifier, a name, and an estimated cost. A material can appear on multiple work orders.

f. Each work order also has a collection of material requirements. A material requirement includes a material, an estimated quantity of the material, and the actual quantity of the material used.

g. The estimated number of hours for a task depends on the work order and task, not on the task alone. Each task of a work order includes an estimated number of hours.

21. For the following problem, define an ERD for the initial requirements and then revise the ERD for the new requirements. Your solution should have an initial ERD, a revised ERD, and a list of design decisions for each ERD. In performing your analysis, you may want to follow the approach presented in Section 6.1.

a. Design a database to assist physical plant personnel in managing assignments of keys to employees. The primary purpose of the database is to ensure proper accounting for all keys.

b. An employee has a unique employee number, a name, a position, and an optional office number.

c. A building has a unique building number, a name, and a location within the campus.

d. A room has a room number, a size (physical dimensions), a capacity, a number of entrances, and a description of equipment in the room. Because each room is located in exactly one building, the identification of a room depends on the identification of a building.

e. Key types (also known as master keys) are designed to open one or more rooms. A room may have one or more key types that open it. A key type has a unique key type number, a date designed, and the employee authorizing the key type. A key type must be authorized before it is created.

f. A copy of a key type is known as a key. Keys are assigned to employees. Each key is assigned to exactly one employee, but an employee can hold multiple keys. The key type number plus a copy number uniquely identify a key. The date the copy was made should be recorded in the database.

   After reviewing your initial design, the physical plant supervisor decides to revise the requirements. Make a separate ERD to show your refinements. Refine your original ERD to support the following new requirements:

g. The physical plant supervisor needs to know not only the current holder of a key but the past holders of a key. For past key holders, the date range that a key was held should be recorded.

h. The physical plant supervisor needs to know the current status of each key: in use by an employee, in storage, or reported lost. If lost, the date reported lost should be stored.

22. Define an ERD that supports the generation of product explosion diagrams, assembly instructions, and parts lists. These documents are typically included in hardware products sold to the public. Your ERD should represent the final products as well as the parts comprising final products. The following points provide more details about the documents.

   a. Your ERD should support the generation of product explosion diagrams as shown in Figure 6.P2 for a wheelbarrow with a hardwood handle. Your ERD should store the containment relationships along with the quantities required for each subpart. For line drawings and geometric position specifications, you can assume that image and position data types are available to store attribute values.

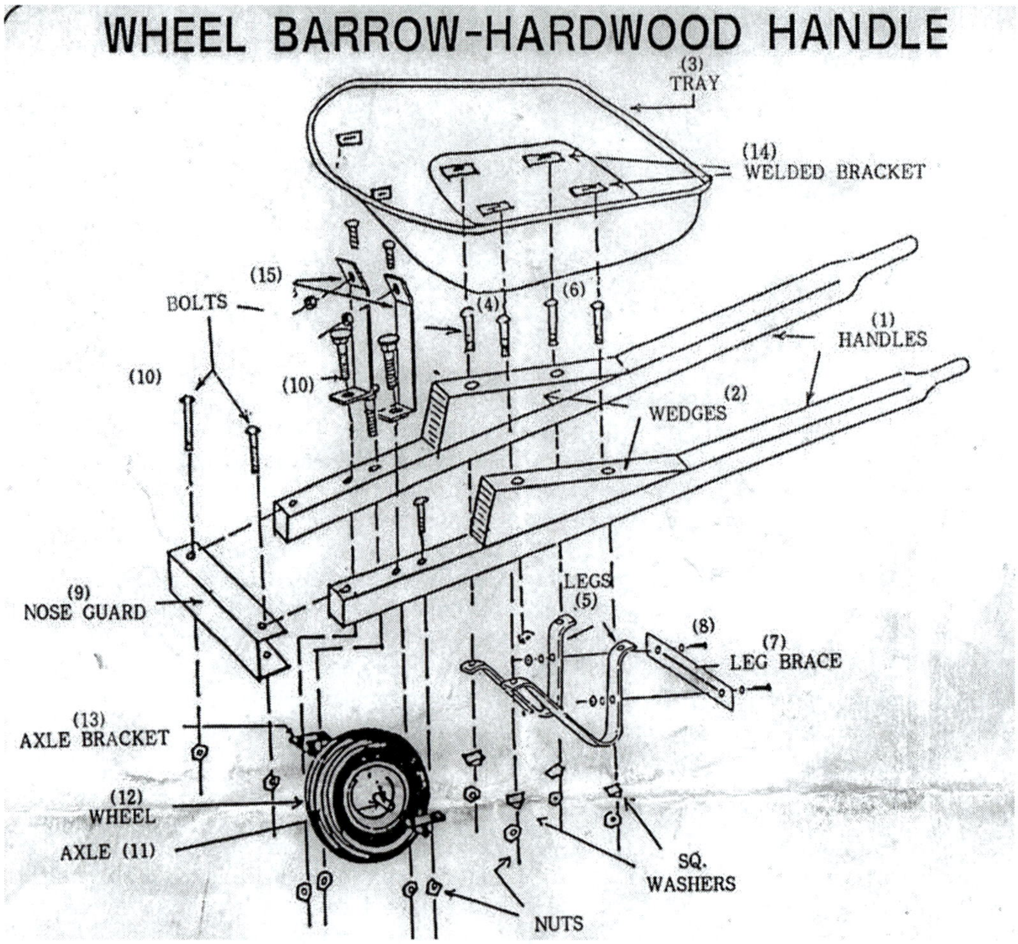

WHEEL BARROW-HARDWOOD HANDLE

Figure 6.P2: Product Explosion Diagram

Your ERD should support the generation of assembly instructions. Each product can have a set of ordered steps for instruction. Table 6-P1 shows some of the assembly instructions for a wheelbarrow. The numbers in the instructions refer to the parts diagram.

Table 6-P1: Sample Assembly Instructions for the Wheelbarrow

Step	Instructions
1	Assembly requires a few hand tools, screw driver, box, or open wrench to fit the nuts.
2	Do NOT wrench-tighten nuts until entire wheelbarrow has been assembled.
3	Set the handles (1) on two boxes or two saw horses (one at either end).
4	Place a wedge (2) on top of each handle and align the bolt holes in the wedge with corresponding bolt holes in the handle.

Your ERD should support the generation of a parts list for each product. Table 6-P2 shows the parts list for the wheelbarrow.

Table 6-P2: Partial Parts List for the Wheelbarrow

Quantity	Part Description
1	Tray
2	Hardwood handle
2	Hardwood wedge
2	Leg

23. For the Expense Report ERD shown in Figure 6.P3, identify and resolve errors and note incompleteness in the specifications. Your solution should include a list of errors and a revised ERD. For each error, identify the type of error (diagram or design) and the specific error within each error type. Note that the ERD may have both diagram and design errors. If you are using the ER Assistant, you can use the Check Diagram feature after checking the diagram rules yourself. Specifications for the ERD appear below:

   a. The Expense Reporting database tracks expense reports and expense report items along with users, expense categories, status codes, and limits on expense category spending.

   b. For each user, the database records the unique user number, the first name, the last name, the phone number, the e-mail address, the spending limit, the organizational relationships among users, and the expense categories (at least one) available to the user. A user can manage other users but have at most one manager. For each expense category available to a user, there is a limit amount.

   c. For each expense category, the database records the unique category number, the category description, the spending limit, and the users permitted to use the expense category. When an expense category is initially created, there may not be related users.

   d. For each status code, the database records the unique status number, the status description, and the expense reports using the status code.

   e. For each expense report, the database records the unique expense report number, the description, the submitted date, the status date, the status code (required), the user number (required), and the related expense items.

   f. For each expense item, the database records the unique item number, the description, the expense date, the amount, the expense category (required), and the expense report number (required).

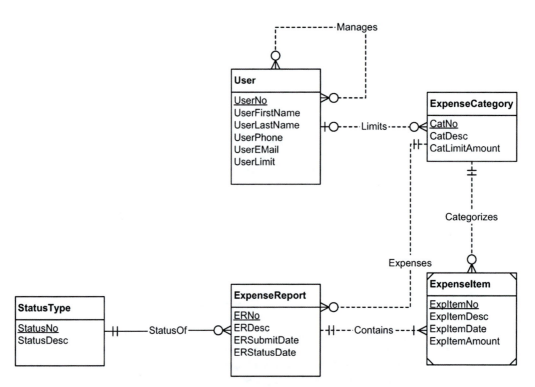

Figure 6.P3: ERD for the Expense Reporting Database

24. For the Intercollegiate Athletic ERD shown in Figure 6.P4, identify and resolve errors and note incompleteness in the specifications. Your solution should include a list of errors and a revised ERD. For each error, identify the type of error (diagram or design) and the specific error within each error type. Note that the ERD may have both diagram and design errors. If you are using the ER Assistant, you can use the Check Diagram feature after checking the diagram rules yourself. Specifications for the ERD are as follows:

    a.   The Intercollegiate Athletic database supports the scheduling and the operation of events along with tracking customers, facilities, locations within facilities, employees, and resources to support events. To schedule an event, a customer initiates an event request with the Intercollegiate Athletic Department. If an event request is approved, one or more event plans are made. Typically, event plans are made for the setup, the operation, and the cleanup of an event. An event plan consists of one or more event plan lines.

    b.   For each event request, the database records the unique event number, the date held, the date requested, the date authorized, the status, an estimated cost, the estimated audience, the facility number (required), and the customer number (required).

    c.   For each event plan, the database records the unique plan number, notes about the plan, the work date, the activity (setup, operation, or cleanup), the employee number (optional), and the event number (required).

    d.   For each event plan line, the database records the line number (unique within a plan number), the plan number (required), the starting time, the ending time, the resource number (required), the location number (required), and the quantity of resources required.

    e.   For each customer, the database records the unique customer number, the name, the address, the contact name, the phone, the e-mail address, and the list of events requested by the customer. A customer is not stored in the database until submitting an event request.

    f.   For each facility, the database records the unique facility number, the facility name, and the list of events in which the facility is requested.

g. For each employee, the database records the unique employee number, the name, the department name, the email address, the phone number, and the list of event plans supervised by the employee.

h. For each location, the database records the related facility number, the location number (unique within a facility), the name, and the list of event plan lines in which the location is used.

i. For each resource, the database records the unique resource number, the name, the rental rate, and the list of event plan lines in which the resource is needed.

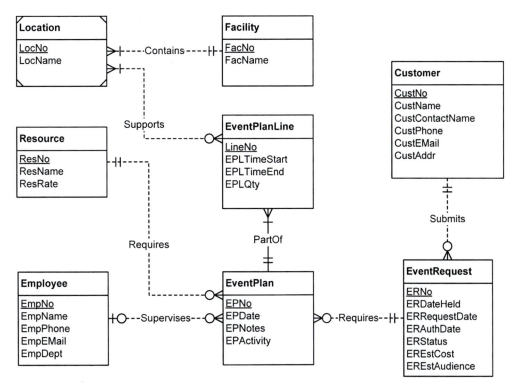

Figure 6.P4: ERD for the Intercollegiate Athletic Database

25. For the Volunteer Information System ERD shown in Figure 6.P5, identify and resolve errors and note incompleteness in the specifications. Your solution should include a list of errors and a revised ERD. For each error, identify the type of error (diagram or design) and the specific error within each error type. Note that the ERD may have both diagram and design errors. If you are using the ER Assistant, you can use the Check Diagram feature after checking the diagram rules yourself. Specifications for the ERD are as follows:

a. The Volunteer Information System supports organizations that need to track volunteers, volunteer areas, events, and hours worked at events. The system will be initially developed for charter schools that have mandatory parent participation as volunteers. Volunteers register as a dual or single-parent family. Volunteer coordinators recruit volunteers for volunteer areas. Event organizers recruit volunteers to work at events. Some events require a schedule of volunteers while other events do not use a schedule. Volunteers work at events and record the time worked.

b. For each family, the database records the unique family number, the first and last name of each parent, the home and business phones, the mailing address (street, city, state, and zip), and an optional e-mail address. For single parent households, information about only one parent is recorded.

c. For each volunteer area, the database records the unique volunteer area, the volunteer area name, the group (faculty senate or parent teacher association) controlling the volunteer area, the family coordinating the volunteer area. In some cases, a family coordinates more than one volunteer area.

    d.   For events, the database records the unique event number, the event description, the event date, the beginning and ending time of the event, the number of required volunteers, the event period and expiration date if the event is a recurring event, and the list of family volunteers for the event. Families can volunteer in advance for a collection of events.

    e.   After completing a work assignment, hours worked are recorded. The database contains the first and last name of the volunteer, the family in which the volunteer represents, the number of hours worked, the optional event, the date worked, the location of the work, and optional comments. The event is optional to allow volunteer hours for activities not considered as events.

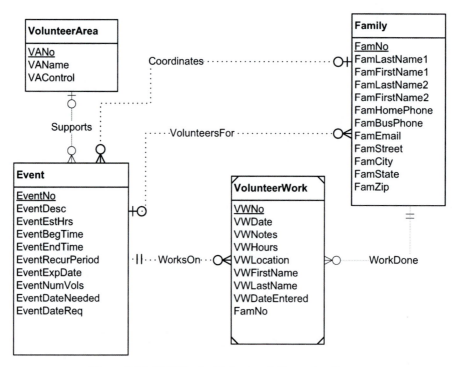

Figure 6.P5: ERD for the Volunteer Information System

26. Define an ERD that supports the generation of television viewing guides, movie listings, sports listings, public access listings, and cable conversion charts. These documents are typically included in television magazines bundled with Sunday newspapers. In addition, these documents are available online. The following points provide more details about the documents.

    a.   A television viewing guide lists the programs available during each time slot of a day as depicted in Figure 6.P6. For each program in a channel/time slot, a viewing guide may include some or all of these attributes: a program title, a television content rating, a description, a rerun status (yes or no), a duration, a closed caption status (yes or no), and a starting time if a program does not begin on a half-hour increment. For each movie, a guide also may include some or all of these attributes: an evaluative rating (number of stars from 1 to 4, with half-star increments), a list of major actors, an optional brief description, a motion picture content rating, and a release year. Public access programs are shown in a public access guide, not in a television viewing guide.

    b.   A movie listing contains all movies shown in a television guide as depicted in Figure 6.P7. For each movie, a listing may include some or all of these attributes: a title, a release year, an evaluative rating, a content rating, a channel abbreviation, a list of days of the week/time combinations, a list of major actors, and a brief description. A movie listing is organized in ascending order by movie titles.

c. A sports listing contains all sports programming in a television guide as depicted in Figure 6.P8. A sports listing is organized by sport and day within a sport. Each item in a sports listing may include some or all of these attributes: an event title, a time, a duration, a channel, an indicator for closed-captioning, an indicator if live, and an indicator if a rerun.

d. A public access listing shows public access programming that does not appear elsewhere in a television guide as depicted in Figure 6.P9. A public access listing contains a list of community organizations (title, area, street address, city, state, zip code, and phone number). After the listing of community organizations, a public access listing contains programming for each day/time slot. Because public access shows do not occupy all time slots and are available on one channel only, there is a list of time slots for each day, not a grid as for a complete television guide. Each public access program has a title and an optional sponsoring community organization.

e. A cable/conversion chart shows the mapping of channels across cable systems as depicted in Figure 6.P10. For each channel, a conversion chart shows a number on each cable system in the local geographic area.

CHANNELS	6 PM	6:30	7 PM	7:30
	CABLE CHANNELS CONTINUED			
68 68	Life Makeover Project		Sixteen *Pepa's Fight* 'TVPG'	
58 7	Ed McMahon's Next Big Star		Candid Camera	
61 61	Home Projects With Rick & Dan			
52 76	◀**Doctor Who** ★★ ('96) 'TVPG'		**The Addams Family** ★★★ ('	
25 25	Home Living - Lamps			
67 67	SoapTalk		Soapnet Special	
22 15 133	Bishop Jakes	Joyce Meyer	C. McClendon	Jack Hayford
57 6	◀**U.S. Marshals** ★★ ('98, Crime drama) *Tommy Lee Jones* 'TV14'			
64 82	**A Face in the Crowd** ★★★ ʸ ('57) *Andy Griffith, Patricia Neal*			
44 44	Beyond Tough		Junkyard Wars	
47 47	🎞 ◀Arena Football (L)		Real TV	Real TV
51 51	◀**The Peacemaker** ★★ ʸ ('97, Action) *George Clooney* 'TV14' (CC)			
59 78	America's Best Waterparks		America's Best Beaches 3	
66 86	Beaver	Beaver	Batman	Batman
33 33	**The Rage: Carrie 2** ★ ʸ ('99) *Emily Bergl, Jason London* (CC)			
45 45	◀Movie	Military Diaries	VH1 Special	
69 69	(:15) **Wall Street** ★★★ ʸ ('87, Drama) *Michael Douglas* 'R'			
10 62	◀**Bull Durham** ★★★ ('88)		Mutant X (R)	

Figure 6.P6: Sample Television Viewing Guide

Movies

A

A.I.: ARTIFICIAL INTELLIGENCE *Science fiction* In the future, a cutting-edge android in the form of a boy embarks on a journey to discover its true nature. *Haley Joel Osment* (PG-13, 2:25) (AS, V) '01 *(Esp.)* **INT June 2** 3:30pm; **6** 10:00am; **8** 8:00am; **11** 5:30pm; **13** 10:00am; **25** 10:00am; **29** 9:00am (CC) ∩, **IN2 June 1** 7:30pm; **8** 6:00am; **10** 6:30am; **11** 3:30pm; **12** 7:30am; **13** 11:00am (CC) ∩, **IN3 June 6** 9:00am, 11:30am, 2:00pm, 4:30pm, 7:00pm, 9:30pm (CC) ∩, **IN4 June 6** 9:00am, 11:30am, 2:00pm, 4:30pm, 7:00pm, 9:30pm

A.K.A. CASSIUS CLAY ★★★ *Documentary* Heavyweight boxing champ Muhammad Ali speaks, visits comic Stepin Fetchit and appears in fight footage. (PG, 1:25) (AS, L, V) '70 *(Esp.)* **TMC June 1** 6:15am; **6** 2:30pm; **19** 6:20am, TMC-W **June 1** 9:15am; **6** 5:30pm; **19** 9:20am

ABANDON SHIP! ★★★ *Adventure* Short rations from a sunken liner force the officer of a packed lifeboat to sacrifice the weak. *Tyrone Power* ⌐ (NR, 1:37) '57 *(Esp.)* TMAX **June 4** 6:05am; **21** 4:40pm; **30** 3:20pm

ABBOTT AND COSTELLO MEET THE KILLER, BORIS KARLOFF ★★½ *Comedy* A hotel detective and bellhop find dead bodies and a fake swami. *Bud Abbott* ⌐ (TVG, 1:30) '49 AMC **June 20** 5:30pm; **21** 7:35am (CC)

ABBOTT AND COSTELLO MEET FRANKENSTEIN ★★★★ *Comedy* The Wolf Man tries to warn a dimwitted porter that Dracula wants his brain for a monster's body. *Bud Abbott* ⌐ (TVG, 1:30) '48 AMC **June 6** 5:30pm (CC)

ABDUCTION OF INNOCENCE: A MOMENT OF TRUTH MOVIE ★★ *Drama* A lumber magnate's teen daughter stands trial for being an accomplice in her own kidnapping. *Katie Wright* (TVPG, 1:45) '96 LIN **June 1** 8:00pm; **2** 9:30am (CC)

THE ABDUCTION OF KARI SWENSON ★★ *Docudrama* A U.S. Olympic biathlete is kidnapped in 1984 by father-and-son Montana mountain men. *Tracy Pollan* (TVPG, 1:45) (V) '87 LIN **June 10** 4:30pm; **11** 6:00am

ABOUT ADAM ★★★ *Romance-comedy* A magnetic young man meets and romances an Irish waitress, then courts and beds the rest of the family. *Stuart Townsend* (R, 1:45) (AS, L) '00 STARZIC **June 22** 8:00pm; **23** 1:10pm; **27** 2:30pm, 10:15pm (CC)

ABOUT SARAH ★★ *Drama* A young woman decides whether to continue her medical career or care for her mentally impaired mother. *Kellie Martin* (TVPG,

discovery. *Ed Harris* (PG-13, 2:47) (AS, L, V) '89 *(Esp.)* ACTION **June 2** 12:05pm, 8:00pm; **3** 6:45am; **13** 12:20pm, 8:00pm; **22** 8:10am, 5:35pm ∩

THE ACCIDENT: A MOMENT OF TRUTH MOVIE ★★ *Docudrama* A teen, charged with manslaughter in a drunken driving crash that killed her best friend, uses alcohol to cope. *Bonnie Root* (TVPG, 1:45) '97 LIN **June 8** 2:45pm (CC)

THE ACCIDENTAL TOURIST ★★★ *Drama* A travel writer takes up with his dog trainer after his wife moves out. *William Hurt* (TVPG, 2:30) (AS, L) '88 FOX-WXIX **June 23** 12:00pm

THE ACCUSED ★★★ *Crime drama* A psychology professor goes to trial for killing a student who tried to seduce her. *Loretta Young* ⌐ (NR, 1:41) '48 TCM **June 8** 10:30am

AN ACT OF LOVE: THE PATRICIA NEAL STORY ★★★ *Docudrama* The actress recovers from a 1965 stroke with help from friends and her husband, writer Roald Dahl. *Glenda Jackson* (NR, 1:40) '81 WE **June 26** 11:10am

ACTIVE STEALTH *Action* When terrorists steal a stealth bomber, the Army calls upon a veteran fighter pilot and his squadron to retrieve it. *Daniel Baldwin* ⌐ (R, 1:35) (AS, L, V) '99 *(Esp.)* AMAX **June 2** 2:45pm; **5** 4:30pm; **7** 8:00pm; **10** 12:10pm; **15** 6:20pm; **18** 8:00pm; **24** 12:50pm; **28** 1:15pm; **30** 1:15pm (CC) ∩

THE ACTRESS ★★½ *Drama* Supported by her mother, a New Englander finally tells her salty father she wants to be an actress. *Spencer Tracy* ⌐ (NR, 1:30) '53

Figure 6.P7: Sample Movie Listing

Sports

8:00pm	**GOLF** Golf Murphy's Irish Open, First Round (R)
11:00am	**GOLF** Golf Murphy's Irish Open, First Round (R)

FRIDAY, JUNE 28

10:00am	**GOLF** Golf Murphy's Irish Open, Second Round (L)
12:00pm	**ESPN** U.S. Senior Open, Second Round (L) (CC)
2:00pm	**ESPN** PGA FedEx St. Jude Classic, Second Round (L) (CC)
3:00pm	**GOLF** Golf ShopRite LPGA Classic, First Round (L)
4:00pm	**ESPN** Golf U.S. Senior Open, Second Round (L) (CC)
5:30pm	**GOLF** Scorecard Report
8:00pm	**GOLF** Golf ShopRite LPGA Classic, First Round (R)
10:00pm	**GOLF** Scorecard Report
11:00pm	**GOLF** Golf Murphy's Irish Open, Second Round (R)

SATURDAY, JUNE 29

10:00am	**GOLF** Golf Murphy's Irish Open, Third Round (L)
3:00pm	**NBC-WLWT** Golf U.S. Senior Open, Third Round (L) (CC)
4:00pm	**ABC-WCPO** PGA FedEx St. Jude Classic, Third Round (L)
4:30pm	**GOLF** Golf ShopRite LPGA Classic, Second Round (L)
7:00pm	**GOLF** Scorecard Report
8:00pm	**GOLF** Haskins Award
8:30pm	**GOLF** Golf ShopRite LPGA Classic, Second Round (R)
10:00pm	**GOLF** Scorecard Report
11:00pm	**GOLF** Haskins Award
11:30pm	**GOLF** Golf Murphy's Irish Open, Third Round (R)

HORSE EVENTS

SUNDAY, JUNE 2

2:00pm	**ESPN2** Equestrian Del Mar National (CC)

WEDNESDAY, JUNE 5

2:00pm	**ESPN2** Wire to Wire

FRIDAY, JUNE 7

5:00pm	**ESPN2** Horse Racing Acorn Stakes (L)

SATURDAY, JUNE 8

2:00pm	**ESPN** Horse Racing Belmont Stakes Special (L) (CC)
5:00pm	**NBC-WLWT** Horse Racing Belmont Stakes (L) (CC)

WEDNESDAY, JUNE 12

2:00pm	**ESPN2** Wire to Wire

SATURDAY, JUNE 15

5:00pm	**CBS-WKRC** Horse Racing Stephen Foster Handicap (L)

WEDNESDAY, JUNE 19

2:00pm	**ESPN2** Wire to Wire

WEDNESDAY, JUNE 26

2:00pm	**ESPN2** Wire to Wire

SATURDAY, JUNE 29

3:00pm	**ESPN2** Budweiser Grand Prix of Devon
5:00pm	**CBS-WKRC** Horse Racing The Mothergoose (L) (CC)
11:00pm	**ESPN2** 2Day at the Races (L)

MARTIAL ARTS

SATURDAY, JUNE 1

10:00pm	**IN2** World Championship Kickboxing Bad to the Bone (L)

MONDAY, JUNE 3

9:00pm	**IN2** World Championship Kickboxing Bad to the Bone (R)

SUNDAY, JUNE 16

9:00pm	**IN1** Ultimate Fighting Championship: Ultimate Royce Gracie

MONDAY, JUNE 17

1:00am	**IN2** Ultimate Fighting Championship: Ultimate Royce Gracie
11:30pm	**IN2** Ultimate Fighting Championship: Ultimate Royce Gracie

Figure 6.P8: Sample Sports Listing

Public Access listings for Channel 24 in all Time Warner franchises in Greater Cincinnati:
Media Bridges Cincinnati, 1100 Race St., Cincinnati 45210. 651-4171.
Waycross Community Media (Forest Park-Greenhills-Springfield Twp.), 2086 Waycross Road, Forest Park 45240. 825-2429.
Intercommunity Cable Regulatory Commission, 2492 Commodity Circle, Cincinnati 45241. 772-4272.
Norwood Community Television, 2020 Sherman Ave., Norwood 45212. 396-5573.

SUNDAY
7 a.m. – Heart of Compassion
7:30 a.m. – Community Pentecostal
8 a.m. – ICRC Programming
8:30 a.m. – ICRC Programming
9 a.m. – St. John Church of Christ
10 a.m. – Beulah Missionary Baptist

MONDAY
6 a.m. – Sonshine Gospel Hour
7 a.m. – Latter Rain Ministry
8 a.m. – Dunamis of Faith
8:30 a.m. – In Jesus' Name
9 a.m. – Happy Gospel Time TV
10 a.m. – Greek Christian Hour
10:30 a.m. – Armor of God
11 a.m. – Delhi Christian Center
Noon – Humanist Perspective
12:30 p.m. – Waterway Hour
1:30 p.m. – Country Gospel Jubilee
2:30 p.m. – Know Your Government
4:30 p.m. – House of Yisrael
5:30 p.m. – Living Vine Presents
6:30 p.m. – Family Dialogue
7 p.m. – Goodwill Talks
8 p.m. – Pastor Nadie Johnson
9 p.m. – Delta Kings Barbershop Show
Midnight – Basement Flava 2
1 a.m. – Total Chaos Hour
2 a.m. – Commissioned by Christ
3 a.m. – From the Heart
3:30 a.m. – Words of Farrakhan
4:30 a.m. – Skyward Bound

11:30 p.m. – Fire Ball Ministry Church of God
12:30 a.m. – Second Peter Pentecostal Church
1:30 a.m. – Road to Glory Land
3:30 a.m. – Shadows of the Cross

WEDNESDAY
6 a.m. – Pure Gospel
8 a.m. – ICRC Programming
8:30 a.m. – Way of the Cross
9 a.m. – Church of Christ Hour
10 a.m. – A Challenge of Faith
10:30 a.m. – Miracles Still Happen
11 a.m. – Deerfield Digest
11:30 a.m. – Bob Schuler
Noon – Friendship Baptist Church
2 p.m. – Business Talk
2:30 p.m. – ICRC Programming
3 p.m. – ICRC Programming
3:30 p.m. – Temple Fitness
4 p.m. – Church of God
5 p.m. – Around Cincinnati
5:30 p.m. – Countering the Silence
6 p.m. – Community Report
6:30 p.m. – ICRC Programming
7 p.m. – Inside Springdale
8 p.m. – ICRC Sports

Figure 6.P9: Sample Public Access Listing

	Time Warner standard	Time Warner upgrade cable ready	Insight	Adelphia Amelia	Fairfield, Middletown Time Warner Hamilton,	Adelphia Delhi
5	5	6	7	5	5	6
9	9	7	8	9	9	10
12	12	13	3	12	12	13
19	3	3	4	3	13	2
25	20	20–	25	25	20	15
48	13	8	13	6	6	8
64	11	11	11	11	11	11
2	–	–	–	–	2	–
7		–	–	–	7	–
14	14	14	14	14	14	14
16	16	16	–	16	16	16
22	–	–	–	–	8	–
43	–	–	–	–	3	–
45	–	–	–	–	10	–
54	21	21	2	–	–	4
A&E	39	39	52	28	27	46
AMC	46	46	31	29	26	40

Figure 6.P10: Sample Conversion Chart

27. Transform the ERD in Figure 6.P11 by adding unlimited history for the *ProdPrice* attribute.

Figure 6.P11: *Product* Entity Type without Price History

28. Transform the ERD in Figure 6.P11 by adding limited history for the *ProdPrice* attribute. The transformed ERD should support the current price and the two most recent prices.

29. Transform the ERD in Figure 6.P12 by adding unlimited history for the *WorksAt* 1-M relationship.

Figure 6.P12: *WorksAt* Relationship without History

30. Transform the ERD in Figure 6.P13 by adding unlimited history for the *Shares* M-N relationship. The Shares relationship represents a timesharing situation in which owners have fractional ownership for a number of consecutive weeks of a property per year.

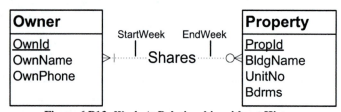

Figure 6.P13: *WorksAt* Relationship without History

Conversion Problems

1. Convert the ERD shown in Figure 6.CP1 into tables. List the conversion rules used and the resulting changes to the tables.

202

Figure 6.CP1: ERD for Conversion Problem 1

2. Convert the ERD shown in Figure 6.CP2 into tables. List the conversion rules used and the resulting changes to the tables.

Figure 6.CP2: ERD for Conversion Problem 2

3. Convert the ERD shown in Figure 6.CP3 into tables. List the conversion rules used and the resulting changes to the tables.

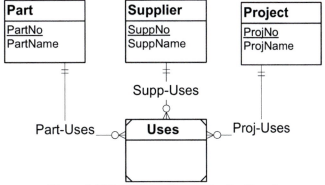

Figure 6.CP3: ERD for Conversion Problem 3

4. Convert the ERD shown in Figure 6.CP4 into tables. List the conversion rules used and the resulting changes to the tables.

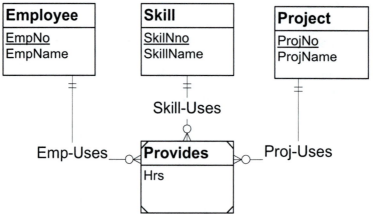

Figure 6.CP4: ERD for Conversion Problem 4

5. Convert the ERD shown in Figure 6.CP5 into tables. List the conversion rules used and the resulting changes to the tables.

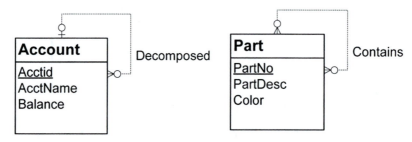

Figure 6.CP5: ERD for Conversion Problem 5

6. Convert the ERD shown in Figure 6.CP6 into tables. List the conversion rules used and the resulting changes to the tables.

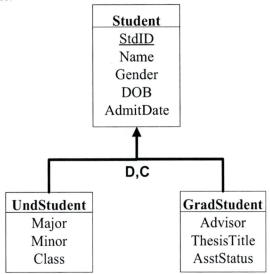

Figure 6.CP6: ERD for Conversion Problem 6

7. Convert the ERD shown in Figure 6.CP7 into tables. List the conversion rules used and the resulting changes to the tables.

Figure 6.CP7: ERD for Conversion Problem 7

8. Convert the ERD shown in Figure 6.CP8 into tables. List the conversion rules used and the resulting changes to the tables.

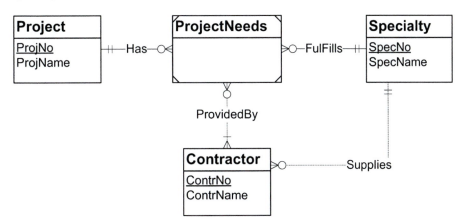

Figure 6.CP8: ERD for Conversion Problem 8

205

9. Convert the ERD shown in Figure 6.CP9 into tables. List the conversion rules used and the resulting changes to the tables.

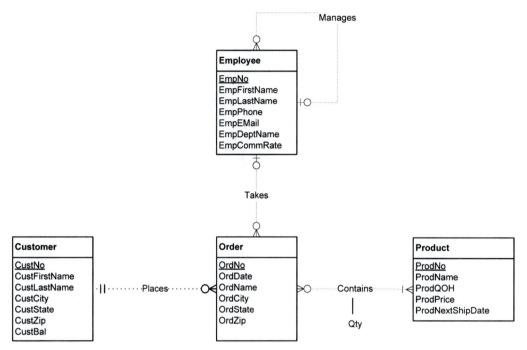

Figure 6.CP9: ERD for Conversion Problem 9

10. Convert the ERD shown in Figure 6.CP10 into tables. List the conversion rules used and the resulting changes to the tables.

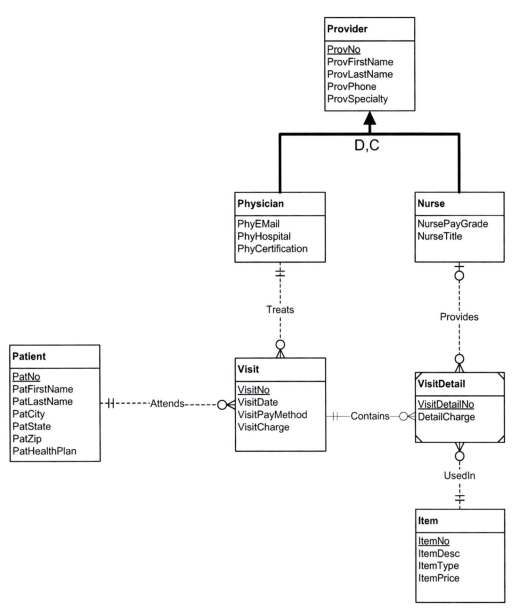

Figure 6.CP10: ERD for Conversion Problem 10

11. Convert the ERD shown in Figure 6.CP11 into tables. List the conversion rules used and the resulting changes to the tables.

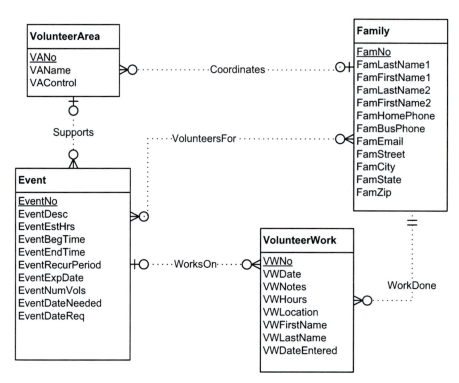

Figure 6.CP11: ERD for Conversion Problem 11

References for Further Study

Chapter 3 of Batini, Ceri, and Navathe (1992) and Chapter 10 of Nijssen and Halpin (1989) provide more details on transformations to refine an ERD. For more details about conversion of generalization hierarchies, consult Chapter 11 of Batini, Ceri, and Navathe. The DBAZine site (www.dbazine.com) and the DevX Database Zone (www.devx.com) have practical advice about database development and data modeling.

7

Normalization of Relational Tables

Learning Objectives

This chapter describes normalization, a technique to eliminate unwanted redundancy in relational tables. After this chapter, the student should have acquired the following knowledge and skills:

- Identify modification anomalies in tables with excessive redundancies
- Define functional dependencies among columns of a table
- Normalize tables by detecting violations of normal forms and applying normalization rules
- Analyze M-way relationships using the concept of independence
- Appreciate the usefulness and limitations of normalization

Overview

Chapters 5 and 6 provided the tools for data modeling, a fundamental skill for database development. You learned about the notation used in entity relationship diagrams, important data modeling patterns, guidelines to avoid common modeling errors, and conversion of entity relationship diagrams (ERDs) into relational tables. You applied this knowledge to construct ERDs for small, narrative problems. This chapter extends your database design skills by presenting normalization techniques to remove redundancy in relational tables.

Redundancies can cause insert, update, and delete operations to produce unexpected side effects known as modification anomalies. This chapter prescribes normalization techniques to remove modification anomalies caused by redundancies. You will learn about functional dependencies, several normal forms, and a procedure to generate tables without redundancies. In addition, you will learn how to analyze M-way relationships for redundancies. This chapter concludes by briefly presenting additional normal forms and discussing the usefulness and limitations of normalization techniques in the database development process.

7.1 Overview of Relational Database Design

After converting an ERD to relational tables, your work is not yet finished. You need to analyze the tables for redundancies that can make the tables difficult to use. This section describes why redundancies can make a table difficult to use and presents an important kind of constraint to analyze redundancies.

7.1.1 Avoidance of Modification Anomalies

A good database design ensures that users can change the contents of a database without unexpected side effects. For example, with a university database, a user should be able to insert a new course without having to simultaneously insert a new offering of the course and a new student enrolled in the course. Likewise, when a student is deleted from the database due to graduation, course data should not be inadvertently lost. These problems are examples of modification anomalies, unexpected side effects that occur when changing the contents of a table with excessive redundancies. A good database design avoids modification anomalies by eliminating excessive redundancies.

> **Modification Anomaly:** an unexpected side effect that occurs when changing the data in a table with excessive redundancies.

To understand more precisely the impact of modification anomalies, let us consider a poorly designed database. Imagine that a university database consists of the single table shown in Table

7-1. Such a poor design[21] makes it easy to identify anomalies. The following list describes some of the problems with this design.

Table 7-1: Sample Data for the Big University Database Table

STDNO	STDCITY	STDCLASS	OFFERNO	OFFTERM	OFFYEAR	ENRGRADE	COURSENO	CRSDESC
S1	SEATTLE	JUN	01	FALL	2008	3.5	C1	DB
S1	SEATTLE	JUN	02	FALL	2008	3.3	C2	VB
S2	BOTHELL	JUN	03	SPRING	2009	3.1	C3	OO
S2	BOTHELL	JUN	02	FALL	2008	3.4	C2	VB

- This table has insertion anomalies. An <u>insertion anomaly</u> occurs when extra data beyond the desired data must be added to the database. For example, to insert a course, it is necessary to know a student and an offering because the combination of *StdNo* and *OfferNo* is the primary key. Remember that a row cannot exist with null values for part of its primary key.
- This table has update anomalies. An <u>update anomaly</u> occurs when it is necessary to change multiple rows to modify only a single fact. For example, if we change the *StdClass* of student S1, two rows must be changed. If S1 was enrolled in 10 classes, 10 rows must be changed.
- This table has deletion anomalies. A <u>deletion anomaly</u> occurs whenever deleting a row inadvertently causes other data to be deleted. For example, if we delete the enrollment of S2 in O3 (third row), we lose the information about offering O3 and course C3.

To deal with these anomalies, users may circumvent them (such as using a default primary key to insert a new course) or database programmers may write code to prevent inadvertent loss of data. A better solution is to modify the table design to remove the redundancies that cause the anomalies.

7.1.2 Functional Dependencies

Functional dependencies are important tools when analyzing a table for excessive redundancies. A functional dependency is a constraint about the database contents. Constraints can be characterized as value-based versus value-neutral (Figure 7.1). A <u>value-based</u> constraint involves a comparison of a column to a constant using a comparison operator such as <, =, or >. For example, age ≥ 21 is an important value-based constraint in a database used to restrict sales of alcohol to minors. A <u>value-neutral</u> constraint involves a comparison of columns. For example, a value-neutral constraint is that retirement age should be greater than current age in a database for retirement planning.

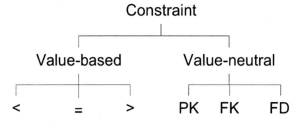

Figure 7.1: Classification of Database Constraints

---

[21] This single-table design is not as extreme as it may seem. Users without proper database training often design a database using a single table.

Primary key (PK) and foreign key (FK) constraints are important kinds of value-neutral constraints. A primary key can take any value as long as it does not match the primary key value in an existing row. A foreign key constraint requires that the value of a column in one table match the value of a primary key in another table.

A functional dependency is another important kind of value-neutral constraint. A funnctional dependency (FD) is a constraint about two or more columns of a table. *X* determines *Y* ($X \to Y$) if there exists at most one value of *Y* for every value of *X*. The word function comes from mathematics where a function gives one value. For example, student number determines city (*StdNo* → *StdCity*) in the university database table if there is at most one city value for every student number. A column appearing on the left-hand side of an FD is called a determinant or, alternatively, an LHS for left-hand side. In this example, *StdNo* is a determinant.

> **Functional Dependency**: a constraint about two or more columns of a table. X determines Y (X → Y) if there exists at most one value of Y for every value of X.

You can also think about functional dependencies as identifying potential candidate keys. By stating that *X → Y*, if *X* and *Y* are placed together in a table without other columns, *X* is a candidate key. Every determinant (LHS) is a candidate key if it is placed in a table with the other columns that it determines. For example, if *StdNo*, *StdCity*, and *StdClass* are placed in a table together and *StdNo → StdCity* and *StdNo → StdClass* then *StdNo* is a candidate key. If there are no other candidate keys, a determinant will become the primary key if it does not allow null values.

Functional Dependency Lists and Diagrams

A simple organization of FDs is to list them, grouped by LHS as shown in Figure 7-2. As you will see, this arrangement facilitates the normalization process.

Table 7-2: List of FDs for the University Database Table

StdNo → StdCity, StdClass
OfferNo → OffTerm, OffYear, CourseNo, CrsDesc
CourseNo → CrsDesc
StdNo, OfferNo → EnrGrade

As an alternative organization, a functional dependency diagram compactly displays the functional dependencies of a particular table. You should arrange FDs to visually group columns sharing the same determinant. In Figure 7.2, it is easy to spot the dependencies where *StdNo* is the determinant. By examining the position and height of lines, you can see that the combination of *StdNo* and *OfferNo* determines *EnrGrade* whereas *OfferNo* alone determines *OffTerm*, *OffYear*, and *CourseNo*. With a large number of FDs, functional dependency diagrams can be difficult to draw and understand. Thus, FD lists are preferred to FD diagrams even though FD lists can be long for a large collection of FDs.

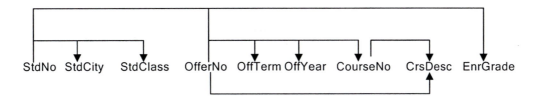

Figure 7.2: Dependency Diagram for the Big University Database Table

Identifying Functional Dependencies

Besides understanding the functional dependency definition and notation, database designers must be able to identify functional dependencies when collecting database requirements. In problem narratives, some functional dependencies can be identified by statements about uniqueness. For example, a user may state that each course offering has a unique offering number along with the year and term of the offering. From this statement, the designer should assert that *OfferNo →* *OffYear* and *OffTerm*. You can also identify functional dependencies in a table design resulting from the conversion of an ERD. Functional dependencies would be asserted for each unique column (primary key or other candidate key) with the unique column as the LHS and other columns in the table on the right-hand side (RHS).

Although functional dependencies derived from statements about uniqueness are easy to identify, functional dependencies derived from statements about 1-M relationships can be confusing to identify. When you see a statement about a 1-M relationship, the functional dependency is derived from the child-to-parent direction, not the parent-to-child direction. For example, the statement "A faculty teaches many offerings but an offering is taught by one faculty," defines a functional dependency from a unique column of offering to a unique column of faculty such as *OfferNo → FacNo*. Novice designers sometimes incorrectly assert that *FacNo* determines a collection of *OfferNo* values. This statement is not correct because a functional dependency must allow at most one associated value, not a collection of values.

> **FDs for 1-M relationships**: assert an FD in the child-to-parent direction of a 1-M relationship. Do not assert an FD for the parent-to-child direction because each LHS value can be associated with at most one RHS value.

Functional dependencies in which the LHS is not a primary or candidate key can also be difficult to identify. These FDs are especially important to identify after converting an ERD to a table design. You should carefully look for FDs in which the LHS is not a candidate key or primary key. You should also consider FDs in tables with a combined primary or candidate key in which the LHS is part of a key, but not the entire key. The presentation of normal forms in Section 7.2 explains that these kinds of FDs can lead to modification anomalies.

Another important consideration in asserting functional dependencies is the minimalism of the LHS. It is important to distinguish when one column alone is the determinant versus a combination of columns. An FD in which the LHS contains more than one column usually represents an M-N relationship. For example, the statement "The order quantity is collected for each product purchased in an order," translates to the FD *OrdNo, ProdNo → OrdQty*. Order quantity depends on the combination of order number and product number, not just one of these columns.

Part of the confusion about the minimalism of the LHS is due to the meaning of columns in the left-hand versus right-hand side of a dependency. To record that student number determines city and class, you can write either *StdNo → StdCity, StdClass* (more compact) or *StdNo →* *StdCity* and *StdNo → StdClass* (less compact). If you assume that the e-mail address is also unique for each student, then you can write *Email → StdCity, StdClass*. You should not write *StdNo, Email → StdCity, StdClass* because these FDs imply that the combination of *StdNo* and *Email* is the determinant. Thus, you should write FDs so that the LHS does not contain unneeded columns[22]. The prohibition against unneeded columns for determinants is the same as the prohibition against unneeded columns in candidate keys. Both determinants and candidate keys must be minimal.

> **Minimal Determinant**: the determinant (column(s) appearing on the LHS of a functional dependency) must not contain extra columns. This minimalism requirement is similar to the minimalism requirement for candidate keys.

---

[22] This concept is more properly known as "full functional dependence." Full functional dependence means that the LHS is minimal.

Eliminating FDs using Sample Data

A functional dependency cannot be proven to exist by examining the rows of a table. However, you can falsify a functional dependency (i.e., prove that a functional dependency does not exist) by examining the rows of a table. For example, in the university database table (Table 7-1) you can conclude that *StdClass* does not determine *StdCity* because there are two rows with the same value for *StdClass* but a different value for *StdCity*. Thus, it is sometimes helpful to examine sample rows in a table to eliminate potential functional dependencies. There are several commercial database design tools that automate the process of eliminating dependencies through examination of sample rows. Ultimately, the database designer must make the final decision about the functional dependencies that exist in a table.

> **Eliminating Potential FDs**: using sample data to eliminate potential FDs. If two rows have the same value for the LHS but different values for the RHS, an FD cannot exist. Some commercial normalization programs use this technique to help a user determine FDs.

To demonstrate the usage of sample data to eliminate potential FDs, the following list explains elimination of FDs with *OffTerm* as the LHS using the sample data in Table 7-1. Note that falsification of an FD requires two rows. Although one would not normally consider FDs with *OffTerm* as a LHS, the elimination technique may be useful for plausible LHS columns such as *OfferNo* and *StdNo*.

OffTerm → *StdNo* is falsified by the first and last rows.
OffTerm → *StdCity* is falsified by the first and last rows.
OffTerm → *StdClass* is not falsified by any pair of rows.
OffTerm → *OfferNo* is falsified by the first and second rows.
OffTerm → *OffYear* is not falsified by any pair of rows.
OffTerm → *EnrGrade* is falsified by the first two rows and the first and last two rows.
OffTerm → *CourseNo* is falsified by the first and second rows.
OffTerm → *CrsDesc* is falsified by the first and second rows.

Since *OffTerm* is not a determinant in any FD, an additional row (row 5) is added in Table 7-2 to falsify FDs not eliminated by rows in Table 7-1. The FDs eliminated with the additional row in Table 7-3 are listed below.

OffTerm → *StdClass* is falsified by all three pairs of rows: <1,5>, <2,5>, and <4,5>.
OffTerm → *OffYear* is falsified by all three pairs of rows: <1,5>, <2,5>, and <4,5>.

Table 7-3: Additional Row in the Sample Data for the Big University Database Table

STDNO	STDCITY	STDCLASS	OFFERNO	OFFTERM	OFFYEAR	ENRGRADE	COURSENO	CRSDESC
S1	SEATTLE	JUN	01	FALL	2008	3.5	C1	DB
S1	SEATTLE	JUN	02	FALL	2008	3.3	C2	VB
S2	BOTHELL	JUN	03	SPRING	2009	3.1	C3	OO
S2	BOTHELL	JUN	02	FALL	2008	3.4	C2	VB
S3	DENVER	SEN	04	FALL	2007	3.0	C3	OO

7.2 Normal Forms

Normalization is the process of removing redundancy in a table so that the table is easier to modify. A number of normal forms have been developed to remove redundancies. A normal form is a rule about allowable dependencies. Each normal form removes certain kinds of redundancies. As shown in Figure 7.3, first normal form (1NF) is the starting point. All tables without repeating groups are in 1NF. 2NF is stronger than 1NF. Only a subset of the 1NF tables is in 2NF. Each successive normal form refines the previous normal form to remove additional kinds of redundancies. Because BCNF (Boyce-Codd Normal Form) is a revised (and stronger) definition for 3NF, 3NF and BCNF are shown in the same part of Figure 7.3.

2NF and 3NF/BCNF are rules about functional dependencies. If the functional dependencies for a table match the specified pattern, the table is in the specified normal form. 3NF/BCNF is the most important in practice because higher normal forms involve other kinds of dependencies that are less common and more difficult to understand. Therefore, most emphasis is given to 3NF/BCNF. Section 7.3 presents 4NF as a way to reason about M-way relationships. Section 7.4 presents 5NF and DKNF (domain key normal form) to show that higher normal forms have been proposed. DKNF is the ultimate normal form, but it remains an ideal rather than a practical normal form.

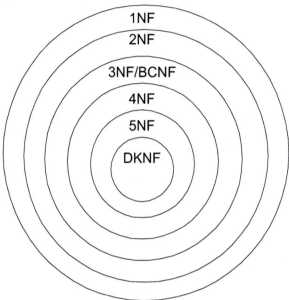

Figure 7.3: Relationship of Normal Forms

7.2.1 First Normal Form

1NF prohibits nesting or repeating groups in tables. A table not in 1NF is unnormalized or nonnormalized. In Table 7-4, the university table is unnormalized because the two rows contain repeating groups or nested tables. To convert an unnormalized table into 1NF, you replace each value of a repeating group with a row. In a new row, you copy the nonrepeating columns. You can see the conversion by comparing Table 7-4 with Table 7-1 (two rows with repeating groups versus four rows without repeating groups).

Table 7-4: Unnormalized University Database Table

STDNO	STDCITY	STDCLASS	OFFERNO	OFFTERM	OFFYEAR	ENRGRADE	COURSENO	CRSDESC
S1	SEATTLE	JUN	01	FALL	2008	3.5	C1	DB
			02	FALL	2008	3.3	C2	VB
S2	BOTHELL	JUN	03	SPRING	2009	3.1	C3	OO
			02	FALL	2008	3.4	C2	VB

Because most commercial DBMSs require 1NF tables[23], you normally do not need to convert tables into 1NF. However, you often need to perform the reverse process (1NF tables to unnormalized tables) for report generation and document representation. As discussed in Chapter

---

[23] Although nested tables have been supported since the SQL:1999 standard with commercial support in Oracle, this feature does not appear important in most business applications. Thus, this chapter does not consider the complications of nested tables on normalization.

10, reports use nesting to show relationships. As discussed in Chapter 18, the eXtensible Markup Language (XML) also uses a hierarchical representation of documents. However, the underlying tables do not have nesting.

7.2.2 Second and Third Normal Forms

The definitions of 2NF and 3NF distinguish between key and nonkey columns[24]. A column is a key column if it is part of a candidate key or a candidate key by itself. Recall that a candidate key is a minimal set of column(s) that has unique values in a table. Minimality means that none of the columns can be removed without losing the uniqueness property. Nonkey columns are any other columns. In Table 7-1, the combination of (*StdNo*, *OfferNo*) is the only candidate key. Other columns such as *StdCity* and *StdClass* are nonkey columns.

The goal of 2NF and 3NF is to produce tables in which every key determines the other columns. An easy way to remember the definitions of both 2NF and 3NF is shown in the following definition.

> **Combined Definition of 2NF and 3NF**: a table is in 3NF if each nonkey column depends on all candidate keys, whole candidate keys, and nothing but candidate keys.[25]

Second Normal Form

To understand this definition, let us break it down to the 2NF and 3NF parts. The 2NF definition uses the first part of the definition as shown in the following definition.

> **2NF Definition**: a table is in 2NF if each nonkey column depends on all candidate keys, not on a subset of any candidate key.

To see if a table is in 2NF, you should look for FDs that violate the definition. An FD in which part of a key determines a nonkey column violates 2NF. If the key contains only one column, the table is in 2NF. Looking at the dependency diagram in Figure 7.2, you can easily detect violations of 2NF. For example, *StdCity* is a nonkey column but *StdNo*, not the entire primary key (combination of *StdNo* and *OfferNo*), determines it. The only FDs that satisfy the 2NF definition are *StdNo*, *OfferNo* → *EnrGrade* and *CourseNo* → *CrsDesc*.

> **2NF Violation**: an FD in which part of key determines a nonkey violates 2NF. An FD containing a single column LHS cannot violate 2NF.

To place the table into 2NF, split the original table into smaller tables that satisfy the 2NF definition. In each smaller table, the entire primary key (not part of the primary key) should determine the nonkey columns. The splitting process involves the project operator of relational algebra. For the university database table, three projection operations split it so that the underlined primary key determines the nonkey columns in each table below.

> **UnivTable1** (<u>StdNo</u>, StdCity, StdClass)
> **UnivTable2** (<u>OfferNo</u>, OffTerm, OffYear, CourseNo, CrsDesc)
> **UnivTable3** (<u>StdNo, OfferNo</u>, EnrGrade)

---

[24] In the literature, key columns are known as prime, and nonkey columns as nonprime.

[25] You can remember this definition by its analogy to the traditional justice oath: "Do you swear to tell the truth, the whole truth, and nothing but the truth, ...".

The splitting process should preserve the original table in two ways. First, the original table should be recoverable by using natural join operations on the smaller tables. Second, the FDs in the original table should be derivable from the FDs in the smaller tables. Technically, the splitting process is known as a nonloss, dependency-preserving decomposition. Some of the references at the end of this chapter explain the theory underlying the splitting process.

After splitting the original table into smaller tables, you should add referential integrity constraints to connect the tables. Whenever a table is split, the splitting column becomes a foreign key in the table in which it is not a primary key. For example, *StdNo* is a foreign key in *UnivTable3* because the original university table was split on this column. Therefore, define a referential integrity constraint stating that *UnivTable3.StdNo* refers to *UnivTable1.StdNo*. The *UnivTable3* table is repeated below with its referential integrity constraints.

UnivTable3 (StdNo, OfferNo, EnrGrade)
    FOREIGN KEY (StdNo) REFERENCES UnivTable1

    FOREIGN KEY (OfferNo) REFERENCES UnivTable2

Third Normal Form

UnivTable2 still has modification anomalies. For example, you cannot add a new course unless the *OfferNo* column value is known. To eliminate the modification anomalies, the definition of 3NF should be applied.

> **3NF Definition:** a table is in 3NF if it is in 2NF and each nonkey column depends only on candidate keys, not on other nonkey columns.

An FD in which one nonkey column determines another nonkey column violates 3NF. In *UnivTable2* above, the FD (*CourseNo* $\rightarrow$ *CrsDesc*) violates 3NF because both columns, *CourseNo* and *CrsDesc* are nonkey. To fix the violation, split *UnivTable2* into two tables, as shown below, and add a foreign key constraint.

UnivTable2-1 (OfferNo, OffTerm, OffYear, CourseNo)
    FOREIGN KEY (CourseNo) REFERENCES UnivTable2-2

UnivTable2-2 (CourseNo, CrsDesc)

An equivalent way to define 3NF is that 3NF prohibits <u>transitive dependencies</u>. A transitive dependency is a functional dependency derived by the law of transitivity. The law of transitivity says that if an object A is related to B and B is related to C, then you can conclude that A is related to C. For example, the < operator obeys the transitive law: A < B and B < C implies that A < C. Functional dependencies, like the < operator, obey the law of transitivity: A $\rightarrow$ B, B $\rightarrow$ C, then A $\rightarrow$ C. In Figure 7.2, *OfferNo* $\rightarrow$ *CrsDesc* is a transitive dependency derived from *OfferNo* $\rightarrow$ *CourseNo* and *CourseNo* $\rightarrow$ *CrsDesc*.

> **Transitive Dependency:** an FD derived by the law of transitivity. Transitive FDs should not be recorded as input to the normalization process.

Because transitive dependencies are easy to overlook, the preferred definition of 3NF does not use transitive dependencies. In addition, you will learn in Section 7.2.4 that you should omit derived dependencies such as transitive dependencies in your analysis.

Combined Example of 2NF and 3NF

The big patient table as depicted in Table 7-5 provides another example for applying your knowledge of 2NF and 3NF. The big patient table contains facts about patients, health care providers, patient visits to a clinic, and diagnoses made by health care providers. The big patient table contains a combined primary key consisting of the combination of *VisitNo* and *ProvNo* (provider number). Like the big university database table depicted in Table 7-1, the big patient

216

table reflects a poor table design with many redundancies. Table 7-6 lists the associated FDs. You should verify that the sample rows in Table 7-5 do not contradict the FDs.

Table 7-5: Sample Data for the Big Patient Table

VISITNO	VISITDATE	**PATNO**	PATAGE	PATCITY	**PATZIP**	PROVNO	PROVSPECIALTY	DIAGNOSIS
V10020	1/13/2009	P1	35	DENVER	80217	D1	INTERNIST	EAR INFECTION
V10020	1/13/2009	P1	35	DENVER	80217	D2	NURSE PRACTITIONER	INFLUENZA
V93030	1/20/2009	P3	17	ENGLEWOOD	80113	D2	NURSE PRACTITIONER	PREGNANCY
V82110	1/18/2009	P2	60	BOULDER	85932	D3	CARDIOLOGIST	MURMUR

Table 7-6: List of FDs for the Big Patient Table

PatNo → PatAge, PatCity, PatZip
PatZip → PatCity
ProvNo → ProvSpecialty
VisitNo → PatNo, VisitDate, PatAge, PatCity, PatZip
VisitNo, ProvNo → Diagnosis

As previously discussed, FDs that violate 2NF involve part of a key determining a nonkey. Many of the FDs in Table 7-6 violate the 2NF definition because the combination of *VisitNo* and *ProvNo* is the primary key. Thus, the FDs with only *VisitNo* or *ProvNo* in the LHS violate 2NF. To alleviate the 2NF violations, split the big patient table so that the violating FDs are associated with separate tables. In the revised list of tables, *PatientTable1* and *PatientTable2* contain the violating FDs. *PatientTable3* retains the remaining columns.

PatientTable1 (ProvNo, ProvSpecialty)
PatientTable2 (VisitNo, VisitDate, PatNo, PatAge, PatCity, PatZip)
PatientTable3 (VisitNo, ProvNo, Diagnosis)
  FOREIGN KEY (VisitNo) REFERENCES PatientTable2

  FOREIGN KEY (ProvNo) REFERENCES PatientTable1

PatientTable1 and *PatientTable3* are in 3NF because there are no nonkey columns that determine other nonkey columns. However, *PatientTable2* violates 3NF because the FDs *PatNo → PatZip, PatAge* and *PatZip → PatCity* involve nonkey columns that determine other nonkey columns. To alleviate the 3NF violations, split *PatientTable2* into three tables as shown in the revised table list. In the revised list of tables, *PatientTable2-1* and *PatientTable2-2* contain the violating FDs, while *PatientTable2-3* retains the remaining columns.

PatientTable2-1 (PatNo, PatAge, PatZip)
  FOREIGN KEY (PatZip) REFERENCES PatientTable2-2

PatientTable2-2 (PatZip, PatCity)
PatientTable2-3 (VisitNo, PatNo, VisitDate)
  FOREIGN KEY (PatNo) REFERENCES PatientTable2-1

Using 2NF and 3NF requires two normalization steps. The normalization process can be performed in one step using Boyce-Codd normal form, as presented in the next subsection.

7.2.3 Boyce-Codd Normal Form

The revised 3NF definition, known as Boyce-Codd normal form (BCNF), is a better definition because it is simpler and covers a special case omitted by the original 3NF definition. The BCNF definition is simpler because it does not refer to 2NF.

BCNF Definition: a table is in BCNF if every determinant is a candidate key.

Violations of BCNF involve FDs in which the determinant (LHS) is not a candidate key. In a poor table design such as the big university database table (sample data in Table 7-1 and FD list in Table 7-2), you can easily detect violations of BCNF. For example, *StdNo* is a determinant but not a candidate key (it is part of a candidate key but not a candidate key itself). The only FD in Table 7-2 that does not violate BCNF is *StdNo, OfferNo → EnrGrade*.

For another example, let us apply the BCNF definition to the FDs of the big patient table shown in Table 7-6. All of the FDs in Table 7-6 violate the BCNF definition except the last FD (*VisitNo, ProvNo → Diagnosis*). All of the other FDs have determinants that are not candidate keys (part of a candidate key in some cases but not an entire candidate key). To alleviate the BCNF violations, split the big patient table into smaller tables. Each determinant should be placed into a separate table along with the columns that it determines. The result is identical to the split for 3NF (see the result of the last 3NF example) with the *PatientTable1*, *PatientTable3*, *PatientTable2-1*, *PatientTable2-2*, and *PatientTable2-3* tables.

Relationship between 3NF and BCNF

Although BCNF and 3NF usually produce the same result, BCNF is a stronger definition than 3NF. Thus, every table in BCNF is by definition in 3NF. BCNF covers two special cases not covered by 3NF: (1) part of a key determines part of a key and (2) a nonkey column determines part of a key. These situations are only possible if there are multiple composite, candidate keys (candidate keys with multiple columns). Analyzing dependencies of tables with multiple composite candidate keys is difficult. Fortunately, tables with multiple, composite candidate keys are not common.

UnivTable4 depicts a table in 3NF but not in BCNF according to the first exception (part of a key determines part of a key). *UnivTable4* (Figure 7.4) has two candidate keys: the combination of *StdNo* and *OfferNo* (the primary key) and the combination of *Email* and *OfferNo*. In the FDs for *UnivTable4* (Figure 7.4), you should note that *StdNo* and *Email* determine each other. Because of the FDs between *StdNo* and *Email*, *UnivTable4* contains a redundancy as *Email* is repeated for each *StdNo*. For example, the first two rows contain the same e-mail address because the *StdNo* value is the same. The following points explain why *UnivTable4* is in 3NF but not in BCNF.

3NF: *UnivTable4* is in 3NF because the only nonkey column (*EnrGrade*) depends on each candidate key (not just part of a candidate key). Since *EnrGrade* is the only nonkey column, it cannot depend on other nonkey columns.

BCNF: The dependencies between *StdNo* and *Email* violate BCNF. Both *StdNo* and *Email* are determinants, but neither is an entire candidate key although each column is part of a candidate key. To eliminate the redundancy, you should split *UnivTable4* into two tables, as shown in Figure 7.4.

UnivTable4			
StdNo	OfferNo	Email	EnrGrade
S1	O1	joe@bigu	3.5
S1	O2	joe@bigu	3.6
S2	O1	mary@bigu	3.8
S2	O3	mary@bigu	3.5

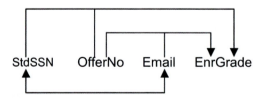

UnivTable4-1 (<u>OfferNo</u>, <u>StdNo</u>, EnrGrade)
　　　FOREIGN KEY (StdNo) REFERENCES UnivTable4-2

UnivTable4-2 (<u>StdNo</u>, Email)

Figure 7.4: Sample Rows, Dependency Diagram, and Normalized Tables for *UnivTable4*

218

UnivTable5 (Figure 7.5) depicts another example of a table with multiple, composite candidate keys. Like *UnivTable4*, *UnivTable5* is in 3NF but not in BCNF, because part of a key determines part of a key. *UnivTable5* has two candidate keys: the combination of *StdNo* and *AdvisorNo* (the primary key) and the combination of *StdNo* and *Major*. *UnivTable5* has a redundancy as *Major* is repeated for each row with the same *AdvisorNo* value. The following points explain why *UnivTable5* is in 3NF but not in BCNF.

> 3NF: *UnivTable5* is in 3NF because *Major* is a key column. *Status* is the only nonkey column. Since *Status* depends on the entire candidate keys (<*StdNo, AdvisorNo*> and <*StdNo, Major*>), *UnivTable5* is in 3NF.
> BCNF: The dependency diagram (Figure 7.5) shows that *AdvisorNo* is a determinant but not a candidate key by itself. Thus, *UnivTable5* is not in BCNF. To eliminate the redundancy, you should split *UnivTable5* into two tables as shown in Figure 7.5.

UNIVTABLE5			
STDNO	ADVISORNO	MAJOR	STATUS
S1	A1	IS	COMPLETED
S1	A2	FIN	PENDING
S2	A1	IS	PENDING
S2	A3	FIN	COMPLETED

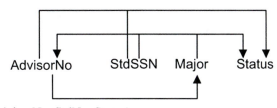

UnivTable5-1 (AdvisorNo, StdNo, Status)
  FOREIGN KEY (AdvisorNo) REFERENCES UnivTable5-2

UnivTable5-2 (AdvisorNo, Major)

Figure 7.5: Sample Rows, Dependency Diagram, and Normalized Tables for *UnivTable5*

These examples demonstrate two points about normalization. First, tables with multiple, composite candidate keys are difficult to analyze. You need to study the dependencies carefully in each example (Figures 7.4 and 7.5) to understand the conclusions about the normal form violations. Second, most tables in 3NF (even ones with multiple composite, candidate keys) are also in BCNF. The examples in Figures 7.4 and 7.5 were purposely constructed to depict the difference between 3NF and BCNF. The importance of BCNF is that it is a simpler definition and can be applied in the procedure described in the next section.

7.2.4 Simple Synthesis Procedure

The simple synthesis procedure can be used to generate tables satisfying BCNF starting with a list of functional dependencies. The word synthesis means that the individual functional dependencies are combined to construct tables. This usage is similar to other disciplines such as music where synthesis involves combining individual sounds to construct larger units such as melodies, scores, and so on.

Figure 7.6 depicts the steps of the simple synthesis procedure. The first two steps eliminate redundancy by removing extraneous columns and derived FDs. The last three steps produce tables for collections of FDs. The tables produced in the last three steps may not be correct if redundant FDs are not eliminated.

1. Eliminate extraneous columns from the LHS of FDs.
2. Remove derived FDs from the FD list.
3. Arrange the FDs into groups with each group having the same determinant.
4. For each FD group, make a table with the determinant as the primary key. Add referential integrity constraints to connect the tables.
5. Merge tables in which one table contains all columns of the other table.
- Choose the primary key of one of the separate tables as the primary of the new, merged table.
- Define a unique constraint for each other primary key that was not designated as the primary key of the new table.

Figure 7.6: Steps of the Simple Synthesis Procedure

Applying the Simple Synthesis Procedure

To understand this procedure, you can apply it to the FDs of the university database table (Table 7-2). In the first step, there are no extraneous columns in the determinants. To demonstrate an extraneous column, suppose there was the FD *StdNo, StdCity → StdClass*. In this FD, if *StdCity* is removed from the left-hand side, then the FD *StdNo → StdClass* still holds. The *StdCity* column is redundant in the FD and should be removed.

To apply the second step, you need to know how FDs can be derived from other FDs. Although there are a number of ways to derive FDs, the most prominent way is through the law of transitivity as stated in the discussion of 3NF (Section 7.2.2). For our purposes here, we will eliminate only transitively derived FDs in step 2. For details about the other ways to derive FDs, you should consult references listed at the end of the chapter.

In the second step, the FD *OfferNo → CrsDesc* is a transitive dependency because *OfferNo → CourseNo* and *CourseNo → CrsDesc* implies *OfferNo → CrsDesc*. Therefore, you should delete this dependency from the list of FDs.

In the third step, you should group the FDs by determinant. From Table 7-2, you can make the following FD groups:

StdNo → StdCity, StdClass
OfferNo → OffTerm, OffYear, CourseNo
CourseNo → CrsDesc
StdNo, OfferNo → EnrGrade

In the fourth step, you replace each FD group with a table having the common determinant as the primary key. Thus, you have four resulting BCNF tables as shown below. You should add table names for completeness.

Student(StdNo, StdCity, StdClass)
Offering(OfferNo, OffTerm, OffYear, CourseNo)
Course(CourseNo, CrsDesc)
Enrollment   (StdNo, OfferNo, EnrGrade)

After defining the tables, you should add referential integrity constraints to connect the tables. To detect the need for a referential integrity constraint, you should look for a primary key in one table appearing in other tables. For example, *CourseNo* is the primary key of *Course* but it also appears in *Offering*. Therefore, you should define a referential integrity constraint indicating that *Offering.CourseNo* refers to *Course.CourseNo*. The tables are repeated below with the addition of referential integrity constraints.

220

Student(<u>StdNo</u>, StdCity, StdClass)
Offering(<u>OfferNo</u>, OffTerm, OffYear, CourseNo)
        FOREIGN KEY (CourseNo) REFERENCES Course
Course(<u>CourseNo</u>, CrsDesc)
Enrollment(<u>StdNo, OfferNo</u>, EnrGrade)
        FOREIGN KEY (StdNo) REFERENCES Student
        FOREIGN KEY (OfferNo) REFERENCES Offering

The fifth step is not necessary because the FDs for this problem are simple. When there are multiple candidate keys for a table, the fifth step is necessary. For example, if *Email* is added as a column, then the FDs *Email* → *StdNo* and *StdNo* → *Email* should be added to the list. Note that the FDs *Email* → *StdCity*, *StdClass* should not be added to the list because these FDs can be transitively derived from the other FDs. As a result of step 3, another group of FDs is added. In step 4, a new table (*Student2*) is added with *Email* as the primary key. Because the *Student* table contains the columns of the *Student2* table, the tables (*Student* and *Student2*) are merged in step 5. One of the candidate keys (*StdNo* or *Email*) is chosen as the primary key. Since *Email* is chosen as the primary key, a unique constraint is defined for *StdNo*.

        Email → *StdNo*
        StdNo → Email

Student2   (<u>Email</u>, StdNo, StdCity, StdClass)

        UNIQUE(StdNo)

As this additional example demonstrates, multiple candidate keys do not violate BCNF. The fifth step of the simple synthesis procedure creates tables with multiple candidate keys because it merges tables. Multiple candidate keys do not violate 3NF either. There is no reason to split a table just because it has multiple candidate keys. Splitting a table with multiple candidate keys can slow query performance due to extra joins.

> **Multiple Candidate Keys**: a common misconception by novice database developers is that a table with multiple candidate keys violates BCNF. Multiple candidate keys do not violate BCNF or 3NF. Thus, you should not split a table just because it has multiple candidate keys.

You can use the simple synthesis procedure to analyze simple dependency structures. Most tables resulting from a conversion of an ERD should have simple dependency structures because the data modeling process has already done much of the normalization process. Most tables should be nearly normalized after the conversion process.

For complex dependency structures, you should use a commercial design tool to perform normalization. To make the synthesis procedure easy to use, some of the details have been omitted. In particular, step 2 can be rather involved because there are more ways to derive dependencies than transitivity. Even checking for transitivity can be difficult with many columns. The full details of step 2 can be found in references cited at the end of the chapter. Even if you understand the complex details, step 2 cannot be done manually for complex dependency structures. For complex dependency structures, you need to use a CASE tool even if you are an experienced database designer.

Another Example Using the Simple Synthesis Procedure

To gain more experience with the Simple Synthesis Procedure, you should understand another example. This example describes a database to track reviews of papers submitted to an academic conference. Prospective authors submit papers for review and possible acceptance in the published conference proceedings. Here are more details about authors, papers, reviews, and reviewers:

- Author information includes the unique author number, the name, the mailing address, and the unique but optional electronic address.
- Paper information includes the primary author, the unique paper number, the title, the abstract, and the review status (pending, accepted, rejected).

- Reviewer information includes the unique reviewer number, the name, the mailing address, and a unique but optional electronic address.
- A completed review includes the reviewer number, the date, the paper number, comments to the authors, comments to the program chairperson, and ratings (overall, originality, correctness, style, and relevance). The combination of reviewer number and paper number identifies a review.

Before beginning the procedure, you must identify the FDs in the problem. The following is a list of FDs for the problem:

> AuthNo → AuthName, AuthEmail, AuthAddress
> AuthEmail → AuthNo
> PaperNo → Primary-AuthNo, Title, Abstract, Status
> RevNo → RevName, RevEmail, RevAddress
> RevEmail → RevNo
> RevNo, PaperNo → Auth-Comm, Prog-Comm, Date, Rating1, Rating2, Rating3, Rating4, Rating5

Because the LHS is minimal in each FD, the first step is finished. The second step is not necessary because there are no transitive dependencies. Note that the FDs *AuthEmail → AuthName, AuthAddress*, and *RevEmail → RevName, RevAddress* can be transitively derived. If any of these FDs were part of the original list, they should be removed. For each of the six FD groups, you should define a table. In the last step, you combine the FD groups with *AuthNo* and *AuthEmail* and *RevNo* and *RevEmail* as determinants. In addition, you should add unique constraints for *AuthEmail* and *RevEmail* because these columns were not selected as the primary keys of the new tables.

> **Author**(AuthNo, AuthName, AuthEmail, AuthAddress)
>   UNIQUE (AuthEmail)
> **Paper**(PaperNo, Primary-Auth, Title, Abstract, Status)
>   FOREIGN KEY (Primary-Auth) REFERENCES Author
> **Reviewer**(RevNo, RevName, RevEmail, RevAddress)
>   UNIQUE (RevEmail)
> **Review**(PaperNo, RevNo, Auth-Comm, Prog-Comm, Date, Rating1, Rating2, Rating3, Rating4, Rating5)
>   FOREIGN KEY (PaperNo) REFERENCES Paper
>   FOREIGN KEY (RevNo) REFERENCES Reviewer

7.3 Refining M-Way Relationships

Beyond BCNF, a remaining concern is the analysis of M-way relationships. Recall that M-way relationships are represented by associative entity types in the Crow's Foot ERD notation. In the conversion process, an associative entity type converts into a table with a combined primary key consisting of three or more components. The concept of independence, underlying 4NF, is an important tool used to analyze M-way relationships. Using the concept of independence, you may find that an M-way relationship should be split into two or more binary relationships to avoid redundancy. In Chapter 12, you will use forms to analyze the need for M-way relationships. The following sections describe the concept of relationship independence and 4NF.

7.3.1 Relationship Independence

Before you study how independence can influence a database design, let us discuss the meaning of independence in statistics. Two variables are statistically independent if knowing something about one variable tells you nothing about another variable. More precisely, two variables are independent if the probability of both variables (the joint probability) can be derived from the probability of each variable alone. For example, one variable may be the age of a rock and another variable may be the age of the person holding the rock. Because the age of a rock, and the age of a person holding the rock are unrelated, these variables are considered independent. However, the age of a person and a person's marital status are related. The value of a person's age influences the probability of being single, married, or divorced. If two variables are independent, it is redundant to store data about how they are related. You can use probabilities about individual variables to derive joint probabilities.

The concept of <u>relationship independence</u> is similar to statistical independence. If two relationships are independent (that is, not related), it is redundant to store data about a third relationship. You can derive the third relationship by combining the two essential relationships through a join operation. If you store the derived relationship, modification anomalies can result. Thus, the essential idea of relationship independence is not to store relationships that can be derived by joining other (independent) relationships.

> **Relationship Independence**: a relationship that can be derived from two independent relationships.

Relationship Independence Example

To clarify relationship independence, consider the associative entity type *Enroll* (Figure 7.7) representing a three-way relationship among students, offerings, and textbooks. The *Enroll* entity type converts to the *Enroll* table (Table 7-7) that consists only of a combined primary key: *StdNo*, *OfferNo*, and *TextNo*.

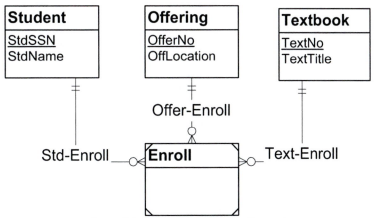

Figure 7.7: M-way Relationship Example

Table 7-7: Sample Rows of the *Enroll* Table

StdNo	OfferNo	TextNo
S1	O1	T1
S1	O2	T2
S1	O1	T2
S1	O2	T1

The design question is whether the *Enroll* table has redundancies. If there is redundancy, modification anomalies may result. The *Enroll* table is in BCNF, so there are no anomalies due to functional dependencies. However, the concept of independence leads to the discovery of redundancies. The *Enroll* table can be divided into three combinations of columns representing three binary relationships: *StdNo-OfferNo* representing the relationship between students and offerings, *OfferNo-TextNo* representing the relationship between offerings and textbooks, and *StdNo-TextNo* representing the relationship between students and textbooks. If any of the binary relationships can be derived from the other two, there is a redundancy.

- The relationship between students and offerings (*StdNo-OfferNo*) cannot be derived from the other two relationships. For example, suppose that textbook T1 is used in two offerings, O1 and O2 and by two students, S1 and S2. Knowledge about these two facts does not determine the relationship between students and offerings. For example, S1 could be enrolled in O1 or perhaps O2.
- Likewise, the relationship between offerings and textbooks (*OfferNo-TextNo*) cannot be derived. A professor's choice for a collection of textbooks cannot be derived by knowing who enrolls in an offering and what textbooks a student uses.
- However, the relationship between students and textbooks (*StdNo-TextNo*) can be derived by the other two relationships. For example, if student S1 is enrolled in offering O1 and offering O1 uses textbook T1, then you can conclude that student S1 uses textbook T1 in offering O1. Because the *Student-Offering* and the *Offering-Textbook* relationships are independent, you know the textbooks used by a student without storing the relationship instances.

Because of this independence, the *Enroll* table and the related associative entity type *Enroll* have redundancy. To remove the redundancy, replace the *Enroll* entity type with two binary relationships (Figure 7.8). Each binary relationship converts to a table as shown in Tables 7-8 and 7-9. The *Enroll* and *Orders* tables have no redundancies. For example, to delete a student's enrollment in an offering (say S1 in O1), only one row must be deleted from Table 7-8. In contrast, two rows must be deleted from Table 7-7.

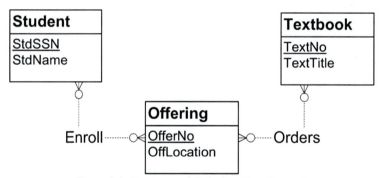

Figure 7.8: Decomposed Relationships Example

Table 7-8: Sample Rows of the Binary *Enroll* Table

StdNo	OfferNo
S1	O1
S1	O2

Table 7-9: Sample Rows of the Binary *Orders* Table

OfferNo	TextNo
O1	T1
O1	T2
O2	T1
O2	T2

If the assumptions change slightly, an argument can be made for an associative entity type representing a three-way relationship. Suppose that the bookstore wants to record textbook purchases by offering and student to estimate textbook demand. Then the relationship between students and textbooks is no longer independent of the other two relationships. Even though a student is enrolled in an offering and the offering uses a textbook, the student may not purchase the textbook (perhaps borrow it) for the offering. In this situation, there is no independence and a three-way relationship is needed. In addition to the M-N relationships in Figure 7.8, there should be a new associative entity type and three 1-M relationships, as shown in Figure 7.9. You need the *Enroll* relationship to record student selections of offerings and the *Orders* relationship to record professor selections of textbooks. The *Purchase* entity type records purchases of textbooks by students in a course offering. However, a purchase cannot be known from the other relationships.

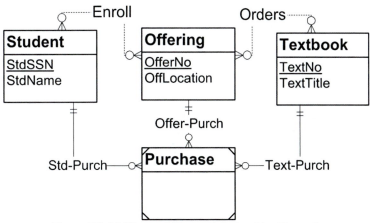

Figure 7.9: M-Way and Binary Relationships Example

7.3.2 Multivalued Dependencies and Fourth Normal Form

In relational database terminology, a relationship that can be derived from other relationships is known as a multivalued dependency (MVD). An MVD involves three columns as described in the following definition. Like in the discussion of relationship independence, the three columns comprise a combined primary key of an associative table. The nonessential or derived relationship involves the columns B and C. The definition states that the nonessential relationship (involving the columns B and C) can be derived from the relationships A-B and A-C. The word <u>multivalued</u> means that A can be associated with a collection of B and C values, not just single values as in a functional dependency.

> **MVD Definition:** The multivalued dependency (MVD) $A \rightarrow\rightarrow B \mid C$ (read A multidetermines B or C) means that
> - A given A value is associated with a collection of B and C values, and
> - B and C are independent given the relationships between A and B and A and C.

MVDs can lead to redundancies because of independence among columns. You can see the redundancy by using a table to depict an MVD as shown in Figure 7.10. If the two rows above the line exist and the MVD $A \rightarrow\rightarrow B \mid C$ is true, then the two rows below the line will exist. The two rows below the line will exist because the relationship between B and C can be derived from the relationships A-B and A-C. In Figure 7.10, value A1 is associated with two B values (B1 and B2) and two C values (C1 and C2). Because of independence, value A1 will be associated with every combination of its related B and C values. The two rows below the line are redundant because they can be derived.

A	B	C
A1	B1	C1
A1	B2	C2
A1	B2	C1
A1	B1	C2

Figure 7.10: Table Representation of an MVD

To apply this concept to the *Enroll* table, consider the possible MVD *OfferNo* →→ *StdNo | TextNo*. In the first two rows of Figure 7.11, offering O1 is associated with students S1 and S2 and textbooks T1 and T2. If the MVD is true, then the two rows below the line will exist. The last two rows do not need to be stored if you know the first two rows and the MVD exists.

OfferNo	StdNo	TextNo
O1	S1	T1
O1	S2	T2
O1	S2	T1
O1	S1	T2

Figure 7.11: Representation of the MVD in the *Enroll* Table

MVDs are generalizations of functional dependencies (FDs). Every FD is an MVD but not every MVD is an FD. An MVD in which a value of *A* is associated with only one value of *B* and one value of *C* is also an FD. In this section, we are interested only in MVDs that are <u>not</u> also FDs. An MVD that is not an FD is known as a <u>nontrivial MVD</u>.

Fourth Normal Form (4NF)

Fourth normal form (4NF) prohibits redundancies caused by multivalued dependencies. As an example, the table *Enroll*(<u>StdNo, OfferNo, TextNo</u>) (Table 7-7) is not in 4NF if the MVD *OfferNo* →→ *StdNo | TextNo* exists. To eliminate the MVD, split the M-way table *Enroll* into the binary tables *Enroll* (Table 7-8) and *Orders* (Table 7-9).

> **4NF Definition**: a table is in 4NF if it does not contain any nontrivial MVDs (MVDs that are not also FDs).

The ideas of MVDs and 4NF are somewhat difficult to understand. The ideas are somewhat easier to understand if you think of an MVD as a relationship that can be derived by other relationships because of independence. Chapter 12 presents another way to reason about M-way relationships using patterns in data entry forms.

7.4 Higher Level Normal Forms

The normalization story does not end with 4NF. Other normal forms have been proposed, but their practicality has not been demonstrated. This section briefly describes two higher normal forms to complete your normalization background.

7.4.1 Fifth Normal Form

Fifth normal form (5NF) applies to M-way relationships like 4NF. Unlike 4NF, 5NF involves situations in which a three-way relationship should be replaced with three binary relationships, not two binary relationships as for 4NF. Because situations in which 5NF applies (as opposed to 4NF) are rare, 5NF is generally not considered a practical normal form. Understanding the details of 5NF requires a lot of intellectual investment, but the return on your study time is rarely applicable.

The example in Figure 7.12 demonstrates a situation in which 5NF could apply. The *Authorization* entity type represents authorized combinations of employees, workstations, and software. This associative entity type has redundancy because it can be divided into three binary relationships as shown in Figure 7.13. If you know employees authorized to use workstations, software licensed for workstations, and employees trained to use software, then you know the valid combinations of employees, workstations, and software. Thus, it is necessary to record the three binary combinations (employee-workstation, software-workstation, and employee-software), not the three-way combination of employee, workstation, and software.

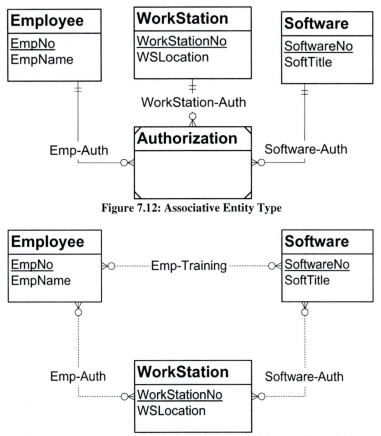

Figure 7.12: Associative Entity Type

Figure 7.13: Replacement of Associative Entity Type with Three Binary Relationships

Whether the situation depicted in Figure 7.13 is realistic is debatable. For example, if software is licensed for servers rather than workstations, the *Software-Auth* relationship may not be necessary. Even though it is possible to depict situations in which 5NF applies, these situations may not exist in real organizations.

7.4.2 Domain Key Normal Form

After reading about so many normal forms, you may be asking questions such as "Where does it stop?" and "Is there an ultimate normal form?" Fortunately, the answer to the last question is yes. In a 1981 paper, Dr. Ronald Fagin proposed domain key normal form (DKNF) as the ultimate normal form. In DKNF, <u>domain</u> refers to a data type: a set of values with allowable operations. A set of values is defined by the kind of values (e.g., whole numbers versus floating-point numbers) and the integrity rules about the values (e.g., values greater than 21). <u>Key</u> refers to the uniqueness property of candidate keys. A table is in DKNF if every constraint on a table can be derived from keys and domains. A table in DKNF cannot have modification anomalies.

Unfortunately, DKNF remains an ideal rather than a practical normal form. There is no known procedure that converts a table into DKNF. In addition, it is not even known what tables can be converted to DKNF. As an ideal, you should try to define tables in which most constraints result from keys and domains. These kinds of constraints are easy to test and understand.

7.5 Practical Concerns about Normalization

After reading this far, you should be well acquainted with the tools of relational database design. Before you are ready to use these tools, some practical advice is useful. This section discusses the role of normalization in the database development process and the importance of thinking carefully about the objective of eliminating modification anomalies.

7.5.1 Role of Normalization in the Database Development Process

There are two different ways to use normalization in the database development process: (1) as a refinement tool or (2) as an initial design tool. In the refinement approach, you perform conceptual data modeling using the Entity Relationship Model and transform the ERD into tables using the conversion rules. Then, you apply normalization techniques to analyze each table: identify FDs, use the simple synthesis procedure to remove redundancies, and analyze a table for independence if the table represents an M-way relationship. Since the primary key determines the other columns in a table, you only need identify FDs in which the primary key is not the LHS.

In the initial design approach, you use normalization techniques in conceptual data modeling. Instead of drawing an ERD, you identify functional dependencies and apply a normalization procedure like the simple synthesis procedure. After defining the tables, you identify the referential integrity constraints and construct a relational model diagram such as that available in Microsoft Access. If needed, an ERD can be generated from the relational database diagram.

This book clearly favors using normalization as a refinement tool, not as an initial design tool. Through development of an ERD, you intuitively group related fields. Much normalization is accomplished in an informal manner without the tedious process of recording functional dependencies. As a refinement tool, there are fewer FDs to specify and less normalization to perform. Applying normalization ensures that candidate keys and redundancies have not been overlooked.

Another reason for favoring the refinement approach is that relationships can be overlooked when using normalization as the initial design approach. 1-M relationships must be identified in the child-to-parent direction. For novice data modelers, identifying relationships is easier when considering both sides of a relationship. For an M-N relationship without attributes, there will not be any functional dependencies that show the need for a table. For example, in a design about textbooks and course offerings, if the relationship between them has no attributes, there are no functional dependencies that relate textbooks and course offerings[26]. In drawing an ERD, however, the need for an M-N relationship becomes clear.

> **Advantages of Normalization as a Refinement Tool**: use normalization to remove redundancies after conversion from an ERD to a table design rather than as an initial design tool.
> - Easier to translate requirements into an ERD than into lists of FDs.
> - Fewer FDs to specify because most FDs are derived from primary keys.
> - Fewer tables to split because normalization performed intuitively during ERD development.
> - Easier to identify relationships especially M-N relationships without attributes.

7.5.2 Analyzing the Normalization Objective

As a design criterion, avoidance of modification anomalies is biased toward database changes. As you have seen, removing anomalies usually results in a database with many tables. A design with many tables makes a database easier to change but more difficult to query. If a database is used predominantly for queries, avoiding modification anomalies may not be an appropriate design goal. Chapter 16 describes databases for decision support in which the primary use is query rather than modification. In this situation, a design that is not fully normalized may be appropriate.

---

[26] An FD can be written with a null right-hand side to represent M-N relationships. The FD for the offering-textbook relationship can be expressed as *TextId, OfferNo* $\rightarrow \varnothing$. However, this kind of FD is awkward to state. It is much easier to define an M-N relationship.

Denormalization is the process of combining tables so that they are easier to query. In addition, physical design goals may conflict with logical design goals. Chapter 8 describes physical database design goals and the use of denormalization as a technique to improve query performance.

Another time to consider denormalization is when an FD is not important. The classic example contains the FDs *Zip → City, State* in a customer table where *City* means the post office city. In some databases, these dependencies may not be important to maintain. If there is not a need to manipulate zip codes independent of customers, the FDs can be safely ignored. However, there are databases in which it is important to maintain a table of zip codes independent of customer information. For example, if a retailer does business in many states and countries, a zip code table is useful to record sales tax rates[27]. If you ignore an FD in the normalization process, you should note that it exists but will not lead to any significant anomalies. Proceed with caution: most FDs will lead to anomalies if ignored.

> **Usage of Denormalization**: consider violating BCNF as a design objective for a table when:
> - An FD is not important to enforce as a candidate key constraint.
> - A database is used predominantly for queries.
> - Query performance requires fewer tables to reduce the number of join operations.

Closing Thoughts

This chapter described how redundancies could make a table difficult to change causing modification anomalies. Avoiding modification anomalies is the goal of normalization techniques. As a prerequisite to normalizing a table, you should list the functional dependencies (FDs). This chapter described two alternative sets of normal forms (either 2NF and 3NF or BCNF) based on functional dependencies. The simple synthesis procedure was presented to analyze functional dependencies and produce tables in BCNF. Providing a complete list of FDs is the most important part of the normalization process. Even if you do not understand the normal forms, you can purchase a CASE tool to perform normalization. CASE tools are not capable of providing a complete list of FDs, however.

This chapter also described an approach to analyze M-way relationships (represented by associative entity types) using the concept of independence. If two relationships are independent, a third relationship can be derived from them. There is no need to store the third relationship. The independence concept is equivalent to multivalued dependency. 4NF prohibits redundancy caused by multivalued dependencies.

This chapter and the data modeling chapters (Chapters 5 and 6) emphasized fundamental skills for database development. After data modeling and normalization are complete, you are ready to implement the design, usually with a relational DBMS. Chapter 8 describes physical database design concepts and practices to facilitate your implementation work on relational DBMSs

Review Concepts

- Redundancies in a table cause modification anomalies.
- Modification anomalies: unexpected side effects when inserting, updating, or deleting
- Functional dependencies: a value neutral constraint similar to a primary key
- Usage of sample data to eliminate possible functional dependencies
- 2NF: nonkey columns dependent on the entire key, not a subset of the key
- 3NF: nonkey columns dependent only on the key, not on other nonkey columns

---

[27] A former database student made this comment about the database of a large computer retailer.

- BCNF: every determinant is a candidate key.
- Simple synthesis procedure: analyze FDs and produce tables in BCNF
- Use the simple synthesis procedure to analyze simple dependency structures
- Use commercial design software to analyze complex dependency structures
- Use relationship independence as a criterion to split M-way relationships into smaller relationships
- MVD: association with collections of values and independence among columns
- MVDs cause redundancy because rows can be derived using independence
- 4NF: no redundancies due to MVDs
- Use normalization techniques as a refinement tool rather than as an initial design tool
- Denormalize a table if FDs do not cause modification anomalies

Questions

1. What is an insertion anomaly?
2. What is an update anomaly?
3. What is a deletion anomaly?
4. What is the cause of modification anomalies?
5. What is a functional dependency?
6. How is a functional dependency like a candidate key?
7. Can a software design tool identify functional dependencies? Briefly explain your answer.
8. What is the meaning of an FD with multiple columns on the right-hand side?
9. Why should you be careful when writing FDs with multiple columns on the left-hand side?
10. What is a normal form?
11. What does 1NF prohibit?
12. What is a key column?
13. What is a nonkey column?
14. What kinds of FDs are not allowed in 2NF?
15. What kinds of FDs are not allowed in 3NF?
16. What is the combined definition of 2NF and 3NF?
17. What kinds of FDs are not allowed in BCNF?
18. What is the relationship between BCNF and 3NF? Is BCNF a stricter normal form than 3NF? Briefly explain your answer.
19. Why is the BCNF definition preferred to the 3NF definition?
20. What are the special cases covered by BCNF but not covered by 3NF?
21. Are the special cases covered by BCNF but not 3NF significant?
22. What is the goal of the simple synthesis procedure?
23. What is a limitation of the simple synthesis procedure?
24. What is a transitive dependency?
25. Are transitive dependencies permitted in 3NF tables? Explain why or why not.
26. Why eliminate transitive dependencies in the FDs used as input to the simple synthesis procedure?
27. When is it necessary to perform the fifth step of the simple synthesis procedure?
28. How is relationship independence similar to statistical independence?
29. What kind of redundancy is caused by relationship independence?
30. How many columns does an MVD involve?
31. What is a multivalued dependency (MVD)?
32. What is the relationship between MVDs and FDs?
33. What is a nontrivial MVD?
34. What is the goal of 4NF?
35. What are the advantages of using normalization as a refinement tool rather than as an initial design tool?
36. Why is 5NF not considered a practical normal form?
37. Why is DKNF not considered a practical normal form?

38. When is denormalization useful? Provide an example to depict when it may be beneficial for a table to violate 3NF.
39. What are the two ways to use normalization in the database development process?
40. Why does this book recommend using normalization as a refinement tool, not as an initial design tool?
41. How many sample rows are necessary to eliminate a possible FD?
42. Explain the pattern in sample data to falsify the FD X → Y.

Problems

Besides the problems presented here, the case study in Chapter 13 provides additional practice. To supplement the examples in this chapter, Chapter 13 provides a complete database design case including conceptual data modeling, schema conversion, and normalization.

1. For the big university database table, list FDs with the column *StdCity* as the determinant that are <u>not</u> true due to the sample data. For each FD, identify the sample rows that contradict it. Remember that it takes two rows to contradict an FD. The sample data are repeated in Table 7-P1 for your reference.

Table 7-P1: Sample Data for the Big University Database Table

STDNO	STDCITY	STDCLASS	OFFERNO	OFFTERM	OFFYEAR	ENRGRADE	COURSENO	CRSDESC
S1	SEATTLE	JUN	O1	FALL	2008	3.5	C1	DB
S1	SEATTLE	JUN	O2	FALL	2008	3.3	C2	VB
S2	BOTHELL	JUN	O3	SPRING	2009	3.1	C3	OO
S2	BOTHELL	JUN	O2	FALL	2008	3.4	C2	VB

2. Following on problem 1, list FDs with the column *StdCity* as the determinant that the sample rows do not violate. For each FD, add one or more sample rows and then identify the sample rows that contradict the FD. Remember that it takes two rows to contradict an FD.
3. For the big patient table, list FDs with the column *PatZip* as the determinant that are <u>not</u> true due to the sample data. Exclude the FD *PatZip* → *PatCity* because it is a valid FD. For the other FDs, identify the sample rows that contradict it. Remember that it takes two rows to contradict an FD. The sample data are repeated in Table 7-P2 for your reference.

Table 7-P2: Sample Data for the Big Patient Table

VISITNO	VISITDATE	**PATNO**	PATAGE	PATCITY	**PATZIP**	PROVNO	PROVSPECIALTY	DIAGNOSIS
V10020	1/13/2009	P1	35	DENVER	80217	D1	INTERNIST	EAR INFECTION
V10020	1/13/2009	P1	35	DENVER	80217	D2	NURSE PRACTITIONER	INFLUENZA
V93030	1/20/2009	P3	17	ENGLEWOOD	80113	D2	NURSE PRACTITIONER	PREGNANCY
V82110	1/18/2009	P2	60	BOULDER	85932	D3	CARDIOLOGIST	MURMUR

4. Following on problem 3, list FDs with the column *PatZip* as the determinant that sample data does not violate. Exclude the FD *PatZip → PatCity* because it is a valid FD. For each FD, add one or more sample rows and then identify the sample rows that contradict the FD. Remember that it takes two rows to contradict an FD.

5. Add sample rows to Table 7-P2 to demonstrate contradictions of the following FDs. Remember that it takes two rows to contradict an FD.

> PatNo → VisitNo
> PatNo → ProvNo
> PatAge → PatZip
> PatAge → PatCity
> PatAge → PatNo

6. Apply the simple synthesis procedure to the FDs of the big patient table. The FDs are repeated in Table 7-P3 for your reference. Show the result of each step in the procedure. Include the primary keys, foreign keys, and other candidate keys in the final list of tables.

Table 7-P3: List of FDs for the Big Patient Table

> PatNo → PatAge, PatCity, PatZip
> PatZip → PatCity
> ProvNo → ProvSpecialty
> VisitNo → PatNo, VisitDate, PatAge, PatCity, PatZip
> VisitNo, ProvNo → Diagnosis

7. The FD diagram in Figure 7.P1 depicts FDs among columns in an order entry database. Figure 7.P1 shows FDs with determinants *CustNo*, *OrderNo*, *ItemNo*, the combination of *OrderNo* and *ItemNo*, the combination of *ItemNo* and *PlantNo*, and the combination of *OrderNo* and *LineNo*. The combination of *OrderNo* and *ItemNo* determines *LineNo*, *QtyOrdered*, and *QtyOutstanding*. In the bottom FDs, the combination of *LineNo* and *OrderNo* determines *ItemNo*, *QtyOrdered*, and *QtyOutstanding*. To test your understanding of dependency diagrams, convert the dependency diagram into a list of dependencies organized by the LHSs.

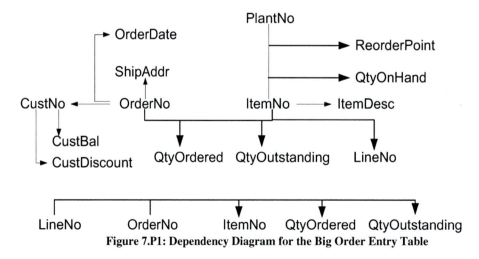

Figure 7.P1: Dependency Diagram for the Big Order Entry Table

8. Using the FD diagram (Figure 7.P1) and the FD list (solution to problem 7) as guidelines, make a table with sample data. There are two candidate keys for the underlying table: the combination of *OrderNo*, *ItemNo*, and *PlantNo* and the combination of *OrderNo*, *LineNo*, and *PlantNo*. Using the sample data, identify insertion, update, and deletion anomalies in the table.

9. Derive 2NF tables starting with the FD list from problem 7 and the table from problem 8.

10. Derive 3NF tables starting with the FD list from problem 7 and the 2NF tables from problem 9.

11. Following on problems 7 and 8, apply the simple synthesis procedure to produce BCNF tables.

12. Modify your table design in problem 11 if the shipping address (*ShipAddr*) column determines customer number (*CustNo*). Do you think that this additional FD is reasonable? Briefly explain your answer.

13. Go back to the original FD diagram in which *ShipAddr* does not determine *CustNo*. How does your table design change if you want to keep track of a master list of shipping addresses for each customer? Assume that you do not want to lose a shipping address when an order is deleted.

14. Using the following FD list for a simplified expense report database, identify insertion, update, and deletion anomalies if all columns are in one table (big expense report table). There are two candidate keys for the big expense report table: *ExpItemNo* (expense item number) and the combination of *CatNo* (category number) and *ERNo* (expense report number). *ExpItemNo* is the primary key of the table.

> ERNo → UserNo, ERSubmitDate, ERStatusDate
> ExpItemNo → ExpItemDesc, ExpItemDate, ExpItemAmt, CatNo, ERNo
> UserNo → UserFirstName, UserLastName, UserPhone, UserEmail
> CatNo → CatName, CatLimit
> ERNo, CatNo → ExpItemNo
> UserEmail → UserNo
> CatName → CatNo

15. Using the FD list in problem 14, identify the FDs that violate 2NF. Using knowledge of the FDs that violate 2NF, design a collection of tables that satisfies 2NF but not 3NF.

16. Using the FD list in problem 14, identify the FDs that violate 3NF. Using knowledge of the FDs that violate 2NF, design a collection of tables that satisfies 3NF.

17. Apply the simple synthesis procedure to produce BCNF tables using the FD list given in problem 14. Show the results of each step in your analysis.

18. Using the following FD list for a simplified graduate student advising database, identify insertion, update, and deletion anomalies if all columns are in one table (big graduate student advising table). There is only one candidate key for the big graduate student advising table: the combination of *PlanNo*, *CourseNo*, and *PaperNo*.

> StdNo → StdName, StdAdmitSems, StdAdmitYear, StdStatus, StdEmail
> StdEmail → StdNo, StdStatus
> CourseNo → CrsDesc, CrsUnits, CrsDeptName, CrsCollName
> PlanNo → PlanDate, PlanAdvName, StdNo, PlanApproval, StdName
> PlanNo, CourseNo → Semester, Year, CreditType, Grade
> PlanNo, PaperNo → DateSubmit, DateDecided, Decision, PaperTitle, StdNo

19. Using the FD list in problem 18, identify the FDs that violate 2NF. Using knowledge of the FDs that violate 2NF, design a collection of tables that satisfies 2NF but not 3NF.

20. Using the FD list in problem 18, identify the FDs that violate 3NF. Using knowledge of the FDs that violate 2NF, design a collection of tables that satisfies 3NF.

21. Apply the simple synthesis procedure to produce BCNF tables using the FD list given in problem 18. Show the results of each step in your analysis.

22. Convert the ERD in Figure 7.P2 into tables and perform further normalization as needed. After converting the ERD to tables, specify FDs for each table. Since the primary key of each table determines the other columns, you should only identify FDs in which the LHS is not the

primary key. If a table is not in BCNF, explain why and split it into two or more tables that are in BCNF.

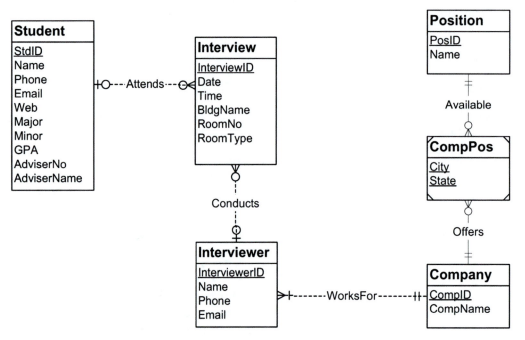

Figure 7.P2: ERD for Problem 22

23. Convert the ERD in Figure 7.P3 into tables and perform further normalization as needed. After the conversion, specify FDs for each table. Since the primary key of each table determines the other columns, you should only identify FDs in which the LHS is not the primary key. If a table is not in BCNF, explain why and split it into two or more tables that are in BCNF.

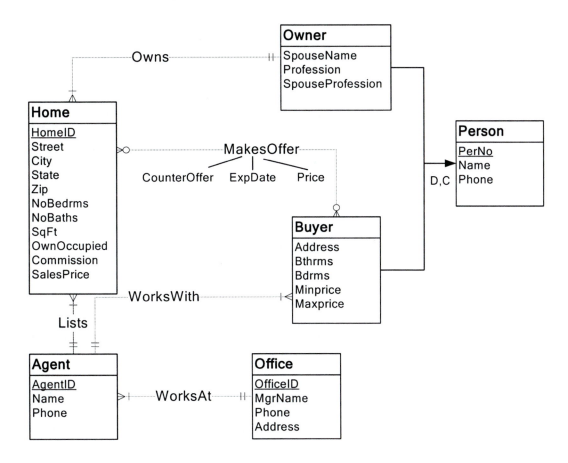

Figure 7.P3: ERD for Problem 23

24. Convert the ERD in Figure 7.P4 into tables and perform further normalization as needed. After the conversion, write down FDs for each table. Since the primary key of each table determines the other columns, you should only identify FDs in which the LHS is not the primary key. If a table is not in BCNF, explain why and split it into two or more tables that are in BCNF. In the *User* entity type, *UserEmail* is unique. In the *ExpenseCategory* entity type, *CatDesc* is unique. In the *StatusType* entity type, *StatusDesc* is unique. For the *ExpenseItem* entity type, the combination of the *Categorizes* and *Contains* relationships are unique.

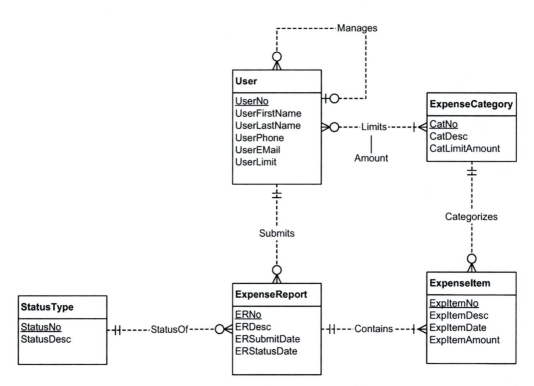

Figure 7.P4: ERD for Problem 24

25. Convert the ERD in Figure 7.P5 into tables and perform further normalization as needed. After the conversion, write down FDs for each table. Since the primary key of each table determines the other columns, you should only identify FDs in which the LHS is not the primary key. If a table is not in BCNF, explain why and split it into two or more tables that are in BCNF. In the *Employee* entity type, each department has one manager. All employees in a department are supervised by the same manager. For the other entity types, *FacName* is unique in *Facility*, *ResName* is unique in *Resource*, and *CustName* and *CustEmail* are unique in *Customer*.

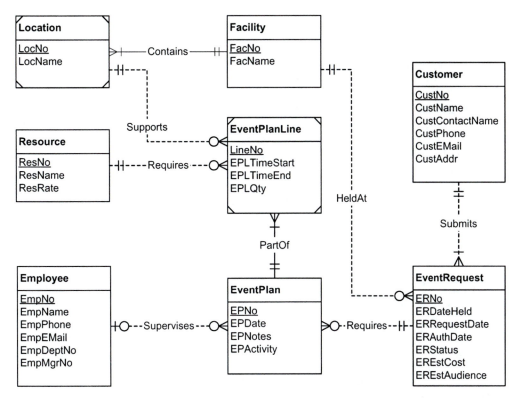

Figure 7.P5: ERD for Problem 25

26. Extend the solution to the problem described in Section 7.2.4 about a database to track submitted conference papers. In the description, underlined parts are new. Write down the new FDs. Using the simple synthesis procedure, design a collection of tables in BCNF. Note dependencies that are not important to the problem and relax your design from BCNF as appropriate. Justify your reasoning.
    * Author information includes a unique author number, a name, a mailing address, and a unique but optional electronic address.
    * Paper information includes the list of authors, the primary author, the paper number, the title, the abstract, the review status (pending, accepted, rejected), and a list of subject categories.
    * Reviewer information includes the reviewer number, the name, the mailing address, a unique but optional electronic address, and a list of expertise categories.
    * A completed review includes the reviewer number, the date, the paper number, comments to the authors, comments to the program chairperson, and ratings (overall, originality, correctness, style, and relevance).
    * The conference organizer should maintain master lists of expertise categories and subject categories. Each category includes a category number and name.
    * Accepted papers are assigned to sessions. Each session has a unique session identifier, a list of papers, a presentation order for each paper, a session title, a session chairperson, a room, a date, a start time, and a duration. Note that each accepted paper can be assigned to only one session.
27. For the following description of an airline reservation database, identify functional dependencies and construct normalized tables. Using the simple synthesis procedure, design a collection of tables in BCNF. Note dependencies that are not important to the problem and relax your design from BCNF as appropriate. Justify your reasoning.

    The Fly by Night Operation is a newly formed airline aimed at the burgeoning market of clandestine travelers (fugitives, spies, con artists, scoundrels, deadbeats, cheating spouses, politicians, etc.). The Fly by Night Operation needs a database to track flights, customers, fares, airplane performance, and personnel assignment. Since the Fly by Night Operation is touted as a "fast way out of town," individual seats are not assigned, and flights of other carriers are not tracked. More specific notes about different parts of the database are listed below:

- Information about a flight includes its unique flight number, its origin, its (supposed) destination, and (roughly) estimated departure and arrival times. To reduce costs, the Fly by Night Operation only has nonstop flights with a single origin and destination.
- Flights are scheduled for one or more dates with an airplane and a crew assigned to each scheduled flight, and the remaining capacity (seats remaining) noted. In a crew assignment, the employee number and the role (e.g., captain, flight attendant) are noted.
- Airplanes have a unique serial number, a model, a capacity, and a next scheduled maintenance date.
- The maintenance record of an airplane includes a unique maintenance number, a date, a description, the serial number of the plane, and the employee responsible for the repairs.
- Employees have a unique employee number, a name, a phone, and a job title.
- Customers have a unique customer number, a phone number, and a name (typically an alias).
- Records are maintained for reservations of scheduled flights including a unique reservation number, a flight number, a flight date, a customer number, a reservation date, a fare, and the payment method (usually cash but occasionally someone else's check or credit card). If the payment is by credit card, a credit card number and an expiration date are part of the reservation record.

28. For the following description of an accounting database, identify functional dependencies and construct normalized tables. Using the simple synthesis procedure, design a collection of tables in BCNF. Note dependencies that are not important to the problem and relax your design from BCNF as appropriate. Justify your reasoning.
    - The primary function of the database is to record entries into a register. A user can have multiple accounts and there is a register for each account.
    - Information about users includes a unique user number, a name, a street address, a city, a state, a zip, and a unique but optional e-mail address.
    - Accounts have attributes including a unique number, a unique name, a start date, a last check number, a type (checking, investment, etc.), a user number, and a current balance (computed). For checking accounts, the bank number (unique), the bank name, and the bank address are also recorded.
    - An entry contains a unique number, a type, an optional check number, a payee, a date, an amount, a description, an account number, and a list of entry lines. The type can have various values including ATM, next check number, deposit, and debit card.
    - In the list of entry lines, the user allocates the total amount of the entry to categories. An entry line includes a category name, a description of the entry line, and an amount.
    - Categories have other attributes not shown in an entry line: a unique category number (name is also unique), a description, a type (asset, expense, revenue, or liability), and a tax-related status (yes or no).
    - Categories are organized in hierarchies. For example, there is a category Auto with subcategorizes Auto:fuel and Auto:repair. Categories can have multiple levels of subcategories.

29. For the ERDs in Figure 7.P6, describe assumptions under which the ERDs correctly depict the relationships among operators, machines, and tasks. In each case, choose appropriate names for the relationships and describe the meaning of the relationships. In part (b) you should also choose the name for the new entity type.

a)

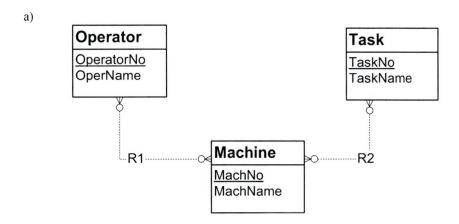

b)

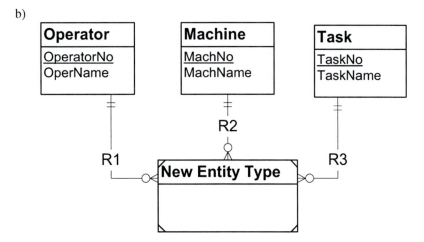

Figure 7.P6: ERDs for Problem 29

30. For the following description of a database to support physical plant operations, identify functional dependencies and construct normalized tables. Using the simple synthesis procedure, design a collection of tables in BCNF. Note dependencies that are not important to the problem and relax your design from BCNF as appropriate. Justify your reasoning.

Design a database to assist physical plant personnel in managing key cards for access to buildings and rooms. The primary purpose of the database is to ensure proper accounting for all key cards.

- A building has a unique building number, a unique name, and a location within the campus.

- A room has a unique room number, a size (physical dimensions), a capacity, a number of entrances, and a description of equipment in the room. Each room is located in exactly one building. The room number includes a building identification and followed by an integer number. For example, room number KC100 identifies room 100 in the King Center (KC) building.

- An employee has a unique employee number, a name, a position, a unique e-mail address, a phone, and an optional room number in which the employee works.

- Magnetically encoded key cards are designed to open one or more rooms. A key card has a unique card number, a date encoded, a list of room numbers that the key card opens, and the number of the employee authorizing the key card. A room may have one or more key cards that open it. A key type must be authorized before it is created.

31. For the ERDs in Figure 7.P7, describe assumptions under which the ERDs correctly depict the relationships among work assignments, tasks, and materials. A work assignment contains the scheduled work for a construction job at a specific location. Scheduled work includes the

tasks and materials needed for the construction job. In each case, choose appropriate names for the relationships and describe the meaning of the relationships. In part (b) you should also choose the name for the new entity type.

a)

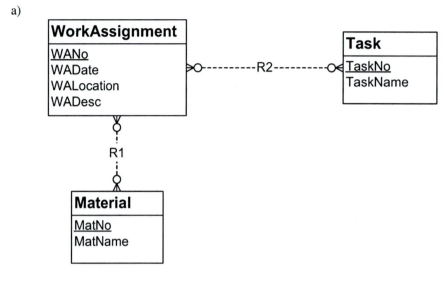

b)

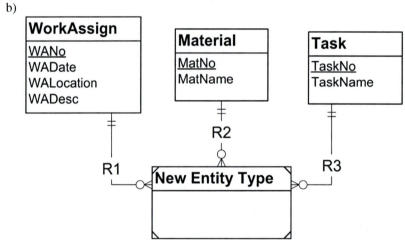

Figure 7.P7: ERDs for Problem 31

32. For the following description of a database to support volunteer tracking, identify functional dependencies and construct normalized tables. Using the simple synthesis procedure, design a collection of tables in BCNF. Note dependencies that are not important to the problem and relax your design from BCNF as appropriate. Justify your reasoning.

Design a database to support organizations that need to track volunteers, volunteer areas, events, and hours worked at events. The system will be initially deployed for charter schools that have mandatory parent participation as volunteers. Volunteers register as a dual- or single-parent family. Volunteer coordinators recruit volunteers for volunteer areas. Event organizers recruit volunteers to work at events. Some events require a schedule of volunteers while other events do not use a schedule. Volunteers work at events and record the time worked.

- For each family, the database records the unique family number, the first and last name of each parent, the home and business phones, the mailing address (street, city, state, and zip), and an optional e-mail address. For single-parent households, information about only one parent is recorded.

- For each volunteer area, the database records the unique volunteer area, the volunteer area name, the group (faculty senate or parent teacher association) controlling the volunteer area, and the family coordinating the volunteer area. In some cases, a family coordinates more than one volunteer area.
- For events, the database records the unique event number, the event description, the event date, the beginning and ending time of the event, the number of required volunteers, the event period and expiration date if the event is a recurring event, the volunteer area, and the list of family volunteers for the event. Families can volunteer in advance for a collection of events.
- After completing a work assignment, hours worked are recorded. The database contains the first and last name of the volunteer, the family the volunteer represents, the number of hours worked, the optional event, the date worked, the location of the work, and optional comments. Usually the volunteer is one of the parents of the family, but occasionally the volunteer is a friend or relative of the family. The event is optional to allow volunteer hours for activities not considered as events.

References for Further Study

The subject of normalization can be much more detailed than described in this chapter. For a more detailed description of normalization, consult computer science books such as Elmasri and Navathe (2004). The simple synthesis procedure was adapted from Hawryszkiewycz (1984). For a classic tutorial on normalization, consult Kent (1983). Fagin (1981) describes domain key normal form, the ultimate normal form. The DBAZine site (www.dbazine.com) and the DevX Database Zone (www.devx.com) have practical advice about database development and normalization.

8

Physical Database Design

Learning Objectives

This chapter describes physical database design, the final phase of the database development process. Physical database design transforms a table design from the logical design phase into an efficient implementation that supports all applications using the database. After this chapter, the student should have acquired the following knowledge and skills:

- Describe the inputs, outputs, and objectives of physical database design
- Appreciate the difficulties of performing physical database design and the need for periodic review of physical database design choices
- List characteristics of sequential, Btree, hash, and bitmap file structures
- Understand the choices made by a query optimizer and the areas in which optimization decisions can be improved
- Understand the trade-offs in index selection and denormalization decisions
- Understand the need for computer-aided tools to assist with physical database design decisions, especially with decisions affected by the query optimization process

Overview

Chapters 5 to 7 covered the conceptual and the logical design phases of database development. You learned about entity relationship diagrams, data modeling practice, schema conversion, and normalization. This chapter extends your database design skills by explaining the process to achieve an efficient implementation of your table design.

To become proficient in physical database design, you need to understand the process and environment. This chapter describes the process of physical database design including the inputs, outputs, and objectives along with two critical parts of the environment, file structures and query optimization. Most of the choices in physical database design relate to characteristics of file structures and query optimization decisions.

After understanding the process and environment, you are ready to perform physical database design. In performing physical database design, you should provide detailed inputs and make choices to balance the needs of retrieval and update applications. This chapter describes the complexity of table profiles and application profiles and their importance for physical design decisions. Index selection is the most important choice of physical database design. This chapter describes trade-offs in index selection and provides index selection rules that you can apply to moderate-size databases. In addition to index selection, this chapter presents denormalization, record formatting, and parallel processing as techniques to improve database performance.

8.1 Overview of Physical Database Design

Decisions in the physical database design phase involve the storage level of a database. Collectively, the storage level decisions are known as the internal schema. This section describes the storage level as well as the objectives, inputs, and outputs of physical database design.

8.1.1 Storage Level of Databases

The storage level is closest to the hardware and operating system. At the storage level, a database consists of physical records (also known as blocks or pages) organized into files. A <u>physical record</u> is a collection of bytes that are transferred between volatile storage in main memory and stable storage on a disk. Main memory is considered volatile storage because the contents of main memory may be lost if a failure occurs. A <u>file</u> is a collection of physical records organized for efficient access. Figure 8.1 depicts relationships between logical records (rows of a table) and physical records stored in a file. Typically, a physical record contains multiple logical records. The size of a physical record is a power of two such as 1,024 (2^{10}) or 4,096 (2^{12}) bytes. A large logical record may be split over multiple physical records. Another possibility is that logical records from more than one table are stored in the same physical record.

> **Physical Record**: collection of bytes that are transferred between volatile storage in main memory and stable storage on a disk. The number of physical record accesses is an important measure of database performance.

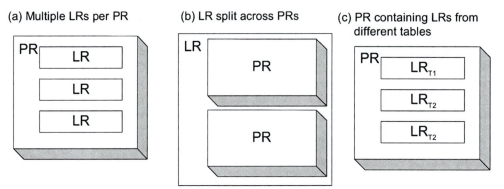

Figure 8.1: Relationships between Logical Records (LR) and Physical Records (PR)

The DBMS and the operating system work together to satisfy requests for logical records made by applications. Figure 8.2 depicts the process of transferring physical and logical records between a disk, DBMS buffers, and application buffers. Normally, the DBMS and the application have separate memory areas known as buffers. When an application makes a request for a logical record, the DBMS locates the physical record containing it. In the case of a read operation, the operating system transfers the physical record from disk to the memory area of the DBMS. The DBMS then transfers the logical record to the application's buffer. In the case of a write operation, the transfer process is reversed.

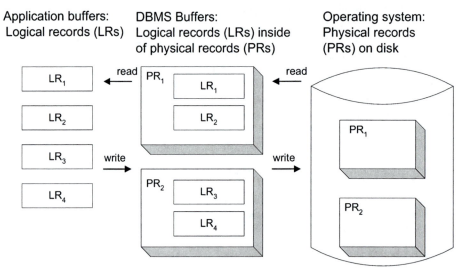

Figure 8.2: Transferring Physical Records

A logical record request may not result in a physical record transfer because of buffering. The DBMS tries to anticipate the needs of applications so that corresponding physical records already reside in the DBMS buffers. A significant difficulty about predicting database performance is the uncertainty about the contents of DBMS buffers. If a DBMS buffer contains a requested logical record, a physical record transfer is not necessary. For example, if multiple applications are accessing the same logical records, the corresponding physical records may reside in the DBMS buffers. Consequently, the uncertainty about the contents of DBMS buffers can make physical database design difficult.

244

8.1.2 Objectives and Constraints

The goal of physical database design is to minimize response time to access and change a database. Because response time is difficult to estimate directly, minimizing computing resources is used as a substitute measure. The resources that are consumed by database processing are physical record transfers, central processing unit (CPU) operations, main memory, and disk space. The latter two resources (main memory and disk space) are considered as constraints rather than resources to minimize. Minimizing main memory and disk space can lead to high response times.

The number of physical record accesses limits the performance of most database applications. A physical record access may involve mechanical movement of a disk including rotation and magnetic head movement. Mechanical movement is generally much slower than electronic switching of main memory. The speed of a disk access is measured in milliseconds (thousandths of a second) whereas a memory access is measured in nanoseconds (billionths of a second). Thus, a physical record access may be many times slower than a main memory access. Reducing the number of physical record accesses will usually improve response time.

CPU usage also can be a factor in some database applications. For example, sorting requires a large number of comparisons and assignments. These operations, performed by the CPU, are many times faster than a physical record access, however. To accommodate both physical record accesses and CPU usage, a weight can be used to combine them into one measure. The weight is usually close to 0 to reflect that many CPU operations can be performed in the time to perform one physical record transfer.

> Combined Measure of Database Performance: *PRA + W * CPU-OP* where
> *PRA* is the number of physical record accesses,
> *CPU-OP* is the number of CPU operations such as comparisons and assignments, and
> *W* is a weight, a real number between 0 and 1.

The objective of physical database design is to minimize the combined measure for all applications using the database. Generally, improving performance on retrieval applications comes at the expense of update applications and vice versa. Therefore, an important theme of physical database design is to balance the needs of retrieval and update applications.

The measures of performance are too detailed to estimate by hand except for simple situations. Complex optimization software calculates estimates using detailed cost formulas. The optimization software is usually part of the SQL compiler. Understanding the nature of the performance measure helps one to interpret choices made by the optimization software.

For most choices in physical database design, the amounts of main memory and disk space are usually fixed. In other words, main memory and disk space are constraints of the physical database design process. As with constraints in other optimization problems, you should consider the effects of changing the given amounts of main memory and disk space. Increasing the amounts of these resources can improve performance. The amount of performance improvement may depend on many factors such as the DBMS, table design, and applications using the database.

8.1.3 Inputs, Outputs, and Environment

Physical database design consists of a number of different inputs and outputs as depicted in Figure 8.3 and summarized in Table 8-1. The starting point is the table design from the logical database design phase. The table and application profiles are used specifically for physical database design. Because these inputs are so critical to the physical database design process, they are discussed in more detail in Section 8.2. The most important outputs are decisions about file structures and data placement. Section 8.5 discusses these decisions in more detail. For simplicity, decisions about other outputs are made separately even though the outputs can be related. For example, file structures are usually selected separately from denormalization decisions even though denormalization decisions can affect file structure decisions. Thus, physical database design is better characterized as a sequence of decision-making processes rather than one large process.

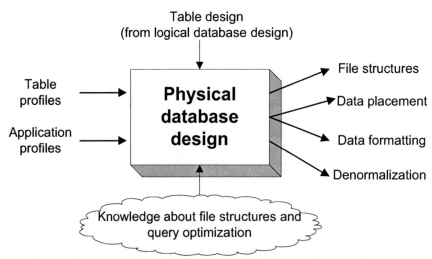

Figure 8.3: Inputs, Outputs, and Environment of Physical Database Design

Table 8-1: Summary of Inputs, Outputs, and Environment of Physical Database Design

Item	Description
Inputs	
Table profiles	Statistics about each table such as the number of rows, unique column values, and distribution of column values
Application profiles	Statistics for each form, report, and query such as the tables accessed/updated, the frequency of access/update, and values used in search requests
Outputs	
File structures	Method of organizing physical records for each table
Data placement	Criteria for arranging physical records in close proximity
Data formatting	Usage of compression and derived data
Denormalization	Combining separate tables into a single table
Environment knowledge	
File structures	Characteristics such as operations supported and cost formulas
Query optimization	Access decisions made by the optimization component for each query

Knowledge about file structures and query optimization are in the environment of physical database design rather than being inputs. The knowledge can be embedded in database design tools. If database design tools are not available, a designer informally uses knowledge about the environment to make physical database decisions. Acquiring the knowledge can be difficult because much of it is specific to each DBMS. Because knowledge of the environment is so crucial in the physical database design process, Sections 8.3 and 8.4 discuss it in more detail.

8.1.4 Difficulties

Before proceeding to learn more details about physical database design, it is important to understand why physical database design is difficult. The difficulty is due to the number of decisions, relationships among decisions, detailed inputs, complex environment, and uncertainty in predicting physical record accesses. These factors are briefly discussed below. In the remainder of this chapter, keep these difficulties in mind.

- The number of possible choices available to the designer can be large. For databases with many columns, the number of possible choices can be too large to evaluate even on large computers.
- Some decisions cannot be made in isolation. For example, file structure decisions for one table can influence the decisions for other tables.

246

- The quality of decisions is limited by the precision of the table and application profiles. However, these inputs can be large and difficult to collect. In addition, the inputs change over time so that periodic revision is necessary.
- The environment knowledge is specific to each DBMS. Much of the knowledge is either a trade secret or too complex to understand in detail.
- The number of physical record accesses is difficult to predict because of uncertainty about the contents of DBMS buffers. The uncertainty arises because the mix of applications accessing the database is constantly changing.

8.2 Inputs of Physical Database Design

Physical database design requires inputs specified in sufficient detail. Inputs specified without enough detail can lead to poor decisions in physical database design and query optimization. This section describes the level of detail recommended for both table profiles and application profiles.

8.2.1 Table Profiles

A table profile summarizes a table as a whole, the columns within a table, and the relationships between tables as shown in Table 8-2. Because table profiles are tedious to construct manually, most DBMSs provide statistics programs to construct them automatically. The designer may need to periodically run the statistics program so that the profiles do not become obsolete. For large databases, table profiles may be estimated on samples of the database. Using the entire database can be too time-consuming and disruptive.

Table 8-2: Typical Components of a Table Profile

Component	Statistics
Table	Number of rows and physical records
Column	Number of unique values, distribution of values, correlation among columns
Relationship	Distribution of the number of related rows

For column and relationship summaries, the distribution conveys the number of rows and related rows for column values. The distribution of values can be specified in a number of ways. A simple way is to assume that the column values are uniformly distributed. Uniform distribution means that each value has an equal number of rows. If the uniform value assumption is made, only the minimum and maximum values are necessary.

A more detailed way to specify a distribution is to use a histogram. A histogram is a two-dimensional graph in which the x-axis represents column ranges and the y-axis represents the number of rows. For example, the first bar in Figure 8.4 means that 9,000 rows have a salary between $10,000 and $50,000. Traditional equal-width histograms do not work well with skewed data because a large number of ranges are necessary to control estimation errors. In Figure 8.4, estimating the number of employee rows using the first two ranges may lead to large estimation errors because more than 97% of employees have salaries less than $80,000. For example, you would calculate about 1,125 rows (12.5% of 9,000) to estimate the number of employees earning between $10,000 and $15,000 using Figure 8.4. However, the actual number of rows is much lower because few employees earn less than $15,000.

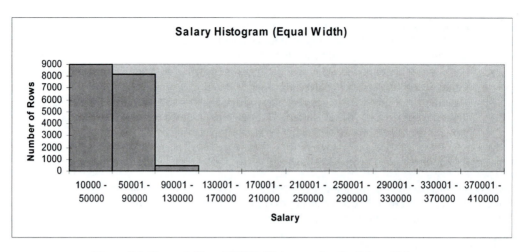

Figure 8.4: Example Equal-Width Histogram for the Salary Column

Because skewed data can lead to poor estimates using traditional (equal-width) histograms, most DBMSs use equal-height histograms as shown in Figure 8.5. In an equal-height histogram, the ranges are determined so that each range has about the same number of rows. Thus the width of the ranges varies, but the height is about the same. Most DBMSs use equal-height histograms because the maximum and expected estimation errors can be controlled by increasing the number of ranges.

Table profiles are used to estimate the combined measure of performance presented in Section 8.1.2. For example, the number of physical records is used to calculate the physical record accesses to retrieve all rows of a table. The distribution of column values is needed to estimate the fraction of rows that satisfy a condition in a query. For example, to estimate the fraction of rows that satisfy the condition, Salary > 45000, you would sum the number of rows in the first three bars of Figure 8.4 and use linear interpolation in the fourth bar.

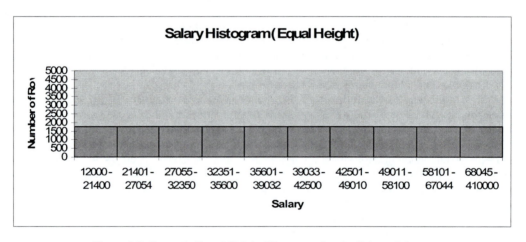

Figure 8.5: Example Equal-Height Histogram for the Salary Column

It is sometimes useful to store more detailed data about columns. If columns are related, errors can be made when estimating the fraction of rows that satisfy conditions connected by logical operators. For example, if the salary and age columns are related, the fraction of rows satisfying the Boolean expression, Salary > 45000 AND Age < 25, cannot be accurately estimated by knowing the distribution of salary and age alone. Data about the statistical relationship between salary and age are also necessary. Because summaries about column relationships are costly to collect and store, many DBMSs assume that columns are independent.

8.2.2 Application Profiles

Application profiles summarize the queries, forms, and reports that access a database as shown in Table 8-3. For forms, the frequency of using the form for each kind of operation (insert, update, delete, and retrieval) should be specified. For queries and reports, the distribution of parameter values encodes the number of times the query/report is executed with various parameter values. Unfortunately, DBMSs are not as helpful to collect application profiles as table profiles. The database designer may need to write specialized software or find third-party software to collect application profiles.

Table 8-3: Typical Components of an Application Profile

Application Type	Statistics
Query	Frequency, distribution of parameter values
Form	Frequency of insert, update, delete, and retrieval operations
Report	Frequency, distribution of parameter values

Table 8-4 depicts profiles for several applications of the university database. The frequency data are specified as an average per unit time period such as per day. Sometimes it is useful to summarize frequencies in more detail. Specifying peak frequencies and variance in frequencies can help avoid problems with peak usage. In addition, importance of applications can be specified as response time limits so that physical designs are biased towards critical applications.

Table 8-4: Example Application Profiles

Application Name	Tables	Operation	Frequency
Enrollment Query	Course, Offering, Enrollment	Retrieval	100 per day during the registration period; 50 per day during the drop/add period
Registration Form	Registration	Insert	1,000 per day during the registration period
Registration Form	Enrollment	Insert	5,000 per day during the registration period; 1,000 per day during drop/add period
Registration Form	Registration	Delete	100 per day during the registration period; 10 per day during the drop/add period
Registration Form	Enrollment	Delete	1,000 per day during the registration period; 500 per day during the drop/add period
Registration Form	Registration, Student	Retrieval	6,000 per day during the registration period; 1,500 per day during the drop/add period
Registration Form	Enrollment, Course, Offering, Faculty	Retrieval	6,000 per day during the registration period; 1,500 per day during the drop/add period
Faculty Workload Report	Faculty, Course, Offering, Enrollment	Retrieval	50 per day during the last week of the academic period; 10 per day otherwise; typical parameters: current year and academic period

249

8.3 File Structures

As mentioned in Section 8.1, selecting among alternative file structures is one of the most important choices in physical database design. In order to choose intelligently, you must understand characteristics of available file structures. This section describes the characteristics of common file structures available in most DBMSs.

8.3.1 Sequential Files

The simplest kind of file structure stores logical records in insertion order. New logical records are appended to the last physical record in the file, as shown in Figure 8.6. Unless logical records are inserted in a particular order and no deletions are made, the file becomes unordered. Unordered files are sometimes known as heap files because of the lack of order.

> **Sequential File**: a simple file organization in which records are stored in insertion order or by key value. Sequential files are simple to maintain and provide good performance for processing large numbers of records.

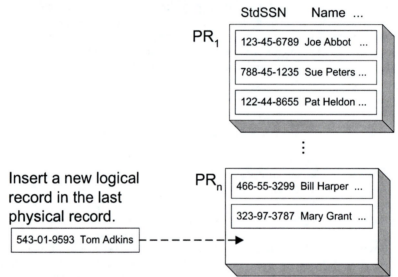

Figure 8.6: Inserting a New Logical Record into an Unordered Sequential File

The primary advantage of unordered sequential files is fast insertion. However, when logical records are deleted, insertion becomes more complicated. For example, if the second logical record in PR_i is deleted, space is available in PR_i. A list of free space must be maintained to tell if a new record can be inserted into the empty space instead of into the last physical record. Alternately, new logical records can always be inserted in the last physical record. However, periodic reorganization to reclaim lost space due to deletions is necessary.

Because ordered retrieval is sometimes needed, ordered sequential files can be preferable to unordered sequential files. Logical records are arranged in key order where the key can be any column, although it is often the primary key. Ordered sequential files are faster when retrieving in key order, either the entire file or a subset of records. The primary disadvantage to ordered sequential files is slow insertion speed. Figure 8.7 demonstrates that records must sometimes be rearranged during the insertion process. The rearrangement process can involve movement of logical records between blocks and maintenance of an ordered list of physical records.

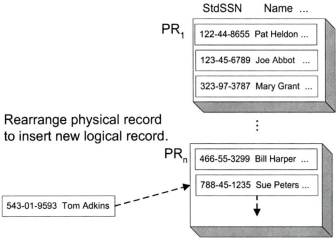

Figure 8.7: Inserting a New Logical Record into an Ordered Sequential File

8.3.2 Hash Files

<u>Hash files,</u> in contrast to sequential files, support fast access of records by primary key value. The basic idea behind hash files is a function that converts a key value into a physical record address. The mod function (remainder division) is a simple hash function. Table 8-5 applies the mod function to the *StdSSN* column values in Figure 8.6. For simplicity, assume that the file capacity is 100 physical records. The divisor for the mod function is 97, a large prime number close to the file capacity. The physical record number is the result of the hash function result plus the starting physical record number, assumed to be 150. Figure 8.8 shows selected physical records of the hash file.

Hash File: a specialized file structure that supports search by key. Hash files transform a key value into an address to provide fast access.

Table 8-5: Hash Function Calculations for StdSSN Values

StdSSN	StdSSN Mod 97	PR Number
122448655	26	176
123456789	39	189
323973787	92	242
466553299	80	230
788451235	24	174
543019593	13	163

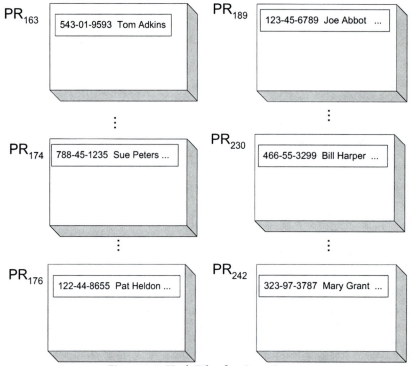

Figure 8.8: Hash File after Insertions

Hash functions may assign more than one key to the same physical record address. A collision occurs when two keys hash to the same physical record address. As long as the physical record has free space, a collision is no problem. However, if the original or home physical record is full, a collision-handling procedure locates a physical record with free space. Figure 8.9 demonstrates the linear probe procedure for collision handling. In the linear probe procedure, a logical record is placed in the next available physical record if its home address is occupied. To retrieve a record by its key, the home address is initially searched. If the record is not found in its home address, a linear probe is initiated.

Home address = Hash function value + Base address

(122448946 mod 97 = 26) + 150

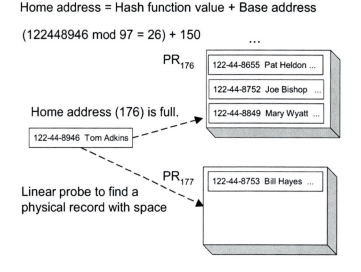

Figure 8.9: Linear Probe Collision Handling during an Insert Operation

The existence of collisions highlights a potential problem with hash files. If collisions do not occur often, insertions and retrievals are very fast. If collisions occur often, insertions and retrievals can be slow. The likelihood of a collision depends on remaining capacity in the hash file. Generally, if the file is less than 70 percent full, collisions do not occur often. However, maintaining a hash file that is only 70 percent full can be a problem if the table grows. If the hash file becomes too full, a reorganization is necessary. A reorganization can be time-consuming and disruptive because a larger hash file is allocated and all logical records are inserted into the new file.

To eliminate reorganizations, dynamic hash files have been proposed. In a dynamic hash file, periodic reorganization is never necessary and search performance does not degrade after many insert operations. However, the average number of physical record accesses to retrieve a record may be slightly higher as compared to a static hash file that is not too full. The basic idea in dynamic hashing is that the size of the hash file grows as records are inserted. For details of the various approaches, consult the references at the end of this chapter.

Another problem with hash files is sequential search. Good hash functions tend to spread logical records uniformly among physical records. Because of gaps between physical records, sequential search may examine empty physical records. For example, to search the hash file depicted in Figure 8.8, 100 physical records must be examined even though only six contain data. Even if the hash file is reasonably full, logical records are spread among more physical records than in a sequential file. Thus, when performing a sequential search, the number of physical record accesses may be higher in a hash file than in a sequential file.

8.3.3 Multiway Tree (Btrees) Files

Sequential files and hash files provide good performance on some operations but poor performance on other operations. Sequential files perform well on sequential search but poorly on key search. Hash files perform well on key search but poorly on sequential search. The multiway tree, or Btree as it is popularly known, is a compromise and widely used file structure. The Btree provides good performance on both sequential search and key search. This section describes characteristics of the Btree, shows examples of Btree operations, and discusses the cost of operations.

Btree File: a popular file structure supported by most DBMSs because it performs well on key search as well as sequential search. A Btree file is a balanced, multiway tree.

Btree Characteristics: What's in a Name?

A Btree is a special kind of tree as depicted in Figure 8.10. A tree is a structure in which each node has at most one parent except for the root or top node. The Btree structure possesses a number of characteristics, discussed in the following list, that make it a useful file structure. Some of the characteristics are possible meanings for the letter B[28] in the name.

---

[28] Another possible meaning for the letter B is Bayer, for the inventor of the Btree, Professor Rudolph Bayer. In a private conversation, Professor Bayer denied naming the Btree after himself or for his employer at the time, Boeing. When pressed, Professor Bayer only said that the B represents the B.

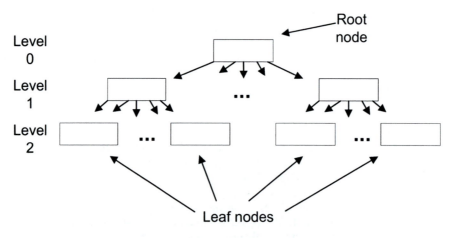

Figure 8.10: Structure of a Btree of Height 3

Balanced: all leaf nodes (nodes without children) reside on the same level of the tree. In Figure 8.10, all leaf nodes are two levels beneath the root. A balanced tree ensures that all leaf nodes can be retrieved with the same access cost.

Bushy: the number of branches from a node is large, perhaps 50 to 200 branches. Multiway, meaning more than two, is a synonym for bushy. The width (number of arrows from a node) and height (number of nodes between root and leaf nodes) are inversely related: increase width, decrease height. The ideal Btree is wide (bushy) but short (few levels).

Block-Oriented: each node in a Btree is a block. To search a Btree, you start in the root node and follow a path to a leaf node containing data of interest. The height of a Btree is important because it determines the number of physical record accesses for searching.

Dynamic: the shape of a Btree changes as logical records are inserted and deleted. Periodic reorganization is never necessary for a Btree. The next subsection describes node splitting and concatenation, the ways that a Btree changes as records are inserted and deleted.

Ubiquitous: the Btree is a widely implemented and used file structure.

Before studying the dynamic nature, let us look more carefully at the contents of a node as depicted in Figure 8.11. Each node consists of pairs with a key value and a pointer (physical record address), sorted by key value. The pointer identifies the physical record that contains the logical record with the key value. Other data in a logical record, besides the key, do not usually reside in the nodes. The other data may be stored in separate physical records or in the leaf nodes.

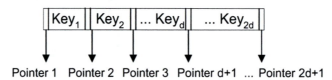

Each nonroot node contains at least half capacity
(d keys and d+1 pointers).

Each nonroot node contains at most full capacity
($2d$ keys and $2d$+1 pointers).

Figure 8.11: Btree Node Containing Keys and Pointers

An important property of a Btree is that each node, except the root, must be at least half full. The physical record size, the key size, and the pointer size determine node capacity. For example, if the physical record size is 4,096 bytes, the key size is 8 bytes, and the pointer size is 8 bytes, the maximum capacity of a node is 256 <key, pointer> pairs. Thus, each node must contain at least 128 pairs. Because the designer usually does not have control over the physical record size and the pointer size, the key size determines the number of branches. Btrees are usually not good for large key sizes due to less branching per node and, hence, taller and less-efficient Btrees.

Node Splitting and Concatenation

Insertions are handled by placing the new key in a nonfull node or by splitting nodes, as depicted in Figure 8.12. In the partial Btree in Figure 8.12(a), each node contains a maximum of four keys. Inserting the key value 55 in Figure 8.12(b) requires rearrangement in the right-most leaf node. Inserting the key value 58 in Figure 8.12(c) requires more work because the right-most leaf node is full. To accommodate the new value, the node is split into two nodes and a key value is moved to the root node. In Figure 8.12(d), a split occurs at two levels because both nodes are full. When a split occurs at the root, the tree grows another level.

Deletions are handled by removing the deleted key from a node and repairing the structure if needed, as demonstrated in Figure 8.13. If the node is still at least half full, no additional action is necessary as shown in Figure 8.13(b). However, if the node is less than half full, the structure must be changed. If a neighboring node contains more than half capacity, a key can be borrowed, as shown in Figure 8.13(c). If a key cannot be borrowed, nodes must be concatenated, as shown in Figure 8.13(d).

Cost of Operations

The height of a Btree is small even for a large table when the branching factor is large. An upper bound or limit on the height (h) of a Btree is

$h \leq ceil(log_d (n+1)/2)$ where
   $ceil$ is the ceiling function ($ceil(x)$ is the smallest integer $\geq x$)
   d is the minimum number of keys in a node
   n is the number of keys to store in the index
   Example: $h \leq 4$ for $n = 1,000,000$ and $d = 42$.

The height dominates the number of physical record accesses in Btree operations. The cost in terms of physical record accesses to find a key is less than or equal to the height. If the row data are not stored in the tree, another physical record access is necessary to retrieve the row data after finding the key. Btrees have logarithmic search cost because the log function dominates the formula for height. Bushy Btrees with a large number of keys in a node can be efficiently searched.

The cost to insert a key includes the cost to locate the nearest key plus the cost to change nodes. In the best case as demonstrated in Figure 8.12(b), the additional cost is one physical record access to change the index record and one physical record access to write the row data. The worst case occurs when a new level is added to the tree, as depicted in Figure 8.12(d). Even in the worst case, the height of the tree still dominates. Another $2h$ write operations are necessary to split the tree at each level.

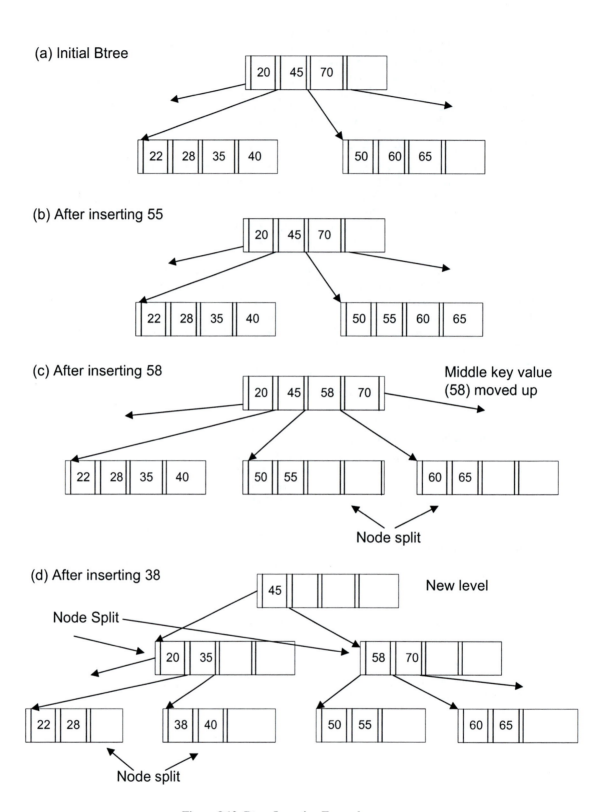

Figure 8.12: Btree Insertion Examples

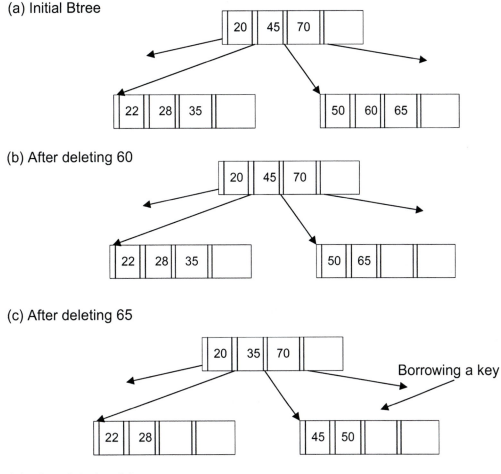

(a) Initial Btree

(b) After deleting 60

(c) After deleting 65

Borrowing a key

(d) After deleting 28

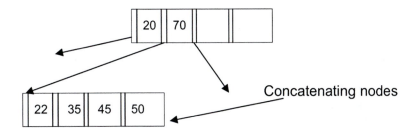

Concatenating nodes

Figure 8.13: Btree Deletion Examples

B+Tree

Sequential searches can be a problem with Btrees. To perform a range search, the search procedure must travel up and down the tree. For example, to retrieve keys in the range 28 to 60 in Figure 8.13(a), the search process starts in the root, descends to the left leaf node, returns to the root, and then descends to the right leaf node. This procedure has problems with retention of physical records in memory. Operating systems may replace physical records if there have not been recent accesses. Because some time may elapse before a parent node is accessed again, the operating system may replace it with another physical record if main memory becomes full. Thus, another physical record access may be necessary when the parent node is accessed again.

To ensure that physical records are not replaced, the B+tree variation is usually implemented. Figure 8.14 shows the two parts of a <u>B+tree</u>. The triangle (index set) represents a normal Btree index. The lower part (sequence set) contains the leaf nodes. All keys reside in the leaf nodes even if a key appears in the index set. The leaf nodes are connected together so that sequential searches do not need to move up the tree. Once the initial key is found, the search process accesses only nodes in the sequence set.

B+tree File: the most popular variation of the Btree. In a B+tree, all keys are redundantly stored in the leaf nodes. The B+tree provides improved performance on sequential and range searches.

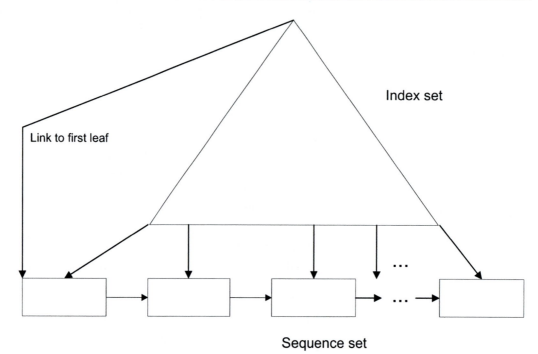

Figure 8.14: B+tree Structure

Index Matching

A Btree can be used to store all data in the nodes (primary file structure) or just pointers to the data records (secondary file structure or index). A Btree is especially versatile as an index because it can be used for a variety of queries. Determining whether an index can be used in a query is known as index matching. When a condition in a WHERE clause references an indexed column, the DBMS must determine if the index can be used. The complexity of a condition determines whether an index can be used. For single-column indexes, an index matches a condition if the column appears alone without functions or operators and the comparison operator matches one of the following items:

- =, >, <, >=, <= (but not <>)
- BETWEEN
- IS NULL
- IN <list of constant values>
- LIKE 'Pattern' in which pattern does not contain a meta character (%, _) as the first part of the pattern

For composite indexes involving more than one column, the matching rules are more complex and restrictive. Composite indexes are ordered by the most significant (first column in the index) to the least significant (last column in the index) column. A composite index matches conditions according to the following rules:

- The first column of the index must have a matching condition.
- Columns match from left (most significant) to right (least significant). Matching stops when the next column in the index is not matched.
- At most, one BETWEEN condition matches. No other conditions match after the BETWEEN condition.
- At most, one IN condition matches an index column. Matching stops after the next matching condition. The second matching condition cannot be IN or BETWEEN.

To depict index matching, Table 8-6 shows examples of matching between indexes and conditions. When matching a composite index, the conditions can be in any order. Because of the restrictive matching rules, composite indexes should be used with caution. It is usually a better idea to create indexes on the individual columns as most DBMSs can combine the results of multiple indexes when answering a query.

Table 8-6: Index Matching Examples

Condition	Index	Matching Notes
C1 = 10	C1	Matches index on C1
C2 BETWEEN 10 AND 20	C2	Matches index on C2
C3 IN (10, 20)	C3	Matches index on C3
C1 <> 10	C1	Does not match index on C1
C4 LIKE 'A%'	C4	Matches index on C4
C4 LIKE '%A'	C4	Does not match index on C4
C1 = 10 AND C2 = 5 AND C3 = 20 AND C4 = 25	(C1,C2,C3,C4)	Matches all columns of the index
C2 = 5 AND C3 = 20 AND C1 = 10	(C1,C2,C3,C4)	Matches the first three columns of the index
C2 = 5 AND C4 = 22 AND C1 = 10 AND C6 = 35	(C1,C2,C3,C4)	Matches the first two columns of the index
C2 = 5 AND C3 = 20 AND C4 = 25	(C1,C2,C3,C4)	Does not match any columns of the index: missing condition on C1
C1 IN (6, 8, 10) AND C2 = 5 AND C3 IN (20, 30, 40)	(C1,C2,C3,C4)	Matches the first two columns of the index: at most one matching IN condition
C2 = 5 AND C1 BETWEEN 6 AND 10	(C1,C2,C3,C4)	Matches the first column of the index: matching stops after the BETWEEN condition

8.3.4 Bitmap Indexes

Btree and hash files work best for columns with unique values. For nonunique columns, Btrees index nodes can store a list of row identifiers instead of an individual row identifier for unique columns. However, if a column has few values, the list of row identifiers can be very long.

As an alternative structure for columns with few values, many DBMSs support <u>bitmap indexes</u>. Figure 8.15 depicts a bitmap column index for a sample *Faculty* table. A bitmap contains a string of bits (0 or 1 values) with one bit for each row of a table. In Figure 8.15, the length of the bitmap is 12 positions because there are 12 rows in the sample *Faculty* table. A record of a bitmap column index contains a column value and a bitmap. A 0 value in a bitmap indicates that the associated row does not have the column value. A 1 value indicates that the associated row has the column value. The DBMS provides an efficient way to convert a position in a bitmap to a row identifier.

Faculty Table

RowId FacNo	...	FacRank
1 098-55-1234		Asst
2 123-45-6789		Asst
3 456-89-1243		Assc
4 111-09-0245		Prof
5 931-99-2034		Asst
6 998-00-1245		Prof
7 287-44-3341		Assc
8 230-21-9432		Asst
9 321-44-5588		Prof
10 443-22-3356		Assc
11 559-87-3211		Prof
12 220-44-5688		Asst

Bitmap Column Index on FacRank

FacRank Bitmap
Asst 110010010001
Assc 001000100100
Prof 000101001010

Figure 8.15: Sample Faculty Table and Bitmap Column Index on FacRank

A variation of the bitmap column index is the bitmap join index. In a bitmap join index, the bitmap identifies rows of a related table, not the table containing the indexed column. Thus, a bitmap join index represents a precomputed join from a column in a parent table to the rows of a child table that join with rows of the parent table.

A join bitmap index can be defined for a join column such as *FacNo* or a nonjoin column such as *FacRank*. Figure 8.16 depicts a bitmap join index for the *FacRank* column in the *Faculty* table to the rows in the sample *Offering* table. The length of the bitmap is 24 bits because there are 24 rows in the sample *Offering* table. A 1 value in a bitmap indicates that a parent row containing the column value joins with the child table in the specified bit position. For example, a 1 in the first bit position of the Asst row of the join index means that a *Faculty* row with the Asst value joins with the first row of the *Offering* table.

Offering Table

RowId	OfferNo	...	FacNo
1	1111		098-55-1234
2	1234		123-45-6789
3	1345		456-89-1243
4	1599		111-09-0245
5	1807		931-99-2034
6	1944		998-00-1245
7	2100		287-44-3341
8	2200		230-21-9432
9	2301		321-44-5588
10	2487		443-22-3356
11	2500		559-87-3211
12	2600		220-44-5688
13	2703		098-55-1234
14	2801		123-45-6789
15	2944		456-89-1243
16	3100		111-09-0245
17	3200		931-99-2034
18	3258		998-00-1245
19	3302		287-44-3341
20	3901		230-21-9432
21	4001		321-44-5588
22	4205		443-22-3356
23	4301		559-87-3211
24	4455		220-44-5688

Bitmap Join Index on FacRank

FacRank	Bitmap
Asst	110010010001110010010001
Assc	001000100100001000100100
Prof	000101001010000101001010

Figure 8.16: Sample Offering Table and Bitmap Join Index on FacRank

> **Bitmap Index**: a secondary file structure consisting of a column value and a bitmap. A bitmap contains one bit position for each row of a referenced table. A bitmap column index references the rows containing the column value. A bitmap join index references the rows of a child table that join with rows of the parent table containing the column. Bitmap indexes work well for stable columns with few values typical of tables in a data warehouse.

Bitmap indexes work well for stable columns with few values. The *FacRank* column would be attractive for a bitmap column index because it contains few values and faculty members do not change rank often. The size of the bitmap is not an important issue because compression techniques can reduce the size significantly. Due to the requirement for stable columns, bitmap indexes are most common for data warehouse tables especially as join indexes. A data warehouse is a decision support database that is mostly used for retrievals and periodic insertion of new data. Chapter 16 discusses the use of bitmap indexes for data warehouse tables.

8.3.5 Summary of File Structures

To help you recall the file structures, Table 8-7 summarizes the major characteristics of each structure. In the first row, hash files can be used for sequential access, but there may be extra physical records because keys are evenly spread among physical records. In the second row, unordered and ordered sequential files must examine on average half the physical records (linear). Hash files examine a constant number (usually close to 1) of physical records, assuming that the file is not too full. Btrees have logarithmic search costs because of the relationship between the height, the log function, and search cost formulas. File structures can store all the data of a table (primary file structure) or store only key data along with pointers to the data records (secondary file structure). A secondary file structure or index provides an alternative path to the data. A bitmap index supports range searches by performing union operations on the bitmaps for each column value in the range.

Table 8-7: Summary of File Structures

	Unordered	Ordered	Hash	B+tree	Bitmap
Sequential search	Y	Y	Extra PRs	Y	N
Key search	Linear	Linear	Constant time	Logarithmic	Y
Range search	N	Y	N	Y	Y
Usage	Primary only	Primary only	Primary or secondary	Primary or secondary	Secondary only

8.3.6 Oracle Storage Concepts and File Structures

To supplement the conceptual presentation of storage concepts, the last part of this section presents selected details about Oracle storage concepts and file structures. Oracle supports a rich collection of file structures to achieve performance objectives.

In Oracle, a database consists of a collection of tablespaces. In the simplest arrangement, a database contains a single tablespace stored in one file. For large databases, a database may contain multiple tablespaces with each tablespace stored on multiple files. A file is a collection of physical records managed by the operating system. Objects such as tables and indexes are stored in files as shown in Figure 8.17. A file is allocated in extents that are collections of contiguous disk blocks. Oracle recommends using uniform extent sizes in a file such as 1 MB.

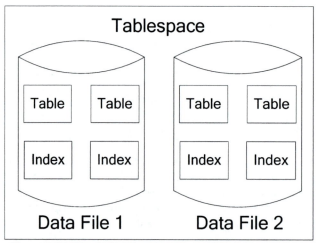

Figure 8.17: Oracle Tablespace, Files, and Database Objects

Oracle has two important parameters to control free space in a data block. As depicted in Figure 8.18, the PCTFREE parameter indicates the minimum percentage of a data block preserved as free space for updates to rows. The PCTFREE parameter provides a high water mark as a block is marked as full for insertions when the PCTFREE limit is reached. After reaching the PCTFREE limit, the PCTUSED parameter indicates the minimum percentage of a block that must be available before new rows are added to the block. Thus, the PCTUSED parameter acts as a low water mark in that a block is marked full until it falls to its PCTUSED limit. The PCTFREE and PCTUSED parameters must sum to less than 100%. For example, PCTFREE of 20% indicates that new rows can be added until a block reaches 80% full. After this point, new rows cannot be added again until the remaining space falls to the PCTUSED value (40%) through deletions.

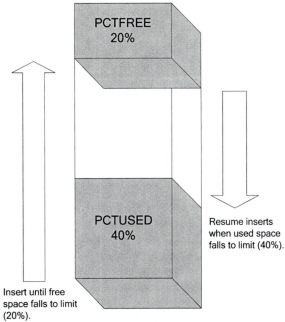

Figure 8.18: Relationship between PCTFREE and PCTUSED Parameters

Oracle provides a variety of file structures to organize disk blocks. For primary storage, Oracle provides unordered, index-organized, and clustered files. An index-organized file is a BTree in which index nodes contain complete rows (key values and non key values). To ensure that an index-organized file is sufficiently bushy, Oracle uses overflow areas to store long rows separate associated index nodes. A clustered file contains rows from two or more tables. Clustering is a specialized structure for closely related tables such as order and order line in which parent and child rows are almost always accessed together. For secondary storage, Oracle provides B+tree, hash, bitmap, and function indexes. A function index uses a function to precompute a column value and store it in the index. A function index is useful for conditions involving a function on a column rather than the column alone.

For large databases, Oracle provides a variety of partitioning options to improve performance and reliability. Partitioning can improve query performance by accessing a subset of partitions, rather than the entire table. Partitioning increases database availability if critical tables and indexes are divided into partitions to reduce the maintenance windows, recovery times, and impact of failures. Partitioning should be done in conjunction with parallel database processing as discussed in Chapter 17. As listed below, Oracle supports various combinations of partitioning for tables and indexes.

A non partitioned table can have partitioned or non portioned indexes.

A partitioned table can have partitioned or non partitioned indexes.

A table can be partitioned by lists of values, range of values, or hash functions.

8.4 Query Optimization

In most relational DBMSs, you do not have the ability to choose the implementation of queries on the physical database. The query optimization component assumes this responsibility. Your productivity increases because you do not need to make these tedious decisions. However, you can sometimes improve optimization decisions if you understand principles of the optimization process. To provide you with an understanding of the optimization process, this section describes the tasks performed and discusses tips to improve optimization decisions.

8.4.1 Translation Tasks

When you submit an SQL statement for execution, the query optimization component translates your query in four phases as shown in Figure 8.19. The first and fourth phases are common to any computer language translation process. The second phase has some unique aspects. The third phase is unique to translation of database languages.

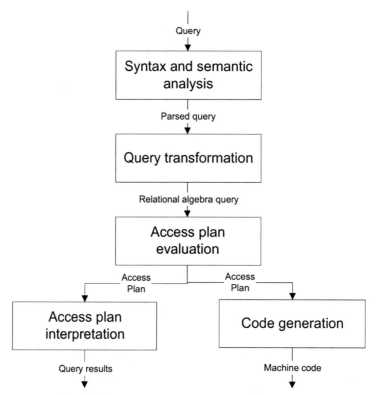

Figure 8.19: Tasks in Database Language Translation

Syntax and Semantic Analysis

The first phase analyzes a query for syntax and simple semantic errors. Syntax errors involve misuse of keywords such as if the FROM keyword was misspelled in Example 8.1. Semantic errors involve misuse of columns and tables. The data language compiler can detect only simple semantic errors involving incompatible data types. For example, a WHERE condition that compares the *CourseNo* column with the *FacSalary* column results in a semantic error because these columns have incompatible data types. To find semantic errors, the DBMS uses table, column, and relationship definitions as stored in the data dictionary.

Example 8.1: Joining three tables (Oracle)
```
SELECT FacName, CourseNo, Enrollment.OfferNo, EnrGrade
  FROM Enrollment, Offering, Faculty
WHERE CourseNo LIKE 'IS%' AND OffYear = 2007
  AND OffTerm = 'FALL'
    AND Enrollment.OfferNo = Offering.OfferNo
    AND Faculty.FacSSN = Offering.FacSSN
```

Query Transformation

The second phase transforms a query into a simplified and standardized format. As with optimizing programming language compilers, database language translators can eliminate redundant parts of a logical expression. For example, the logical expression (OffYear = 2008 AND OffTerm = 'WINTER') OR (OffYear = 2008 AND OffTerm = 'SPRING') can be simplified to OffYear = 2008 AND (OffTerm = 'WINTER' OR OffTerm = 'SPRING'). Join simplification is unique to database languages. For example, if Example 8.1 contained a join with the *Student* table, this table could be eliminated if no columns or conditions involving the *Student* table are used in the query.

264

The standardized format is usually based on relational algebra. The relational algebra operations are rearranged so that the query can be executed faster. Typical rearrangement operations are described below. Because the query optimization component performs this rearrangement, you do not have to be careful about writing your query in an efficient way.

- Restriction operations are combined so that they can be tested together.
- Projection and restriction operations are moved before join operations to eliminate unneeded columns and rows before expensive join operations.
- Cross product operations are transformed into join operations if a join condition exists in the WHERE clause.

Access Plan Evaluation

The third phase generates an access plan to implement the rearranged relational algebra query. An access plan indicates the implementation of a query as operations on files, as depicted in Figure 8.18. In an access plan, the leaf nodes are individual tables in the query, and the arrows point upward to indicate the flow of data. The nodes above the leaf nodes indicate decisions about accessing individual tables. In Figure 8.20, Btree indexes are used to access individual tables. The first join combines the *Enrollment* and the *Offering* tables. The Btree file structures provide the sorting needed for the merge join algorithm. The second join combines the result of the first join with the *Faculty* table. The intermediate result must be sorted on *FacSSN* before the merge join algorithm can be used. Figure 8.21 shows a variation of the access plan in Figure 8.20 in which the join order is changed.

Access Plan: a tree that encodes decisions about file structures to access individual tables, the order of joining tables, and the algorithm to join tables.

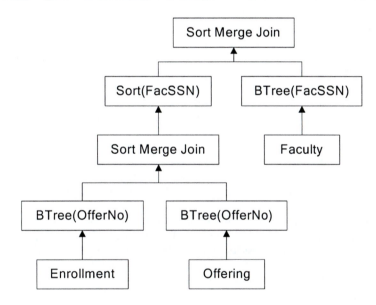

Figure 8.20: Access Plan for Example 8.1

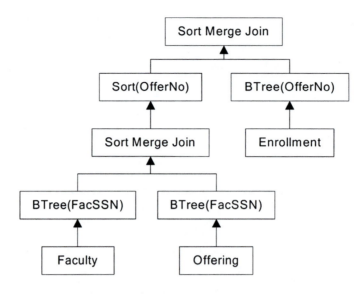

Figure 8.21: Alternative Access Plan for Example 8.1

Access plans vary by join orders, file structures, and join algorithms. For join order, the optimization component only considers feasible join orders in which the next join does not share a table with the previous joins in a join order. For example, if a query involves four tables (T1 to T2) with three joins (T1-T2, T2-T3, and T3-T4), some feasible join orders are <T1-T2, T2-T3, T3-T4> and <T3-T4, T2-T3, T1-T2>. The join order < T1-T2, T3-T4, T2-T3> is not feasible because the first two joins do not share a common table. For file structures, the optimization component considers primary and secondary file structures. For secondary file structures, a WHERE condition must match an index. Some optimization components can consider set operations (intersection for conditions connected by AND and union for conditions connected by OR) to combine the results of multiple indexes on the same table.

Most optimization components use a small set of join algorithms. Table 8-8 summarizes common join algorithms employed by optimization components. For each join operation in a query, the optimization component considers each supported join algorithm. For the nested loops and the hybrid algorithms, the optimization component must also choose the outer table and the inner table. All algorithms except the star join involve two tables at a time. The star join can combine any number of tables matching the star pattern (a child table surrounded by parent tables in 1-M relationships). The nested loops algorithm can be used with any join operation, not just an equi-join operation.

The query optimization component uses cost formulas to evaluate access plans. Each operation in an access plan has a corresponding cost formula that estimates the physical record accesses and CPU operations. The cost formulas use table profiles to estimate the number of rows in a result. For example, the number of rows resulting from a WHERE condition can be estimated using distribution data such as a histogram. The query optimization component chooses the access plan with the lowest cost.

The query optimization component evaluates a large number of access plans. The number of join orders is the dominant element in determining the number of access plans. In most queries, the number of joins is one less than the number of tables in the query. In this situation, an upper bound on the number of join orders with N tables is $(N-1)!$ where ! indicates the factorial function. The factorial function has explosive growth as it grows faster than exponential functions. The factorial function overstates the number of join orders because it includes infeasible join orders. As the number of joins increases, the number of feasible join orders approaches the total number of join orders. Figure 8.22 plots the number of tables to the number of access plans using the factorial function as an upper limit for the number of join orders. Note that the scale of the y-axis is power of 10. So for a query with 10 tables, the number of access plans is more than 10^6.

Table 8-8: Summary of Common Join Algorithms

Algorithm	Requirements	When to Use
Nested loops	Choose outer table and inner table; can be used for all joins	Appropriate when restrictive conditions on the outer table with an index on the join column of the inner table or when all pages of the inner table fit into memory
Sort merge	Both tables must be sorted (or use an index) on the join columns; only used for equi-joins	Appropriate if sort cost is small or if a clustered join index exists
Hybrid join	Combination of sort merge and nested loops; outer table must be sorted (or use a join column index); inner table must have an index on the join column; only used for equi-joins	Performs better than sort merge when there is a nonclustering index (see the next section) on the join column of the inner table
Hash join	Internal hash file built for both tables; only used for equi-joins	Hash join performs better than sort merge when the tables are not sorted or clustered indexes do not exist
Star join	Join multiple tables in which there is one child table related to multiple parent tables in 1-M relationships; bitmap join index required on each parent table; only used for equi-joins	Useful for tables matching the star pattern with bitmap join indexes especially when there are highly selective conditions on the parent tables; widely used to optimize data warehouse queries (see Chapter 16)

The number of access plans indicates that query optimization can consume considerable resources. Query optimization components use many heuristics to reduce the number of plans evaluated. Still, evaluating access plans can involve a significant amount of time when a query contains more than eight to ten tables.

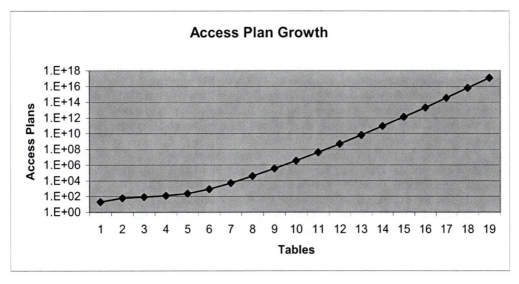

Figure 8.22: Access Plan Growth by Number of Tables

Access Plan Execution

The last phase executes the selected access plan. The query optimization component either generates machine code or interprets the access plan. Execution of machine code results in faster response than interpreting an access plan. However, most DBMSs interpret access plans because of the variety of hardware supported. The performance difference between interpretation and machine code execution is usually not significant for most users.

8.4.2 Improving Optimization Decisions

Even though the query optimization component performs its role automatically, the database administrator also has a role to play. The database administrator should review access plans of poorly performing queries and updates. Enterprise DBMSs typically provide graphical displays of access plans to facilitate review. Graphical displays are essential because text displays of hierarchical relationships are difficult to read.

To improve poor decisions in access plans, some enterprise DBMSs allow hints that influence the choice of access plans. For example, Oracle allows hints to choose the optimization goal, the file structures to access individual tables, the join algorithm, and the join order. Hints should be used with caution because they override the judgment of the optimizer. Hints with join algorithms and join orders are especially problematic because of the subtlety of these decisions. Overriding the judgment of the optimizer should only be done as a last resort after determining the cause of poor performance. In many cases, the database administrator can fix problems with table profile deficiencies and query coding style to improve performance rather than override the judgment of the optimizer.

Table Profile Deficiencies

The query optimization component needs detailed and current statistics to evaluate access plans. Statistics that are not detailed enough or outdated can lead to the choice of poor access plans. Most DBMSs provide control over the level of detail of statistics and the currency of the statistics. Some DBMSs even allow dynamic database sampling at optimization time but normally this level of data currency is not needed.

If statistics are not collected for a column, most DBMSs use the uniform value assumption to estimate the number of rows. Using the uniform value assumption often leads to sequential file access rather than Btree access if the column has significant skew in its values. For example, consider a query to list employees with salaries greater than $100,000. If the salary range is $10,000 to $2,000,000, about 95 percent of the employee table should satisfy this condition using the uniform value assumption. For most companies, however, few employees would have a salary greater than $100,000. Using the estimate from the uniform value assumption, the optimizer will choose a sequential file instead of a Btree to access the employee table. The estimate would not improve much using an equal-width histogram because of the extreme skew in salary values.

An equal-height histogram will provide much better estimates. To improve estimates using an equal-height histogram, the number of ranges should be increased. For example with 10 ranges, the maximum error is about 10% and the expected error is about 5%. To decrease the maximum and expected estimation errors by 50%, the number of ranges should be doubled. A database administrator should increase the number of ranges if estimation errors for the number of rows cause poor choices for accessing individual tables.

A hint can be useful for conditions involving parameter values. If the database administrator knows that the typical parameter values result in the selection of few rows, a hint can be used to force the optimization component to use an index.

In addition to detailed statistics about individual columns, an optimization component sometimes needs detailed statistics on combinations of columns. If a combination of columns appears in the WHERE clause of a query, statistics on the column combination are important if the columns are not independent. For example, employee salaries and positions are typically related. A WHERE clause with both columns such as `EmpPosition = 'Janitor' AND Salary > 50000` would likely have few rows that satisfy both conditions. An optimization component with no knowledge of the relationship among these columns would be likely to significantly overestimate the number of rows in the result.

Most optimization components assume that combinations of columns are statistically independent to simplify the estimation of the number of rows. Unfortunately, few DBMSs maintain statistics on combinations of columns. If a DBMS does not maintain statistics on column combinations, a database designer may want to use hints to override the judgment of the DBMS when a joint condition in a WHERE clause generates few rows. Using a hint could force the optimization component to combine indexes when accessing a table rather than using a sequential table scan.

Query Coding Practices

Poorly written queries can lead to slow query execution. The database administrator should review poorly performing queries looking for coding practices that lead to slow performance. The remainder of this subsection explains the coding practices that can lead to poorly performing queries. Table 8-9 provides a convenient summary of the coding practices.

- You should not use functions on indexable columns as functions eliminate the opportunity to use an index. You should be especially aware of implicit type conversions even if a function is not used. An implicit type conversion occurs if the data type of a column and the associated constant value do not match. For example the condition, `OffYear = '2007'` causes an implicit conversion of the *OffYear* column to a character data type. The conversion eliminates the possibility of using an index on *OffYear*.

- Queries with extra join operations will slow performance. The execution speed of a query is primarily determined by the number of join operations so eliminating unnecessary join operations may significantly decrease execution time.

- For queries involving 1-M relationships in which there is a condition on the join column, you should make the condition on the parent table rather than the child table. The condition on the parent table can significantly reduce the effort in joining the tables.

- For queries involving the HAVING clause, eliminate conditions that do not involve aggregate functions. Conditions involving simple comparisons of columns in the GROUP BY clause belong in the WHERE clause, not the HAVING clause. Moving these conditions to the WHERE clause will eliminate rows sooner, thus providing faster execution.

- You should avoid Type II nested queries (see Chapter 9), especially when the nested query performs grouping with aggregate calculations. Many DBMSs perform poorly as query optimization components often do not consider efficient ways to implement Type II nested queries. You can improve query execution speed can improve by replacing a Type II nested query with a separate query.

- Queries with complex views can lead to poor performance because an extra query may be executed. Chapter 10 describes view processing with some guidelines for limiting the complexity of views.

- The optimization process can be time-consuming, especially for queries containing more than seven or eight tables. To reduce optimization time, most DBMSs save access plans to avoid the time-consuming phases of the translation process. Query binding is the process of associating a query with an access plan. Most DBMSs rebind automatically if a query changes or the database changes (file structures, table profiles, data types, etc.). Chapter 11 discusses query binding for dynamic SQL statements inside of a computer program.

Query Binding: associating an access plan with an SQL statement. Binding can reduce execution time for complex queries because the time-consuming phases of the translation process are not performed after the initial binding occurs.

8.5 Index Selection

Index selection is the most important decision available to the physical database designer. However, it also can be one of the most difficult decisions. As a designer, you need to understand the difficulty of index selection and the limitations of performing index selection without an automated tool. This section helps you gain this knowledge by defining the index selection problem, discussing trade-offs in selecting indexes, and presenting index selection rules for moderate-size databases.

Table 8-9: Summary of Coding Practices

Coding Practice	Recommendation	Performance Issue
Functions on columns in conditions	Avoid functions on columns	Eliminates possible usage of index
Implicit type conversions	Use constants with data types matching the corresponding columns	Eliminates possible usage of index
Extra join operations	Eliminate unnecessary join operations by looking for tables that do not involve conditions or columns	Execution time is primarily determined by the number of join operations.
Conditions on join columns	Conditions on join columns should use the parent table not the child table.	Reducing the number of rows in the parent table will decrease execution time of join operations.
Row conditions in the HAVING clause	Move row conditions in the HAVING clause to the WHERE clause	Row conditions in the WHERE clause allow reduction in the intermediate result size.
Type II nested queries with grouping (Chapter 9)	Convert Type II nested queries into separate queries.	Query optimization components often do not consider efficient ways to implement Type II nested queries.
Queries using complex views (Chapter 10)	Rewrite queries using complex views to eliminate view references	An extra query may be executed.
Rebinding of queries (Chapter 11)	Ensure that queries in a stored procedure are bound once.	Repetitive binding involves considerable overhead for complex queries.

8.5.1 Problem Definition

Index selection involves two kinds of indexes, clustering and nonclustering. In a <u>clustering</u> <u>index</u>, the order of the rows is close to the index order. Close means that physical records containing rows will not have to be accessed more than one time if the index is accessed sequentially. Figure 8.23 shows the sequence set of a B+tree index pointing to associated rows inside physical records. Note that for a given node in the sequence set, most associated rows are clustered inside the same physical record. Ordering the row data by the index column is a simple way to make a clustered index.

Index: a secondary file structure that provides an alternative path to the data. In a clustering index, the order of the data records is close to the index order. In a nonclustering index, the order of the data records is unrelated to the index order.

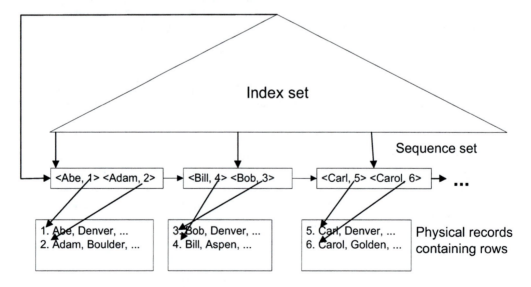

Figure 8.23: Clustering Index Example

270

In contrast, a <u>nonclustering index</u> does not have this closeness property. In a nonclustered index, the order of the rows is not related to the index order. Figure 8.24 shows that the same physical record may be repeatedly accessed when using the sequence set. The pointers from the sequence set nodes to the rows cross many times, indicating that the index order is different from the row order.

Index selection involves choices about clustered and nonclustered indexes, as shown in Figure 8.25. It is usually assumed that each table is stored in one file. The SQL statements indicate the database work to be performed by applications. The weights should combine the frequency of a statement with its importance. The table profiles must be specified in the same level of detail as required for query optimization.

Index Selection Problem: for each table, select at most one clustering index and zero or more nonclustering indexes.

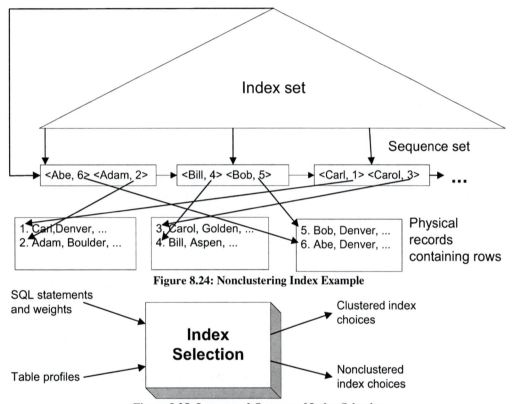

Figure 8.24: Nonclustering Index Example

Figure 8.25: Inputs and Outputs of Index Selection

Usually, the index selection problem is restricted to Btree indexes and separate files for each table. The references at the end of the chapter provide details about using other kinds of indexes (such as hash indexes) and placing data from multiple tables in the same file. However, these extensions make the problem more difficult without adding much performance improvement. The extensions are useful only in specialized situations.

8.5.2 Trade-offs and Difficulties

The best selection of indexes balances faster retrieval with slower updates. A nonclustering index can improve retrievals by providing fast access to selected records. In Example 8.2, a nonclustering index on either the *OffYear*, *OffTerm*, or *CourseNo* columns may be useful if relatively few rows satisfy the associated condition in the query. Usually, less than 5 percent of the rows must satisfy a condition for a nonclustering index to be useful. It is unlikely that any of the conditions in Example 8.2 will yield such a small fraction of the rows.

For optimizers that support multiple index access for the same table, nonclustering indexes can be useful even if a single index by itself does not provide high enough selectivity of rows. For example, the number of rows after applying the conditions on *CourseNo*, *OffYear*, and *OffTerm* should be small, perhaps 20 to 30 rows. If an optimizer can accurately estimate the number of rows, indexes on the three columns can be combined to access the *Offering* rows. Thus, the ability to use multiple indexes on the same table increases the usefulness of nonclustering indexes.

A nonclustering index can also be useful in a join if one table in the join has a small number of rows in the result. For example, if only a few *Offering* rows meet all three conditions in Example 8.2, a nonclustering index on the *Faculty.FacNo* column may be useful when joining the *Faculty* and *Offering* tables.

Example 8.2 (Oracle): Join of the Faculty and Offering Tables

```
SELECT FacName, CourseNo, OfferNo
 FROM Offering, Faculty
 WHERE CourseNo LIKE 'IS%' AND OffYear = 2007
   AND OffTerm = 'FALL'
   AND Faculty.FacNo = Offering.FacNo
```

A clustering index can improve retrievals under more situations than a nonclustering index. A clustering index is useful in the same situations as a nonclustering index except that the number of resulting rows can be larger. For example, a clustering index on either the *CourseNo*, *OffYear*, or *OffTerm* columns may be useful if perhaps 20 percent of the rows satisfy the associated condition in the query.

A clustering index can also be useful on joins because it avoids the need to sort. For example, using clustering indexes on the *Offering.FacNo* and *Faculty.FacNo* columns, the *Offering* and *Faculty* tables can be joined by merging the rows from each table. Merging rows is often a fast way to join tables if the tables do not need to be sorted (clustered indexes exist).

The cost to maintain indexes as a result of INSERT, UPDATE, and DELETE statements balances retrieval improvements. INSERT and DELETE statements affect all indexes of a table. Thus, many indexes on a table are not preferred if the table has frequent insert and delete operations. UPDATE statements affect only the columns listed in the SET clause. If UPDATE statements on a column are frequent, the benefit of an index is usually lost.

Clustering index choices are more sensitive to maintenance than nonclustering index choices. Clustering indexes are more expensive to maintain than nonclustering indexes because the data file must be changed similar to an ordered sequential file. For nonclustering indexes, the data file can be maintained as an unordered sequential file.

Difficulties of Index Selection

Index selection is difficult to perform well for a variety of reasons as explained in this subsection. If you understand the reasons that index selection is difficult, you should gain insights into the computer-aided tools to help in the selection process for large databases. Enterprise DBMSs and some outside vendors provide computer-aided tools to assist with index selection.

- Application weights are difficult to specify. Judgments that combine frequency and importance can make the result subjective.
- Distribution of parameter values is sometimes needed. Many SQL statements in reports and forms use parameter values. If parameter values vary from being highly selective to not very selective, selecting indexes is difficult.
- The behavior of the query optimization component must be known. Even if an index appears useful for a query, the query optimization component must use it. There may be subtle reasons why the query optimization component does not use an index, especially a nonclustering index.
- The number of choices is large. Even if indexes on combinations of columns are ignored, the theoretical number of choices is exponential in the number of columns (2^{NC} where NC is the number of columns). Although many of these choices can be easily eliminated, the number of practical choices is still quite large.

- Index choices can be interrelated. The interrelationships can be subtle, especially when choosing indexes to improve join performance. The selection of a clustering index on a parent table can influence the selection on a related child table.

An index selection tool can help with the last three problems. A good tool should use the query optimization component to derive cost estimates for each query under a given choice of indexes. However, a good tool cannot help alleviate the difficulty of specifying application profiles and parameter value distributions. Other tools may be provided to specify and capture application profiles.

Oracle SQL Access Advisor

The Oracle SQL Access Advisor performs a variety of physical design tasks including index selection. The SQL Access Advisor makes recommendations for indexes (B+tree, bitmap, hash, and function) using a workload specification. To ensure realistic recommendations, the SQL Access Advisor uses the Oracle optimization component to determine the impact of index choices on a workload. Workloads can be provided by a DBA or collected from database operations. A workload specification involves a collection of SQL statements. For each SQL statement, a specification includes the frequency, priority, optimizer cost, rows retrieved, memory usage, CPU time, and disk reads. Workload specifications can be stored and reused throughout the history of a database.

8.5.3 Selection Rules

Despite the difficulties previously discussed, you usually can avoid poor index choices by following some simple rules. You also can use the rules as a starting point for a more careful selection process.

Rule 1: A primary key is a good candidate for a clustering index.

Rule 2: To support joins, consider indexes on foreign keys. A nonclustering index on a foreign key is a good idea when there are important queries with highly selective conditions on the related primary key table. A clustering index is a good choice when most joins use a parent table with a clustering index on its primary key, and the queries do not have highly selective conditions on the parent table.

Rule 3: A column with many values may be a good choice for a nonclustering index if it is used in equality conditions. The term *many values* means that a column is almost unique.

Rule 4: A column used in highly selective range conditions is a good candidate for a nonclustering index.

Rule 5: A combination of columns used together in query conditions may be good candidates for nonclustering indexes if the joint conditions return few rows, the DBMS optimizer supports multiple index access, and the columns are stable. Individual indexes should be created on each column.

Rule 6: A frequently updated column is not a good index candidate.

Rule 7: Volatile tables (lots of insertions and deletions) should not have many indexes.

Rule 8: Stable columns with few values are good candidates for bitmap indexes if the columns appear in WHERE conditions.

Rule 9: Avoid indexes on combinations of columns. Most optimization components can use multiple indexes on the same table. An index on a combination of columns is not as flexible as multiple indexes on individual columns of the table.

Applying the Selection Rules

Let us apply these rules to the *Student, Enrollment,* and *Offering* tables of the university database. Table 8-10 lists summaries of the table profiles. More detail about column and relationship distributions can be encoded in histograms. Table 8-11 lists SQL statements and frequencies for these tables. The names beginning with $ represent parameters supplied by a user. The frequencies assume a student population of 30,000, in which students enroll in an average of four offerings per term. After a student graduates or leaves the university, the *Student* and *Enrollment* rows are archived.

Table 8-10: Table Profiles

Table	Number of Rows	Column (Number of Unique Values)
Student	30,000	StdSSN (PK), StdLastName (29,000), StdAddress (20,000), StdCity (500), StdZip (1,000), StdState (50), StdMajor (100), StdGPA (400)
Enrollment	300,000	StdSSN (30,000), OfferNo (2,000), EnrGrade (400)
Offering	10,000	OfferNo (PK), CourseNo (900), OffTime (20), OffLocation (500), FacSSN (1,500), OffTerm (4), OffYear (10), OffDays (10)
Course	1,000	CourseNo (PK), CrsDesc (1,000), CrsUnits (6)
Faculty	2,000	FacSSN (PK), FacLastName (1,900), FacAddress (1,950), FacCity (50), FacZip (200), FacState (3), FacHireDate (300), FacSalary (1,500), FacRank (10), FacDept (100)

Table 8-11: SQL Statements and Frequencies for Several University Database Tables

SQL Statement	Frequency	Comments
1. INSERT INTO Student …	7,500/year	Beginning of year
2. INSERT INTO Enrollment …	120,000/term	During registration
3. INSERT INTO Offering …	1,000/year	Before scheduling deadline
4. DELETE Student WHERE StdSSN = $X	8,000/year	After separation
5. DELETE Offering WHERE OfferNo = $X	1,000/year	End of year
6. DELETE Enrollment WHERE OfferNo = $X AND StdSSN = $Y	64,000/year	End of year
7. SELECT * FROM Student WHERE StdGPA > $X AND StdMajor = $Y	1,200/year	$X is usually very large or small
8. SELECT * FROM Student WHERE StdSSN = $X	30,000/term	

9. SELECT * FROM Offering
   WHERE OffTerm = $X AND OffYear = $Y
   AND CourseNo LIKE $Z
	60,000/term	Few rows in result

10. SELECT * FROM Offering, Enrollment
   WHERE StdSSN = $X AND OffTerm = $Y
   AND OffYear = $Z
   AND Offer.OfferNo =
Enrollment.OfferNo
	30,000/term	Few rows in result

11. UPDATE Student SET StdGPA = $X WHERE StdSSN = $Y	30,000/term	Updated at end of reporting form
12. UPDATE Enrollment SET EnrGrade = $X WHERE StdSSN = $Y AND OfferNo = $Z	120,000/term	Part of grade reporting form
13. UPDATE OfferNo SET FacSSN = $X WHERE OfferNo = $Y	500/year	

14. SELECT FacSSN, FacFirstName,
FacLastName
   FROM Faculty
   WHERE FacRank = $X AND FacDept = $Y
	1,000/term	Most occurring during registration

15. SELECT *
   FROM Student, Enrollment, Offering
   WHERE Offer.OfferNo = $X
   AND Student.StdSSN =
Enrollment.StdSSN
   AND Offer.OfferNo =
Enrollment.OfferNo
	4,000/year	Most occurring beginning of semester

Table 8-12 lists index choices according to the index selection rules. Only a few indexes are recommended because of the frequency of maintenance statements and the absence of highly selective conditions on columns other than the primary key. In queries 9 and 10, although the individual conditions on *OffTerm* and *OffYear* are not highly selective, the joint condition may be reasonably selective to recommend bitmap indexes, especially in query 9 with the additional condition on *CourseNo*. There is an index on *StdGPA* because parameter values should be very high or low, providing high selectivity with few rows in the result. A more detailed study of the *StdGPA* index may be necessary because it has a considerable amount of update activity. Even though not suggested by the SQL statements, the *StdLastName* and *FacLastName* columns also may be good index choices because they are almost unique (a few duplicates) and reasonably stable. If there are additional SQL statements that use these columns in conditions, nonclustered indexes should be considered.

Table 8-12: Index Selections for the University Database Tables

Column	Index Kind	Rule
Student.StdNo	Clustering	1
Student.StdGPA	Nonclustering	4
Offering.OfferNo	Clustering	1
Enrollment.OfferNo	Clustering	2
Faculty.FacRank	Bitmap	8
Faculty.Dept	Bitmap	8
Offering.OffTerm	Bitmap	8
Offering.OffYear	Bitmap	8

Although SQL:2006 does not support statements for indexes, most DBMSs support index statements. In Example 8.3, the word following the INDEX keyword is the name of the index. The CREATE index statement also can be used to create an index on a combination of columns by listing multiple columns in the parentheses. The Oracle CREATE INDEX statement cannot be used to create a clustered index. To create a clustered index, Oracle provides the ORGANIZATION INDEX clause as part of the CREATE TABLE statement.

Example 8.3: Oracle CREATE INDEX statements

```
CREATE UNIQUE INDEX StdNoIndex ON Student (StdNo)
CREATE INDEX StdGPAIndex ON Student (StdGPA)
CREATE UNIQUE INDEX OfferNoIndex ON Offering (OfferNo)
CREATE INDEX EnrollOfferNoIndex ON Enrollment (OfferNo)
CREATE BITMAP INDEX OffYearIndex ON Offering (OffYear)
CREATE BITMAP INDEX OffTermIndex ON Offering (OffTerm)
CREATE BITMAP INDEX FacRankIndex ON Faculty (FacRank)
CREATE BITMAP INDEX FacDeptIndex ON Faculty (FacDept)
```

8.6 Additional Choices in Physical Database Design

Although index selection is the most important decision of physical database design, there are other decisions that can significantly improve performance. This section discusses two decisions, denormalization and record formatting, that can improve performance in selected situations. Next, this section presents parallel processing to improve database performance, an increasingly popular alternative. Finally, several ways to improve performance related to specific kinds of processing are briefly discussed.

8.6.1 Denormalization

Denormalization combines tables so that they are easier to query. After combining tables, the new table may violate a normal form such as BCNF. Although some of the denormalization techniques do not lead to violations in a normal form, they still make a design easier to query and more difficult to update. Denormalization should always be done with extreme care because a normalized design has important advantages. Chapter 7 described one situation for denormalization: ignoring a functional dependency if it does not lead to significant modification anomalies. This section describes additional situations under which denormalization may be justified.

> Normalized Designs
> - Have better update performance.
> - Require less coding to enforce integrity constraints.
> - Support more indexes to improve query performance.

Repeating Groups

A repeating group is a collection of associated values such as sales history, lines of an order, or payment history. The rules of normalization force repeating groups to be stored in a child table separate from the associated parent table. For example, the lines of an order are stored in an order line table, separate from a related order table. If a repeating group is always accessed with its associated parent table, denormalization may be a reasonable alternative.

Figure 8.26 shows a denormalization example of quarterly sales data. Although the denormalized design does not violate BCNF, it is less flexible for updating than the normalized design. The normalized design supports an unlimited number of quarterly sales as compared to only four quarters of sales results for the denormalized design. However, the denormalized design does not require a join to combine territory and sales data.

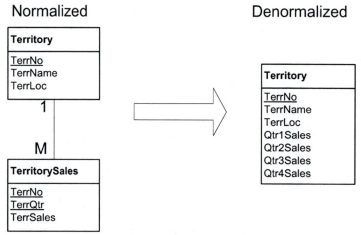

Figure 8.26: Denormalizing a Repeating Group

Generalization Hierarchies

Following the conversion rule for generalization hierarchies in Chapter 6 can result in many tables. If queries often need to combine these separate tables, it may be reasonable to store the separate tables as one table. Figure 8.27 demonstrates denormalization of the *Emp*, *HourlyEmp*, and *SalaryEmp* tables. They have 1-1 relationships because they represent a generalization hierarchy. Although the denormalized design does not violate BCNF, the combined table may waste space because of null values. However, the denormalized design avoids the outer join operator to combine the tables.

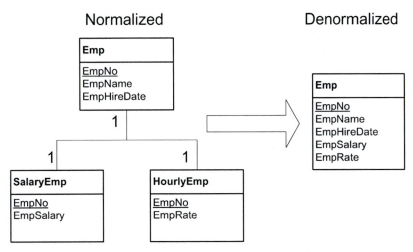

Figure 8.27: Denormalizing a Generalization Hierarchy

Codes and Meanings

Normalization rules require that foreign keys be stored alone to represent 1-M relationships. If a foreign key represents a code, the user often requests an associated name or description in addition to the foreign key value. For example, the user may want to see the state name in addition to the state code. Storing the name or description column along with the code violates BCNF, but it eliminates some join operations. If the name or description column is not changed often, denormalization may be a reasonable choice. Figure 8.28 demonstrates denormalization for the *Dept* and *Emp* tables. In the denormalized design, the *DeptName* column has been added to the *Emp* table.

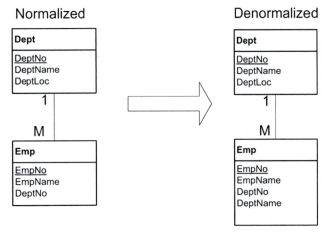

Figure 8.28: Denormalizing to Combine Code and Meaning Columns

8.6.2 Record Formatting

Record formatting decisions involve compression and derived data. With an increasing emphasis on storing complex data types such as audio, video, and images, compression is becoming an important issue. In some situations, there are multiple compression alternatives available. Compression is a trade-off between input-output and processing effort. Compression reduces the number of physical records transferred but may require considerable processing effort to compress and decompress the data.

   Decisions about derived data involve trade-offs between query and update operations. For query purposes, storing derived data reduces the need to retrieve data needed to calculate the derived data. However, updates to the underlying data require additional updates to the derived data. Storing derived data to reduce join operations may be reasonable. Figure 8.29 demonstrates derived data in the *Order* table. If the total amount of an order is frequently requested, storing the derived column *OrdAmt* may be reasonable. Calculating order amount requires a summary or aggregate calculation of related *OrdLine* and *Product* rows to obtain the *Qty* and *ProdPrice* columns. Storing the *OrdAmt* column avoids two join operations.

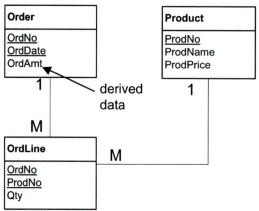

Figure 8.29: Storing Derived Data to Improve Query Performance

8.6.3 Parallel Processing

Retrieval and modification performance can be improved significantly through parallel processing. Retrievals involving many records can be improved by reading physical records in parallel. For example, a report to summarize daily sales activity may read thousands of records from several tables. Parallel reading of physical records can reduce significantly the execution time of the report. In addition, performance can be improved significantly for batch applications with many write operations and read/write of large logical records such as images.

As a response to the potential performance improvements, many DBMSs provide parallel processing capabilities. Chapter 17 describes architectures for parallel database processing. The presentation here is limited to an important part of any parallel database processing architecture, Redundant Arrays of Independent Disks (RAID)[29]. The RAID controller (Figure 8.30) enables an array of disks to appear as one large disk to the DBMS. For very high performance, a RAID controller can control as many as 90 disks. Because of the controller, RAID storage requires no changes in applications and queries. However, the query optimization component may be changed to account for the effect of parallel processing on access plan evaluation.

> **RAID**: a collection of disks (a disk array) that operates as a single disk. RAID storage supports parallel read and write operations with high reliability.

Striping is an important concept for RAID storage. Striping involves the allocation of physical records to different disks. A stripe is the set of physical records that can be read or written in parallel. Normally, a stripe contains a set of adjacent physical records. Figure 8.31 depicts an array of four disks that allows the reading or writing of four physical records in parallel.

---

[29] RAID originally was an acronym for Redundant Arrays of Inexpensive Disks. Because prices of disk drives have fallen dramatically since the invention of the RAID idea (1988), inexpensive has been replaced by independent.

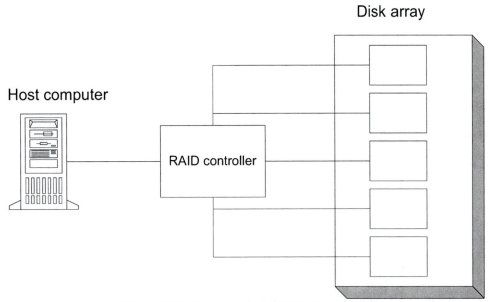

Figure 8.30: Components of a RAID Storage System

Each stripe consists of four adjacent physical records. Three stripes are shown separated by dotted lines.

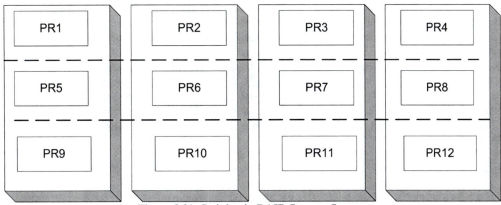

Figure 8.31: Striping in RAID Storage Systems

To utilize RAID storage, a number of architectures have emerged. The architectures, known as RAID-X, support parallel processing with varying amounts of performance and reliability. Reliability is an important issue because the mean time between failures (a measure of disk drive reliability) decreases as the number of disk drives increases. To combat reliability concerns, RAID architectures incorporate redundancy using mirrored disks, error-correcting codes, and spare disks. Here are RAID architectures that provide varying amounts of performance and reliability.

- <u>RAID-1</u>: involves a full mirror or redundant array of disks to improve reliability. Each physical record is written to both disk arrays in parallel. Read operations from separate queries can access a disk array in parallel to improve performance across queries. RAID-1 involves the most storage overhead as compared to other RAID architectures.
- <u>RAID-5</u>: uses both data and error-correcting pages (known as parity pages) to improve reliability. Read operations can be performed in parallel on stripes. Write operations involve a data page and an error-correcting page on another disk. To reduce disk contention, the error-correcting pages are randomly located across disks. RAID-5 uses storage space more efficiently than RAID-1 but can involve slower write times because

of the error-correcting pages. Thus, RAID-1 is often preferred for highly volatile parts of a database.

- Advanced architectures use a two-dimensional arrangement of mirroring and striping. A mirror of striped volumes tolerates failure to one volume because a volume is chosen and then used like striped RAID. At a higher cost, striping of mirrored volumes provides even higher reliability because it does not fail until one disk in each stripe fails.

Beyond these basic architectures, the RAID naming convention incorporates the number of data disks, parity disks, and spares. For example, 5+1+1 involves 5 data disks, 1 parity disk, and 1 hot spare disk.

To increase capacity beyond RAID and to remove the reliance on storage devices attached to a server, Storage Area Networks (SANs) have been developed. A SAN is a specialized high-speed network that connects storage devices and servers. The goal of SAN technology is to integrate different types of storage subsystems into a single system and to eliminate the potential bottleneck of a single server controlling storage devices. Many large organizations are using SANs to integrate storage systems for operational databases, data warehouses, archival storage of documents, and traditional file systems.

8.6.4 Other Ways to Improve Performance

There are a number of other ways to improve database performance that are related to a specific kind of processing. For transaction processing (Chapter 15), you can add computing capacity (faster and more processors, memory, and hard disk) and make trade-offs in transaction design. For data warehouses (Chapter 16), you can add computing capacity and design new tables with derived data. For distributed database processing (Chapter 17), you can allocate processing and data to various computing locations. Data can be allocated by partitioning a table vertically (column subset) and horizontally (row subset) to locate data close to its usage. These design choices are discussed in the respective chapters in Part 7.

In addition to tuning performance for specific processing requirements, you also can improve performance by utilizing options specific to a DBMS. Fragmentation is an important concern in database storage as it is with any disk storage. Most DBMSs provide guidelines and tools to monitor and control fragmentation. In addition, most DBMSs have options for file structures that can improve performance. You must carefully study the specific DBMS to understand these options. It may take several years of experience and specialized education to understand options of a particular DBMS. However, the payoff of increased salary and demand for your knowledge can be worth the study.

Closing Thoughts

This chapter has described the nature of the physical database design process and details about the inputs, environment, and design decisions. Physical database design involves details closest to the operating system such as movement of physical records. The objective of physical database design is to minimize certain computing resources (physical record accesses and processing effort) without compromising the meaning of the database. Physical database design is a difficult process because the inputs can be difficult to specify, the environment is complex, and the number of choices can be overwhelming.

To improve your proficiency in performing physical database design, this chapter described details about the inputs and the environment of physical database design. This chapter described table profiles and application profiles as inputs that must be specified in sufficient detail to achieve an efficient design. The environment consists of file structures and the query optimization component of the DBMS. For file structures, this chapter described characteristics of sequential, hash, Btree, and bitmap structures used by many DBMSs. For query optimization, this chapter described the tasks of query optimization and tips to produce better optimization results.

After establishing the background for the physical database design process, the inputs, and the environment, this chapter described decisions about index selection, denormalization, and record formatting. For index selection, this chapter described trade-offs between retrieval and update applications and presented rules for selecting indexes. For denormalization and data formatting, this chapter presented a number of situations when they are useful.

This chapter concludes the database development process. After completing these steps, you should have an efficient table design that represents the needs of an organization. To complete your understanding of the database development process, Chapter 13 provides a detailed case study in which to apply the ideas in preceding parts of this book.

Review Concepts

- Relationship between physical records and logical records
- Objective of physical database design
- Difficulties of physical database design
- Level of detail in table and application profiles
- Equal-height histograms to specify column distributions
- Characteristics of sequential, hash, and Btree file structures
- Possible meanings of the letter *B* in the name *Btree*: balanced, bushy, block-oriented
- Bitmap indexes for stable columns with few values
- Bitmap join indexes for frequent join operations using conditions on stable nonjoin columns
- Oracle storage terminology: tablespace, file, and extent
- Oracle storage parameters to control free space in a block: PCTFREE and PCTUSED
- Tasks of data language translation
- The usage of cost formulas and table profiles to evaluate access plans
- The importance of table profiles with sufficient detail for access plan evaluation
- Coding practices to avoid poorly executing queries
- The difference between clustered and nonclustered indexes
- Trade-offs in selecting indexes
- Index selection rules to avoid poor index choices
- Denormalization to improve join performance
- Record formatting to reduce physical record accesses and improve query performance
- RAID storage to provide parallel processing for retrievals and updates
- RAID architectures to provide parallel processing with high reliability
- Storage Area Networks (SANs) to integrate storage subsystems and to eliminate reliance upon server-attached storage devices

Questions

1. What is the difference between a physical record access and a logical record access?
2. Why is it difficult to know when a logical record access results in a physical record access?
3. What is the objective of physical database design?
4. What computing resources are constraints rather than being part of the objective of physical database design?
5. What are the contents of table profiles?
6. What are the contents of application profiles?
7. Describe two ways to specify distributions of columns used in table and application profiles.
8. Why do most enterprise DBMSs use equal-height histograms to represent column distributions instead of equal-width histograms?
9. What is a file structure?
10. What is the difference between a primary and a secondary file structure?
11. Describe the uses of sequential files for sequential search, range search, and key search.
12. What is the purpose of a hash function?
13. Describe the uses of hash files for sequential search, range search, and key search.
14. What is the difference between a static hash file and a dynamic hash file?
15. Define the terms *balanced*, *bushy*, and *block-oriented* as they relate to Btree files.
16. Briefly explain the use of node splits and concatenations in the maintenance of Btree files.

17. What does it mean to say that Btrees have logarithmic search cost?
18. What is the difference between a Btree and a B+tree?
19. What is a bitmap?
20. How does a DBMS use a bitmap?
21. What are the components of a bitmap index record?
22. What is the difference between a bitmap column index and a bitmap join index?
23. When should bitmap indexes be used?
24. What is the difference between a primary and secondary file structure?
25. What does it mean to say that an index matches a column?
26. Why should composite indexes be used sparingly?
27. What happens in the query transformation phase of database language translation?
28. What is an access plan?
29. What is a multiple index scan?
30. How are access plans evaluated in query optimization?
31. Why does the uniform value assumption sometimes lead to poor access plans?
32. What does it mean to bind a query?
33. What join algorithm can be used for all joins operations?
34. For what join algorithms must the optimization component choose the outer and inner tables?
35. What join algorithm can combine more than two tables at a time?
36. When is the sort merge algorithm a good choice for combining tables?
37. When is the hash join algorithm a good choice for combining tables?
38. What is an optimizer hint? Why should hints be used cautiously?
39. Identify a situation in which an optimizer hint should not be used.
40. Identify a situation in which an optimizer hint may be appropriate.
41. What is the difference between a clustering and a nonclustering index?
42. When is a nonclustering index useful?
43. When is a clustering index useful?
44. What is the relationship of index selection to query optimization?
45. What are the trade-offs in index selection?
46. Why is index selection difficult?
47. When should you use the index selection rules?
48. Why should you be careful about denormalization?
49. Identify two situations when denormalization may be useful.
50. What is RAID storage?
51. For what kinds of applications can RAID storage improve performance?
52. What is striping in relation to RAID storage?
53. What techniques are used in RAID storage to improve reliability?
54. What are the advantages and disadvantages of RAID-1 versus RAID-5?
55. What is a Storage Area Network (SAN)?
56. What is the relationship of a SAN to RAID storage?
57. What are the trade-offs in storing derived data?
58. What processing environments also involve physical database design decisions?
59. What are some DBMS-specific concerns for performance improvement?
60. What is an implicit type conversion? Why may implicit type conversions cause poor query performance?
61. Why do unnecessary joins cause poor query performance?
62. Why should row conditions in the HAVING clause be moved to the WHERE clause?
63. How are the Oracle PCTFREE and PCTUSED parameters used to control free space in a data block?
64. What is the relationship among the Oracle storage terminology tablespace, file, and extent?
65. In Oracle, can a database object such as a table be stored in more than one file? (Hint: you can find the answer in the Oracle Database Concepts document.)
66. In Oracle, what is an indexed-organized file structure?

Problems

Besides the problems presented here, the case study in Chapter 13 provides additional practice. To supplement the examples in this chapter, Chapter 13 provides a complete database design case including physical database design.

1. Use the following data to perform the indicated calculations. Show formulas that you used to perform the calculations.

> Row size = 100 bytes
> Number of rows = 100,000
> Primary key size = 6 bytes
> Physical record size = 4,096 bytes
> Pointer size = 4 bytes
> Floor(X) is the largest integer less than or equal to X.
> Ceil(X) is the smallest integer greater than or equal to X.

   1.1. Calculate the number of rows that can fit in a physical record. Assume that only complete rows can be stored (use the Floor function).
   1.2. Calculate the number of physical records necessary for a sequential file. Assume that physical records are filled to capacity except for the last physical record (use the Ceil function).
   1.3. If an unordered sequential file is used, calculate the number of physical record accesses on the average to retrieve a row with a specified key value.
   1.4. If an ordered sequential file is used, calculate the number of physical record accesses on the average to retrieve a row with a specified key value. Assume that the key exists in the file.
   1.5. Calculate the average number of physical record accesses to find a key that does not exist in an unordered sequential file and an ordered sequential file.
   1.6. Calculate the number of physical records for a static hash file. Assume that each physical record of the hash file is 70 percent full.
   1.7. Calculate the maximum branching factor on a node in a Btree. Assume that each record in a Btree consists of <key value, pointer> pairs.
   1.8. Using your calculation from problem 1.7, calculate the maximum height of a Btree index.
   1.9. Calculate the maximum number of physical record accesses to find a node in the Btree with a specific key value.

2. Answer query optimization questions for the following SQL statement:
   SELECT * FROM Customer
   WHERE CustCity = 'DENVER' AND CustBalance > 5000
   AND CustState = 'CO'

   2.1. Show four access plans for this query assuming that nonclustered indexes exist on the columns CustCity, CustBalance, and CustState. There is also a clustered index on the primary key column, CustNo.
   2.2. Using the uniform value assumption, estimate the fraction of rows that satisfy the condition on CustBalance. The smallest balance is 0 and the largest balance is $10,000.
   2.3. Using the following histogram, estimate the fraction of rows that satisfy the condition on CustBalance.

Histogram for *CustBalance*

Range	Rows
0 – 100	1,000
101 – 250	950
251 – 500	1,050
501 – 1,000	1,030
1,001 – 2,000	975
2,001 – 4,500	1,035
4,501 –	1,200

1. Answer query optimization questions for the following SQL statement

   SELECT OrdNo, OrdDate, Vehicle.ModelNo
   FROM Customer, Order, Vehicle
   WHERE CustBalance > 5000
   AND Customer.CustNo = Vehicle.CustNo
   AND Vehicle.SerialNo = Order.SerialNo

   1.1. List the possible orders to join the Customer, Order, and Vehicle tables.
   1.2. For one of these join orders, make an access plan. Assume that Btree indexes only exist for the primary keys, Customer.CustNo, Order.OrdNo, and Vehicle.SerialNo.

2. For the following tables and SQL statements, select indexes that balance retrieval and update requirements. For each table, justify your choice using the rules discussed in Section 8.5.3.

Customer(<u>CustNo</u>, CustName, CustCity, CustState, CustZip, CustBal)

Order(<u>OrdNo</u>, OrdDate, *CustNo*)

    FOREIGN KEY CustNo REFERENCES Customer

OrdLine(<u>*OrdNo, ProdNo*</u>, OrdQty)

    FOREIGN KEY OrdNo REFERENCES Order

    FOREIGN KEY ProdNo REFERENCES Product

Product(<u>ProdNo</u>, ProdName, ProdColor, ProdPrice)

SQL Statement	Frequency
1. INSERT INTO Customer …	100/day
2. INSERT INTO Product …	100/month
3. INSERT INTO Order …	3,000/day
4. INSERT INTO OrdLine …	9,000/day
5. DELETE Product WHERE ProdNo = $X	100/year
6. DELETE Customer WHERE CustNo = $X	1,000/year
7. SELECT * FROM Order, Customer WHERE OrdNo = $X AND Order.CustNo = Customer.CustNo	300/day
8. SELECT * FROM OrdLine, Product WHERE OrdNo = $X AND OrdLine.ProdNo = Product.ProdNo	300/day
9. SELECT * FROM Customer, Order, OrdLine, Product WHERE CustName = $X AND OrdDate = $Y AND Customer.CustNo = Order.CustNo AND Order.OrdNo = OrdLine.OrdNo AND Product.ProdNo = OrdLine.ProdNo	500/day
10. UPDATE OrdLine SET OrdQty = $X WHERE OrdNo = $Y	300/day
11. UPDATE Product SET ProdPrice = $X WHERE ProdNo = $Y	300/month

4.1. For the Customer table, what columns are good choices for the clustered index? Nonclustered indexes?

4.2. For the Product table, what columns are good choices for the clustered index? Nonclustered indexes?

4.3. For the Order table, what columns are good choices for the clustered index? Nonclustered indexes?

4.4. For the OrdLine table, what columns are good choices for the clustered index? Nonclustered indexes?

5. Indexes on combinations of columns are not as useful as indexes on individual columns. Consider a combination index on two columns, CustState and CustCity, where CustState is the primary ordering and CustCity is the secondary ordering. For what kinds of conditions can the index be used? For what kinds of conditions is the index not useful?

6. For query 9 in problem 4, list the possible join orders considered by the query optimization component.

7. For the following tables of a financial planning database, identify possible uses of denormalization and derived data to improve performance. In addition, identify denormalization and derived data already appearing in the tables. The tables track financial assets held and trades made by customers. A trade involves a purchase or sale of a specified quantity of an asset by a customer. Assets include stocks and bonds. The *Holding* table contains the <u>net</u> quantity of each asset held by a customer. For example, if a customer has purchased 10,000 shares of IBM and sold 4,000, the *Holding* table shows a net quantity of 6,000. A frequent query is to list the most recent valuation for each asset held by a customer. The most recent valuation is the net quantity of the asset times the most recent price.

Customer(<u>CustNo</u>, CustName, CustAddress, CustCity, CustState, CustZip, CustPhone)
Asset(<u>AssetNo</u>, SecName, LastClose)
Stock(<u>AssetNo</u>, OutShares, IssShares)
Bond(<u>AssetNo</u>, BondRating, FacValue)
PriceHistory(<u>AssetNo</u>, <u>PHistDate</u>, PHistPrice)
    FOREIGN KEY AssetNo REFERENCES Asset
Holding(<u>CustNo</u>, <u>AssetNo</u>, NetQty)
    FOREIGN KEY CustNo REFERENCES Customer
    FOREIGN KEY AssetNo REFERENCES Asset
Trade(<u>TradeNo</u>, CustNo, AssetNo, TrdQty, TrdPrice, TrdDate, TrdType, TrdStatus)
    FOREIGN KEY CustNo REFERENCES Customer
    FOREIGN KEY AssetNo REFERENCES Asset

8. Rewrite the following SQL statement to improve its performance on most DBMSs. Use the tips in Section 8.4.2 to rewrite the statement. The Oracle SQL statement uses the financial trading database shown in problem 7. The purpose of the statement is to list the customer number and the name of customers and the sum of the amount of their completed October 2008 buy trades. The amount of a trade is the quantity (number of shares) times the price per share. A customer should be in the result if the sum of the amount of his/her completed October 2008 buy trades exceeds by 25 percent the sum of the amount of his/her completed September 2008 buy trades.

```
SELECT Customer.Custno, CustName,
       SUM(TrdQty * TrdPrice) AS SumTradeAmt
  FROM Customer, Trade
  WHERE Customer.CustNo = Trade.CustNo
    AND TrdDate BETWEEN '1-Oct-2008' AND '31-Oct-2008'
  GROUP BY Customer.CustNo, CustName
  HAVING TrdType = 'BUY' AND SUM(TrdQty * TrdPrice) >
    ( SELECT 1.25 * SUM(TrdQty * TrdPrice) FROM Trade
      WHERE TrdDate BETWEEN '1-Sep-2008' AND '30-Sep-2008'
        AND TrdType = 'BUY'
        AND Trade.CustNo = Customer.CustNo )
```

9. Rewrite the following SELECT statement to improve its performance on most DBMSs. Use the tips in Section 8.4.2 to rewrite the statement. The Oracle SQL statement uses the financial trading database shown in problem 7. Note that the *CustNo* column uses the integer data type.

```
SELECT Customer.CustNo, CustName,
       TrdQty * TrdPrice, TrdDate, SecName
  FROM Customer, Trade, Asset
  WHERE Customer.CustNo = Trade.CustNo
    AND Trade.AssetNo = Asset.AssetNo
    AND TrdType = 'BUY' AND Trade.CustNo = '10001'
    AND TrdDate BETWEEN '1-Oct-2008' AND '31-Oct-2008'
```

10. For the following conditions and indexes, indicate if the index matches the condition.

- Index on TrdDate: TrdDate BETWEEN '1-Oct-2008' AND '31-Oct-2008'
- Index on CustPhone: CustPhone LIKE '(303)%'
- Index on TrdType: TrdType <> 'BUY'
- Bitmap column index on BondRating: BondRating IN ('AAA', 'AA', 'A')
- Index on <CustState, CustCity, CustZip>:
  CustState = 'CO' AND CustCity = 'Denver'
  CustState IN ('CO', 'CA') AND CustCity LIKE '%er'
  CustState IN ('CO', 'CA') AND CustZip LIKE '8%'
  CustState = 'CO' AND CustCity IN ('Denver', 'Boulder') AND CustZip LIKE '8%'

11. For the sample *Customer* and *Trade* tables below, construct bitmap indexes as indicated.
Bitmap column index on *Customer.CustState*
Join bitmap index on *Customer.CustNo* to the *Trade* table
Bitmap join index on *Customer.CustState* to the *Trade* table

Customer Table

RowID	CustNo	...	CustState
1	113344		CO
2	123789		CA
3	145789		UT
4	111245		NM
5	931034		CO
6	998245		CA
7	287341		UT
8	230432		CO
9	321588		CA
10	443356		CA
11	559211		UT
12	220688		NM

Trade Table

RowID	TradeNo	...	CustNo
1	1111		113344
2	1234		123789
3	1345		123789
4	1599		145789
5	1807		145789
6	1944		931034
7	2100		111245
8	2200		287341
9	2301		287341
10	2487		230432
11	2500		443356
12	2600		559211
13	2703		220688
14	2801		220688
15	2944		220688
16	3100		230432
17	3200		230432
18	3258		321588
19	3302		321588
20	3901		559211
21	4001		998245
22	4205		998245
23	4301		931034
24	4455		443356

12. For the following tables and SQL statements, select indexes (clustering and nonclustering) that balance retrieval and update requirements. For each table, justify your choice using the rules discussed in Section 8.5.3.

Customer(<u>CustNo</u>, CustName, CustAddress, CustCity, CustState, CustZip, CustPhone)
Asset(<u>AssetNo</u>, AssetName, AssetType)
PriceHistory(<u>AssetNo</u>, <u>PHistDate</u>, PHistPrice)
    FOREIGN KEY AssetNo REFERENCES Asset
Holding(<u>CustNo</u>, <u>AssetNo</u>, NetQty)
    FOREIGN KEY CustNo REFERENCES Customer
    FOREIGN KEY AssetNo REFERENCES Asset
Trade(<u>TradeNo</u>, CustNo, AssetNo, TrdQty, TrdPrice, TrdDate, TrdType, TrdStatus)
    FOREIGN KEY CustNo REFERENCES Customer
    FOREIGN KEY AssetNo REFERENCES Asset

SQL Statement	Frequency
1. INSERT INTO Customer …	100/day
2. INSERT INTO Asset …	100/quarter
3. INSERT INTO Trade …	10,000/day
4. INSERT INTO Holding …	200/day
5. INSERT INTO PriceHistory …	5,000/day
5. DELETE Asset WHERE AssetNo = $X	300/year
6. DELETE Customer WHERE CustNo = $X	3,000/year
7. SELECT * FROM Holding, Customer, Asset, PriceHistory WHERE CustNo = $X AND Holding.CustNo = Customer.CustNo AND Holding.AssetNo = Asset.AssetNo AND Asset.AssetNo = PriceHistory.AssetNo AND PHistDate = $Y	15,000/month

287

```
 8. SELECT * FROM Trade                                        1,000/day
      WHERE TradeNo = $X
 9. SELECT * FROM Customer, Trade, Asset                       10,000/month
      WHERE Customer.CustNo = $X
        AND TrdDate BETWEEN $Y AND $Z
        AND Customer.CustNo = Trade.CustNo
        AND Trade.AssetNo = Asset.AssetNo
10. UPDATE Trade SET TrdStatus = $X                            1,000/day
      WHERE TradeNo = $Y
11. UPDATE Holding SET NetQty = $X                             10,000/day
      WHERE CustNo = $Y AND AssetNo = $Z
12. SELECT * FROM Customer WHERE CustZip = $X                  500/day
        AND CustPhone LIKE $Y%
13. SELECT * FROM Trade WHERE TrdStatus = $X                   10/day
        AND TrdDate = $Y
14. SELECT * FROM Asset WHERE AssetName LIKE $X%              500/day
```

13. For the workload of problem 12, are there any SELECT statements in which a DBA might want to use optimizer hints? Please explain the kind of hint that could be used and your reasoning for using it.

14. Investigate tools for managing access plans of an enterprise DBMS. You should investigate tools for textual display of access plans, graphical display of access plans, and hints to influence the judgment of the optimizer.

15. Investigate the database design tools of an enterprise DBMS or CASE tool. You should investigate command-level tools and graphical tools for index selection, table profiles, and application profiles.

16. Investigate the query optimization component of an enterprise DBMS or CASE tool. You should investigate the access methods for single table access, join algorithms, and usage of optimizer statistics.

17. Show the state of the Btree in Figure 8P.1 after insertion of the following keys: 115, 142, 111, 134, 170, 175, 127, 137, 108, and 140. The Btree has a maximum key capacity of 4. Show the node splits that occur while inserting the keys. You may use the interactive Btree tool on the website http://sky.fit.qut.edu.au/~maire/baobab/baobab.html for help with this problem.

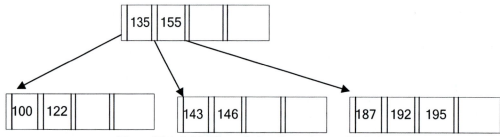

Figure 8P.1: Initial Btree Before Insertions and Deletions

18. Following on problem 17, show the state of the Btree after deleting the following keys: 108, 111, and 137. Show the node concatenations and key borrowings after deleting the keys. You may use the interactive Btree tool on the website http://sky.fit.qut.edu.au/~maire/baobab/baobab.html for help with this problem.

19. List the feasible join orders for joining tables T1, T2, T3, T4, and T5 on join conditions T1.T1No = T2.T1No, T2.T2No = T3.T2No, T3.T3No = T4.T3No, and T4.T4No = T5.T4No. How many infeasible join orders exist?

20. Use the following data to perform the indicated calculations. Show formulas that you used to perform the calculations.

Row size = 180 bytes
Number of rows = 2,000,000
Primary key size = 8 bytes

Physical record size = 4,096 bytes

Pointer size = 8 bytes

Floor(X) is the largest integer less than or equal to *X*.

Ceil(X) is the smallest integer greater than or equal to *X*.

20.1. Calculate the number of rows that can fit in a physical record. Assume that only complete rows can be stored (use the Floor function).

20.2. Calculate the number of physical records necessary for a sequential file. Assume that physical records are filled to capacity except for the last physical record (use the Ceil function).

20.3. If an unordered sequential file is used, calculate the number of physical record accesses on the average to retrieve a row with a specified key value.

20.4. If an ordered sequential file is used, calculate the number of physical record accesses on the average to retrieve a row with a specified key value. Assume that the key exists in the file.

20.5. Calculate the average number of physical record accesses to find a key that does not exist in an unordered sequential file and an ordered sequential file.

20.6. Calculate the number of physical records for a static hash file. Assume that each physical record of the hash file is 70 percent full.

20.7. Calculate the maximum branching factor on a node in a Btree. Assume that each record in a Btree consists of <key value, pointer> pairs.

20.8. Using your calculation from problem 20.7, calculate the maximum height of a Btree index.

20.9. Calculate the maximum number of physical record accesses to find a node in the Btree with a specific key value.

References for Further Study

The subject of physical database design can be much more detailed and mathematical than described in this chapter. For a more detailed description of file structures and physical database design, consult computer science books such as Elmasri and Navathe (2007) and Teorey (1999). For detailed tutorials about query optimization, consult Chaudhuri (1998), Jarke and Koch (1984) and Mannino, Chu, and Sager (1988). Finkelstein, Schkolnick, and Tiberio (1988) describe DBDSGN, an index selection tool for SQL/DS, an IBM relational DBMS. Chaudhuri. and Narasayya (1997, 2001) describe tools for index selection and statistics management for Microsoft SQL Server. Shasha and Bonnet (2003) provide more details about physical database design decisions. For details about physical database design for a specific DBMS, you should consult online documentation for the specific product. The Physical Database Design section of the online list of Web Resources provides links to physical database design tools and sources of practical advice about physical database design.

9

Advanced Query Formulation with SQL

Learning Objectives

This chapter extends your query formulation skills by explaining advanced table matching problems involving the outer join, difference, and division operators. Other parts of the SELECT statement are demonstrated to explain these advanced matching problems. In addition, the subtle effects of null values are explained to help you interpret query results involving null values. After this chapter, you should have acquired the following knowledge and skills:

- Recognize Type I nested queries for joins and understand the associated conceptual evaluation process
- Recognize Type II nested queries and understand the associated conceptual evaluation process
- Recognize problems involving the outer join, difference, and division operators
- Adapt example SQL statements to matching problems involving the outer join, difference, and division operators
- Understand the effect of null values on conditions, aggregate calculations, and grouping

Overview

As the first chapter in Part 5 of the textbook, this chapter builds on material covered in Chapter 4. Chapter 4 provided a foundation for query formulation using SQL. Most importantly, you learned an important subset of the SELECT statement and usage of the SELECT statement for problems involving joins and grouping. This chapter extends your knowledge of query formulation to advanced matching problems. To solve these advanced matching problems, additional parts of the SELECT statement are introduced.

This chapter continues with the learning approaches of Chapter 4: provide many examples to imitate and problem-solving guidelines to help you reason through difficult problems. You first will learn to formulate problems involving the outer join operator using new keywords in the FROM clause. Next you will learn to recognize nested queries and apply them to formulate problems involving the join and difference operators. Then you will learn to recognize problems involving the division operator and formulate them using the GROUP BY clause, nested queries in the HAVING clause, and the COUNT function. Finally, you will learn the effect of null values on simple conditions, compound conditions with logical operators, aggregate calculations, and grouping.

The presentation in this chapter covers additional features in Core SQL:2006, especially features not part of SQL-92. All examples execute in recent versions of Microsoft Access (2002 and beyond) and Oracle (9i and beyond) except where noted.

9.1 Outer Join Problems

One of the powerful but sometimes confusing aspects of the SELECT statement is the number of ways to express a join. In Chapter 4, you formulated joins using the cross product style and the join operator style. In the cross product style, you list the tables in the FROM clause and the join conditions in the WHERE clause. In the join operator style, you write join operations directly in the FROM clause using the INNER JOIN and ON keywords.

The major advantage of the join operator style is that problems involving the outer join operator can be formulated. Outer join problems cannot be formulated with the cross product style except with proprietary SQL extensions. This section demonstrates the join operator style for outer join problems and combinations of inner and outer joins. In addition, the proprietary outer join extension of older Oracle versions (8i and previous versions) is shown in Appendix 9C. For your reference, the relationship diagram of the university database is repeated from Chapter 4 (see Figure 9.1).

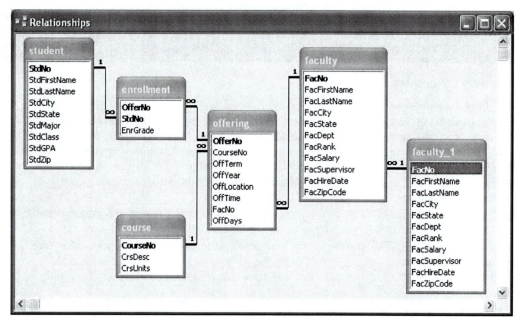

Figure 9.1: Relationship Window for the University Database

9.1.1 SQL Support for Outer Join Problems

A join between two tables generates a table with the rows that match on the join column(s). The outer join operator generates the join result (the matching rows) plus the nonmatching rows. A <u>one-sided outer join</u> generates a new table with the matching rows plus the nonmatching rows from <u>one</u> of the tables. For example, it can be useful to see all offerings listed in the output even if an offering does not have an assigned faculty.

> **One-Sided Outer Join**: an operator that generates the join result (the matching rows) plus the nonmatching rows from one of the input tables. SQL supports the one-sided outer join operator through the LEFT JOIN and RIGHT JOIN keywords.

SQL uses the LEFT JOIN and RIGHT JOIN keywords[30] to produce a one-sided outer join. The LEFT JOIN keyword creates a result table containing the matching rows and the nonmatching rows of the left table. The RIGHT JOIN keyword creates a result table containing the matching rows and the nonmatching rows of the right table. Thus, the result of a one-sided outer join depends on the direction (RIGHT or LEFT) and the position of the table names. Examples 9.1 and 9.2 demonstrate one-sided outer joins using both the LEFT and RIGHT keywords. The result rows with blank values for certain columns are nonmatched rows.

---

[30] The full SQL keywords are LEFT OUTER JOIN and RIGHT OUTER JOIN. The SQL:2006 standard and most DBMSs allow omission of the OUTER keyword.

Example 9.1 (Access): One-Sided Outer Join using LEFT JOIN

For offerings beginning with IS in the associated course number, retrieve the offer number, the course number, the faculty number, and the faculty name. Include an offering in the result even if the faculty is not yet assigned. The Oracle[31] counterpart of this example uses % instead of * as the wild card character.

```
SELECT OfferNo, CourseNo, Offering.FacNo, Faculty.FacNo,
       FacFirstName, FacLastName
  FROM Offering LEFT JOIN Faculty
       ON Offering.FacNo = Faculty.FacNo
  WHERE CourseNo LIKE 'IS*'
```

OfferNo	CourseNo	Offering.FacNo	Faculty.FacNo	FacFirstName	FacLastName
1111	IS320				
2222	IS460				
1234	IS320	098-76-5432	098-76-5432	LEONARD	VINCE
3333	IS320	098-76-5432	098-76-5432	LEONARD	VINCE
4321	IS320	098-76-5432	098-76-5432	LEONARD	VINCE
4444	IS320	543-21-0987	543-21-0987	VICTORIA	EMMANUEL
8888	IS320	654-32-1098	654-32-1098	LEONARD	FIBON
9876	IS460	654-32-1098	654-32-1098	LEONARD	FIBON
5679	IS480	876-54-3210	876-54-3210	CRISTOPHER	COLAN
5678	IS480	987-65-4321	987-65-4321	JULIA	MILLS

Example 9.2 (Access): One-Sided Outer Join using RIGHT JOIN

For offerings beginning with "IS" in the associated course number, retrieve the offer number, the course number, the faculty number, and the faculty name. Include an offering in the result even if the faculty is not yet assigned. The result is identical to Example 9.1. The Oracle counterpart of this example uses % instead of * as the wild card character.

```
SELECT OfferNo, CourseNo, Offering.FacNo, Faculty.FacNo,
       FacFirstName, FacLastName
  FROM Faculty RIGHT JOIN Offering
       ON Offering.FacNo = Faculty.FacNo
  WHERE CourseNo LIKE 'IS*'
```

A <u>full outer join</u> generates a table with the matching rows plus the nonmatching rows from both tables. Typically, a full outer join is used to combine two similar but not union compatible tables. For example, the *Student* and *Faculty* tables are similar because they contain information about university people. However, they are not union compatible. They have common columns such as first name, last name, and city but also unique columns such as GPA and salary. Occasionally, you will need to write a query that combines both tables. For example, find all university people within a certain city. A full outer join is used in such problems.

> **Full Outer Join**: an operator that generates the join result (the matching rows) plus the nonmatching rows from both input tables. SQL supports the full outer join operator through the FULL JOIN keyword.

---

[31] Appendix 9C shows the proprietary notation used in Oracle 8i for outer joins.

SQL:2006 provides the FULL JOIN keyword as demonstrated in Example 9.3. Note the null values in both halves (*Student* and *Faculty*) of the result.

Example 9.3 (SQL:2006 and Oracle 9i and beyond): Full Outer Join

Combine the *Faculty* and *Student* tables using a full outer join. List the Social Security number, the name (first and last), the salary (faculty only), and the GPA (students only) in the result. This SQL statement does not execute in Microsoft Access.

```
SELECT FacNo, FacFirstName, FacLastName, FacSalary,
       StdNo, StdFirstName, StdLastName, StdGPA
  FROM Faculty FULL JOIN Student
       ON Student.StdNo = Faculty.FacNo
```

FacNo	FacFirstName	FacLastName	FacSalary	StdNo	StdFirstName	StdLastName	StdGPA
				123456789	HOMER	WELLS	3
				124567890	BOB	NORBERT	2.7
				234567890	CANDY	KENDALL	3.5
				345678901	WALLY	KENDALL	2.8
				456789012	JOE	ESTRADA	3.2
				567890123	MARIAH	DODGE	3.6
				678901234	TESS	DODGE	3.3
				789012345	ROBERTO	MORALES	2.5
				890123456	LUKE	BRAZZI	2.2
				901234567	WILLIAM	PILGRIM	3.8
098765432	LEONARD	VINCE	35000				
543210987	VICTORIA	EMMANUEL	120000				
654321098	LEONARD	FIBON	70000				
765432109	NICKI	MACON	65000				
876543210	CRISTOPHER	COLAN	40000	876543210	CRISTOPHER	COLAN	4
987654321	JULIA	MILLS	75000				

Some DBMSs (such as Microsoft Access and Oracle 8i) do not directly support the full outer join operator. In these systems, a full outer join is formulated by taking the union of two one-sided outer joins using the steps shown below. The SELECT statement implementing these steps is shown in Example 9.4. Appendix 9C contains the Oracle 8i counterpart of Example 9.4.

1. Construct a right join of *Faculty* and *Student* (nonmatched rows of *Student*).
2. Construct a left join of *Faculty* and *Student* (nonmatched rows of *Faculty*).
3. Construct a union of these two temporary tables. Remember when using the UNION operator, the two table arguments must be "union compatible": each corresponding column from both tables must have compatible data types. Otherwise, the UNION operator will not work as expected.

Example 9.4 (Access): Full Outer Join Using a Union of Two One-Sided Outer Joins

Combine the *Faculty* and *Student* tables using a full outer join. List the social security number, the name (first and last), the salary (faculty only), and the GPA (students only) in the result. The result is identical to Example 9.3.

```
SELECT FacNo, FacFirstName, FacLastName, FacSalary,
       StdNo, StdFirstName, StdLastName, StdGPA
  FROM Faculty RIGHT JOIN Student
       ON Student.StdNo = Faculty.FacNo
          UNION
SELECT FacNo, FacFirstName, FacLastName, FacSalary,
       StdNo, StdFirstName, StdLastName, StdGPA
  FROM Faculty LEFT JOIN Student
       ON Student.StdNo = Faculty.FacNo
```

9.1.2 Mixing Inner and Outer Joins

Inner and outer joins can be mixed as demonstrated in Examples 9.5 and 9.6. For readability, it is generally preferred to use the join operator style rather than to mix the join operator and cross product styles.

Example 9.5 (Access): Mixing a One-Sided Outer Join and an Inner Join

Combine columns from the *Faculty*, *Offering*, and *Course* tables for information systems courses (IS in the beginning of the course number) offered in 2008. Include a row in the result even if there is not an assigned instructor. The Oracle counterpart of this example uses % instead of * as the wild card character.

```
SELECT OfferNo, Offering.CourseNo, OffTerm, CrsDesc,
       Faculty.FacNo, FacFirstName, FacLastName
  FROM ( Faculty RIGHT JOIN Offering
       ON Offering.FacNo = Faculty.FacNo )
     INNER JOIN Course
       ON Course.CourseNo = Offering.CourseNo
WHERE Course.CourseNo LIKE 'IS*' AND OffYear = 2008
```

OfferNo	CourseNo	OffTerm	CrsDesc	FacNo	FacFirstName	FacLastName
1111	IS320	SUMMER	FUNDAMENTALS OF BUSINESS PROGRAMMING			
3333	IS320	SPRING	FUNDAMENTALS OF BUSINESS PROGRAMMING	098-76-5432	LEONARD	VINCE
4444	IS320	WINTER	FUNDAMENTALS OF BUSINESS PROGRAMMING	543-21-0987	VICTORIA	EMMANUEL
5678	IS480	WINTER	FUNDAMENTALS OF DATABASE MANAGEMENT	987-65-4321	JULIA	MILLS
5679	IS480	SPRING	FUNDAMENTALS OF DATABASE MANAGEMENT	876-54-3210	CRISTOPHER	COLAN
8888	IS320	SUMMER	FUNDAMENTALS OF BUSINESS PROGRAMMING	654-32-1098	LEONARD	FIBON
9876	IS460	SPRING	SYSTEMS ANALYSIS	654-32-1098	LEONARD	FIBON

Example 9.6 (Access): Mixing a One-Sided Outer Join and Two Inner Joins

List the rows of the *Offering* table where there is at least one student enrolled, in addition to the requirements of Example 9.5. Remove duplicate rows when there is more than one student enrolled in an offering. The Oracle counterpart of this example uses % instead of * as the wild card character.

```
SELECT DISTINCT Offering.OfferNo, Offering.CourseNo,
       OffTerm, CrsDesc, Faculty.FacNo, FacFirstName,
       FacLastName
FROM ( ( Faculty RIGHT JOIN Offering
     ON Offering.FacNo = Faculty.FacNo )
   INNER JOIN Course
     ON Course.CourseNo = Offering.CourseNo )
   INNER JOIN Enrollment
     ON Offering.OfferNo = Enrollment.OfferNo
WHERE Offering.CourseNo LIKE 'IS*' AND OffYear = 2008
```

OfferNo	CourseNo	OffTerm	CrsDesc	FacNo	FacFirstName	FacLastName
5678	IS480	WINTER	FUNDAMENTALS OF DATABASE MANAGEMENT	987-65-4321	JULIA	MILLS
5679	IS480	SPRING	FUNDAMENTALS OF DATABASE MANAGEMENT	876-54-3210	CRISTOPHER	COLAN
9876	IS460	SPRING	SYSTEMS ANALYSIS	654-32-1098	LEONARD	FIBON

When mixing inner and outer joins, you should be careful about the order of combining operations. Some DBMSs such as Microsoft Access claim that outer joins must precede inner joins. In Examples 9.5 and 9.6, the one-sided outer join operations precede the inner join operations as indicated by the position of the parentheses. However, the claims in the Access documentation are not always enforced. For example, Example 9.6a returns the same results as Example 9.6.

Example 9.6a (Access): Mixing a On e-Sided Outer Join an d Two Inner J oins with the Outer Join Performed Last

List the rows of the *Offering* table where there is at least one student enrolled, in addition to the requirements of Example 9.5. Remove duplicate rows when there is more than one student enrolled in an offering. The Oracle counterpart of this example uses % instead of * as the wild card character. The result is identical to Example 9.6.

```
SELECT DISTINCT Offering.OfferNo, Offering.CourseNo,
       OffTerm, CrsDesc, Faculty.FacNo, FacFirstName,
       FacLastName
FROM Faculty RIGHT JOIN
   ( ( Offering INNER JOIN Course
     ON Course.CourseNo = Offering.CourseNo )
   INNER JOIN Enrollment
     ON Offering.OfferNo = Enrollment.OfferNo )
     ON Offering.FacNo = Faculty.FacNo
WHERE Offering.CourseNo LIKE 'IS*' AND OffYear = 2008
```

9.2 Understanding Nested Queries

A nested query or subquery is a query (SELECT statement) inside a query. A nested query typically appears as part of a condition in the WHERE or HAVING clauses. Nested queries also can be used in the FROM clause. Nested queries can be used like a procedure (Type I nested query) in which the nested query is executed one time or like a loop (Type II nested query) in which the nested query is executed repeatedly. This section demonstrates examples of both kinds of nested queries and explains problems in which they can be applied.

9.2.1 Type I Nested Queries

Type I nested queries are like procedures in a programming language. A Type I nested query evaluates *one* time and produces a table. The nested (or inner) query does not reference the outer query. Using the IN comparison operator, a Type I nested query can be used to express a join. In Example 9.7, the nested query on the *Enrollment* table generates a list of qualifying student number values. A row is selected in the outer query on *Student* if the student number is an element of the nested query result.

> **Type I Nested Query**: a nested query in which the inner query does not reference any tables used in the outer query. Type I nested queries can be used for some join problems and some difference problems.

Example 9.7: Using a Type I Nested Query to Perform a Join

List the student number, name, and major of students who have a high grade (≥ 3.5) in a course offering.

```
SELECT StdNo, StdFirstName, StdLastName, StdMajor
 FROM Student
WHERE Student.StdNo IN
 ( SELECT StdNo FROM Enrollment
    WHERE EnrGrade >= 3.5  )
```

StdNo	StdFirstName	StdLastName	StdMajor
123-45-6789	HOMER	WELLS	IS
124-56-7890	BOB	NORBERT	FIN
234-56-7890	CANDY	KENDALL	ACCT
567-89-0123	MARIAH	DODGE	IS
789-01-2345	ROBERTO	MORALES	FIN
890-12-3456	LUKE	BRAZZI	IS
901-23-4567	WILLIAM	PILGRIM	IS

Type I nested queries should be used only when the result does not contain any columns from the tables in the nested query. In Example 9.7, no columns from the *Enrollment* table are used in the result. In Example 9.8, the join between the *Student* and *Enrollment* tables cannot be performed with a Type I nested query because *EnrGrade* appears in the result.

Example 9.8: Combining a Type I Nested Query and the Join Operator Style

Retrieve the name, city, and grade of students who have a high grade (≥ 3.5) in a course offered in fall 2007.

```
SELECT StdFirstName, StdLastName, StdCity, EnrGrade
 FROM Student INNER JOIN Enrollment
       ON Student.StdNo = Enrollment.StdNo
WHERE EnrGrade >= 3.5 AND Enrollment.OfferNo IN
 ( SELECT OfferNo FROM Offering
    WHERE OffTerm = 'FALL' AND OffYear = 2007 )
```

StdFirstName	StdLastName	StdCity	EnrGrade
CANDY	KENDALL	TACOMA	3.5
MARIAH	DODGE	SEATTLE	3.8
HOMER	WELLS	SEATTLE	3.5
ROBERTO	MORALES	SEATTLE	3.5

It is possible to have multiple levels of nested queries although this practice is not encouraged because the statements can be difficult to read. In a nested query, you can have another nested query using the IN comparison operator in the WHERE clause. In Example 9.9, the nested query on the *Offering* table has a nested query on the *Faculty* table. No *Faculty* columns are needed in the main query or in the nested query on *Offering*.

Example 9.9: Using a Type I Nested Query inside Another Type I Nested Query

Retrieve the name, city, and grade of students who have a high grade (≥ 3.5) in a course offered in fall 2007 taught by Leonard Vince.

```
SELECT StdFirstName, StdLastName, StdCity, EnrGrade
 FROM Student, Enrollment
 WHERE Student.StdNo = Enrollment.StdNo
   AND EnrGrade >= 3.5 AND Enrollment.OfferNo IN
   ( SELECT OfferNo FROM Offering
       WHERE OffTerm = 'FALL' AND OffYear = 2007
       AND FacNo IN
        ( SELECT FacNo  FROM Faculty
          WHERE FacFirstName = 'LEONARD'
           AND FacLastName = 'VINCE' )   )
```

StdFirstName	StdLastName	StdCity	EnrGrade
CANDY	KENDALL	TACOMA	3.5
MARIAH	DODGE	SEATTLE	3.8
HOMER	WELLS	SEATTLE	3.5
ROBERTO	MORALES	SEATTLE	3.5

The Type I style gives a visual feel to a query. You can visualize a Type I subquery as navigating between tables. Visit the table in the subquery to collect join values that can be used to select rows from the table in the outer query. The use of Type I nested queries is largely a matter of preference. Even if you do not prefer this join style, you should be prepared to interpret queries written by others with Type I nested queries.

The DELETE statement provides another use of a Type I nested query. A Type I nested query is useful when the deleted rows are related to other rows, as demonstrated in Example 9.10. Using a Type I nested query is the standard way to reference related tables in DELETE statements. Chapter 4 demonstrated the join operator style inside a DELETE statement, a proprietary extension of Microsoft Access. For your reference, Example 9.11 shows a DELETE statement using the join operator style that removes the same rows as Example 9.10.

Example 9.10: DELETE Statement Using a Type I Nested Query

Delete offerings taught by Leonard Vince. Three Offering rows are deleted. In addition, this statement deletes related rows in the *Enrollment* table because the ON DELETE clause is set to CASCADE.

```
DELETE FROM Offering
 WHERE Offering.FacNo IN
  ( SELECT FacNo FROM Faculty
    WHERE FacFirstName = 'LEONARD'
      AND FacLastName = 'VINCE' )
```

Example 9.11 (Access only): DELETE Statement Using INNER JOIN Operation

Delete offerings taught by Leonard Vince. Three *Offering* rows are deleted. In addition, this statement deletes related rows in the *Enrollment* table because the ON DELETE clause is set to CASCADE.

```
DELETE Offering.*
 FROM Offering INNER JOIN Faculty
      ON Offering.FacNo = Faculty.FacNo
 WHERE FacFirstName = 'LEONARD'
   AND FacLastName = 'VINCE'
```

9.2.2 Limited SQL Formulations for Difference Problems

You should recall from Chapter 3 that the difference operator combines tables by finding the rows of a first table not in a second table. A typical usage of the difference operator is to combine two tables with some similar columns but not entirely union compatible. For example, you may want to find faculty who are not students. Although the *Faculty* and *Student* tables contain some compatible columns, the tables are not union compatible. The placement of the word *not* in the problem statement indicates that the result contains rows only in the *Faculty* table, not in the *Student* table. This requirement involves a difference operation.

> **Difference Problems**: problem statements involving the difference operator often have a *not* relating two nouns in a sentence. For example, "students who are not faculty" and "employees who are not customers" are problem statements involving a difference operator.

Some difference problems can be formulated using a Type I nested query with the NOT IN operator. As long as the comparison among tables involves a single column, a Type I nested query can be used. In Example 9.12, a Type I nested query can be used because the comparison only involves a single column from the *Faculty* table (*FacNo*).

Example 9.12: Using a Type I Nested Query for a Difference Problem

Retrieve the Social Security number, name (first and last), department, and salary of faculty who are <u>not</u> students.

```
SELECT FacNo, FacFirstName, FacLastName, FacDept,
       FacSalary
 FROM Faculty
 WHERE FacNo NOT IN
  ( SELECT StdNo FROM Student )
```

FacNo	FacFirstName	FacLastName	FacDept	FacSalary
098-76-5432	LEONARD	VINCE	MS	$35,000.00
543-21-0987	VICTORIA	EMMANUEL	MS	$120,000.00
654-32-1098	LEONARD	FIBON	MS	$70,000.00
765-43-2109	NICKI	MACON	FIN	$65,000.00
987-65-4321	JULIA	MILLS	FIN	$75,000.00

Another formulation approach for some difference problems involves a one-sided outer join operator to generate a table with only nonmatching rows. The IS NULL comparison operator can remove rows that match, as demonstrated in Example 9.13. However, this formulation cannot be used when there are conditions to test on the excluded table (*Student* in Example 9.13). If there are conditions to test on the *Student* table (such as on student class), another SQL formulation approach must be used.

Example 9.13: One-Sided Outer Join with Only Nonmatching Rows

Retrieve the student number, name, department, and salary of faculty who are *not* students. The result is identical to Example 9.12.

```
SELECT FacNo, FacFirstName, FacLastName, FacSalary
  FROM Faculty LEFT JOIN Student
       ON Faculty.FacNo = Student.StdNo
 WHERE Student.StdNo IS NULL
```

Although SQL:2006 does have a difference operator (the EXCEPT keyword), it is sometimes not convenient because only the common columns can be shown in the result. Example 9.14 does not provide the same result as Example 9.12 because the columns unique to the *Faculty* table (*FacDept* and *FacSalary*) are not in the result. Another query that uses the first result must be formulated to retrieve the unique *Faculty* columns.

Example 9.14 (Oracle): Difference Query

Show faculty who are *not* students (pure faculty). Only show the common columns in the result. Note that Microsoft Access does not support the EXCEPT keyword. Oracle uses the MINUS keyword instead of EXCEPT. The result is identical to Example 9.12 except for *FacCity* and *FacState* instead of *FacDept* and *FacSalary*.

```
SELECT FacNo AS PerNo, FacFirstName AS FirstName,
       FacLastName AS LastName, FacCity AS City,
       FacState AS State
  FROM Faculty
       MINUS
SELECT StdNo AS PerNo, StdFirstName AS FirstName,
       StdLastName AS LastName, StdCity AS City,
       StdState AS State
  FROM Student
```

Difference Problems Cannot Be Solved with Inequality Joins

It is important to note that difference problems such as Example 9.12 cannot be solved with a join alone. Example 9.12 requires that every row of the *Student* table be searched to select a faculty row. In contrast, a join selects a faculty row when the first matching student row is found. To contrast difference and join problems, examine Example 9.15. Although it looks correct, it is does not provide the desired result. Every faculty row will be in the result because there is at least one student row that does not match every faculty row.

Example 9.15: Inequality Join

Erroneous formulation for the problem "Retrieve the faculty number, name (first and last), and rank of faculty who are *not* students." The result contains all faculty rows.

```
SELECT DISTINCT FacNo, FacFirstName, FacLastName,
                FacRank
  FROM Faculty, Student
  WHERE Student.StdNo <> Faculty.FacNo
```

To understand Example 9.15, you can use the conceptual evaluation process discussed in Chapter 4 (Section 4.3). The result tables show the cross product (Table 9-3) of Tables 9-1 and 9-2 followed by the rows that satisfy the WHERE condition (Table 9-4). Notice that only one row of the cross product is deleted. The final result (Table 9-5) contains all rows of Table 9-2.

Table 9-1: Sample Student Table

StdNo	StdFirstName	StdLastName	StdMajor
123-45-6789	HOMER	WELLS	IS
124-56-7890	BOB	NORBERT	FIN
234-56-7890	CANDY	KENDALL	ACCT

Table 9-2: Sample Faculty Table

FacNo	FacFirstName	FacLastName	FacRank
098-76-5432	LEONARD	VINCE	ASST
543-21-0987	VICTORIA	EMMANUEL	PROF
876-54-3210	CRISTOPHER	COLAN	ASST

Table 9-3: Cross Product of the Sample *Student* and *Faculty* Tables

FacNo	FacFirstName	FacLastName	FacRank	StdNo	StdFirstName	StdLastName	StdMajor
098-76-5432	LEONARD	VINCE	ASST	123-45-6789	HOMER	WELLS	IS
098-76-5432	LEONARD	VINCE	ASST	124-56-7890	BOB	NORBERT	FIN
098-76-5432	LEONARD	VINCE	ASST	876-54-3210	CRISTOPHER	COLAN	IS
543-21-0987	VICTORIA	EMMANUEL	PROF	123-45-6789	HOMER	WELLS	IS
543-21-0987	VICTORIA	EMMANUEL	PROF	124-56-7890	BOB	NORBERT	FIN
543-21-0987	VICTORIA	EMMANUEL	PROF	876-54-3210	CRISTOPHER	COLAN	IS
876-54-3210	CRISTOPHER	COLAN	ASST	123-45-6789	HOMER	WELLS	IS
876-54-3210	CRISTOPHER	COLAN	ASST	124-56-7890	BOB	NORBERT	FIN
876-54-3210	CRISTOPHER	COLAN	ASST	876-54-3210	CRISTOPHER	COLAN	IS

Table 9-4: Restriction of Table 9-3 to Eliminate Matching Rows

FacNo	FacFirstName	FacLastName	FacRank	StdNo	StdFirstName	StdLastName	StdMajor
098-76-5432	LEONARD	VINCE	ASST	123-45-6789	HOMER	WELLS	IS
098-76-5432	LEONARD	VINCE	ASST	124-56-7890	BOB	NORBERT	FIN
098-76-5432	LEONARD	VINCE	ASST	876-54-3210	CRISTOPHER	COLAN	IS
543-21-0987	VICTORIA	EMMANUEL	PROF	123-45-6789	HOMER	WELLS	IS
543-21-0987	VICTORIA	EMMANUEL	PROF	124-56-7890	BOB	NORBERT	FIN
543-21-0987	VICTORIA	EMMANUEL	PROF	876-54-3210	CRISTOPHER	COLAN	IS
876-54-3210	CRISTOPHER	COLAN	ASST	123-45-6789	HOMER	WELLS	IS
876-54-3210	CRISTOPHER	COLAN	ASST	124-56-7890	BOB	NORBERT	FIN

Table 9-5: Projection of Table 9-4 to Eliminate *Student* Columns

FacNo	FacFirstName	FacLastName	FacRank
098-76-5432	LEONARD	VINCE	ASST
543-21-0987	VICTORIA	EMMANUEL	PROF
876-54-3210	CRISTOPHER	COLAN	ASST

Summary of Limited Formulations for Difference Problems

This section has discussed three SQL formulations for difference problems. Each formulation has limitations as noted in Table 9-6. In practice, the one-sided outer join approach is the most restrictive as many problems involve conditions on the excluded table. Section 9.2.3 presents a more general formulation without the restrictions noted in Table 9-6.

Table 9-6: Limitations of SQL Formulations for Difference Problems

SQL Formulation	Limitations
Type I nested query with the NOT IN operator	Only one column for comparing rows of the two tables
One-sided outer join with an IS NULL condition	No conditions (except the IS NULL condition) on the excluded table
Difference operation using the EXCEPT or MINUS keywords	Result must contain only union-compatible columns

9.2.3 Using Type II Nested Queries for Difference Problems

Although Type II nested queries provide a more general solution for difference problems, they are conceptually more complex than Type I nested queries. Type II nested queries have two distinguishing features. First, Type II nested queries reference one or more columns from an outer query. Type II nested queries are sometimes known as correlated subqueries because they reference columns used in outer queries. In contrast, Type I nested queries are not correlated with outer queries. In Example 9.16, the nested query contains a reference to the *Faculty* table used in the outer query.

302

Example 9.16: Using a Type II Nested Query for a Difference Problem

Retrieve the faculty number, the name (first and last), the department, and the salary of faculty who are *not* students.

```
SELECT FacNo, FacFirstName, FacLastName, FacDept,
       FacSalary
  FROM Faculty
  WHERE NOT EXISTS
   ( SELECT * FROM Student
       WHERE Student.StdNo = Faculty.FacNo )
```

FacNo	FacFirstName	FacLastName	FacDept	FacSalary
098-76-5432	LEONARD	VINCE	MS	$35,000.00
543-21-0987	VICTORIA	EMMANUEL	MS	$120,000.00
654-32-1098	LEONARD	FIBON	MS	$70,000.00
765-43-2109	NICKI	MACON	FIN	$65,000.00
987-65-4321	JULIA	MILLS	FIN	$75,000.00

The second distinguishing feature of Type II nested queries involves execution. A Type II nested query executes one time for *each* row in the outer query. In this sense, a Type II nested query is similar to a nested loop that executes one time for each execution of the outer loop. In each execution of the inner loop, variables used in the outer loop are used in the inner loop. In other words, the inner query uses one or more values from the outer query in each execution.

> **Type II Nested Query**: a nested query in which the inner query references a table used in the outer query. Because a Type II nested query executes for each row of its outer query, Type II nested queries are more difficult to understand and execute than Type I nested queries.

To help you understand Example 9.16, Table 9-9 traces the execution of the nested query using Tables 9-7 and 9-8. The EXISTS operator is true if the nested query returns one or more rows. In contrast, the NOT EXISTS operator is true if the nested query returns 0 rows. Thus, a faculty row in the outer query is selected only if there are no matching student rows in the nested query. For example, the first two rows in Table 9-7 are selected because there are no matching rows in Table 9-8. The third row is *not* selected because the nested query returns one row (the third row of Table 9-7).

Table 9-7: Sample *Faculty* Table

FacNo	FacFirstName	FacLastName	FacRank
098-76-5432	LEONARD	VINCE	ASST
543-21-0987	VICTORIA	EMMANUEL	PROF
876-54-3210	CRISTOPHER	COLAN	ASST

Table 9-8: Sample *Student* Table

StdNo	StdFirstName	StdLastName	StdMajor
123-45-6789	HOMER	WELLS	IS
124-56-7890	BOB	NORBERT	FIN
876-54-3210	CRISTOPHER	COLAN	IS

Table 9-9: Execution Trace of Nested Query in Example 9.16

FacNo	Result of subquery execution	NOT EXISTS
098-76-5432	0 rows retrieved	true
543-21-0987	0 rows retrieved	true
876-54-3210	1 row retrieved	false

NOT EXISTS operator: a table comparison operator often used with Type II nested queries. NOT EXISTS is true for a row in an outer query if the inner query returns no rows and false if the inner query returns one or more rows.

Example 9.17 shows another formulation that clarifies the meaning of the NOT EXISTS operator. Here, a faculty row is selected if the number of rows in the nested query is 0. Using the sample tables (Tables 9-7 and 9-8), the nested query result is 0 for the first two faculty rows.

Example 9.17: Using a Type II Nested Query with the COUNT Function

Retrieve the faculty number, the name, the department, and the salary of faculty who are *not* students. The result is the same as Example 9.16.

```
SELECT FacNo, FacFirstName, FacLastName, FacDept,
       FacSalary
 FROM Faculty
 WHERE 0 =
  ( SELECT COUNT(*) FROM Student
      WHERE Student.StdNo = Faculty.FacNo )
```

More Difficult Difference Problems

More difficult difference problems combine a difference operation with join operations. For example, consider the query to list students who took all of their information systems (IS) offerings in winter 2008 from the same instructor. The query results should include students who took only one offering as well as students who took more than one offering.
- Construct a list of students who have taken IS courses in winter 2008 (a join operation).
- Construct another list of students who have taken IS courses in winter 2008 from more than one instructor (a join operation).
- Use a difference operation (first student list minus the second student list) to produce the result.

Conceptualizing a problem in this manner forces you to recognize that it involves a difference operation. If you recognize the difference operation, you can make a formulation in SQL involving a nested query (Type II with NOT EXISTS or Type I with NOT IN) or the EXCEPT keyword. Example 9.18 shows a NOT EXISTS solution in which the outer query retrieves a student row if the student does not have an offering from a *different* instructor in the inner query.

Example 9.18 (Access): More Difficult Difference Problem Using a Type II Nested Query

List the student number and the name of students who took all of their information systems offerings in winter 2008 from the same instructor. Include students who took only one offering as well as students who took more than one offering. Note that in the nested query, the columns *Enrollment.StdNo* and *Offering.FacNo* refer to the outer query.

```
SELECT DISTINCT Enrollment.StdNo, StdFirstName,
                  StdLastName
FROM Student, Enrollment, Offering
WHERE Student.StdNo = Enrollment.StdNo
   AND Enrollment.OfferNo = Offering.OfferNo
   AND CourseNo LIKE 'IS*' AND OffTerm = 'WINTER'
     AND OffYear = 2008 AND NOT EXISTS
         ( SELECT * FROM Enrollment E1, Offering O1
           WHERE E1.OfferNo = O1.OfferNo
             AND Enrollment.StdNo = E1.StdNo
               AND O1.CourseNo LIKE 'IS*'
             AND O1.OffYear = 2008
             AND O1.OffTerm = 'WINTER'
               AND Offering.FacNo <> O1.FacNo )
```

StdNo	StdFirstName	StdLastName
123-45-6789	HOMER	WELLS
234-56-7890	CANDY	KENDALL
345-67-8901	WALLY	KENDALL
456-78-9012	JOE	ESTRADA
567-89-0123	MARIAH	DODGE

Example 9.18 (Oracle): More Difficult Difference Problem Using a Type II Nested Query

List the student number and name of the students who took all of their information systems offerings in winter 2008 from the same instructor. Include students who took only one offering as well as students who took more than one offering.

```
SELECT DISTINCT Enrollment.StdNo, StdFirstName,
                  StdLastName
FROM Student, Enrollment, Offering
WHERE Student.StdNo = Enrollment.StdNo
   AND Enrollment.OfferNo = Offering.OfferNo
   AND CourseNo LIKE 'IS%' AND OffTerm = 'WINTER'
     AND OffYear = 2008 AND NOT EXISTS
         ( SELECT * FROM Enrollment E1, Offering O1
           WHERE E1.OfferNo = O1.OfferNo
             AND Enrollment.StdNo = E1.StdNo
               AND O1.CourseNo LIKE 'IS%'
             AND O1.OffYear = 2008
             AND O1.OffTerm = 'WINTER'
               AND Offering.FacNo <> O1.FacNo )
```

Example 9.19 shows a second example using the NOT EXISTS operator to solve a complex difference problem. Conceptually this problem involves a difference operation between two sets: the set of all faculty members and the set of faculty members teaching in the specified term. The difference operation can be implemented by selecting a faculty in the outer query list if the faculty does not teach an offering during the specified term in the inner query result.

Example 9.19: Another Difference Problem Using a Type II Nested Query

List the name (first and last) and department of faculty who are *not* teaching in winter term 2008.
```
        SELECT DISTINCT FacFirstName, FacLastName, FacDept
        FROM Faculty
        WHERE NOT EXISTS
          ( SELECT * FROM Offering
             WHERE Offering.FacNo = Faculty.FacNo
               AND OffTerm = 'WINTER' AND OffYear = 2008 )
```

FacFirstName	FacLastName	FacDept
CRISTOPHER	COLAN	MS
LEONARD	FIBON	MS
LEONARD	VINCE	MS

Example 9.20 shows a third example using the NOT EXISTS operator to solve a complex difference problem. In this problem, the word *only* connecting different parts of the sentence indicates a difference operation. Conceptually this problem involves a difference operation between two sets: the set of all faculty members teaching in winter 2008 and the set of faculty members teaching in winter 2008 in addition to teaching in another term. The difference operation can be implemented by selecting a faculty teaching in winter 2008 in the outer query if the same faculty does not teach an offering in a different term in the nested query.

Example 9.20: Another Difference Problem Using a Type II Nested Query

List the name (first and last) and department of faculty who are *only* teaching in winter term 2008.

```
SELECT DISTINCT FacFirstName, FacLastName, FacDept
  FROM Faculty F1, Offering O1
  WHERE F1.FacNo = O1.FacNo
    AND OffTerm = 'WINTER' AND OffYear = 2008
    AND NOT EXISTS
  ( SELECT * FROM Offering O2
      WHERE O2.FacNo = F1.FacNo
        AND ( OffTerm <> 'WINTER' OR OffYear <> 2008 ) )
```

FacFirstName	FacLastName	FacDept
EMMANUEL	VICTORIA	MS
MILLS	JULIA	FIN

9.2.4 Nested Queries in the FROM Clause

So far, you have seen nested queries in the WHERE clause with certain comparison operators (IN and EXISTS) as well as with traditional comparison operators when the nested query produces a single value such as the count of the number of rows. Similar to the usage in the WHERE clause, nested queries also can appear in the HAVING clause as demonstrated in the next section. Nested queries in the WHERE and the HAVING clauses have been part of the SQL design since its initial design.

In contrast, nested queries in the FROM clause were supported beginning with SQL:1999. The design of SQL:1999 began a philosophy of consistency in language design. Consistency means that wherever an object is permitted, an object expression should be permitted. In the FROM clause, this philosophy means that wherever a table is permitted, a table expression (a nested query) should be allowed. Nested queries in the FROM clause are not as widely used as nested queries in the WHERE and HAVING clauses. The remainder of this section demonstrates some specialized uses of nested queries in the FROM clause.

One usage of nested queries in the FROM clause is to compute an aggregate function within an aggregate function (nested aggregates). SQL does not permit an aggregate function inside another aggregate function. A nested query in the FROM clause overcomes the prohibition against nested aggregates as demonstrated in Example 9.21. Without a nested query in the FROM clause, two queries would be necessary to produce the output. In Access, the nested query would be a stored query. In Oracle, the nested query would be a view (see Chapter 10 for an explanation of views).

Example 9.21: Using a Nested Query in the FROM Clause

List the course number, the course description, the number of offerings, and the average enrollment across offerings.

```
SELECT T.CourseNo, T.CrsDesc, COUNT(*) AS NumOfferings,
       Avg(T.EnrollCount) AS AvgEnroll
FROM
  ( SELECT Course.CourseNo, CrsDesc,
           Offering.OfferNo, COUNT(*) AS EnrollCount
    FROM Offering, Enrollment, Course
    WHERE Offering.OfferNo = Enrollment.OfferNo
      AND Course.CourseNo = Offering.CourseNo
    GROUP BY Course.CourseNo, CrsDesc, Offering.OfferNo
      ) T
GROUP BY T.CourseNo, T.CrsDesc
```

CourseNo	CrsDesc	NumOfferings	AvgEnroll
FIN300	FUNDAMENTALS OF FINANCE	1	2
FIN450	PRINCIPLES OF INVESTMENTS	1	2
FIN480	CORPORATE FINANCE	1	3
IS320	FUNDAMENTALS OF BUSINESS PROGRAMMING	2	6
IS460	SYSTEMS ANALYSIS	1	7
IS480	FUNDAMENTALS OF DATABASE MANAGEMENT	2	5.5

Another usage of a nested query in the FROM clause is to compute aggregates from multiple groupings. Without a nested query in the FROM clause, a query can contain aggregates from only one grouping. For example, multiple groupings are needed to summarize the number of students per offering and the number of resources per offering. This query would be useful if the design of the university database was extended with a *Resource* table and an associative table (*ResourceUsage*) connected to the *Offering* and the *Resource* tables via 1-M relationships. The query would require two nested queries in the FROM clause, one to retrieve the enrollment count for offerings and the other to retrieve the resource count for offerings.

In Access, a nested query in the FROM clause can compensate for the inability to use the DISTINCT keyword inside aggregate functions. For example, the DISTINCT keyword is necessary to compute the number of distinct courses taught by faculty as shown in Example 9.22. To produce the same results in Access, a nested query in the FROM clause is necessary as shown in Example 9.23. The nested query in the FROM clause uses the DISTINCT keyword to eliminate duplicate course numbers. Section 9.3.3 contains additional examples using nested queries in the FROM clause to compensate for the DISTINCT keyword inside the COUNT function.

Example 9.22 (Oracle): Using the DISTINCT Keyword inside the COUNT Function

List the faculty number, the last name, and the number of unique courses taught.

```
SELECT Faculty.FacNo, FacLastName,
       COUNT(DISTINCT CourseNo) AS NumPreparations
 FROM Faculty, Offering
 WHERE Faculty.FacNo = Offering.FacNo
 GROUP BY Faculty.FacNo, FacLastName
```

FacNo	FacLastName	NumPreparations
098-76-5432	VINCE	1
543-21-0987	EMMANUEL	1
654-32-1098	FIBON	2
765-43-2109	MACON	2
876-54-3210	COLAN	1
987-65-4321	MILLS	2

Example 9.23: Using a Nested Qu ery in the FROM Clause Instea d of the DISTINCT Keyword inside the COUNT Function

List the faculty number, the last name, and the number of unique courses taught. The result is identical to Example 9.22. Although this SELECT statement executes in Access and Oracle, you should use the statement in Example 9.22 in Oracle because it will execute faster.

```
SELECT T.FacNo, T.FacLastName,
       COUNT(*) AS NumPreparations
FROM
  ( SELECT DISTINCT Faculty.FacNo, FacLastName, CourseNo
     FROM Offering, Faculty
     WHERE Offering.FacNo = Faculty.FacNo ) T
GROUP BY T.FacNo, T.FacLastName
```

9.3 Formulating Division Problems

Division problems can be some of the most difficult problems. Because of the difficulty, the divide operator of Chapter 3 is briefly reviewed. After this review, this section discusses some easier division problems before moving to more advanced problems.

9.3.1 Review of the Divide Operator

To review the divide operator, consider a simplified university database consisting of three tables: *Student1* (Table 9-10), *Club* (Table 9-11), and *StdClub* (Table 9-12) showing student membership in clubs. The divide operator is typically applied to linking tables showing M-N relationships. The *StdClub* table links the *Student1* and *Club* tables: a student may belong to many clubs and a club may have many students.

Table 9-10: *Student1* Table Listing

StdNo	SName	SCity
S1	JOE	SEATTLE
S2	SALLY	SEATTLE
S3	SUE	PORTLAND

Table 9-11: *Club* Table Listing

ClubNo	CName	CPurpose	CBudget	CActual
C1	DELTA	SOCIAL	$1,000.00	$1,200.00
C2	BITS	ACADEMIC	$500.00	$350.00
C3	HELPS	SERVICE	$300.00	$330.00
C4	SIGMA	SOCIAL		$150.00

Table 9-12: *StdClub* **Table Listing**

StdNo	ClubNo
S1	C1
S1	C2
S1	C3
S1	C4
S2	C1
S2	C4
S3	C3

The divide operator builds a table consisting of the values of one column (*StdNo*) that match *all* of the values in a specified column (*ClubNo*) of a second table (*Club*). A typical division problem is to list the students who belong to *all* clubs. The resulting table contains only student S1 because S1 is associated with all four clubs.

> **Divide**: an operator of relational algebra that combines rows from two tables. The divide operator produces a table in which values of a column from one input table are associated with all the values from a column of the second table.

Division is more conceptually difficult than join because division matches on all of the values whereas join matches on a single value. If this problem involved a join, it would be stated as "list students who belong to *any* club." The key difference is the word *any* versus *all*. Most division problems can be written with adjectives *every* or *all* between a verb phrase representing a table and a noun representing another table. In this example, the phrase "students who belong to all clubs" fits this pattern. Another example is "students who have taken every course."

9.3.2 Simple Division Problems

There are a number of ways to perform division in SQL. Some books describe an approach using Type II nested queries. Because this approach can be difficult to understand if you have not had a course in logic, a different approach is used here. The approach here uses the COUNT function with a nested query in the HAVING clause.

The basic idea is to compare the number of students associated with a club in the *StdClub* table with the number of clubs in the *Club* table. To perform this operation, group the *StdClub* table on *StdNo* and compare the number of rows in each *StdNo* group with the number of rows in the *Club* table. You can make this comparison using a nested query in the HAVING clause as shown in Example 9.24.

Example 9.24: Simplest Division Problem

List the student number of students who belong to all of the clubs.

```
SELECT StdNo
  FROM StdClub
  GROUP BY StdNo
  HAVING COUNT(*) = ( SELECT COUNT(*) FROM Club )
```

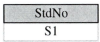

StdNo
S1

Note that the COUNT(*) on the left-hand side tallies the number of rows in the *StdNo* group. The right-hand side contains a nested query with only a COUNT(*) in the result. The nested query is Type I because there is no connection to the outer query. Therefore, the nested query only executes one time and returns a single row with a single value (the number of rows in the *Club* table).

Now let us examine some variations of the first problem. The most typical variation is to retrieve students who belong to a subset of the clubs rather than all of the clubs. For example, retrieve students who belong to all of the social clubs. To accomplish this change, you should modify Example 9.24 by including a WHERE condition in both the outer and the nested query. Instead of counting all *Student1* rows in a *StdNo* group, count only the rows where the club's purpose is social. Compare this count to the number of social clubs in the *Club* table. Example 9.25 shows these modifications.

Example 9.25: Division Problem to Find a Subset Match

List the student number of students who belong to all of the social clubs.

```
SELECT StdNo
 FROM StdClub, Club
 WHERE StdClub.ClubNo = Club.ClubNo
   AND CPurpose = 'SOCIAL'
 group by StdNo
 having count(*) =
   ( SELECT COUNT(*) FROM Club
     WHERE CPurpose = 'SOCIAL' )
```

StdNo
S1
S2

Other variations are shown in Examples 9.26 and 9.27. In Example 9.26, a join between *StdClub* and *Student* is necessary to obtain the student name. Example 9.27 reverses the previous problems by looking for clubs rather than students.

Example 9.26: Division Problem with Joins

List the student number and the name of students who belong to all of the social clubs.

```
SELECT Student1.StdNo, SName
 FROM StdClub, Club, Student1
 WHERE StdClub.ClubNo = Club.ClubNo
   AND Student1.StdNo = StdClub.StdNo
   AND CPurpose = 'SOCIAL'
 GROUP BY Student1.StdNo, SName
 HAVING COUNT(*) =
   ( SELECT COUNT(*) FROM Club
     WHERE CPurpose = 'SOCIAL' )
```

StdNo	SName
S1	JOE
S2	SALLY

Example 9.27: Another Division Problem

List the club numbers of clubs that have all of the Seattle students as members.

```
SELECT ClubNo
 FROM StdClub, Student1
 WHERE Student1.StdNo = StdClub.StdNo
   AND SCity = 'SEATTLE'
 GROUP BY ClubNo
 HAVING COUNT(*) =
   ( SELECT COUNT(*) FROM Student1
     WHERE SCity = 'SEATTLE' )
```

ClubNo
C1
C4

9.3.3 Advanced Division Problems

Example 9.28 (using the original university database tables) depicts another complication of division problems in SQL. Before tackling this additional complication, let us examine a simpler problem. Example 9.28 can be formulated with the same technique as shown in Section 9.3.2. First, join the *Faculty* and *Offering* tables, select rows matching the WHERE conditions, and group the result by faculty name (first and last). Then, compare the count of the rows in each faculty *name* group with the number of fall 2007, information systems offerings from the *Offering* table.

Example 9.28 (Access): Division Problem with a Join

List faculty number and the name (first and last) of faculty who teach all of the fall 2007, information systems offerings.

```
SELECT Faculty.FacNo, FacFirstName, FacLastName
 FROM Faculty, Offering
 WHERE Faculty.FacNo = Offering.FacNo
   AND OffTerm = 'FALL' AND CourseNo LIKE 'IS*'
   AND OffYear = 2007
 GROUP BY Faculty.FacNo, FacFirstName, FacLastName
 HAVING COUNT(*) =
   ( SELECT COUNT(*) FROM Offering
     WHERE OffTerm = 'FALL' AND OffYear = 2007
       AND CourseNo LIKE 'IS*' )
```

FacNo	FacFirstName	FacLastName
098-76-5432	LEONARD	VINCE

Example 9.28 (Oracle): Division Problem with a Join

List faculty number and the name (first and last) of faculty who teach all of the fall 2007, information systems offerings.

```
SELECT Faculty.FacNo, FacFirstName, FacLastName
 FROM Faculty, Offering
 WHERE Faculty.FacNo = Offering.FacNo
   AND OffTerm = 'FALL' AND CourseNo LIKE 'IS%'
   AND OffYear = 2007
 GROUP BY Faculty.FacNo, FacFirstName, FacLastName
 having count(*) =
   ( SELECT COUNT(*) FROM Offering
     WHERE OffTerm = 'FALL' AND OffYear = 2007
       AND CourseNo LIKE 'IS%' )
```

Example 9.28 is not particularly useful because it is unlikely that any instructors have taught every offering. Rather, it is more useful to retrieve instructors who have taught one offering of every course as demonstrated in Example 9.29. Rather than counting the rows in each group, count the unique *CourseNo* values. This change is necessary because *CourseNo* is not unique in the *Offering* table. There can be multiple rows with the same *CourseNo*, corresponding to a situation where there are multiple offerings for the same course. The solution only executes in Oracle because Access does not support the DISTINCT keyword in aggregate functions. Example 9.30 shows an Access solution using two nested queries in FROM clauses. The second nested query occurs inside the nested query in the HAVING clause. Appendix 9.A shows an alternative to nested queries in the FROM clause using multiple SELECT statements.

Example 9.29 (Oracle): Division Problem with DISTINCT inside COUNT

List the faculty number and the name (first and last) of faculty who teach at least one section of all of the fall 2007 information systems courses.

```
SELECT Faculty.FacNo, FacFirstName, FacLastName
 FROM Faculty, Offering
 WHERE Faculty.FacNo = Offering.FacNo
   AND OffTerm = 'FALL' AND CourseNo LIKE 'IS%'
   AND OffYear = 2007
 GROUP BY Faculty.FacNo, FacFirstName, FacLastName
 having count(distinct CourseNo) =
   ( SELECT COUNT(DISTINCT CourseNo) FROM Offering
       WHERE OffTerm = 'FALL' AND OffYear = 2007
         AND CourseNo LIKE 'IS%' )
```

FacNo	FacFirstName	FacLastName
098-76-5432	LEONARD	VINCE

Example 9.30 (Access): Division Problem Using Nested Queries in the FROM Clauses instead of the DISTINCT Keyword inside the COUNT Function

List the faculty number and the name (first and last) of faculty who teach at least one section of all of the fall 2007 information systems courses. The result is the same as Example 9.29.

```
SELECT FacNo, FacFirstName, FacLastName
 from
   (SELECT DISTINCT Faculty.FacNo, FacFirstName,
           FacLastName, CourseNo
     FROM Faculty, Offering
     WHERE Faculty.FacNo = Offering.FacNo
       AND OffTerm = 'FALL' AND OffYear = 2007
       AND CourseNo LIKE 'IS*' )
 GROUP BY FacNo, FacFirstName, FacLastName
 having count(*) =
   ( SELECT COUNT(*) FROM
     ( SELECT DISTINCT CourseNo
         FROM Offering
         WHERE OffTerm = 'FALL' AND OffYear = 2007
         AND CourseNo LIKE 'IS*' ) )
```

Example 9.31 is another variation of the technique used in Example 9.29. The DISTINCT keyword is necessary so that students taking more than one offering from the same instructor are not counted twice. Note that the DISTINCT keyword is not necessary for the nested query because only rows of the *Student* table are counted. Example 9.32 shows an Access solution using a nested query in the FROM clause.

Example 9.31 (Oracle): Another Division Problem with DISTINCT inside COUNT

List the faculty who have taught all seniors in their fall 2007 information systems offerings.

```
SELECT Faculty.FacNo, FacFirstName, FacLastName
 FROM Faculty, Offering, Enrollment, Student
 WHERE Faculty.FacNo = Offering.FacNo
   AND OffTerm = 'FALL' AND CourseNo LIKE 'IS%'
   AND OffYear = 2007 AND StdClass = 'SR'
   AND Offering.OfferNo = Enrollment.OfferNo
   AND Student.StdNo = Enrollment.StdNo
 GROUP BY Faculty.FacNo, FacFirstName, FacLastName
 having count(distinct Student.StdNo) =
   ( SELECT COUNT(*) FROM Student
     WHERE StdClass = 'SR' );
```

FacNo	FacFirstName	FacLastName
098-76-5432	LEONARD	VINCE

Example 9.32 (Access): Another Division Proble m Using Nested Querie s in the FROM Clauses Instead of the DISTINCT Keyword inside the COUNT Function

List the faculty who have taught all seniors in their fall 2007 information systems offerings. The result is identical to Example 9.31.

```
SELECT FacNo, FacFirstName, FacLastName
 from
   ( SELECT DISTINCT Faculty.FacNo, FacFirstName,
           FacLastName, Student.StdNo
     FROM Faculty, Offering, Enrollment, Student
     WHERE Faculty.FacNo = Offering.FacNo
       AND OffTerm = 'FALL' AND CourseNo LIKE 'IS*'
       AND OffYear = 2007 AND StdClass = 'SR'
       AND Offering.OfferNo = Enrollment.OfferNo
       AND Student.StdNo = Enrollment.StdNo )
 GROUP BY FacNo, FacFirstName, FacLastName
 having count(*) =
   ( SELECT COUNT(*) FROM Student
     WHERE StdClass = 'SR' );
```

9.4 Null Value Considerations

The last section of this chapter does not involve difficult matching problems or new parts of the SELECT statement. Rather, this section presents interpretation of query results when tables contain null values. These effects have largely been ignored until this section to simplify the presentation. Because most databases use null values, you need to understand the effects to attain a deeper understanding of query formulation.

Null values affect simple conditions involving comparison operators, compound conditions involving logical operators, aggregate calculations, and grouping. As you will see, some of the null value effects are rather subtle. Because of these subtle effects, a good table design minimizes, although it usually does not eliminate, the use of null values. The null effects described in this section are specified in the SQL standards (1992 through 2006). Because specific DBMSs may provide different results, you may need to experiment with your DBMS.

9.4.1 Effect on Simple Conditions

Simple conditions involve a comparison operator, a column or column expression, and a constant, column, or column expression. A simple condition results in a null value if either column (or column expression) in a comparison is null. A row qualifies in the result if the simple condition evaluates to true for the row. Rows evaluating to false or null are discarded. Example 9.33 depicts a simple condition evaluating to null for one of the rows.

Example 9.33: Simple Condition Using a Column with Null Values

List the clubs (Table 9-11) with a budget greater than $200. The club with a null budget (C4) is omitted because the condition evaluates as a null value.

```
SELECT *
FROM Club
WHERE CBudget > 200
```

ClubNo	CName	CPurpose	CBudget	CActual
C1	DELTA	SOCIAL	$1,000.00	$1,200.00
C2	BITS	ACADEMIC	$500.00	$350.00
C3	HELPS	SERVICE	$300.00	$330.00

A more subtle result can occur when a simple condition involves two columns and at least one column contains null values. If neither column contains null values, every row will be in the result of either the simple condition or the opposite (negation) of the simple condition. For example, if < is the operator of a simple condition, the opposite condition contains ≥ assuming the columns remain in the same positions. If at least one column contains null values, some rows will not appear in the result of either the simple condition or its negation. More precisely, rows containing null values will be excluded in both results, as demonstrated in Examples 9.34 and 9.35.

Example 9.34: Simple Condition Involving Two Columns

List the clubs with the budget greater than the actual spending. The club with a null budget (C4) is omitted because the condition evaluates to null.

```
SELECT *
FROM Club
WHERE CBudget > CActual
```

ClubNo	CName	CPurpose	CBudget	CActual
C2	BITS	ACADEMIC	$500.00	$350.00

Example 9.35: Opposite Condition of Example 9.32

List the clubs with the budget less than or equal to the actual spending. The club with a null budget (C4) is omitted because the condition evaluates to null.

```
SELECT *
FROM Club
WHERE CBudget <= CActual
```

ClubNo	CName	CPurpose	CBudget	CActual
C1	DELTA	SOCIAL	$1,000.00	$1,200.00
C3	HELPS	SERVICE	$300.00	$330.00

9.4.2 Effect on Compound Conditions

Compound conditions involve one or more simple conditions connected by the logical or Boolean operators AND, OR, and NOT. Like simple conditions, compound conditions evaluate to true, false, or null. A row is selected if the entire compound condition in the WHERE clause evaluates to true.

To evaluate the result of a compound condition, the SQL:2006 standard uses truth tables with three values. A truth table shows how combinations of values (true, false, and null) combine with the Boolean operators. Truth tables with three values define a three-valued logic. Tables 9-13 through 9-15 depict truth tables for the AND, OR, and NOT operators. The internal cells in these tables are the result values. For example, the first internal cell (True) in Table 9-13 results from the AND operator applied to two conditions with true values. You can test your understanding of the truth tables using Examples 9.36 and 9.37.

Table 9-13: AND Truth Table

AND	True	False	Null
True	True	False	Null
False	False	False	False
Null	Null	False	Null

Table 9-14: OR Truth Table

OR	True	False	Null
True	True	True	True
False	True	False	Null
Null	True	Null	Null

Table 9-15: NOT Truth Table

NOT	True	False	Null
	False	True	Null

Example 9.36: Evaluation of a Compound OR Condition with a Null Value

List the clubs with the budget less than or equal to the actual spending or the actual spending less than $200. The club with a null budget (C4) is included because the second condition evaluates to true.

```
SELECT *
 FROM Club
 WHERE CBudget <= CActual  OR  CActual < 200
```

ClubNo	CName	CPurpose	CBudget	CActual
C1	DELTA	SOCIAL	$1,000.00	$1,200.00
C3	HELPS	SERVICE	$300.00	$330.00
C4	SIGMA	SOCIAL		$150.00

Example 9.37: Evaluation of a Compound AND Condition with a Null Value

List the clubs (Table 9-11) with the budget less than or equal to the actual spending and the actual spending less than $500. The club with a null budget (C4) is not included because the first condition evaluates to null.

```
SELECT *
 FROM Club
 WHERE CBudget <= CActual  AND  CActual < 500
```

ClubNo	CName	CPurpose	CBudget	CActual
C3	HELPS	SERVICE	$300.00	$330.00

9.4.3 Effect on Aggregate Calculations and Grouping

Null values are ignored in aggregate calculations. Although this statement seems simple, the results can be subtle. For the COUNT function, COUNT(*) returns a different value than COUNT(column) if the column contains null values. COUNT(*) always returns the number of rows. COUNT(column) returns the number of non-null values in the column. Example 9.38 demonstrates the difference between COUNT(*) and COUNT(column).

Example 9.38: COUNT Function with Null Values

List the number of rows in the *Club* table and the number of values in the *CBudget* column.

```
SELECT COUNT(*) AS NumRows,
       COUNT(CBudget) AS NumBudgets
  FROM Club
```

NumRows	NumBudgets
4	3

An even more subtle effect can occur if the SUM or AVG functions are applied to a column with null values. Without regard to null values, the following equation is true: SUM(Column1) + SUM(Column2) = SUM(Column1 + Column2). With null values in at least one of the columns, the equation may not be true because a calculation involving a null value yields a null value. If Column1 has a null value in one row, the plus operation in SUM(Column1 + Column2) produces a null value for that row. However, the value of Column2 in the same row is counted in SUM(Column2). Example 9.39 demonstrates this subtle effect using the minus operator instead of the plus operator.

Example 9.39: SUM Function with Null Values

Using the *Club* table, list the sum of the budget values, the sum of the actual values, the difference of the two sums, and the sum of the differences (budget – actual). The last two columns differ because of a null value in the *CBudget* column. Parentheses enclose negative values in the result.

```
SELECT SUM(CBudget) AS SumBudget,
       SUM(CActual) AS SumActual,
       SUM(CBudget)-SUM(CActual) AS SumDifference,
       SUM(CBudget-CActual) AS SumOfDifferences
  FROM Club
```

SumBudget	SumActual	SumDifference	SumOfDifferences
$1,800.00	$2,030.00	($230.00)	($80.00)

Null values also can affect grouping operations performed in the GROUP BY clause. The SQL standard stipulates that all rows with null values are grouped together. The grouping column shows null values in the result. In the university database, this kind of grouping operation is useful to find course offerings without assigned professors, as demonstrated in Example 9.40.

Example 9.40: Grouping on a Column with Null Values

For each faculty number in the *Offering* table, list the number of offerings. In Microsoft Access and Oracle, an Offering row with a null *FacNo* value displays as a blank. In Access, the null row displays before the non-null rows as shown below. In Oracle, the null row displays after the non-null rows.

```
SELECT FacNo, COUNT(*) AS NumRows
  FROM Offering
  GROUP BY FacNo
```

FacNo	NumRows
	2
098-76-5432	3
543-21-0987	1
654-32-1098	2
765-43-2109	2
876-54-3210	1
987-65-4321	2

Closing Thoughts

Chapter 9 has presented advanced query formulation skills with an emphasis on complex matching between tables and a wider subset of SQL. Complex matching problems include the outer join with its variations (one-sided and full) as well as problems requiring the difference and division operators of relational algebra. In addition to new kinds of problems and new parts of the SELECT statement, this chapter explained the subtle effects of null values to provide a deeper understanding of query formulation.

Two new parts of the SELECT statement were covered. The keywords LEFT, RIGHT, and FULL as part of the join operator style support outer join operations. Nested queries are a query inside another query. To understand the effect of a nested query, look for tables used in both an outer and an inner query. If there are no common tables, the nested query executes one time (Type I nested query). Otherwise, the nested query executes one time for each row of the outer query (Type II nested query). Type I nested queries are typically used to formulate joins as part of the SELECT and DELETE statements. Type I nested queries with the NOT IN operator and Type II nested queries with the NOT EXISTS operator are useful for problems involving the difference operator. Type I nested queries in the HAVING clause are useful for problems involving the division operator.

Although advanced query skills are not as widely applied as the fundamental skills covered in Chapter 4, they are important when required. You may gain a competitive edge by mastering these advanced query formulation skills.

Chapters 4 and 9 have covered important query formulation skills and a large part of the SELECT statement of SQL. Despite this significant coverage, there is still much left to learn. There are even more complex matching problems and other parts of the SELECT statement that were not described. You are encouraged to extend your skills by consulting the references cited at the end of the chapter. In addition, you have not learned how to apply your query formulation skills to building applications. Chapter 10 applies your skills to building applications with views, while Chapter 11 applies your skills to stored procedures and triggers.

Review Concepts

- Formulating one-sided outer joins with Access and Oracle (9i and beyond)
  ```
  SELECT OfferNo, CourseNo, Offering.FacNo, Faculty.FacNo,
          FacFirstName, FacLastName
      FROM Offering LEFT JOIN Faculty
      ON Offering.FacNo = Faculty.FacNo
      WHERE CourseNo = 'IS480'
  ```
- Formulating full outer joins using the FULL JOIN keyword (SQL:2006 and Oracle 9i and beyond)
  ```
  SELECT FacNo, FacFirstName, FacLastName, FacSalary,
          StdNo, StdFirstName, StdLastName, StdGPA
      FROM Faculty FULL JOIN Student
      ON Student.StdNo = Faculty.FacNo
  ```
- Formulating full outer joins by combining two one-sided outer joins in Access
  ```
  SELECT FacNo, FacFirstName, FacLastName, FacSalary,
          StdNo, StdFirstName, StdLastName, StdGPA
      FROM Faculty RIGHT JOIN Student
      ON Student.StdNo = Faculty.FacNo
                                          UNION
  SELECT FacNo, FacFirstName, FacLastName, FacSalary,
          StdNo, StdFirstName, StdLastName, StdGPA
      FROM Faculty LEFT JOIN Student
      ON Student.StdNo = Faculty.FacNo
  ```
- Mixing inner and outer joins (Access and Oracle 9i and beyond)
  ```
  SELECT OfferNo, Offering.CourseNo, OffTerm, CrsDesc,
          Faculty.FacNo, FacFirstName, FacLastName
      FROM ( Faculty RIGHT JOIN Offering
      ON Offering.FacNo = Faculty.FacNo )
                                          INNER JOIN Course
      ON Course.CourseNo = Offering.CourseNo
      WHERE OffYear = 2006
  ```
- Understanding that conditions in the WHERE or HAVING clause can use SELECT statements in addition to scalar (individual) values
- Identifying Type I nested queries by the IN keyword and the lack of a reference to a table used in an outer query
- Using a Type I nested query to formulate a join
  ```
  SELECT DISTINCT StdNo, StdFirstName, StdLastName,
                  StdMajor
      FROM Student
      WHERE Student.StdNo IN
      ( SELECT StdNo FROM Enrollment
      WHERE EnrGrade >= 3.5  )
  ```
- Using a Type I nested query inside a DELETE statement to test conditions on a related table
  ```
  DELETE FROM Offering
      WHERE Offering.FacNo IN
      ( SELECT FacNo FROM Faculty
      WHERE FacFirstName = 'LEONARD'
          AND FacLastName = 'VINCE' )
  ```
- Not using a Type I nested query for a join when a column from the nested query is needed in the final query result
- Identifying problem statements involving the difference operator: the words *not* or *only* relating two nouns in a sentence
- Limited SQL formulations for difference problems: Type I nested queries with the NOT IN operator, one-sided outer join with an IS NULL condition, and difference operation using the EXCEPT or MINUS keywords

- Using a Type I nested query with the NOT IN operator for difference problems involving a comparison of a single column

```
SELECT FacNo, FacFirstName, FacLastName, FacDept,
          FacSalary
     FROM Faculty
     WHERE FacNo NOT IN
     ( SELECT StdNo FROM Student )
```

- Identifying Type II nested queries by a reference to a table used in an outer query
- Using Type II nested queries with the NOT EXISTS operator for complex difference problems

```
SELECT FacNo, FacFirstName, FacLastName, FacDept,
          FacSalary
     FROM Faculty
     WHERE NOT EXISTS
     ( SELECT * FROM Student
     WHERE Student.StdNo = Faculty.FacNo )
```

- Using a nested query in the FROM clause to compute nested aggregates or aggregates for more than one grouping

```
SELECT T.CourseNo, T.CrsDesc, COUNT(*) AS NumOfferings,
          Avg(T.EnrollCount) AS AvgEnroll
     FROM
     ( SELECT Course.CourseNo, CrsDesc,
          Offering.OfferNo, COUNT(*) AS EnrollCount
     FROM Offering, Enrollment, Course
     WHERE Offering.OfferNo = Enrollment.OfferNo
          AND Course.CourseNo = Offering.CourseNo
     GROUP BY Course.CourseNo, CrsDesc, Offering.OfferNo
     ) T
     GROUP BY T.CourseNo, T.CrsDesc
```

- Identifying problem statements involving the division operator: the word every or all connecting different parts of a sentence
- Using the count method to formulate division problems

```
SELECT StdNo
     FROM StdClub
     GROUP BY StdNo
     HAVING COUNT(*) = ( SELECT COUNT(*) FROM Club )
```

- Evaluating a simple condition containing a null value in a column expression
- Using three-valued logic and truth tables to evaluate compound conditions with null values
- Understanding the result of aggregate calculations with null values
- Understanding the result of grouping on a column with null values

Questions

1. Explain a situation when a one-sided outer join is useful.
2. Explain a situation when a full outer join is useful.
3. How do you interpret the meaning of the LEFT and RIGHT JOIN keywords in the FROM clause?
4. What is the interpretation of the FULL JOIN keywords in the FROM clause?
5. How do you perform a full outer join in SQL implementations (such as Microsoft Access and Oracle 8i) that do not support the FULL JOIN keywords?
6. What is a nested query?
7. What is the distinguishing feature about the appearance of Type I nested queries?
8. What is the distinguishing feature about the appearance of Type II nested queries?
9. How many times is a Type I nested query executed as part of an outer query?
10. How is a Type I nested query like a procedure in a program?
11. How many times is a Type II nested query executed as part of an outer query?
12. How is a Type II nested query like a nested loop in a program?

319

13. What is the meaning of the IN comparison operator?
14. What is the meaning of the EXISTS comparison operator?
15. What is the meaning of the NOT EXISTS comparison operator?
16. When can you not use a Type I nested query to perform a join?
17. Why is a Type I nested query a good join method when you need a join in a DELETE statement?
18. Why does SQL:2006 permit nested queries in the FROM clause?
19. Identify two situations in which nested queries in the FROM clause are necessary.
20. How do you detect that a problem involves a division operation?
21. Explain the "count" method for formulating division problems.
22. Why is it sometimes necessary to use the DISTINCT keyword inside the COUNT function for division problems?
23. What is the result of a simple condition when a column expression in the condition evaluates to null?
24. What is a truth table?
25. How many values do truth tables have in the SQL:2006 standard?
26. How do you use truth tables to evaluate compound conditions?
27. How do null values affect aggregate calculations?
28. Explain why the following equation may not be true if Column1 or Column2 contains null values: `SUM(Column1) - SUM(Column2) = SUM(Column1 - Column2)`
29. How are null values handled in a grouping column?
30. In Access, how do you compensate for the lack of the DISTINCT keyword inside the COUNT function?
31. When can you use a Type I nested query with the NOT IN operator to formulate a difference operation in SQL?
32. When can you use a one-sided outer join with an IS NULL condition to formulate a difference operation in SQL?
33. When can you use a MINUS operation in SQL to formulate a difference operation in SQL?
34. What is the most general way to formulate difference operations in SQL statements?

Problems

The problems use the tables of the Order Entry database introduced in the Problems section of Chapter 4. When formulating the problems, remember that the *EmpNo* foreign key in the *OrderTbl* table allows null values. An order does not have an associated employee if taken over the Internet.

1. Using a Type I nested query, list the customer number, name (first and last), and city of each customer who has a balance greater than $150 and placed an order in February 2008.
2. Using a Type II nested query, list the customer number, name (first and last), and city of each customer who has a balance greater than $150 and placed an order in February 2008.
3. Using two Type I nested queries, list the product number, the name, and the price of products with a price greater than $150 that were ordered on January 23, 2008.
4. Using two Type I nested queries and another join style, list the product number, name, and price of products with a price greater than $150 that were ordered in January 2008 by customers with balances greater than $400.
5. List the order number, order date, employee number, and employee name (first and last) of orders placed on January 23, 2008. List the order even if there is not an associated employee.
6. List the order number, order date, employee number, employee name (first and last), customer number, and customer name (first and last) of orders placed on January 23, 2008. List the order even if there is not an associated employee.
7. List all the people in the database. The resulting table should have all columns of the *Customer* and *Employee* tables. Match the *Customer* and *Employee* tables on first and last

names. If a customer does not match any employees, the columns pertaining to the *Employee* table will be blank. Similarly for an employee who does not match any customers, the columns pertaining to the *Customer* table will be blank.

8. For each Ink Jet product ordered in January 2008, list the order number, order date, customer number, customer name (first and last), employee number (if present), employee name (first and last), quantity ordered, product number, and product name. Include products containing Ink Jet in the product name. Include both Internet (no employee) and phone orders (taken by an employee).

9. Using a Type II nested query, list the customer number and name of Colorado customers who have not placed orders in February 2008.

10. Repeat problem 9 using a Type I nested query with a NOT IN condition instead of a nested query. If the problem cannot be formulated in this manner, provide an explanation indicating the reason.

11. Repeat problem 9 using the MINUS keyword. Note that Access does not support the MINUS keyword. If the problem cannot be formulated in this manner, provide an explanation indicating the reason.

12. Repeat problem 9 using a one-sided outer join and an IS NULL condition. If the problem cannot be formulated in this manner, provide an explanation indicating the reason.

13. Using a Type II nested query, list the employee number, first name, and last name of employees in the (720) area code who have not taken orders. An employee is in the (720) area code if the employee phone number contains the string (720) in the beginning of the column value.

14. Repeat problem 13 using a Type I nested query with a NOT IN condition instead of a nested query. If the problem cannot be formulated in this manner, provide an explanation indicating the reason. (Hint: you need to think carefully about the effect of null values in the *OrderTbl.EmpNo* column.)

15. Repeat problem 9 using a one-sided outer join and an IS NULL condition. If the problem cannot be formulated in this manner, provide an explanation indicating the reason.

16. Repeat problem 9 using the MINUS keyword. Note that Access does not support the MINUS keyword. If the problem cannot be formulated in this manner, provide an explanation indicating the reason.

17. List the order number and order date of orders containing only one product with the words Ink Jet in the product description.

18. List the customer number and name (first and last) of customers who have ordered products only manufactured by Connex. Include only customers who have ordered at least one product manufactured by Connex. Remove duplicate rows from the result.

19. List the order number and order date of orders containing every product with the words Ink Jet in the product description.

20. List the product number and name of products contained on every order placed on January 7, 2008 through January 9, 2008.

21. List the customer number and name (first and last) of customers who have ordered every product manufactured by ColorMeg, Inc. in January 2008.

22. Using a Type I nested query, delete orders placed by customer Betty Wise in January 2008. The CASCADE DELETE action will delete related rows in the *OrdLine* table.

23. Using a Type I nested query, delete orders placed by Colorado customers that were taken by Landi Santos in January 2008. The CASCADE DELETE action will delete related rows in the *OrdLine* table.

24. List the order number and order date of orders in which any part of the shipping address (street, city, state, and zip) differs from the customer's address.

25. List the employee number and employee name (first and last) of employees who have taken orders in January 2008 from every Seattle customer.

26. For Colorado customers, compute the average amount of their orders. The average amount of a customer's orders is the sum of the amount (quantity ordered times the product price) on each order divided by the number of orders. The result should include the customer number, customer last name, and average order amount.

27. For Colorado customers, compute the average amount of their orders and the number of orders placed. The result should include the customer number, customer last name,

average order amount, and number of orders placed. In Access, this problem is especially difficult to formulate.

28. For Colorado customers, compute the number of unique products ordered. If a product is purchased on multiple orders, it should be counted only one time. The result should include the customer number, customer last name, and number of unique products ordered.

29. For each employee with a commission less than 0.04, compute the number of orders taken and the average number of products per order. The result should include the employee number, employee last name, number of orders taken, and the average number of products per order. In Access, this problem is especially difficult to formulate as a single SELECT statement.

30. For each Connex product, compute the number of unique customers who ordered the product in January 2008. The result should include the product number, product name, and number of unique customers.

Null Value Problems

The following problems are based on the *Product* and *Employee* tables of the Order Entry database. The tables are repeated below for your convenience. The *ProdNextShipDate* column contains the next expected shipment date for the product. If the value is null, a new shipment has not been arranged. A shipment may not be scheduled for a variety of reasons, such as the large quantity on hand or unavailability of the product from the manufacturer. In the *Employee* table, the commission rate can be null indicating a commission rate has not been assigned. A null value for *SupEmpNo* indicates that the employee has no superior.

Product

ProdNo	ProdName	ProdMfg	ProdQOH	ProdPrice	ProdNextShipDate
P0036566	17 inch Color Monitor	ColorMeg, Inc.	12	$169.00	2/20/2008
P0036577	19 inch Color Monitor	ColorMeg, Inc.	10	$319.00	2/20/2008
P1114590	R3000 Color Laser Printer	Connex	5	$699.00	1/22/2008
P1412138	10 Foot Printer Cable	Ethlite	100	$12.00	
P1445671	8-Outlet Surge Protector	Intersafe	33	$14.99	
P1556678	CVP Ink Jet Color Printer	Connex	8	$99.00	1/22/2008
P3455443	Color Ink Jet Cartridge	Connex	24	$38.00	1/22/2008
P4200344	36-Bit Color Scanner	UV Components	16	$199.99	1/29/2008
P6677900	Black Ink Jet Cartridge	Connex	44	$25.69	
P9995676	Battery Back-up System	Cybercx	12	$89.00	2/1/2008

Employee

EmpNo	EmpFirstName	EmpLastName	EmpPhone	EmpEMail	SupEmpNo	EmpCommRate
E1329594	Landi	Santos	(303) 789-1234	LSantos@bigco.com	E8843211	0.02
E8544399	Joe	Jenkins	(303) 221-9875	JJenkins@bigco.com	E8843211	0.02
E8843211	Amy	Tang	(303) 556-4321	ATang@bigco.com	E9884325	0.04
E9345771	Colin	White	(303) 221-4453	CWhite@bigco.com	E9884325	0.04
E9884325	Thomas	Johnson	(303) 556-9987	TJohnson@bigco.com		0.05
E9954302	Mary	Hill	(303) 556-9871	MHill@bigco.com	E8843211	0.02
E9973110	Theresa	Beck	(720) 320-2234	TBeck@bigco.com	E9884325	

1. Identify the result rows in the following SELECT statement. Both Access and Oracle versions of the statement are shown.

```
Access:
SELECT *
   FROM Product
   WHERE ProdNextShipDate = #1/22/2008#

Oracle:
SELECT *
   FROM Product
   WHERE ProdNextShipDate = '22-Jan-2008';
```

2. Identify the result rows in the following SELECT statement:

```
Access:
SELECT *
   FROM Product
   WHERE ProdNextShipDate = #1/22/2008#
      AND ProdPrice < 100

Oracle:
SELECT *
   FROM Product
   WHERE ProdNextShipDate = '22-Jan-2008'
      AND ProdPrice < 100;
```

3. Identify the result rows in the following SELECT statement:

```
Access:
SELECT *
   FROM Product
   WHERE ProdNextShipDate = #1/22/2008#
      OR ProdPrice < 100

Oracle:
SELECT *
   FROM Product
   WHERE ProdNextShipDate = '22-Jan-2008'
      OR ProdPrice < 100;
```

4. Determine the result of the following SELECT statement:

```
SELECT COUNT(*) AS NumRows,
       COUNT(ProdNextShipDate) AS NumShipDates
   FROM Product
```

5. Determine the result of the following SELECT statement:

```
SELECT ProdNextShipDate, COUNT(*) AS NumRows
  FROM Product
  GROUP BY ProdNextShipDate
```

6. Determine the result of the following SELECT statement:

```
SELECT ProdMfg, ProdNextShipDate, COUNT(*) AS NumRows
  FROM Product
  GROUP BY ProdMfg, ProdNextShipDate
```

7. Determine the result of the following SELECT statement:

```
SELECT ProdNextShipDate, ProdMfg, COUNT(*) AS NumRows
  FROM Product
  GROUP BY ProdNextShipDate, ProdMfg
```

8. Identify the result rows in the following SELECT statement:

```
SELECT EmpFirstName, EmpLastName
  FROM Employee
  WHERE EmpCommRate > 0.02
```

9. Determine the result of the following SELECT statement:

```
SELECT SupEmpNo, AvG(EmpCommRate) AS AvgCommRate
  FROM Employee
  GROUP BY SupEmpNo
```

10. Determine the result of the following SELECT statement. The statement computes the average commission rate of subordinate employees. The result includes the employee number, first name, and last name of the supervising employee as well as the average commission amount of the subordinate employees.

```
SELECT Emp.SupEmpNo, Sup.EmpFirstName, Sup.EmpLastName,
       AvG(Emp.EmpCommRate) AS AvgCommRate
FROM Employee Emp, Employee Sup
WHERE Emp.SupEmpNo = Sup.EmpNo
  GROUP BY Emp.SupEmpNo, Sup.EmpFirstName,
Sup.EmpLastName
```

11. Using your knowledge of null value evaluation, explain why these two SQL statements generate different results for the Order Entry Database. You should remember that null values are allowed for *OrderTbl.EmpNo*.

```
SELECT EmpNo, EmpLastName, EmpFirstName
FROM Employee
WHERE EmpNo NOT IN
( SELECT EmpNo FROM OrderTbl WHERE EmpNo IS NOT NULL )

SELECT EmpNo, EmpLastName, EmpFirstName
FROM Employee
WHERE EmpNo NOT IN
( SELECT EmpNo FROM OrderTbl )
```

References for Further Study

Most textbooks for the business student do not cover query formulation and SQL in as much detail as here. For advanced SQL coverage beyond the coverage in this chapter, you should consult the summary of SQL books at www.ocelot.ca/books.htm. For new features in SQL:1999, you should read Melton and Simon (2001). Groff and Weinberg (1999) cover the various notations for outer joins available in commercial DBMSs. The DBAZine site (www.dbazine.com) and the DevX.com Database Zone (www.devx.com) have plenty of practical advice about query formulation and SQL. For product-specific SQL advice, the DataBased Advisor site (my.advisor.com/pub/DataBasedAdvisor) features forums and articles about a number of DBMSs including Microsoft SQL Server and Microsoft Access. Oracle documentation can be found at the Oracle Technet site (www.oracle.com/technology).

Appendix 9.A: Usage of Multiple Statements in Microsoft Access

In Microsoft Access, you can use multiple SELECT statements instead of nested queries in the FROM clause. Using multiple statements can provide simpler formulation in some cases than using nested queries in the FROM clause. For example, instead of using DISTINCT inside COUNT as in Example 9.29, you can use a stored query with the DISTINCT keyword following the SELECT keyword. In Example 9A.1, the first stored query (Temp9A-1) finds the unique combinations of faculty name and course number. Note the use of the DISTINCT keyword to eliminate duplicates. The second stored query (Temp9A-2) finds the unique course numbers in the *Offering* table. The final query combines the two stored queries. Note that you can use stored queries similar to the way tables are used. Simply use the stored query name in the FROM clause.

Example 9A.1: Using Stored Queries Instead of Nested Queries in the FROM Clause

List the name of faculty who teach in at least one section of all fall 2007 information systems courses. The result is identical to that in Example 9.29.

Temp9A-1:
```
SELECT DISTINCT Faculty.FacNo, FacFirstName,
               FacLastName, CourseNo
 FROM Faculty, Offering
 WHERE Faculty.FacNo = Offering.FacNo
   AND OffTerm = 'FALL' AND OffYear = 2007
   AND CourseNo LIKE 'IS*'
```
Temp9A-2:
```
SELECT DISTINCT CourseNo
 FROM Offering
 WHERE OffTerm = 'FALL' AND OffYear = 2007
   AND CourseNo LIKE 'IS*'

SELECT FacNo, FacFirstName, FacLastName
 FROM [Temp9A-1]
 GROUP BY FacNo, FacFirstName, FacLastName
 having count(*) = ( select count(*) from [Temp9A-2] )
```

Appendix 9.B: SQL:2006 Syntax Summary

This appendix summarizes the SQL:2006 syntax for nested SELECT statements (subqueries) and outer join operations presented in Chapter 9. For the syntax of other variations of the nested SELECT and outer join operations not presented in Chapter 9, consult an SQL reference book. Nested SELECT statements can be used in the FROM clause and the WHERE clause of the SELECT, UPDATE, and DELETE statements. The conventions used in the syntax notation are identical to those used at the end of Chapter 3.

BExpanded Syntax for Nested Queries in the FROM Clause

```
<Table-Specification>:
    { <Simple-Table>    |   -- defined in Chapter 4
      <Join-Operation>  |   -- defined in Chapter 4
      <Simple-Select> [ [ AS ] AliasName ] }
            -- <Simple-Select> is defined in Chapter 4
```

Expanded Syntax for Row Conditions

```
<Row-Condition>:
{ <Simple-Condition> |    -- defined in Chapter 4
  <Compound-Condition> |  -- defined in Chapter 4
  <Exists-Condition>   |
  <Element-Condition>  }

<Exists-Condition>:  [ NOT ] EXISTS <Simple-Select>

<Simple-Select>: -- defined in Chapter 4

<Element-Condition>:
 <Scalar-Expression> <Element-Operator>( <Simple-Select>
)

<Element-Operator>:
 { = | < | > | >= | <= | <> | [ NOT ] IN }

<Scalar-Expression>: -- defined in Chapter 4
```

Expanded Syntax for Group Conditions

```
<Simple-Group-Condition>:  -- Last choice is new
{ <Column-Expression> ComparisonOperator
      <Column-Experssion>  |
  <Column-Expression> [ NOT ] IN ( Constant* )  |
  <Column-Expression> BETWEEN <Column-Expression>
      AND <Column-Expression> |
  <Column-Expression> IS [NOT] NULL  |
  ColumnName [ NOT ] LIKE StringPattern |
  <Exists-Condition>  |
  <Column-Expression> <Element-Operator> <Simple-Select> }
}
<Column-Expression>: -- defined in Chapter 4
```

Expanded Syntax for Outer Join Operations

```
<Join-Operation>:
  { <Simple-Table> <Join-Operator> <Simple-Table>
    ON <Join-Condition>   |
    { <Simple-Table> | <Join-Operation> } <Join-Operator>
      { <Simple-Table> | <Join-Operation> }
      ON <Join-Condition>   |
    ( <Join-Operation> )   }

<Join-Operator>:
{ [ INNER ] JOIN        |
  LEFT [ OUTER ] JOIN    |
  RIGHT [ OUTER ] JOIN   |
  FULL [ OUTER ] JOIN    }
```

Appendix 9.C: Oracle 8i Notation for Outer Joins

Until the Oracle 9i release, Oracle used a proprietary extension for one-sided outer joins. To express a one-sided outer join in Oracle 8i SQL, you need to use the notation (+) as part of a join condition in the WHERE clause. You place the (+) notation just after the join column of the null table, that is, the table with null values in the result. In contrast, the SQL:2006 LEFT and RIGHT keywords are placed after the table in which nonmatching rows are preserved in the result. The Oracle 8i formulations of Examples 9.1, 9.2, 9.4, 9.5, and 9.6 demonstrate the (+) notation.

Example 9.1 (Oracle 8i): One-Sided Outer Join with Outer Join Symbol on the Right Side of a Join Condition

The (+) notation is placed after the *Faculty.FacNo* column in the join condition because *Faculty* is the null table in the result.

```
SELECT OfferNo, CourseNo, Offering.FacNo, Faculty.FacNo,
       FacFirstName, FacLastName
 FROM Faculty, Offering
 WHERE Offering.FacNo = Faculty.FacNo (+)
   AND CourseNo LIKE 'IS%'
```

Example 9.2 (Oracle 8i): One-Sided Outer Join with Outer Join Symbol on the Left Side of a Join Condition

The (+) notation is placed after the *Faculty.FacNo* column in the join condition because *Faculty* is the null table in the result.

```
SELECT OfferNo, CourseNo, Offering.FacNo, Faculty.FacNo,
       FacFirstName, FacLastName
 FROM Faculty, Offering
 WHERE Faculty.FacNo (+) = Offering.FacNo
   AND CourseNo LIKE 'IS%'
```

Example 9.4 (Oracle 8i): Full Outer Join Using a Union of Two One-Sided Outer Joins

Combine the *Faculty* and *Student* tables using a full outer join. List the Social Security number, the name (first and last), the salary (faculty only), and the GPA (students only) in the result.

```
SELECT FacNo, FacFirstName, FacLastName, FacSalary,
       StdNo, StdFirstName, StdLastName, StdGPA
 FROM Faculty, Student
 WHERE Student.StdNo = Faculty.FacNo (+)
                                                    UNION
SELECT FacNo, FacFirstName, FacLastName, FacSalary,
       StdNo, StdFirstName, StdLastName, StdGPA
 FROM Faculty, Student
 WHERE Student.StdNo (+) = Faculty.FacNo
```

Example 9.5 (Oracle 8i): Mixing a One-Sided Outer Join and an Inner Join

Combine columns from the *Faculty*, *Offering*, and *Course* tables for IS courses offered in 2008. Include a row in the result even if there is not an assigned instructor.

```
SELECT OfferNo, Offering.CourseNo, OffTerm, CrsDesc,
       Faculty.FacNo, FacFirstName, FacLastName
  FROM Faculty, Offering, Course
  WHERE Offering.FacNo = Faculty.FacNo (+)
    AND Course.CourseNo = Offering.CourseNo
    AND Course.CourseNo LIKE 'IS%' AND OffYear = 2008
```

Example 9.6 (Oracle 8i): Mixing a One-Sided Outer Join and Two Inner Joins

List the rows of the *Offering* table where there is at least one student enrolled, in addition to the requirements of Example 9.6. Remove duplicate rows when there is more than one student enrolled in an offering.

```
SELECT DISTINCT Offering.OfferNo, Offering.CourseNo,
       OffTerm, CrsDesc, Faculty.FacNo, FacFirstName,
       FacLastName
  FROM Faculty, Offering, Course, Enrollment
  WHERE Offering.FacNo = Faculty.FacNo (+)
    AND Course.CourseNo = Offering.CourseNo
                                                 AND
Offering.OfferNo = Enrollment.OfferNo
    AND Course.CourseNo LIKE 'IS%' AND OffYear = 2008
```

It should be noted that the proprietary extension of Oracle is inferior to the SQL:2006 notation. The proprietary extension does not allow specification of the order of performing outer joins. This limitation can be problematic on difficult problems involving more than one outer join. Thus, you should use the SQL:2006 outer join syntax although later Oracle versions (9i and beyond) still support the proprietary extension using the (+) symbol.

10

Application Development with Views

Learning Objectives

This chapter describes underlying concepts for views and demonstrates usage of views in forms and reports. After this chapter, the student should have acquired the following knowledge and skills:

- Write CREATE VIEW statements
- Write queries that use views
- Understand basic ideas about the modification and materialization approaches for processing queries with views
- Apply rules to determine if single-table and multiple-table views are updatable
- Determine data requirements for hierarchical forms
- Write queries that provide data for hierarchical forms
- Formulate queries that provide input for hierarchical reports

Overview

Chapters 3, 4, and 9 provided the foundation for understanding relational databases and formulating queries in SQL. Most importantly, you gained practice with a large number of examples, acquired problem-solving skills for query formulation, and learned different parts of SQL. This chapter shows you how to apply your query formulation skills to building applications with views.

This chapter emphasizes views as the foundation for building database applications. Before discussing the link between views and database applications, essential background is provided. You will learn the motivation for views, the CREATE VIEW statement, and usage of views in SELECT and data manipulation (INSERT, UPDATE, and DELETE) statements. Most view examples in Sections 10.2 and 10.3 are supported in both Microsoft Access and Oracle. After this background, you will learn to use views for hierarchical forms and reports. You will learn the steps for analyzing data requirements culminating in views to support the data requirements.

The presentation in Sections 10.1 and 10.2 covers features in Core SQL:2006 that were part of SQL-92. Some of the features of updatable views in Sections 10.3 and 10.4 are specific to Microsoft Access due to the varying support among DBMSs and the strong support available in Access.

10.1 Background

A <u>view</u> is a virtual or derived table. Virtual means that a view behaves like a base table but no physical table exists. A view can be used in a query like a base table. However, the rows of a view do not exist until they are derived from base tables. This section describes why views are important and how to define them in SQL.

> **View**: a table derived from base or physical tables using a query.

10.1.1 Motivation

Views provide the external level of the Three Schema Architecture described in Chapter 1. The Three Schema Architecture promotes <u>data independence</u> to reduce the impact of database definition changes on applications that use a database. Because database definition changes are common, reducing the impact of database definition changes is important to control the cost of software maintenance. Views support compartmentalization of database requirements so that database definition changes do not affect applications using a view. If an application accesses the database through a view, most changes to the conceptual schema will not affect the application. For example, if a table name used in a view changes, the view definition must be changed but applications using the view do not have to be changed.

<u>Simplification</u> of tasks is another important benefit of views. Many queries can be easier to formulate if a view is used rather than base tables. Without a view, a SELECT statement may

involve two, three, or more tables and require grouping if summary data are needed. With a view, the SELECT statement can just reference a view without joins or grouping. Training users to write single table queries is much easier than training them to write multiple table queries with grouping.

Views provide simplification similar to macros in programming languages and spreadsheets. A macro is a named collection of commands. Using a macro removes the burden of specifying the commands. In a similar manner, using a view removes the burden of writing the underlying query.

Views also provide a flexible level of <u>security</u>. Restricting access by views is more flexible than restrictions for columns and tables because a view is any derived part of a database. Data not in the view are hidden from the user. For example, you can restrict a user to selected departments, products, or geographic regions in a view. Security using tables and columns cannot specify conditions and computations, which can be done in a view. A view even can include aggregate calculations to restrict users to row summaries rather than individual rows.

The only drawback to views can be performance. For most views, using the views instead of base tables directly will not involve a significant performance penalty. For some complex views, using the views can involve a significant performance penalty as opposed to using the base tables directly. The performance penalty can vary by DBMS. Before using complex views, you are encouraged to compare performance to using the base tables directly.

10.1.2 View Definition

Defining a view is no more difficult than writing a query. SQL provides the CREATE VIEW statement in which the view name and the underlying SELECT statement must be specified, as shown in Examples 10.1 and 10.2. In Oracle, the CREATE VIEW statement executes directly. In Microsoft Access, the CREATE VIEW statement can be used in SQL-92 query mode[32]. In SQL-89 query mode, the SELECT statement part of the examples can be saved as a stored query to achieve the same effect as a view. You create a stored query simply by writing it and then supplying a name when saving it.

Example 10.1: Define a Single Table View

Define a view named IS_View consisting of students majoring in IS.

```
CREATE VIEW IS_View AS
  SELECT * FROM Student
  WHERE StdMajor = 'IS'
```

StdNo	StdFirstName	StdLastName	StdCity	StdState	StdZip	StdMajor	StdClass	StdGPA
123-45-6789	HOMER	WELLS	SEATTLE	WA	98121-1111	IS	FR	3.00
345-67-8901	WALLY	KENDALL	SEATTLE	WA	98123-1141	IS	SR	2.80
567-89-0123	MARIAH	DODGE	SEATTLE	WA	98114-0021	IS	JR	3.60
876-54-3210	CRISTOPHER	COLAN	SEATTLE	WA	98114-1332	IS	SR	4.00
890-12-3456	LUKE	BRAZZI	SEATTLE	WA	98116-0021	IS	SR	2.20
901-23-4567	WILLIAM	PILGRIM	BOTHELL	WA	98113-1885	IS	SO	3.80

Example 10.2: Define a Multiple Table View

Define a view named MS_View consisting of offerings taught by faculty in the Management Science department.

```
CREATE VIEW MS_View AS
  SELECT OfferNo, Offering.CourseNo, CrsUnits, OffTerm,
         OffYear, Offering.FacNo, FacFirstName,
```

---

[32] SQL-89 is the default query mode in Microsoft Access 2002 and 2003. The query mode can be changed using the Tables/Query tab in the Options window (Tools→Options …).

```
                FacLastName, OffTime, OffDays
        FROM Faculty, Course, Offering
        WHERE FacDept = 'MS'
          AND Faculty.FacNo = Offering.FacNo
          AND Offering.CourseNo = Course.CourseNo
```

OfferNo	CourseNo	CrsUnits	OffTerm	OffYear	FacNo	FacFirstName	FacLastName	OffTime	OffDays
1234	IS320	4	FALL	2007	098-76-5432	LEONARD	VINCE	10:30 AM	MW
3333	IS320	4	SPRING	2008	098-76-5432	LEONARD	VINCE	8:30 AM	MW
4321	IS320	4	FALL	2007	098-76-5432	LEONARD	VINCE	3:30 PM	TTH
4444	IS320	4	WINTER	2008	543-21-0987	VICTORIA	EMMANUEL	3:30 PM	TTH
8888	IS320	4	SUMMER	2008	654-32-1098	LEONARD	FIBON	1:30 PM	MW
9876	IS460	4	SPRING	2008	654-32-1098	LEONARD	FIBON	1:30 PM	TTH
5679	IS480	4	SPRING	2008	876-54-3210	CRISTOPHER	COLAN	3:30 PM	TTH

In the CREATE VIEW statement, a list of column names enclosed in parentheses can follow the view name. A list of column names is required when you want to rename one or more columns from the names used in the SELECT clause. The column list is omitted in MS_View because there are no renamed columns. The column list is required in Example 10.3 to rename the aggregate calculation (COUNT(*)) column. If one column is renamed, the entire list of column names must be given.

Example 10.3: Define a View with Renamed Columns

Define a view named Enrollment_View consisting of offering data and the number of students enrolled.

```
CREATE VIEW  Enrollment_View
 (OfferNo, CourseNo, Term, Year, Instructor, NumStudents)
 AS
 SELECT Offering.OfferNo, CourseNo, OffTerm, OffYear,
        FacLastName, COUNT(*)
  FROM Offering, Faculty, Enrollment
  WHERE  Offering.FacNo  =  Faculty.FacNo
    AND Offering.OfferNo  =  Enrollment.OfferNo
    GROUP BY Offering.OfferNo, CourseNo, OffTerm, OffYear,
        FacLastName
```

OfferNo	CourseNo	Term	Year	Instructor	NumStudents
1234	IS320	FALL	2007	VINCE	6
4321	IS320	FALL	2007	VINCE	6
5555	FIN300	WINTER	2008	MACON	2
5678	IS480	WINTER	2008	MILLS	5
5679	IS480	SPRING	2008	COLAN	6
6666	FIN450	WINTER	2008	MILLS	2
7777	FIN480	SPRING	2008	MACON	3
9876	IS460	SPRING	2008	FIBON	7

10.2 Using Views for Retrieval

This section shows examples of queries that use views and explains processing of queries with views. After showing examples in Section 10.2.1, two methods to process queries with views are described in Section 10.2.2.

333

10.2.1 Using Views in SELECT Statements

Once a view is defined, it can be used in SELECT statements. You simply use the view name in the FROM clause and the view columns in other parts of the statement. You can add other conditions and select a subset of the columns as demonstrated in Examples 10.4 and 10.5.

Example 10.4 (Oracle): Query Using a Multiple Table View

List the spring 2008 courses in MS_View.

```
SELECT OfferNo, CourseNo, FacFirstName, FacLastName,
       OffTime, OffDays
FROM MS_View
WHERE OffTerm = 'SPRING' AND OffYear = 2008
```

OfferNo	CourseNo	FacFirstName	FacLastName	OffTime	OffDays
3333	IS320	LEONARD	VINCE	8:30 AM	MW
9876	IS460	LEONARD	FIBON	1:30 PM	TTH
5679	IS480	CRISTOPHER	COLAN	3:30 PM	TTH

Example 10.5 (Oracle): Query Using a Grouping View

List the spring 2008 offerings of IS courses in the Enrollment_View. In Access, you need to substitute the * for % as the wildcard symbol.

```
SELECT OfferNo, CourseNo, Instructor, NumStudents
FROM Enrollment_View
WHERE Term = 'SPRING' AND Year = 2008
  AND CourseNo LIKE 'IS%'
```

OfferNo	CourseNo	Instructor	NumStudents
5679	IS480	COLAN	6
9876	IS460	FIBON	7

Both queries are much easier to write than the original queries. A novice user can probably write both queries with just a little training. In contrast, it may take many hours of training for a novice user to write queries with multiple tables and grouping.

According to SQL:2006, a view can be used in any query. In practice, most DBMSs have some limitations on view usage in queries. For example, some DBMSs do not support the queries[33] shown in Examples 10.6 and 10.7.

Example 10.6 (Oracle): Grouping Query Using a View Derived from a Grouping Query

List the average number of students by instructor name using *Enrollment_View*.

```
SELECT Instructor, AVG(NumStudents) AS AvgStdCount
FROM Enrollment_View
GROUP BY Instructor
```

Instructor	AvgStdCount
COLAN	6
FIBON	7
MACON	2.5
MILLS	3.5
VINCE	6

---

[33] Microsoft Access 97 through 2007 and Oracle 8i through 11g all support Examples 10.6 and 10.7.

334

Example 10.7 (Oracle): Joining a Base Table with a View Derived from a Grouping Query
List the offering number, instructor, number of students, and course units using the
Enrollment_View view and the *Course* table.

```
SELECT OfferNo, Instructor, NumStudents, CrsUnits
  FROM Enrollment_View, Course
  WHERE Enrollment_View.CourseNo = Course.CourseNo
    AND NumStudents < 5
```

OfferNo	Instructor	NumStudents	CrsUnits
5555	MACON	2	4
6666	MILLS	2	4
7777	MACON	3	4

10.2.2 Processing Queries with View References

To process queries that reference a view, the DBMS can use either a materialization or
modification strategy. <u>View materialization</u> requires the storage of view rows. The simplest way
to store a view is to build the view from the base tables on demand (when the view query is
submitted). Processing a query with a view reference requires that a DBMS execute two queries,
as depicted in Figure 10.1. A user submits a query using a view (Query$_v$). The query defining the
view (Query$_d$) is executed and a temporary view table is created. Figure 10.1 depicts this action
by the arrow into the view. Then, the query using the view is executed using the temporary view
table.

      View materialization is usually not the preferred strategy because it requires the DBMS
to execute two queries. However, on certain queries such as Examples 10.6 and 10.7,
materialization may be necessary. In addition, materialization is preferred in data warehouses in
which retrievals dominate. In a data warehouse environment, views are periodically refreshed
from base tables rather than materialized on demand. Chapter 16 discusses materialized views
used in data warehouses.

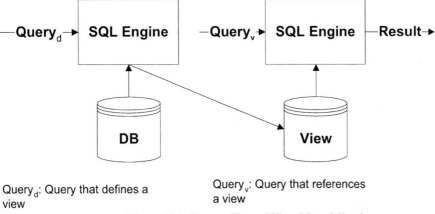

Query$_d$: Query that defines a
view

Query$_v$: Query that references
a view

Figure 10.1: Process Flow of View Materialization

View Materialization: a method to process a query on a view by executing the query directly on the stored view. The stored view can be materialized on demand (when the view query is submitted) or periodically rebuilt from the base tables. For databases with a mixture of retrieval and update activity, materialization usually is not an efficient way to process a query on a view.

In an environment with a mix of update and retrieval operations, <u>view modification</u> usually provides better performance than materialization because the DBMS only executes one query. Figure 10.2 shows that a query using a view is modified or rewritten as a query using base tables only; then the modified query is executed using the base tables. The modification process happens automatically without any user knowledge or action. In most DBMSs, the modified query cannot be seen even if you want to review it.

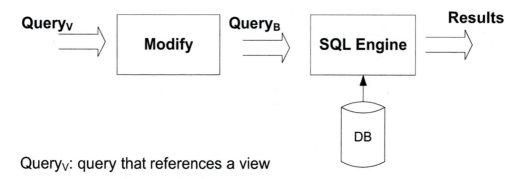

Query$_V$: query that references a view

Query$_B$: modification of Query$_V$ such that references to the view are replaced by references to base tables.

Figure 10.2: Process Flow of View Modification

View Modification: a method to process a query on a view involving the execution of only one query. A query using a view is translated into a query using base tables by replacing references to the view with its definition. For databases with a mixture of retrieval and update activity, modification provides an efficient way to process a query on a view.

As a view modification example, consider the transformation shown from Example 10.8 to Example 10.9. When you submit a query using a view, the reference to the view is replaced with the definition of the view. The view name in the FROM clause is replaced by base tables. In addition, the conditions in the WHERE clause are combined using the Boolean AND with the conditions in the query defining the view. The underlined parts in Example 10.9 indicate substitutions made in the modification process.

Example 10.8: Query Using MS_View

```
SELECT OfferNo, CourseNo, FacFirstName, FacLastName,
       OffTime, OffDays
FROM MS_View
WHERE OffTerm = 'SPRING' AND OffYear = 2008
```

OfferNo	CourseNo	FacFirstName	FacLastName	OffTime	OffDays
3333	IS320	LEONARD	VINCE	8:30 AM	MW
9876	IS460	LEONARD	FIBON	1:30 PM	TTH
5679	IS480	CRISTOPHER	COLAN	3:30 PM	TTH

Example 10.9: Modification of Example 10.8

Example 10.8 is modified by replacing references to MS_View with base table references.

```
SELECT OfferNo, Course.CourseNo, FacFirstName,
       FacLastName, OffTime, OffDays
  FROM Faculty, Course, Offering
  WHERE FacDept = 'MS'
    AND Faculty.FacNo = Offering.FacNo
      AND Offering.CourseNo = Course.CourseNo
      AND OffTerm = 'SPRING' AND OffYear = 2008
```

Some DBMSs perform additional simplification of modified queries to remove unnecessary joins. For example, the *Course* table is not needed because there are no conditions and columns from the *Course* table in Example 10.9. In addition, the join between the *Offering* and the *Course* tables is not necessary because every *Offering* row is related to a *Course* row (null is not allowed). As a result the modified query can be simplified by removing the *Course* table. Simplification will result in a faster execution time, as the most important factor in execution time is the number of tables.

Example 10.10: Further Simplification of Example 10.9

Simplify by removing the *Course* table because it is not needed in Example 10.9.

```
SELECT OfferNo, CourseNo, FacFirstName, FacLastName,
       OffTime, OffDays
  FROM Faculty, Offering
  WHERE FacDept = 'MS'
    AND Faculty.FacNo = Offering.FacNo
      AND OffTerm = 'SPRING' AND OffYear = 2008
```

10.3 Updating Using Views

Depending on its definition, a view can be read-only or updatable. A read-only view can be used in SELECT statements as demonstrated in Section 10.2. All views are at least read-only. A read-only view cannot be used in queries involving INSERT, UPDATE, and DELETE statements. A view that can be used in modification statements as well as SELECT statements is known as an updatable view. This section describes rules for defining both single-table and multiple-table updatable views.

> **Updatable View:** a view that can be used in SELECT statements as well as UPDATE, INSERT, and DELETE statements. Views that can be used only with SELECT statements are known as read-only views.

10.3.1 Single-Table Updatable Views

An updatable view allows you to insert, update, or delete rows in the underlying base tables by performing the corresponding operation on the view. Whenever a modification is made to a view row, a corresponding operation is performed on the base table. Intuitively, this means that the rows of an updatable view correspond in a one-to-one manner with rows from the underlying base tables. If a view contains the primary key of the base table, then each view row matches a base table row. A single-table view is updatable if it satisfies the following three rules that include the primary key requirement.

Rules for Single-Table Updatable Views

The view includes the primary key of the base table.
All required fields (NOT NULL) of the base table without a default value are in the view.
The view's query does not include the GROUP BY or DISTINCT keywords.

Following these rules, *Fac_View1* (Example 10.11) is updatable while *Fac_View2* (Example 10.12) and *Fac_View3* (Example 10.13) are read-only. *Fac_View1* is updatable assuming the missing *Faculty* columns are not required. *Fac_View2* violates Rules 1 and 2 while *Fac_View3* violates all three rules making both views read-only.

Example 10.11: Single-Table Updatable View
Create a row and column subset view with the primary key.

```
CREATE VIEW Fac_View1 AS
   SELECT FacNo, FacFirstName, FacLastName, FacRank,
          FacSalary, FacDept, FacCity, FacState, FacZipCode
   FROM Faculty
   WHERE FacDept = 'MS'
```

FacNo	FacFirstName	FacLastName	FacRank	FacSalary	FacDept	FacCity	FacState	FacZipCode
098-76-5432	LEONARD	VINCE	ASST	35000.00	MS	SEATTLE	WA	98111-9921
543-21-0987	VICTORIA	EMMANUEL	PROF	120000.00	MS	BOTHELL	WA	98011-2242
654-32-1098	LEONARD	FIBON	ASSC	70000.00	MS	SEATTLE	WA	98121-0094
876-54-3210	CRISTOPHER	COLAN	ASST	40000.00	MS	SEATTLE	WA	98114-1332

Example 10.12: Single Table Read-Only View
Create a row and column subset without the primary key.

```
CREATE VIEW Fac_View2 AS
   SELECT FacDept, FacRank, FacSalary
   FROM Faculty
   WHERE FacSalary > 50000
```

FacDept	FacRank	FacSalary
MS	PROF	120000.00
MS	ASSC	70000.00
FIN	PROF	65000.00
FIN	ASSC	75000.00

Example 10.13: Single table read-only view
Create a grouping view with faculty department and average salary.

```
CREATE View Fac_View3 (FacDept, AvgSalary) AS
   SELECT FacDept, AVG(FacSalary)
   FROM Faculty
   WHERE FacRank = 'PROF'
   GROUP BY FacDept
```

FacDept	AvgSalary
FIN	65000
MS	120000

Because *Fac_View1* is updatable, it can be used in INSERT, UPDATE, and DELETE statements to change the *Faculty* table. In Chapter 4, you used these statements to change rows in base tables. Examples 10.14 through 10.16 demonstrate that these statements can be applied to views to change rows of the underlying base tables. Note that modifications to views are subject to the integrity rules of the underlying base tables. For example, the insertion in Example 10.14 is rejected if another *Faculty* row has 999-99-8888 as the faculty number. When deleting rows in a view or changing the primary key column, the rules on referenced rows apply (Section 3.4). For example, the deletion in Example 10.16 is rejected if the *Faculty* row with *FacNo* 098-76-5432 has related rows in the *Offering* table and the delete action for the *Faculty-Offering* relationship is set to RESTRICT.

Example 10.14: Insert Operation on Updatable View

Insert a new faculty row into the MS department.

```
INSERT INTO Fac_View1
   (FacNo, FacFirstName, FacLastName, FacRank, FacSalary,
    FacDept, FacCity, FacState, FacZipCode)
   VALUES ('999-99-8888', 'JOE', 'SMITH', 'PROF', 80000,
           'MS', 'SEATTLE', 'WA', '98011-011')
```

Example 10.15: Update Operation on Updatable View

Give assistant professors in Fac_View1 a 10 percent raise.

```
UPDATE Fac_View1
   SET FacSalary = FacSalary * 1.1
   WHERE FacRank = 'ASST'
```

Example 10.16: Delete Operation on Updatable View

Delete a specific faculty member from Fac_View1.

```
DELETE FROM Fac_View1
   WHERE FacNo = '999-99-8888'
```

View Updates with Side Effects

Some modifications to updatable views can be problematic, as demonstrated in Example 10.17 and Tables 10-1 and 10-2. The update statement in Example 10.17 changes the department of the last row (Victoria Emmanuel) in the view and the corresponding row in the base table. Upon regenerating the view, however, the changed row disappears (Table 10-2). The update has the side effect of causing the row to disappear from the view. This kind of side effect can occur whenever a column in the WHERE clause of a view definition is changed by an UPDATE statement. Example 10.17 updates the *FacDept* column, the column used in the WHERE clause of the definition of the *Fac_View1* view.

Example 10.17: Update Operation on Updatable View with a Side Effect

Change the department of highly paid faculty members to the finance department.

```
UPDATE Fac_View1
   SET FacDept = 'FIN'
   WHERE FacSalary > 100000
```

Table 10-1: Fac_View1 before Update

FacNo	FacFirstName	FacLastName	FacRank	FacSalary	FacDept	FacCity	FacState	FacZipCode
098-76-5432	LEONARD	VINCE	ASST	35000.00	MS	SEATTLE	WA	98111-9921
543-21-0987	VICTORIA	EMMANUEL	PROF	120000.00	MS	BOTHELL	WA	98011-2242
654-32-1098	LEONARD	FIBON	ASSC	70000.00	MS	SEATTLE	WA	98121-0094
876-54-3210	CRISTOPHER	COLAN	ASST	40000.00	MS	SEATTLE	WA	98114-1332

Table 10-2: Fac_View1 after Example 10.17 Update

FacNo	FacFirstName	FacLastName	FacRank	FacSalary	FacDept	FacCity	FacState	FacZipCode
098-76-5432	LEONARD	VINCE	ASST	35000.00	MS	SEATTLE	WA	98111-9921
654-32-1098	LEONARD	FIBON	ASSC	70000.00	MS	SEATTLE	WA	98121-0094
876-54-3210	CRISTOPHER	COLAN	ASST	40000.00	MS	SEATTLE	WA	98114-1332

Because this side effect can be confusing to a user, the WITH CHECK OPTION clause can be used to prevent updates with side effects. If the WITH CHECK OPTION is specified in the CREATE VIEW statement (Example 10.18), INSERT or UPDATE statements that do not satisfy the WHERE clause are rejected. The update in Example 10.17 would be rejected if *Fac_View1* contained a CHECK OPTION clause because changing *FacDept* to 'FIN' contradicts the WHERE condition with *FacDept* = 'MS'.

Example 10.18 (Oracle): Single-Table Updatable View Using the WITH CHECK OPTION
Create a row and column subset view with the primary key. The WITH CHECK OPTION is not supported in Access.

```
CREATE VIEW Fac_View1_Revised AS
  SELECT FacNo, FacFirstName, FacLastName, FacRank,
         FacSalary, FacDept, FacCity, FacState, FacZipCode
  FROM Faculty
  WHERE FacDept = 'MS'
WITH CHECK OPTION
```

WITH CHECK OPTION: a clause in the CREATE VIEW statement that prevents side effects when updating a view. The WITH CHECK OPTION clause prevents UPDATE and INSERT statements that violate a view's WHERE clause.

10.3.2 Multiple-Table Updatable Views

It may be surprising but some multiple-table views are also updatable. A multiple-table view may correspond in a one-to-one manner with rows from more than one table if the view contains the primary key of each table. Because multiple-table views are more complex than single-table views, there is not wide agreement on updatability rules for multiple-table views.

Some DBMSs do not support updatability for any multiple-table views. Other systems support updatability for a large number of multiple-table views. In this section, the updatability rules in Microsoft Access are described as they support a wide range of multiple-table views. In addition, the rules for updatable views in Access are linked to the presentation of hierarchical forms in Section 10.4.

To complement the presentation of the Access updatability rules, Appendix 10.B describes the rules for updatable join views in Oracle. The rules for updatable join views in Oracle are similar to Microsoft Access although Oracle is more restrictive on the allowable manipulation operations and the conditions required for updatable tables.

In Access, multiple-table queries that support updates are known as 1-M updatable queries. A 1-M updatable query involves two or more tables with one table playing the role of the parent or 1 table and another table playing the role of the child or M table. For example, in a query involving the *Course* and the *Offering* tables, *Course* plays the role of the parent table and *Offering* the child table. To make a 1-M query updatable, follow these rules:

Rules for 1-M Updatable Views

- The query includes the primary key of the child table.
- For the child table, the query contains all required columns (NOT NULL) without default values.
- The query does not include the GROUP BY clause or the DISTINCT keyword.
- The join column of the parent table should be unique (either a primary key or a unique constraint).
- The query contains the foreign key column(s) of the child table.
- The query includes the primary key and required columns of the parent table if the view supports insert operations on the parent table. Update operations are supported on the parent table even if the query does not contain the primary key of the parent table.

Using these rules, Course_Offering_View1 (Example 10.19) and Faculty_Offering_View1 (Example 10.21) are updatable. Course_Offering_View2 (Example 10.20) is not updatable because *Offering.CourseNo* (the foreign key in the child table) is missing.

In the SELECT statements, the join operator style (INNER JOIN keywords) is used because Microsoft Access requires it for 1-M updatable queries.

Example 10.19 (Access): 1-M Updatable Query
Create a 1-M updatable query (saved as Course_Offering_View1) with a join between the *Course* and the *Offering* tables. This query supports insert operations on both the *Course* and *Offering* tables as the primary key and required columns of the parent table are in the result.

```
Course_Offering_View1:
   SELECT Course.CourseNo, CrsDesc, CrsUnits,
          Offering.OfferNo, OffTerm, OffYear,
          Offering.CourseNo, OffLocation, OffTime, FacNo,
          OffDays
     FROM Course INNER JOIN Offering
          ON Course.CourseNo = Offering.CourseNo
```

Example 10.20 (Access): Multiple-Table Read-Only Query
This query (saved as Course_Offering_View2) is read-only because it does not contain *Offering.CourseNo*.

```
Course_Offering_View2:
   SELECT CrsDesc, CrsUnits, Offering.OfferNo,
          Course.CourseNo, OffTerm, OffYear, OffLocation,
          OffTime, FacNo, OffDays
     FROM Course INNER JOIN Offering
          ON Course.CourseNo = Offering.CourseNo
```

Example 10.21 (Access): 1-M Updatable Query
Create a 1-M updatable query (saved as Faculty_Offering_View1) with a join between the *Faculty* and the *Offering* tables. This query supports update operations on both tables (*Offering* and *Faculty*) but only insert operations on the *Offering* table.

```
Faculty_Offering_View1:
   SELECT Offering.OfferNo, Offering.FacNo, CourseNo,
          OffTerm, OffYear, OffLocation, OffTime,
OffDays,
          FacFirstName, FacLastName, FacDept
     FROM Faculty INNER JOIN Offering
          ON Faculty.FacNo = Offering.FacNo
```

Inserting Rows in 1-M Updatable Queries

Inserting a new row in a 1-M updatable query is more involved than inserting a row in a single-table view. This complication occurs because there is a choice about the tables that support insert operations. Rows from the child table only or both the child and parent tables can be inserted as a result of a view update. To insert a row into the child table, supply only the values needed to insert a row into the child table as demonstrated in Example 10.22. Note that the value for *Offering.CourseNo* and *Offering.FacNo* must match existing rows in the *Course* and the *Faculty* tables, respectively.

Example 10.22 (Access): Inserting a Row into the Child Table as a Result of a View Update
Insert a new row into *Offering* as a result of using Course_Offering_View1.

```
INSERT INTO Course_Offering_View1
  ( Offering.OfferNo, Offering.CourseNo, OffTerm, OffYear,
    OffLocation, OffTime, FacNo,OffDays )
  VALUES ( 7799, 'IS480', 'SPRING', 2008, 'BLM201',
           #1:30PM#, '098-76-5432', 'MW' )
```

To insert a row into both tables (parent and child tables), the view must include the primary key and the required columns of the parent table. If the view includes these columns, supplying values for all columns inserts a row into both tables as demonstrated in Example 10.23. Supplying values for just the parent table inserts a row only into the parent table as demonstrated in Example 10.24. In both examples, the value for *Course.CourseNo* must <u>not</u> match an existing row in *Course*.

Example 10.23 (Access): Inserting a Row into Both Tables as a result of a View Update
Insert a new row into Course and Offering as a result of using Course_Offering_View1.

```
INSERT INTO Course_Offering_View1
  ( Course.CourseNo, CrsUnits, CrsDesc, Offering.OfferNo,
    OffTerm, OffYear, OffLocation, OffTime, FacNo,
    OffDays )
  VALUES ( 'IS423', 4, 'OBJECT ORIENTED COMPUTING', 8877,
           'SPRING', 2008, 'BLM201', #3:30PM#,
           '123-45-6789', 'MW' )
```

Example 10.24 (Access): Inserting a Row into the Parent Table as a Result of a View Update
Insert a new row into the *Course* table as a result of using the Course_Offering_View1.

```
INSERT INTO Course_Offering_View1
  ( Course.CourseNo, CrsUnits, CrsDesc)
  VALUES ( 'IS481', 4, 'ADVANCED DATABASE' )
```

1-M Updatable Queries with More than Two Tables

Queries involving more than two tables also can be updatable. The same rules apply to 1-M updatable queries with more than two tables. However, you should apply the rules to each join in the query. For example, if a query has three tables (two joins) then apply the rules to both joins. In Faculty_Offering_Course_View1 (Example 10.25), *Offering* is the child table in both joins. Thus, the foreign keys (*Offering.CourseNo* and *Offering.FacNo*) must be in the query result. In the Faculty_Offering_Course_Enrollment_View1 (Example 10.26), *Enrollment* is the child table in one join and *Offering* is the child table in the other two joins. The primary key of the *Offering* table is not needed in the result unless *Offering* rows should be inserted using the view. The query in Example 10.26 supports inserts on the *Enrollment* table and updates on the other tables.

Example 10.25 (Access): 1-M Updatable Query with Three Tables

```
Faculty_Offering_Course_View1:
  SELECT CrsDesc, CrsUnits, Offering.OfferNo,
         Offering.CourseNo, OffTerm, OffYear,
OffLocation,
         OffTime, Offering.FacNo, OffDays, FacFirstName,
         FacLastName
    FROM ( Course INNER JOIN Offering
         ON Course.CourseNo = Offering.CourseNo )
         INNER JOIN Faculty
         ON Offering.FacNo = Faculty.FacNo
```

Example 10.26 (Access): 1-M Updatable Query with Four Tables

```
Faculty_Offering_Course_Enrollment_View1:
  SELECT CrsDesc, CrsUnits, Offering.CourseNo,
         Offering.FacNo, FacFirstName, FacLastName,
         OffTerm, OffYear, OffLocation, OffTime, OffDays,
         Enrollment.OfferNo, Enrollment.StdNo,
         Enrollment.EnrGrade
    FROM ( ( Course INNER JOIN Offering
         ON Course.CourseNo = Offering.CourseNo )
       INNER JOIN Faculty
         ON Offering.FacNo = Faculty.FacNo )
       INNER JOIN Enrollment
         ON Enrollment.OfferNo = Offering.OfferNo
```

The specific rules about which insert, update, and delete operations are supported on 1-M updatable queries are more complex than what is described here. The purpose here is to demonstrate that multiple-table views can be updatable and the rules can be complex. The Microsoft Access documentation provides a complete description of the rules.

The choices about updatable tables in a 1-M updatable query can be confusing especially when the query includes more than two tables. Typically, only the child table should be updatable, so the considerations in Examples 10.23 and 10.24 do not apply. The choices are usually dictated by the needs of data entry forms, which are presented in the next section.

10.4 Using Views in Hierarchical Forms

One of the most important benefits of views is that they are the building blocks for applications. Data entry forms, a cornerstone of most database applications, support retrieval and modification of tables. Data entry forms are formatted so that they are visually appealing and easy to use. In contrast, the standard formatting of query results may not appeal to most users. This section describes the hierarchical form, a powerful kind of data entry form, and the relationships between views and hierarchical forms.

10.4.1 What Is a Hierarchical Form?

A form is a document used in a business process. A form is designed to support a business task such as processing an order, registering for a class, or making an airline reservation. Hierarchical forms support business tasks with a fixed and a variable part. The fixed part of a hierarchical form is known as the main form, while the variable (repeating) part is known as the subform. For example, a hierarchical form for course offerings (Figure 10.3) shows course data in the main form and offering data in the subform. A hierarchical form for class registration (Figure 10.4) shows registration and student data in the main form and enrollment in course offerings in the subform. The billing calculation fields below the subform are part of the main form. In each form, the subform can display multiple records while the main form shows only one record.

> **Hierarchical Form:** a formatted window for data entry and display using a fixed (main form) and a variable (subform) part. One record is shown in the main form and multiple, related records are shown in the subform.

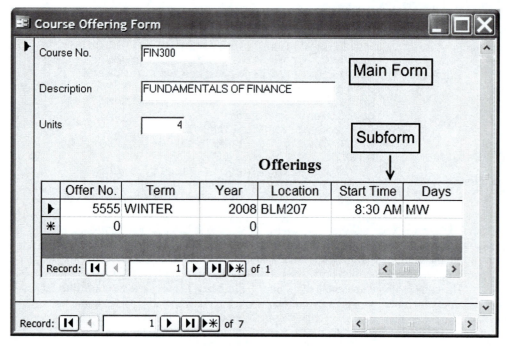

Figure 10.3: Example Course Offering Form

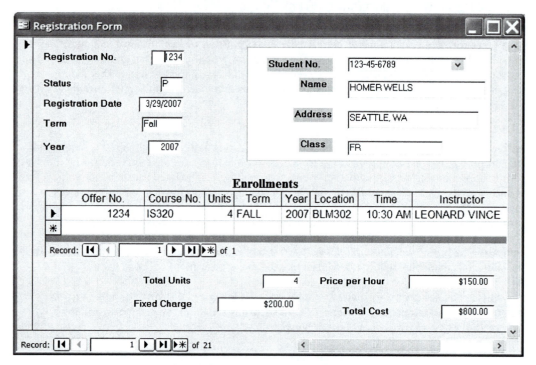

Figure 10.4: Example Registration Form

Hierarchical forms can be part of a system of related forms. For example, a student information system may have forms for student admissions, grade recording, course approval, course scheduling, and faculty assignments to courses. These forms may be related indirectly through updates to the database or directly by sending data between forms. For example, updates to a database made by processing a registration form are used at the end of a term by a grade recording form. This chapter emphasizes the data requirements of individual forms, an important skill of application development. This skill complements other application development skills such as user interface design and workflow design.

10.4.2 Relationship between Hierarchical Forms and Tables

Hierarchical forms support operations on 1-M relationships. A hierarchy or tree is a structure with 1-M relationships. Each <u>1-M relationship</u> has a parent (the 1 table) and child (the M table). A hierarchical form allows the user to insert, update, delete, and retrieve records in both tables of a 1-M relationship. A hierarchical form is designed to manipulate (display, insert, update, and delete) the parent table in the main form and the child table in the subform. In essence, a hierarchical form is a convenient interface for operations on a 1-M relationship.

   As examples, consider the hierarchical forms shown in Figures 10.3 and 10.4. In the Course Offering Form (Figure 10.3), the relationship between the *Course* and *Offering* tables enables the form to display a *Course* row in the main form and related *Offering* rows in the subform. The Registration Form (Figure 10.4) operates on the *Registration* and *Enrollment* tables as well as the 1-M relationship between these tables. The *Registration* table is a new table in the university database. Figure 10.5 shows a revised relationship diagram.

   To better support a business process, it is often useful to display other information in the main form and the subform. Other information (outside of the parent and the child tables) is usually for display purposes. Although it is possible to design a form to allow columns from other tables to be changed, the requirements of a particular business process may not warrant it. For example, the Registration Form (Figure 10.4) contains columns from the *Student* table in the main form so that a user can be authenticated. Likewise, columns from the *Offering*, *Faculty*, and *Course* tables are shown in the subform so that a user can make an informed enrollment choice. If a business process permits columns from other tables to be changed, this task is usually done using another form.

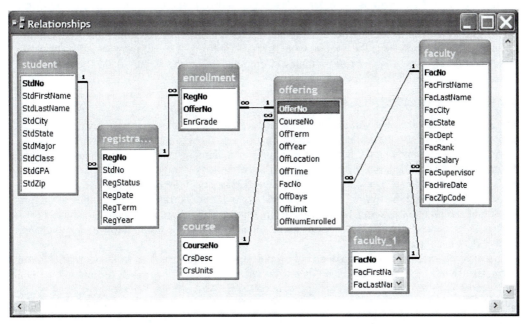

Figure 10.5: Relationships in the Revised University Database

10.4.3 Query Formulation Skills for Hierarchical Forms

To implement a hierarchical form, you should make decisions for each step listed below. These steps help to clarify the relationship between a form and its related database tables. In addition, these steps can be used directly to implement the form in some DBMSs such as Microsoft Access.

1. Identify the 1-M relationship manipulated by the form.
2. Identify the join or linking columns for the 1-M relationship.
3. Identify the other tables in the main form and the subform.
4. Determine the updatability of the tables in the hierarchical form.
5. Write queries for the main form and the subform.

Step 1: Identify the 1-M Relationship

The most important decision is matching the form to a 1-M relationship in the database. If you are starting from a picture of a form (such as Figure 10.3 or 10.4), look for a relationship that has columns from the parent table in the main form and columns from the child table in the subform. Usually, the parent table contains the primary key of the main form. In Figure 10.3, the Course No field is the primary key of the main form so the *Course* table is the parent table. In Figure 10.4, the Registration No. field is the primary key of the main form, so the *Registration* table is the parent table. If you are performing the form design and layout yourself, decide on the 1-M relationship before you sketch the form layout.

Step 2: Identify the Linking Columns

If you can identify the 1-M relationship, identifying the linking columns is usually easy. The linking columns are simply the join columns from both tables (parent and child) in the relationship. In the Course Offering Form, the linking columns are *Course.CourseNo* and *Offering.CourseNo*. In the Registration Form, the linking columns are *Registration.RegNo* and *Enrollment.RegNo*. It is important to remember that the linking columns connect the main form to the subform. With this connection, the subform only shows rows that match the value in the linking column of the main form. Without this connection, the subform displays all rows, not just the rows related to the record displayed in the main form.

Step 3: Determine Other Tables

In addition to the 1-M relationship, other tables can be shown in the main form and the subform to provide a context to a user. If you see columns from other tables, you should note those tables so that you can use them in step 5 when writing queries for the form. For example, the Registration Form includes columns from the *Student* table in the main form. The subform includes columns from the *Offering*, *Faculty*, and *Course* tables. Computed columns, such as Total Units, are not a concern until the form is implemented.

Step 4: Determine Updatable Tables

The fourth step requires that you understand the tables that can be changed when using the form. Typically, there is only one table in the main form and one table in the subform that should be changed as the user enters data. In the Registration Form, the *Registration* table is changed when the user manipulates the main form and the *Enrollment* table is changed when the user manipulates the subform. Typically the tables identified in step 3 are read-only. The *Student*, *Offering*, *Faculty*, and the *Course* tables are read-only in the Registration subform. For some form fields that are not updatable in a hierarchical form, buttons can be used to transfer to another form to change the data. For example, a button can be added to the main form to allow a user to change student data in another form.

Sometimes the main form does not support updates to any tables. In the Course Offering Form, the *Course* table is not changed when using the main form. The reason for making the main form read-only is to support the course approval process. Most universities require a separate approval process for new courses using a separate form. The Course Offering Form is designed only for adding offerings to existing courses. If a university does not have this constraint, the main form can be used to change the *Course* table.

As part of designing a hierarchical form, you should clearly understand the requirements of the underlying business process. These requirements should then be transformed into decisions about which tables are affected by user actions in the form such as updating a field or inserting a new record.

Step 5: Write Form Queries

The last step integrates decisions made in the other steps. You should write a query for the main form and a query for the subform. These queries must support updates to the tables you identified in step 4. You should follow the rules for formulating updatable views (both single-table and multiple-table) given in Section 10.3. Some DBMSs may require that you use a CREATE VIEW statement for these queries while other DBMSs may allow you to type the SELECT statements directly.

Tables 10-3 and 10-4 summarize the responses for steps 1 to 4 for the Course Offering and Registration forms. For step 5, examples 10.27 to 10.30 show queries for the main forms and subforms of Figures 5.3 and 5.4. In Example 10.29, the *Address* form field (Figure 10.4) is derived from the *StdCity* and *StdState* columns. In Example 10.30, the primary key of the *Offering* table is not needed because the query does not support insert operations on the *Offering* table. The query only supports insert operations on the *Enrollment* table. Note that all examples conform to the Microsoft Access (97 to 2003 versions) rules for 1-M updatable queries.

Table 10-3: Summary of Query Formulation Steps for the Course Offering Form

Step	Response
1	*Course* (parent table), *Offering* (child table)
2	Course.CourseNo, Offering.CourseNo
3	Only data from the *Course* and *Offering* tables
4	Insert, update, and delete operations on the *Offering* table in the subform

Example 10.27 (Access): Query for the Main Form of the Course Offering Form
```
SELECT CourseNo, CrsDesc, CrsUnits FROM Course
```

Example 10.28 (Access): Query for the Subform of the Course Offering Form
```
SELECT * FROM Offering
```

Table 10-4: Summary of Query Formulation Steps for the Registration Form

Step	Response
1	*Registration* (parent table), *Enrollment* (child table)
2	Registration.RegNo, Enrollment. RegNo
3	Data from the *Student* table in the main form and the *Offering*, *Course*, and *Faculty* tables in the subform
4	Insert, update, and delete operations on the *Registration* table in the main form and the *Enrollment* table in the subform

Example 10.29 (Access): Query for the Main Form of the Registration Form
```
SELECT RegNo, RegTerm, RegYear, RegDate,
       Registration.StdNo, RegStatus, StdFirstName,
       StdLastName, StdClass, StdCity, StdState
  FROM Registration INNER JOIN Student
   ON Registration.StdNo = Student.StdNo
```

Example 10.30 (Access): Query for the Subform of the Registration Form
```
SELECT RegNo, Enrollment.OfferNo, Offering.CourseNo,
OffTime,
        OffLocation, OffTerm, OffYear, Offering.FacNo,
          FacFirstName, FacLastName, CrsDesc, CrsUnits
   FROM ( ( Enrollment INNER JOIN Offering
            ON Enrollment.OfferNo = Offering.OfferNo )
        INNER JOIN Faculty
            ON Faculty.FacNo = Offering.FacNo )
        INNER JOIN Course
            ON Course.CourseNo = Offering.CourseNo
```

In the subform query for the Registration Form (Example 10.30), there is one other issue. The subform query will display an *Offering* row only if there is an associated *Faculty* row. If you want the subform to display *Offering* rows regardless of whether there is an associated *Faculty* row, a one-sided outer join should be used, as shown in Example 10.31. You can tell if an outer join is needed by looking at example copies of the form. If you can find offerings listed without an assigned faculty, then you need a one-sided outer join in the query.

Example 10.31 (Access): Revised Subform Query with a One-Sided Outer Join
```
SELECT RegNo, Enrollment.OfferNo, Offering.CourseNo,
        OffTime, OffLocation, OffTerm, OffYear,
         Offering.FacNo, FacFirstName, FacLastName,
        CrsDesc, CrsUnits
   FROM ( ( Enrollment INNER JOIN Offering
            ON Enrollment.OfferNo = Offering.OfferNo)
        INNER JOIN Course
            ON Offering.CourseNo = Course.CourseNo )
        LEFT JOIN Faculty
            ON Faculty.FacNo = Offering.FacNo
```

As another example, Table 10-5 summarizes responses to the query formulation steps for the Faculty Assignment Form shown in Figure 10.6. The goal of this form is to support administrators in assigning faculty to course offerings. The 1-M relationship for the form is the relationship from the *Faculty* table to the *Offering* table. This form cannot be used to insert new *Faculty* rows or change data about *Faculty*. In addition, this form cannot be used to insert new *Offering* rows. The only update operation supported by this form is to change the *Faculty* assigned to teach an existing *Offering*. To update the assigned faculty in the subform, the linking column (Offering.FacNo) must appear in the subform. Examples 10.32 and 10.33 show the main form and the subform queries.

Table 10-5: Summary of Query Formulation Steps for the Faculty Assignment Form

Step	Response
1	*Faculty* (parent table), *Offering* (child table)
2	Faculty.FacNo, Offering.FacNo
3	Data from the *Course* table in the subform
4	Update Offering.FacNo

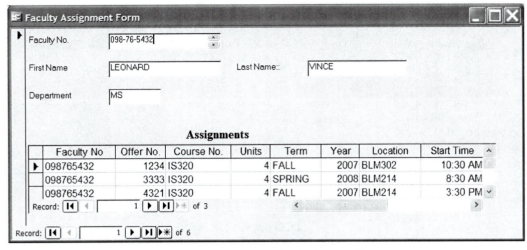

Figure 10.6: Example Faculty Assignment Form

Example 10.32 (Access): Main Form Query for the Faculty Assignment Form

```
SELECT FacNo, FacFirstName, FacLastName, FacDept
FROM Faculty
```

Example 10.33 (Access): Subform Query for the Faculty Assignment Form

```
SELECT OfferNo, Offering.CourseNo, FacNo, OffTime,
       OffDays, OffLocation, CrsUnits
FROM Offering INNER JOIN COURSE
       ON Offering.CourseNo = Course.CourseNo
```

10.5 Using Views in Reports

Besides being the building blocks of data entry forms, views are also the building blocks of reports. A report is a stylized presentation of data appropriate to a selected audience. A report is similar to a form in that both use views and present the data much differently than it appears in the base tables. A report differs from a form in that a report does not change the base tables while a form can make changes to the base tables. This section describes the hierarchical report, a powerful kind of report, and the relationship between views and hierarchical reports.

10.5.1 What is a Hierarchical Report?

Hierarchical reports (also known as control break reports) use nesting or indentation to provide a visually appealing format. The Faculty Schedule Report (Figure 10.7) shows data arranged by department, faculty name, and term. Each indented field is known as a group. The nesting of the groups indicates the sorting order of the report. The innermost line in a report is known as the detail line. In the Faculty Schedule Report, detail lines show the course number, offering number, and other details of the assigned course. The detail lines also can be sorted. In the Faculty Schedule Report, the detail lines are sorted by course number.

> **Hierarchical Report**: a formatted display of a query using indentation to show grouping and sorting.

349

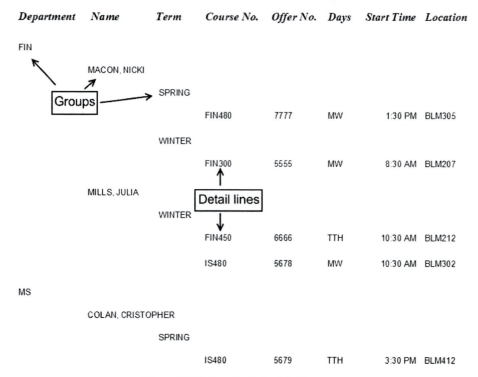

Figure 10.7: Faculty Schedule Report

The major advantage of hierarchical reports is that users can grasp more readily the meaning of data that are sorted and arranged in an indented manner. The standard output of a query (a datasheet) is difficult to inspect when data from multiple tables is in the result. For example, compare the Faculty Schedule Report with the datasheet (Figure 10.8) showing the same information. It can be distracting to see the department, faculty name, and term repeated.

FacDept	FacLastName	FacFirstName	OffTerm	CourseNo	OfferNo	OffLocation	OffTime	OffDays
FIN	MACON	NICKI	SPRING	FIN480	7777	BLM305	1:30 PM	MW
FIN	MACON	NICKI	WINTER	FIN300	5555	BLM207	8:30 AM	MW
FIN	MILLS	JULIA	WINTER	FIN450	6666	BLM212	10:30 AM	TTH
FIN	MILLS	JULIA	WINTER	IS480	5678	BLM302	10:30 AM	MW
MS	COLAN	CRISTOPHER	SPRING	IS480	5679	BLM412	3:30 PM	TTH
MS	EMMANUEL	VICTORIA	WINTER	IS320	4444	BLM302	3:30 PM	TTH
MS	FIBON	LEONARD	SPRING	IS460	9876	BLM307	1:30 PM	TTH
MS	VINCE	LEONARD	FALL	IS320	4321	BLM214	3:30 PM	TTH
MS	VINCE	LEONARD	FALL	IS320	1234	BLM302	10:30 AM	MW
MS	VINCE	LEONARD	SPRING	IS320	3333	BLM214	8:30 AM	MW

Figure 10.8: Datasheet Showing the Contents of the Faculty Schedule Report

To improve appearance, hierarchical reports can show summary data in the detail lines, computed columns, and calculations after groups. The detail lines in Figure 10.9 show the enrollment (number of students enrolled) in each course offering taught by a professor. In SQL, the number of students is computed with the COUNT function. The columns Percent Full ((Enrollment/Limit) * 100%) and Low Enrollment (a true/false value) are computed. A check box is a visually appealing way to display true/false columns. Many reports show summary calculations after each group. In the Faculty Work Load Report, summary calculations show the total units and students as well as average percentage full of course offerings.

Faculty Work Load Report for the 2007-2008 Academic Year

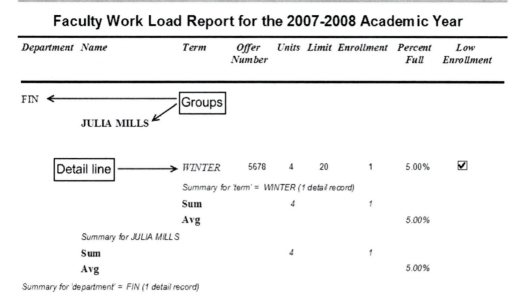

Figure 10.9: Faculty Work Load Report

10.5.2 Query Formulation Skills for Hierarchical Reports

Formulating queries for reports is similar to formulating queries for forms. In formulating a query for a report, you should (1) match fields in the report to database columns, (2) determine the needed tables, and (3) identify the join conditions. Most report queries will involve joins and possibly one-sided outer joins. More difficult queries involving difference and division operations are not common. These steps can be followed to formulate the query, shown in Example 10.34, for the Faculty Schedule Report (Figure 10.7).

In some ways, formulating queries for hierarchical reports is easier than for hierarchical forms. Queries for reports do not need to be updatable (they usually are read-only). In addition, there is only one query for a report as opposed to two or more queries for a hierarchical form.

Example 10.34: Query for the Faculty Scheduling Report

```
SELECT Faculty.FacNo, Faculty.FacFirstName, FacLastName,
       Faculty.FacDept, Offering.OfferNo,
       Offering.CourseNo, Offering.OffTerm,
       Offering.OffYear, Offering.OffLocation,
       Offering.OffTime, Offering.OffDays
FROM Faculty, Offering
WHERE Faculty.FacNo = Offering.FacNo
  AND ( ( Offering.OffTerm = 'FALL'
  AND Offering.OffYear = 2007 )
   OR ( Offering.OffTerm = 'WINTER'
  AND Offering.OffYear = 2008 )
   OR ( Offering.OffTerm = 'SPRING'
  AND Offering.OffYear = 2008 ) )
```

The major query formulation issue for hierarchical reports is the <u>level</u> of the output. Sometimes there is a choice between whether the query's output contains individual rows or groups of rows. A rule of thumb is that the query should produce data for detail lines on the report. The query for the Faculty Work Load Report (Example 10.35) groups the data and counts the number of students enrolled. The query directly produces data for detail lines on the report. If the query produced one row per student enrolled in a course (a finer level of detail), then the report must calculate the number of students enrolled. With most reporting tools, it is easier to perform aggregate calculations in the query when the detail line of the report shows only summary data.

Query Formulation Tip for Hierarchical Reports: the query for a report should produce data for the detail lines of the report. If the detail lines in a report contain summary data, the query should usually contain summary data.

The other calculations (*PercentFull* and *LowEnrollment*) in Example 10.35 can be performed in the query or report with about the same effort. Note that the field *OffLimit* is a new column in the *Offering* table. It shows the maximum number of students that can enroll in a course offering.

Example 10.35: Query for the Faculty Work Load Report with summary data in detail lines

```
SELECT Offering.OfferNo, FacFirstName, FacLastName,
       FacDept, OffTerm, CrsUnits, OffLimit,
       Count(Enrollment.RegNo) AS NumStds,
       NumStds/Offlimit AS PercentFull,
       (NumStds/Offlimit) < 0.25 AS LowEnrollment
  FROM Faculty, Offering, Course, Enrollment
  WHERE Faculty.FacNo = Offering.FacNo
    AND Course.CourseNo = Offering.CourseNo
    AND Offering.OfferNo = Enrollment.OfferNo
    AND ( ( Offering.OffTerm = 'FALL'
    AND Offering.OffYear = 2007 )
     OR ( Offering.OffTerm = 'WINTER'
          AND Offering.OffYear = 2008 )
     OR ( Offering.OffTerm = 'SPRING'
    AND Offering.OffYear = 2008 ) )
  GROUP BY Offering.OfferNo, FacFirstName, FacLastName,
           FacDept, OffTerm, CrsUnits, OffLimit
```

Closing Thoughts

This chapter has described views, which are virtual tables derived from base tables with queries. The important concepts about views are the motivation for views and the usage of views in database application development. The major benefit of views is data independence. Changes to base table definitions usually do not impact applications that use views. Views can also simplify queries written by users as well as provide a flexible unit for security control. To effectively use views, you need to understand the difference between read-only and updatable views. A read-only view can be used in a query just like a base table. All views are at least read-only, but only some views are updatable. With an updatable view, changes to rows in the view are propagated to the underlying base tables. Both single-table and multiple-table views can be updatable. The most important determinant of updatability is that a view contains primary keys of the underlying base tables.

Views have become the building blocks of database applications because form and report tools use views. Data entry forms support retrieval and changes to a database. Hierarchical forms manipulate 1-M relationships in a database. To define a hierarchical form, you need to identify the 1-M relationship and define updatable views for the fixed (main form) and variable (subform) part of the form. Hierarchical reports provide a visually appealing presentation of data. To define a hierarchical report, you need to identify grouping levels and formulate a query to produce data for the detail lines of the report.

This chapter continues Part 5 by emphasizing application development with relational databases. In Chapter 9, you extended your query formulation skills and understanding of relational databases begun in the Part 2 chapters. This chapter stressed the application of query formulation skills in building applications based on views. Chapter 11 demonstrates the usage of queries in stored procedures and triggers to customize and extend database applications. To cement your understanding of application development with views, you need to use a relational DBMS especially to build forms and reports. It is only by applying the concepts to an actual database application that you will really learn the concepts.

Review Concepts

- Benefits of views: data independence, simplified query formulation, security
- View definition in SQL:
  ```
  CREATE VIEW IS_Students AS
       SELECT * FROM Student WHERE StdMajor = 'IS'
  ```
- Using a view in a query:
  ```
  SELECT StdFirstName, StdLastName, StdCity, StdGPA
       FROM IS_Students
       WHERE StdGPA >= 3.7
  ```
- Using an updatable view in INSERT, UPDATE, and DELETE statements:
  ```
  UPDATE IS_Students
       SET StdGPA = 3.5
       WHERE StdClass = 'SR'
  ```
- View modification: DBMS service to process a query on a view involving the execution of only one query. A query using a view is translated into a query using base tables by replacing references to the view with its definition.
- View materialization: DBMS service to process a query on a view by executing the query directly on the stored view. The stored view can be materialized on demand (when the view query is submitted) or periodically rebuilt from the base tables.
- Typical usage of view modification for databases that have a mix of update and retrieval operations
- Updatable view: a view that can be used in SELECT statements as well as UPDATE, INSERT, and DELETE statements.
- Rules for defining single-table updatable views: primary key and required columns
- WITH CHECK option to prevent view updates with side effects
- Rules for defining multiple-table updatable views: primary key and required columns of each updatable table along with foreign keys of the child tables
- 1-M updatable queries for developing data entry forms in Microsoft Access
- Components of a hierarchical form: main form and subform
- Hierarchal forms providing a convenient interface for manipulating 1-M relationships
- Query formulation steps for hierarchical forms: identify the 1-M relationship, identify the linking columns, identify other tables on the form, determine updatability of tables, write the form queries
- Writing updatable queries for the main form and the subform
- Hierarchical report: a formatted display of a query using indentation to show grouping and sorting
- Components of hierarchical reports: grouping fields, detail lines, and group summary calculations.
- Writing queries for hierarchical reports: provide data for detail lines

Questions

1. How do views provide data independence?
2. How can views simplify queries written by users?
3. How is a view like a macro in a spreadsheet?
4. What is view materialization?
5. What is view modification?
6. When is modification preferred to materialization for processing view queries?
7. What is an updatable view?
8. Why are some views read-only?
9. What are the rules for single-table updatable views?
10. What are the rules for 1-M updatable queries in Microsoft Access? multiple-table updatable views?
11. What is the purpose of the WITH CHECK clause?
12. What is a hierarchical form?

13. Briefly describe how a hierarchical form can be used in a business process that you know about. For example, if you know something about order processing, describe how a hierarchical form can support this process.
14. What is the difference between a main form and a subform?
15. What is the purpose of linking columns in hierarchical forms?
16. Why should you write updatable queries for a main form and a subform?
17. Why are tables used in a hierarchical form even when the tables cannot be changed as a result of using the form?
18. What is the first step of the query formulation process for hierarchical forms?
19. What is the second step of the query formulation process for hierarchical forms?
20. What is the third step of the query formulation process for hierarchical forms?
21. What is the fourth step of the query formulation process for hierarchical forms?
22. What is the fifth step of the query formulation process for hierarchical forms?
23. Provide an example of a hierarchical form in which the main form is not updatable. Explain the business reason that determines the read-only status of the main form.
24. What is a hierarchical report?
25. What is a grouping column in a hierarchical report?
26. How do you identify grouping columns in a report?
27. What is a detail line in a hierarchical report?
28. What is the relationship of grouping columns in a report to sorting columns?
29. Why is it often easier to write a query for a hierarchical report than for a hierarchical form?
30. What does it mean that a query should produce data for the detail line of a hierarchical report?
31. Do commercial DBMSs agree on the rules for updatable multiple-table views? If no, briefly comment on the level of agreement about rules for updatable multiple-table views.
32. What side effects can occur when a user changes the row of an updatable view? What is the cause of such side effects?

Problems

The problems use the extended order entry database depicted in Figure 10.P1 and Table 10-P1. Oracle CREATE TABLE statements for the new tables and the revised *Product* table follow Table 10-P1. This database extends the order entry database used in the problems of Chapters 3 and 9 with three tables: (1) *Supplier*, containing the list of suppliers for products carried in inventory; (2) *Purchase*, recording the general details of purchases to replenish inventory; and (3) *PurchLine*, containing the products requested on a purchase. In addition, the extended order entry database contains a new 1-M relationship (*Supplier* to *Product*) that replaces the *Product.ProdMfg* column in the original database.

In addition to the revisions noted in the previous paragraph, you should be aware of several assumptions made in the design of the Extended Order Entry Database:

- The design makes the simplifying assumption that there is only one supplier for each product. This assumption is appropriate for a single retail store that orders directly from manufacturers.
- The 1-M relationship from *Supplier* to *Purchase* supports the purchasing process. In this process, a user designates the supplier before selecting items to order from the supplier. Without this relationship, the business process and associated data entry forms would be more difficult to implement.

Table 10-P1: Explanations of Selected Columns in the Revised Order Entry Database

Column Name	Description
PurchDate	Date of making the purchase
PurchPayMethod	Payment method for the purchase (Credit, PO, or Cash)
PurchDelDate	Expected delivery date of the purchase

SuppDiscount	Discount provided by the supplier
PurchQty	Quantity of product purchased
PurchUnitCost	Unit cost of the product purchased

```
CREATE TABLE Product
(       ProdNo              CHAR(8),
        ProdName            VARCHAR2(50)
                            CONSTRAINT ProdNameRequired NOT NULL,
        SuppNo              CHAR(8)
                            CONSTRAINT SuppNo1Required NOT NULL,
        ProdQOH             INTEGER DEFAULT 0,
        ProdPrice           DECIMAL(12,2) DEFAULT 0,
        ProdNextShipDate    DATE,
CONSTRAINT PKProduct PRIMARY KEY (ProdNo),
CONSTRAINT SuppNoFK1 FOREIGN KEY (SuppNo) REFERENCES Supplier
    ON DELETE CASCADE )
```

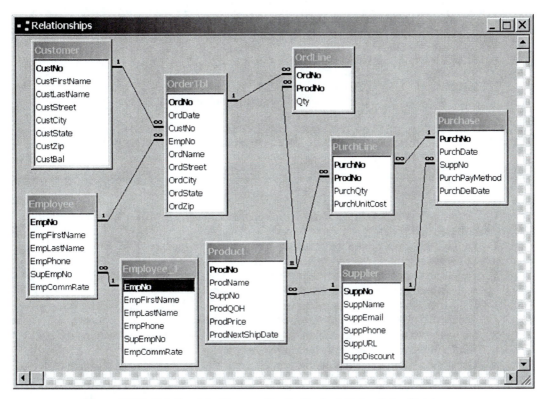

Figure 10.P1: Relationship Diagram for the Revised Order Entry Database

```
CREATE TABLE Supplier
(       SuppNo              CHAR(8),
        SuppName            VARCHAR2(30)
                            CONSTRAINT SuppNameRequired NOT NULL,
        SuppEmail           VARCHAR2(50),
        SuppPhone           CHAR(13),
        SuppURL             VARCHAR2(100),
        SuppDiscount        DECIMAL(3,3),
  CONSTRAINT PKSupplier PRIMARY KEY (SuppNo) )
```

```
CREATE TABLE Purchase
(       PurchNo             CHAR(8),
        PurchDate           DATE
                            CONSTRAINT PurchDateRequired NOT NULL,
        SuppNo              CHAR(8)
                            CONSTRAINT SuppNo2Required NOT NULL,
        PurchPayMethod      CHAR(6) DEFAULT 'PO',
        PurchDelDate        DATE,
  CONSTRAINT PKPurchase PRIMARY KEY (PurchNo) ,
  CONSTRAINT SuppNoFK2 FOREIGN KEY (SuppNo) REFERENCES Supplier )
```

```
CREATE TABLE PurchLine
(       ProdNo          CHAR(8),
        PurchNo         CHAR(8),
        PurchQty        INTEGER DEFAULT 1
                        CONSTRAINT PurchQtyRequired NOT NULL,
        PurchUnitCost DECIMAL(12,2),
CONSTRAINT PKPurchLine PRIMARY KEY (PurchNo, ProdNo),
CONSTRAINT FKPurchNo FOREIGN KEY (PurchNo) REFERENCES Purchase
    ON DELETE CASCADE,
CONSTRAINT FKProdNo2 FOREIGN KEY (ProdNo) REFERENCES Product )
```

1. Define a view containing products from supplier number S3399214. Include all *Product* columns in the view.
2. Define a view containing the details of orders placed in January 2008. Include all *OrderTbl* columns, *OrdLine.Qty*, and the product name in the view.
3. Define a view containing the product number, name, price, and quantity on hand along with the number of orders in which the product appears.
4. Using the view defined in problem 1, write a query to list the products with a price greater than $300. Include all view columns in the result.
5. Using the view defined in problem 2, write a query to list the rows containing the words Ink Jet in the product name. Include all view columns in the result.
6. Using the view defined in problem 3, write a query to list the products in which more than five orders have been placed. Include the product name and the number of orders in the result.
7. For the query in problem 4, modify the query so that it uses base tables only.
8. For the query in problem 5, modify the query so that it uses base tables only.
9. For the query in problem 6, modify the query so that it uses base tables only.
10. Is the view in problem 1 updatable? Explain why or why not.
11. Is the view in problem 2 updatable? Explain why or why not. What database tables can be changed by modifying rows in the view?
12. Is the view in problem 3 updatable? Explain why or why not.
13. For the view in problem 1, write an INSERT statement that references the view. The effect of the INSERT statement should add a new row to the *Product* table.
14. For the view in problem 1, write an UPDATE statement that references the view. The effect of the UPDATE statement should modify the *ProdQOH* column of the row added in problem 13.

15. For the view in problem 1, write a DELETE statement that references the view. The effect of the DELETE statement should remove the row added in problem 13.

16. Modify the view definition of problem 1 to prevent side effects. Use a different name for the view than the name used in problem 1. Note that the WITH CHECK option cannot be specified in Microsoft Access using the SQL window.

17. Write an UPDATE statement for the view in problem 1 to modify the *SuppNo* of the row with *ProdNo* of P6677900 to S4420948. The UPDATE statement should be rejected by the revised view definition in problem 16 but accepted by the original view definition in problem 1. This problem cannot be done in Access using the SQL window.

18. Define a 1-M updatable query involving the *Customer* and the *OrderTbl* tables. The query should support updates to the *OrderTbl* table. The query should include all columns of the *OrderTbl* table and the name (first and last), street, city, state, and zip of the *Customer* table. Note that this problem is specific to Microsoft Access.

19. Define a 1-M updatable query involving the *Customer* table, the *OrderTbl* table, and the *Employee* table. The query should support updates to the *OrderTbl* table. Include all rows in the *OrderTbl* table even if there is a null employee number. The query should include all columns of the *OrderTbl* table, the name (first and last), street, city, state, and zip of the *Customer* table, and the name (first and last) and phone of the *Employee* table. Note that this problem is specific to Microsoft Access.

20. Define a 1-M updatable query involving the *OrdLine* and the *Product* tables. The query should support updates to the *OrdLine* table. The query should include all columns of the *OrdLine* table and the name, the quantity on hand, and the price of the *Product* table. Note that this problem is specific to Microsoft Access.

21. Define a 1-M updatable query involving the *Purchase* and the *Supplier* tables. The query should support updates and inserts to the *Product* and the *Supplier* tables. Include the necessary columns so that both tables are updatable. Note that this problem is specific to Microsoft Access.

22. For the sample Simple Order Form shown in Figure 10.P2, answer the five query formulation questions discussed in Section 10.4.3. The form supports manipulation of the heading and the details of orders.

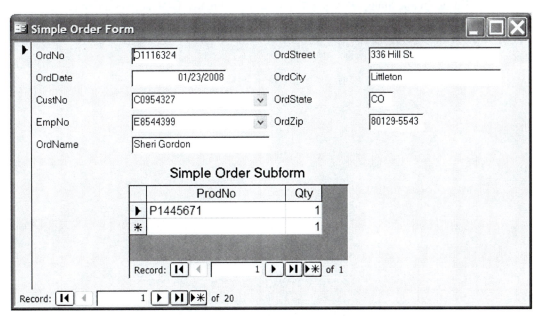

Figure 10.P2: Simple Order Form

23. For the sample Order Form shown in Figure 10.P3, answer the five query formulation questions discussed in Section 10.4.3. Like the Simple Order Form depicted in Figure 10.P2, the Order Form supports manipulation of the heading and the details of orders. In addition, the Order Form displays data from other tables to provide a context for the user when completing an order. The Order Form supports both phone (an employee taking the

order) and Web (without an employee taking the order) orders. The subform query should compute the Amount field as `Qty*ProdPrice`. Do not compute the Total Amount field in either the main form query or the subform query. It is computed in the form.

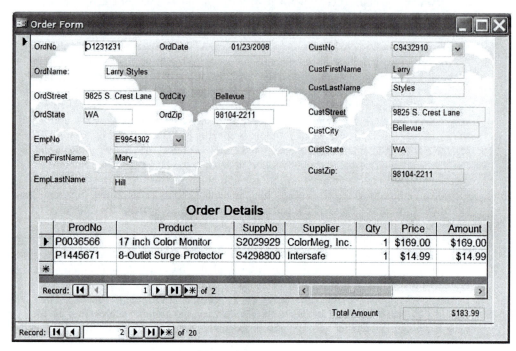

Figure 10.P3: Order Form

24. Modify your answer to problem 23 assuming that the Order Form supports only phone orders, not Web orders.

25. For the sample Simple Purchase Form shown in Figure 10.P4, answer the five query formulation questions discussed in Section 10.4.3. The form supports manipulation of the heading and the details of purchases.

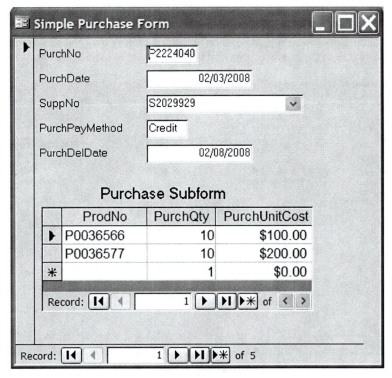

Figure 10.P4: Simple Purchase Form

26. For the sample Purchase Form shown in Figure 10.P5, use the five query formulation steps presented in Section 10.4.3. Like the Simple Purchase Form depicted in Figure 10.P4, the Purchase Form supports manipulation of the heading and the details of purchases. In addition, the Purchase Form displays data from other tables to provide a context for the user when completing a purchase. The subform query should compute the Amount field as `PurchQty*PurchUnitCost`. Do not compute the Total Amount field in either the main form query or the subform query. It is computed in the form.

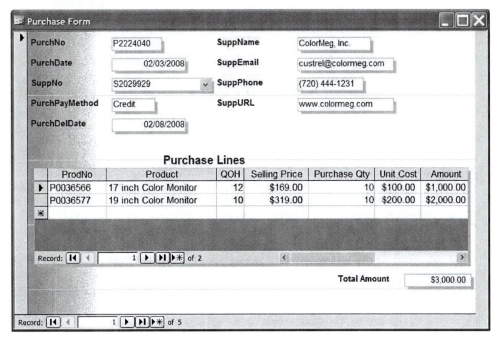

Figure 10.P5: Purchase Form

27. For the sample Supplier Form shown in Figure 10.P6, use the five query formulation steps presented in Section 10.4.3. The main form supports the manipulation of supplier data while the subform supports the manipulation of only the product number and the product name of the products provided by the supplier in the main form.

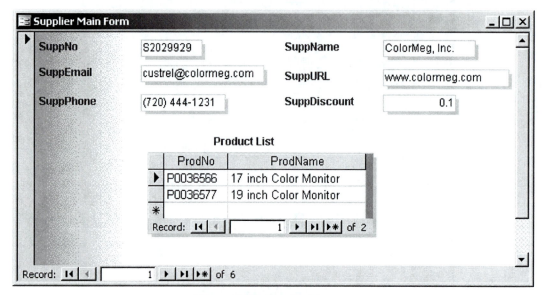

Figure 10.P6: Supplier Form

28. For the Order Detail Report, write a SELECT statement to produce the data for the detail lines. The grouping column in the report is *OrdNo*. The report should list the orders for customer number O2233457 in January 2008.

Order Detail Report

Order Number	Order Date	Product No	Qty	Price	Amount
O2233457	1/12/2008	P1441567	1	$14.99	$14.99
		P0036577	2	$319.00	$638.00
Total Order Amount				$652.99	
O4714645	1/11/2008	P9995676	2	$89.00	$178.00
		P0036566	1	$369.00	$369.00
Total Order Amount				$547.00	

29. For the sample Order Summary Report, write a SELECT statement to produce the data for the detail lines. The Zip Code report field is the first five characters of the *CustZip* column. The grouping field in the report is the first five characters of the *CustZip* column. The Order Amount Sum report field is the sum of the quantity times the product price. Limit the report to year 2008 orders. You should also include the month number in the SELECT statement so that the report can be sorted by the month number instead of the Month report field. Use the following expressions to derive computed columns used in the report:

- In Microsoft Access, the expression left(CustZip, 5) generates the Zip Code report field. In Oracle, the expression substr(CustZip, 1, 5) generates the Zip Code report field.

360

- In Microsoft Access, the expression format(OrdDate, "mmmm yyyy") generates the Year report field. In Oracle, the expression to_char(OrdDate, 'MONTH YYYY') generates the Year report field.
- In Microsoft Access, the expression month(OrdDate) generates the Month report field. In Oracle, the expression to_number(to_char(OrdDate, 'MM')) generates the Month report field.

Order Summary Report

Zip Code	Month	Order Line Count	Order Amount Sum
80111	January 2008	10	$1,149
	February 2008	21	$2,050
Summary of 80111		31	$3,199
80113	January 2008	15	$1,541
	February 2008	11	$1,450
Summary of 80113		31	$2,191

30. Revise the Order Summary Report to list the number of orders and the average order amount instead of the Order Line Count and Order Amount Sum. The revised report appears below. You will need to use a SELECT statement in the FROM clause or write two statements to produce the data for the detail lines.

Order Summary Report

Zip Code	Month	Order Count	Order Amount Average
80111	January 2008	5	$287.25
	February 2008	10	$205.00
Summary of 80111		15	$213.27
80113	January 2008	5	$308.20
	February 2008	4	$362.50
Summary of 80113		9	$243.44

31. For the Purchase Detail Report, write a SELECT statement to produce the data for the detail lines. The grouping column in the report is *PurchNo*. The report should list the orders for supplier number S5095332 in February 2008.

Purchase Detail Report

Purch Number	Purch Date	Product No	Qty	Cost	Amount
P2345877	2/11/2008	P1441567	1	$11.99	$11.99
		P0036577	2	$229.00	$458.00
Total Purchase Amount				$469.99	.
P4714645	2/10/2008	P9995676	2	$69.00	$138.00
		P0036566	1	$309.00	$309.00

Total Purchase Amount

$447.00

32. For the sample Purchase Summary Report, write a SELECT statement to produce the data for the detail lines. The Area Code report field is the second through fourth characters of the *SuppPhone* column. The grouping field in the report is the second through fourth characters of the *SuppPhone* column. The Purchase Amount Sum report field is the sum of the quantity times the product price. Limit the report to year 2008 orders. You should also include the month number in the SELECT statement so that the report can be sorted by the month number instead of the Month report field. Use the following expressions to derive computed columns used in the report:

- In Microsoft Access, the expression `mid(SuppPhone, 2, 3)` generates the Area Code report field. In Oracle, the expression `substr(SuppPhone, 2, 3)` generates the Area Code report field.
- In Microsoft Access, the expression `format(PurchDate, "mmmm yyyy")` generates the Year report field. In Oracle, the expression `to_char(PurchDate, 'MONTH YYYY')` generates the Year report field.
- In Microsoft Access, the expression `month(PurchDate)` generates the Month report field. In Oracle, the expression `to_number(to_char(PurchDate, 'MM'))` generates the Month report field.

Purchase Summary Report

Area Code	Month	Purch Line Count	Purch Amount Sum
303	January 2008	20	$1,149
	February 2008	11	$2,050
Summary of 303		31	$3,199
720	January 2008	19	$1,541
	February 2008	11	$1,450
Summary of 720		30	$2,191

33. Revise the Purchase Summary Report to list the number of purchases and the average purchase amount instead of the Purchase Line Count and Purchase Amount Sum. The

1. revised report appears below. You will need to use a SELECT statement in the FROM clause or write two statements to produce the data for the detail lines.

Purchase Summary Report

Area Code		Month	Purchase Count	Average Purchase Amount
303	January 2008	8		$300.00
	February 2008	12		$506.50
Summary of 303		20		$403.25
720	January 2008	6		$308.20
	February 2008	3		$362.50
Summary of 720		9		$243.44

34. Define a view containing purchases from supplier names Connex or Cybercx. Include all *Purchase* columns in the view.
35. Define a view containing the details of purchases placed in February 2008. Include all *Purchase* columns, *PurchLine.PurchQty*, *PurchLine.PurchUnitCost*, and the product name in the view.
36. Define a view containing the product number, name, price, and quantity on hand along with the sum of the quantity purchased and the sum of the purchase cost (unit cost times quantity purchased).
37. Using the view defined in problem 34, write a query to list the purchases made with payment method PO. Include all view columns in the result.
38. Using the view defined in problem 35, write a query to list the rows containing the words Printer in the product name. Include all view columns in the result.
39. Using the view defined in problem 36, write a query to list the products in which the total purchase cost is greater than $1,000. Include the product name and the total purchase cost in the result.
40. For the query in problem 37, modify the query so that it uses base tables only.
41. For the query in problem 38, modify the query so that it uses base tables only.
42. For the query in problem 39, modify the query so that it uses base tables only.

References for Further Study

The DBAZine site (www.dbazine.com) and the DevX.com Database Zone (www.devx.com) have plenty of practical advice about query formulation and SQL. For product-specific SQL advice, the DataBased Advisor site (my.advisor.com/pub/DataBasedAdvisor) features forums and articles about a number of DBMSs including Microsoft SQL Server and Microsoft Access. Oracle documentation can be found at the Oracle Technet site (www.oracle.com/technology). In Chapter 10, Date (2003) provides additional details of view updatability issues especially related to multiple-table views. Melton and Simon (2001) describe updatable query specifications in SQL:1999.

Appendix 10.A: SQL:2006 Syntax Summary

This appendix summarizes the SQL:2006 syntax for the CREATE VIEW statement presented in Chapter 10 and a simple companion statement (DROP VIEW). The conventions used in the syntax notation are identical to those used at the end of Chapter 3.

CREATE VIEW Statement

```
CREATE VIEW ViewName [ ( ColumnName* ) ]
  AS  <Select-Statement>
  [ WITH CHECK OPTION ]


<Select-Statement>:  -- defined in Chapter 4 and extended in Chapter 9
```

DROP VIEW Statement

```
DROP VIEW ViewName  [ { CASCADE | RESTRICT } ]
  -- CASCADE deletes the view and any views that use its definition.
  -- RESTRICT means that the view is not deleted if any views use its definition.
```

Appendix 10.B: Rules for Updatable Join Views in Oracle

In recent Oracle versions (9i to 11g), a join view contains one or more tables or views in its defining FROM clause. Fundamental to updatable join views is the concept of a <u>key preserving table</u>. A join view preserves a table if every candidate key of the table can be a candidate key of the join result table. This statement means that the rows of an updatable join view can be mapped in a 1-1 manner with each key preserved table. In a join involving a 1-M relationship, the child table could be key preserved because each child row is associated with at most one parent row. Using the definition of a key preserving table, a join view is updatable if it satisfies the following conditions:

It does not contain the DISTINCT keyword, the GROUP BY clause, aggregation functions, or set operations (UNION, MINUS, and INTERSECT).
It contains at least one key preserving table.
The CREATE VIEW statement does not contain the WITH CHECK OPTION.

An updatable join view supports insert, update, and delete operations on one underlying table per manipulation statement. The updatable table is the key preserving table. An UPDATE statement can modify (in the SET clause) only columns of one key preserving table. An INSERT statement can add values for columns of one key preserved table. An INSERT statement cannot contain columns from nonkey preserving tables. Rows can be deleted as long as the join view contains only one key preserving table. Join views with more than one key preserving table do not support DELETE statements.

11

Stored Procedures and Triggers

Learning Objectives

This chapter explains the motivation and design issues for stored procedures and triggers and provides practice writing them using PL/SQL, the database programming language of Oracle. After this chapter, the student should have acquired the following knowledge and skills:

- Explain the reasons for writing stored procedures and triggers
- Understand the design issues of language style, binding, database connection, and result processing for database programming languages
- Write PL/SQL procedures
- Understand the classification of triggers
- Write PL/SQL triggers
- Understand trigger execution procedures

Overview

Chapter 10 provided details about application development with views. You learned about defining user views, updating base tables with views, and using views in forms and reports. This chapter augments your database application development skills with stored procedures and triggers. Stored procedures provide reuse of common code, while triggers provide rule processing for common tasks. Together, stored procedures and triggers support customization of database applications and improved productivity in developing database applications.

To become skilled in database application development as well as in database administration, you need to understand stored procedures and triggers. Since both stored procedures and triggers are coded in a database programming language, this chapter first provides background about the motivation and design issues for database programming languages as well as specific details about PL/SQL, the proprietary database programming language of Oracle.

After the background about database programming languages and PL/SQL, this chapter then presents stored procedures and triggers. For stored procedures, you will learn about the motivation and coding practices for simple and more advanced procedures. For triggers, you will learn about the classification of triggers, trigger execution procedures, and coding practices for triggers.

The presentation of PL/SQL details in Sections 11.1 to 11.3 assumes that you have had a previous course in computer programming using a business programming language such as Visual Basic or Java. If you would like a broader treatment of the material without the computer programming details, you should read Sections 11.1.1, 11.1.2, 11.3.1, and the introductory material in Section 11.2 before the beginning of Section 11.2.1. In addition, the trigger examples in Section 11.3.2 mostly involve SQL statements so that you can understand the triggers without detailed knowledge of PL/SQL statements.

For continuity, all examples about stored procedures and triggers use the revised university database of Chapter 10. Figure 11.1 shows the Access relationship window of the revised university database for convenient reference.

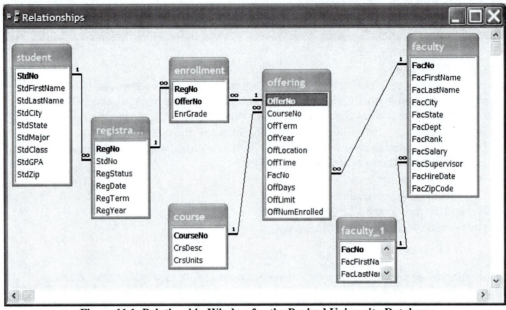

Figure 11.1: Relationship Window for the Revised University Database

11.1 Database Programming Languages and PL/SQL

After learning about the power of nonprocedural access and application development tools, you might think that procedural languages are not necessary for database application development. However, these tools despite their power are not complete solutions for commercial database application development. This section presents the motivation for database programming languages, design issues for database programming languages, and details about PL/SQL, the database programming language of Oracle.

11.1.1 Motivation for Database Programming Languages

A database programming language is a procedural language with an interface to one or more DBMSs. The interface allows a program to combine procedural statements with database access, usually nonprocedural database access. This subsection discusses three primary motivations (customization, batch processing, and complex operations) for using a database programming language and two secondary motivations (efficiency and portability).

> **Database Programming Language**: a procedural language with an interface to one or more DBMSs. The interface allows a program to combine procedural statements with nonprocedural database access.

Customization

Most database application development tools support customization. Customization is necessary because no tool provides a complete solution for the development of complex database applications. Customization allows an organization to use the built-in power of a tool along with customized code to change the tool's default actions and to add new actions beyond those supported by the tool.

To support customized code, most database application development tools use event-driven coding. In this coding style, an event triggers the execution of a procedure. An event model includes events for user actions such as clicking a button, as well as internal events such as before a database record is updated. An event procedure may access the values of controls on forms and reports as well as retrieve and update database rows. Event procedures are coded using a database programming language, often a proprietary language provided by a DBMS vendor. For commercial application development, event coding is common.

Batch Processing

Despite the growth of online database processing, batch processing continues to be an important way to process database work. For example, check processing typically is a batch process in which a clearinghouse bank processes large groups or batches of checks during nonpeak hours. Batch processing usually involves a delay from the occurrence of an event to its capture in a database. In the check processing case, checks are presented for payment to a merchant but not processed by a clearinghouse bank until later. Some batch processing applications such as billing statement preparation involves a cutoff time not a time delay. Batch processing in situations involving time delays and time cutoffs can provide significant economies of scale to offset the drawback of less timely data. Even with the continued growth of commercial Web commerce, batch processing will remain an important method of processing database work.

Application development for batch processing involves writing computer programs in a database programming language. Since few development tools support batch processing, coding can be detailed and labor intensive. The programmer typically must write code to read input data, perform database manipulation, and create output records to show the processing result.

Complex Operations

Nonprocedural database access by definition does not support all possible database retrievals. The design of a nonprocedural language involves a trade-off between amount of code and computational completeness. To allow general-purpose computation, a procedural language is necessary. To reduce coding, nonprocedural languages support compact specification of important and common operations. The SELECT statement of SQL supports the operations of relational algebra along with ordering and grouping. To perform database retrievals beyond the operations of relational algebra, coding in a database programming language is necessary.

The transitive closure is an important operation not supported by most SQL implementations. This operation is important for queries involving self-referencing relationships. For example, to retrieve all employees managed directly or indirectly using a self-referencing relationship, the transitive closure operator is needed. This operation involves self-join operations, but the number of self-join operations depends on the depth (number of layers of subordinates) in an organization chart. Although the WITH RECURSIVE clause for transitive closure operations was introduced in SQL:1999, most DBMSs have not implemented this feature. With most DBMSs, transitive closure operations must be coded using a database programming language. To code a transitive closure operation, a self-join query must be repetitively executed inside a loop until the query returns an empty result.

Other Motivations

Efficiency and portability are two additional reasons for using a database programming language. When distrust in optimizing database compilers was high (until the mid-1990s), efficiency was a primary motivation for using a database programming language. To avoid inefficiencies of optimizing compilers, some DBMS vendors supported record-at-a-time access with the programmer determining the access plan for complex queries. As confidence has grown in optimizing database compilers, the efficiency need has become less important. However, with complex Web applications and immature Web development tools, efficiency has become an important issue in some applications. As Web development tools mature, efficiency should become a less important issue.

Portability can be important in some environments. Most application development tools and database programming languages are proprietary. If an organization wants to remain vendor neutral, an application can be built using a nonproprietary programming language (such as Java) along with a standard database interface. If just DBMS neutrality is desired (not neutrality from an application development tool), some application development tools allow connection with a variety of DBMSs through standard database interfaces such as the Open Database Connectivity (ODBC) and the Java Database Connectivity (JDBC). Portability is a particular concern for Web database access in which an application must be compatible with many types of servers and browsers.

11.1.2 Design Issues

Before undertaking the study of any database programming language, you should understand design issues about integrating a procedural language with a nonprocedural language. Understanding the issues will help you differentiate among the many languages in the marketplace and understand the features of a specific language. Each DBMS usually provides several alternatives for database programming languages. This section discusses the design issues of language style, binding, database connection, and result processing with an emphasis on the design choices first specified in SQL:1999 and refined in SQL:2003 and SQL:2006. Many DBMS vendors are adapting to the specifications in SQL:2006.

Language Style

SQL:2006 provides two language styles for integrating a procedural language with SQL. A statement-level interface involves changes to the syntax of a host programming language to accommodate embedded SQL statements. The host language contains additional statements to establish database connections, execute SQL statements, use the results of an SQL statement, associate programming variables with database columns, handle exceptions in SQL statements, and manipulate database descriptors. Statement-level interfaces are available for standard and proprietary languages. For standard languages such as Java and Visual Basic, some DBMSs provide a precompiler to process the statements before invoking the programming language compiler. Most DBMSs also provide proprietary languages such as the Oracle language PL/SQL with a statement-level interface to support embedded SQL.

> **Statement-Level Interface**: a language style for integrating a programming language with a nonprocedural language such as SQL. A statement-level interface involves changes to the syntax of a host programming language to accommodate embedded SQL statements.

The SQL:2006 specification defines the Persistent Stored Modules (SQL/PSM) language as a database programming language. Because SQL/PSM was defined after many DBMS vendors already had widely used proprietary languages, most DBMS vendors do not conform to the SQL/PSM standard. However, the SQL/PSM standard has influenced the design of proprietary database programming languages such as Oracle PL/SQL.

The second language style provided by SQL:2006 is known as a call-level interface (CLI). The SQL:2006 CLI contains a set of procedures and a set of type definitions for SQL data types. The procedures provide similar functionality to the additional statements in a statement-level interface. The SQL:2006 CLI is more difficult to learn and use than a statement-level interface. However, the SQL:2006 CLI is portable across host languages, whereas the statement-level interface is not portable and not supported for all programming languages.

> **Call-Level Interface (CLI)**: a language style for integrating a programming language with a nonprocedural language such as SQL. A CLI includes a set of procedures and a set of type definitions for manipulating the results of SQL statements in computer programs.

The most widely used call-level interfaces are the Open Database Connectivity (ODBC) supported by Microsoft and the Java Database Connectivity (JDBC) supported by Oracle. Because both Microsoft and Oracle have cooperated with the SQL standards efforts, the most recent versions of these proprietary CLIs are compatible to the SQL:2006 CLI. Because of the established user bases, these interfaces probably will continue to be more widely used than the SQL:2006 CLI.

Binding

Binding for a database programming language involves the association of an SQL statement with its access plan. Recall from Chapter 8 that the SQL compiler determines the best access plan for an SQL statement after a detailed search of possible access plans. Static binding involves the determination of the access plan at compile time. Because the optimization process can consume considerable computing resources, it is desirable to determine the access plan at compile time and then reuse the access plan for repetitively executed statements. However, in some applications, the data to retrieve cannot be predetermined. In these situations, dynamic binding is necessary in which the access plan for a statement is determined when the statement is executed during run-time of the application. Even in these dynamic situations, it is useful to reuse the access plan for a statement if the statement is repetitively executed by the application.

SQL:2006 specifies both static and dynamic binding to support a range of database applications. A statement-level interface can support both static and dynamic binding. Embedded SQL statements have static binding. Dynamic SQL statements are supported by the SQL:2006 EXECUTE statement that contains an SQL statement as an input parameter. If a dynamic statement is repetitively executed by an application, the SQL:2006 PREPARE statement supports reuse of the access plan. The SQL:2006 CLI supports only dynamic binding. If a dynamic statement is repetitively executed by an application, the SQL:2006 CLI provides the Prepare() procedure to reuse the access plan.

Database Connection

A database connection identifies the database used by an application. A database connection can be implicit or explicit. For procedures and triggers stored in a database, the connection is implicit. The SQL statements in triggers and procedures implicitly access the database that contains the triggers and procedures.

In programs external to a database, the connection is explicit. SQL:2006 contains the CONNECT statement and other related statements for statement-level interfaces and the Connect() procedure and related procedures in the CLI. A database is identified by a Web address or a database identifier that contains a Web address. Using a database identifier relieves the database programmer from knowing the specific Web address for a database as well as providing the server administrator more flexibility to relocate a database to a different location on a server.

Result Processing

To process the results of SQL statements, database programming languages must resolve differences in data types and processing orientation. The data types in a programming language may not correspond exactly to the standard SQL data types. To resolve this problem, the database interface provides statements or procedures to map between the programming language data types and the SQL data types.

The result of a SELECT statement can be one row or a collection of rows. For SELECT statements that return at most one row (for example, retrieval by primary key), the SQL:2006 specification allows the result values to be stored in program variables. In the statement-level interface, SQL:2006 provides the USING clause to store result values in program variables. The SQL:2006 CLI provides for implicit storage of result values using predefined descriptor records that can be accessed in a program.

For SELECT statements that return more than one row, a cursor must be used. A cursor allows storage and iteration of a set of records returned by a SELECT statement. A cursor is similar to a dynamic array in which the array size is determined by the size of the query result. For statement-level interfaces, SQL:2006 provides statements to declare cursors, open and close cursors, position cursors, and retrieve values from cursors. The SQL:2006 CLI provides procedures with similar functionality to the statement-level interface. Section 11.2.3 presents details about cursors for PL/SQL.

> **Cursor**: a construct in a database programming language that allows storage and iteration of a set of records returned by a SELECT statement. A cursor is similar to a dynamic array in which the array size is determined by the size of the query result.

11.1.3 PL/SQL Statements

Programming Language/Structured Query Language (PL/SQL) is a proprietary database programming language for the Oracle DBMS. Since its introduction in 1992, Oracle has steadily added features to PL/SQL so that it has the features of a modern programming language as well as a statement-level interface for SQL. Because PL/SQL is a widely used language among Oracle developers and Oracle is a widely used enterprise DBMS, this chapter uses PL/SQL to depict stored procedures and triggers.

To prepare you to read and code stored procedures and triggers, this section presents examples of PL/SQL statements. After reading this section, you should understand the structure of PL/SQL statements and be able to write PL/SQL statements using the example statements as guidelines. This section shows enough PL/SQL statement examples to allow you to read and write stored procedures and triggers of modest complexity after you complete the chapter. However, this section depicts neither all PL/SQL statements nor all statement variations.

This section is not a tutorial about computer programming. To follow the remainder of this chapter, you should have taken a previous course in computer programming or have equivalent experience. You will find that PL/SQL statements are similar to statements in other modern programming languages such as Java and Visual Basic.

Basics of PL/SQL

PL/SQL statements contain reserved words and symbols, user identifiers, and constant values. Reserved words in PL/SQL are not case sensitive. Reserved symbols include the semicolon (;) for terminating statements as well as operators such as + and −. User identifiers provide names for variables, constants, and other PL/SQL constructs. User identifiers like reserved words are not case sensitive. The following list defines restrictions on user identifiers:

- Must have a maximum of 30 characters.
- Must begin with a letter.
- Allowable characters are letters (upper- or lower-case), numbers, the dollar sign, the pound symbol (#), and the underscore.
- Must not be identical to any reserved word or symbol.
- Must not be identical to other identifiers, table names, or column names.

A PL/SQL statement may contain constant values for numbers and character strings along with certain reserved words. The following list provides background about PL/SQL constants:

- Numeric constants can be whole numbers (100), numbers with a decimal point (1.67), negative numbers (-150.15), and numbers in scientific notation (3.14E7).
- String constants are surrounded in single quotation marks such as 'this is a string'. Do not use single quotation marks to surround numeric or Boolean constants. String constants are case sensitive so that 'This is a string' is a different value than 'this is a string'. To use a single quotation mark in a string constant, you should use two single quotation marks as 'today''s date'.
- Boolean constants are the TRUE and FALSE reserved words.
- The reserved word NULL can be used as a number, string, or Boolean constant. For strings, two single quotation marks '' without anything inside denote the NULL value.
- PL/SQL does not provide date constants. You should use the To_Date function to convert a string constant to a date value.

Variable Declaration and Assignment Statements

A variable declaration contains a variable name (a user identifier), a data type, and an optional default value. Table 11-1 lists common PL/SQL data types. Besides using the predefined types, a variable's type can be a user defined-type created with a TYPE statement. A default value can be indicated with the DEFAULT keyword or the assignment (:=) symbol. The DECLARE keyword should precede the first variable declaration as shown in Example 11.1.

Example 11.1: PL/SQL Variable Declarations
Lines beginning with double hyphens are comments.

```
DECLARE
    aFixedLengthString      CHAR(6) DEFAULT 'ABCDEF';
    aVariableLengthString   VARCHAR2(30);
    anIntegerVariable       INTEGER := 0;
    aFixedPrecisionVariable DECIMAL(10,2);
    -- Uses the SysDate function for the default value
    aDateVariable           DATE DEFAULT SysDate;
```

Table 11-1: Summary of Common PL/SQL Data Types

Category	Data Types	Comments
String	CHAR(L), VARCHAR2(L)	CHAR for fixed length strings, VARCHAR2 for variable length strings; L for the maximum length
Numeric	INTEGER, SMALLINT, POSITIVE, NUMBER(W,D), DECIMAL(W,D), FLOAT, REAL	W for the width; D for the number of digits to the right of the decimal point
Logical	BOOLEAN	TRUE, FALSE values
Date	DATE	Stores both date and time information including the century, the year, the month, the day, the hour, the minute, and the second. A date occupies 7 bytes.

For variables associated with columns of a database table, PL/SQL provides anchored declarations. Anchored declarations relieve the programmer from knowing the data types of database columns. An anchored declaration includes a fully-qualified column name followed by the keyword %TYPE. Example 11.2 demonstrates anchored variable declarations using columns from the revised university database of Chapter 10. The last anchored declaration involves a variable using the type associated with a previously defined variable.

Example 11.2: PL/SQL Anchored Variable Declarations

```
DECLARE
    anOffTerm Offering.OffTerm%TYPE;
    anOffYear Offering.OffYear%TYPE;
    aCrsUnits Course.CrsUnits%TYPE;
    aSalary1 DECIMAL(10,2);
    aSalary2 aSalary1%TYPE;
```

Oracle also provides structured data types for combining primitive data types. Oracle supports variable length arrays (VARRAY), tables (TABLE), and records (RECORD) for combining data types. For information about the structured data types, you should consult the online Oracle documentation such as the PL/SQL User's Guide.

Assignment statements involve a variable, the assignment symbol (:=), and an expression on the right. Expressions can include combinations of constants, variables, functions, and operators. When evaluated, an expression produces a value. Example 11.3 demonstrates assignment statements with various expression elements.

Example 11.3: PL/SQL Assignment Examples
It is assumed that variables used in the examples have been previously declared. Lines beginning with double hyphens are comments.

```
aFixedLengthString := 'XYZABC';
-- || is the string concatenation function
aVariableLengthString := aFixedLengthString || 'ABCDEF';
anIntegerVariable := anAge + 1;
aFixedPrecisionVariable := aSalary * 0.10;
-- To_Date is the date conversion function
aDateVariable := To_Date('30-Jun-2008');
```

Conditional Statements

PL/SQL provides the IF and CASE statements for conditional decision making. In an IF statement, a logical expression or condition evaluating to TRUE, FALSE, or NULL, follows the IF keyword. Conditions include comparison expressions using the comparison operators (Table 11-2) connected using the logical operators AND, OR, and NOT. Parentheses can be used to clarify the order of evaluation in complex conditions. When mixing the AND and OR operators, you should use parentheses to clarify the order of evaluation. Conditions are evaluated using the three-valued logic described in Chapter 9 (Section 9.4).

Table 11-2: List of PL/SQL Comparison Operators

Operator	Meaning
=	Equal to
<>	Not equal to
>	Greater than
<	Less than
>=	Greater than or equal to
<=	Less than or equal to

As in other languages, the PL/SQL IF statement has multiple variations. Example 11-4 depicts the first variation known as the IF-THEN statement. Any number of statements can be used between the THEN and END IF keywords. Example 11-5 depicts the second variation known as the IF-THEN-ELSE statement. This statement allows a set of alternative statements if the condition is false. The third variation (IF-THEN-ELSIF) depicted in Example 11-6 allows a condition for each ELSIF clause along with a final ELSE clause if all conditions are false.

```
IF-THEN Statement:
IF condition THEN
   sequence of statements
END IF;
```

```
IF-THEN-ELSE Statement:
IF condition THEN
   sequence of statements 1
ELSE
   sequence of statements 2
END IF;
```

```
IF-THEN-ELSIF Statement:
IF condition1 THEN
   sequence of statements 1
ELSIF condition2 THEN
   sequence of statements 2
ELSIF conditionN THEN
   sequence of statements N
ELSE
   sequence of statements N+1
END IF;
```

Example 11.4: IF-THEN Statement Examples

It is assumed that variables used in the examples have been previously declared.

```
IF aCrsUnits > 3 THEN
    CourseFee := BaseFee + aCrsUnits * VarFee;
END IF;


IF anOffLimit > NumEnrolled OR CourseOverRide = TRUE THEN
    NumEnrolled := NumEnrolled + 1;
    EnrDate := SysDate;
END IF;
```

Example 11.5: IF-THEN-ELSE Statement Examples

It is assumed that variables used in the examples have been previously declared.

```
IF aCrsUnits > 3 THEN
    CourseFee := BaseFee + ((aCrsUnits - 3) * VarFee);
ELSE
    CourseFee := BaseFee;
END IF;


IF anOffLimit > NumEnrolled OR CourseOverRide = TRUE THEN
    NumEnrolled := NumEnrolled + 1;
    EnrDate := SysDate;
ELSE
    Enrolled := FALSE;
END IF;
```

Example 11.6: IF-THEN-ELSIF Statement Examples

It is assumed that variables used in the examples have been previously declared.

```
IF anOffTerm = 'Fall' AND Enrolled := TRUE THEN
    FallEnrolled := FallEnrolled + 1;
ELSIF anOffTerm = 'Spring' AND Enrolled := TRUE THEN
    SpringEnrolled := SpringEnrolled + 1;
ELSE
    SummerEnrolled := SummerEnrolled + 1;
END IF;


IF aStdClass = 'FR' THEN
    NumFR := NumFR + 1;
    NumStudents := NumStudents + 1;
ELSIF aStdClass = 'SO' THEN
    NumSO := NumSO + 1;
    NumStudents := NumStudents + 1;
ELSIF aStdClass = 'JR' THEN
    NumJR := NumJR + 1;
    NumStudents := NumStudents + 1;
ELSIF aStdClass = 'SR' THEN
    NumSR := NumSR + 1;
    NumStudents := NumStudents + 1;
END IF;
```

The CASE statement uses a selector instead of condition. A selector is an expression whose value determines a decision. Example 11.7 shows a CASE statement corresponding to the second part of Example 11.6. The CASE statement was first introduced in PL/SQL for Oracle 9i. Previous Oracle versions give a syntax error for Example 11.7.

Example 11.7: CASE Statement Example Corresponding to the Second Part of Example 11-6
It is assumed that variables used in the example have been previously declared.

```
CASE aStdClass
  WHEN 'FR' THEN
    NumFR := NumFR + 1;
    NumStudents := NumStudents + 1;
  WHEN 'SO' THEN
    NumSO := NumSO + 1;
    NumStudents := NumStudents + 1;
  WHEN 'JR' THEN
    NumJR := NumJR + 1;
    NumStudents := NumStudents + 1;
  WHEN 'SR' THEN
    NumSR := NumSR + 1;
    NumStudents := NumStudents + 1;
END CASE;
```

```
CASE Statement:
CASE selector
  WHEN expression1 THEN sequence of statements 1
  WHEN expression2 THEN sequence of statements 2
  WHEN expressionN THEN sequence of statements N
  [ ELSE sequence of statements N+1 ]
END CASE;
```

Iteration Statements

PL/SQL contains three iteration statements along with a statement to terminate a loop. The FOR LOOP statement iterates over a range of integer values, as shown in Example 11.8. The WHILE LOOP statement iterates until a stopping condition is false, as shown in Example 11.9. The LOOP statement iterates until an EXIT statement ceases termination, as shown in Example 11.10. Note that the EXIT statement can also be used in the FOR LOOP and the WHILE LOOP statements to cause early termination of a loop.

Example 11.8: FOR LOOP Statement Example
It is assumed that variables used in the example have been previously declared.

```
FOR Idx IN 1 .. NumStudents LOOP
    TotalUnits := TotalUnits + (Idx * aCrsUnits);
END LOOP;
```

Example 11.9: WHILE LOOP statement corresponding to Example 11.8

```
Idx := 1;
WHILE Idx <= NumStudents LOOP
    TotalUnits := TotalUnits + (Idx * aCrsUnits);
    Idx := Idx + 1;
END LOOP;
```

Example 11.10: LOOP statement corresponding to Example 11.8

```
Idx := 1;
LOOP
    TotalUnits := TotalUnits + (Idx * aCrsUnits);
    Idx := Idx + 1;
    EXIT WHEN Idx > NumStudents;
END LOOP;
```

```
FOR LOOP Statement:
FOR variable IN BeginExpr .. EndExpr LOOP
  sequence of statements
END LOOP;
```

```
WHILE LOOP Statement:
WHILE condition LOOP
  sequence of statements
END LOOP;
```

```
LOOP Statement:
LOOP
  sequence of statements containing an EXIT statement
END LOOP;
```

11.1.4 Executing PL/SQL Statements in Anonymous Blocks

PL/SQL is a block structured language. You will learn about named blocks in Section 11.2. This section introduces anonymous blocks so that you can execute statement examples in SQL *Plus, the most widely used tool for the execution of PL/SQL statements. Anonymous blocks also are useful for testing procedures and triggers. Before presenting anonymous blocks, a brief introduction to SQL *Plus is provided.

To use SQL *Plus, you need an Oracle login name and password. Authentication to SQL *Plus is different than authentication to your operating system. After connecting to SQL *Plus, you will see the SQL> prompt. At the prompt, you can enter SQL statements, PL/SQL blocks, and SQL *Plus commands. Table 11-3 lists common SQL *Plus commands. To terminate an individual statement or SQL *Plus command, you use a semicolon at the end of the statement or command. To terminate a collection of statements or commands, you should use a slash (/) on a line by itself.

Table 11-3: List of Common SQL *Plus Commands

Command	Example and Meaning
CONNECT	CONNECT UserName@DatabaseId/Password opens a connection to DatabaseId for UserName with Password.
DESCRIBE	DESCRIBE TableName lists the columns of TableName.
EXECUTE	EXECUTE Statement executes the PL/SQL statement.
HELP	HELP ColumnName describes ColumnName.
SET	SET SERVEROUTPUT ON causes the results of PL/SQL statements to be displayed.
SHOW	SHOW ERRORS causes compilation errors to be displayed.
SPOOL	SPOOL FileName causes the output to be written to FileName. SPOOL OFF stops spooling to a file.
/	Use on a line by itself to terminate a collection of statements or SQL *Plus commands

A PL/SQL block contains an optional declaration section (DECLARE keyword), an executable section (BEGIN keyword), and an optional exception section (EXCEPTION keyword). This section depicts anonymous blocks containing declaration and executable sections. Section 11.2 depicts the exception section.

```
Block Structure:
[ DECLARE
  sequence of declarations ]
BEGIN
  sequence of statements
[ EXCEPTION
  sequence of statements to respond to exceptions ]
END;
```

To demonstrate anonymous blocks, Example 11.11 computes the sum and product of integers 1 to 10. The Dbms_Output.Put_Line procedure displays the results. The Dbms_Output package contains procedures and functions to read and write lines in a buffer. Example 11.12 modifies Example 11.11 to compute the sum of the odd numbers and the product of the even numbers.

Example 11.11: Anonymous Block to Compute the Sum and the Product
The first line (SET command) and the last line (/) are not part of
the anonymous block.

```
    DECLARE
      aFixedLengthString       CHAR(6) DEFAULT 'ABCDEF';
      aVariableLengthString    VARCHAR2(30);
      anIntegerVariable        INTEGER := 0;
      aFixedPrecisionVariable  DECIMAL(10,2);
      -- Uses the SysDate function for the default value
      aDateVariable            DATE DEFAULT SysDate;
```

Example 11.12: Anonymous Block to Compute the Sum of the Even Numbers and the Product of the Even Numbers
The SET command is not necessary if it was used for Example 11.11 in the same session of SQL
*Plus.

```
    SET SERVEROUTPUT ON;
    DECLARE
      TmpSum      INTEGER;
      TmpProd     INTEGER;
      Idx         INTEGER;
    BEGIN
      -- Initialize temporary variables
      TmpSum := 0;
      TmpProd := 1;
      -- Use a loop to compute the sum of the even numbers and
      -- the product of the odd numbers.
      -- Mod(X,Y) returns the integer remainder of X/Y.
      FOR Idx IN 1 .. 10 LOOP
         IF Mod(Idx,2) = 0 THEN -- even number
            TmpSum := TmpSum + Idx;
         ELSE
            TmpProd := TmpProd * Idx;
         END IF;
      END LOOP;
      -- Display the results
      Dbms_Output.Put_Line('Sum is ' || To_Char(TmpSum));
      Dbms_Output.Put_Line('Product is ' || To_Char(TmpProd));
    END;
    /
```

11.2 Stored Procedures

With background about database programming languages and PL/SQL, you are now ready to learn
about stored procedures. Programming languages have supported procedures since the early days
of business computing. Procedures support the management of complexity by allowing computing
tasks to be divided into manageable chunks. A database procedure is like a programming language
procedure except that it is managed by the DBMS, not the programming environment. The
following list explains the reasons for a DBMS to manage procedures:

- A DBMS can compile the programming language code along with the SQL statements in
  a stored procedure. In addition, a DBMS can detect when the SQL statements in a
  procedure need to be recompiled due to changes in database definitions.
- Stored procedures allow flexibility for client-server development. The stored procedures
  are saved on a server and not replicated on each client. In the early days of client-server
  computing, the ability to store procedures on a server was a major motivation for stored
  procedures. With the development of distributed objects on the Web, this motivation is
  not as important now because there are other technologies for managing stored
  procedures on remote servers.

- Stored procedures allow for the development of more complex operators and functions than supported by SQL. Chapter 18 describes the importance of specialized procedures and functions in object-oriented databases.
- Database administrators can manage stored procedures with the same tools for managing other parts of a database application. Most importantly, stored procedures are managed by the security system of the DBMS.

This section covers PL/SQL procedures, functions, and packages. Some additional parts of PL/SQL (cursors and exceptions) are shown to demonstrate the utility of stored procedures. Testing scripts assume that the university tables are populated according to the data on the textbook's website.

11.2.1 PL/SQL Procedures

In PL/SQL, a procedure is a named block with an optional set of parameters. Each parameter contains a parameter name, a usage (IN, OUT, IN OUT), and a data type. An input parameter (IN) should not be changed inside a procedure. An output parameter (OUT) is given a value inside a procedure. An input-output parameter (IN OUT) should have a value provided outside a procedure but can be changed inside a procedure. The data type specification should not include any constraints such as length. For example, for a string parameter you should use the data type VARCHAR2. You do not provide a length in the specification of the data type for a parameter.

```
Procedure Structure:
CREATE [OR REPLACE] PROCEDURE ProcedureName
   [ ( Parameter1, …, ParameterN ) ]
IS
   [ sequence of declarations ]
BEGIN
   sequence of statements
[ EXCEPTION
   sequence of statements to respond to exceptions ]
END;
```

As a simple example, the procedure pr_InsertRegistration in Example 11.13 inserts a row into the Registration table of the university database. The input parameters provide the values to insert. The Dbms_Output.Put_Line procedure call displays a message that the insert was successful. In the testing code that follows the CREATE PROCEDURE statement, the ROLLBACK statement eliminates the effect of any SQL statements. ROLLBACK statements are useful in testing code when database changes should not be permanent.

Example 11.13: Procedure to Insert a Row into the Registration Table along with Code to Test the Procedure

```
CREATE OR REPLACE PROCEDURE pr_InsertRegistration
(aRegNo IN Registration.RegNo%TYPE,
 aStdNo IN Registration.StdNo%TYPE,
 aRegStatus IN Registration.RegStatus%TYPE,
 aRegDate IN Registration.RegDate%TYPE,
 aRegTerm IN Registration.RegTerm%TYPE,
 aRegYear IN Registration.RegYear%TYPE) IS
-- Create a new registration
BEGIN
INSERT INTO Registration
   (RegNo, StdNo, RegStatus, RegDate, RegTerm, RegYear)
VALUES
   (aRegNo, aStdNo, aRegStatus, aRegDate, aRegTerm,
    aRegYear);

dbms_output.put_line('Row added to Registration table');
END;
/

-- Testing code
SET SERVEROUTPUT ON;
-- Number of rows before the procedure execution
SELECT COUNT(*) FROM Registration;

BEGIN
pr_InsertRegistration
   (1275,'901-23-4567','F',To_Date('27-Feb-2008'),'Spring',
    2008);
END;
/
-- Number of rows after the procedure execution
SELECT COUNT(*) FROM Registration;
-- Delete the inserted row using the ROLLBACK statement
ROLLBACK;
```

To enable reuse of pr_InsertRegistration by other procedures, you should replace the output display with an output parameter indicating the success or failure of the insertion. Example 11.14 modifies Example 11.13 to use an output parameter. The OTHERS exception catches a variety of errors such as a violation of a primary key constraint or a foreign key constraint. You should use the OTHERS exception when you do not need specialized code for each kind of exception. To catch a specific error, you should use a predefined exception (Table 11-4) or create a user-defined exception. A later section contains an example of a user-defined exception. After the procedure, the script includes test cases for a successful insert as well as a primary key constraint violation.

Example 11.14: Procedure to Insert a Row into the Registration Table Along with Code to Test the Procedure

```
CREATE OR REPLACE PROCEDURE pr_InsertRegistration
(aRegNo IN Registration.RegNo%TYPE,
 aStdNo IN Registration.StdNo%TYPE,
 aRegStatus IN Registration.RegStatus%TYPE,
 aRegDate IN Registration.RegDate%TYPE,
 aRegTerm IN Registration.RegTerm%TYPE,
 aRegYear IN Registration.RegYear%TYPE) IS
-- Create a new registration
BEGIN
INSERT INTO Registration
   (RegNo, StdNo, RegStatus, RegDate, RegTerm, RegYear)
VALUES
   (aRegNo, aStdNo, aRegStatus, aRegDate, aRegTerm,
```

```
      aRegYear);

   dbms_output.put_line('Row added to Registration table');
   END;
   /


   -- Testing code
   SET SERVEROUTPUT ON;
   -- Number of rows before the procedure execution
   SELECT COUNT(*) FROM Registration;

   BEGIN
   pr_InsertRegistration
     (1275,'901-23-4567','F',To_Date('27-Feb-2008'),'Spring',
      2008);
   END;
   /
   -- Number of rows after the procedure execution
   SELECT COUNT(*) FROM Registration;
   -- Delete the inserted row using the ROLLBACK statement
   ROLLBACK;
```

Table 11-4: List of Common Predefined PL/SQL Exceptions

Exception When	Raised
Cursor_Already_Open	Attempt to open a cursor that has been previously opened
Dup_Val_On_Index	Attempt to store a duplicate value in a unique index
Invalid_Cursor	Attempt to perform an invalid operation on a cursor such as closing a cursor that was not previously opened
No_Data_Found	SELECT INTO statement returns no rows
Rowtype_Mismatch	Attempt to assign values with incompatible data types between a cursor and a variable
Timeout_On_Resource	Timeout34 occurs such as when waiting for an exclusive lock
Too_Many_Rows	SELECT INTO statement returns more than one row

11.2.2 PL/SQL Functions

Functions should return values instead of manipulating output variables and having side effects such as inserting rows into a table. You should always use a procedure if you want to have more than one result and/or have a side effect. Functions should be usable in expressions, meaning that a function call can be replaced by the value it returns. A PL/SQL function is similar to a procedure in that both contain a parameter list. However, a function should use only input parameters. After the parameter list, the return data type is defined without any constraints such as length. In the function body, the sequence of statements should include a RETURN statement to generate the function's output value.

---

[34] Chapter 15 explains the usage of timeouts with transaction locking to prevent deadlocks.

Procedures versus Functions: use a procedure if the code should have more than one result or a side effect. Functions should be usable in expressions, meaning that a function call can be replaced by the value it returns. To enable functions to be used in expressions, functions should only use input parameters.

As a simple example, the function fn_RetrieveStdName in Example 11.15 retrieves the name of a student given the student number. The predefined exception No_Data_Found is true if the SELECT statement does not return at least one row. The SELECT statement uses the INTO clause to associate the variables with the database columns. The INTO clause can be used only when the SELECT statement returns at most one row. If an INTO clause is used when a SELECT statement returns more than one row, an exception is generated. The Raise_Application_Error procedure displays an error message and an error number. This predefined procedure is useful to handle unexpected errors.

Example 11.15: Function to Retrieve the Student Name Given the Student Number
```
CREATE OR REPLACE FUNCTION fn_RetrieveStdName
(aStdNo IN Student.StdNo%type) RETURN VARCHAR2 IS
-- Retrieves the student name (concatenate first and last
-- name) given a student number. If the student does
-- not exist, return null.
aFirstName Student.StdFirstName%TYPE;
aLastName Student.StdLastName%TYPE;

BEGIN

SELECT StdFirstName, StdLastName
 INTO aFirstName, aLastName
 FROM Student
 WHERE StdNo = aStdNo;

RETURN(aLastName || ', ' || aFirstName);

EXCEPTION
-- No_Data_Found is raised if the SELECT statement
returns no data.
 WHEN No_Data_Found THEN
   RETURN(NULL);

 WHEN OTHERS THEN
   raise_application_error(-20001, 'Database error');

END;
/
-- Testing code
SET SERVEROUTPUT ON;
DECLARE
aStdName VARCHAR2(50);
```

```
BEGIN
-- This call should display a student name.
aStdName := fn_RetrieveStdName('901-23-4567');
IF aStdName IS NULL THEN
    dbms_output.put_line('Student not found');
ELSE
    dbms_output.put_line('Name is ' || aStdName);
END IF;

-- This call should not display a student name.
aStdName := fn_RetrieveStdName('905-23-4567');
IF aStdName IS NULL THEN
    dbms_output.put_line('Student not found');
ELSE
    dbms_output.put_line('Name is ' || aStdName);
END IF;
END;
/
```

Example 11.16 shows a function with a more complex query than the function in Example 11.15. The testing code contains two cases to test for an existing student and a nonexisting student along with a SELECT statement that uses the function in the result. An important benefit of functions is that they can be used in expressions in SELECT statements.

Example 11.16: Function to Compute the Weighted GPA Given the Student Number and Year

```
CREATE OR REPLACE FUNCTION fn_RetrieveStdName
(aStdNo IN Student.StdNo%type) RETURN VARCHAR2 IS
-- Retrieves the student name (concatenate first and last
-- name) given a student number. If the student does
-- not exist, return null.
aFirstName Student.StdFirstName%TYPE;
aLastName Student.StdLastName%TYPE;

BEGIN

SELECT StdFirstName, StdLastName
 INTO aFirstName, aLastName
 FROM Student
 WHERE StdNo = aStdNo;

RETURN(aLastName || ', ' || aFirstName);

EXCEPTION
-- No_Data_Found is raised if the SELECT statement
returns no data.
 WHEN No_Data_Found THEN
  RETURN(NULL);

 WHEN OTHERS THEN
   raise_application_error(-20001, 'Database error');

END;
/
-- Testing code
SET SERVEROUTPUT ON;
DECLARE
aStdName VARCHAR2(50);
```

383

```
BEGIN
-- This call should display a student name.
aStdName := fn_RetrieveStdName('901-23-4567');
IF aStdName IS NULL THEN
    dbms_output.put_line('Student not found');
ELSE
    dbms_output.put_line('Name is ' || aStdName);
END IF;

-- This call should not display a student name.
aStdName := fn_RetrieveStdName('905-23-4567');
IF aStdName IS NULL THEN
    dbms_output.put_line('Student not found');
ELSE
    dbms_output.put_line('Name is ' || aStdName);
END IF;
END;
/
```

11.2.3 Using Cursors

The previous procedures and functions are rather simple as they involve retrieval of a single row. More complex procedures and functions involve iteration through multiple rows using a cursor. PL/SQL provides cursor declaration (explicit or implicit), a specialized FOR statement for cursor iteration, cursor attributes to indicate the status of cursor operations, and statements to perform actions on explicit cursors. PL/SQL supports static cursors in which the SQL statement is known at compile-time as well as dynamic cursors in which the SQL statement is not determined until run-time.

Example 11.17 depicts an implicit cursor to return the class rank of a student in an offering. Implicit cursors are not declared in the DECLARE section. Instead, implicit cursors are declared, opened, and iterated inside a FOR statement. In Example 11.17, the FOR statement iterates through each row of the SELECT statement using the implicit cursor EnrollRec. The SELECT statement sorts the result in descending order by enrollment grade. The function exits the FOR statement when the StdNo value matches the parameter value. The class rank is incremented only when the grade changes so that two students with the same grade have the same rank.

> **Implicit PL/SQL Cursor:** a cursor that is neither explicitly declared nor explicitly opened. Instead a special version of the FOR statement declares, opens, iterates, and closes a locally named SELECT statement. An implicit cursor cannot be referenced outside of the FOR statement in which it is declared.

Example 11.17: Using an Implicit Cursor to Determine the Class Rank of a Given Student and Offering
```
CREATE OR REPLACE FUNCTION fn_DetermineRank
(aStdNo IN Student.StdNo%TYPE, anOfferNo IN
Offering.OfferNo%TYPE)
    RETURN INTEGER IS
-- Determines the class rank given a StdNo and OfferNo.
-- Uses an implicit cursor.
-- If the student or offering do not exist, return 0.
TmpRank INTEGER :=0;
PrevEnrGrade Enrollment.EnrGrade%TYPE := 9.9;
FOUND BOOLEAN := FALSE;

BEGIN
-- Loop through implicit cursor
```

```
FOR EnrollRec IN
  ( SELECT Student.StdNo, EnrGrade
     FROM Student, Registration, Enrollment
     WHERE Enrollment.OfferNo = anOfferNo
       AND Student.StdNo = Registration.StdNo
       AND Registration.RegNo = Enrollment.RegNo
     ORDER BY EnrGrade DESC ) LOOP

    IF EnrollRec.EnrGrade < PrevEnrGrade THEN
    -- Increment the class rank when the grade changes
        TmpRank := TmpRank + 1;
        PrevEnrGrade := EnrollRec.EnrGrade;
    END IF;
    IF EnrollRec.StdNo = aStdNo THEN
        Found := TRUE;
        EXIT;
    END IF;
END LOOP;

IF Found THEN
  RETURN(TmpRank);
ELSE
  RETURN(0);
END IF;

EXCEPTION
WHEN OTHERS THEN
    raise_application_error(-20001, 'Database error');

END;
/
-- Testing code
SET SERVEROUTPUT ON;
-- Execute query to see test data
SELECT Student.StdNo, EnrGrade
 FROM Student, Registration, Enrollment
 WHERE Enrollment.OfferNo = 5679
   AND Student.StdNo = Registration.StdNo
   AND Registration.RegNo = Enrollment.RegNo
 ORDER BY EnrGrade DESC;

-- Test script
DECLARE
aRank INTEGER;
BEGIN
-- This call should return a rank of 6.
aRank := fn_DetermineRank('789-01-2345', 5679);
IF aRank > 0 THEN
    dbms_output.put_line('Rank is ' || to_char(aRank));
ELSE
    dbms_output.put_line('Student is not enrolled.');
END IF;

-- This call should return a rank of 0.
aRank := fn_DetermineRank('789-01-2005', 5679);
IF aRank > 0 THEN
    dbms_output.put_line('Rank is ' || to_char(aRank));
ELSE
```

```
            dbms_output.put_line('Student is not enrolled.');
      END IF;
      END;
      /
```

Example 11.18 depicts a procedure with an explicit cursor to return the class rank and the grade of a student in an offering. The explicit cursor EnrollCursor in the CURSOR statement contains offer number as a parameter. Explicit cursors must use parameters for nonconstant search values in the associated SELECT statement. The OPEN, FETCH, and CLOSE statements replace the FOR statement of Example 11.17. After the FETCH statement, the condition EnrollCursor%NotFound tests for the empty cursor.

> **Explicit PL/SQL Cursor**: a cursor that is declared with the CURSOR statement in the DECLARE section. Explicit cursors are usually manipulated by the OPEN, CLOSE, and FETCH statements. Explicit cursors can be referenced anyplace inside the BEGIN section.

Example 11.18: Using an Explicit Cursor to Determine the Class Rank and Grade of a Given Student and Offering

```
      CREATE OR REPLACE PROCEDURE pr_DetermineRank
      (aStdNo IN Student.StdNo%TYPE, anOfferNo IN
       Offering.OfferNo%TYPE,
       OutRank OUT INTEGER, OutGrade OUT
      Enrollment.EnrGrade%TYPE ) IS
      -- Determines the class rank and grade for a given
      -- student number and OfferNo using an explicit cursor.
      -- If the student or offering do not exist, return 0.
      TmpRank INTEGER :=0;
      PrevEnrGrade Enrollment.EnrGrade%TYPE := 9.9;
      Found BOOLEAN := FALSE;
      TmpGrade Enrollment.EnrGrade%TYPE;
      TmpStdNo Student.StdNo%TYPE;
      -- Explicit cursor
      CURSOR EnrollCursor (tmpOfferNo Offering.OfferNo%TYPE) IS
         SELECT Student.StdNo, EnrGrade
           FROM Student, Registration, Enrollment
           WHERE Enrollment.OfferNo = anOfferNo
             AND Student.StdNo = Registration.StdNo
             AND Registration.RegNo = Enrollment.RegNo
           ORDER BY EnrGrade DESC;

      BEGIN
      -- Open and loop through explicit cursor
      OPEN EnrollCursor(anOfferNo);
      LOOP
         FETCH EnrollCursor INTO TmpStdNo, TmpGrade;
         EXIT WHEN EnrollCursor%NotFound;
         IF TmpGrade < PrevEnrGrade THEN
         -- Increment the class rank when the grade changes
            TmpRank := TmpRank + 1;
            PrevEnrGrade := TmpGrade;
         END IF;
         IF TmpStdNo = aStdNo THEN
            Found := TRUE;
            EXIT;
         END IF;
      END LOOP;

      CLOSE EnrollCursor;
      IF Found THEN
```

386

```
      OutRank := TmpRank;
      OutGrade := PrevEnrGrade;
    ELSE
      OutRank := 0;
      OutGrade := 0;
    END IF;

    EXCEPTION
    WHEN OTHERS THEN
      raise_application_error(-20001, 'Database error');
    END;
    /
    -- Testing code
    SET SERVEROUTPUT ON;
    -- Execute query to see test data
    SELECT Student.StdNo, EnrGrade
     FROM Student, Registration, Enrollment
     WHERE Student.StdNo = Registration.StdNo
       AND Registration.RegNo = Enrollment.RegNo
       AND Enrollment.OfferNo = 5679
     ORDER BY EnrGrade DESC;

    -- Test script
    DECLARE
    aRank INTEGER;
    aGrade Enrollment.EnrGrade%TYPE;
    BEGIN
    -- This call should produce a rank of 6.
    pr_DetermineRank('789-01-2345', 5679, aRank, aGrade);
    IF aRank > 0 THEN
     dbms_output.put_line('Rank is ' || to_char(aRank) ||
       '.');
     dbms_output.put_line('Grade is ' || to_char(aGrade) ||
       '.');
    ELSE
     dbms_output.put_line('Student is not enrolled.');
    END IF;

    -- This call should produce a rank of 0.
    pr_DetermineRank('789-01-2005', 5679, aRank, aGrade);
    IF aRank > 0 THEN
     dbms_output.put_line('Rank is ' || to_char(aRank) ||
       '.');
     dbms_output.put_line('Grade is ' || to_char(aGrade) ||
       '.');
    ELSE
     dbms_output.put_line('Student is not enrolled.');
    END IF;
    END;
    /
```

PL/SQL supports a number of cursor attributes as listed in Table 11-5. When used with an explicit cursor, the cursor name precedes the cursor attribute. When used with an implicit cursor, the SQL keyword precedes the cursor attribute. For example, SQL%RowCount denotes the number of rows in an implicit cursor. The implicit cursor name is not used.

Table 11-5: List of Common Cursor Attributes

Cursor Attribute	Value
%IsOpen	True if cursor is open
%Found	True if cursor is not empty following a FETCH statement
%NotFound	True if cursor is empty following a FETCH statement
%RowCount	Number of rows fetched. After each FETCH, the RowCount is incremented

11.2.4 PL/SQL Packages

Packages support a larger unit of modularity than procedures or functions. A package may contain procedures, functions, exceptions, variables, constants, types, and cursors. By grouping related objects together, a package provides easier reuse than individual procedures and functions. Oracle provides many predefined packages such as the DBMS_Output package containing groups of related objects. In addition, a package separates a public interface from a private implementation to support reduced software maintenance efforts. Changes to a private implementation do not affect the usage of a package through its interface. Chapter 18 on object databases provides more details about the benefits of larger units of modularity.

A package interface contains the definitions of procedures and functions along with other objects that can be specified in the DECLARE section of a PL/SQL block. All objects in a package interface are public. Example 11.19 demonstrates the interface for a package combining some of the procedures and functions presented in previous sections.

```
Package Interface Structure:
CREATE [OR REPLACE] PACKAGE PackageName IS
[ Constant, variable, and type declarations ]
[ Cursor declarations ]
[ Exception declarations ]
[ Procedure definitions ]
[ Function definitions ]
END PackageName;
```

Example 11.19: Package Interface Containing Related Procedures and Functions for the University Database

```
CREATE OR REPLACE PACKAGE pck_University IS
PROCEDURE pr_DetermineRank
 (aStdNo IN Student.StdNo%TYPE, anOfferNo IN
  Offering.OfferNo%TYPE,
  OutRank OUT INTEGER, OutGrade OUT
Enrollment.EnrGrade%TYPE );
FUNCTION fn_ComputeWeightedGPA
 (aStdNo IN Student.StdNo%TYPE, aYear IN
Offering.OffYear%TYPE)
   RETURN NUMBER;
END pck_University;
/
```

A package implementation or body contains the private details of a package. For each object in the package interface, the package body must define an implementation. In addition, private objects can be defined in a package body. Private objects can be used only inside the package body. External users of a package cannot access private objects. Example 11.20 demonstrates the body for the package interface in Example 11.19. Note that each procedure or function terminates with an END statement containing the procedure or function name. Otherwise the procedure and function implementations are identical to creating a procedure or function outside of a package.

```
Package Body Structure:
CREATE [OR REPLACE] PACKAGE BODY PackageName IS
[ Variable and type declarations ]
[ Cursor declarations ]
[ Exception declarations ]
[ Procedure implementations ]
[ Function implementations ]
[ BEGIN sequence of statements ]
[ EXCEPTION exception handling statements ]
END PackageName;
```

Example 11.20: Package Body Containing Implementations of Procedures and Functions

```
CREATE OR REPLACE PACKAGE BODY pck_University IS
PROCEDURE pr_DetermineRank
 (aStdNo IN Student.StdNo%TYPE, anOfferNo IN
  Offering.OfferNo%TYPE,
  OutRank OUT INTEGER, OutGrade OUT
Enrollment.EnrGrade%TYPE ) IS
-- Determines the class rank and grade for a given
-- student number and OfferNo using an explicit cursor.
-- If the student or offering do not exist, return 0.
TmpRank INTEGER :=0;
PrevEnrGrade Enrollment.EnrGrade%TYPE := 9.9;
Found BOOLEAN := FALSE;
TmpGrade Enrollment.EnrGrade%TYPE;
TmpStdNo Student.StdNo%TYPE;
-- Explicit cursor
CURSOR EnrollCursor (tmpOfferNo Offering.OfferNo%TYPE) IS
   SELECT Student.StdNo, EnrGrade
    FROM Student, Registration, Enrollment
    WHERE Enrollment.OfferNo = anOfferNo
      AND Student.StdNo = Registration.StdNo
      AND Registration.RegNo = Enrollment.RegNo
    ORDER BY EnrGrade DESC;

BEGIN
-- Open and loop through explicit cursor
OPEN EnrollCursor(anOfferNo);
LOOP
    FETCH EnrollCursor INTO TmpStdNo, TmpGrade;
    EXIT WHEN EnrollCursor%NotFound;
    IF TmpGrade < PrevEnrGrade THEN
    -- Increment the class rank when the grade changes
       TmpRank := TmpRank + 1;
       PrevEnrGrade := TmpGrade;
    END IF;
    IF TmpStdNo = aStdNo THEN
       Found := TRUE;
       EXIT;
    END IF;
END LOOP;

CLOSE EnrollCursor;
IF Found THEN
  OutRank := TmpRank;
  OutGrade := PrevEnrGrade;
ELSE
  OutRank := 0;
  OutGrade := 0;
END IF;
```

```
EXCEPTION
WHEN OTHERS THEN
  raise_application_error(-20001, 'Database error');
END pr_DetermineRank;

FUNCTION fn_ComputeWeightedGPA
(aStdNo IN Student.StdNo%TYPE, aYear IN
 Offering.OffYear%TYPE)
    RETURN NUMBER IS
-- Computes the weighted GPA given a student number and
-- year. Weighted GPA is the sum of units times the grade
-- divided by the total units.
-- If the student does not exist, return null.
WeightedGPA NUMBER;

BEGIN

SELECT SUM(EnrGrade*CrsUnits)/SUM(CrsUnits)
 INTO WeightedGPA
 FROM Student, Registration, Enrollment, Offering, Course
 WHERE Student.StdNo = aStdNo
   AND Offering.OffYear = aYear
   AND Student.StdNo = Registration.StdNo
   AND Registration.RegNo = Enrollment.RegNo
   AND Enrollment.OfferNo = Offering.OfferNo
   AND Offering.CourseNo = Course.CourseNo;

RETURN(WeightedGPA);

EXCEPTION
 WHEN no_data_found THEN
  RETURN(NULL);

 WHEN OTHERS THEN
  raise_application_error(-20001, 'Database error');

END fn_ComputeWeightedGPA;
END pck_University;
/
```

To use the objects in a package, you need to use the package name before the object name. In Example 11.21, you should note that the package name (pck_University) precedes the procedure and function names.

Example 11.21: Script to Use the Procedures and Functions of the University Package

```
SET SERVEROUTPUT ON;
DECLARE
aRank INTEGER;
aGrade Enrollment.EnrGrade%TYPE;
aGPA NUMBER;
BEGIN
-- This call should produce a rank of 6.
pck_University.pr_DetermineRank('789-01-2345', 5679,
 aRank, aGrade);
IF aRank > 0 THEN
 dbms_output.put_line('Rank is ' || to_char(aRank) ||
  '.');
 dbms_output.put_line('Grade is ' || to_char(aGrade) ||
  '.');
ELSE
```

```
  dbms_output.put_line('Student is not enrolled.');
END IF;
-- This call should display a weighted GPA.
aGPA := pck_University.fn_ComputeWeightedGPA
  ('901-23-4567', 2008);
IF aGPA IS NULL THEN
 dbms_output.put_line('Row not found');
ELSE
 dbms_output.put_line('Weighted GPA is ' ||
  to_char(aGPA));
END IF;
END;
/
```

11.3 Triggers

Triggers are rules managed by a DBMS. Because a trigger involves an event, a condition, and a sequence of actions, it also is known as an event-condition-action rule. Writing the action part or trigger body is similar to writing a procedure or a function except that a trigger has no parameters. Triggers are executed by the rule system of the DBMS not by explicit calls as for procedures and functions. Triggers officially became part of SQL:1999 although most DBMS vendors implemented triggers long before the release of SQL:1999.

> **Trigger**: a rule that is stored and executed by a DBMS. Because a trigger involves an event, a condition, and a sequence of actions, it also is known as an event-condition-action rule.

This section covers Oracle triggers with background about SQL:2006 triggers. The first part of this section discusses the reasons that triggers are important parts of database application development and provides a classification of triggers. The second part demonstrates trigger coding in PL/SQL. The final part presents the trigger execution procedures of Oracle and SQL:2006.

11.3.1 Motivation and Classification of Triggers

Triggers are widely implemented in DBMSs because they have a variety of uses in business applications. The following list explains typical uses of triggers.

- Complex integrity constraints: Integrity constraints that cannot be specified by constraints in CREATE TABLE statements. A typical restriction on constraints in CREATE TABLE statements is that columns from other tables cannot be referenced. Triggers allow reference to columns from multiple tables to overcome this limitation. An alternative to a trigger for a complex constraint is an assertion discussed in Chapter 14. However, most DBMSs do not support assertions so triggers are the only choice for complex integrity constraints.
- Transition constraints: Integrity constraints that compare the values before and after an update occurs. For example, you can write a trigger to enforce the transition constraint that salary increases do not exceed 10 percent.
- Update propagation: Update derived columns in related tables such as to maintain perpetual inventory balance or the seats remaining on a scheduled flight.
- Exception reporting: Create a record of unusual conditions as an alternative to rejecting a transaction. A trigger can also send a notification in an e-mail message. For example, instead of rejecting a salary increase of 10 percent, a trigger can create an exception record and notify a manager to review the salary increase.
- Audit trail: Create a historical record of a transaction such as a history of automated teller usage.
- Generalization hierarchy simulation: Perform update propagation to maintain generalization hierarchy relationships and enforce generalization hierarchy constraints. Although SQL:2006 supports generalization hierarchies for tables, many DBMSs do not support generalization hierarchies. Triggers can be written to support generalization

hierarchies converted into a table design as specified by the Generalization Hierarchy Rule (see Section 6.4.3).

SQL:2006 classifies triggers by granularity, timing, and applicable event. For granularity, a trigger can involve each row affected by an SQL statement or an entire SQL statement. Row triggers are more common than statement triggers. For timing, a trigger can fire before or after an event. Typically, triggers for constraint checking fire before an event, while triggers updating related tables and performing other actions fire after an event. For applicable event, a trigger can apply to INSERT, UPDATE, and DELETE statements. Update triggers should specify a list of applicable columns.

Because the SQL:1999 trigger specification was defined in response to vendor implementations, most trigger implementations varied from the original specification in SQL:1999 and the revised specification in SQL:2006. Oracle supports most parts of the specification while adding proprietary extensions. An important extension is the INSTEAD OF trigger that fires in place of an event, not before or after an event. Oracle also supports data definition events and other database events. Microsoft SQL Server provides statement triggers with access to row data in place of row triggers. Thus, most DBMSs support the spirit of the SQL:2006 trigger specification in trigger granularity, timing, and applicable events but do not adhere strictly to the SQL:2006 trigger syntax.

11.3.2 Oracle Triggers

An Oracle trigger contains a trigger name, a timing specification, an optional referencing clause, an optional granularity, an optional WHEN clause, and a PL/SQL block for the body as explained in the following list:

- The timing specification involves the keywords BEFORE, AFTER, or INSTEAD OF along with a triggering event using the keywords INSERT, UPDATE, or DELETE. With the UPDATE event, you can specify an optional list of columns. To specify multiple events, you can use the OR keyword. Oracle also supports data definition and other database events, but these events are beyond the scope of this chapter.
- The referencing clause allows alias names for the old and new data that can be referenced in a trigger.
- The granularity is specified by the FOR EACH ROW keywords. If you omit these keywords, the trigger is a statement trigger.
- The WHEN clause restricts when a trigger fires or executes. Because Oracle has numerous restrictions on conditions in WHEN clauses, the WHEN clause is used infrequently.
- The body of a trigger looks like other PL/SQL blocks except that triggers have more restrictions on the statements in a block.

```
Oracle Trigger Structure:
CREATE [OR REPLACE] TRIGGER TriggerName
TriggerTiming TriggerEvent
[ Referencing clause ]
[ FOR EACH ROW ]
[ WHEN ( Condition ) ]
[ DECLARE sequence of declarative statements ]
BEGIN sequence of statements
[ EXCEPTION exception handling statements ]
END;
```

Introductory Triggers and Testing Code

To start on some simple Oracle triggers, Examples 11.22 through 11.24 contain triggers that fire respectively on every INSERT, UPDATE, and DELETE statement on the Course table. Example 11.25 demonstrates a trigger with a combined event that fires for every action on the Course table.

The triggers in Examples 11.22 through 11.25 have no purpose except to depict a wide range of trigger syntax as explained in the following list.

- A common naming scheme for triggers identifies the table name, the triggering actions (I for INSERT, U for UPDATE, and D for DELETE), and the timing (B for BEFORE and A for AFTER). For example, the last part of the trigger name (DIUA) in Example 11.25 denotes the DELETE, INSERT, and UPDATE events along with the AFTER timing.
- In Example 11.25, the OR keyword in the trigger event specification supports compound events involving more than one event.
- There is no referencing clause as the default names for the old (:OLD) and the new (:NEW) row are used in the trigger bodies.

Example 11.22: Trigger That Fires for INSERT statements on the Course Table Along with Testing Code to Fire the Trigger

```
CREATE OR REPLACE TRIGGER tr_Course_IA
AFTER INSERT
ON Course
FOR EACH ROW
BEGIN
    -- No references to OLD row because only NEW exists
for INSERT
    dbms_output.put_line('Inserted Row');
    dbms_output.put_line('CourseNo: ' || :NEW.CourseNo);
    dbms_output.put_line('Course Description: ' ||
     :NEW.CrsDesc);
    dbms_output.put_line('Course Units: ' ||
     To_Char(:NEW.CrsUnits));
END;
/
-- Testing statements
SET SERVEROUTPUT ON;
INSERT INTO Course (CourseNo, CrsDesc, CrsUnits)
 VALUES ('IS485','Advanced Database Management',4);

ROLLBACK;
```

Example 11.23: Trigger That Fires for Every UPDATE Statement on the Course Table Along with Testing Code to Fire the Trigger

```
CREATE OR REPLACE TRIGGER tr_Course_UA
AFTER UPDATE
ON Course
FOR EACH ROW
BEGIN
    dbms_output.put_line('New Row Values');
    dbms_output.put_line('CourseNo: ' || :NEW.CourseNo);
    dbms_output.put_line('Course Description: ' ||
     :NEW.CrsDesc);
    dbms_output.put_line('Course Units: ' ||
      To_Char(:NEW.CrsUnits));

    dbms_output.put_line('Old Row Values');
    dbms_output.put_line('CourseNo: ' || :OLD.CourseNo);
    dbms_output.put_line('Course Description: ' ||
     :OLD.CrsDesc);
    dbms_output.put_line('Course Units: ' ||
      To_Char(:OLD.CrsUnits));
END;
/
-- Testing statements
SET SERVEROUTPUT ON;
-- Add row so it can be updated
INSERT INTO Course (CourseNo, CrsDesc, CrsUnits)
 VALUES ('IS485','Advanced Database Management',4);

UPDATE Course
 SET CrsUnits = 3
 WHERE CourseNo = 'IS485';

ROLLBACK;
```

Example 11.24: Trigger That Fires for Every DELETE Statement on the Course Table Along with Testing Code to Fire the Trigger

```
CREATE OR REPLACE TRIGGER tr_Course_DA
AFTER DELETE
ON Course
FOR EACH ROW
BEGIN
    -- No references to NEW row because only OLD exists
for DELETE
    dbms_output.put_line('Deleted Row');
    dbms_output.put_line('CourseNo: ' || :OLD.CourseNo);
    dbms_output.put_line('Course Description: ' ||
     :OLD.CrsDesc);
    dbms_output.put_line('Course Units: ' ||
      To_Char(:OLD.CrsUnits));
END;
/
-- Testing statements
SET SERVEROUTPUT ON;
-- Insert row so that it can be deleted
INSERT INTO Course (CourseNo, CrsDesc, CrsUnits)
 VALUES ('IS485','Advanced Database Management',4);

DELETE FROM Course
 WHERE CourseNo = 'IS485';

ROLLBACK;
```

Example 11.25: Trigger with a Combined Event That Fires for Every action on the Course Table Along with testing Code to Fire the Trigger

```
CREATE OR REPLACE TRIGGER tr_Course_DIUA
AFTER INSERT OR UPDATE OR DELETE
ON Course
FOR EACH ROW
BEGIN
    dbms_output.put_line('Inserted Table');
    dbms_output.put_line('CourseNo: ' || :NEW.CourseNo);
    dbms_output.put_line('Course Description: ' ||
     :NEW.CrsDesc);
    dbms_output.put_line('Course Units: ' ||
     To_Char(:NEW.CrsUnits));

    dbms_output.put_line('Deleted Table');
    dbms_output.put_line('CourseNo: ' || :OLD.CourseNo);
    dbms_output.put_line('Course Description: ' ||
     :OLD.CrsDesc);
    dbms_output.put_line('Course Units: ' ||
     To_Char(:OLD.CrsUnits));
END;
/
-- Testing statements
SET SERVEROUTPUT ON;
INSERT INTO Course (CourseNo, CrsDesc, CrsUnits)
 VALUES ('IS485','Advanced Database Management',4);
UPDATE Course
 SET CrsUnits = 3
 WHERE CourseNo = 'IS485';
DELETE FROM Course
 WHERE CourseNo = 'IS485';

ROLLBACK;
```

Triggers, unlike procedures, cannot be tested directly. Instead, you should use SQL statements that cause the triggers to fire. When the trigger in Example 11.25 fires for an INSERT statement, the old values are null. Likewise, when the trigger fires for a DELETE statement, the new values are null. When the trigger fires for an UPDATE statement, the old and new values are not null unless the table had null values before the update.

BEFORE ROW Trigger for Constraint Checking

BEFORE ROW triggers typically are used for complex integrity constraints because BEFORE ROW triggers should not contain SQL manipulation statements. For example, enrolling in an offering involves a complex integrity constraint to ensure that a seat exists in the related offering. Example 11.26 demonstrates a BEFORE ROW trigger to ensure that a seat remains when a student enrolls in an offering. The trigger ensures that the number of students enrolled in the offering is less than the limit. The testing code inserts students and modifies the number of students enrolled so that the next insertion raises an error. The trigger uses a user-defined exception to handle the error.

Example 11.26: Trigger to Ensure That a Seat Remains in an Offering

```
CREATE OR REPLACE TRIGGER tr_Enrollment_IB
-- This trigger ensures that the number of enrolled
-- students is less than the offering limit.
BEFORE INSERT
ON Enrollment
```

```
            FOR EACH ROW
            DECLARE
                anOffLimit Offering.OffLimit%TYPE;
                anOffNumEnrolled Offering.OffNumEnrolled%TYPE;
                -- user defined exception declaration
                NoSeats EXCEPTION;
                ExMessage VARCHAR(200);
            BEGIN
                SELECT OffLimit, OffNumEnrolled
                    INTO anOffLimit, anOffNumEnrolled
                    FROM Offering
                    WHERE Offering.OfferNo = :NEW.OfferNo;

                IF anOffNumEnrolled >= anOffLimit THEN
                    RAISE NoSeats;
                END IF;
            EXCEPTION
                WHEN NoSeats THEN
                    -- error number between -20000 and -20999
                    ExMessage := 'No seats remaining in offering ' ||
                                 to_char(:NEW.OfferNo) || '.';
                    ExMessage := ExMessage || 'Number enrolled: ' ||
                                 to_char(anOffNumEnrolled) || '. ';
                    ExMessage := ExMessage || 'Offering limit: ' ||
                                 to_char(anOffLimit);
                    Raise_Application_Error(-20001, ExMessage);
            END;
            /
            -- Testing statements
            SET SERVEROUTPUT ON;
            -- See offering limit and number enrolled
            SELECT OffLimit, OffNumEnrolled
             FROM Offering
             WHERE Offering.OfferNo = 5679;
            -- Insert the last student
            INSERT INTO Enrollment (RegNo, OfferNo, EnrGrade)
             VALUES (1234,5679,0);

            -- update the number of enrolled students
            UPDATE Offering
             SET OffNumEnrolled = OffNumEnrolled + 1
             WHERE OfferNo = 5679;

            -- See offering limit and number enrolled
            SELECT OffLimit, OffNumEnrolled
             FROM Offering
             WHERE Offering.OfferNo = 5679;
            -- Insert a student beyond the limit
            INSERT INTO Enrollment (RegNo, OfferNo, EnrGrade)
             VALUES (1236,5679,0);

            ROLLBACK;
```

AFTER ROW Trigger for Update Propagation

The testing code for the BEFORE ROW trigger in Example 11.26 includes an UPDATE statement to increment the number of students enrolled. An AFTER trigger can automate this task as shown in Example 11.27. The triggers in Examples 11.26 and 11.27 work in tandem. The BEFORE ROW trigger ensures that a seat remains in the offering. The AFTER ROW trigger then updates the related Offering row.

Example 11.27: Trigger to Update the Number of Enrolled Students in an Offering

```
CREATE OR REPLACE TRIGGER tr_Enrollment_IA
-- This trigger updates the number of enrolled
-- students in the related Offering row.
AFTER INSERT
ON Enrollment
FOR EACH ROW
BEGIN
   UPDATE Offering
    SET OffNumEnrolled = OffNumEnrolled + 1
    WHERE OfferNo = :NEW.OfferNo;
EXCEPTION
  WHEN OTHERS THEN
    RAISE_Application_Error(-20001, 'Database error');
END;
/
-- Testing statements
SET SERVEROUTPUT ON;
-- See the offering limit and number enrolled
SELECT OffLimit, OffNumEnrolled
 FROM Offering
 WHERE Offering.OfferNo = 5679;
-- Insert the last student
INSERT INTO Enrollment (RegNo, OfferNo, EnrGrade)
VALUES (1234,5679,0);

-- See the offering limit and number enrolled
SELECT OffLimit, OffNumEnrolled
 FROM Offering
 WHERE Offering.OfferNo = 5679;

ROLLBACK;
```

Combining Trigger Events to Reduce the Number of Triggers

The triggers in Examples 11.26 and 11.27 involve insertions to the Enrollment table. Additional triggers are needed for updates to the Enrollment.OfferNo column and deletions of Enrollment rows.

As an alternative to separate triggers for events on the same table, one large BEFORE trigger and one large AFTER trigger can be written. Each trigger contains multiple events as shown in Examples 11.28 and 11.29. The action part of the trigger in Example 11.29 uses the keywords INSERTING, UPDATING, and DELETING to determine the triggering event. The script in Example 11.30 is rather complex because it tests two complex triggers.

Example 11.28: Trigger to Ensure That a Seat Remains in an Offering When Inserting or Updating an Enrollment Row

```
-- Drop the previous trigger to avoid interactions
DROP TRIGGER tr_Enrollment_IB;
CREATE OR REPLACE TRIGGER tr_Enrollment_IUB
-- This trigger ensures that the number of enrolled
-- students is less than the offering limit.
BEFORE INSERT OR UPDATE OF OfferNo
ON Enrollment
FOR EACH ROW
DECLARE
    anOffLimit Offering.OffLimit%TYPE;
    anOffNumEnrolled Offering.OffNumEnrolled%TYPE;
    NoSeats EXCEPTION;
  ExMessage   VARCHAR(200);
```

```
                SELECT OffLimit, OffNumEnrolled
                  INTO anOffLimit, anOffNumEnrolled
                  FROM Offering
                  WHERE Offering.OfferNo = :NEW.OfferNo;

            IF anOffNumEnrolled >= anOffLimit THEN
               RAISE NoSeats;
            END IF;
          EXCEPTION
            WHEN NoSeats THEN
              -- error number between -20000 and -20999
               ExMessage := 'No seats remaining in offering ' ||
                            to_char(:NEW.OfferNo) || '.';
               ExMessage := ExMessage || 'Number enrolled: ' ||
                            to_char(anOffNumEnrolled) || '. ';
               ExMessage := ExMessage || 'Offering limit: ' ||
                            to_char(anOffLimit);
               raise_application_error(-20001, ExMessage);
          END;
```

Example 11.29: Trigger to Update the Number of Enrolled Students in an Offering When Inserting, Updating, or Deleting an Enrollment Row

```
          -- Drop the previous trigger to avoid interactions
          DROP TRIGGER tr_Enrollment_IA;
          CREATE OR REPLACE TRIGGER tr_Enrollment_DIUA
          -- This trigger updates the number of enrolled
          -- students the related offering row.
          AFTER INSERT OR DELETE OR UPDATE of OfferNo
          ON Enrollment
          FOR EACH ROW
          BEGIN
           -- Increment the number of enrolled students for insert
           -- and update
           IF INSERTING OR UPDATING THEN
              UPDATE Offering
                SET OffNumEnrolled = OffNumEnrolled + 1
                WHERE OfferNo = :NEW.OfferNo;
           END IF;
          -- Decrease the number of enrolled students for delete,
          update
          IF UPDATING OR DELETING THEN
              UPDATE Offering
                SET OffNumEnrolled = OffNumEnrolled - 1
                WHERE OfferNo = :OLD.OfferNo;
          END IF;

          EXCEPTION
            WHEN OTHERS THEN
               raise_application_error(-20001, 'Database error');
          END;
```

Example 11.30: Script to Test the Triggers in Examples 11.28 and 11.29

```
          -- Test case 1
          -- See the offering limit and number enrolled
          SELECT OffLimit, OffNumEnrolled
           FROM Offering
           WHERE Offering.OfferNo = 5679;
          -- Insert the last student
          INSERT INTO Enrollment (RegNo, OfferNo, EnrGrade)
           VALUES (1234,5679,0);
          -- See the offering limit and the number enrolled
```

```
SELECT OffLimit, OffNumEnrolled
 FROM Offering
 WHERE Offering.OfferNo = 5679;

-- Test case 2
-- Insert a student beyond the limit: exception raised
INSERT INTO Enrollment (RegNo, OfferNo, EnrGrade)
 VALUES (1236,5679,0);
-- Transfer a student to offer 5679: exception raised
UPDATE Enrollment
 SET OfferNo = 5679
 WHERE RegNo = 1234 AND OfferNo = 1234;

-- Test case 3
-- See the offering limit and the number enrolled before
-- update
SELECT OffLimit, OffNumEnrolled
 FROM Offering
 WHERE Offering.OfferNo = 4444;
-- Update a student to a non full offering
UPDATE Enrollment
 SET OfferNo = 4444
 WHERE RegNo = 1234 AND OfferNo = 1234;
-- See the offering limit and the number enrolled after
-- update
SELECT OffLimit, OffNumEnrolled
 FROM Offering
 WHERE Offering.OfferNo = 4444;

-- Test case 4
-- See the offering limit and the number enrolled before
-- delete
SELECT OffLimit, OffNumEnrolled
 FROM Offering
 WHERE Offering.OfferNo = 1234;
-- Delete an enrollment
DELETE Enrollment
 WHERE OfferNo = 1234;
-- See the offering limit and the number enrolled
SELECT OffLimit, OffNumEnrolled
 FROM Offering
 WHERE Offering.OfferNo = 1234;

-- Erase all changes
ROLLBACK;
```

There is no clear preference for many smaller triggers or fewer larger triggers. Although smaller triggers are easier to understand than larger triggers, the number of triggers is a complicating factor to understand interactions among triggers. The next subsection explains trigger execution procedures to clarify issues of trigger interactions.

Additional BEFORE ROW Trigger Examples

BEFORE triggers can also be used for transition constraints and data standardization. Example 11.31 depicts a trigger for a transition constraint. The trigger contains a WHEN clause to restrict the trigger execution. Example 11.32 depicts a trigger to enforce uppercase usage for the faculty name columns. Although BEFORE triggers should not perform updates with SQL statements, they can change the new values as the trigger in Example 11.32 demonstrates.

Example 11.31: Trigger to Ensure That a Salary Increase Does Not Exceed 10 percent

Note that the NEW and OLD keywords should not be preceded by a colon (:) when used in a WHEN condition.

```
CREATE OR REPLACE TRIGGER tr_FacultySalary_UB
-- This trigger ensures that a salary increase does
-- not exceed 10%.
BEFORE UPDATE OF FacSalary
ON Faculty
FOR EACH ROW
WHEN (NEW.FacSalary > 1.1 * OLD.FacSalary)
DECLARE
SalaryIncreaseTooHigh EXCEPTION;
ExMessage VARCHAR(200);
BEGIN
    RAISE SalaryIncreaseTooHigh;
EXCEPTION
  WHEN SalaryIncreaseTooHigh THEN
    -- error number between -20000 and -20999
      ExMessage := 'Salary increase exceeds 10%. ';
      ExMessage := ExMessage || 'Current salary: ' ||
                  to_char(:OLD.FacSalary) || '. ';
      ExMessage := ExMessage || 'New salary: ' ||
                  to_char(:NEW.FacSalary) || '.';
      Raise_Application_Error(-20001, ExMessage);
END;
/
SET SERVEROUTPUT ON;
-- Test case 1: salary increase of 5%
UPDATE Faculty
 SET FacSalary = FacSalary * 1.05
 WHERE FacNo = '543-21-0987';
SELECT FacSalary FROM Faculty
 WHERE FacNo = '543-21-0987';
-- Test case 2: salary increase of 20% should generate
-- an error.
UPDATE Faculty
 SET FacSalary = FacSalary * 1.20
 WHERE FacNo = '543-21-0987';
ROLLBACK;
```

Example 11.32: Trigger to Change the Case of the Faculty First Name and Last Name

```
CREATE OR REPLACE TRIGGER tr_FacultyName_IUB
-- This trigger changes the case of FacFirstName and
-- FacLastName.
BEFORE INSERT OR UPDATE OF FacFirstName, FacLastName
ON Faculty
FOR EACH ROW
BEGIN
   :NEW.FacFirstName := Upper(:NEW.FacFirstName);
   :NEW.FacLastName := Upper(:NEW.FacLastName);
END;
/
-- Testing statements
UPDATE Faculty
 SET FacFirstName = 'Joe', FacLastName = 'Smith'
 WHERE FacNo = '543-21-0987';
-- Display the changed faculty name.
SELECT FacFirstName, FacLastName
 FROM Faculty
 WHERE FacNo = '543-21-0987';
ROLLBACK;
```

AFTER ROW Trigger for Exception Reporting

The trigger in Example 11.31 implements a hard constraint in that large raises (greater than 10 percent) are rejected. A more flexible approach is a soft constraint in which a large raise causes a row to be written to an exception table. The update succeeds but an administrator can review the exception table at a later point to take additional action. A message can also be sent to alert the administrator to review specific rows in the exception table.

Example 11.33 depicts a trigger to implement a soft constraint for large employee raises. The AFTER trigger timing is used because a row should only be written to the exception table if the update succeeds. As demonstrated in the next section, AFTER ROW triggers only execute if there are no errors encountered in integrity constraint checking.

Example 11.33: CREATE TABLE Statement for the Exception Table and Trigger

Insert a Row into an Exception Table when a Salary Increase Exceeds 10 Percent. Note that LogTable must be created before creating the trigger. The SEQUENCE is an Oracle object that maintains unique values. The expression LogSeq.NextVal generates the next value of the sequence.

```
-- Create exception table and sequence
CREATE TABLE LogTable
(ExcNo              INTEGER       PRIMARY KEY,
 ExcTrigger         VARCHAR2(25)  NOT NULL,
 ExcTable           VARCHAR2(25)  NOT NULL,
 ExcKeyValue        VARCHAR2(15)  NOT NULL,
 ExcDate            DATE DEFAULT SYSDATE NOT NULL,
 ExcTe              VARCHAR2(255) NOT NULL );

CREATE SEQUENCE LogSeq INCREMENT BY 1;

CREATE OR REPLACE TRIGGER tr_FacultySalary_UA
-- This trigger inserts a row into LogTable when
-- when a raise exceeds 10%.
AFTER UPDATE OF FacSalary
ON Faculty
FOR EACH ROW
WHEN (NEW.FacSalary > 1.1 * OLD.FacSalary)
DECLARE
    SalaryIncreaseTooHigh EXCEPTION;
    ExMessage VARCHAR(200);
BEGIN
    RAISE SalaryIncreaseTooHigh;
EXCEPTION
  WHEN SalaryIncreaseTooHigh THEN
    INSERT INTO LogTable
      (ExcNo, ExcTrigger, ExcTable, ExcKeyValue, ExcDate,
ExcText)
        VALUES (LogSeq.NextVal, 'TR_ FacultySalary_UA',
'Faculty', to_char(:New.FacNo), SYSDATE,
        'Salary raise greater than 10%');
END;
```

```
/
SET SERVEROUTPUT ON;
-- Test case 1: salary increase of 5%
UPDATE Faculty
  SET FacSalary = FacSalary * 1.05
  WHERE FacNo = '543-21-0987';
SELECT FacSalary FROM Faculty
  WHERE FacNo = '543-21-0987';
SELECT * FROM LogTable;

-- Test case 2: salary increase of 20% should generate
-- an exception.
UPDATE Faculty
  SET FacSalary = FacSalary * 1.20
  WHERE FacNo = '543-21-0987';
SELECT FacSalary FROM Faculty
  WHERE FacNo = '543-21-0987';
SELECT * FROM LogTable;
ROLLBACK;
```

Triggers to Simulate Operations on a Generalization Hierarchy

The traditional relational model does not directly support generalization hierarchies as presented in Chapters 5 and 6. Even though SQL:2006 has added support for generalization hierarchies among tables (see Chapter 18), most DBMSs including Oracle do not support this part of the SQL:2006 specification. Because generalization hierarchies are a specialized but useful feature, it is important to provide some level of support.

In Oracle, triggers can provide a level of support for generalization hierarchies using the INSTEAD OF event for views. An INSTEAD OF trigger is used in place of a manipulation event (INSERT, UPDATE, or DELETE) on a view. INSTEAD OF triggers can only be used with views, typically to support view updates. INSTEAD OF triggers are also useful for operations on tables related by generalization relationships as an INSTEAD OF trigger can map an operation to more than one base table.

Before presenting the trigger example, some additional tables and views are needed. The Generalization Hierarchy Rule (see Section 6.4.3) is applied to convert the student generalization hierarchy in Figure 11.2 into tables as shown in Example 11.34. The Generalization Hierarchy Rule generates one table per entity type with the primary key replicated in each table. Thus the subtype tables contain the primary key plus the specialized columns specific to the subtype table. Example 11.35 contains two views combining the parent and subtype tables. These views will be used in INSTEAD OF triggers to map manipulation actions on the views to the underlying base tables.

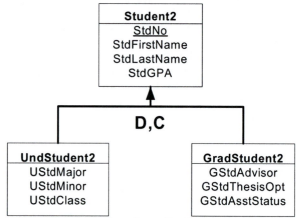

Figure 11.2: ERD for Student Generalization Hierarchy

Example 11.34: CREATE TABLE Statements for the Student Generalization Hierarchy.
The table names use the number 2 to avoid conflicts with other table names.

402

```
-- Student2 is the parent table in the generalization
hierarchy
CREATE TABLE Student2(
 StdNo CHAR(11),
 StdFirstName VARCHAR2(20) not null,
 StdLastName VARCHAR2(30) not null,
 StdGPA DECIMAL(3,2),
 CONSTRAINT Student2PK PRIMARY KEY (StdNo) );
-- UndStudent2 is a child table in the generalization
-- hierarchy.
CREATE TABLE UndStudent2(
 StdNo CHAR(11),
 UStdMajor CHAR(6),
 UStdMinor CHAR(6),
 UStdClass CHAR(2),
 CONSTRAINT UndStudent2PK PRIMARY KEY (StdNo),
 CONSTRAINT UndStudent2FK FOREIGN KEY(StdNo)
  REFERENCES Student2 ON DELETE CASCADE );
-- GradStudent2 is a child table in the generalization
-- hierarchy.
CREATE TABLE GradStudent2(
 StdNo CHAR(11),
 GStdAdvisor VARCHAR2(20),
 GStdThesisOpt CHAR(10) DEFAULT 'NONTHESIS',
 -- NONTHESIS or THESIS
 GStdAsstStatus CHAR(6) DEFAULT 'NONE', -- NONE, TA, RA
 CONSTRAINT GradStudent2PK PRIMARY KEY (StdNo),
 CONSTRAINT GradStudent2FK FOREIGN KEY(StdNo)
   REFERENCES Student2 ON DELETE CASCADE );
```

Example 11.35: CREATE VIEW Statements for Views Used to Manipulate the Student Generalization Hierarchy.

```
-- View for undergraduate students
CREATE VIEW AllUndStudent AS
  SELECT Student2.StdNo, StdFirstName, StdLastName,
        StdGPA, UStdMajor, UStdMinor, UStdClass
    FROM Student2, UndStudent2
    WHERE Student2.StdNo = UndStudent2.Stdno;
-- View for graduate students
CREATE VIEW AllGradStudent AS
  SELECT Student2.StdNo, StdFirstName, StdLastName,
        StdGPA, GStdAdvisor, GStdThesisOpt,
        GStdAsstStatus
    FROM Student2, GradStudent2
    WHERE Student2.StdNo = GradStudent2.Stdno;
```

To insert a row into a child table in a generalization hierarchy, a row should be added to the parent table. Example 11.36 contains INSTEAD OF triggers that insert rows in the child and parent tables. For example, the tr_UndStudent_II trigger inserts a row into the UndStudent2 and Student2 tables. The testing code in Example 11.37 contains INSERT statements for each view. The INSTEAD OF trigger executes in place of the INSERT statements. Note that INSTEAD OF triggers are proprietary to Oracle.

Example 11.36: Triggers to Insert Rows in Child and Parent Tables of the Student Generalization Hierarchy.

```
-- Insert trigger for undergraduate students
CREATE OR REPLACE TRIGGER tr_AllUndStudent_II
INSTEAD OF INSERT ON AllUndStudent
FOR EACH ROW
BEGIN
-- Insert into parent (Student2)
```

```
        INSERT INTO Student2 (StdNo, StdFirstName, StdLastName,
          StdGPA)
         VALUES(:New.StdNo,:New.StdFirstName,:New.StdLastName,
           :New.StdGPA);
        -- Insert into child (UndStudent2)
        INSERT INTO UndStudent2 (StdNo, UStdMajor, UStdMinor,
          UStdClass)
         VALUES(:New.StdNo, :New.UStdMajor, :New.UStdMinor,
               :New.UStdClass);
        EXCEPTION
         WHEN OTHERS THEN
          raise_application_error(-20001,
             'DB error in tr_UndStudent_II');
        END;
        -- Insert trigger for graduate students
        CREATE OR REPLACE TRIGGER tr_AllGradStudent_II
        INSTEAD OF INSERT ON AllGradStudent
        FOR EACH ROW
        BEGIN
        -- Insert into parent (Student2)
        INSERT INTO Student2 (StdNo, StdFirstName,
          StdLastName, StdGPA)
         VALUES(:New.StdNo,:New.StdFirstName,:New.StdLastName,
           :New.StdGPA);
        -- Insert into child (UndStudent2)
        INSERT INTO GradStudent2(StdNo,GStdAdvisor,GStdThesisOpt,
                                 GStdAsstStatus)
         VALUES(:New.StdNo,:New.GStdAdvisor,:New.GStdThesisOpt,
               :New.GStdAsstStatus);
        EXCEPTION
         WHEN OTHERS THEN
          raise_application_error(-20001,
             'DB error in tr_GradStudent_II');
        END;
```

Example 11.37: Testing Code for INSTEAD OF INSERT Triggers

```
        -- Test cases for tr_UndStudent_II
        INSERT INTO AllUndStudent
          (StdNo,StdFirstName,StdLastName,StdGPA,UStdMajor,
          UStdMinor, UStdClass)
         VALUES('123-45-6789', 'HOMER', 'WELLS', 3.00, 'IS',
               'ACCT','FR');
        INSERT INTO AllUndStudent
          (StdNo, stdFirstName, stdLastName, stdGPA, UStdMajor,
          UStdMinor, UStdClass)
         VALUES('234-56-7890', 'CANDY', 'KENDALL', 2.70, 'FIN',
               'IS','JR');
        -- SELECT statements to verify insertions
        SELECT * FROM AllUndStudent;
        SELECT * FROM Student2;
        SELECT * FROM UndStudent2;
        -- Test cases for tr_GradStudent_II
        INSERT INTO AllGradStudent
          (StdNo, StdFirstName, StdLastName, StdGPA, GStdAdvisor,
          GStdThesisOpt, GStdAsstStatus)
         VALUES ('345-67-8901','WALLY','KENDALL', 2.80, 'Jones',
          'NONTHESIS', 'NONE');
        INSERT INTO AllGradStudent
          (StdNo, StdFirstName, StdLastName, StdGPA, GStdAdvisor,
          GStdThesisOpt, GStdAsstStatus)
```

```
                VALUES ('456-78-9012','JOE','ESTRADA', 3.20, 'Jones',
                        'THESIS', 'RA');
                -- SELECT statements to verify insertions
                SELECT * FROM AllGradStudent;
                SELECT * FROM Student2;
                SELECT * FROM GradStudent2;
                ROLLBACK;
```

The student generalization hierarchy has a disjointness constraint so that a student cannot simultaneously be both an undergraduate and graduate student. Example 11.38 contains a modified trigger to check for membership in the other child table of the generalization hierarchy. In the original trigger in Example 11.36, inserting the same row in the other child (GradStudent2) using the AllGradStudent view will fail because a row already exists in the parent table (Student2).

Example 11.38: Modification of Trigger in Example 11.36
Ensure that an Undergraduate Student is not in the GradStudent Table along with Testing Code.

Example 11.37: Testing Code for INSTEAD OF INSERT Triggers
```
                -- Test cases for tr_UndStudent_II
                INSERT INTO AllUndStudent
                  (StdNo,StdFirstName,StdLastName,StdGPA,UStdMajor,
                  UStdMinor, UStdClass)
                  VALUES('123-45-6789', 'HOMER', 'WELLS', 3.00, 'IS',
                        'ACCT','FR');
                INSERT INTO AllUndStudent
                  (StdNo, stdFirstName, stdLastName, stdGPA, UStdMajor,
                  UStdMinor, UStdClass)
                  VALUES('234-56-7890', 'CANDY', 'KENDALL', 2.70, 'FIN',
                        'IS','JR');
                -- SELECT statements to verify insertions
                SELECT * FROM AllUndStudent;
                SELECT * FROM Student2;
                SELECT * FROM UndStudent2
                -- Test cases for tr_GradStudent_II
                INSERT INTO AllGradStudent
                  (StdNo, StdFirstName, StdLastName, StdGPA, GStdAdvisor,
                  GStdThesisOpt, GStdAsstStatus)
                  VALUES ('345-67-8901','WALLY','KENDALL', 2.80, 'Jones',
                  'NONTHESIS', 'NONE');
                INSERT INTO AllGradStudent
                  (StdNo, StdFirstName, StdLastName, StdGPA, GStdAdvisor,
                  GStdThesisOpt, GStdAsstStatus)
                  VALUES ('456-78-9012','JOE','ESTRADA', 3.20, 'Jones',
                        'THESIS', 'RA');
                -- SELECT statements to verify insertions
                SELECT * FROM AllGradStudent;
                SELECT * FROM Student2;
                SELECT * FROM GradStudent2;
                ROLLBACK;
```

Another trigger is needed to manage updates. Updates to a view should be directed to the appropriate base table. Example 11.39 contains an INSTEAD OF UPDATE trigger to direct updates to the appropriate table (Student2 or UndStudent2). A similar trigger is necessary to direct graduate student updates to the Student2 or GradStudent2 table. Note that Oracle does not allow column specification in INSTEAD OF UPDATE triggers. In BEFORE and AFTER triggers, it is good coding practice for UPDATE triggers to specify the column.

Example 11.39: INSTEAD OF UPDATE Trigger
Update either Student2 or UndStudent2 table along with Testing Code.
```
                -- Update trigger for UndStudent
```

```
-- Cannot specify column list for INSTEAD of UPDATE
-- triggers
CREATE OR REPLACE TRIGGER tr_AllUndStudent_UI
INSTEAD OF UPDATE ON AllUndStudent
FOR EACH ROW
BEGIN
-- Update UndStudent2
  IF UPDATING('UStdMajor') THEN
    UPDATE UndStudent2
    SET UStdMajor = :NEW.UStdMajor
    WHERE StdNo = :OLD.StdNo;
  END IF;
  IF UPDATING('UStdMinor') THEN
    UPDATE UndStudent2
    SET UStdMinor = :NEW.UStdMinor
    WHERE StdNo = :OLD.StdNo;
  END IF;
  IF UPDATING('UStdClass') THEN
    UPDATE UndStudent2
    SET UStdClass = :NEW.UStdClass
    WHERE StdNo = :OLD.StdNo;
  END IF;
-- Update Student2
  IF UPDATING('StdGPA') THEN
    UPDATE Student2
    SET StdGPA = :NEW.StdGPA
    WHERE StdNo = :OLD.StdNo;
  END IF;
  IF UPDATING('StdFirstName') THEN
    UPDATE Student2
    SET StdFirstName = :NEW.StdFirstName
    WHERE StdNo = :OLD.StdNo;
  END IF;
  IF UPDATING('StdLastName') THEN
    UPDATE Student2
    SET StdLastName = :NEW.StdLastName
    WHERE StdNo = :OLD.StdNo;
  END IF;
EXCEPTION
  WHEN OTHERS THEN
    raise_application_error(-20001,
     'DB error in tr_UStdMajor_UI');
END;
/
-- Trigger testing statements
-- Insert data: depends on tr_UndStudent_II
INSERT INTO AllUndStudent
 (StdNo, StdFirstName, StdLastName, StdGPA, UStdMajor,
 UStdMinor, UStdClass)
 VALUES ('123-45-6789','HOMER','WELLS',3.00,'IS',
         'ACCT','FR');
INSERT INTO AllUndStudent
 (StdNo, StdFirstName, StdLastName, StdGPA, UStdMajor,
 UStdMinor, UStdClass)
 VALUES ('234-56-7890','CANDY','KENDALL', 2.70,'FIN',
         'IS','JR');
-- Update statements
UPDATE AllUndStudent
 SET UStdMajor = 'MGMT'
 WHERE StdNo = '123-45-6789';
UPDATE AllUndStudent
```

```
    SET StdGPA = 3.1
     WHERE StdNo = '234-56-7890';
    -- View results
    SELECT * FROM AllUndStudent;
    SELECT * FROM Student2;
    SELECT * FROM UndStudent2;
    ROLLBACK;
```

11.3.3 Understanding Trigger Execution

As the previous subsection demonstrated, individual triggers are usually easy to understand. Collectively, however, triggers can be difficult to understand especially in conjunction with integrity constraint enforcement and database actions. To understand the collective behavior of triggers, integrity constraints, and database manipulation actions, you need to understand the execution procedure used by a DBMS. Although SQL:2006 specifies a trigger execution procedure, most DBMSs do not adhere strictly to it. Therefore, this subsection emphasizes the Oracle trigger execution procedure with comments about the differences between the Oracle and the SQL:2006 execution procedures.

> **Trigger Execution Procedure**: specifies the order of execution among the various kinds of triggers, integrity constraints, and database manipulation statements. Trigger execution procedures can be complex because the actions of a trigger may fire other triggers.

Simplified Trigger Execution Procedure

The trigger execution procedure applies to data manipulation statements (INSERT, UPDATE, and DELETE). Before this procedure begins, Oracle determines the applicable triggers for an SQL statement. A trigger is applicable to a statement if the trigger contains an event that matches the statement type. To match an UPDATE statement with a column list, at least one column in the triggering event must be in the list of columns updated by the statement. After determining the applicable triggers, Oracle executes triggers in the order of BEFORE STATEMENT, BEFORE ROW, AFTER ROW, and AFTER STATEMENT. An applicable trigger does not execute if its WHEN condition is not true.

Simplified Oracle Trigger Execution Procedure
1. Execute the applicable BEFORE STATEMENT triggers.
a. For each row affected by the SQL manipulation statement:
b. Execute the applicable BEFORE ROW triggers.
c. Perform the data manipulation operation on the row.
2. Perform integrity constraint checking.
3. Execute the applicable AFTER ROW triggers.
4. Perform deferred integrity constraint checking.
5. Execute the applicable AFTER statement triggers.

The trigger execution procedure of Oracle differs slightly from the SQL:2006 execution procedure for overlapping triggers. Two triggers with the same timing, granularity, and applicable table overlap if an SQL statement may cause both triggers to fire. For example a BEFORE ROW trigger with the UPDATE ON Customer event overlaps with a BEFORE ROW trigger with the UPDATE OF CustBal ON Customer event. Both triggers fire when updating the CustBal column. For overlapping triggers, Oracle specifies that the execution order is arbitrary. For SQL:2006, the execution order depends on the time in which the trigger is defined. Overlapping triggers are executed in the order in which the triggers were created.

> **Overlapping Triggers**: two or more triggers with the same timing, granularity, and applicable table. The triggers overlap if an SQL statement may cause both triggers to fire. You should not depend on a particular firing order for overlapping triggers.

Trigger overlap is subtle for UPDATE triggers. Two UPDATE triggers on the same table can overlap even if the triggers involve different columns. For example, UPDATE triggers on OffLocation and OffTime overlap if an UPDATE statement changes both columns. For UPDATE statements changing only one column, the triggers do not overlap.

As demonstrated in the Simple Trigger Execution Procedure, most constraint checking occurs after executing the applicable BEFORE ROW triggers but before executing the applicable AFTER ROW triggers. Deferred constraint checking is performed at the end of a transaction. Chapter 15 on transaction management presents SQL statements for deferred constraint checking. In most applications, few constraints are declared with deferred checking.

Trigger Execution Procedure with Recursive Execution

Data manipulation statements in a trigger complicate the simplified execution procedure. Data manipulation statements in a trigger may cause other triggers to fire. Consider the AFTER ROW trigger in Example 11.29 that fires when an Enrollment row is added. The trigger updates the OffNumEnrolled column enrolled in the related Offering row. Suppose there is another trigger on the OffNumEnrolled column of the Offering table that fires when the OffNumEnrolled column becomes large (say within two of the limit). This second trigger should fire as a result of the first trigger firing when an offering becomes almost full.

When a data manipulation statement is encountered in a trigger, the trigger execution procedure is recursively executed. Recursive execution means that a procedure calls itself. In the previous example, the trigger execution procedure is recursively executed when a data manipulation statement is encountered in the trigger in Example 11.29. In the Oracle execution procedure, steps 2.1 and 2.4 may involve recursive execution of the procedure. In the SQL:2006 execution procedure, only step 2.4 may involve recursive execution because SQL:2006 prohibits data manipulation statements in BEFORE ROW triggers.

Actions on referenced rows also complicate the simplified execution procedure. When deleting or updating a referenced row, the foreign key constraint can specify actions (CASCADE, SET NULL, and SET DEFAULT) on related rows. For example, a foreign key constraint containing ON DELETE CASCADE for Offering.CourseNo means that deletion of a Course row causes deletion of the related Offering rows. Actions on referenced rows can cause other triggers to fire leading to recursive execution of the trigger execution procedure in step 2.3 for both Oracle and SQL:2006. Actions on referenced rows are performed as part of constraint checking in step 2.3.

With these complications that cause recursive execution, the full trigger execution procedure is presented below. Most DBMSs such as Oracle limit the recursion depth in steps 2.1, 2.3, and 2.4.

Oracle Trigger Execution Procedure with Recursive Execution
1. Execute the applicable BEFORE STATEMENT triggers.
2. For each row affected by the SQL manipulation statement
   a. Execute the applicable BEFORE ROW triggers. Recursively execute the procedure for data manipulation statements in a trigger.
   b. Perform the data manipulation operation on the row.
   c. Perform integrity constraint checking. Recursively execute the procedure for actions on referenced rows.
   d. Execute the applicable AFTER ROW triggers. Recursively execute the procedure for data manipulation statements in a trigger.
3. Perform deferred integrity constraint checking.
4. Execute the applicable AFTER statement triggers.

The full execution procedure shows considerable complexity when executing a trigger. To control complexity among a collection of triggers, you should follow these guidelines:
- Define triggers for general purpose business rules, not rules specific to a given application.
- Avoid data manipulation statements in BEFORE triggers.
- Limit data manipulation statements in AFTER triggers to statements that are likely to succeed.
- For triggers that fire on UPDATE statements, always list the columns in which the trigger applies.
- Ensure that overlapping triggers do not depend on a specific order to fire. In most DBMSs, the firing order is arbitrary. Even if the order is not arbitrary (as in SQL:2006), it is risky to depend on a specific firing order.
- Be cautious about triggers on tables affected by actions on referenced rows. These triggers will fire as a result of actions on the parent tables.

Mutating Table Errors

Oracle has a restriction on trigger execution that can impede the development of specialized triggers. In trigger actions, Oracle prohibits SQL statements on the table in which the trigger is defined or on related tables affected by DELETE CASCADE actions. The underlying trigger table and the related tables are known as mutating tables. For example on a trigger for the Registration table, Oracle prohibits SQL statements on the Registration table as well as on the Enrollment table if the Enrollment table contains a foreign key constraint on Enrollment.RegNo with the ON DELETE CASCADE action. If a trigger executes an SQL statement on a mutating table, a run-time error occurs.

For most triggers, you can avoid mutating table errors by using row triggers with new and old values. In specialized situations, you must redesign a trigger to avoid a mutating table error. One situation involves a trigger to enforce an integrity constraint involving other rows of the same table. For example, a trigger to ensure that no more than five rows contain the same value for a column would have a mutating table error. Another example would be a trigger that ensures that a row cannot be deleted if it is the last row associated with a parent table. A second situation involves a trigger for a parent table that inserts rows into a child table if the child table has a foreign key constraint with ON DELETE CASCADE.

To write triggers in these situations, you will need a more complex solution. For complete details, you should consult some websites that show solutions to avoid mutating table errors. The Oracle documentation mentions the following three approaches:
1. Write a package and a collection of triggers that use procedures in the package. The package maintains a private array that contains the old and new values of the mutating table. Typically, you will need a BEFORE STATEMENT trigger to initialize the private array, an AFTER ROW trigger to insert into the private array, and an AFTER STATEMENT trigger to enforce the integrity constraint using the private array.

2. Create a view and use an INSTEAD OF trigger for the view. View triggers do not have any mutating table restrictions.
3. Write a compound trigger, a new feature in Oracle 11g. A compound trigger can have multiple timings, BEFORE STATEMENT, BEFORE ROW, AFTER ROW, and AFTER STATEMENT. A compound trigger is an alternative to the package solution in point 1 above.

Closing Thoughts

This chapter has augmented your knowledge of database application development with details about database programming languages, stored procedures, and triggers. Database programming languages are procedural languages with an interface to one or more DBMSs. Database programming languages support customization, batch processing, and complex operations beyond the SQL SELECT statement as well as improved efficiency and portability in some cases. The major design issues in a database programming language are language style, binding, database connections, and result processing. This chapter presented background about PL/SQL, a widely used database programming language available as part of Oracle.

After learning about database programming languages and PL/SQL, the chapter presented stored procedures. Stored procedures provide modularity like programming language procedures. Stored procedures managed by a DBMS provide additional benefits including reuse of access plans, dependency management, and security control by the DBMS. You learned about PL/SQL procedure coding through examples demonstrating procedures, functions, exception processing, and embedded SQL containing single row results and multiple row results with cursors. You also learned about PL/SQL packages that group related procedures, functions, and other PL/SQL objects.

The final part of the chapter covered triggers for business rule processing. A trigger involves an event, a condition, and a sequence of actions. You learned the varied uses for triggers as well as a classification of triggers by granularity, timing, and applicable event. After this background material, you learned about coding Oracle triggers using PL/SQL statements in a trigger body. To provide understanding about the complexity of large collections of triggers, you learned about trigger execution procedures specifying the order of execution among various kinds of triggers, integrity constraints, and SQL statements.

The material in this chapter is important for both application developers and database administrators. Stored procedures and triggers can be a significant part of large applications, perhaps as much as 25 percent of the code. Application developers use database programming languages to code stored procedures and triggers, while database administrators provide oversight in the development process. In addition, database administrators may write stored procedures and triggers to support the process of database monitoring. Thus, database programming languages, stored procedures, and triggers are important tools for careers in both application development and database administration.

Review Concepts

- Primary motivation for database programming languages: customization, batch processing, and complex operations
- Secondary motivation for database programming languages: efficiency and portability
- Statement-level interface to support embedded SQL in a programming language
- Call-level interface to provide procedures to invoke SQL statements in a programming language
- Popularity of proprietary call-level interfaces (ODBC and JDBC) instead of the SQL:2006 call-level interface
- Support for static and dynamic binding of SQL statements in statement-level interfaces
- Support for dynamic binding with access plan reuse for repetitive executions in call-level interfaces
- Implicit versus explicit database connections
- Usage of cursors to integrate set-at-a-time processing of SQL with record-at-a-time processing of programming languages
- PL/SQL data types and variable declaration
- Anchored variable declaration in PL/SQL

- Conditional statements in PL/SQL: IF-THEN, IF-THEN-ELSE, IF-THEN-ELSIF, and CASE
- Looping statements in PL/SQL: FOR LOOP, WHILE LOOP, and LOOP with an EXIT statement
- Anonymous blocks to execute PL/SQL statements and test stored procedures and triggers
- Motivations for stored procedures: compilation of access plans, flexibility in client-server development, implementation of complex operators, and convenient management using DBMS tools for security control and dependency management
- Specification of parameters in PL/SQL procedures and functions
- Exception processing in PL/SQL procedures and functions
- Using static cursors in PL/SQL procedures and functions
- Implicit versus explicit cursors in PL/SQL
- PL/SQL packages to group related procedures, functions, and other objects
- Public versus private specification of packages
- Motivation for triggers: complex integrity constraints, transition constraints, update propagation, exception reporting, audit trails, and support for generalization hierarchies
- Trigger granularity: statement versus row-level triggers
- Trigger timing: before or after an event
- Trigger events: INSERT, UPDATE, or DELETE as well as compound events with combinations of these events
- SQL:2006 trigger specification versus proprietary trigger syntax
- Oracle BEFORE ROW triggers for complex integrity constraints, transition constraints, and data entry standardization
- Oracle AFTER ROW triggers for update propagation and exception reporting
- Oracle INSTEAD OF triggers that execute in place of manipulation operations on views
- The order of trigger execution in a trigger execution procedure: BEFORE STATEMENT, BEFORE ROW, AFTER ROW, AFTER STATEMENT
- The order of integrity constraint enforcement in a trigger execution procedure
- Arbitrary execution order for overlapping triggers
- Recursive execution of a trigger execution procedure for data manipulation statements in a trigger body and actions on referenced rows

Questions

1. What is a database programming language?
2. Why is customization an important motivation for database programming languages?
3. How do database programming languages support customization?
4. Why is batch processing an important motivation for database programming languages?
5. Why is support for complex operations an important motivation for database programming languages?
6. Why is efficiency a secondary motivation for database programming languages, not a primary motivation?
7. Why is portability a secondary motivation for database programming languages, not a primary motivation?
8. What is a statement-level interface?
9. What is a call-level interface?
10. What is binding for a database programming language?
11. What is the difference between dynamic and static binding?
12. What is the relationship between language style and binding?
13. What SQL:2006 statements and procedures support explicit database connections?
14. What differences must be resolved to process the results of an SQL statement in a computer program?
15. What is a cursor?
16. What statements and procedures does SQL:2006 provide for cursor processing?
17. Why study PL/SQL?

18. Explain case sensitivity in PL/SQL. Why are most elements case insensitive?
19. What is an anchored variable declaration?
20. What is a logical expression?
21. What conditional statements are provided by PL/SQL?
22. What iteration statements are provided by PL/SQL?
23. Why use an anonymous block?
24. Why should a DBMS manage stored procedures rather than a programming environment?
25. What are the usages of a parameter in a stored procedure?
26. What is the restriction on the data type in a parameter specification?
27. Why use predefined exceptions and user-defined exceptions?
28. Why use the OTHERS exception?
29. How does a function differ from a procedure?
30. What are the two kinds of cursor declaration in PL/SQL?
31. What is the difference between a static and a dynamic cursor in PL/SQL?
32. What is a cursor attribute?
33. How are cursor attributes referenced?
34. What is the purpose of a PL/SQL package?
35. Why separate the interface from the implementation in a PL/SQL package?
36. What does a package interface contain?
37. What does a package implementation contain?
38. What is an alternative name for a trigger?
39. What are typical uses for triggers?
40. How does SQL:2006 classify triggers?
41. Why do most trigger implementations differ from the SQL:2006 specification?
42. How are compound events specified in a trigger?
43. How are triggers tested?
44. Is it preferable to write many smaller triggers or fewer larger triggers?
45. What is a trigger execution procedure?
46. What is the order of execution for various kinds of triggers?
47. What is an overlapping trigger? What is the execution order of overlapping triggers?
48. What situations lead to recursive execution of the trigger execution procedure?
49. List at least two ways to reduce the complexity of a collection of triggers.
50. What is a mutating table error in an Oracle trigger?
51. How are mutating table errors avoided?
52. What are typical uses of BEFORE ROW triggers?
53. What are typical uses of AFTER ROW triggers?
54. What is the difference between a hard constraint and a soft constraint?
55. What kind of trigger can be written to implement a soft constraint?
56. How does the Oracle trigger execution procedure differ from the SQL:2006 execution procedure for recursive execution?
57. What is an INSTEAD OF trigger?
58. Why are INSTEAD OF triggers useful to support operations on generalization hierarchies?

Problems

Each problem uses the revised order entry database shown in Chapter 10. For your reference, Figure 11.P1 shows a relationship window for the revised order entry database. More details about the revised database can be found in the Chapter 10 problems.

The problems provide practice with PL/SQL coding and development of procedures, functions, packages, and triggers. In addition, some problems involve anonymous blocks and scripts to test the procedures, functions, packages, and triggers.

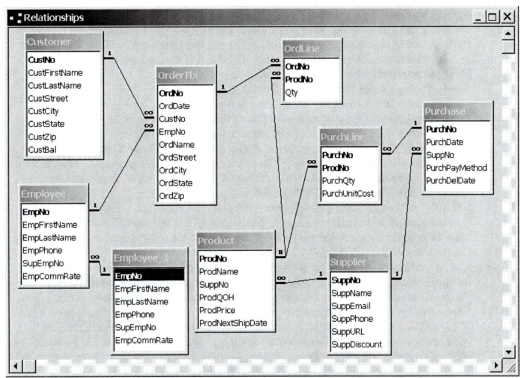

Figure 11.P1: Relationship Diagram for the Revised Order Entry Database

1. Write a PL/SQL anonymous block to calculate the number of days in a nonleap year. Your code should loop through the months of the year (1 to 12) using a FOR LOOP. You should use an IF-THEN-ELSIF statement to determine the number of days to add for the month. You can group months together that have the same number of days. Display the number of days after the loop terminates.

2. Revise problem 1 to calculate the number of days in a leap year. If working in Oracle 9i or beyond, use a CASE statement instead of an IF-THEN-ELSIF statement. Note that you cannot use a CASE statement in Oracle 8i.

3. Write a PL/SQL anonymous block to calculate the future value of $1,000 at 8 percent interest, compounded annually for 10 years. The future value at the end of year i is the amount at the beginning of the year plus the beginning amount times the yearly interest rate. Use a WHILE LOOP to calculate the future value. Display the future amount after the loop terminates.

4. Write a PL/SQL anonymous block to display the price of product number P0036577. Use an anchored variable declaration and a SELECT INTO statement to determine the price. If the price is less than $100, display a message that the product is a good buy. If the price is between $100 and $300, display a message that the product is competitively priced. If the price is greater than $300, display a message that the product is feature laden.

5. Write a PL/SQL procedure to insert a new row into the Product table using input parameters for the product number, product name, product price, next ship date, quantity on hand, and supplier number. For a successful insert, display an appropriate message. If

413

an error occurs in the INSERT statement, raise an exception with an appropriate error message.

6. Revise problem 5 to generate an output value instead of displaying a message about a successful insert. In addition, the revised procedure should catch a duplicate primary key error. If the user tries to insert a row with an existing product number, your procedure should raise an exception with an appropriate error message.

7. Write testing scripts for the procedures in problems 5 and 6. For the procedure in problem 6, your script should test for a primary key violation and a foreign key violation.

8. Write a PL/SQL function to determine if the most recent order for a given customer number was sent to the customer's billing address. The function should return TRUE if each order address column (street, city, state, and zip) is equal to the corresponding customer address column. If any address column is not equal, return false. The most recent order has the largest order date. Return NULL if the customer does not exist or there are no orders for the customer.

9. Create a testing script for the PL/SQL function in problem 8.

10. Create a procedure to compute the commission amount for a given order number. The commission amount is the commission rate of the employee taking the order times the amount of the order. The amount of an order is the sum of the product of the quantity of a product ordered times the product price. If the order does not have a related employee (a Web order), the commission is zero. The procedure should have an output variable for the commission amount. The output variable should be null if an order does not exist.

11. Create a testing script for the PL/SQL procedure in problem 10.

12. Create a function to check the quantity on hand of a product. The input parameters are a product number and a quantity ordered. Return FALSE if the quantity on hand is less than the quantity ordered. Return TRUE if the quantity on hand is greater than or equal to the quantity ordered. Return NULL if the product does not exist.

13. Create a procedure to insert an order line. Use the function from problem 12 to check for adequate stock. If there is not sufficient stock, the output parameter should be FALSE. Raise an exception if there is an insertion error such as a duplicate primary key.

14. Create testing scripts for the function in problem 12 and the procedure in problem 13.

15. Write a function to compute the median of the customer balance column. The median is the middle value in a list of numbers. If the list size is even, the median is the average of the two middle values. For example, if there are 18 customer balances, the median is the average of the ninth and tenth balances. You should use an implicit cursor in your function. You may want to use the Oracle SQL functions Trunc and Mod in writing your function. Write a test script for your function. Note that this function does not have any parameters. Do not use parentheses in the function declaration or in the function invocation when a function does not have parameters.

16. Revise the function in problem 15 with an explicit cursor using the CURSOR, the OPEN, the FETCH, and the CLOSE statements. Write a test script for your revised function.

17. Create a package containing the function in problem 15, the procedure in problem 13, the procedure in problem 10, the function in problem 8, and the procedure in problem 6. The function in problem 12 should be private to the package. Write a testing script to execute each public object in the package. You do not need to test each public object completely. One execution per public object is fine because you previously tested the procedures and functions outside the package.

18. Write an AFTER ROW trigger to fire for every action on the Customer table. In the trigger, display the new and old customer values every time that the trigger fires. Write a script to test the trigger.

19. Write a trigger for a transition constraint on the Employee table. The trigger should prevent updates that increase or decrease the commission rate by more than 10 percent. Write a script to test your trigger.

20. Write a trigger to remove the prefix http:// in the column Supplier.SuppURL on insert and update operations. Your trigger should work regardless of the case of the prefix http://. You need to use Oracle SQL functions for string manipulation. You should study Oracle SQL functions such as SubStr, Lower, and LTrim. Write a script to test your trigger.

21. Write a trigger to ensure that there is adequate stock when inserting a new OrdLine row or updating the quantity of an OrdLine row. On insert operations, the ProdQOH of the related Product row should be greater than or equal to the quantity in the new row. On update operations, the ProdQOH should be greater than or equal to the difference in the quantity (new quantity minus old quantity).

22. Write a trigger to propagate updates to the Product table after an operation on the OrdLine table. For insertions, the trigger should decrease the quantity on hand by the order quantity. For updates, the trigger should decrease the quantity on hand by the difference between the new order quantity minus the old order quantity. For deletions, the trigger should increase the quantity on hand by the old order quantity.

23. Write a script to test the triggers from problems 21 and 22.

24. Write a trigger to propagate updates to the Product table after insert operations on the PurchLine table. The quantity on hand should increase by the purchase quantity. Write a script to test the trigger.

25. Write a trigger to propagate updates to the Product table after update operations on the PurchLine table. The quantity on hand should increase by the difference between the new purchase quantity and the old purchase quantity. Write a script to test the trigger.

26. Write a trigger to propagate updates to the Product table after delete operations on the PurchLine table. The quantity on hand should decrease by the old purchase quantity. Write a script to test the trigger.

27. Write a trigger to propagate updates to the Product table updates to the ProdNo column of the PurchLine table. The quantity on hand of the old product should decrease while the quantity on hand of the new product should increase. Write a script to test the trigger.

28. Suppose that you have an UPDATE statement that changes both the ProdNo column and the PurchQty column of the PurchLine table. What triggers (that you wrote in previous problems) fire for such an UPDATE statement? If more than one trigger fires, why do the triggers overlap and what is the firing order? Modify the overlapping triggers and prepare a test script so that you can determine the firing order. Does the Oracle trigger execution procedure guarantee the firing order?

29. For the UPDATE statement in problem 28, do the triggers that you created in previous problems work correctly? Write a script to test your triggers for such an UPDATE statement. If the triggers do not work correctly, rewrite them so that they work correctly for an UPDATE statement on both columns as well as UPDATE statements on the individual columns. Write a script to test the revised triggers. Hint: you need to specify the column in the UPDATING keyword in the trigger body. For example, you can specify UPDATING('PurchQty') to check if the PurchQty column is being updated.

30. Can you devise another solution to the problem of UPDATE statements that change both ProdNo and PurchQty? Is it reasonable to support such UPDATE statements in online applications?

31. Write a trigger to implement a hard constraint on the Product.ProdPrice column. The trigger should prevent updates that increase or decrease the value more than 15 percent. Write a script to test the trigger.

32. Write a trigger to implement a soft constraint on the Product.ProdPrice column. The trigger should insert a row into an exception table for updates that increase or decrease the value more than 15 percent. You should use the exception table shown in Example 11.33. Write a script to test the trigger.

33. Convert the employee generalization hierarchy shown in Figure 11.P2 into a table design using the Generalization Hierarchy Rule (see Section 6.4.3).

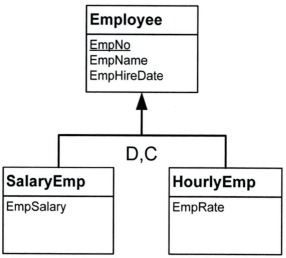

Figure 11.P2: Generalization Hierarchy for Employees

34. Define two views for the table design of the employee generalization hierarchy view. The first view (salary employee view) should contain all rows and columns (direct and inherited) of salaried employees. The second view (hourly employee view) should contain all rows and columns (direct and inherited) of hourly employees.

35. Write triggers and associated testing code to insert rows into the salary and hourly employee views. You should use INSTEAD OF INSERT triggers to map the view operations into base table operations.

36. Modify the INSTEAD OF INSERT trigger from problem 35 on the salary employee view to enforce the disjointness constraint. Write testing code for the modified trigger.

37. As an alternative to the modification of the INSTEAD OF INSERT trigger in problem 36, write a trigger on the SalaryEmp table to enforce the disjointness constraint. Write testing code for the new trigger. Does the trigger fire when inserting a row in the salary employee view? Please explain your answer.

38. Write a trigger and associated testing code for updating columns of the salary employee view. You should use an INSTEAD OF UPDATE trigger to map the view operations into base table operations.

39. Do you need to write a trigger to enforce the completeness constraint for a generalization hierarchy? Please explain your answer. Try to write a trigger to explain your answer.

References for Further Study

The Oracle Technology Network (www.oracle.com/technology) contains a wealth of material about PL/SQL, stored procedures, and triggers. The PL/SQL User's Guide provides details about PL/SQL and stored procedures. The Oracle SQL Reference provides details about triggers as well as descriptions of predefined functions such as Mod and SubStr. More details and examples can be found in the Oracle Concepts and the Oracle Application Developers Guide. Melton and Simon (2001) describe triggers in SQL:1999.

Appendix 11.A: SQL:2006 Syntax Summary

This appendix summarizes the SQL:2006 syntax for the trigger statement. The conventions used in the syntax notation are identical to those used at the end of Chapter 3.

Trigger Statement

```
CREATE TRIGGER TriggerName
 <TriggerTiming> <TriggerEvent> ON TableName
 [ REFERENCING <AliasClause> [ <AliasClause> ] ]
 [ <GranularityClause> [ WHEN ( <Row-Condition> ) ] ]
 <ActionBlock>

<TriggerTiming>: { BEFORE | AFTER }

<TriggerEvent>: { INSERT | DELETE |
  UPDATE [ OF ColumnName* ] }

<AliasClause>: { <RowAlias> | <TableAlias> }

<RowAlias>:
  { OLD [ROW] [AS] AliasName |
    NEW [ROW] [AS] AliasName }

<TableAlias>:
  { OLD TABLE [AS] AliasName |
    NEW TABLE [AS] AliasName }

<GranularityClause>: FOR EACH { ROW | STATEMENT }
```

12

View Design and Integration

Learning Objectives

This chapter describes the practice of designing user views and combining user views into a complete conceptual design. After this chapter, the student should have acquired the following knowledge and skills:

- Understand the motivation for view design and integration
- Analyze a form and construct an ERD to represent it
- Determine an integration strategy for a database development effort
- Perform both incremental and parallel integration approaches
- Recognize and resolve synonyms and homonyms in the view integration process

Overview

Chapters 5, 6, and 7 provided tools for data modeling and normalization, fundamental skills for database design. You applied this knowledge to construct entity relationship diagrams (ERDs) for modest-size problems, convert ERDs into relational tables, and normalize the tables. This chapter extends your database design skills by demonstrating an approach to analyze views and integrate user views into a complete, conceptual schema. This approach is an applications-oriented approach appropriate for designing complex databases.

To become a good database designer, you need to extend your skills to larger problems. To motivate you about the importance of extending your skills, this chapter describes the nature of large database development projects. This chapter then presents a methodology for view design with an emphasis on constructing an ERD to represent a data entry form. Forms can provide important sources of requirements for database design. You will learn to analyze individual forms, construct an ERD, and check the ERD for consistency against the form. Because of the emphasis on views and forms, this chapter logically follows Chapter 10 on application development with views. While studying this chapter, you may want to review important concepts from Chapter 10, such as updatable views.

After the presentation of view design, this chapter describes the process of view integration, combining ERDs representing individual views. You will learn about the incremental and parallel integration approaches, determination of an integration strategy by analyzing relationships among forms, and application of the integration process using both the incremental and parallel approaches.

12.1 Motivation for View Design and Integration

The complexity of a database reflects the complexity of the underlying organization and the functions that a database supports. Many factors can contribute to the complexity of an organization. Size is certainly an important determinant of complexity. Size can be measured in many ways such as by sales volume, the number of employees, the number of products, and the number of countries in which an organization operates. Size alone is not the only determinant, however. Other factors that contribute to organizational complexity are the regulatory environment, the competitive environment, and the organizational structure. For example, the areas of payroll and personnel can be tremendously complex because of the number of employee types, varied compensation packages, union agreements, and government regulations.

Large organizations have many databases with individual databases supporting groups of functions such as payroll, personnel, accounting, material requirements, and so on. These individual databases can be very complex, as measured by the size of the ERDs. An ERD for a large database can have hundreds of entity types and relationships. When converted to a relational database, the database can have hundreds to perhaps thousands of tables. A large ERD is difficult to inspect visually because it can fill an entire wall. Other measures of complexity involve the use of a database through forms, reports, stored procedures, and triggers. A large database can have hundreds to thousands of forms, reports, stored procedures, and triggers.

Designing large databases is a time-consuming and labor-intensive process. The design effort often involves collecting requirements from many different groups of users. Requirements can be notoriously difficult to capture. Users often need to experience a system to clarify their requirements. Because of the volume of requirements and the difficulty of capturing requirements, a large database design effort can involve a team of designers. Coordination among designers is an important part of the database design effort.

To manage complexity, the *divide and conquer* strategy is used in many areas of computing. Dividing a large problem allows smaller problems to be independently solved. The solutions to the smaller problems are then combined into a solution for the entire problem.

View design and integration (Figure 12.1) supports management of the complexity of a database design effort. In view design, an ERD is constructed for each group of users. The requirements can come in many formats such as interviews, documentation of an existing system, and proposed forms and reports. A view is typically small enough for a single person to design. Multiple designers can work on views covering different parts of a database. The view integration process merges the views into a complete, conceptual schema. Integration involves recognizing and resolving conflicts. To resolve conflicts, it is sometimes necessary to revise conflicting views. Compromise is an important part of conflict resolution in the integration process.

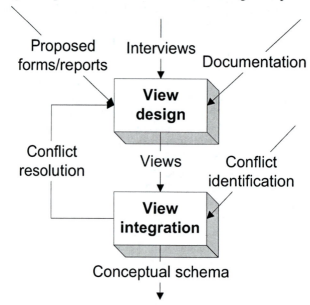

Figure 12.1: Overview of View Design and Integration

The remaining sections of this chapter provide details about the view design and integration activities. A special emphasis is given to data entry forms as a source of requirements.

12.2 View Design with Forms

Forms can provide an important source of requirements for database design. Because of familiarity, users can effectively communicate many requirements through the forms they use. To aid you in using forms as database requirements, this section describes a procedure to design views using data entry forms. The procedure enables you to analyze the data requirements of a form. After the form analysis procedure, application of the procedure to forms with M-way relationships is discussed.

12.2.1 Form Analysis

In using forms for database design, you reverse the traditional database development process. In the traditional process, a database design precedes application development. With a form-driven approach to database design, forms are defined before or concurrently with the database design. Forms may exist in paper format or as part of an existing system. The form definition does not need to be as complete as required after the database design is complete. For example, it is not necessary to define the entire set of events for user interaction with a form until later in the development process. Initially, form definition can involve a sketch on a word processor (Figure 12.2) or drawing tool. In addition, you may need several sample instances of a form.

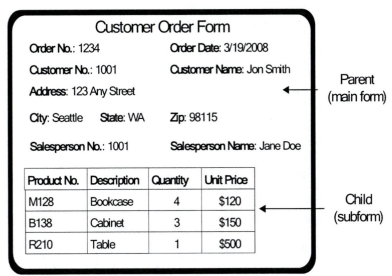

Figure 12.2: Sample Customer Order Form

The use of forms in view design does not preclude requirements in other formats such as interviews and documentation of an existing system. You should use all kinds of requirements in the view design process. As an important source of requirements, forms should be analyzed carefully.

In form analysis (Figure 12.3), you create an entity relationship diagram to represent a form. The resulting ERD is a view of the database. The ERD should be general enough to support the form and other anticipated processing. The backtracking in Figure 12.3 shows that the form analysis process can return to previous steps. It is not necessary to perform the steps sequentially. In particular, if any problems are found in the last step, other steps must be repeated to correct the problems. The remainder of this section explains the form analysis steps in more detail and applies the form analysis process to example forms.

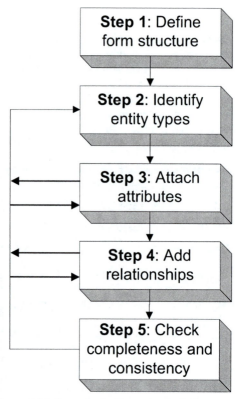

Figure 12.3: Steps in the Form Analysis Process

Step 1: Define Form Structure

In the first step, you construct a hierarchy that depicts the form structure. Most forms consist of a simple hierarchy where the main form is the parent and the subform is the child. For example, Figure 12.4 depicts the structure of the customer order form in Figure 12.2. A rectangle (parent or child) in the hierarchy diagram is called a node. Complex forms can have more nodes (parallel subforms) and more levels (subforms inside subforms) in the hierarchy. For example, an automotive service order form may have a subform (child) showing part charges and another subform (child) showing labor charges. Complex forms such as a service order form are not as common because they can be difficult for users to understand.

As part of making the form structure, you should identify keys within each node in the hierarchy. In Figure 12.4, node keys are underlined. In the parent node, the node key value is unique among all form instances. In the child node, the node key value is unique within the parent node. For example, a product number is unique on an order. However, two orders may use the same product number.

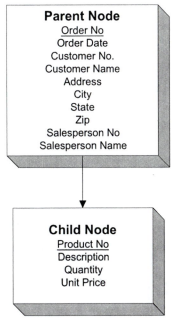

Figure 12.4: Hierarchical Structure for the Customer Order Form

Step 2: Identify Entity Types

In the second step, you may split each node in the hierarchical structure into one or more entity types. Typically, each node in the hierarchical structure represents more than one entity type. You should look for form fields that can be primary keys of an entity type in the database. You should make an entity type if the form field is a potential primary key and there are other associated fields in the form. Equivalently, you group form fields into entity types using functional dependencies (FDs). All form fields determined by the same field(s) should be placed together in the same entity type.

As an example of step 2, there are three entity types in the parent node of Figure 12.4 as shown in Figure 12.5: *Customer* identified by *Customer No*, *Order* identified by *Order No*, and *Salesperson* identified by *Salesperson No*. The parent node key (*Order No*) usually designates an entity type. *Customer No* and *Salesperson No* are good choices because there are other associated fields (*Customer Name* and *Salesperson Name*). In the child node, there is one entity type: *Product* designated by *Product No* because *Product No* can be a primary key with other associated fields.

Figure 12.5: Entity Types for the Customer Order Form

Step 3: Attach Attributes

In the third step, you attach attributes to the entity types identified in the previous step. It is usually easy to associate form fields with the entity types. You should group together fields that are associated with the primary keys found in step 2. Sometimes the proximity of fields can provide clues to their grouping: form fields close together often belong in the same entity type. In this example, group the fields as shown in Figure 12.6. *Order* with *Order No* and *Order Date*, *Customer* with *Customer No*, *Customer Name*, *Address*, *City*, *State*, and *Zip*, *Salesperson* with *Salesperson No* and *Salesperson Name*, and *Product* with *Product No*, *Description*, and *Unit Price*.

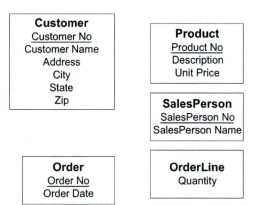

Figure 12.6: Attributes Added to the Entity Types of Figure 12.5

If you are observant, you might notice that *Quantity* does not seem to belong to *Product* because the combination of *Order No* and *Product No* determines *Quantity*. You can create a new entity type (*OrderLine*) with *Quantity* as an attribute. If you miss this entity type, *Quantity* can be made an attribute of a relationship in the next step. In addition, the *Unit Price* attribute can be considered an attribute of the *OrderLine* entity type if the historical price rather than the current price of a product is tracked.

Step 4: Add Relationships

In the fourth step, you connect entity types with relationships and specify cardinalities. Table 12-1 summarizes rules about connecting entity types. You should begin with the entity type containing the primary key of the form. Let us call this the form entity type. Make the form entity type the center of the ERD. Typically, several relationships connect the form entity type to other entity types derived from the parent and the child nodes. In Figure 12.5, *Order* is the form entity type.

Table 12-1: Rules to Connect Entity Types

1.	Place the form entity type in the center of the ERD.
2.	Add relationships between the form entity type and other entity types derived from the parent node. The relationships are usually 1-M.
3.	Add a relationship to connect the form entity type to an entity type in the child node.
4.	Add relationships to connect entity types derived from the child node if not already connected.

After identifying the form entity type, you should add 1-M relationships with other entity types derived from fields in the main form. This leaves us with *Order* connected to *Customer* and *SalesPerson* through 1-M relationships as shown in Figure 12.7. You should verify that the same customer can make many orders and the same salesperson can take many orders by examining additional form instances and talking to knowledgeable users.

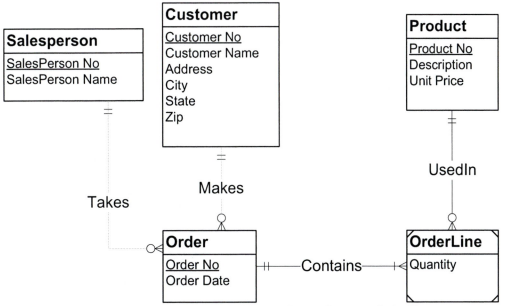

Figure 12.7: Entity Relationship Diagram for the Customer Order Form

Next you should connect the entity types derived from fields in the subform. *Product* and *OrderLine* can be connected by a 1-M relationship. An order line contains one product, but the same product may appear in order lines of different forms.

To finish the relationships, you need to connect an entity type derived from main form fields with an entity type derived from subform fields. Typically, the relationship will connect the form entity type (*Order*) with an entity type derived from the child node. This relationship can be 1-M or M-N. In Figure 12.7, you can assume that an order can be associated with many products. If you examine other order form instances, you could see the same product associated with different orders. Therefore, a product can be associated with many orders. Here, it is important to note that *Quantity* is not associated with either *Product* or *Order* but with the combination. The combination can be considered a relationship or entity type. In Figure 12.7, *OrderLine* is an entity type. Figure 12.8 shows an alternative representation as an M-N relationship.

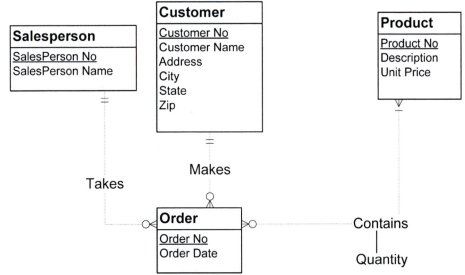

Figure 12.8: Alternative ERD for the Customer Order Form

Step 5: Check Completeness and Consistency

In the fifth step, you check the ERD for consistency and completeness with the form structure. The ERD should adhere to the diagram rules defined in Chapter 5 (Section 5.4.2). For example, the ERD should contain minimum and maximum cardinalities for all relationships, a primary key for all entity types, and a name for all relationships.

For consistency, the form structure provides several constraints on the relationship cardinalities as summarized in Table 12-2. The first rule is necessary because only one value is displayed on the form. For example, there is only one value displayed for the customer number, name, and so on. As an example of the first rule, the maximum cardinality is one in the relationship from *Order* to *Customer* and from *Order* to *Salesperson*. The second rule ensures that there is a 1-M relationship from the parent to the child node. A given record in the parent node can be related to many records in the child node. As an example of the second rule, the relationship from *Order* to *OrderLine* has a maximum cardinality of M. In the alternative ERD (Figure 12.8), the maximum cardinality is M from *Order* to *Product*.

Table 12-2: Consistency Rules for Relationship Cardinalities

1. In at least one direction, the maximum cardinality should be one for relationships connecting entity types derived from the same node (parent or child).
2. In at least one direction, the maximum cardinality should be greater than one for relationships connecting entity types derived from nodes on different levels of the form hierarchy.

After following the steps of form analysis, you also can explore transformations as discussed in Chapter 6 (Section 6.2). The attribute to entity type transformation is often useful. If the form only displays a primary key, you may not initially create an entity type. For example, if only the salesperson number is displayed, you may not create a separate salesperson entity type. You can ask the user whether other data about a salesperson should be maintained. If yes, transform the salesperson number into an entity type.

Another Form Analysis Example

The Invoice Form (Figure 12.9) provides another example for form analysis. A customer receives an invoice form along with the products ordered. In the main form, an invoice contains fields to identify the customer and the order. In the subform, an invoice identifies the products and the quantities shipped, ordered, and backordered. The quantity backordered equals the quantity ordered less the quantity shipped. Corresponding to this form, Figure 12.10 shows the hierarchical structure.

Invoice Form						
Customer No.: 1273				Invoice No.: 06389		
Name: Contemporary Designs				**Date:** 3/28/2008		
Address: 123 Any Street				Order No.: 61384		
City: Seattle		State: WA		Zip: 98105		
Product No.	Description	Qty. Ord.	Qty. Ship	Qty. Back.	Unit Price	Total Price
B381	Cabinet	2	2		150.00	300.00
R210	Table	1	1		500.00	500.00
M128	Bookcase	4	2	2	200.00	400.00
				Total Amount		$1200.00
				Discount		60.00
				Amount Due		$1140.00

Figure 12.9: Sample Invoice Form

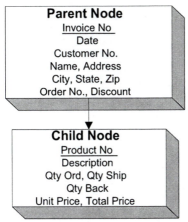

Figure 12.10: Hierarchical Structure for the Invoice Form

Figure 12.11 shows the result of steps 2 and 3 for the Customer Invoice form. The asterisks denote computed fields. *Invoice*, *Customer*, and *Order* are derived from the parent node. *Product* and *ShipLine* are derived from the child node. If you miss *ShipLine*, you can add it later as a relationship.

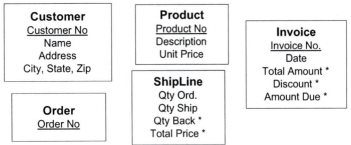

Figure 12.11: Entity Types for the Invoice Form

Figure 12.12 displays the ERD for the Invoice Form. The *SentTo* and *ShipFor* relationships connect entity types from the parent node. The *ShipsIn* relationship connects an entity type in the parent node (*Invoice*) with an entity type in the child node (*ShipLine*). Figure 12.13 shows an alternative ERD with the *ShipLine* entity type replaced by an M-N relationship.

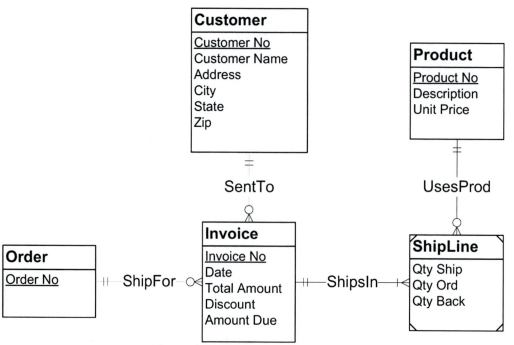

Figure 12.12: ERD for the Invoice Form

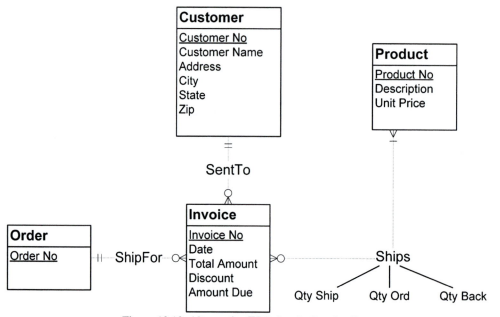

Figure 12.13: Alternative ERD for the Invoice Form

12.2.2 Analysis of M-Way Relationships Using Forms

Chapter 7 described the concept of relationship independence as a way to reason about the need for M-way relationships. This section describes a more application-oriented way to reason about M-way relationships. You can use data entry forms to help determine if an M-way associative entity type is needed to represent an M-way relationship involving three or more entity types. Data entry forms provide a context to understand M-way relationships. Without the context of a form, it can be difficult to determine that an M-way relationship is necessary as opposed to binary relationships.

An M-way relationship may be needed if a form shows a data entry pattern involving three entity types. Typically, one entity type resides on the main form and the other two entity

428

types reside on the subform. Figure 12.14 shows a form with a project in the main form and part-supplier combinations (two entity types) in the subform. This form can be used to purchase parts for a particular project (localized purchasing). Because purchasing decisions are made by projects, both Part No. and Supplier No. can be updated in the subform. Figure 12.15 shows an ERD for this form. An associative entity type involving purchase, part, and supplier is necessary because a purchase can involve many combinations of parts and suppliers.

Project Purchasing Form			
Purchase No.: P1234		Purchase Date: 3/19/2008	
Project No.: PR1		Project Manager: Jon Smith	
Part No.	Supplier No.	Quantity	Unit Price
M128	S100	4	$120
M128	S101	3	$150
R210	S102	1	$500

Figure 12.14: Sample Project Purchasing Form

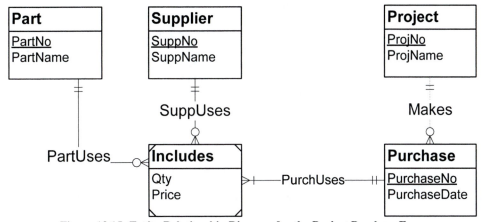

Figure 12.15: Entity Relationship Diagram for the Project Purchase Form

As an alternative to localized purchasing for each project, some organizations may prefer centralized purchasing. Figure 12.16 shows a form to support centralized purchasing with the supplier in the main form and related parts (one entity type) in the subform. The ERD in Figure 12.17 shows a binary relationship between *Purchase* and *Part*. To allocate parts to projects, there is another form with the project in the main form and the parts used by the project in the subform. The ERD for the other form would need a binary relationship between project and part.

Purchasing Form		
Purchase No.: P1234	Purchase Date: 3/19/2008	
Supplier No.: S101	**Supplier Name:** Anytime Supply	
Part No.	Quantity	Unit Price
M128	4	$120
M129	3	$150
R210	1	$500

Figure 12.16: Sample Purchasing Form

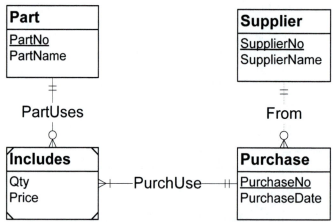

Figure 12.17: Entity Relationship Diagram for the Purchasing Form

Even if there are two or more entity types in a subform, binary relationships may suffice if only one entity type is updatable. In Figure 12.14, both Supplier No. and Part No. are updatable in the subform. Thus, an M-way relationship is necessary. As a counter example, Figure 12.18 shows a form for course registration. The subform shows primary keys of the *Offering*, *Faculty*, and *Course* entity types, but only *Offering* is updatable in the subform. Faculty No. and Course No. are read-only. The selection of a faculty member and the course corresponding to the offering are made in other forms. Thus, the ERD only contains binary relationships as Figure 12.19 shows.

Registration No.: 1273					Date: 5/15/2008	
Quarter: Fall					Year: 2008	
Student No: 123489					Student Name: Sue Thomas	
Offer No.	Course No.	Days	Time	Location	Faculty No.	Faculty Name
1234	IS480	MW	10:30	BLM211	1111	Sally Hope
3331	IS460	MW	8:30	BLM411	2121	George Jetstone
2222	IS470	MW	1:30	BLM305	1111	Sally Hope

Figure 12.18: Registration Form

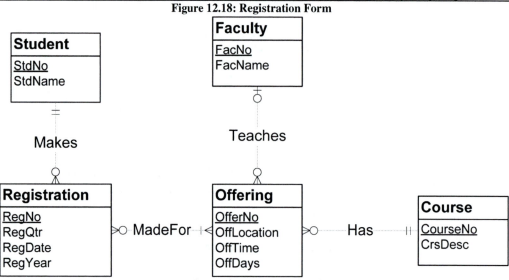

Figure 12.19: Entity Relationship Diagram for the Registration Form

12.3 View Integration

With a large database project, even skilled database designers need tools to manage the complexity of the design process. Together, view design and integration can help you manage a large database design project by allowing a large effort to be split into smaller parts. In the last section, you studied a method to design an ERD representing the data requirements of a form.

430

This section describes the process to combine individual views into a complete database design. Two approaches for view integration are presented along with an example of each approach.

12.3.1 Incremental and Parallel Integration Approaches

The incremental and parallel approaches are opposite ways to perform view integration. In the incremental approach (Figure 12.20), a view and partially integrated ERD are merged in each integration step. Initially, the designer chooses a view and constructs an ERD for it. For subsequent views, the designer performs integration while analyzing the next view. The view design and integration processes are performed jointly for each view after the first one. This approach is incremental as a partially integrated ERD is produced after each step. This approach is also binary as the current view is analyzed along with the partially integrated ERD.

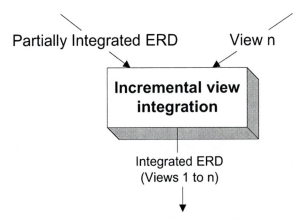

Figure 12.20: Incremental Integration Process

In the parallel approach (Figure 12.21), ERDs are produced for each view and then the view ERDs are merged. The integration occurs in one large step after all views are analyzed. This approach is parallel because different designers can perform view designs at the same time. Integration can be more complex in the parallel approach because integration is postponed until all views are complete. The integration occurs in one step when all views are integrated to produce the final ERD.

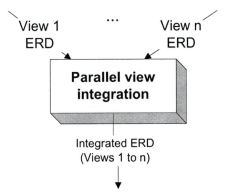

Figure 12.21: Parallel Integration Process

Both approaches have advantages and disadvantages. The incremental approach has more integration steps, but each integration step is smaller. The parallel approach postpones integration until the end when a large integration effort may be necessary. The incremental approach is well suited to closely related views. For example, the order and the invoice forms are closely related because an order precedes an invoice. The parallel approach works well on large projects with views that are not closely related. Independent teams can work on different parts of a design in parallel. On a large project with many database designers, the parallel approach supports more independent work.

Determining an Integration Strategy

The incremental and parallel approaches are typically combined in a large database design project. An <u>integration strategy</u> (Figure 12.22) specifies a mix of incremental and parallel approaches to integrate a set of views. To choose an integration strategy, you divide the views into subsets (say *n* subsets). For each subset of views, the incremental approach is followed. You should choose subsets of views so that the views in a subset are closely related. Views in different subsets should not be closely related. Incremental integration across subsets of views can proceed in parallel. After an integrated ERD is produced for each subset of views, a parallel integration produces the final, integrated ERD. If the ERDs from each subset of views do not overlap much, the final integration should not be difficult. If there is significant overlap among the subset of views, incremental integration can be used to combine the ERDs from the view subsets.

> **Integration Strategy**: a mix of incremental and parallel approaches to integrate a set of views. The views are divided into subsets. For each subset of views, incremental integration is used. Parallel integration is applied to the ERDs resulting from integrating the view subsets.

As an example, consider a database to support a consulting firm. The database should support marketing to potential customers, billing on existing projects, and conducting work on projects. The database design effort can be divided into three parts (marketing, billing, and working). A separate design team may work incrementally on each part. If the marketing part has requirements for customer contacts and promotions, two incremental ERDs should be produced. After working independently, the teams can perform a parallel integration to combine their work.

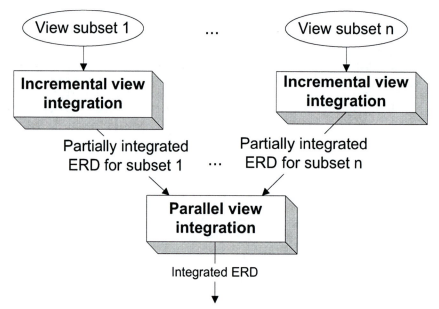

Figure 12.22: Outline of a General Integration Strategy

Precedence Relationships among Forms

To help determine an integration strategy, you should identify precedence relationships among forms. Form A precedes form B if form A must be completed before form B is used. Form A typically provides some data used in form B. For example, the invoice form (Figure 12.9) uses the quantity of each product ordered (from the order form) to determine the quantity to ship. A good rule of thumb is to place forms with precedence relationships in the same view subset. Thus, the invoice and order forms should be in the same subset of views.

To further depict the use of precedence relationships, let us extend the order and invoice example. Figure 12.23 shows precedence relationships among forms for a custom manufacturing company. The product design form contains data about the components of a product. The product

432

manufacturing form contains data about the sequence of physical operations necessary to manufacture a product. The customer and product forms contain data only about customers and products, respectively. The precedence relationships indicate that instances of the customer and product forms must be complete before an order is taken. Likewise, the product and product design forms must be completed before a manufacturing form is completed.

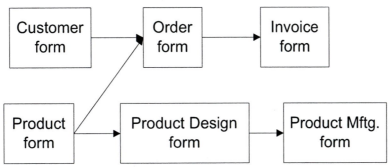

Figure 12.23: Precedence Relationships among Forms

Using these precedence relationships, the forms can be divided into two groups: (1) an ordering process consisting of the customer, product, order, and invoice forms and (2) a manufacturing process consisting of the product, product design, and product manufacturing forms.

Resolving Synonyms and Homonyms

In any integration approach, resolution of synonyms and homonyms is a very important issue. A synonym is a group of words that are spelled differently but have the same meaning. For example, OrdNo, Order Number, and ONO are likely synonyms. Synonyms occur when different parts of an organization use different vocabulary to describe the same concepts. This situation is especially common if a database did not exist before the design effort.

A homonym is a group of words that have the same sound and often the same spelling but have different meanings. In database design, homonyms arise because of context of usage. For example, two forms may show an address field. In one form, the address may represent the street address while in the other form, it represents the street, city, state, and zip. Even when both address fields represent the street address, they may not be the same. One form might contain the billing address while the other form contains the shipping address.

Standardizing a vocabulary is a major part of database development. To standardize a vocabulary, you must resolve synonyms and homonyms. The use of naming standards and a corporate data dictionary can aid in the identification and resolution of synonyms and homonyms. You can create and maintain a corporate data dictionary with a CASE tool. Some CASE tools help with the enforcement of naming standards. Even with these tools, recognizing synonyms and homonyms can be difficult. The most important point is to be alert for their existence. Resolving them is easier: rename synonyms the same (or establish an official list of synonyms) and rename homonyms differently.

Resolution of Synonyms and Homonyms: A synonym is a group of words that are spelled differently but have the same meaning. A homonym is a group of words that have the same sound and often the same spelling but have different meanings. The use of naming standards and a corporate data dictionary can aid in the identification and resolution of synonyms and homonyms.

12.3.2 View Integration Examples

This section depicts the incremental and parallel approaches to view integration using the customer order and invoice forms. The final result is identical with both approaches, but the path to this result is different.

Incremental Integration Example

To demonstrate the incremental integration approach, let us integrate the customer invoice form (Figure 12.9) with the ERD from Figure 12.7. The hierarchical structure of the invoice form is shown in Figure 12.10. You can start by adding an entity for invoice with invoice number and date. As steps 2 and 3 are performed (Figure 12.11), it is useful to see how the entity types should be merged into the existing ERD (Figure 12.7). The other form fields that match existing entity types are listed below.

- Order No. matches the *Order* entity type.
- Customer No., Customer Name, Address, City, State, and Zip match the *Customer* entity type.
- Product No., Description, and Unit Price match the *Product* entity type.

As you match form fields to existing entity types, you should check for synonyms and homonyms. For example, it is not clear that *Address*, *City*, *State*, and *Zip* fields have the same meaning in the two forms. Certainly these fields have the same general meaning. However, it is not clear whether a customer might have a different address for ordering purposes than for shipping purposes. You may need to conduct additional interviews and examine additional form instances to resolve this issue. If you determine that the two sets of fields are homonyms (an order may be billed to one address and shipped to another), there are a number of data modeling alternatives as listed below.

- Revise the *Customer* entity type with two sets of address fields: billing address fields and shipping address fields. This solution restricts the customer to having only a single shipping address. If more than one shipping address is possible, this solution is not feasible.
- Add shipping address fields to the *Invoice* entity type. This solution supports multiple shipping addresses per customer. However, if an invoice is deleted, the shipping address is lost.
- Create a new entity type (*ShipAddress*) with the shipping address fields. This solution supports multiple shipping addresses per customer. It may require overhead to gather the shipping addresses. If shipping addresses are maintained separate from invoices, this solution is the best.

The integrated ERD in Figure 12.24 uses the second alternative. In a real problem, more information should be gathered from the users before making the decision.

In the incremental integration process, the usual process of connecting entity types (step 4 of Figure 12.3) should be followed. For example, there is an M cardinality relating an entity type derived from the parent node with an entity type derived from the child node. The maximum cardinality in *ShipsIn* from *Invoice* to *ShipLine* satisfies this constraint. Note that *ShipLine* could be represented as an M-N relationship instead of as an entity type with two 1-M relationships.

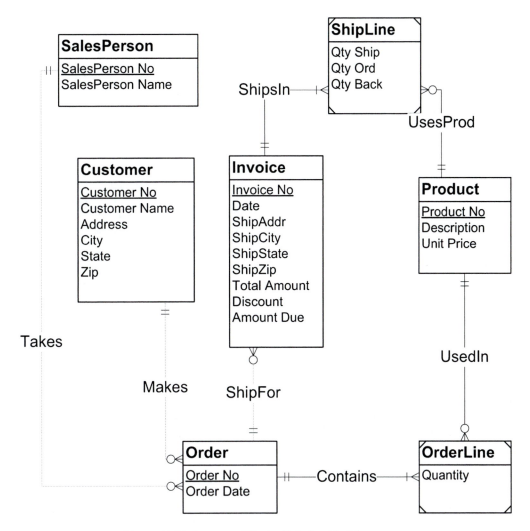

Figure 12.24: Integrated Entity Relationship Diagram

As another point of interest from Figure 12.24, there is no relationship from *Invoice* to *Customer*. At first thought, a relationship may seem necessary because customer data appears on the main form of an invoice. If the invoice customer can be different from the order customer, a relationship between *Invoice* and *Customer* is needed. If the customer on an order is the same as the customer on the related invoice, a relationship is not needed. The customer for an invoice can be found by navigating from *Invoice* to *Order* and *Order* to *Customer*. In Figure 12.24, the assumption is that the order customer and the invoice customer are identical.

Parallel Integration Example

To demonstrate the parallel integration process, let us integrate the customer invoice form (Figure 12.9) with the order form (Figure 12.2). The major difference between the parallel and incremental approaches is that integration occurs later in the parallel approach. Thus, the first step is to construct an ERD for each form using the steps of form analysis described previously. In the ERD for the invoice form (Figure 12.12), *Invoice* is directly connected to both *Customer* and *Order*. The direct connection follows the practice of making the form entity type (*Invoice*) the center of the diagram.

The integration process merges the order form ERD (Figure 12.7) with the invoice form ERD (Figure 12.12) to produce the ERD shown in Figure 12.24. The final ERD should be the same whether you use the incremental or the parallel approach.

Again, a major integration issue is the resolution of homonyms for the address fields. In the two ERDs (Figures 12.7 and 12.12), the *Customer* entity type contains the address fields. Working independently on the two forms, it is easy to overlook the two uses of the address fields:

billing and shipping. Unless you note that the address fields in the invoice form are for shipping purposes, you may not notice that the fields are homonyms.

Another integration issue is the connections among *Invoice*, *Order*, and *Customer*. In Figure 12.7, *Customer* is directly connected to *Order*, but in Figure 12.12, *Order* and *Customer* are not directly connected by a relationship. The integration process must resolve this difference. The relationship between *Order* and *Customer* is needed because orders precede invoices. A relationship between *Invoice* and *Customer* is not needed if the customer shown on an invoice is the same customer shown on the associated order. Assuming that the customer on an order is identical to the customer on the associated invoices, *Invoice* is not directly connected to *Customer* in Figure 12.24.

These two integration examples depict the advantage of the incremental integration approach over the parallel approach. Conflicts due to different uses of fields and timing (orders precede invoices) are resolved sooner in the incremental approach. In the parallel approach, such conflicts are not detected until the final step. This discussion conveys the sentiment discussed earlier: incremental integration is most appropriate when integrating closely related views.

Closing Thoughts

This chapter has described view design and integration, an important skill for designing large databases. Large databases can involve ERDs with hundreds of entity types and relationships. In addition to the large size of the ERDs, there are often hundreds of forms, reports, stored procedures, and triggers that will use the database. View design and integration helps manage the complexity of such large database design efforts.

This chapter emphasized forms in the view design process. Forms are an important source of requirements because they are common and easily communicated. A five-step procedure was given to analyze a form. The result of the form analysis process is an ERD that captures the data requirements of the form. This chapter also described how the form analysis process could help detect the need for M-way associative entity types in an ERD.

This chapter described two approaches to view integration. In the incremental approach, a view and the partially integrated ERD are merged in each integration step. In the parallel approach, ERDs are produced for each view, and then the individual ERDs are merged. The incremental approach works well for closely related views, while the parallel approach works well for unrelated views. This chapter discussed how to determine an integration strategy to combine the incremental and parallel approaches. In any integration approach, resolving synonyms and homonyms is critical. This chapter demonstrated that forms provide a context to resolve synonyms and homonyms.

This chapter concludes your study of the first two phases (conceptual data modeling and logical database design) of database development and provides a link between application development and database development. After completing these steps, you should have a high-quality relational database design: a design that represents the needs of the organization and is free of unwanted redundancies. Chapter 13 provides a detailed case study to apply the ideas in Parts 2 to 5 of this book.

Review Concepts

- Measures of organizational and database complexity
- Characteristics of large database design efforts
- Inputs and outputs of view design and view integration
- Importance of forms as sources of database requirements
- Five steps of form analysis
- Form structure: nodes and node keys
- Rules for adding relationships in form analysis
- Rules to check cardinalities for consistency in form analysis
- Using form analysis to detect the need for M-way relationships
- Using the incremental and parallel integration approaches
- Integration strategy: a mix of incremental and parallel approaches to integrate a set of views

- Using precedence relationships among forms to determine an integration strategy
- Detection of synonyms and homonyms during view integration

Questions

1. What factors influence the size of a conceptual schema?
2. What are measures of conceptual database design complexity?
3. How does the view design and integration process help to manage the complexity of large database design efforts?
4. What is the goal of form analysis?
5. What level of detail should be provided for form definitions to support the form analysis process?
6. What are node keys in a form structure?
7. How do nodes in a form structure correspond to main forms and subforms?
8. What is the form entity type?
9. Why does the ERD for a form often have a different structure than the form?
10. Why is it recommended to place the form entity type in the center of the ERD?
11. Explain the first consistency rule in Table 12-2.
12. Explain the second consistency rule in Table 12-2.
13. What pattern in a data entry form may indicate the need for an M-way relationship?
14. How many integration steps are necessary to perform incremental integration with 10 views?
15. How many view design steps are necessary to perform parallel integration with 10 views?
16. In the incremental integration approach, why are view design and integration performed together?
17. When is the incremental integration approach appropriate?
18. When is the parallel integration approach appropriate?
19. What is an integration strategy?
20. When does a form depend on another form?
21. What criteria can you use to decide how to group views in an integration strategy?
22. What is a synonym in view integration?
23. What is a homonym in view integration?
24. Why do synonyms and homonyms occur when designing a database?
25. How can using forms in database design help you to detect synonyms and homonyms?

Problems

Besides the problems presented here, the case studies in this book's website provide additional practice. To supplement the examples in this chapter, Chapter 13 provides a complete database design case including view design and integration.

1. Perform form analysis for the Simple Order Form (problem 22 of Chapter 10). Your solution should include a hierarchical structure for the form, an ERD that represents the form, and design justifications. Ignore the database design in Chapter 10 when performing the analysis. In your analysis, you can assume that an order must contain at least one product.

2. Perform form analysis for the Order Form (problem 23 of Chapter 10). Your solution should include a hierarchical structure for the form, an ERD that represents the form, and design justifications. Ignore the database design in Chapter 10 when performing the analysis. Here are a number of additional points to supplement the sample form shown in problem 23 of Chapter 10:
   - In all additional form instances, customer data appears on the main form.
   - In some additional form instances, the employee data does not appear on the main form.
   - In some additional form instances, the price for the same product varies. For example, the price for product P0036566 is $169.00 on some instances and $150.00 on other instances.

- The supplier number cannot be updated on the subform. In addition, the supplier number and name are identical for all instances of the subform with the same product number.

3. Perform form analysis for the Simple Purchase Form (problem 25 of Chapter 10). Your solution should include a hierarchical structure for the form, an ERD that represents the form, and design justifications. Ignore the database design in Chapter 10 when performing the analysis. Here are a number of additional points to supplement the sample form shown in problem 25 of Chapter 10:
   - The purchase unit price can vary across form instances containing the same product number.
   - A purchase must contain at least one product.

4. Perform form analysis for the Purchase Form (problem 26 of Chapter 10). Your solution should include a hierarchical structure for the form, an ERD that represents the form, and design justifications. Ignore the database design in Chapter 10 when performing the analysis. Here are a number of additional points to supplement the sample form shown in problem 26 of Chapter 10:
   - In all additional form instances, supplier data appears on the main form.
   - The selling price can vary across form instances containing the same product number.
   - The unit cost and QOH are identical across subform instances for a given product.

5. Perform form analysis for the Supplier Form (problem 27 of Chapter 10). Your solution should include a hierarchical structure for the form, an ERD that represents the form, and design justifications. Ignore the database design in Chapter 10 when performing the analysis. In analyzing the form, you can assume that a given product only appears on one Supplier Form instance.

6. Perform parallel integration using the ERDs that you created in problems 2, 4, and 5. Ignore the database design in Chapter 10 when performing the analysis. In performing the integration, you should assume that every product on a purchase form must come from the same supplier. In addition, you should assume that a Supplier Form instance must be completed before products can be ordered or purchased.

7. Perform form analysis on the Project Staffing Form that follows. Projects have a manager, a start date, an end date, a category, a budget (hours and dollars), and a list of staff assigned. For each staff assigned, the available hours and the assigned hours are shown.

Project Staffing Form			
Project ID: PR1234 Category: Auditing Budget Hours: 170 Begin Date: 6/1/2008	Project Name: A/P testing **Manager:** Scott Jones Budget Dollars: $10,000 **End Date:** 6/30/2008		
Staff ID	Staff Name	Avail. Hours	Assigned Hours
S128	Rob Scott	10	10
S129	Sharon Store	20	5
S130	Sue Kendall	20	15

8. Perform incremental integration using the ERD from problem 7 and the Program Form that follows. A project is divided into a number of programs. Each program is assigned to one employee. An employee can be assigned to a program only if the employee has been assigned to the project.

Program Form			
Staff ID: S128 Project ID: PR1234	**Name:** Rob Scott Project Manager: Scott Jones		
Program ID	Hours	Status	Due Date
PR1234-1	10	completed	6/25/2008
PR1234-2	10	pending	6/27/2008
PR1234-3	20	pending	6/15/2008

9. Perform incremental integration using the ERD from problem 8 and the Timesheet Form that follows. The Timesheet Form allows an employee to record hours worked on various programs during a time period.

Timesheet Form			
Timesheet ID: TS100 Total Hours: 18 Staff ID: S128 Begin Date: 5/1/2008	Time Period No.: 5 **Name:** Rob Scott **End Date:** 5/31/2008		
Program ID	Hours	Pay Type	Date
PR1234-1	4	regular	5/2/2008
PR1234-1	6	overtime	5/2/2008
PR1234-2	8	regular	5/3/2008

10. Define an integration strategy for the Project Staffing, Program, and Timesheet forms. Briefly justify your integration strategy.

References for Further Study

View design and integration is covered in more detail in specialized books on database design. The best reference on view design and integration is Batini, Ceri, and Navathe (1992). Other database design books such as Nijssen and Halpin (1989) and Teorey (1999) also cover view design and integration. More details about the methodology for form analysis and view integration can be found in Choobineh, Mannino, Konsynski, and Nunamaker (1988) and Choobineh, Mannino, and Tseng (1992). Batra (1997) provides a more recent update to this work on form analysis.

13

Database Development for Student Loan Limited

Learning Objectives

This chapter applies the knowledge and skills presented in the chapters of Parts 2 to 6 to a moderate-size case. After this chapter, the student should have acquired the following knowledge and skills:

- Perform conceptual data modeling for a comparable case
- Refine an ERD using conversion and normalization for a comparable case
- Estimate a workload on a table design of moderate size
- Perform index selection for a comparable case
- Specify the data requirements for applications in a comparable case

Overview

The chapters of Parts 2 to 6 have provided knowledge and techniques about the database development process and database application development. For the database development process, you learned about using the Entity Relationship Model (Chapters 5 and 6), refining a conceptual schema through conversion and normalization (Chapters 6 and 7), the view modeling and view integration processes for large conceptual data modeling efforts (Chapter 12), and finding an efficient implementation (Chapter 8). In addition, you learned about the broad context of database development (Chapter 2). For application development, you learned about query formulation (Chapters 3 and 9), application development with views (Chapter 10), and stored procedures and triggers to customize database applications (Chapter 11).

  This chapter applies the specific development techniques of other chapters to a moderate-size case. By carefully following the case and its solution, you should reinforce your design skills, gain insights about the database development process, and obtain a model for database development of comparable cases.

  This chapter presents a case derived from discussions with information systems professionals of a large commercial processor of student loans. Servicing student loans is a rather complex business owing to the many different kinds of loans, changing government regulations, and numerous billing conditions. To adapt the case for this chapter, many details have been omitted. The database for the actual information system is more than 150 tables. The case presented here preserves the essential concepts of student loan processing but is understandable in one chapter. You should find the case challenging and informative. You might even learn how to have your student loans forgiven!

13.1 Case Description

This section describes the purpose and environment of student loan processing as well as the workflow of a proposed system for Student Loan Limited. In addition to the details in this section, Appendix 13.A contains a glossary of fields contained in the forms and reports.

13.1.1 Overview

The Guaranteed Student Loan (GSL) program was created to help students pay for their college education. GSL loans are classified according to subsidy status: (1) subsidized, in which the federal government pays interest accruing during school years and (2) unsubsidized, in which the federal government does not pay interest accruing during school years. On unsubsidized loans, the interest accruing during school years is added to the principal when repayment begins. Repayment of loans begins about six months after separation from school. A given student can receive multiple GSL loans with each loan possibly having a different interest rate and subsidy status.

  To support the GSL program, different organizations may play the role of lender, guarantor, and service provider. Students apply for loans from lenders, including banks, savings and loans, and credit unions. The U.S. Department of Education makes loans possible by guaranteeing repayment if certain conditions are met. Lenders ensure that applicants are eligible for the GSL program. The <u>service provider</u> tracks student status, calculates repayment schedules, and collects payments. The <u>guarantor</u> ensures that loans are serviced properly by monitoring the work of the service provider. If a loan enters claim (nonpayment) status and the loan has not been serviced according to Department of Education guidelines, the guarantor can become liable. To reduce their risk, lenders usually do not service or guarantee their loans. Instead, lenders typically contract with a service provider and guarantor.

Student Loan Limited is a leading service provider for GSL and other types of student loans. Student Loan Limited currently uses a legacy system with older file technology. The firm wants to switch to a client-server architecture using a relational DBMS. The new architecture should allow them to respond to new regulations easier as well as to pursue new business such as the direct lending program.

13.1.2 Flow of Work

Processing of student loans follows the pattern shown in Figure 13.1. Students apply for a loan from a lender. In the approval process, the lender usually identifies a guarantor. If the loan is approved, the student signs a promissory note that describes the interest rate and the repayment terms. After the promissory note is signed, the lender sends a loan origination form to Student Loan Limited. Student Loan Limited then disburses funds as specified in the loan origination form. Typically, funds are disbursed in each period of an academic year.

Upon separating from school (graduation or leaving school), the repayment process begins. Shortly after a student separates from school, Student Loan Limited sends a disclosure letter. A disclosure letter provides an estimate of the monthly payment required to repay an outstanding loan by the end of the payment period. The student receives one disclosure letter per note except if the notes have been consolidated into a single note. Notes are consolidated if the interest rate, subsidy status, and repayment period are similar.

Several months after separation, Student Loan Limited sends the first bill. For convenience, Student Loan Limited sends one consolidated statement even if the student has multiple outstanding loans. With most students, Student Loan Limited processes periodic bills and payments until all loans are repaid. If a student becomes delinquent, collection activities begin. If collection is successful, the student returns to the billing-payment cycle. Otherwise, the loan enters claim (default) and may be given to a collection agency.

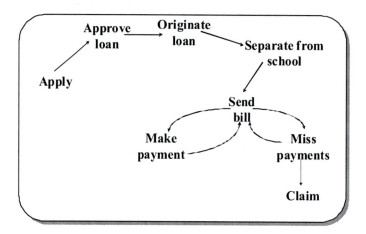

Figure 13.1: Loan Processing Work Flow

Loan Origination Form

The Loan Origination Form, an electronic document sent from a lender, triggers involvement of Student Loan Limited. Figures 13.2 and 13.3 depict sample forms with student, loan, and disbursement data. An origination form includes only one loan identified by a unique loan number. Each time a loan is approved, the lender sends a new loan origination form. The disbursement method can be electronic funds transfer (EFT) or check. If the disbursement method is EFT (Figure 13.2), the routing number, the account number, and the financial institution must be given. The disbursement plan shows the date of disbursement, the amount, and any fees. Note that the note value is the sum of the amounts disbursed plus the fees. Fees typically amount to 6 percent of the loan.

Loan Origination Form			
Loan No. L101		Date	6 Sept. 2006
Student No.		S100	
Name		Sam Student	
Address		15400 Any Street	
City, State, Zip		Anytown, USA 00999	
Phone (341) 555-2222		Date of Birth 11/11/1987	
Expected Graduation		May 2008	
Institution ID: U100		**Institution Name**: University of Colorado	
Address		1250 14th Street, Suite 700	
City, State, Zip		Denver CO 80217	
Disbursement Method		*EFT* **X** *Check*	
Routing No. R10001		Account No. A111000	
Disbursement Bank		Any Student Bank USA	
Lender No. LE100		Lender Name Any Bank USA	
Guarantor No. G100		**Guarantor Name** Any Guarantor USA	
Note Value: $10000		**Subsidized**: Yes **Rate:** 8.5%	
Disbursement Plan			
Date	Amount	Origination Fee	Guarantee Fee
30 Sept. 2006	$3,200	$100	$100
30 Dec. 2006	$3,200	$100	$100
30 Mar. 2006	$3,000	$100	$100

Figure 13.2: Sample Loan Origination Form

Loan Origination Form			
Loan No. L100		Date	7 Sept. 2007
Student No.		S100	
Name		Sam Student	
Address		15400 Any Street	
City, State, Zip		Anytown, USA 00999	
Phone (341) 555-2222		Date of Birth 11/11/1987	
Expected Graduation		May 2008	
Institution Id: U100		**Instituition Name**: University of Colorado	
Address		1250 14th Street, Suite 700	
City, State, Zip		Denver CO 80217	
Disbursement Method		*EFT* *Check* **X**	
Routing No. --		Account No. --	
Disbursement Bank		--	
Lender No. LE100		Lender Name Any Bank USA	
Guarantor No. G100		**Guarantor Name** Any Guarantor USA	
Note Value: $10000		Subsidized: No Rate: 8.0%	
		Disbursement Plan	
Date	Amount	Origination Fee	Guarantee Fee
29 Sept. 2007	$3,200	$100	$100
30 Dec. 2007	$3,200	$100	$100
28 Mar. 2007	$3,000	$100	$100

Figure 13.3: Sample Loan Origination Form

Disclosure Letter

After a student graduates but before repayment begins, Student Loan Limited is required to send disclosure letters for each outstanding loan. Typically, disclosure letters are sent about 60 days after a student separates from school. In some cases, more than one disclosure letter per loan may be sent at different times. A disclosure letter includes fields for the amount of the loan, amount of the monthly payment, number of payments, interest rate, total finance charge, and due date of the first and last payments. In the sample disclosure letter (Figure 13.4), the fields in the form letter are underlined. Student Loan Limited is required to retain copies of disclosure letters in case the guarantor needs to review the loan processing of a student.

```
Disclosure Letter

1 July 2008

Subject: Loan L101

Dear Ms. Student,

According to our records, your guaranteed student loan enters repayments status in
        September 2008.  The total amount that you borrowed was $10,000.  Your
        payment schedule includes 120 payments with an interest rate of 8.5%.  Your
        estimated finance charge is $4,877.96.  Your first payment will be due on October
        31, 2008.  Your monthly payment will be $246.37.  Your last payment is due
        September 30, 2018.

Sincerely,

Anne Administrator, Student Loan Limited
```

Figure 13.4: Sample Disclosure Letter

Statement of Account

About six months after a student separates, Student Loan Limited sends the first bill. For most students, additional bills follow monthly. In Student Loan Limited vocabulary, a bill is known as a Statement of Account. Figures 13.5 and 13.6 depict sample statements. The top half of a statement contains the unique statement number, amount due, due date, amount paid, and payment method (EFT or check). If the payment method is by check (Figure 13.5), the student returns the statement to Student Loan Limited with the check enclosed. In this case, the amount paid is completed either by the student when the bill is returned or by data entry personnel of Student Loan Limited when the statement is processed. If the payment method is EFT (Figure 13.6), the amount paid is shown on the statement along with the date that the transfer will be made. The date paid is completed by Student Loan Limited when a payment is received. The lower half of a statement lists the status of each loan. For each loan, the loan number, outstanding balance, and interest rate are shown.

```
Statement of Account
Statement No.        B100              Date              1 Oct. 2008
Student No.          S100              Name              Sam Student
Street               123 Any Street    Zip               00011
City                 Any City          State             Any State
Amount Due           $246.37           Due Date          31 Oct. 2008
Payment Method       Check X   EFT     Amount Enclosed
Loan Summary
Loan No.             Balance          Rate
L100                 $10,000          8.5%
L101                 $10,000          8.2%
For Office Use Only
Date Paid:
```

Figure 13.5: Sample Statement of Account for Check Payment

```
Statement of Account
Statement No.        B101              Date              1 Nov. 2008
Student No.          S100              Name              Sam Student
Street               123 Any Street    Zip               00011
City                 Any City          State             Any State
Amount Due           $246.37           Due Date          30 Nov. 2008
Payment Method       Check  EFT  X     Amount Enclosed
Note: $246.37 will be deducted from your account on 30 Nov. 2008
Loan Summary
Loan No.             Balance           Rate
L100                 $9,946.84         8.5%
L101                 $9,944.34         8.2%
For Office Use Only
Date Paid:
```

Figure 13.6: Sample Statement of Account for EFT Payment

After a payment is received, Student Loan Limited applies the principal amount of the payment to outstanding loan balances. The payment is apportioned among each outstanding loan according to an associated payment schedule. If a student pays more than the specified amount, the extra amount may be applied in a number of ways, such as the loan with the highest interest rate is reduced first or all outstanding loans are reduced equally. The method of applying extra amounts is determined by the Department of Education's policy. As with most government policies, it is subject to change. Applications of a payment to loan balances can be seen by comparing two consecutive statements. Figures 13.5 and 13.6 show that $53.16 of the October 2008 payment was applied to loan L100.

Loan Activity Report

After the end of each year, Student Loan Limited sends each student a report summarizing all loan activity. For each loan, the report (Figure 13.7) shows the loan balance at the beginning of the year, the total amount applied to reduce the principal, the total interest paid, and the loan balance at the end of the year. Student Loan Limited is required to retain copies of loan activity reports in case the guarantor needs to review the loan processing of a student.

```
Loan Activity Report
                                        Date              1 Feb. 2009
Student No.          S100              Name              Sam Student
Street               123 Any Street    Zip               00011
City                 Any City          State             Any State
Payment Summary for 2005
Loan No.     Beg. Balance   Principal        Interest         Ending
                                                              Balance
L100         $10,000        160.60           211.37           $9,839.40
L101         $10,000        168.12           203.85           $9,831.88
For Office Use Only
Date Paid:
```

Figure 13.7: Sample Loan Activity Report

New Technology

To reduce paper, Student Loan Limited is interested in imaging the documents (disclosure letters and loan activity reports) required by guarantors. After imaging the documents, they would like to store recent documents in the student loan database and older documents in archival storage.

13.2 Conceptual Data Modeling

The conceptual data modeling phases use the incremental integration approach because the case is not too large and the forms are related. Incremental integration begins with the loan origination form because it triggers involvement of Student Loan Limited with a loan.

13.2.1 ERD for the Loan Origination Form

The Loan Origination Form contains two nodes, as shown in Figure 13.8. The child node contains the repeating disbursement fields. The *Loan* entity type is the center of the ERD as shown in Figure 13.9. The surrounding entity types (*Guarantor, Lender, Institution*, and *Student*) and associated relationships are derived from the parent node. The minimum cardinality is 0 from *Loan* to *Guarantor* because some loans do not have a guarantor (lender performs role). The *DisburseLine* entity type and associated relationship are derived from the child node. Table 13-1 shows assumptions corresponding to the annotations in Figure 13.9.

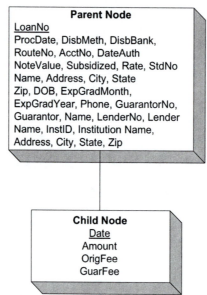

Figure 13.8: Structure of the Loan Origination Form

446

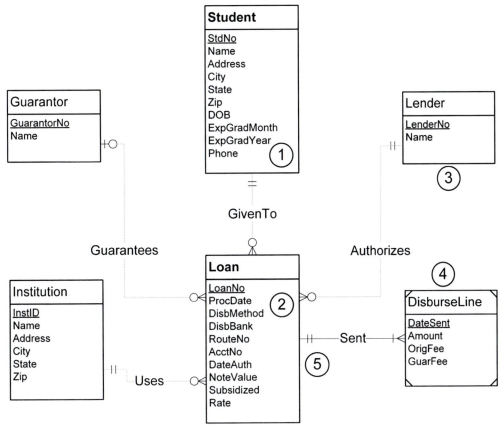

Figure 13.9: ERD for the Loan Origination Form

Table 13-1: Assumptions for the ERD in Figure 13.9

Annotation Number	Explanation
1	The expected graduation fields can be combined into one field or kept as two fields.
2	Routing number (*RouteNo*), account number (*AcctNo*), and disbursement bank (*DisbBank*) are required if the disbursement method is EFT. Otherwise, they are not used.
3	There would probably be other data about lenders and guarantors that is stored. Because the form only shows the identifying number and name, the ERD does not include extra attributes.
4	*DisburseLine* is identification dependent on *Loan*. Because *DisburseLine.DateSent* is a local key, there cannot be two disbursements of the same loan on the same date. The primary key of *DisburseLine* is a concatenation of *LoanNo* and *DateSent*.
5	The sum of the amount, the origination fee, and the guarantee fee in the disbursement plan should equal the note value.

13.2.2 Incremental Integration after Adding the Disclosure Letter

The disclosure letter contains only a single node (Figure 13.10) because it has no repeating groups. Figure 13.11 shows the integrated ERD, with corresponding assumptions shown in Table 13-2. The ERD in Figure 13.11 assumes that images can be stored in the database. Therefore, the particular fields of a disclosure letter are not stored. The unique *LetterNo* field has been added as a convenient identifier of a disclosure letter. If images cannot be stored in the database, some of the fields in the disclosure letter may need to be stored because they are difficult to compute.

447

```
                    Parent Node
              LoanNo, DateSent
              StdName, RepayDate,
              AmtBorrowed, NumPayments,
              IntRate, EstFinCharge
              FirstPayDate, MonthPayment,
              LastPayDate
```

Figure 13.10: Structure of the Disclosure Letter

Table 13-2: Assumptions for the ERD in Figure 13.11

Annotation Number	Explanation
1	The relationship between *DiscLetter* and *Loan* allows multiple letters per loan. As stated in the case, multiple disclosure letters may be sent for the same loan.
2	The *Image* field contains a scanned image of the letter. The guarantor may require a copy of the letter if the loan is audited. As an alternative to storing the image, an indicator of the physical location could be stored if imaging technology is not used.
3	The minimum cardinality of 0 is needed because a payment plan is not created until a student has separated from school.

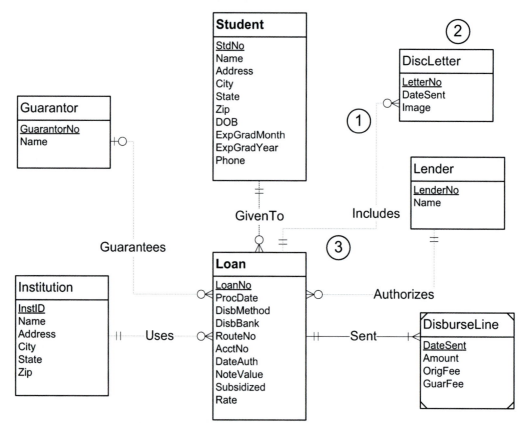

Figure 13.11: ERD after Adding the Disclosure Letter

13.2.3 Incremental Integration after Adding the Statement of Account

The statement of account contains both parent and child nodes (Figure 13.12) because it has a repeating group. Figure 13.13 shows the integrated ERD with corresponding assumptions shown in Table 13-3. The *Applied* relationship in Figure 13.13 represents the parent-child relationship in the form hierarchy. The minimum cardinality is 0 from *Loan* to *Statement* because a loan does not have any amounts applied until after it enters payment status.

448

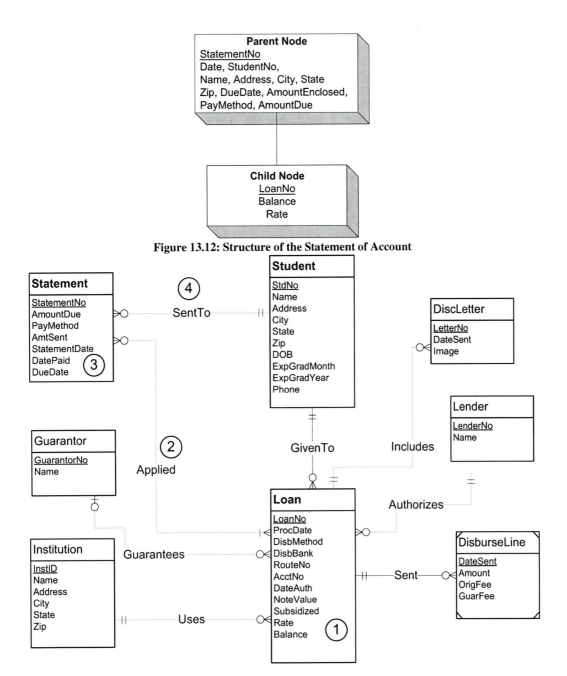

Parent Node
StatementNo
Date, StudentNo,
Name, Address, City, State
Zip, DueDate, AmountEnclosed,
PayMethod, AmountDue

Child Node
LoanNo
Balance
Rate

Figure 13.12: Structure of the Statement of Account

Statement
StatementNo
AmountDue
PayMethod
AmtSent
StatementDate
DatePaid ③
DueDate

④ SentTo

Student
StdNo
Name
Address
City
State
Zip
DOB
ExpGradMonth
ExpGradYear
Phone

DiscLetter
LetterNo
DateSent
Image

Lender
LenderNo
Name

Guarantor
GuarantorNo
Name

② Applied

GivenTo

Includes

Authorizes

Institution
InstID
Name
Address
City
State
Zip

Guarantees

Uses

Loan
LoanNo
ProcDate
DisbMethod
DisbBank
RouteNo
AcctNo
DateAuth
NoteValue
Subsidized
Rate ①
Balance

Sent

DisburseLine
DateSent
Amount
OrigFee
GuarFee

Figure 13.13: ERD after Adding the Statement of Account

449

Table 13-3: Assumptions for the ERD in Figure 13.13

Annotation Number	Explanation
1	*Balance* is added as a field to reflect the loan summary on a statement. The balance reflects the last payment made on a loan.
2	The *Applied* relationship is created at the same time as the statement. However, the principal and interest fields are not updated until after a payment is received. The attributes (*Principal*, *Interest*, *CumPrincipal*, and *CumInterest*) of the applied relationship are not shown in the diagram to reduce clutter. *CumPrinicipal* and *CumInterest* are derived columns that facilitate the Loan Activity Report.
3	If the payment method is EFT, other attributes such as routing number and account number might be needed in *Statement*. Since these attributes are not shown in a statement, they are omitted from the *Statement* entity type.
4	The *SentTo* relationship is redundant. It can be derived from the *Applied* and *GivenTo* relationships. If time to derive the *SentTo* relationship is not onerous, it can be dropped.

13.2.4 Incremental Integration after Adding the Loan Activity Report

The loan activity report contains both parent and child nodes (Figure 13.14) because it has a repeating group. Figure 13.15 shows the integrated ERD with corresponding assumptions shown in Table 13-4. Like the ERD for the disclosure letter (Figure 13.11), the ERD in Figure 13.15 assumes that images can be stored in the database. Therefore, the particular fields of a loan activity report are not stored. The unique *ReportNo* field has been added as a convenient identifier of an activity report. If images cannot be stored in the database, some of the fields in the loan activity report may need to be stored because they are difficult to compute.

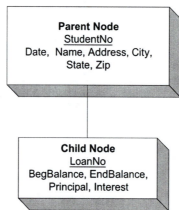

Parent Node
StudentNo
Date, Name, Address, City, State, Zip

Child Node
LoanNo
BegBalance, EndBalance, Principal, Interest

Figure 13.14: Structure of the Loan Activity Report

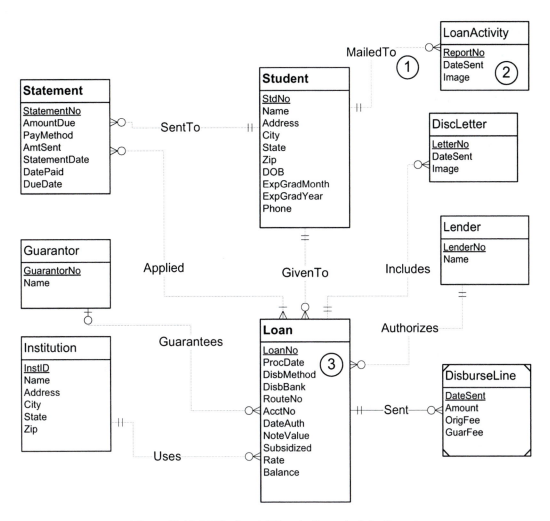

Figure 13.15: ERD after Adding the Loan Activity Report

Table 13-4: Assumptions for the ERD in Figure 13.15

Annotation Number	Explanation
1	The *LoanActivity* entity type is not directly related to the *Loan* entity type because it is assumed that an activity report summarizes all loans of a student.
2	The *Image* field contains a scanned image of the report. The guarantor may require a copy of the report if the loan is audited. As an alternative to storing the image, an indicator of the physical location could be stored if imaging technology is not used.
3	To make the calculations easier, fields for annual principal and interest could be added to the *Loan* entity type. These fields would be updated after every payment is received. These fields should be considered during physical database design.

13.3 Refining the Conceptual Schema

After building a conceptual ERD, you refine it by applying conversion rules to produce an initial table design and using normalization rules to remove excessive redundancies from your initial table design. This section describes refinements of the conceptual ERD that produce a good table design for Student Loan Limited

13.3.1 Schema Conversion

The conversion can be performed using the first four rules (Chapter 6) as listed in Table 13-5. The optional 1-M relationship rule (Rule 5) could be applied to the *Guarantees* relationship. However, the number of loans without guarantors appears small so the 1-M relationship rule is used instead. The generalization hierarchy rule (Rule 6) is not needed because the ERD (Figure 13.9) does not have any generalization hierarchies. The conversion result is shown in Table 13-6 (primary keys underlined and foreign keys italicized) and Figure 13.16 (graphical depiction of tables, primary keys, and foreign keys).

Table 13-5: Rules Used to Convert the ERD of Figure 13.15

Conversion Rule	Objects	Comments
Entity type rule	Student, Statement, Loan, DiscLetter, LoanActivity, Lender, Guarantor, Institution, DisburseLine tables	Primary keys in each table are identical to entity types except for *DisburseLine*
1-M relationship rule	Loan.StdNo, Loan.GuarantorNo, Loan.LenderNo, LoanActivity.StdNo, DiscLetter.LoanNo, Statement.StdNo, DisburseLine.LoanNo, Loan.InstID	Foreign key columns and referential integrity constraints added
M-N relationship rule	Applies table	Combined primary key: *StatementNo, LoanNo*
Identification dependency rule	Primary key (*LoanNo, DateSent*)	*LoanNo* added to primary key of *DisburseLine* table

Table 13-6: List of Tables after Conversion

Student(<u>StdNo</u>, Name, Address, Phone, City, State, Zip, ExpGradMonth, ExpGradYear, DOB)
Lender(<u>LenderNo</u>, Name)
Guarantor(<u>GuarantorNo</u>, Name)
Instituition(<u>InstID</u>, Name, Address, City, State, Zip)
Loan(<u>LoanNo</u>, ProcDate, DisbMethod, DisbBank, RouteNo, AcctNo, DateAuth, NoteValue, Subsidized, Rate, Balance, *StdNo*, *InstID*, *GuarantorNo*, *LendNo*)
DiscLetter(<u>LetterNo</u>, DateSent, Image, *LoanNo*)
LoanActivity(<u>ReportNo</u>, DateSent, Image, *StdNo*)
DisburseLine(*<u>LoanNo</u>*, <u>DateSent</u>, Amount, OrigFee, GuarFee)
Statement(<u>StatementNo</u>, AmtDue, PayMethod, AmtSent, StatementDate, DatePaid, DueDate, *StdNo*)
Applied(*<u>LoanNo</u>*, *<u>StatementNo</u>*, Principal, Interest, CumPrincipal, CumInterest)

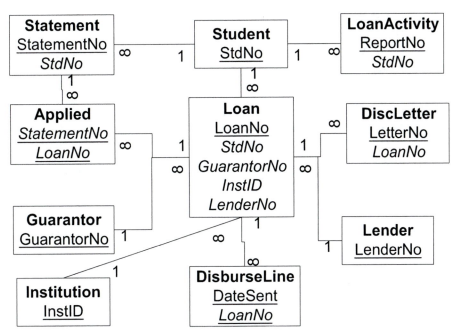

Figure 13.16: Relational Model Diagram for the Initial Table Design

13.3.2 Normalization

The tables resulting from the conversion process may still have redundancy. To eliminate redundancy, you should list the FDs for each table and apply the normalization rules or the simple synthesis procedure. Table 13-7 lists the FDs for each table.

Table 13-7: List of FDs

Table	FDs
Student	StdNo → Name, Address, City, State, Zip, ExpGradMonth, ExpGradYear, DOB, Phone Zip → State
Lender	LenderNo → Name
Guarantor	GuarantorNo → Name
Institution	InstID → Name, Address, City, State, Zip; Zip → City, State
Loan	LoanNo → ProcDate, DisbMethod, DisbBank, RouteNo, AcctNo, DateAuth, NoteValue, Subsidized, Rate, Balance, StdNo, InstID, GuarantorNo, LenderNo; RouteNo → DisbBank
Discletter	LetterNo → DateSent, Image, LoanNo; LoanNo, DateSent → LetterNo, Image
LoanReport	ReportNo → DateSent, Image, StdNo; StdNo, DateSent → ReportNo, Image
DisburseLine	LoanNo, DateSent → Amount, OrigFee, GuarFee
Statement	StatementNo → AmtDue, PayMethod, AmtSent, StatementDate, DatePaid, DueDate, StdNo
Applied	LoanNo, StatementNo → Principal, Interest, CumPrincipal, CumInterest

Because most FDs involve a primary key on the left-hand side, there is not much normalization work. However, the *Loan*, *Student*, and *Institution* tables violate BCNF as these tables have determinants that are not candidate keys. The *DiscLetter* and *LoanReport* tables do not violate BCNF because all determinants are candidate keys. For the tables violating BCNF, here are explanations and options about splitting the tables:

- *Student* is not in BCNF because of the FD with *Zip*. If Student Loan Limited wants to update zip codes independently of students, a separate table should be added.

453

- *Loan* is not in BCNF because of the FD involving *RouteNo*. If Student Loan Limited wants to update banks independently of loans, a separate table should be created.
- *Institution* is not in BCNF because of the FDs with *Zip*. If Student Loan Limited wants to update zip codes independently of institutions, a separate table should be added. Only one zip table is needed for both *Student* and *Institution*.

In the revised table design (Figure 13.17), the *ZipCode* table and the *Bank* table are added to remove redundancies. Appendix 13.B shows CREATE TABLE statements with the revised list of tables. Delete and update actions are also included in Appendix 13.B. For most foreign keys, deletions are restricted because the corresponding parent and child tables are not closely related. For example, deletions are restricted for the foreign key *Loan.InstID* because the *Institution* and *Loan* tables are not closely related. In contrast, deletions cascade for the foreign key *DisburseLine.LoanNo* because disbursement lines are identification dependent on the related loan. Deletions also cascade for the foreign key *Applied.StatementNo* because applied rows represent statement lines that have no meaning without the statement. The update action of most foreign keys was set to cascade to allow easy changing of primary key values.

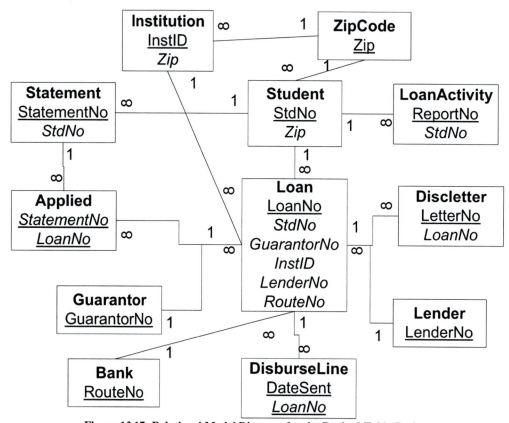

Figure 13.17: Relational Model Diagram for the Revised Table Design

13.4 Physical Database Design and Application Development

After producing a good table design, you are ready to implement the database. This section describes physical database design decisions including index selection, derived data, and denormalization for the Student Loan Limited database. Before describing these decisions, table and application profiles are defined. After physical database design decisions are presented, application development of some forms and reports is depicted as a cross-check on database development.

13.4.1 Application and Table Profiles

To clarify anticipated usage of the database, the documents described in Section 13.1 are split into database access applications as summarized in Table 13-8. Three separate applications are associated with the Loan Origination Form. Verifying data involves retrievals to ensure that the student, lender, institution, and guarantor exist. If a student does not exist, a new row is added. Creating a loan involves inserting a row in the *Loan* table and multiple rows in the *DisburseLine* table. For the other documents, there is an application to create the document and retrieve the document. For statements of account, there is also an application to update the *Applied* and *Loan* tables when payments are received.

Table 13-8: Application Characteristics

Application	Tables	Conditions
Verify data (for loan origination)	Student, Lender, Institution, Guarantor	StdNo = $X; LenderNo = $Y; InstID = $Z; GuarantorNo = $W
Create loan (for loan origination)	Loan, DisburseLine	1 row inserted in *Loan*; multiple rows inserted in *DisburseLine*
Create student (for loan origination)	Student	1 row inserted
Create disclosure letter	Student, Loan, DiscLetter	Insert row in *DiscLetter*; retrieve rows from *Student* and *Loan* (*LoanNo* = $X)
Display disclosure letter	DiscLetter	LoanNo = $X
Create loan activity report	Student, Loan, LoanActivity, Applied, Statement	Insert row in *LoanActivity*; retrieve rows from *Student* (*StdNo* = $X) and *Statement* (*DatePaid* in past year)
Display loan activity report	LoanActivity	*StdNo* = $X
Create statement of account	Statement	1 row inserted in *Statement*; multiple rows inserted in *Applied*
Display statement of account	Statement, Student, Applied, Loan	*StdNo* = $X AND *DateSent* = $Y; sometimes using *StatementNo* = $Z
Apply payment	Applied, Statement, Loan	*Applied* rows updated; *LoanNo* = $X AND *StatementNo* = $Y; *Balance* updated in the *Loan* table

To make physical database design decisions, the relative importance of applications must be specified. The frequencies in Table 13-9 assume 100,000 new loans per year and 100,000 students in repayment per year. The loan origination applications and the statement of account applications dominate the workload. The coarse frequencies (per year) are sufficient to indicate the relative importance of applications. A finer specification (e.g., by month or day) may be needed to schedule work such as to arrange for batch processing instead of online processing. For example, applications involving loan origination forms may be processed in batch instead of online.

Table 13-9: Application Frequencies

Application	Frequency	Comments
Verify data	100,000/year	Most activity at beginning of term
Create loan	100,000/year	Most activity at beginning of term
Create student	20,000/year	Most students are repeat
Create disclosure letter	50,000/year	Spread evenly throughout year
Display disclosure letter	5,000/year	Spread evenly throughout year
Create loan activity report	30,000/year	End-of-year processing
Display loan activity report	5,000/year	Spread evenly throughout year
Create statement of account	100,000/year	Once per month
Display statement of account	10,000/year	Spread evenly throughout year
Apply payment	100,000/year	Spread evenly throughout month

After defining the application profiles, table profiles can be defined. The volume of modification activity (inserts, updates, deletes) can help in the estimation of table profiles. In addition, you should use statistics from existing systems and interviews with key application personnel to help make the estimates. Table 13-10 provides an overview of the profiles. More detail about column distributions and relationship distributions can be added after the system is partially populated.

Table 13-10: Table Profiles

Table	Number of Rows	Column (Number of Unique Values)
Student	100,000	*StdNo* (PK), *Name* (99,000), *Address* (90,000), *City* (1,000), *Zip* (1,000), *DOB* (365), *ExpGradMonth* (12), *ExpGradYear* (10)
Loan	300,000	*LoanNo* (PK), *ProcDate* (350), *DisbMethod* (3), *DisbBank* (3,000), *RouteNo* (3,000), *AcctNo* (90,000), *DateAuth* (350), *NoteValue* (1,000), *Subsidized* (2), *Rate* (1,000), *Balance* (10,000), *StdNo* (100,000), *InstID* (2,000), *GuarantorNo* (100), *LenderNo* (2,000)
Institution	2,000	*InstID* (PK), *Name* (2,000), *Address* (2,000), *City* (500), *State* (50), *Zip* (500)
DiscLetter	1,000,000	*LetterNo* (PK), *DateSent* (350), *Image* (1,000,000), *LoanNo* (300,000)
Statement	2,000,000	*StatementNo* (PK), *AmtDue* (100,000), *PayMethod* (3), *AmtSent* (200,000), *StatementDate* (350), *DatePaid* (350), *DueDate* (350), *StdNo* (100,000)
Guarantor	100	GuarantorNo (PK), Name (100)
Bank	3,000	*RouteNo* (PK), *DisbBank* (3,000)
DisburseLine	900,000	*LoanNo* (300,000), *DateSent* (350), *Amount* (5,000), *OrigFee* (5,000), *GuarFee* (5,000)
Applied	6,000,000	*LoanNo* (300,000), *StatementNo* (2,000,000), *Principal* (100,000), *Interest* (1,000,000)
ZipCode	1,000	*Zip* (PK), *State* (50)
Lender	2,000	*LenderNo* (PK), *Name* (2,000)

13.4.2 Index Selection

You can select indexes using the application profiles and the rules described in Chapter 8. To clarify the selection process, let us consider retrieval needs before manipulation needs. Recall that rules 1 through 5 (Chapter 8) involve the selection of indexes for retrieval needs. The following list discusses useful index choices for retrieval purposes:

- Indexes on the primary keys of the *Student*, *Lender*, *Guarantor*, *Institution*, *DiscLetter*, *LoanActivity*, *Statement*, and *Bank* tables support the verify loan, display disclosure letter, display activity report, and display statement of account applications.

- A nonclustering index on student name may be a good choice to support the retrieval of statements of account and the loan activity reports.
- To support joins, nonclustering indexes on foreign keys *Loan.StdNo*, *Statement.StdNo*, *Applied.LoanNo*, and *Applied.StatementNo* may be useful. For example, an index on *Loan.StdNo* facilitates joining the *Student* and the *Loan* tables when given a specific *StdNo* value.

Because the *Applied* and *Loan* tables have lots of modifications, you should proceed with caution about indexes on the component fields. Some mitigating factors may offset the impact of the modification activity, however. The updates in the apply payment application do not affect the foreign key fields in these tables. Batch processing can reduce the impact of the insertions on the *Loan* and the *Applied* tables. The create loan and create statement of account applications may be performed in batch because loan origination forms are received in batch and statements of account can be produced in batch. If the indexes are too much of a burden for batch processing, it may be possible to drop the indexes before batch processing and re-create them after finishing.

Table 13-11 shows index choices based on the previous discussion. The choices assume that foreign key indexes on the *Applied* and the *Loan* tables do not impede insertion activity. Further investigation is necessary to determine the impact of indexes on insertions in the *Loan* and the *Applied* tables.

Table 13-11: Index Selections for the Revised Table Design

Column	Index Kind	Rule
Student.StdNo	Clustering	1
Student.Name	Nonclustering	3
Statement.StatementNo	Clustering	1
DiscLetter.LetterNo	Clustering	1
Loan.LoanNo	Clustering	1
Institution.InstID	Clustering	1
Guarantor.GuarantorNo	Clustering	1
Lender.LenderNo	Clustering	1
LoanActivity.ReportNo	Clustering	1
ZipCode.Zip	Clustering	1
Bank.RouteNo	Clustering	1
Statement.StdNo	Nonclustering	2
Loan.StdNo	Nonclustering	2
Applied.StatementNo	Clustering	2
Applied.LoanNo	Nonclustering	2

13.4.3 Derived Data and Denormalization Decisions

There are some derived data in the revised table design. The *CumPrincipal* and *CumInterest* columns are derived in the *Applied* table. The *DiscLetter* and the *LoanActivity* tables have lots of derived data in the *Image* columns. In all of these cases, the derived data seem justified because of the difficulty of computing it.

Denormalization may be useful for some foreign keys. If users frequently request the name along with the foreign key, denormalization may be useful for the foreign keys in the *Loan* table. For example, storing both *LenderNo* and *Lender.Name* in the *Loan* table violates BCNF, but it may reduce joins between the *Loan* and the *Lender* tables. The usage of the database should be monitored carefully to determine whether the *Loan* table should be denormalized by adding name columns in addition to the *LenderNo*, *GuarantorNo*, *InstID*, and *RouteNo* columns. If performance can be significantly improved, denormalization is a good idea because the *Lender*, *Guarantor*, *Institution*, and *Bank* tables are relatively static.

13.4.4 Other Implementation Decisions

There are a number of implementation decisions that involve the database development process. Because these decisions can have a large impact on the success of the loan servicing system, they are highlighted in this section.

- Smooth conversion from the old system to the new system is an important issue. One impediment to smooth conversion is processing volumes. Sometimes processing volumes in a new system can be much larger than in the old system. One way to alleviate potential performance problems is to execute the old and the new systems in parallel with more work shifted to the new system over time.
- An important part of the conversion process involves the old data. Converting the old data to the new format is not usually difficult except for data quality concerns. Sometimes, the poor quality of old data causes many rejections in the conversion process. The conversion process needs to be sensitive to rejecting poor-quality data because rejections can require extensive manual corrections.
- The size of the image data (loan activity reports and disclosure letters) can impact the performance of the database. Archival of the image data can improve performance for images that are infrequently retrieved.

13.4.5 Application Development

To complete the development of the database, you should implement the forms and reports used in the database design requirements. Implementing the forms and reports provides a cross-check on the conceptual and logical design phases. Your table design should support queries for each form and report. Often, limitations in a table design appear as a result of implementing forms and reports. After implementing the forms and reports, you should use them under typical workloads to ensure adequate performance. It is likely that you will need to adjust your physical design to achieve acceptable performance.

This section demonstrates implementation of the data requirements for some of the forms and reports in Section 13.1 along with a trigger for maintenance of derived data. The implementation of the data requirements for the other forms and reports are left as end-of-chapter problems.

Data Requirements for the Loan Origination Form

The following list provides answers to the five data requirement steps including the main form and subform queries. For reference, Figures 13.2 and 13.3 show instances of the Loan Origination Form.

- Identify the 1-M relationship manipulated by the form: The 1-M relationship connects the *Loan* table to the *DisburseLine* table.
- Identify the join or linking columns for the 1-M relationship: *Loan.LoanNo* and *DisburseLine.LoanNo* are the linking columns.
- Identify the other tables in the main form and the subform: In addition to the *Loan* table, the main form contains the *Student* table, the *Instituition* table, the *Bank* table, the *Lender* table, and the *Guarantor* table. The subform does not contain additional tables beyond the *DisburseLine* table.
- Determine the updatability of the tables in the hierarchical form: The *Loan* table in the main form and the *DisburseLine* table in the subform are updatable. The other tables are read-only. Separate forms should be provided to update the other tables that appear in the main form.
- Write the main form query: The one-sided outer join with the *Bank* table preserves the Loan table. The one-sided outer join allows the bank data optionally to appear on the form. The bank data appears on the form when the disbursement method is electronic. The SELECT statement retrieves some additional columns that do not appear on the form such as *Bank.RouteNo*. These additional columns do not affect the updatability of the query.

```
SELECT Loan.*, Student.*, Institution.*, Bank.*,
       Institution.*, Lender.*
FROM (((( Student INNER JOIN Loan
       ON Student.StdNo = Loan.StdNo )
   INNER JOIN Institution
       ON Institution.InstId = Loan.InstId )
   INNER JOIN Lender ON Lender.LenderNo = Loan.LenderNo )
   INNER JOIN Guarantor
       ON Guarantor.GuarantorNo = Loan.GuarantorNo )
   LEFT JOIN Bank ON Bank.RouteNo = Loan.RouteNo
```

Write the subform query:

        SELECT DisburseLine.*
        FROM DisburseLine

Data Requirements for the Loan Activity Report

The report query is difficult to formulate because each line of the Loan Activity Report shows the beginning and the ending loan balances. Two rows in the *Applied* and the *Statement* tables must be used to calculate the beginning and the ending loan balances. The ending loan balance is calculated as the note value of the loan minus the cumulative principal payment reflected on the last *Applied* row in the report year. The beginning loan balance is calculated as the note value of the loan minus the cumulative principal payment reflected on the last *Applied* row in the year prior to the report year. To determine the last *Applied* row for a given year, the *Applied* table is joined to the *Statement* row having the largest *DatePaid* in the year. The nested queries in the WHERE clause retrieve the *Statement* rows with the maximum *DatePaid* for the report year and the year prior to the report. The identifier *EnterReportYear* is the parameter for the report year. The **Year** function is a Microsoft Access function that retrieves the year part of a date.

```
SELECT Student.StdNo, Name, Address, Phone, City, State,
       Zip, Loan.LoanNo, NoteValue, ACurr.CumPrincipal,
       ACurr.CumInterest, APrev.CumPrincipal
 FROM Student, Loan, Applied ACurr, Applied APrev,
       Statement SCurr, Statement SPrev
 WHERE Student.StdNo = Loan.StdNo
   AND Loan.LoanNo = SCurr.LoanNo
   AND SCurr.StatementNo = ACurr.StatementNo
   AND ACurr.LoanNo = Loan.LoanNo
   AND SCurr.DatePaid =
   ( SELECT MAX(DatePaid) FROM Statement
      WHERE Year(DatePaid) = EnterReportYear )
   AND Loan.LoanNo = SPrev.LoanNo
   AND SPrev.StatementNo = APrev.StatementNo
   AND APrev.LoanNo = Loan.LoanNo
   AND SPrev.DatePaid =
   ( SELECT MAX(DatePaid) FROM Statement
      WHERE Year(DatePaid) = EnterReportYear - 1 )
```

This report query demonstrates the need for the computed columns *CumPrincipal* and *CumInterest*. The report query would be very difficult to formulate without these derived columns.

Derived Data Maintenance

AFTER ROW triggers can be defined to maintain the derived columns in the *Loan* and the *Applied* tables. The code below shows an Oracle trigger to maintain the *Loan.Balance* column after creating an *Applied* row. The triggers to maintain the *Applied.CumPrincipal* and *Applied.CumInterest* columns would involve mutating table considerations in Oracle. Because solutions to triggers with mutating tables were not shown in Chapter 11, the solution to maintain these columns will not be shown here either. The solution involves either an INSTEAD OF trigger with a view or an Oracle package with a collection of triggers.

```
CREATE OR REPLACE TRIGGER tr_Applied_IA
-- This trigger updates the Balance column
-- of the related Loan row.
AFTER INSERT
ON Applied
FOR EACH ROW
BEGIN
   UPDATE Loan
     SET Balance = Balance - :NEW.Principal
     WHERE LoanNo = :NEW.LoanNo;
EXCEPTION
  WHEN OTHERS THEN
     RAISE_Application_Error(-20001, 'Database error');
END;
```

Closing Thoughts

This chapter presented a moderate-size case study as a capstone of the database development process. The Student Loan Limited case described a significant subset of commercial student loan processing including accepting loans from lenders, notifying students of repayment, billing and processing payments, and reporting loan status. The case solution integrated techniques presented in the chapters of Parts 2 to 6. The solution depicted models and documentation produced in the conceptual modeling, logical database design, and physical database design phases as well as data requirements for forms, reports, and triggers.

After careful reading of this chapter, you are ready to tackle database development for a real organization. You are encouraged to work cases available through the textbook's website to solidify your understanding of the database development process. This case, although presenting a larger, more integrated problem than the other chapters, is still not comparable to performing database development for a real organization. For a real organization, requirements are often ambiguous, incomplete, and inconsistent. Deciding on the database boundary and modifying the database design in response to requirement changes are crucial to long-term success. Monitoring the operation of the database allows you to improve performance as dictated by database usage. These challenges make database development a stimulating intellectual activity.

Review Concepts

- Guaranteed Student Loan (GSL) program providing subsidized and unsubsidized loans
- Roles of students, lenders, service providers, guarantors, and government regulators in the GSL program
- Workflow for processing student loans involving loan applications, loan approval, load origination, separation from school, and loan repayment
- Important documents for loan processing: the loan origination form, the disclosure letter, the statement of account, and the loan activity report
- Conceptual data modeling: incremental integration strategy for the loan origination form, the disclosure letter, the statement of account, and the loan activity report
- Converting the ERD using the basic conversion rules
- Removing normal form violations in the *Loan*, *Student*, and *Institution* tables
- Specification of table and application profiles for physical database design

- Applying the index selection rules for clustering indexes on primary keys and nonclustering indexes on foreign keys
- Using denormalization for the *Loan* table
- Specifying data requirements for the loan origination form and the loan activity report to cross-check the result of the conceptual data modeling and logical design phases
- Writing triggers to maintain derived data in the *Loan* and *Applied* tables

Questions

1. Why is the student application process not considered in the conceptual design phase?
2. Why is the incremental integration approach used to analyze the requirements?
3. Why is the Loan Origination Form analyzed first?
4. How is the note value field on the Loan Origination Form related to other data on the form?
5. Explain how the 1-M relationship in the Loan Origination Form is represented in the ERD of Figure 13.9.
6. What is the primary key of the *DisburseLine* entity type in Figure 13.9?
7. What data are contained in the image attribute of the *DiscLetter* entity type in Figure 13.11?
8. Explain how the 1-M relationship in the statement of account is represented in the ERD of Figure 13.13.
9. Why is the optional 1-M relationship rule (Rule 5 of Chapter 9) not used to convert the ERD of Figure 13.15?
10. Explain how the *Authorizes* relationship in Figure 13.15 is converted in Figure 13.16.
11. Explain how the identification dependency in Figure 13.15 is converted in Figure 13.16.
12. Explain how the *Applied* relationship in Figure 13.15 is converted in Figure 13.16.
13. Explain why the *DiscLetter* table is in BCNF.
14. Discuss a possible justification for violating BCNF with the *Student* table depicted in Table 13-7.
15. Why decompose the documents into multiple database applications as depicted in Table 13-8?
16. Explain the difference between batch and online processing of loan origination forms. Why is batch processing feasible for loan origination forms?
17. How can batch processing reduce the impact of maintaining indexes?
18. Explain why a clustered index is recommended for the *Applied.StatementNo* column.
19. Explain why a nonclustered index is recommended for the *Applied.LoanNo* column.
20. Explain the relationship between the *Loan.NoteValue* column and the *Amount, OrigFee,* and *GuarFee* columns in the *DisburseLine* table.

Problems

The following problems involve extensions to the Student Loan Limited case. For additional cases of similar complexity, visit this book's website.

1. Use the optional 1-M relationship rule to convert the *Guarantees* relationship in Figure 13.15. Modify the relational model diagram in Figure 13.16 with the conversion change.
2. Simplify the ERD for the loan origination form (Figure 13.9) by combining the *Loan* entity type with entity types associated with a loan (*Lender* and *Guarantor*). What transformation (see Chapter 6) is used to combine the entity types? What transformation can be used to split bank attributes (*RouteNo* and *DisbBank*) into a separate entity type?
3. Modify the ERD in Figure 13.15 to reflect a change in the relationship between an activity report and associated loans of a student. The assumption in the case is that an activity report summarizes all of a student's loans. The new assumption is that an activity report may summarize only a subset of a student's loans.
4. Explain how denormalization can be used to combine the *LoanActivity* and the *Student* tables. Do the same for the *DiscLetter* and the *Loan* tables.
5. Student Loan Limited has decided to enter the direct lending business. A direct lending loan is similar to a guaranteed student loan except there is neither a lender nor a guarantor

for a direct lending loan. Due to the lack of a lender and guarantor, there are no origination and guarantee fees. However, there is a service fee of about 3 percent per note value. In addition, a student may choose income-contingent repayment after separating from school. If a student chooses income contingent repayment, the terms of the loan and payment amount are revised.

    a.   Modify the ERD in Figure 13.15 to reflect these new requirements.

    b.   Convert the ERD changes to a table design. Show your conversion result as a modification to the relational database diagram in Figure 13.16.

6.   Student Loan Limited cannot justify the expense of imaging software and hardware. Therefore, the database design must be modified. The *Image* columns in the *DiscLetter* and the *LoanActivity* tables cannot be stored. Instead, the data stored inside the image columns must be stored or computed on demand.

    a.   Make recommendations for storing or computing the underlined fields in a disclosure letter. Modify the table design as necessary. Consider update and retrieval trade-offs in your recommendation.

    b.   Make recommendations for storing or computing the fields in a loan activity report. Modify the table design as necessary. Consider update and retrieval trade-offs in your recommendation.

7.   Write a SELECT statement to indicate the data requirements for the disclosure letter depicted in Figure 13.4.

8.   Use the five steps presented in Chapter 10 to specify the data requirements for the Statement of Account form depicted in Figure 13.5.

9.   What are issues involving enforcement of the relationship between the *Loan.NoteValue* column and the *Amount*, *OrigFee*, and *GuarFee* columns in the *DisburseLine* table?

10.   Why would an Oracle trigger to maintain the *Applied.CumPrincipal* and *Applied.CumInterest* columns involve mutating table considerations?

Appendix 13.A: Glossary of Form and Report Fields

Appendix 13.A provides a brief description of the fields found on the documents presented in Section 13.1. The field names are the captions from the associated document.

Loan Origination Form

Loan No.: unique alphanumeric value that identifies a Loan Origination Form
Date: date that the Loan Origination Form was completed
Student No.: unique alphanumeric value that identifies a student
Name: name of student applying
Address: street address of student applying
City, State, Zip: concatenation of the student's city, state, and zip code
Phone: phone number including area code of the student applying
Date of Birth: birth date of student applying
Expected Graduation: month and year of expected graduation
Institution ID: federal identification number of the university or school
Institution Name: name of the university or school
Address: street address of the university or school
City, State, Zip: concatenation of the institution's city, state, and zip code
Disbursement Method: the method used to distribute funds to the student applicant; the values can be EFT (electronic funds transfer) or check.
Routing No.: unique alphanumeric value that identifies a bank to disburse the funds; only used if disbursement method is EFT.
Account No.: unique alphanumeric value that identifies an account of the student applicant; Account No. is only guaranteed to be unique within the student's bank (identified by routing number).
Disbursement Bank: name of the bank from which the funds are disbursed; used only if the disbursement method is EFT.
Lender No.: unique alphanumeric value that identifies the financial institution lending funds to the student applicant.
Lender Name: name of the financial institution lending to the student applicant
Guarantor No.: unique alphanumeric value that identifies the financial institution ensuring the loan is properly serviced.
Guarantor Name: name of the guaranteeing financial institution
Note Value: amount (in dollars) borrowed by the student applicant; note value is equal to the sum of the disbursement amounts and the fees (origination and guarantee).
Subsidized: yes/no value indicating whether the government pays the interest while the student is in school
Rate: interest rate on the loan
Date: disbursement date; this is the Date field under Disbursement Plan.
Amount: disbursement amount in dollars
Origination Fee: fee (in dollars) charged by the lending institution
Guarantee Fee: fee (in dollars) charged by the guarantor

Disclosure Letter

Date: date (1 July 2005) that the letter was sent to the student applicant
Loan No: loan number of the associated loan
Last Name: title and last name (Mr. Student) of student applicant
Repayment Starting: month and year (September 2005) when loans enter repayment status
Amount Borrowed: sum of amounts ($10,000) borrowed in all loans covered by payment plan
Number of Payments: estimated number of scheduled payments (120) to retire the amount borrowed
Interest Rate: weighted average percentage rate (8.5 percent) of loans covered by the payment plan
Finance Charge: estimated finance charge ($4,877.96) if amount borrowed is repaid according to the payment plan

Payment Amount: amount of payment ($246.37) required for each month (except perhaps for the last month). If a student does not pay this amount each month, the student will be in arrears unless other arrangements are made.

First Payment Date: date (October 31, 2005) when the first payment is due if the payment plan is followed.

Last Payment Date: date (September 30, 2015) when the last payment is due if the payment plan is followed.

Statement of Account

Statement No: unique alphanumeric value (B100) that identifies the statement of account form

Date: date that the statement was sent

Student No.: unique alphanumeric value that identifies a student

Name: name of student applying

Address: street address of student applicant (part of the mailing address)

City: city of the student applicant (part of the mailing address)

State: two-letter state abbreviation of the student applicant (part of the mailing address)

Zip: five- or nine-digit zip code of the student applicant (part of the mailing address)

Amount Due: amount (in dollars) that the student should remit

Due Date: date when repayment should be received by Student Loan Limited. A late penalty may be assessed if the amount is received at a later date.

Payment Method: check or EFT

Amount Enclosed: amount (in dollars) sent with the payment. If payment method is EFT, the applicant does not complete this field.

Loan No.: unique alphanumeric value that identifies a loan of the applicant

Balance: outstanding loan balance (in dollars) before repayment

Rate: percentage interest rate applying to the loan

Date Paid: date when the payment is received; this field should be completed by staff at Student Loan Limited

Loan Activity Report

Date: date that the report was prepared

Student No.: unique alphanumeric value that identifies a student

Name: name of student applying

Street: street address of student applicant (part of the mailing address)

City: city of the student applicant (part of the mailing address)

State: two-letter state abbreviation of the student applicant (part of the mailing address)

Zip: five- or nine-digit zip code of the student applicant (part of the mailing address)

Loan No.: unique alphanumeric value that identifies a loan of the applicant

Beg. Balance: outstanding loan balance (in dollars) at beginning of year

Principal: total amount of payments applied to principal

Interest: total amount of payments applied to interest

Ending Balance: outstanding loan balance (in dollars) at the end of year after applying payments

Appendix 13.B: CREATE TABLE Statements

Appendix 13.B contains CREATE TABLE statements for the tables resulting from the conversion and normalization process described in Section 13.3. The CREATE TABLE statements conform to SQL:2006 syntax.

```
CREATE TABLE Student
( StdNo            CHAR(10),
  Name             CHAR(30)
                   CONSTRAINT StdNameRequired NOT NULL,
  Address          VARCHAR(50)
                   CONSTRAINT StdAddressRequired NOT NULL,
  Phone            CHAR(9),
  City             CHAR(30)
                   CONSTRAINT StdCityRequired NOT NULL,
  Zip              CHAR(9)        CONSTRAINT StdZipRequired NOT NULL,
  ExpGradMonth     SMALLINT,
  ExpGradYear      INTEGER,
  DOB              DATE           CONSTRAINT StdDOBRequired NOT NULL,
CONSTRAINT FKZip1 FOREIGN KEY (Zip) REFERENCES ZipCode
  ON DELETE RESTRICT
  ON UPDATE CASCADE,
CONSTRAINT PKStudent PRIMARY KEY (StdNo) )
```

```
CREATE TABLE Lender
( LenderNo  INTEGER,
  Name      CHAR(30)     CONSTRAINT LendNameRequired NOT NULL,
CONSTRAINT PKLender PRIMARY KEY (LenderNo) )
```

```
CREATE TABLE Guarantor
( GuarantorNo     CHAR(10),
  Name            CHAR(30)   CONSTRAINT GrnNameRequired NOT NULL,
CONSTRAINT PKGuarantor PRIMARY KEY (GuarantorNo) )
```

```
CREATE TABLE Institution
( InstID   CHAR(10),
  Name     CHAR(30)     CONSTRAINT InstNameRequired NOT NULL,
  Address  VARCHAR(50)  CONSTRAINT InstAddressRequired NOT NULL,
  City     CHAR(30)     CONSTRAINT InstCityRequired NOT NULL,
  Zip      CHAR(9)      CONSTRAINT InstZipRequired NOT NULL,
CONSTRAINT FKZip2 FOREIGN KEY (Zip) REFERENCES ZipCode
  ON DELETE RESTRICT
  ON UPDATE CASCADE,
CONSTRAINT PKInstitution PRIMARY KEY (InstID) )
```

```
CREATE TABLE ZipCode
( Zip        CHAR(9),
  State      CHAR(2) CONSTRAINT ZipStateRequired NOT NULL,
CONSTRAINT PKZipCode PRIMARY KEY (Zip) )
```

```
CREATE TABLE Loan
( LoanNo          CHAR(10),
  ProcDate        DATE
                  CONSTRAINT LoanProcDateRequired NOT NULL,
  DisbMethod      CHAR(6)
                  CONSTRAINT LoanDisbMethodRequired NOT NULL,
  RouteNo         CHAR(10),
  AcctNo          CHAR(10),
```

```
      DateAuth        INTEGER
                      CONSTRAINT LoanDateAuthRequired NOT NULL,
      NoteValue       DECIMAL(10,2)
                      CONSTRAINT LoanNoteValueRequired NOT NULL,
      Subsidized      BOOLEAN
                      CONSTRAINT LoanSubsidizedRequired NOT NULL,
      Rate            FLOAT      CONSTRAINT LoanRateRequired NOT NULL,
      Balance         DECIMAL(10,2),
      StdNo           CHAR(10) CONSTRAINT LoanStdNoRequired NOT NULL,
      InstID          CHAR(10) CONSTRAINT LoanInstIdRequired NOT NULL,
      GuarantorNo     CHAR(10),
      LenderNo        CHAR(10) CONSTRAINT LoanLenderNoRequired NOT NULL,
CONSTRAINT FKStdNo1 FOREIGN KEY (StdNo) REFERENCES Student
   ON DELETE RESTRICT
   ON UPDATE CASCADE,
CONSTRAINT FKInstID FOREIGN KEY (InstID) REFERENCES Institution
   ON DELETE RESTRICT
   ON UPDATE CASCADE,
CONSTRAINT FKGuarantorNo FOREIGN KEY (GuarantorNo)
         REFERENCES Guarantor
   ON DELETE RESTRICT
   ON UPDATE CASCADE,
CONSTRAINT FKLenderNo FOREIGN KEY (LenderNo) REFERENCES Lender
   ON DELETE RESTRICT
   ON UPDATE CASCADE,
CONSTRAINT FKRouteNo FOREIGN KEY (RouteNo) REFERENCES Bank
   ON DELETE RESTRICT
   ON UPDATE CASCADE,
CONSTRAINT PKLoan PRIMARY KEY (LoanNo) )
```

```
CREATE TABLE Bank
( RouteNo    CHAR(10),
  Name       CHAR(30)    CONSTRAINT BankNameRequired NOT NULL,
CONSTRAINT PKBank PRIMARY KEY (RouteNo) )
```

```
CREATE TABLE DisburseLine
( LoanNo     CHAR(10),
  DateSent   DATE,
  Amount     DECIMAL(10,2)   CONSTRAINT DLAmountRequired NOT NULL,
  OrigFee    DECIMAL(10,2)   CONSTRAINT DLOrigFeeRequired NOT NULL,
  GuarFee    DECIMAL(10,2)   CONSTRAINT DLGuarFeeRequired NOT NULL,
CONSTRAINT FKLoanNo1 FOREIGN KEY (LoanNo) REFERENCES Loan
  ON DELETE CASCADE
  ON UPDATE CASCADE,
CONSTRAINT PKDisburseLine PRIMARY KEY (LoanNo, DateSent) )
```

```
CREATE TABLE DiscLetter
( LetterNo   INTEGER,
  DateSent   DATE           CONSTRAINT DLDateSentRequired NOT NULL,
  Image      BLOB           CONSTRAINT DLImageRequired NOT NULL,
  LoanNo     CHAR(10)       CONSTRAINT DLLoanNoRequired NOT NULL,
 CONSTRAINT FKLoanNo2 FOREIGN KEY (LoanNo) REFERENCES Loan
    ON DELETE RESTRICT
    ON UPDATE CASCADE,
 CONSTRAINT PKDiscLetter PRIMARY KEY (LetterNo) )
```

```
CREATE TABLE LoanActivity
( ReportNo   INTEGER,
  DateSent   DATE        CONSTRAINT LADateSentRequired NOT NULL,
  Image      BLOB        CONSTRAINT LAImageRequired NOT NULL,
  StdNo      CHAR(10)    CONSTRAINT LAStdNoRequired NOT NULL,
CONSTRAINT FKStdNo2 FOREIGN KEY (StdNo) REFERENCES Student
  ON DELETE RESTRICT
  ON UPDATE CASCADE,
CONSTRAINT PKLoanActivity PRIMARY KEY (ReportNo) )
```

```
CREATE TABLE Statement
( StatementNo    CHAR(10),
  StatementDate  DATE
                 CONSTRAINT StmtDateRequired NOT NULL,
  PayMethod      CHAR(6)
                 CONSTRAINT StmtPayMethodRequired NOT NULL,
  StdNo          CHAR(10)
                 CONSTRAINT StmtStdNoRequired NOT NULL,
  AmtDue         DECIMAL(10,2)
                 CONSTRAINT StmtAmtDuetRequired NOT NULL,
  DueDate        DATE
                 CONSTRAINT StmtDueDateRequired NOT NULL,
  AmtSent        DECIMAL(10,2),
  DatePaid       DATE,
CONSTRAINT FKStdNo3 FOREIGN KEY (StdNo) REFERENCES Student
  ON DELETE RESTRICT
  ON UPDATE CASCADE,
CONSTRAINT PKStatement PRIMARY KEY (StatementNo) )
```

```
CREATE TABLE Applied
( LoanNo         CHAR(10),
  StatementNo    CHAR(10),
  Principal      DECIMAL(10,2)
                 CONSTRAINT AppPrincipal NOT NULL,
  Interest       DECIMAL(10,2)   CONSTRAINT AppInterest NOT NULL,
  CumPrincipal   DECIMAL(10,2)
                 CONSTRAINT AppCumPrincipal NOT NULL,
  CumInterest    DECIMAL(10,2)
                 CONSTRAINT AppCumInterest NOT NULL,
CONSTRAINT FKLoanNo3 FOREIGN KEY (LoanNo) REFERENCES Loan
  ON DELETE RESTRICT
  ON UPDATE CASCADE,
CONSTRAINT FKStatementNo FOREIGN KEY (StatementNo)
  REFERENCES Statement
  ON DELETE CASCADE
  ON UPDATE CASCADE,
CONSTRAINT PKApplied PRIMARY KEY (LoanNo, StatementNo) )
```

Data and Database Administration

Learning Objectives

This chapter provides an overview of the responsibilities and tools of database specialists known as data administrators and database administrators. After this chapter, the student should have acquired the following knowledge and skills:

- Compare and contrast the responsibilities of database administrators and data administrators
- Control databases using SQL statements for security and integrity
- Manage stored procedures and triggers
- Understand the roles of data dictionary tables and the information resource dictionary
- Describe the data planning process
- Understand the process to select and evaluate DBMSs
- Gain insights about the processing environments in which database technology is used

Overview

Utilizing the knowledge and skills in Parts 1 through 6, you should be able to develop databases and implement applications that use the databases. You learned about query formulation, conceptual data modeling, relational database design, physical database design, application development with views, stored procedures, triggers, and database development using requirements represented as views. Part 7 complements these knowledge and skill areas by exploring issues and skills involved in managing databases in different processing environments. This chapter describes the responsibilities and tools of data specialists (data administrators and database administrators) and provides an introduction to the different processing environments for databases.

Before learning the details of the processing environments, you need to understand the organizational context in which databases exist and learn tools and processes for managing databases. This chapter first discusses an organizational context for databases. You will learn about database support for management decision making, the goals of information resource management, and the responsibilities of data and database administrators. After explaining the organizational context, this chapter presents new tools and processes to manage databases. You will learn SQL statements for security and integrity, management of triggers and stored procedures, and data dictionary manipulation as well as processes for data planning and DBMS selection. This chapter concludes with an introduction to the different processing environments that will be presented in more detail in the other chapters of Part 7.

14.1 Organizational Context for Managing Databases

This section reviews management decision-making levels and discusses database support for decision making at all levels. After this background, this section describes the function of information resource management and the responsibilities of data specialists to manage information resources.

14.1.1 Database Support for Management Decision Making

Databases support business operations and management decision making at various levels. Most large organizations have developed many <u>operational databases</u> to help conduct business efficiently. Operational databases directly support major functions such as order processing, manufacturing, accounts payable, and product distribution. The reasons for investing in an operational database are typically faster processing, larger volumes of business, and reduced personnel costs.

Operational Database: a database to support the daily functions of an organization.

As organizations achieve improved operations, they begin to realize the decision-making potential of their databases. Operational databases provide the raw materials for management decision making as depicted in Figure 14.1. Lower-level management can obtain exception and problem reports directly from operational databases. However, much value must be added to leverage the operational databases for middle and upper management. The operational databases must be cleaned, integrated, and summarized to provide value for tactical and strategic decision making. Integration is necessary because operational databases often are developed in isolation without regard for the information needs of tactical and strategic decision making.

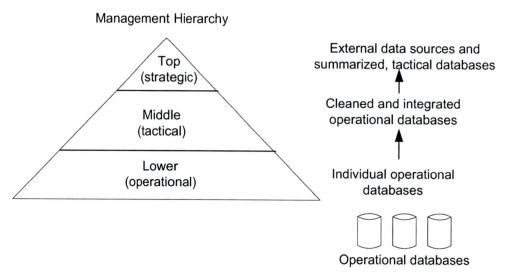

Figure 14.1: Database Support for Management Levels

Table 14-1 provides examples of management decisions and data requirements. Lower-level management deals with short-term problems related to individual transactions. Periodic summaries of operational databases and exception reports assist operational management. Middle management relies on summarized data that are integrated across operational databases. Middle management may want to integrate data across different departments, manufacturing plants, and retail stores. Top management relies on the results of middle management analysis and external data sources. Top management needs to integrate data so that customers, products, suppliers, and other important entities can be tracked across an entire organization. In addition, external data must be captured and then integrated with internal data.

Table 14-1: Examples of Management Decision Making

Level	Example Decisions	Data Requirements
Top	Identify new markets and products; plan growth; reallocate resources across divisions	Economic and technology forecasts; news summaries; industry reports; medium-term performance reports
Middle	Choose suppliers; forecast sales, inventory, and cash; revise staffing levels; prepare budgets	Historical trends; supplier performance; critical path analysis; short-term and medium-term plans
Lower	Schedule employees; correct order delays; find production bottlenecks; monitor resource usage	Problem reports; exception reports; employee schedules; daily production results; inventory levels

14.1.2 Information Resource Management to Knowledge Management

As a response to the challenges of leveraging operational databases and information technology for management decision making, the philosophy of information resource management has arisen. Information resource management involves processing, distributing, and integrating information throughout an organization. A key element of information resource management is the control of information life cycles (Figure 14.2). Each level of management decision making and business operations has its own information life cycle. For effective decision making, the life cycles must be integrated to provide timely and consistent information. For example, information life cycles for operations provide input to life cycles for management decision making.

Information Life Cycle: the stages of information transformation in an organization. Each entity has its own information life cycle that should be managed and integrated with the life cycles of other entities.

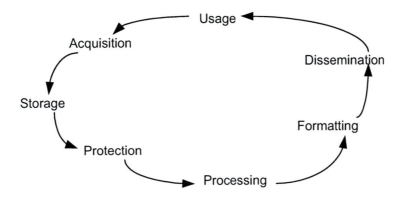

Figure 14.2: Typical Stages of an Information Life Cycle

Data quality is a particular concern for information resource management because of the impact of data quality on management decision making. As discussed in Chapter 2, data quality involves a number of dimensions such as correctness, timeliness, consistency, completeness, and reliability. Often the level of data quality that suffices for business operations may be insufficient for decision making at upper levels of management. This conflict is especially true for the consistency dimension. For example, inconsistency of customer identification across operational databases can impair decision making at the upper management level. Information resource management emphasizes a long-term, organizationwide perspective on data quality to ensure support for management decision making.

In recent years, there has been a movement to extend information resource management into knowledge management. Traditionally, information resource management has emphasized technology to support predefined recipes for decision making rather than the ability to react to a constantly changing business environment. To succeed in today's business environment, organizations must emphasize fast response and adaptation rather than planning. To meet this challenge organizations should develop systems that facilitate knowledge creation rather than information management. For knowledge creation, a greater emphasis is on human information processing and organization dynamics to balance the technology emphasis, as shown in Figure 14.3.

Knowledge Management: applying information technology with human information processing capabilities and organization processes to support rapid adaptation to change.

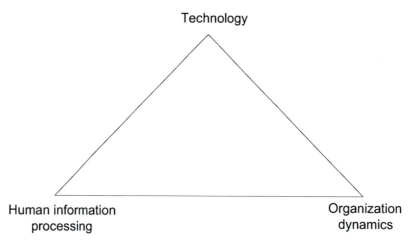

Figure 14.3: Three Pillars of Knowledge Management

This vision for knowledge management provides a context for the use of information technology to solve business problems. The best information technology will fail if not aligned with the human and organization elements. Information technology should amplify individual intellectual capacity, compensate for limitations in human processing, and support positive organization dynamics.

14.1.3 Responsibilities of Data Administrators and Database Administrators

As part of controlling information resources, new management responsibilities have arisen. The data administrator (DA) is a middle- or upper-management position with broad responsibilities for information resource management. The database administrator (DBA) is a support role with responsibilities related to individual databases and DBMSs. Table 14-2 compares the responsibilities of data administrators and database administrators. The data administrator views the information resource in a broader context than the database administrator. The data administrator considers all kinds of data whether stored in relational databases, files, Web pages, or external sources. The database administrator typically considers only data stored in databases.

Table 14-2: Responsibilities of Data Administrators and Database Administrators

Position	Responsibilities
Data administrator	Develops an enterprise data model
	Establishes interdatabase standards and policies about naming, data sharing, and data ownership
	Negotiates contractual terms with information technology vendors
	Develops long-range plans for information technology
Database administrator	Develops detailed knowledge of individual DBMSs
	Consults on application development
	Performs data modeling, logical database design, and physical database design
	Enforces data administration standards
	Monitors database performance
	Performs technical evaluation of DBMSs
	Creates security, integrity, and rule-processing statements
	Devises standards and policies related to individual databases and DBMSs

472

Development of an <u>enterprise data model</u> is one of the most important responsibilities of the data administrator. An enterprise data model provides an integrated model of all databases of an organization. Because of its scope, an enterprise data model is less detailed than the individual databases that it encompasses. The enterprise data model concentrates on the major subjects in operational databases rather the full details. An enterprise data model can be developed for data planning (what databases to develop) or decision support (how to integrate and summarize existing databases). Section 14.3 describes the details of data planning while Chapter 16 describes the details of developing an enterprise data model for decision support. The data administrator is usually heavily involved in both efforts.

> **Enterprise Data Model**: a conceptual data model of an organization. An enterprise data model can be used for data planning or decision support.

Large organizations may offer much specialization in data administration and database administration. For data administration, specialization can occur by task and environment. On the task side, data administrators can specialize in planning versus policy establishment. On the environment side, data administrators can specialize in environments such as decision support, operations, and nontraditional data such as images, text, and video. For database administration, specialization can occur by DBMS, task, and environment. Because of the complexities of learning a DBMS, DBAs typically specialize in one product. Task specialization is usually divided between data modeling, application development support, and performance evaluation. Environment specialization is usually divided between transaction processing and data warehouses.

In large organizations, various titles are used for database specialists. The following list explains some common titles used in large organizations.

- Database architect: primarily specializes in data modeling and logical database design
- System DBA: interfaces with system administration and analyzes database impact on hardware and operating system
- Application DBA: specializes in management and usage of procedural objects including triggers, stored procedures, and transaction design
- Senior DBA: a highly experienced DBA who supervises junior DBAs and provides expert trouble shooting
- Performance DBA: specializes in physical database design and performance tuning
- Data warehouse administrator: specializes in operation and development of data warehouse

In small organizations, the boundary between data administration and database administration is fluid. There may not be separate positions for data administrators and database administrators. The same person may perform duties from both positions. As organizations grow, specialization usually develops so that separate positions are created.

14.2 Tools of Database Administration

To fulfill the responsibilities mentioned in the previous section, database administrators use a variety of tools. You already have learned about tools for data modeling, logical database design, view creation, physical database design, triggers, and stored procedures. Some of the tools are SQL statements (CREATE VIEW and CREATE INDEX) while others are part of CASE tools for database development. This section presents additional tools for security, integrity, and data dictionary access and discusses management of stored procedures and triggers.

14.2.1 Security

Security involves protecting a database from unauthorized access and malicious destruction. Because of the value of data in corporate databases, there is strong motivation for unauthorized users to gain unauthorized access to corporate databases. Competitors have strong motivation to access sensitive information about product development plans, cost-saving initiatives, and customer profiles. Lurking criminals want to steal unannounced financial results, business transactions, and sensitive customer data such as credit card numbers. Social deviants and terrorists can wreck havoc by intentionally destroying database records. With growing use of the Web to conduct business, competitors, criminals, and social deviants have even more opportunity to compromise database security.

Database Security: protecting databases from unauthorized access and malicious destruction.

Security is a broad subject involving many disciplines. There are legal and ethical issues about who can access data and when data can be disclosed. There are network, hardware, operating system, and physical controls that augment the controls provided by DBMSs. There are also operational problems about passwords, authentication devices, and privacy enforcement. These issues are not further addressed because they are beyond the scope of DBMSs and database specialists. The remainder of this subsection emphasizes access control approaches and SQL statements for authorization rules.

For access control, DBMSs support creation and storage of authorization rules and enforcement of authorization rules when users access a database. Figure 14.4 depicts the interaction of these elements. Database administrators create <u>authorization rules</u> that define who can access which parts of a database for what operations. Enforcement of authorization rules involves authenticating the user and ensuring that authorization rules are not violated by access requests (database retrievals and modifications). Authentication occurs when a user first connects to a DBMS. Authorization rules must be checked for each access request.

Authorization Rules: define authorized users, allowable operations, and accessible parts of a database. The database security system stores authorization rules and enforces them for each database access.

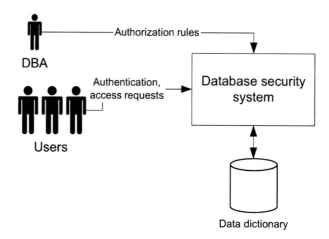

Figure 14.4: Database Security System

The most common approach to authorization rules is known as <u>discretionary access control</u>. In discretionary access control, users are assigned access rights or privileges to specified parts of a database. For precise control, privileges are usually specified for views rather than tables or fields. Users can be given the ability to read, update, insert, and delete specified parts of a database. To simplify the maintenance of authorization rules, privileges can be assigned to groups or roles rather than individual users. Because roles are more stable than individual users, authorization rules that reference roles require less maintenance than rules referencing individual users. Users are assigned to roles and given passwords. During the database login process, the database security system authenticates users and notes the roles to which they belong.

Discretionary Access Control: users are assigned access rights or privileges to specified parts of a database. Discretionary access control is the most common kind of security control supported by commercial DBMSs.

Mandatory access controls are less flexible than discretionary access controls. In mandatory control approaches, each object is assigned a classification level and each user is given a clearance level. A user can access an object if the user's clearance level provides access to the classification level of the object. Typical clearance and classification levels are confidential, secret, and top secret. Mandatory access control approaches primarily have been applied to highly sensitive and static databases for national defense and intelligence gathering. Because of the limited flexibility of mandatory access controls, only a few DBMSs support them. DBMSs that are used in national defense and intelligence gathering must support mandatory controls, however.

> **Mandatory Access Control**: a database security approach for highly sensitive and static databases. A user can access a database element if the user's clearance level provides access to the classification level of the element.

In addition to access controls, DBMSs support encryption of databases. Encryption involves the encoding of data to obscure their meaning. An encryption algorithm changes the original data (known as the plaintext). To decipher the data, the user supplies an encryption key to restore the encrypted data (known as the ciphertext) to its original (plaintext) format. Two of the most popular encryption algorithms are the Data Encryption Standard and the Public-Key Encryption algorithm. Because the Data Encryption Standard can be broken by massive computational power, the Public-Key Encryption algorithm has become the preferred approach.

SQL:2006 Security Statements

SQL:2006 supports discretionary authorization rules using the CREATE/DROP ROLE statements and the GRANT/REVOKE statements. When a role is created, the DBMS grants the role to either the current user or current role. In Example 14.1, the ISFaculty and ISAdvisor roles are granted to the current user while the ISAdministrator role is granted to the role of the current user. The WITH ADMIN clause means that a user assigned the role can assign the role to others. The WITH ADMIN option should be used sparingly because it provides wide latitude to the role. A role can be dropped with the DROP ROLE statement.

Example 14.1 (SQL:2006): CREATE ROLE Statement Examples

```
CREATE ROLE ISFaculty;
CREATE ROLE ISAdministrator WITH ADMIN CURRENT_ROLE;
CREATE ROLE ISAdvisor;
```

In a GRANT statement, you specify the privileges (see Table 14-3), the object (table, column, or view), and the list of authorized users (or roles). In Example 14.2, SELECT access is given to three roles (ISFaculty, ISAdvisor, ISAdministrator) while UPDATE access is given only to the ISAdministrator. Individual users must be assigned to roles before they can access the *ISStudentGPA* view.

Example 14.2 (SQL:2006): View Definition, GRANT, and REVOKE Statements

```
CREATE VIEW ISStudentGPA AS
   SELECT StdNo, StdFirstName, StdLastName, StdGPA
     FROM Student
     WHERE StdMajor = 'IS';
-- Grant privileges to roles
GRANT SELECT ON ISStudentGPA
   TO ISFaculty, ISAdvisor, ISAdministrator;
GRANT UPDATE ON ISStudentGPA.StdGPA TO ISAdministrator;
-- Assign users to roles
GRANT ISFaculty TO Mannino;
GRANT ISAdvisor TO Olson;
GRANT ISAdministrator TO Smith WITH GRANT OPTION;

REVOKE SELECT ON ISStudentGPA FROM ISFaculty RESTRICT;
```

Table 14-3: Explanation of Common SQL:2006 Privileges

Privilege	Explanation
SELECT	Query the object; can be specified for individual columns
UPDATE	Modify the value; can be specified for individual columns
INSERT	Add a new row; can be specified for individual columns
DELETE	Delete a row; cannot be specified for individual columns
TRIGGER	Create a trigger on a specified table
REFERENCES	Reference columns of a given table in integrity constraints
EXECUTE	Execute the stored procedure

The GRANT statement can also be used to assign users to roles as shown in the last three GRANT statements in Example 14.2. In addition to granting the privileges in Table 14-3, a user can be authorized to pass privileges to other users using the WITH GRANT OPTION keyword. In the last GRANT statement of Example 14.2, user Smith can grant the ISAdministrator role to other users. The WITH GRANT option should be used sparingly because it provides wide latitude to the user.

To remove an access privilege, the REVOKE statement is used. In the last statement of Example 14.2, the SELECT privilege is removed from ISFaculty. The RESTRICT clause means the privilege is revoked only if the privilege has not been granted to the specified role by more than one user.

Security in Oracle and Access

Oracle 11g extends the SQL:2006 security statements with the CREATE USER statement, predefined roles, and additional privileges. In SQL:2006, user creation is an implementation issue. Since Oracle does not rely on the operating system for user creation, it provides the CREATE USER statement. Oracle provides predefined roles for highly privileged users including the CONNECT role to create tables in a schema, the RESOURCE role for creating tables and application objects such as stored procedures, and the DBA role for managing databases. For privileges, Oracle distinguishes between system privileges (independent of object) and object privileges. Granting system privileges usually is reserved for highly secure roles because of the far-reaching nature of system privileges as shown in Table 14-4. The ORACLE object privileges are similar to the SQL:2006 privileges except that Oracle provides more objects than SQL:2006, as shown in Table 14-5.

Table 14-4: Explanation of Common Oracle System Privileges

System Privilege	Explanation
CREATE X, CREATE ANY X	Create objects of kind X in one's schema[35]; CREATE ANY allows creating objects in other schemas
ALTER X, ALTER ANY X	Alter objects of kind X in one's schema; ALTER ANY X allows altering objects in other schemas
INSERT ANY, DELETE ANY, UPDATE ANY, SELECT ANY	Insert, delete, update, and select from a table in any schema
DROP X, DROP ANY X	DROP objects of kind X in one's schema; DROP ANY allows dropping of objects in other schemas
ALTER SYSTEM, ALTER DATABASE, ALTER SESSION	Issue ALTER SYSTEM commands, ALTER DATABASE commands, and ALTER SESSION commands
ANALYZE ANY	Analyze any table, index, or cluster

Table 14-5: Mapping between Common Oracle Privileges and Objects

Privilege/Object	Table	View	Sequence [36]	Procedure, Function, Package, Library, Operator, IndexType	Materialized View[37]
ALTER	X		X		
DELETE	X	X			X
EXECUTE				X	
INDEX	X				
INSERT	X	X			X
REFERENCES	X	X			
SELECT	X	X	X		X
UPDATE	X	X			X

In addition to extensions to the standard SQL security statements, Oracle provides advanced security features (security policies, auditing, and profiles) with no counterpart in the SQL:2006 specification. Security policies support dynamic restrictions for fine-grained control to the row and column level. Security restrictions based on views alone cannot be customized to the individual user level without a large number of views, one per user. Security policies in Oracle support dynamic generation of conditions so that access can be restricted based on individual user characteristics such as customer numbers and employee departments. Oracle provides auditing to record user database actions. Auditing can be triggered by combinations of user name, statement type, time, and database object. In addition, security policies can trigger auditing when specified

---

[35] A schema is a collection of related tables and other Oracle objects that are managed as a unit.
[36] A sequence is a collection of values maintained by Oracle. Sequences typically are used for system-generated primary keys.
[37] A materialized view is stored rather than derived. Materialized views are useful in data warehouses as presented in Chapter 16.

elements in an Oracle database are accessed or changed. Profiles specify resource limits for roles and users. Profiles can restrict CPU time, memory usage, data block accesses, idle time, elapsed time, and concurrent sessions.

Most DBMSs allow authorization restrictions by application objects such as forms and reports in addition to the database objects permissible in the GRANT statement. These additional security constraints are usually specified in proprietary interfaces or in application development tools, rather than in SQL. For example, Microsoft Access 2003 allows definition of authorization rules through the User and Group Permissions window as shown in Figure 14.5. Permissions for database objects (tables and stored queries) as well as application objects (forms and reports) can be specified using this window. In addition, Access SQL supports the GRANT/REVOKE statements similar to the SQL:2006 statements as well as the CREATE/DROP statements for users and groups.

Figure 14.5: User and Group Permissions Window in Microsoft Access 2003

14.2.2 Integrity Constraints

You have already seen integrity constraints presented in previous chapters. In Chapter 3, you were introduced to primary keys, foreign keys, candidate keys, and non-null constraints along with the corresponding SQL syntax. In Chapter 5, you studied cardinality constraints and generalization hierarchy constraints. In Chapter 7, you studied functional and multivalued dependencies as part of the normalization process. Chapter 8 described indexes that can be used to enforce primary and candidate key constraints efficiently. Chapter 11 presented triggers that can be used to specify complex integrity constraints. This subsection describes additional kinds of integrity constraints and the corresponding SQL syntax.

SQL Domains

In Chapter 3, standard SQL data types were defined. A data type indicates the kind of data (character, numeric, yes/no, etc.) and permissible operations (numeric operations, string operations, etc.) for columns using the data type. SQL:2006 provides a limited ability to define new data types using the CREATE DOMAIN statement. A domain can be created as a subset of a standard data type. Example 14.3 demonstrates the CREATE DOMAIN statement along with usage of the new domains in place of standard data types. The CHECK clause defines a constraint for the domain limiting the domain to a subset of the standard data type.

Example 14.3 (SQL:2006): CREATE DOMAIN Statements and Usage of the Domains

```
CREATE DOMAIN StudentClass AS CHAR(2)
  CHECK ( VALUE IN ('FR', 'SO', 'JR', 'SR') )

CREATE DOMAIN CourseUnits AS SMALLINT
  CHECK ( VALUE BETWEEN 1 AND 9 )
```

In the CREATE TABLE statement for the *Student* table, the domain can be referenced in the *StdClass* column.

```
StdClass    StudentClass   NOT NULL
```

In the CREATE TABLE statement for the *Course* table, the domain can be referenced in the *CrsUnits* column.

```
CrsUnits    CourseUnits    NOT NULL
```

SQL:2006 provides a related feature known as a distinct type. Like a domain, a distinct type is based on a primitive type. Unlike a domain, a distinct type cannot have constraints. However, the SQL specification provides improved type checking for distinct types as compared to domains. A column having a distinct type can be compared only with another column using the same distinct type. Example 14.4 demonstrates distinct type definitions and a comparison among columns based on the types.

Example 14.4 (SQL:2006): Distinct Types and Usage of the Distinct Types

```
-- USD distinct type and usage in a table definition
CREATE DISTINCT TYPE USD AS DECIMAL(10,2);
USProdPrice   USD

CREATE DISTINCT TYPE Euro AS DECIMAL(10,2);
EuroProdPrice  Euro

-- Type error: columns have different distinct types
USProdPrice > EuroProdPrice
```

For object-oriented databases, SQL:2006 provides user-defined types, a more powerful capability than domains or distinct types. User-defined data types can be defined with new operators and functions. In addition, user-defined data types can be defined using other user-defined data types. Chapter 18 describes user-defined data types as part of the presentation of the object-oriented features of SQL:2006. Because of the limitations, most DBMSs no longer support domains and distinct types. For example Oracle 11g supports user-defined types but does not support domains or distinct types.

CHECK Constraints in the CREATE TABLE Statement

When a constraint involves row conditions on columns of the same table, a CHECK constraint may be used. CHECK constraints are specified as part of the CREATE TABLE statement as shown in Example 14.5. For easier traceability, you should always name constraints. When a constraint violation occurs, most DBMSs will display the constraint name.

Example 14.5 (SQL:2006): CHECK Constraint Clauses
Here is a CREATE TABLE statement with CHECK constraints for the valid GPA range and
upper-class students (juniors and seniors) having a declared (non-null) major.

```
CREATE TABLE Student
( StdNo           CHAR(11),
  StdFirstName    VARCHAR(50)
                  CONSTRAINT StdFirstNameRequired NOT NULL,
  StdLastName     VARCHAR(50)
                  CONSTRAINT StdLastNameRequired NOT NULL,
  StdCity         VARCHAR(50)
                  CONSTRAINT StdCityRequired NOT NULL,
  StdState        CHAR(2)
                  CONSTRAINT StdStateRequired NOT NULL,
  StdZip          CHAR(9)
                  CONSTRAINT StdZipRequired NOT NULL,
  StdMajor        CHAR(6),
  StdClass        CHAR(6),
  StdGPA          DECIMAL(3,2),
  CONSTRAINT PKStudent PRIMARY KEY (StdSSN),
  CONSTRAINT ValidGPA CHECK ( StdGPA BETWEEN 0 AND 4 ),
  CONSTRAINT MajorDeclared CHECK
    ( StdClass IN ('FR','SO') OR StdMajor IS NOT NULL ) )
```

Although CHECK constraints are widely supported, most DBMSs limit the conditions
inside CHECK constraints. The SQL:2006 specification allows any condition that could appear in
a SELECT statement including conditions that involve SELECT statements. Most DBMSs do not
permit conditions involving SELECT statements in a CHECK constraint. For example, Oracle 11g
prohibits SELECT statements in CHECK constraints as well as references to columns from other
tables. For these complex constraints, assertions may be used (if supported by the DBMS) or
triggers if assertions are not supported.

SQL:2006 Assertions

SQL:2006 assertions are more powerful than constraints about domains, columns, primary keys,
and foreign keys. Unlike CHECK constraints, assertions are not associated with a specific table.
An assertion can involve a SELECT statement of arbitrary complexity. Thus, assertions can be
used for constraints involving multiple tables and statistical calculations, as demonstrated in
Examples 14.6 through 14.8. However, complex assertions should be used sparingly because they
can be inefficient to enforce. There may be more efficient ways to enforce assertions such as
through event conditions in a form and stored procedures. As a DBA, you are advised to
investigate the event programming capabilities of application development tools before using
complex assertions.

Example 14.6 (SQL:2006): CREATE ASSERTION Statement.
This assertion statement ensures that each faculty has a course load between three and nine units.

```
CREATE ASSERTION FacultyWorkLoad
  CHECK (NOT EXISTS
    ( SELECT Faculty.FacNo, OffTerm, OffYear
      FROM Faculty, Offering, Course
      WHERE Faculty.FacNo = Offering.FacNo
        AND Offering.CourseNo = Course.CourseNo
      GROUP BY Faculty.FacNo, OffTerm, OffYear
      HAVING SUM(CrsUnits) < 3 OR SUM(CrsUnits) > 9 ) )
```

Example 14.7 (SQL:2006): CREATE ASSERTION Statement.
This assertion statement ensures that no two courses are offered at the same time and place. The
conditions involving the *OffTime* and *OffDays* columns should be refined to check for any overlap,
not just equality. Because these refinements would involve string and date functions specific to a
DBMS, they are not shown.

```
CREATE ASSERTION OfferingConflict
  CHECK (NOT EXISTS
    ( SELECT O1.OfferNo
       FROM Offering O1, Offering O2
       WHERE O1.OfferNo <> O2.OfferNo
         AND O1.OffTerm = O2.OffTerm
         AND O1.OffYear = O2.OffYear
         AND O1.OffDays = O2.OffDays
         AND O1.OffTime = O2.OffTime
         AND O1.OffLocation = O2.OffLocation  ) )
```

Example 14.8 (SQL:2006): Assertion Statement to Ensure that Full-Time Students Have at Least Nine Units

```
CREATE ASSERTION FullTimeEnrollment
  CHECK (NOT EXISTS
    ( SELECT Enrollment.RegNo
       FROM Registration, Offering, Enrollment, Course
       WHERE Offering.OfferNo = Enrollment.OfferNo
         AND Offering.CourseNo = Course.CourseNo
         AND Offering.RegNo = Registration.RegNo
         AND RegStatus = 'F'
       GROUP BY Enrollment.RegNo
       HAVING SUM(CrsUnits) >= 9 ) )
```

Assertions are checked after related modification operations complete. For example, the *OfferingConflict* assertion in Example 14.7 would be checked for each insertion of an *Offering* row and for each change to one of the columns in the WHERE clause of the assertion. In some cases, an assertion should be delayed until other statements complete. The keyword DEFERRABLE can be used to allow an assertion to be tested at the end of a transaction rather than immediately. Deferred checking is an issue with transaction design discussed in Chapter 15.

Assertions are not widely supported because assertions overlap with triggers. An assertion is a limited kind of trigger with an implicit condition and action. Because assertions are simpler than triggers, they are usually easier to create and more efficient to execute. However, no major relational DBMS supports assertions so triggers must be used in places where assertions would be more appropriate.

14.2.3 Management of Triggers and Stored Procedures

In Chapter 11, you learned about the concepts and coding details of stored procedures and triggers. Although a DBA writes stored procedures and triggers to help manage databases, the primary responsibilities for a DBA are to manage stored procedures and triggers, not to write them. The DBA's responsibilities include setting standards for coding practices, monitoring dependencies, and understanding trigger interactions.

For coding practices, a DBA should consider documentation standards, parameter usage, and content, as summarized in Table 14-6. Documentation standards may include naming standards, explanations of parameters, and descriptions of pre- and post-conditions of procedures. Parameter usage in procedures and functions should be monitored. Functions should use only input parameters and not have side effects. For content, triggers should not perform integrity checking that can be coded as declarative integrity constraints (CHECK constraints, primary keys, foreign keys, ...). To reduce maintenance, triggers and stored procedures should reference the data types of associated database columns. In Oracle, this practice involves anchored data types. Because most application development tools support triggers and event procedures for forms and reports, the choice between a database trigger/procedure versus an application trigger/procedure is not always clear. A DBA should participate in setting standards that provide guidance between using database triggers and procedures as opposed to application triggers and event procedures.

Table 14-6: Summary of Coding Practice Concerns for a DBA

Coding Practice Area	Concerns
Documentation	Procedure and trigger naming standards; explanation of parameters; comments describing pre- and post-conditions
Parameter usage	Only input parameters for functions; no side effects for functions
Trigger and procedure content	Do not use triggers for standard integrity constraints; usage of anchored data types for variables; standards for application triggers and event procedures versus database triggers and procedures

A stored procedure or trigger depends on the tables, views, procedures, and functions that it references as well as on access plans created by the SQL compiler. When a referenced object changes, its dependents should be recompiled. In Figure 14.6, trigger X needs recompilation if changes are made to the access plan for the UPDATE statement in the trigger body. Likewise, the procedure needs recompilation if the access plan for the SELECT statement becomes outdated. Trigger X may need recompilation if changes are made to table A or to procedure pr_LookupZ. Most DBMSs maintain dependencies to ensure that stored procedures and triggers work correctly. If a procedure or trigger uses an SQL statement, most DBMSs will automatically recompile the procedure or trigger if the associated access plan becomes obsolete.

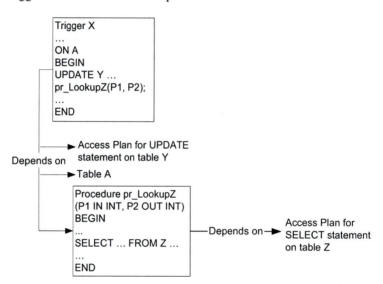

Figure 14.6: Dependencies among Database Objects

A DBA should be aware of the limitations of DBMS-provided tools for dependency management. Table 14-7 summarizes the dependency management issues of access plan obsolescence, modification of referenced objects, and deletion of referenced objects. For access plans, a DBA should understand that manual recompilation may be necessary if optimizer statistics become outdated. For remotely stored procedures and functions, a DBA can choose between timestamp and signature dependency maintenance. With timestamp maintenance, a DBMS will recompile a dependent object for any change in referenced objects. Timestamp maintenance may lead to excessive recompilation because many changes to referenced objects do not require recompilation of the dependent objects. Signature maintenance involves recompilation when a signature (parameter name or usage) changes. A DBA also should be aware that a DBMS will not recompile a procedure or trigger if a referenced object is deleted. The dependent procedure or trigger will be marked as invalid because recompilation is not possible.

Table 14-7: Summary of Dependency Concerns for a DBA

Dependency Area	Concerns
Access plan obsolescence	DBMS should automatically recompile. DBA may need to recompile when optimizer statistics become outdated.
Modification of referenced objects	DBMS should automatically recompile. DBA should choose between timestamp and signature maintenance for remote procedures and functions.
Deletion of referenced objects	DBMS marks procedure/trigger as invalid if referenced objects are deleted.

Trigger interactions were discussed in Chapter 11 as part of trigger execution procedures. Triggers interact when one trigger fires other triggers and when triggers overlap leading to firing in arbitrary order. A DBA can use trigger analysis tools provided by a DBMS vendor or manually analyze trigger interactions if no tools are provided. A DBA should require extra testing for interacting triggers. To minimize trigger interaction, a DBA should implement guidelines like those summarized in Table 14-8.

Table 14-8: Summary of Guidelines to Control Trigger Complexity

Guideline	Explanation
BEFORE ROW triggers	Do not use data manipulation statements in BEFORE ROW triggers to avoid firing other triggers.
UPDATE triggers	Use a list of columns for UPDATE triggers to reduce trigger overlap.
Actions on referenced rows	Be cautious about triggers on tables affected by actions on referenced rows. These triggers will fire as a result of actions on the parent tables.
Overlapping triggers	Do not depend on a specific firing order.

14.2.4 Data Dictionary Manipulation

The data dictionary is a special database that describes individual databases and the database environment. The data dictionary contains data descriptors called metadata that define the source, use, value, and meaning of data. DBAs typically deal with two kinds of data dictionaries to track the database environment. Each DBMS provides a data dictionary to track tables, columns, assertions, indexes, and other objects managed by the DBMS. Independent CASE tools provide a data dictionary known as the information resource dictionary that tracks a broader range of objects relating to information systems development. This subsection provides details about both kinds of data dictionaries.

Metadata: data that describe other data including the source, use, value, and meaning of the data.

Catalog Tables in SQL:2006 and Oracle

SQL:2006 contains catalog tables in the Definition_Schema as summarized in Table 14-9. The Definition_Schema contains one or more catalog tables corresponding to each object that can be created in an SQL data definition or data control statement. The base catalog tables in the Definition_Schema are not meant to be accessed in applications. For access to metadata in applications, SQL:2006 provides the Information_Schema that contains views of the base catalog tables of the Definition_Schema.

Table 14-9: Summary of Important Catalog Tables in SQL:2006

Table	Contents
USERS	One row for each user
DOMAINS	One row for each domain
DOMAIN_CONSTRAINTS	One row for each domain constraint on a table
TABLES	One row for each table and view
VIEWS	One row for each view
COLUMNS	One row for each column
TABLE_CONSTRAINTS	One row for each table constraint
REFERENTIAL_CONSTRAINTS	One row for each referential constraint

The SQL:2006 Definition_Schema and Information_Schema have few implementations because most DBMSs already had proprietary catalog tables long before the standard was released. Thus, you will need to learn the catalog tables of each DBMS with which you work. Typically, a DBMS may have hundreds of catalog tables. However, for any specific task such as managing triggers, a DBA needs to use a small number of catalog tables. Table 14-10 lists some of the most important catalog tables of Oracle.

Table 14-10: Common Catalog Tables for Oracle

Table Name	Contents
USER_CATALOG	Contains basic data about each table and view defined by a user.
USER_OBJECTS	Contains data about each object (functions, procedures, indexes, triggers, assertions, etc.) defined by a user. This table contains the time created and the last time changed for each object.
USER_TABLES	Contains extended data about each table such as space allocation and statistical summaries.
USER_TAB_COLUMNS	Contains basic and extended data for each column such as the column name, the table reference, the data type, and a statistical summary.
USER_VIEWS	Contains the SQL statement defining each view.

A DBA implicitly modifies catalog tables when using data definition commands such as the CREATE TABLE statement. The DBMS uses the catalog tables to process queries, authorize users, check integrity constraints, and perform other database processing. The DBMS consults the catalog tables before performing almost every action. Thus, the integrity of the catalog tables is crucial to the operation of the DBMS. Only the most-authorized users should be permitted to modify the catalog tables. To improve security and reliability, the data dictionary is usually a separate database stored independently of user databases.

A DBA can query the catalog tables through proprietary interfaces and SELECT statements. Proprietary interfaces such as the Table Definition window of Microsoft Access and the Oracle Enterprise Manager are easier to use than SQL but are not portable across DBMSs. SELECT statements provide more control over the information retrieved than do proprietary interfaces.

Information Resource Dictionary

An information resource dictionary contains a much broader collection of metadata than does a data dictionary for a DBMS. An information resource dictionary (IRD) contains metadata about individual databases, computerized and human processes, configuration management, version control, human resources, and the computing environment. Conceptually, an IRD defines metadata used throughout the information systems life cycle. Both DBAs and DAs can use an IRD to manage information resources. In addition, other information systems professionals can use an IRD during selected tasks in the information systems life cycle.

Information Resource Dictionary: a database of metadata that describes the entire information systems life cycle. The information resource dictionary system manages access to an IRD.

Because of its broader role, an IRD is not consulted by a DBMS to conduct operations. Rather, an <u>information resource dictionary system (IRDS)</u> manages an IRD. Many CASE tools can use the IRDS to access an IRD as depicted in Figure 14.7. CASE tools can access an IRD directly through the IRDS or indirectly through the import/export feature. The IRD has an open architecture so that CASE tools can customize and extend its conceptual schema.

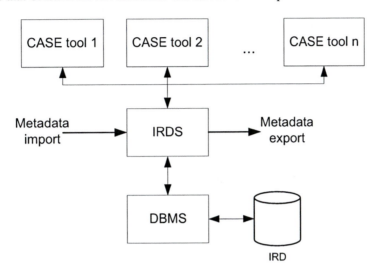

Figure 14.7: IRDS Architecture

There are two primary proposals for the IRD and the IRDS. The IRD and the IRDS were originally developed as standards by the International Standards Organization (ISO) in the early 1990s. The implementation of the standards, however, was limited. Microsoft and Texas Instruments jointly developed the Microsoft Repository, which supported many of the goals of the IRD and the IRDS although it did not conform to the standard. However, the Microsoft Repository has been phased out after initially gaining some acceptance among CASE tool vendors.

As an alternative to the IRD and IRDS, the Object Management Group (OMG) developed the Model Driven Architecture (MDA) in the early 2000s. The MDA provides an open specification that supports the formal modeling of all aspects of the software life cycle including business processes, software architectures, data warehousing, metadata repositories, tool integration and even the software development process itself. The MDA uses multiple standards, including the Unified Modeling Language (UML), the Meta-Object Facility (MOF), XML Metadata Interchange (XMI), Enterprise Distributed Object Computing (EDOC), the Software Process Engineering Metamodel (SPEM), and the Common Warehouse Metamodel (CWM). The OMG relies on commercial and open source developers to implement tools for the MDA. However, the MDA has not gained enough commercial acceptance to be considered an important standard.

Thus, the IRD and IRDS remain idealized concepts without a widely accepted commercial standard. Data specialists must deal with proprietary data dictionary interfaces in commercial CASE tools to compliment the dictionary tables available with enterprise DBMSs.

14.3 Processes for Database Specialists

This section describes processes performed by data administrators and database administrators. Data administrators perform data planning as part of the information systems planning process.

Both data administrators and database administrators may perform tasks in the process of selecting and evaluating DBMSs. This section presents the details of both processes.

14.3.1 Data Planning

Despite the vast sums of money spent on information technology, many organizations feel disappointed in the payoff. Many organizations have created islands of automation that support local objectives but not the global objectives for the organization. The islands-of-automation approach can lead to a misalignment of the business and information technology objectives. One result of the misalignment is the difficulty in extracting the decision-making value from operational databases.

As a response to problems with islands of automation, many organizations perform a detailed planning process for information technology and systems. The planning process is known under various names such as information systems planning, business systems planning, information systems engineering, and information systems architecture. All of these approaches provide a process to achieve the following objectives:

- Evaluation of current information systems with respect to the goals and objectives of the organization
- Determination of the scope and the timing of developing new information systems and utilization of new information technology
- Identification of opportunities to apply information technology for competitive advantage

Information Systems Planning: the process of developing enterprise models of data, processes, and organizational roles. Information systems planning evaluates existing systems, identifies opportunities to apply information technology for competitive advantage, and plans new systems.

The information systems planning process involves the development of enterprise models of data, processes, and organizational roles, as depicted in Figure 14.8. In the first part of the planning process, broad models are developed. Table 14-11 shows the initial level of detail for the data, process, and organization models. Because the enterprise data model is usually more stable than the process model, it is usually developed first. To integrate these models, interaction models are developed as shown in Table 14-11. If additional detail is desired, the process and the data models are further expanded. These models should reflect the current information systems infrastructure as well as planned future directions.

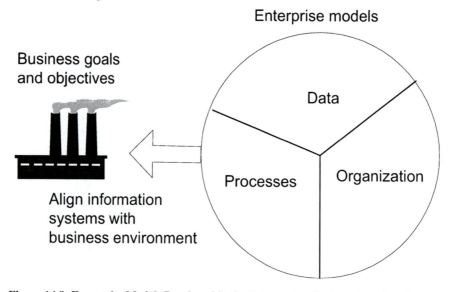

Figure 14.8: Enterprise Models Developed in the Information Systems Planning Process

Table 14-11: Level of Detail of Enterprise Models

Model	Levels of Detail
Data	Subject model (initial level), entity model (detailed level)
Process	Functional areas and business processes (initial level), activity model (detailed level)
Organization	Role definitions and role relationships
Data-process interaction	Matrix and diagrams showing data requirements of processes
Process-organization interaction	Matrix and diagrams showing role responsibilities
Data-organization	Matrix and diagrams showing usage of data by roles

Data administrators play an important part in the development of information system plans. Data administrators conduct numerous interviews to develop the enterprise data model and coordinate with other planning personnel to develop the interaction models. To improve the likelihood that plans will be accepted and used, data administrators should involve senior management. By emphasizing the decision-making potential of integrated information systems, senior management will be motivated to support the planning process.

14.3.2 Selection and Evaluation of Database Management Systems

Selection and evaluation of a DBMS can be a very important task for an organization. DBMSs provide an important part of the computing infrastructure. As organizations strive to conduct electronic commerce over the Internet and extract value from operational databases, DBMSs play an even greater role. The selection and evaluation process is important because of the impacts of a poor choice. The immediate impacts may be slow database performance and loss of the purchase price. A poorly performing information system can cause lost sales and higher costs. The longer-term impacts are high switching costs. To switch DBMSs, an organization may need to convert data, recode software, and retrain employees. The switching costs can be much larger than the original purchase price.

Selection and Evaluation Process

The selection and evaluation process involves a detailed assessment of an organization's needs and features of candidate DBMSs. The goal of the process is to determine a small set of candidate systems that will be investigated in more detail. Because of the detailed nature of the process, a DBA performs most of the tasks. Therefore, a DBA needs a thorough knowledge of DBMSs to perform the process.

Figure 14.9 depicts the steps of the selection and evaluation process. In the first step, a DBA conducts a detailed analysis of the requirements. Because of the large number of requirements, it is helpful to group them. Table 14-12 lists major groupings of requirements while Table 14-13 shows some individual requirements in one group. Each individual requirement should be classified as essential, desirable, or optional to the requirement group. In some cases, several levels of requirements may be necessary. A DBA should be able to objectively measure individual requirements in the candidate systems.

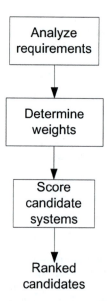

Figure 14.9: Overview of the Selection and Evaluation Process

Table 14-12: Some Major Requirement Groups

Category
Data definition (conceptual)
Nonprocedural retrieval
Data definition (internal)
Application development
Procedural language
Concurrency control
Recovery management
Parallel database processing
Distributed database support
Vendor support
Query optimization

Table 14-13: Some Detailed Requirements for the Conceptual Data Definition Category

Requirement (Importance)	Explanation
Entity integrity (essential)	Declaration and enforcement of primary keys
Candidate keys (desirable)	Declaration and enforcement of candidate keys
Referential integrity (essential)	Declaration and enforcement of referential integrity
Referenced rows (desirable)	Declaration and enforcement of rules for referenced rows
Standard data types (essential)	Support for whole numbers (several sizes), floating-point numbers (several sizes), fixed-point numbers, fixed-length strings, variable-length strings, and dates (date, time, and timestamp)
User-defined data types (desirable)	Support for new data types or a menu of optional data types
User interface (desirable)	Graphical user interface to manipulate dictionary tables
General assertions (optional)	Declaration and enforcement of multitable constraints

After determining the groupings, the DBA should assign weights to the major requirement groups and score candidate systems. With more than a few major requirement groups, assigning consistent weights is very difficult. The DBA needs a tool to help assign consistent weights and to score candidate systems. Unfortunately, no analytical method for weight assignment and system scoring has achieved widespread usage. To encourage the use of analytical methods for weight assignment and scoring, one promising approach is depicted.

The <u>Analytic Hierarchy Process</u> provides a simple approach that achieves a reasonable level of consistency. Using the Analytic Hierarchy Process, a DBA assigns weights to pairwise combinations of requirement groups. For example, a DBA should assign a weight that represents the importance of conceptual data definition as compared to nonprocedural retrieval. The Analytic Hierarchy Process provides a nine-point scale with interpretations shown in Table 14-14. Table 14-15 applies the scale to rank some of the requirement groups in Table 14-12. For consistency, if entry $A_{ij} = x$, then $A_{ji} = 1/x$. In addition, the diagonal elements in Table 14-15 should always be 1. Thus, it is necessary to complete only half the rankings in Table 14-15. The final row in the matrix shows column sums used to normalize weights and determine importance values.

Analytic Hierarchy Process: a decision theory technique to evaluate problems with multiple objectives. The process supports the selection and evaluation process by allowing a systematic assignment of weights to requirements and scores to features of candidate DBMSs.

Table 14-14: Interpretation of Rating Values for Pairwise Comparisons

Ranking Value of A_{ij}	Meaning
1	Requirements i and j are equally important.
3	Requirement i is slightly more important than requirement j.
5	Requirement i is significantly more important than requirement j.
7	Requirement i is very significantly more important than requirement j.
9	Requirement i is extremely more important than requirement j.

Table 14-15: Sample Weights for Some Requirement Groups

	Data Definition (Conceptual)	Nonprocedural Retrieval	Application Development	Concurrency Control
Data Definition (conceptual)	1	1/5 (0.20)	1/3 (0.33)	1/7 (0.14)
Nonprocedural Retrieval	5	1	3	1/3 (0.33)
Application Development	3	1/3 (0.33)	1	1/5 (0.20)
Concurrency Control	7	3	5	1
Column Sum	16	4.53	9.33	1.67

After assigning pairwise weights to the requirement groups, the weights are combined to determine an importance weight for each requirement group. The cell values are normalized by dividing each cell by its column sum as shown in Table 14-16. The final importance value for each requirement group is the average of the normalized weights in each row as shown in Table 14-17.

Importance weights must be computed for each subcategory of requirement groups in the same manner as for requirement groups. For each subcategory, pairwise weights are assigned before normalizing the weights and computing final importance values.

After computing importance values for the requirements, candidate DBMSs are assigned scores. Scoring candidate DBMSs can be complex because of the number of individual requirements and the need to combine individual requirements into an overall score for the requirement group. As the first part of the scoring process, a DBA should carefully investigate the features of each candidate DBMS.

Table 14-16: Normalized Weights for Some Requirement Groups

	Data Definition (Conceptual)	Nonprocedural Retrieval	Application Development	Concurrency Control
Data Definition (conceptual)	0.06	0.04	0.04	0.08
Nonprocedural Retrieval	0.31	0.22	0.32	0.20
Application Development	0.19	0.07	0.11	0.12
Concurrency Control	0.44	0.66	0.54	0.60

Table 14-17: Importance Values for Some Requirement Groups

Requirement Group	Importance
Data Definition (conceptual)	0.06
Nonprocedural Retrieval	0.26
Application Development	0.12
Concurrency Control	0.56

Many approaches have been proposed to combine individual feature scores into an overall score for the requirement group. The Analytic Hierarchy Process supports pairwise comparisons among candidate DBMSs using the rating values in Table 14-14. The interpretations change slightly to reflect comparisons among candidate DBMSs rather than the importance of requirement groups. For example, a value 3 should be assigned if DBMS i is slightly better than DBMS j. For each requirement subcategory, a comparison matrix should be created to compare the candidate DBMSs. Scores for each DBMS are computed by normalizing the weights and computing the row averages as for requirement groups.

After scoring the candidate DBMSs for each requirement group, the final scores are computed by combining the requirement group scores with the importance of requirement groups. For details about computing the final scores, you should consult the references at the end of the chapter about the Analytic Hierarchy Process.

Final Selection Process

After the selection and evaluation process completes, the top two or three candidate DBMSs should be evaluated in more detail. Benchmarks can be used to provide a more detailed evaluation of candidate DBMSs. A benchmark is a workload to evaluate the performance of a system or product. A good benchmark should be relevant, portable, scalable, and understandable. Because developing good benchmarks requires significant expertise, most organizations should not attempt to develop a benchmark. Fortunately, the Transaction Processing Council (TPC) has developed a number of standard, domain-specific benchmarks as summarized in Table 14-18. Each benchmark was developed over an extended time period with input from a diverse group of contributors.

Benchmark: a workload to evaluate the performance of a system or product. A good benchmark should be relevant, portable, scalable, and understandable.

Table 14-18: Summary of TPC Benchmarks

Benchmark	Description	Performance Measures
TPC-C	Online order entry benchmark	Transactions per minute, price per transactions per minute
TPC-H	Decision support for ad hoc queries	Composite queries per hour, price per composite queries per hour
TPC-App	Business-to-business transaction processing with application and Web services	Web service interactions per second (SIPS) per application server, total SIPS, price per SIPS
TPC-E	Transaction workload of a brokerage firm	Transactions per second, price per transactions per second

A DBA can use the TPC results for each benchmark to obtain reasonable estimates about the performance of a particular DBMS in a specific hardware/software environment. The TPC performance results involve total system performance, not just DBMS performance so that results are not inflated when a customer uses a DBMS in a specific hardware/software environment. To facilitate price performance trade-offs, the TPC publishes the performance measure along with price/performance for each benchmark. The price covers all cost dimensions of an entire system environment including workstations, communications equipment, system software, computer system or host, backup storage, and three years' maintenance cost. The TPC audits the benchmark results prior to publication to ensure that vendors have not manipulated the results.

To augment the published TPC results, an organization may want to evaluate a DBMS on a trial basis. Customized benchmarks can be created to gauge the efficiency of a DBMS for its intended usage. In addition, the user interface and the application development capabilities can be evaluated by building small applications.

The final phase of the selection process may involve nontechnical considerations performed by data administrators along with senior management and legal staff. Assessment of each vendor's future prospects is important because information systems can have a long life. If the underlying DBMS does not advance with the industry, it may not support future initiatives and upgrades to the information systems that use it. Because of the high fixed and variable costs (maintenance fees) of a DBMS, negotiation is often a critical element of the final selection process. The final contract terms along with one or two key advantages often make the difference in the final selection.

Open source DBMS software is a recent development that complicates the selection and evaluation process. Open source DBMS software has uncertainty in licensing and future prospects but obvious purchase price advantages over commercial DBMS software. With open source software, the lack of profit incentives may hinder product updates and lead to software license changes to obtain product updates. For example, MySQL, the most popular open source DBMS, recently changed its licensing so that commercial users will typically pay licensing fees. Despite these uncertainties, many organizations utilize open source DBMS software especially for non-mission-critical systems.

14.4 Managing Database Environments

DBMSs operate in several different processing environments. Data specialists must understand the environments to ensure adequate database performance and set standards and policies. This section provides an overview of the processing environments with an emphasis on the tasks performed by database administrators and data administrators. The other chapters in Part 7 provide the details of the processing environments.

14.4.1 Transaction Processing

Transaction processing involves the daily operations of an organization. Every day, organizations process large volumes of orders, payments, cash withdrawals, airline reservations, insurance claims, and other kinds of transactions. DBMSs provide essential services to perform transactions in an efficient and reliable manner. Organizations such as banks with automatic tellers, airlines with online reservation systems, and universities with online registration could not function without reliable and efficient transaction processing. With exploding interest to conduct business over the Internet, the importance of transaction processing will grow even larger.

Data specialists have many responsibilities for transaction processing, as listed in Table 14-19. Data administrators may perform planning responsibilities involving infrastructure and disaster recovery. Database administrators usually perform the more detailed tasks such as consulting on transaction design and monitoring performance. Because of the importance of transaction processing, database administrators often must be on call to troubleshoot problems. Chapter 15 presents the details of transaction processing for concurrency control and recovery management. After you read Chapter 15, you may want to review Table 14-19 again.

Table 14-19: Responsibilities of Database Specialists for Transaction Processing

Area	Responsibilities
Transaction design	Consult about design to balance integrity and performance; educate about design issues and DBMS features
Performance monitoring	Monitor transaction performance and troubleshoot performance problems; modify resource levels to improve performance
Transaction processing infrastructure	Determine resource levels of disks, memory, RAID devices, and servers for efficient and reliable processing
Disaster recovery	Provide contingency plans for various kinds of database failures

14.4.2 Data Warehouse Processing

Data warehousing involves the decision support side of databases. Because many organizations have not been able to use operational databases directly to support management decision making, the idea of a data warehouse was conceived. A data warehouse is a central database in which enterprisewide data are stored to facilitate decision support activities by user departments. Data from operational databases and external sources are extracted, cleaned, integrated, and then loaded into a data warehouse. Because the data warehouse contains historical data, most activity involves retrievals of summarized data.

Data specialists have many responsibilities for data warehouses, as listed in Table 14-20. Data administrators may perform planning responsibilities involving the data warehouse architecture and the enterprise data model. Database administrators usually perform the more detailed tasks such as performance monitoring and consulting. To support a large data warehouse, additional software products separate from a DBMS may be necessary. A selection and evaluation process should be conducted to choose the most appropriate product. Chapter 16 presents the details of data warehouses. After you read Chapter 16, you may want to review Table 14-20 again.

Table 14-20: Responsibilities of Database Specialists for Data Warehouses

Area	Responsibilities
Data warehouse usage	Educate and consult about application design and DBMS features for data warehouse processing
Performance monitoring	Monitor data warehouse loading performance and troubleshoot integrity problems; modify resource levels to improve performance
Data warehouse refresh	Determine the frequency of refreshing the data warehouse and the schedule of activities to refresh the data warehouse
Data warehouse architecture	Determine architecture to support decision-making needs; select database products to support architecture; determine resource levels for efficient processing
Enterprise data model	Provide expertise about operational database content; determine conceptual data model for the data warehouse; promote data quality to support data warehouse development

14.4.3 Distributed Environments

DBMSs can operate in distributed environments to support both transaction processing and data warehouses. In distributed environments, DBMSs can provide the ability to distribute processing and data among computers connected by a network. For distributed processing, a DBMS may allow the distribution of functions provided by the DBMS as well as application processing to be distributed among different computers in a network. For distributed data, a DBMS may allow tables to be stored and possibly replicated at different computers in a network. The ability to distribute processing and data provides the promise of improved flexibility, scalability, performance, and reliability. However, these improvements only can be obtained through careful design.

Data specialists have many responsibilities for distributed database environments, as shown in Table 14-21. Data administrators usually perform planning responsibilities involving setting goals and determining architectures. Because distributed environments do not increase functionality, they must be justified by improvements in the underlying applications. Database administrators perform more detailed tasks such as performance monitoring and distributed database design. To support distributed environments, other software products along with major extensions to a DBMS may be necessary. A selection and evaluation process should be conducted to choose the most appropriate products. Chapter 17 presents the details of distributed processing and distributed data. After you read Chapter 17, you may want to review Table 14-21 again.

Table 14-21: Responsibilities of Database Specialists for Distributed Environments

Area	Responsibilities
Application development	Educate and consult about impacts of distributed environments for transaction processing and data warehouses
Performance monitoring	Monitor performance and troubleshoot problems with a special emphasis on distributed environment
Distributed environment architectures	Identify goals for distributed environments; choose distributed processing, parallel database, and distributed database architectures to meet goals; select additional software products to support architectures
Distributed environment design	Design distributed databases; determine resource levels for efficient processing

14.4.4 Object Database Management

Object DBMSs support additional functionality for transaction processing and data warehouse applications. Many information systems use a richer set of data types than provided by relational DBMSs. For example, many financial databases need to manipulate time series, a data type not provided by most relational DBMSs. With the ability to convert any kind of data to a digital format, the need for new data types is even more pronounced. Business databases often need to integrate traditional data with nontraditional data based on new data types. For example, information systems for processing insurance claims must manage traditional data such as account numbers, claim amounts, and accident dates as well as nontraditional data such as images, maps, and drawings. Because of these needs, existing relational DBMSs have been extended with object capabilities and new object DBMSs have been developed.

Data specialists have many responsibilities for object databases as shown in Table 14-22. Data administrators usually perform planning responsibilities involving setting goals and determining architectures. Database administrators perform more detailed tasks such as performance monitoring, consulting, and object database design. An object DBMS can be a major extension to an existing relational DBMS or a new DBMS. A selection and evaluation process should be conducted to choose the most appropriate product. Chapter 18 presents the details of object DBMSs. After you read Chapter 18, you may want to review Table 14-22 again.

Table 14-22: Responsibilities of Database Specialists for Object Databases

Area	Responsibilities
Application development	Educate and consult about creating new data types, inheritance for data types and tables, and other object features
Performance monitoring	Monitor performance and troubleshoot problems with new data types
Object database architectures	Identify goals for object DBMSs; choose object database architectures
Object database design	Design object databases; select data types; create new data types

Closing Thoughts

This chapter has described the responsibilities, tools, and processes used by data specialists to manage databases and support management decision making. Many organizations provide two roles for managing information resources. Data administrators perform broad planning and policy setting, while database administrators perform detailed oversight of individual databases and DBMSs. To provide a context to understand the responsibilities of these positions, this chapter discussed the philosophy of information resource management that emphasizes information technology as a tool for processing, distributing, and integrating information throughout an organization.

This chapter described a number of tools to support database administrators. Database administrators use security rules to restrict access and integrity constraints to improve data quality. This chapter described security rules and integrity constraints along with associated SQL:2006 syntax. For triggers and stored procedures, this chapter described managerial responsibilities of DBAs to complement the coding details in Chapter 11. The data dictionary is an important tool for managing individual databases as well as integrating database development with information systems development. This chapter presented two kinds of data dictionaries: catalog tables used by DBMSs and the information resource dictionary used by CASE tools.

Database specialists need to understand two important processes to manage information technology. Data administrators participate in a detailed planning process that determines new directions for information systems development. This chapter described the data planning process as an important component of the information systems planning process. Both data administrators and database administrators participate in the selection and evaluation of DBMSs. Database administrators perform the detailed tasks while data administrators often make final selection decisions using the detailed recommendations. This chapter described the steps of the selection and evaluation process and the tasks performed by database administrators and data administrators in the process.

This chapter provides a context for the other chapters in Part 7. The other chapters provide details about different database environments including transaction processing, data warehouses, distributed environments, and object DBMSs. This chapter has emphasized the responsibilities, tools, and processes of database specialists for managing these environments. After completing the other chapters in Part 7, you are encouraged to reread this chapter to help you integrate the details with the management concepts and techniques.

Review Concepts

- Information resource management: management philosophy to control information resources and apply information technology to support management decision-making
- Database administrator: support position for managing individual databases and DBMSs
- Data administrator: management position with planning and policy responsibilities for information technology
- Discretionary access controls for assigning access rights to groups and users

- Mandatory access controls for highly sensitive and static databases used in intelligence gathering and national defense
- SQL CREATE/DROP ROLE statements and GRANT/REVOKE statements for discretionary authorization rules

```
CREATE ROLE ISFaculty

GRANT SELECT ON ISStudentGPA
        TO ISFaculty, ISAdvisor, ISAdministrator

REVOKE SELECT ON ISStudentGPA FROM ISFaculty
```

- Oracle 11g system and object privileges for discretionary access control
- Advanced Oracle security tools for fine grained control of data access, auditing, and resource limitations
- SQL CREATE DOMAIN statement for data type constraints

```
    CREATE DOMAIN StudentClass AS CHAR(2)
        CHECK (VALUE IN ('FR', 'SO', 'JR', 'SR') )
```

- SQL distinct types for improved type checking
- Limitations of SQL domains and distinct types compared to user-defined data types
- SQL CREATE ASSERTION statement for complex integrity constraints

```
CREATE ASSERTION OfferingConflict
        CHECK (NOT EXISTS
        ( SELECT O1.OfferNo
        FROM Offering O1, Offering O2
        WHERE O1.OfferNo <> O2.OfferNo
            AND O1.OffTerm = O2.OffTerm
            AND O1.OffYear = O2.OffYear
            AND O1.OffDays = O2.OffDays
            AND O1.OffTime = O2.OffTime
            AND O1.OffLocation = O2.OffLocation  ) )
```

- CHECK constraints in the CREATE TABLE statement for constraints involving row conditions on columns of the same table

```
CREATE TABLE Student
( StdSSN           CHAR(11),
     StdFirstName VARCHAR(50)
                 CONSTRAINT StdFirstNameRequired NOT NULL,
     StdLastName  VARCHAR(50)
                 CONSTRAINT StdLastNameRequired NOT NULL,
     StdCity      VARCHAR(50)
                 CONSTRAINT StdCityRequired NOT NULL,
     StdState     CHAR(2)
                 CONSTRAINT StdStateRequired NOT NULL,
     StdZip       CHAR(9)
                 CONSTRAINT StdZipRequired NOT NULL,
     StdMajor     CHAR(6),
     StdClass     CHAR(6),
     StdGPA       DECIMAL(3,2),
CONSTRAINT PKStudent PRIMARY KEY (StdSSN),
CONSTRAINT ValidGPA CHECK ( StdGPA BETWEEN 0 AND 4 ),
CONSTRAINT MajorDeclared CHECK
        ( StdClass IN ('FR','SO') OR StdMajor IS NOT NULL ) )
```

- Management of trigger and procedure coding practices: documentation standards, parameter usage, and content
- Management of object dependencies: access plan obsolescence, modification of referenced objects, deletion of referenced objects
- Controlling trigger complexity: identifying trigger interactions, minimizing trigger actions that can fire other triggers, no dependence on a specific firing order for overlapping triggers
- Catalog tables for tracking the objects managed by a DBMS

- Information resource dictionary for managing the information systems development process
- Development of an enterprise data model as an important part of the information systems planning process
- Selection and evaluation process for analyzing organization needs and DBMS features
- Using a tool such as the Analytic Hierarchy Process for consistently assigning importance weights and scoring candidate DBMSs
- Using standard, domain benchmark results to gauge the performance of DBMSs
- Responsibilities of database specialists for managing transaction processing, data warehouses, distributed environments, and object DBMSs

Questions

1. Why is it difficult to use operational databases for management decision making?
2. How must operational databases be transformed for management decision making?
3. What are the phases of the information life cycle?
4. What does it mean to integrate information life cycles?
5. What data quality dimension is important for management decision making but not for operational decision making?
6. How does knowledge management differ from information resource management?
7. What are the three pillars of knowledge management?
8. What kind of position is the data administrator?
9. What kind of position is the database administrator?
10. Which position (data administrator versus database administrator) takes a broader view of information resources?
11. What is an enterprise data model?
12. For what reasons is an enterprise data model developed?
13. What kinds of specialization are possible in large organizations for data administrators and database administrators?
14. What is discretionary access control?
15. What is mandatory access control?
16. What kind of database requires mandatory access control?
17. What are the purposes of the GRANT and REVOKE statements in SQL?
18. Why should authorization rules reference roles instead of individual users?
19. Why do authorization rules typically use views rather than tables or columns?
20. What are the two uses of the GRANT statement?
21. Why should a DBA cautiously use the WITH ADMIN clause in the CREATE ROLE statement and the WITH GRANT OPTION clause in the GRANT statement?
22. What is the difference between system privileges and object privileges in Oracle? Provide an example of a system privilege and an object privilege.
23. What other disciplines does computer security involve?
24. What is the purpose of the CREATE DOMAIN statement? Compare and contrast an SQL domain with a distinct type.
25. What additional capabilities does SQL:2006 add for user-defined types as compared to domains?
26. What is the purpose of assertions in SQL?
27. What does it mean to say that an assertion is deferrable?
28. What are alternatives to SQL assertions? Why would you use an alternative to an assertion?
29. What are the coding issues about which a DBA should be concerned?
30. How does a stored procedure or trigger depend on other database objects?
31. What are the responsibilities for a DBA for managing dependencies?
32. What is the difference between timestamp and signature dependency maintenance?
33. List at least three ways that a DBA can control trigger interactions.
34. What kind of metadata does a data dictionary contain?
35. What are catalog tables? What kind of catalog tables are managed by DBMSs?

36. What is the difference between the Information_Schema and the Definition_Schema in SQL:2006?
37. Why is it necessary to learn the catalog tables of a specific DBMS?
38. How does a DBA access catalog tables?
39. What is the purpose of an information resource dictionary?
40. What functions does an information resource dictionary system perform?
41. What are the purposes of information systems planning?
42. Why is the enterprise data model developed before the process model?
43. Why is the selection and evaluation process important for DBMSs?
44. What are some difficulties in the selection and evaluation process for a complex product like a DBMS?
45. What are the steps in the selection and evaluation process?
46. How is the Analytic Hierarchy Process used in the selection and evaluation process?
47. What responsibilities does the database administrator have in the selection and evaluation process?
48. What responsibilities does the data administrator have in the selection and evaluation process?
49. What are the responsibilities of database administrators for transaction processing?
50. What are responsibilities of database administrators for managing data warehouses?
51. What are the responsibilities of database administrators for managing databases in distributed environments?
52. What are the responsibilities of database administrators for managing object databases?
53. What are the responsibilities of data administrators for transaction processing?
54. What are the responsibilities of data administrators for managing data warehouses?
55. What are the responsibilities of data administrators for managing databases in distributed environments?
56. What are the responsibilities of data administrators for managing object databases?
57. What are the characteristics of a good benchmark?
58. Why does the Transaction Processing Council publish total system performance measures rather than component measures?
59. Why does the Transaction Processing Council publish price/performance results?
60. How does the Transaction Processing Council ensure that benchmark results are relevant and reliable?
61. What is the status of standards and implementations of the Information Resource Dictionary?
62. Briefly describe the Model Driven Architecture (MDA) and its current status.
63. What are the choices for information resource tools beyond the dictionary tables provided by an enterprise DBMS?
64. Briefly describe the advanced tools provided by Oracle for data security.

Problems

Due to the nature of this chapter, the problems are more open-ended than other chapters. More detailed problems appear at the end of the other chapters in Part 7.

1. Prepare a short presentation (6 to 12 slides) about the TPC-C benchmark. You should provide details about its history, database design, application details, and recent results.
2. Prepare a short presentation (6 to 12 slides) about the TPC-H benchmark. You should provide details about its history, database design, application details, and recent results.
3. Prepare a short presentation (6 to 12 slides) about the TPC-E benchmark. You should provide details about its history, database design, application details, and recent results.
4. Prepare a short presentation (6 to 12 slides) about the TPC-App benchmark. You should provide details about its history, database design, application details, and recent results.
5. Compare and contrast the software licenses for MySQL and another open source DBMS product.
6. Develop a list of detailed requirements for nonprocedural retrieval. You should use Table 14-13 as a guideline.

1. Provide importance weights for your list of detailed requirements from problem 6 using the AHP criteria in Table 14-4.
2. Normalize the weights and compute the importance values for your detailed requirements using the importance weights from problem 7.
3. Write named CHECK constraints for the following integrity rules. Modify the CREATE TABLE statement to add the named CHECK constraints.

```
CREATE TABLE Customer
( CustNo            CHAR(8),
  CustFirstName     VARCHAR2(20)
                    CONSTRAINT CustFirstNameRequired NOT NULL,
  CustLastName      VARCHAR2(30)
                    CONSTRAINT CustLastNameRequired NOT NULL,
  CustStreet        VARCHAR2(50),
  CustCity          VARCHAR2(30),
  CustState         CHAR(2),
  CustZip           CHAR(10),
  CustBal           DECIMAL(12,2) DEFAULT 0,
CONSTRAINT PKCustomer PRIMARY KEY (CustNo)  )
```

- Customer balance is greater than or equal to 0.
- Customer state is one of CO, CA, WA, AZ, UT, NV, ID, or OR.

4. Write named CHECK constraints for the following integrity rules. Modify the CREATE TABLE statement to add the named CHECK constraints.

```
CREATE TABLE Purchase
(     PurchNo           CHAR(8),
      PurchDate         DATE
                        CONSTRAINT PurchDateRequired NOT NULL,
      SuppNo            CHAR(8)
                        CONSTRAINT SuppNo2Required NOT NULL,
      PurchPayMethod    CHAR(6) DEFAULT 'PO',
      PurchDelDate      DATE,
  CONSTRAINT PKPurchase PRIMARY KEY (PurchNo),
  CONSTRAINT SuppNoFK2 FOREIGN KEY (SuppNo) REFERENCES Supplier )
```

- Purchase delivery date is either later than the purchase date or null.
- Purchase payment method is not null when purchase delivery date is not null.
- Purchase payment method is PO, CC, DC, or null.

5. In this problem, you should create a view, several roles, and then grant specific kinds of access of the view to the roles.
   - Create a view of the *Supplier* table in the extended Order Entry Database introduced in the problems section of Chapter 10. The view should include all columns of the *Supplier* table for suppliers of printer products (*Product.ProdName* column containing the word "Printer"). Your view should be named "PrinterSupplierView."
   - Define three roles: PrinterProductEmp, PrinterProductMgr, and StoreMgr.
   - Grant the following privileges of PrinterSupplierView to PrinterProductEmp: retrieval of all columns except supplier discount.
   - Grant the following privileges of PrinterSupplierView to PrinterProductMgr: retrieval and modification of all columns of PrinterSupplierView except supplier discount.
   - Grant the following privileges of PrinterSupplierView to StoreMgr: retrieval for all columns, insert, delete, and modification of supplier discount.

12. Identify important privileges in an enterprise DBMS for data warehouses and database statistics. The privileges are vendor specific so you need to read the documentation of an enterprise DBMS.
13. Identify and briefly describe dictionary tables for database statistics in an enterprise DBMS. The dictionary tables are vendor specific so you need to read the documentation of an enterprise DBMS.
14. Write a short summary (one page) about DBA privileges in an enterprise DBMS. Identify predefined roles and/or user accounts with DBA privileges and the privileges granted to these roles.

References for Further Study

The book by Jay Louise Weldon (1981) remains the classic book on database administration despite its age. Mullin (2002) provides a more recent comprehensive reference about database administration. The Information Resource Management section of the online list of Web resources provides links to information resource management and knowledge management sources. Numerous SQL books provide additional details about the security and integrity features in SQL. Inmon (1986) and Martin (1982) have written detailed descriptions of information systems planning. Castano et al. (1995) is a good reference for additional details about database security. For more details about the Analytic Hierarchy Process mentioned in Section 14.3.2, you should consult Saaty (1988) and Zahedi (1986). Su et al. (1987) describe the Logic Scoring of Preferences, an alternative approach to DBMS selection. The Transaction Processing Council (www.tpc.org) provides an invaluable resource about domain-specific benchmarks for DBMSs. Details about the Model Development Architecture (MDA) can be found at the website of the Object Management Group (www.omg.org).

Appendix 14.A: SQL:2006 Syntax Summary

This appendix summarizes the SQL:2006 syntax for the CREATE/DROP ROLE statements, the GRANT/REVOKE statements, the CREATE DOMAIN statement, and the CREATE ASSERTION statement as well as the CHECK constraint clause of the CREATE TABLE statement. The conventions used in the syntax notation are identical to those used at the end of Chapter 3.

CREATE and DROP ROLE Statements

```
CREATE ROLE RoleName
  [ WITH ADMIN UserName { CURRENT_USER | CURRENT_ROLE } ]

DROP ROLE RoleName
```

GRANT and REVOKE Statements

```
-- GRANT statement for privileges
GRANT { <Privilege>* | ALL PRIVILEGES } ON ObjectName
  TO UserName* [ WITH GRANT OPTION ]

<Privilege>:
   { SELECT [ (ColumnName*) ] |
     DELETE    |
     INSERT [ (ColumnName*) ]        |
     REFERENCES [ (ColumnName*) ]  |
     UPDATE [ (ColumnName*) ]
     USAGE  |
     TRIGGER  |
     UNDER  |
     EXECUTE }

-- GRANT statement for roles
GRANT RoleName*
  TO UserName* [ WITH ADMIN OPTION ]

-- REVOKE statement for privileges
REVOKE [ GRANT OPTION FOR ] <Privilege>*
  ON ObjectName FROM UserName*
  [ GRANTED BY { CURRENT_USER | CURRENT_ROLE } ]
  { CASCADE | RESTRICT }

-- REVOKE statement for roles
REVOKE [ ADMIN OPTION FOR ] RoleName*
  FROM UserName*
  [ GRANTED BY { CURRENT_USER | CURRENT_ROLE } ]
  { CASCADE | RESTRICT }
```

CREATE DOMAIN and DROP DOMAIN Statements

```
CREATE DOMAIN DomainName DataType
  [ CHECK ( <Domain-Condition> ) ]

<Domain-Condition>:
   { VALUE <Comparison-Operator> Constant |
     VALUE BETWEEN Constant AND Constant  |
     VALUE IN ( Constant* )   }

<Comparison-Operator>:
   { = | < | > | <= | >= | <> }

DROP DOMAIN DomainName { CASCADE | RESTRICT }
```

CREATE ASSERTION and DROP ASSERTION Statements

```
CREATE ASSERTION AssertionName
  CHECK ( <Group-Condition> )

<Group-Condition>: -- initially defined in Chapter 4 and
extended in Chapter 9

DROP ASSERTION AssertionName { CASCADE | RESTRICT }
```

CHECK Constraint Clause in the CREATE TABLE Statement

```
CREATE TABLE  TableName
  ( <Column-Definition>*  [ ,  <Table-Constraint>*  ]  )

<Column-Definition>: ColumnName DataType
[ DEFAULT { DefaultValue | USER | NULL } ]
[ <Embedded-Column-Constraint>+ ]

-- Check constraint can be used as an embedded column
-- constraint or as a table constraint.

<Embedded-Column-Constraint>:
  { [ CONSTRAINT ConstraintName ] NOT NULL      |
    [ CONSTRAINT ConstraintName ] UNIQUE        |
    [ CONSTRAINT ConstraintName ] <Check-Constraint> |
    [ CONSTRAINT ConstraintName ] PRIMARY KEY   |
    [ CONSTRAINT ConstraintName ] FOREIGN KEY
        REFERENCES TableName [ ( ColumnName ) ]
        [ ON DELETE  <Action-Specification> ]
        [ ON UPDATE  <Action-Specification> ] }

<Table-Constraint>: [ CONSTRAINT ConstraintName ]
  { <Primary-Key-Constraint>  |
    <Foreign-Key-Constraint>  |
    <Uniqueness-Constraint>   |
    <Check-Constraint>  }

<Primary-Key-Constraint>: PRIMARY KEY ( ColumnName* )

<Foreign-Key-Constraint>: FOREIGN KEY ( ColumnName* )
    REFERENCES TableName [( ColumnName* )]
    [ ON DELETE  <Action-Specification> ]
    [ ON UPDATE  <Action-Specification> ]

<Action-Specification>: { CASCADE | SET NULL |
    SET DEFAULT | RESTRICT }

<Uniqueness-Constraint>: UNIQUE ( ColumnName* )

<Check-Constraint>: CHECK ( <Row-Condition> )

<Row-Condition>: -- defined in Chapter 4
```

15

Transaction Management

Learning Objectives

This chapter describes transaction management features to support concurrent usage of a database and recovery from failures. After this chapter, the student should have acquired the following knowledge and skills:

- Explain the ACID transaction properties and the concepts of recovery and concurrency transparency
- Understand the role of locking to prevent interference problems among multiple users
- Understand the role of recovery tools to deal with database failures
- Understand transaction design issues that affect performance
- Describe the relationship of workflow management to transaction management

Overview

Chapter 14 presented a context for managing databases and an overview of the different processing environments for databases. You learned about the responsibilities of database specialists and the tools and processes used by database specialists. The most prevalent and important database environment is transaction processing that supports the daily operations of an organization. This chapter begins the details of Part 7 by describing DBMS support for transaction processing.

      This chapter presents a broad coverage of transaction management. Before you can understand DBMS support for transaction processing, you need a more detailed understanding of transaction concepts. This chapter describes properties of transactions, SQL statements to define transactions, and properties of transaction processing. After learning about transaction concepts, you are ready to study concurrency control and recovery management, two major services to support transaction processing. For concurrency control, this chapter describes the objective, interference problems, and tools of concurrency control. For recovery management, this chapter describes failure types, recovery tools, and recovery processes.

      Besides knowing the transaction management services provided by a DBMS, you should understand the issues of transaction design. This chapter describes important issues of transaction design including hot spots, transaction boundaries, isolation levels, and integrity constraint enforcement. To broaden your background, you should understand how database transactions fit into the larger context of collaborative work. The final section describes workflow management and contrasts it with transaction management in DBMSs.

15.1 Basics of Database Transactions

Transaction processing involves the operating side of databases. Whereas operations management involves the production of physical goods, transaction management involves the control of information goods or transactions. Transaction management, like management of physical goods, is enormously important to modern organizations. Organizations such as banks with automatic tellers, airlines with online reservation systems, and universities with online registration could not function without reliable and efficient transaction processing. Large organizations now conduct thousands of transactions per minute. With continued growth in electronic commerce, the importance of transaction processing will increase.

      In common discourse, a transaction is an interaction among two or more parties for the conduct of business such as buying a car from a dealership. Database transactions have a more precise meaning. A database transaction involves a collection of operations that must be processed as one unit of work. Transactions should be processed reliably so that there is no loss of data due to multiple users and system failures. To help you grasp this more precise meaning, this section presents examples of transactions and defines properties of transactions.

> **Transaction:** a unit of work that should be processed reliably. DBMSs provide recovery and concurrency control services to process transactions efficiently and reliably.

15.1.1 Transaction Examples

A transaction is a user-defined concept. For example, making an airline reservation may involve reservations for the departure and return. To a traveler, the combination of the departure and the return is a transaction, not the departure and the return separately. If a departure and return are considered separately, a traveler may make a departure without obtaining a desired return flight. The implication for DBMSs is that a transaction is a user- defined set of database operations. A transaction can involve any number of reads and writes to a database. To provide the flexibility of user-defined transactions, DBMSs cannot restrict transactions to only a specified number of reads and writes to a database.

An information system may have many different kinds of transactions. Table 15-1 depicts transactions of an order entry system. At any point in time, customers may be conducting business with each of these transactions. For example, many customers may be placing orders while other customers check on the status of their orders. As an additional example of transactions in an information system, Table 15-2 depicts typical transactions in a university payroll system. Some of the transactions are periodic while others are one-time events.

Table 15-1: Typical Transactions in an Order Entry System

Transaction	Description
Add order	Customer places a new order.
Update order	Customer changes details of an existing order.
Check status	Customer checks the status of an order.
Payment	Payment received from a customer.
Shipment	Goods sent to a customer.

Table 15-2: Typical Transactions in University Payroll System

Transaction	Description
Hire employee	Employee begins service with the university.
Pay employee	Periodic payment made to employee for service.
Submit time record	Hourly employees submit a record of hours worked.
Reappointment	Employee is assigned a new position.
Evaluation	Periodic performance evaluation
Termination	Employee leaves employment at the university.

SQL Statements to Define Transactions

To define a transaction, you can use some additional SQL statements. Figure 15.1 depicts additional SQL statements to define the prototypical automatic teller machine (ATM) transaction. The START TRANSACTION[38] and COMMIT statements define the statements in a transaction. Any other SQL statements between them are part of the transaction. Typically, a transaction involves a number of SELECT, INSERT, UPDATE, and DELETE statements. In Figure 15.1, an actual transaction would have valid SQL statements for the lines beginning with SELECT, UPDATE, and INSERT. Valid programming language statements would be substituted for lines with pseudo code such as "Display greeting."

---

[38] SQL: 2006 specifies the START TRANSACTION and COMMIT statements. Some DBMSs use the keyword BEGIN instead of START. Some DBMSs such as Oracle do not use a statement to explicitly start a transaction. A new transaction begins with the next SQL statement following a COMMIT statement.

```
START TRANSACTION
Get account number, pin, type, and amount
SELECT account number, type, and balance
If balance is sufficient then
            UPDATE account by posting debit
            UPDATE account by posting credit
            INSERT history row
            Display final message and issue cash
Else
            Write error message
End If
On Error: ROLLBACK
COMMIT
```

Figure 15.1: Pseudocode for an ATM Transaction

Besides the START TRANSACTION and COMMIT statements, the ROLLBACK statement may be used. ROLLBACK is like an undo command in a word processor in that the effects of user actions are removed. Unlike an undo command, ROLLBACK applies to a sequence of actions not just a single action. Thus, a ROLLBACK statement causes all effects of a transaction to be removed. The database is restored to the state before the transaction was executed.

A ROLLBACK statement can be used in several contexts. One situation is to allow a user to cancel a transaction. A second situation is to respond to errors. In this situation, the ROLLBACK statement can be used as part of exception-handling statements such as the "On Error" line in Figure 15.1. Exception-handling statements are part of programming languages such as Java and Visual Basic. Exception handling allows unanticipated errors such as communication errors to be processed separately from the normal logic of the transaction.

As you will learn later in this chapter, transactions should be designed to have short duration. To shorten the duration of the ATM transaction, the user interaction can be placed outside of the transaction. In the ATM transaction, the START TRANSACTION statement can be placed after the first three lines to remove user interaction. Long-running transactions can cause excessive waiting among concurrent users of a database. However, the UPDATE and INSERT statements must remain in the same transaction because these statements are part of the same unit of work. Section 15.4.1 discusses issues related to removing user interaction time from a transaction. Sometimes, user interaction time should remain part of a transaction.

Other Transaction Examples

Figures 15.2 and 15.3 depict transactions for an airline reservation and online shopping purchase. In both examples, the transaction consists of more than one database action (read or write). In the airline reservation, two flight rows must be updated along with a reservation row. In a more complex airline reservation involving multiple flights per part (departure or return), more flight rows must be updated. In the online shopping purchase, product rows are updated and order detail rows are inserted.

```
START TRANSACTION
Get reservation preferences
SELECT departure and return flight rows
if reservation is acceptable then
            Get payment method and details
            UPDATE seats remaining of departure flight row
            UPDATE seats remaining of return flight row
            INSERT reservation row
            Send receipt to customer
End If
On Error: ROLLBACK
COMMIT
```

Figure 15.2: Pseudocode for an Airline Reservation Transaction

```
START TRANSACTION
Place product selections in shopping cart
If checking out then
     Get account and payment details
     SELECT account row
            For each product row
                 UPDATE QOH of product row
                 INSERT order detail row
                 Send message to shipping department
     End For
Send confirmation message to customer
End If
On Error: ROLLBACK
COMMIT
```

Figure 15.3: Pseudocode for an Online Shopping Transaction

15.1.2 Transaction Properties

DBMSs ensure that transactions obey certain properties. The most important and widely known properties are the ACID properties (atomic, consistent, isolated, and durable) as presented the following list.

- *Atomic* means that a transaction cannot be subdivided. Either all the work in the transaction is completed or nothing is done. For example, the ATM transaction will not debit an account without also crediting a corresponding account. The atomic property implies that partial changes made by a transaction must be undone if the transaction aborts.
- *Consistent* means that if applicable constraints are true before the transaction starts, the constraints will be true after the transaction terminates. For example, if a user's account is balanced before a transaction, then the account is balanced after the transaction. Otherwise, the transaction is rejected and no changes take effect.
- *Isolated* means that transactions do not interfere with each other except in allowable ways. A transaction should never overwrite changes made by another transaction. In addition, a transaction may be restricted from interfering in other ways such as not viewing the temporary changes made by other transactions. For example, your significant other will not know that you are withdrawing money until your ATM transaction completes.
- *Durable* means that any changes resulting from a transaction are permanent. No failure will erase any changes after a transaction terminates. For example, if a bank's computer experiences a failure five minutes after a transaction completes, the results of the transaction are still recorded on the bank's database.

To ensure that transactions meet the ACID properties, DBMSs provide certain services that are transparent to database developers (programmers and analysts). In common usage, transparency means that you can see through an object, rendering its inner details invisible. For DBMSs, transparency means that the inner details of transaction services are invisible. Transparency is very important because services that ensure ACID transactions are difficult to implement. By providing these services, DBMSs improve the productivity of database programmers and analysts.

DBMSs provide two services, recovery transparency and concurrency transparency, to ensure that transactions obey the ACID properties. Recovery involves actions to deal with failures such as communication errors and software crashes. Concurrency involves control of interference among multiple, simultaneous users of the database. The following discussion provides details about transparency for recovery and concurrency.

- *Recovery transparency* means that the DBMS automatically restores a database to a consistent state after a failure. For example, if a communication failure occurs during an ATM transaction, the effects of the transaction are automatically removed from the database. On the other hand, if the DBMS crashes three seconds after an ATM transaction completes, the details of the transaction remain permanent.
- *Concurrency transparency* means that users perceive the database as a single-user system even though there may be many simultaneous users. For example, even though many users may try to reserve a popular flight using a reservation transaction, the DBMS ensures that users do not overwrite each other's work.

Even though the inner details of concurrency and recovery are not visible to a user, these services are not free. Recovery and concurrency control involve overhead that may require additional resources and careful monitoring to reach an acceptable level of performance. The DBA must be aware of the resource implications of these services and understand the tools to monitor performance. More computing resources such as memory, disk space, and parallel processing may be necessary to improve performance. Performance monitoring is required to ensure adequate performance. The DBA should monitor key indicators of performance and change parameter settings to alleviate performance problems.

In addition to resources and monitoring, the selection of a DBMS can be crucial to achieve acceptable transaction processing performance. The purchase price of a DBMS often depends on the level of transaction services provided. Most DBMS products have different editions to support workgroups to entire enterprises. DBMS editions can vary by the number of concurrent transactions supported, parallel processing services provided, and recovery services available. DBMSs that support large numbers of concurrent users with very high availability can be costly.

Transaction design is another reason for understanding details of concurrency control and recovery. Even if a good DBMS is selected and adequate resources are devoted to transaction processing, poor transaction design can lead to performance problems. To achieve a satisfactory transaction design, you should have background about concurrency control and recovery as well as understand transaction design principles, as discussed in the following sections.

15.2 Concurrency Control

Most organizations cannot function without multiuser databases. For example, airline, retail, banking, and help desk databases can have thousands of users simultaneously trying to conduct business. Multiple users can access these databases concurrently, that is, at the same time. If access was restricted to only one user at a time, little work would be accomplished and most users would take their business elsewhere. However, concurrent users cannot be permitted to interfere with each other. This section defines the objective, problems, and tools of concurrency control.

15.2.1 Objective of Concurrency Control

The objective of concurrency control is to maximize transaction throughput while preventing interference among multiple users. Transaction throughput, the number of transactions processed per time unit, is a measure of the amount of work performed by a DBMS. Typically, transaction throughput is reported in transactions per minute. In a high-volume environment such as electronic commerce, DBMSs may need to process hundreds of thousands of transactions per minute. In 2008, the Transaction Processing Council (www.tpc.org) reported top results for the TPC-C benchmark (an order entry benchmark) of more than four million of transactions per minute.

From a user's perspective, transaction throughput is related to response time. Higher transaction throughput means lower response times. Users are typically unwilling to wait more than a few seconds for completion of a transaction.

> **Transaction Throughput**: the number of transactions processed per time interval. It is an important measure of transaction processing performance.

If there is no interference, the result of executing concurrent transactions is the same as executing the same transactions in some sequential order. Sequential execution means that one transaction completes before another one executes, thus ensuring no interference. Executing transactions sequentially would result in low throughput and high waiting times. Thus, DBMSs allow transactions to execute simultaneously while ensuring the results are the same as though executed sequentially.

Transactions executing concurrently cannot interfere unless they are manipulating common data. Essentially, the same transaction order must be maintained for each common database item. For example, if transaction i writes database item A before transaction j writes database item A, then transaction j cannot write item B before transaction i writes item B. If transaction j writes item B before transaction i, a concurrency control violation has occurred. This informal definition of correct concurrent execution will be clarified in Section 15.2.2 with presentation of specific concurrency control problems.

Most concurrent transactions manipulate only small amounts of common data. For example, in an airline reservation, two users can simultaneously enter new reservation rows because the reservation rows are unique for each customer. However, interference can occur on the seats-remaining column of a flight table. For popular flights, many users may want to decrement the value of the seats-remaining column. It is critical that the DBMS control concurrent updating of this column in popular flight rows.

A hot spot is common data that multiple users try to change simultaneously. Essentially, a hot spot represents a scarce resource that users must queue to access. Typical hot spots are the seats-remaining for popular flights, the quantity-on-hand of popular inventory items, and the seats-taken in popular course offerings. In an ideal world, DBMSs would only track hot spots. Unfortunately, hot spots can be difficult to know in advance so DBMSs track access to all parts of a database.

> **Hot Spot**: common data that multiple users try to change. Without adequate concurrency control, users may interfere with each other on hot spots.

Interference on hot spots can lead to lost data and poor decision making. The following sections describe interference problems and tools to prevent them.

15.2.2 Interference Problems

There are three problems that can result because of simultaneous access to a database: (1) lost update, (2) uncommitted dependency, and (3) inconsistent retrieval. This section defines each problem and presents examples of their occurrence.

Lost Update

Lost update is the most serious interference problem because changes to a database are inadvertently lost. In a _lost update_, one user's update overwrites another user's update, as depicted by the timeline of Figure 15.4. The timeline shows two concurrent transactions trying to update the seats remaining (*SR*) field of the same flight record. Assume that the value of *SR* is 10 before the transactions begin. After time T_2, both transactions have stored the value of 10 for *SR* in local buffers as a result of the read operations. After time T_4, both transactions have made changes to their local copy of *SR*. However, each transaction changes the value to 9, unaware of the activity of the other transaction. After time T_6, the value of *SR* on the database is 9. But the value after finishing both transactions should be 8, not 9! One of the changes has been lost.

Transaction A	Time	Transaction B
Read SR (10)	T_1	
	T_2	Read SR (10)
If SR > 0 then SR = SR -1	T_3	
	T_4	If SR > 0 then SR = SR -1
Write SR (9)	T_5	
	T_6	Write SR (9)

Figure 15.4: Example Lost Update Problem

Lost Update: a concurrency control problem in which one user's update overwrites another user's update.

Some students become confused about the lost update problem because of the actions performed on local copies of the data. The calculations at times T_3 and T_4 are performed in memory buffers specific to each transaction. Even though transaction A has changed the value of *SR*, transaction B performs the calculation with its own local copy of *SR* having a value of 10. The write operation performed by transaction A is not known to transaction B unless transaction B reads the value again.

A lost update involves two or more transactions trying to change (write to) the same part of the database. As you will see in the next two problems, two transactions can also conflict if only one is changing the database.

Uncommitted Dependency

An _uncommitted dependency_ occurs when one transaction reads data written by another transaction before the other transaction commits. An uncommitted dependency is also known as a dirty read because it is caused by one transaction reading dirty (uncommitted) data. In Figure 15.5, transaction A reads the *SR* field, changes its local copy of the *SR* field, and writes the new value back to the database. Transaction B then reads the changed value. Before transaction A commits, however, an error is detected and transaction A issues a rollback. The rollback could have been issued as a result of the user canceling the transaction or as a result of a failure. The value used by transaction B is now a phantom value. The real *SR* value is now 10 because A's change was not permanent. Transaction B may use its value (9) to make an erroneous decision. For example, if *SR*'s value was 1 before transaction A began, transaction B might be denied a reservation.

Transaction A	Time	Transaction B
Read SR (10)	T_1	
SR = SR - 1	T_2	
Write SR (9)	T_3	
	T_4	Read SR (9)
Rollback	T_5	

Figure 15.5: Example Dirty Read Problem

Uncommitted Dependency: a concurrency control problem in which one transaction reads data written by another transaction before the other transaction commits. If the second transaction aborts, the first transaction may rely on data that will no longer exist.

Because data are not permanent until a transaction commits, a conflict can occur even though only one transaction writes to the database. An uncommitted dependency involves one transaction writing and another transaction reading the same part of the database. However, an uncommitted dependency cannot cause a problem unless a rollback occurs. The third problem also involves conflicts when only one transaction writes to a database.

Problems Involving Inconsistent Retrievals

The last problem involves situations in which interference causes inconsistency among multiple retrievals of a subset of data. All inconsistent retrieval problems involve one transaction reading and the second transaction changing the same part of the database. The incorrect summary problem is the most significant problem involving inconsistent retrievals. An incorrect summary[39] occurs when a transaction calculating a summary function, reads some values before another transaction changes the values but reads other values after another transaction changes the values. In Figure 15.6, transaction B reads SR_1 after transaction A changes the value but reads SR_2 before transaction A changes the value. For consistency, transaction B should use all the values either before or after they are changed by other transactions.

Incorrect Summary: a concurrency control problem in which a transaction reads several values, but another transaction updates some of the values while the first transaction is still executing.

A second problem involving inconsistent retrievals is known as the phantom read problem. A phantom read problem occurs when a transaction executes a query with row conditions. Then, another transaction inserts or modifies data that the query would retrieve. Finally, the original transaction executes the same query again. The second query execution retrieves different records than the first execution. The new and changed rows are phantom because they did not exist in the result of the first query execution.

---

[39] An incorrect summary is also known as an inconsistent analysis.

Transaction A	Time	Transaction B
Read SR_1 (10)	T_1	
$SR_1 = SR_1 - 1$	T_2	
Write SR_1 (9)	T_3	
	T_4	Read SR_1 (9)
	T_5	Sum = Sum + SR_1
	T_6	Read SR_2 (5)
	T_7	Sum = Sum + SR_2
Read SR_2 (5)	T_8	
$SR_2 = SR_2 - 1$	T_9	
Write SR_2 (4)	T_{10}	

Figure 15.6: Example Incorrect Summary Problem

A third problem involving inconsistent retrievals is known as the nonrepeatable read problem. A <u>nonrepeatable read problem</u> occurs when a transaction reads the same value more than one time. In between reading the data item, another transaction modifies the data item. The second retrieval contains a different value than the first retrieval because of the change made by the other transaction.

The nonrepeatable read and phantom read problems are slightly different. A nonrepeatable read problem would occur if another user changed the value of a column of a query row so that the query returns a different value in the next execution. A phantom read problem would occur if a new row is inserted that matches a condition in a query so that the query retrieves an additional row in the next execution. The key difference is the row condition requirement for the phantom read problem.

15.2.3 Concurrency Control Tools

This section describes two tools, locks and the two-phase locking protocol, used by most DBMSs to prevent the three interference problems discussed in the previous section. In addition to the two tools, the deadlock problem is presented because a deadlock can be a negative byproduct resulting from lock usage. This section closes by briefly discussing optimistic concurrency control approaches that do not use locks.

Locks

Locks provide a way to prevent other users from accessing a database item in use. A database item can be a row, block, a subset of rows, or even an entire table. Before accessing a database item, a lock must be obtained. Other users must wait if trying to obtain a conflicting lock on the same item. Table 15-3 shows conflicts for two kinds of locks. A <u>shared</u> (S) lock must be obtained before reading a database item, whereas an <u>exclusive</u> (X) lock must be obtained before writing. As shown in Table 15-3, any number of users can hold a shared lock on the same item. However, only one user can hold an exclusive lock.

Lock: a fundamental tool of concurrency control. A lock on a database item prevents other transactions from performing conflicting actions on the same item.

Table 15-3: Locking Conflicts

| User 1 Holds | User 2 Requests | |
	S Lock	X Lock
S Lock	Lock granted	User 2 waits
X Lock	User 2 waits	User 2 waits

The concurrency control manager is the part of the DBMS responsible for managing locks. The concurrency control manager maintains a hidden[40] table to record locks held by various transactions. A lock record contains a transaction identifier, a record identifier, a kind, and a count, as explained in Table 15-4. In the simplest scheme, the kind is either shared or exclusive, as discussed previously. Most DBMSs have other kinds of locks to improve efficiency and allow for more concurrent access. The concurrency control manager performs two operations on lock records. The <u>lock</u> operator adds a row to the lock table whereas the <u>unlock</u> operator or release operator deletes a row from the lock table.

Table 15-4: Fields in a Lock Record

Field Name	Description
Transaction identifier	Unique identifier for a transaction
Record identifier	Identifies the record to be locked
Kind	Indicates the intended usage of the locked record
Count	Number of other users holding this kind of lock

Locking Granularity

<u>Locking granularity</u> is one complication about locks. Granularity refers to the size of the database item locked. Most DBMSs can hold locks for different granularities, as depicted in Figure 15.7. The entire database is the coarsest lock that can be held. If an exclusive lock is held on the entire database, no other users can access the database until the lock is released. On the other extreme, an individual column is the finest lock that can be held. Locks also can be held on parts of the database not generally seen by users. For example, locks can be held on indexes and blocks (physical records).

Locking Granularity: the size of the database item locked. Locking granularity is a trade-off between waiting time (amount of concurrency permitted) and overhead (number of locks held).

---

[40] The lock table is hidden from all users except the internal concurrency control manager. Under special circumstances, the database administrator can access the lock table.

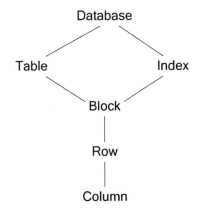

Figure 15.7: Typical Levels of Locking Granularity

Locking granularity is a trade-off between overhead and waiting. Holding locks at a fine level decreases waiting among users but increases system overhead because more locks must be obtained. Holding locks at a coarser level reduces the number of locks but increases the amount of waiting. In some DBMSs, the concurrency control manager tries to detect the pattern of usage and promotes locks if needed. For example, the concurrency control manager initially can grant row locks to a transaction in anticipation that only a few rows will be locked. If the transaction continues to request locks, the concurrency control component can promote the row locks to a lock on a subset of rows or the entire table.

To alleviate blocking caused by locking coarse items as shared or exclusive, <u>intent locks</u> are often used. Intent locks support more concurrency on coarse items than shared or exclusive locks. Intent locks also allow efficient detection of conflicts among locks on items of varying granularity. To support read and write at lower levels of granularity, three kinds of intent locks are used: (1) intention shared when intending to read lower-level items, (2) intention exclusive when intending to write lower-level items, and (3) shared intention exclusive when intending to read and write lower-level items. For example, a transaction should request an intention shared lock on a table for which it intends to read rows of the table. The intention shared lock on the table only conflicts with exclusive locks on the table or smaller grained items.

Intent Lock: a lock on a large database item (such as a table) indicating intention to lock smaller items contained in the larger item. Intent locks alleviate blocking when locking coarse items and allow efficient detection of conflicts among locks on items of varying granularity.

Deadlocks

Using locks to prevent interference problems can lead to deadlocks. A <u>deadlock</u> is a problem of mutual waiting. One transaction has a resource that a second transaction needs, and the second transaction holds a resource that the first transaction needs. Figure 15.8 depicts a deadlock among two transactions trying to purchase two popular electronic goods (say a video game controller and a GPS device). Transaction A obtains an exclusive lock on the product row containing electronic good 1. The second transaction obtains an exclusive lock on the product row containing electronic good 2. Transaction A then tries to obtain an exclusive lock on the row containing electronic good 2 but is blocked because transaction B holds an exclusive lock. Likewise, transaction B must wait to obtain an exclusive lock on the row containing electronic good 1. Deadlocks can involve more than two transactions, but the pattern is more complex.

Transaction A	Time	Transaction B
XLock Pr_1	T_1	
	T_2	XLock Pr_2
XLock Pr_2 (wait)	T_3	
	T_4	XLock Pr_1 (wait)

Figure 15.8: Example Deadlock Problem

To control deadlocks, most enterprise DBMSs perform deadlock detection. Deadlocks can be detected by looking for cyclic patterns of mutual waiting. In practice, most deadlocks involve two or three transactions. Because deadlock detection can involve significant computation time, deadlock detection is only performed at periodic intervals or triggered by waiting transactions. For example, deadlock detection for Figure 15.8 could be performed when transaction B is forced to wait. When a deadlock is detected, the transaction with the latest start time (transaction B in Figure 15.8) is usually forced to restart.

Some DBMSs use a simpler time-out policy to control deadlocks. In a time-out policy, the concurrency control manager aborts (with a ROLLBACK statement) any transaction waiting for more than a specified time. Note that a time-out policy may abort transactions that are not deadlocked. The time-out interval should be set large enough so that few non deadlocked transactions will wait that long.

Deadlock: a problem of mutual waiting that can occur when using locks. If a deadlock is not resolved, the involved transactions will wait forever. A DBMS can control deadlocks through detection or a timeout policy.

Two-Phase Locking Protocol

To ensure that lost update problems do not occur, the concurrency control manager requires that all transactions follow the Two-Phase Locking (2PL) protocol. *Protocol* is a fancy word for a group behavior rule. A protocol binds all members of a group to behave in a specified manner. For human communication, Robert's Rules of Order require that all meeting participants follow certain rules. For data communication, protocols ensure that messages have a common format that both sender and receiver can recognize. For concurrency control, all transactions must follow the 2PL protocol to ensure that concurrency control problems do not occur. Two-phase locking has three conditions as listed in the note in the margin.

Definition of 2PL
(1) Before reading or writing to a data item, the transaction must acquire the applicable lock to the data item.
(2) Wait if a conflicting lock is held on the data item.
(3) After releasing a lock, the transaction does not acquire any new locks.

The first two conditions follow from the usage of locks as previously explained. The third condition is subtler. If new locks are acquired after releasing locks, two transactions can obtain and release locks in a pattern in which a concurrency control problem occurs.

The third condition is usually simplified so that at least exclusive locks are held until the end of the transaction. At commit time, locks of a transaction are released. Figure 15.9 graphically depicts the 2PL protocol with the simplified third condition. At the beginning of the transaction (BOT), a transaction has no locks. A growing phase ensues in which the transaction acquires locks but never releases any locks. At the end of the transaction (EOT), the shrinking phase occurs in which all locks are released together. Simplifying the definition of 2PL makes the protocol easier to enforce and obviates the difficult problem of predicting when a transaction may release locks.

To provide flexibility between concurrency control problems permitted and potential waiting, most DBMSs relax the 2PL protocol to permit some locks to be released before the end of a transaction. Section 15.4.2 presents the concept of isolation levels to determine the level of interference tolerated.

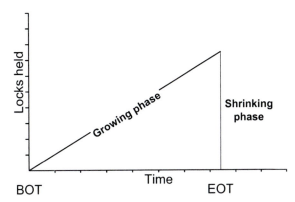

Figure 15.9: Growing and Shrinking Phases of 2PL

Optimistic Approaches

The use of locks and 2PL is a pessimistic approach to concurrency control. Locking assumes that every transaction conflicts. If contention is only for relatively few hot spots, then locking may require excessive overhead.

Optimistic concurrency control approaches assume that conflicts are rare. If conflicts are rare, it is more efficient to check for conflicts rather than manage a large number of locks. In optimistic approaches, transactions are permitted to access the database without acquiring locks. Instead, the concurrency control manager checks whether a conflict has occurred. The check can be performed either just before a transaction commits or after each read and write. By reviewing the relative time of reads and writes, the concurrency control manager can determine whether a conflict has occurred. If a conflict occurs, the concurrency control manager issues a rollback and restarts the offending transaction.

Despite the appeal of optimistic approaches, most organizations use 2PL even though some enterprise DBMSs support optimistic approaches. The performance of optimistic approaches depends on the frequency of conflicts. If conflicts increase, the performance of optimistic approaches decreases. Even if conflicts are rare, optimistic approaches can have more variability because the penalty for conflicts is larger in optimistic approaches. Pessimistic approaches resolve conflicts by waiting. Optimistic approaches resolve conflicts by rolling back and restarting. Restarting a transaction may delay a transaction more than waiting for a resource to be released.

15.3 Recovery Management

Recovery management is a service to restore a database to a consistent state after a failure. This section describes the kinds of failures to prevent, the tools of recovery management, and the recovery processes that use the tools.

15.3.1 Data Storage Devices and Failure Types

From the perspective of database failures, volatility is an important characteristic of data storage devices. Main memory is volatile because it loses its state if power is lost. In contrast, a hard disk is nonvolatile because it retains its state if power is lost. This distinction is important because DBMSs cannot depend on volatile memory to recover data after failures. Even nonvolatile devices are not completely reliable. For example, certain failures make the contents of a hard disk unreadable. To achieve high reliability, DBMSs may replicate data on several kinds of nonvolatile storage media such as a hard disk, magnetic tape, and optical disk. Using a combination of nonvolatile devices improves reliability because different kinds of devices usually have independent failure rates.

Some failures affect main memory only, while others affect both volatile and nonvolatile memory. Table 15-5 shows four kinds of failures along with their effect and frequency. The first two kinds of failures affect the memory of one executing transaction. Transaction code should check for error conditions such as an invalid account number or cancellation of the transaction by the user. A program-detected failure usually leads to aborting the transaction with a specified message to the user. The SQL ROLLBACK statement can abort a transaction if an abnormal condition occurs. Recall that the ROLLBACK statement causes all changes made by the transaction to be removed from the database. Program-detected failures are usually the most common and least harmful.

Table 15-5: Failure Types, Effects, and Frequency

Type	Effect	Frequency
Program-detected	Local (1 transaction)	Most frequent
Abnormal termination	Local (1 transaction)	Moderate frequency
System failure	Global (all active transactions)	Not frequent
Device failure	Global (all active and past transactions)	Least frequent

Abnormal termination has an effect similar to a program-detected failure but a different cause. The transaction aborts, but the error message is often unintelligible to the user. Abnormal termination can be caused by events such as transaction time-out, communication line failure, or programming error (for example, dividing by zero). The ON ERROR statement in Figure 15.1 detects abnormal termination. A ROLLBACK statement removes any effects of the terminated transaction on the database.

The last two kinds of failures have more serious consequences but are usually far less common. A system failure is an abnormal termination of the operating system. An operating system failure affects all executing transactions. A device failure such as a disk crash affects all executing transactions and all committed transactions whose work is recorded on the disk. A device failure can take hours to recover while a system crash can take minutes.

15.3.2 Recovery Tools

The recovery manager uses redundancy and control of the timing of database writes to restore a database after a failure. Three tools discussed in this section, transaction log, checkpoint, and database backup, are forms of redundancy. The last tool (force writing) allows the recovery manager to control when database writes are recorded. This section explains the nature of these tools, while the next section explains how these tools are used in recovery processes.

Transaction Log

A transaction log provides a history of database changes. Every change to a database is also recorded in the log. The log is a hidden table not available to normal users. A typical log (Table 15-6) contains a unique log sequence number (LSN), a transaction identifier, a database action, a time, a row identifier, a column name, and values (old and new). For insert operations, the column name * denotes all columns with the new value containing an entire row of values. The old and new values are sometimes called the before and after images, respectively. If the database action is insert, the log only contains the new values. Similarly, if the database action is delete, the log only contains the old values. Besides insert, update, and delete actions, log records are created for the beginning and ending of a transaction.

Transaction Log: a table that contains a history of database changes. The recovery manager uses the log table to recover from failures.

Table 15-6: Example Transaction Log for an ATM Transaction

LSN	TransNo	Action	Time	Table	Row	Column	Old	New
1	101001	START	10:29					
2	101001	UPDATE	10:30	Acct	10001	AcctBal	100	200
3	101001	UPDATE	10:30	Acct	15147	AcctBal	500	400
4	101001	INSERT	10:32	Hist	25045	*		<1002, 500, ...>
5	101001	COMMIT	10:33					

The recovery manager can perform two operations on the log. In an undo operation, the database reverts to a previous state by substituting the old value for whatever value is stored in the database. In a redo operation, the recovery component reestablishes a new state by substituting the new value for whatever value is stored in the database. To undo (redo) a transaction, the undo (redo) operation is applied to all log records of a specified transaction except for the start and commit records.

A log can add considerable storage overhead. In an environment of large transaction volumes, 100 gigabytes of log records can be generated each day. Because of this large size, many organizations have both an online log stored on disk and an archive log stored on tape or optical disk. The online log is usually divided into two parts (current and next) to manage online log space. Given the role of the log in the recovery process, the integrity of the log is crucial. Enterprise DBMSs can maintain redundant logs to provide nonstop processing in case of a log failure.

Checkpoint

The purpose of a checkpoint is to reduce the time to recover from failures. At periodic times, a checkpoint record is written to the log to record all active transactions. In addition, all log buffers as well as some database buffers are written to disk. At restart time, the recovery manager relies on the checkpoint log record and knowledge of log and database page writes to reduce the amount of restart work.

Checkpoint: the act of writing a checkpoint record to the log and writing log and some database buffers to disk. All transaction activity ceases while a checkpoint occurs. The checkpoint interval should be chosen to balance restart time with checkpoint overhead.

The checkpoint interval is defined as the period between checkpoints. The interval can be expressed as a time (such as five minutes) or as a size parameter such as the number of committed transactions, the number of log pages, or the number of database pages. The checkpoint interval is a design parameter. A small interval reduces restart work but causes more overhead to record checkpoints. A large interval reduces checkpoint overhead but increases restart work. A typical checkpoint interval might be 10 minutes for large transaction volumes.

Recording a checkpoint may involve considerable disruption in transaction processing as all transaction activity ceases while a checkpoint occurs. No new transactions can begin and existing transactions cannot initiate new operations during a checkpoint. The length of the disruption depends on the type of checkpoint used. In a cache-consistent checkpoint, buffer pages (log pages and dirty database pages) remaining in memory are written to disk and then the checkpoint record is written to the log. A page is dirty if it has been changed by a transaction.

To reduce the disruption caused by cache-consistent checkpoints, some DBMSs support either fuzzy checkpoints or incremental checkpoints. In a fuzzy checkpoint, the recovery manager only writes dirty database pages older than the previous checkpoint. Since most dirty database pages should have already been written to disk before the checkpoint, a fuzzy checkpoint should write fewer database pages than a cache consistent checkpoint. At restart time, the recovery manager uses the two most recent fuzzy checkpoint records in the log. Thus, fuzzy checkpoints involve less overhead than cache-consistent checkpoints but may require more restart work.

In an incremental checkpoint, no database pages are written to disk. Instead, dirty database pages are periodically written to disk in ascending age order. At checkpoint time, the log position of the oldest dirty data page is recorded to provide a starting point for recovery. The amount of restart work can be controlled by the frequency of writing dirty data pages.

Figure 15.10 provides a convenient summary of the three types of checkpoints. Enterprise DBMSs may provide a choice among more than one type of checkpoint. The trend is to use more resource efficient checkpoints (fuzzy and incremental) at the cost of somewhat longer restart times.

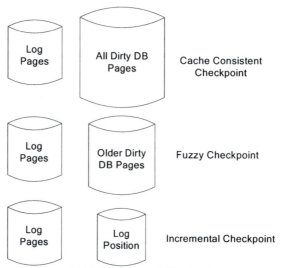

Figure 15.10: Summary of Checkpoint Types

Force Writing

The ability to control the timing of database page transfers to nonvolatile storage is known as force writing. Without the ability to control the timing of write operations to nonvolatile storage, reliable recovery is not possible. Force writing means that the DBMS, not the operating system, controls when data are written to nonvolatile storage. Normally, when a program issues a write command, the operating system puts the data in a buffer. For efficiency, the data are not written to disk until the buffer is full. Typically, there is some small delay between arrival of data in a buffer and transferring the buffer to disk. With force writing, the operating system allows the DBMS to control when the buffer is written to disk.

> **Force Writing**: the ability to control the timing of database page transfers to nonvolatile storage. This ability is fundamental to recovery management.

The recovery manager uses force writing at checkpoint time and the end of a transaction. At checkpoint time, in addition to inserting a checkpoint record, all log and some database buffers are force written to disk. This force writing can add considerable overhead to the checkpoint process. At the end of a transaction, the recovery manager force writes any log records of a transaction remaining in memory.

Database Backup

A backup is a copy of all or part of a disk. The backup is used when the disk containing the database or log is damaged. For high reliability and faster restart processing, backups can be made on independent disk drives as well as sequential media such as magnetic tape. Periodically, a backup should be made for both the database and the log. To save time, most backup schedules include less frequent massive backups to copy the entire contents of a disk and more frequent incremental backups to copy only the changed part.

15.3.3 Recovery Processes

The recovery process depends on the kind of failure. Recovery from a device failure is simple but can be time-consuming, as listed below:

- The database is restored from the most recent backup.
- Then, the recovery manager applies the redo operator to all committed transactions after the backup. Because the backup may be several hours to days old, the log must be consulted to restore transactions committed after the backup.
- The recovery process finishes by restarting incomplete transactions.

For local failures and system failures, the recovery process depends on when database changes are recorded on disk. Database changes can be recorded before the commit (immediate update) or after the commit (deferred update). The amount of work and the use of log operations (undo and redo) depend on the timing of database updates. The remainder of this section describes recovery processes for local and system failures under each scenario.

Immediate Update

In the <u>immediate update approach</u>, database updates are written to the disk when they occur. Database writes may also occur at checkpoint time depending on the checkpoint algorithm. Database writes must occur after writes of the corresponding log records. This usage of the log is known as the <u>write ahead log protocol</u>. If log records were written after corresponding database records, recovery would not be possible if a failure occurred between the time of writing the database records and the log records. To support the write ahead log protocol, the recovery manager maintains a table of log sequence numbers for each database page in a buffer. A database page cannot be written to disk if its associated log sequence number is larger than the sequence number of the last log record written to disk.

> **Immediate Update Approach**: database updates are written to disk when they occur but after the corresponding log updates. To restore a database, both undo and redo operations may be needed.

Recovery from a local failure is easy because only a single transaction is affected. All log records of the transaction are found by searching the log backwards. The undo operation is then applied to each log record of the transaction. If a failure occurs during the recovery process, the undo operation is applied again. The effect of applying the undo operator multiple times is the same as applying undo one time. After completing the undo operations, the recovery manager may offer the user the chance to restart the aborted transaction.

Recovery from a system failure is more difficult because all active users are affected. To help you understand recovery from a system failure, Figure 15.11 shows the progress of a number of transactions with respect to the commit time, the most recent checkpoint, and the failure. Each transaction represents a class of transactions. For example, transaction class T1 represents transactions started and finished before the checkpoint (and the failure). No other kinds of transactions are possible.

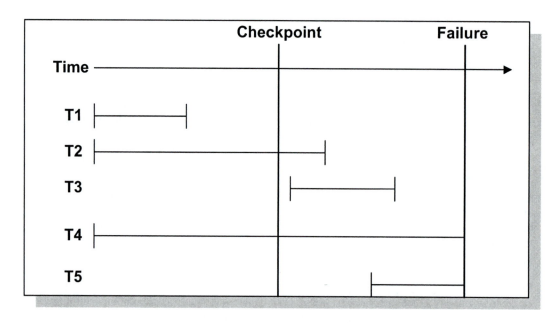

Figure 15.11: Transaction Timeline

The immediate update approach may involve both undo and redo operations, as summarized in Table 15-7. To understand the amount of work necessary, remember that log records are stable at checkpoint time and end of transaction and database changes are stable at checkpoint time. Although other database writes occur when a buffer fills, the timing of other writes is unpredictable. T1 transactions require no work because both log and database changes are stable before the failure. T2 transactions must be redone from the checkpoint because only database changes prior to the checkpoint are stable. T3 transactions must be redone entirely because database changes are not guaranteed to be stable even though some changes may be recorded on disk. T4 and T5 transactions must be undone entirely because some database changes after the checkpoint may be recorded on disk.

Table 15-7: Summary of Restart Work for the Immediate Update Approach

Class	Description	Restart Work
T1	Finished before CP	None
T2	Started before CP; finished before failure	Redo forward from the most recent checkpoint
T3	Started after CP; finished before failure	Redo forward from the most recent checkpoint
T4	Started before CP; not yet finished	Undo backwards from most recent log record
T5	Started after CP; not yet finished	Undo backwards from most recent log record

Deferred Update

In the deferred update approach, database updates are written to disk only after a transaction commits. No database writes occur at checkpoint time except for already committed transactions. The advantage of the deferred update approach is that undo operations are not necessary. However, it may be necessary to perform more redo operations than in the immediate update approach.

Deferred Update Approach: database updates are written only after a transaction commits. To restore a database, only redo operations are used.

Local failures are handled without any restart work in the deferred update approach. Because no database changes occur until after a transaction commits, the transaction is aborted without any undo work. The recovery manager typically would provide the user with the option of restarting the transaction.

System failures also can be handled without undo operations as depicted in Table 15-8. T4 and T5 transactions (not yet committed) do not require undo operations because no database changes are written to disk until after a transaction commits. T2 and T3 transactions (committed after the checkpoint) require redo operations because it is not known whether all database changes are stable. T2 transactions (started before the checkpoint) must be redone from the first log record rather than just from the checkpoint as in the immediate update approach. Thus, the deferred update approach requires more restart work for T2 transactions than does the immediate update approach. However, the deferred update approach requires no restart work for T4 and T5 transactions, while the immediate update approach must undo T4 and T5 transactions.

Table 15-8: Summary of Restart Work for the Deferred Update Approach

Class	Description	Restart Work
T1	Finished before CP	None
T2	Started before CP; finished before failure	Redo forward from the first log record
T3	Started after CP; finished before failure	Redo forward from the first log record
T4	Started before CP; not yet finished	None
T5	Started after CP; not yet finished	None

Recovery Example

Tables 15-7 and 15-8 although depicting the kind of restart work necessary, do not depict the sequence of log operations. To help you understand the log operations generated at restart time, Table 15-9 shows an example log including checkpoint records. The checkpoint action includes a list of active transactions at the time of the checkpoint. To simplify the restart process, cache consistent checkpoints are assumed.

Table 15-10 lists the log operations for the immediate update approach. The immediate update approach begins in the rollback phase. In step 1, the recovery manager adds transaction 4 to the uncommitted list and applies the undo operator to LSN 20. Likewise in step 4, the recovery manager adds transaction 3 to the uncommitted list and applies the undo operator to LSN 17. In step 5, the recovery manager adds transaction 2 to the committed list because the log record contains the COMMIT action. In step 6, the recovery manager takes no action because redo operations will be applied in the roll forward phase. In step 11, the roll backward phase ends because the START record for the last transaction on the uncommitted list has been encountered. In the roll forward phase, the recovery manager uses redo operations for each log record of active transactions.

Table 15-9: Example Transaction Log

LSN	TransNo	Action	Time	Table	Row	Column	Old	New
1	1	START	10:29					
2	1	UPDATE	10:30	Acct	10	Bal	100	200
3		CKPT(1)	10:31					
4	1	UPDATE	10:32	Acct	25	Bal	500	400
5	2	START	10:33					
6	2	UPDATE	10:34	Acct	11	Bal	105	205
7	1	INSERT	10:35	Hist	101	*		<1, 400,...>
8	2	UPDATE	10:36	Acct	26	Bal	100	200
9	2	INSERT	10:37	Hist	102	*		<2, 200,...>
10	3	START	10:38					
11	3	UPDATE	10:39	Acct	10	Bal	100	200
12		CKPT(1,2,3)	10:40					
13	3	UPDATE	10:41	Acct	25	Bal	500	400
14	1	COMMIT	10:42					
15	2	UPDATE	10:43	Acct	29	Bal	200	300
16	2	COMMIT	10:44					
17	3	INSERT	10:45	Hist	103	*		<3, 400,...>
18	4	START	10:46					
19	4	UPDATE	10:47	Acct	10	Bal	100	200
20	4	INSERT	10:48	Hist	104	*		<3, 200,...>

Table 15-10: Restart Work Using the Immediate Update Approach

Step Number	LSN	Actions
1	20	Undo; add 4 to the uncommitted list
2	19	Undo
3	18	Remove 4 from the uncommitted list
4	17	Undo, add 3 to the uncommitted list
5	16	Add 2 to the committed list
6	15	No action
7	14	Add 1 to the committed list
8	13	Undo
9	12	Note that 3 remains uncommitted
10	11	Undo
11	10	Remove 3 from the uncommitted list
12		Roll forward phase: begin reading the log at the most recent checkpoint record (LSN = 12)
13	14	Remove 1 from the committed list
14	15	Redo
15	16	Remove 2 from the committed list; stop because the committed list is empty

Table 15-11 lists the log operations for the deferred update approach. The recovery manager begins by reading the log backwards as in the immediate update approach. In step 1, the recovery manager ignores log records 20 through 17 because they involve transactions that did not commit before the failure. In steps 2 and 4, the recovery manager notes that transactions 1 and 2 have committed and will need to be redone during the roll forward phase. In step 3, the recovery manager takes no action because a redo operation will be taken later during the roll forward phase. The roll backward phase continues until START records are found for all committed transactions. In the roll forward phase, the recovery manager uses redo operations for each action of transactions on the committed list. The roll forward phase ends when the recovery manager finds the COMMIT record of the last transaction on the committed list.

Table 15-11: Restart Work Using the Deferred Update Approach

Step Number	LSN	Actions
1	20,19,18,17	No action because the transactions cannot be complete
2	16	Add 2 to the committed and incomplete lists
3	15	No action; redo during the roll forward phase
4	14	Add 1 to the committed and incomplete lists
5	13	No action because the transaction cannot be complete
6	12	Note that START records have not been found for 1 and 2
7	11,10	No action because the transaction cannot be complete
8	9,8,7,6	No action; redo during the roll forward phase
9	5	Remove 2 from the incomplete list (START record found)
10	4	No action; redo during the roll forward phase
11	3	Note that START record has not been found for 1
12	2	No action. Redo during the roll forward phase
13	1	Remove 1 from the incomplete list; begin the roll forward phase
14	2	Redo
15	4	Redo
16	6	Redo
17	7	Redo
18	8	Redo
19	9	Redo
20	14	Remove 1 from the committed list
21	15	Redo
22	16	Remove 2 from the committed list; end the roll forward phase

Recovery Features in Oracle 11g

To depict the recovery features used in an enterprise DBMS, highlights of the recovery manager in Oracle 11g are presented. Oracle uses the immediate update process with incremental checkpoints. No database writes occur at checkpoint time as database writes are periodically written to disk in ascending age order. The log sequence number corresponding to the oldest dirty database page is written to disk to identify the starting point for restart.

Incremental checkpoints involve a trade-off between the frequency of writing dirty database pages versus restart time. More frequent writes slow transaction throughput but decrease restart time. To control this trade-off, Oracle provides a parameter known as the Mean Time to Recover (MTTR) defined as the expected time (in seconds) to recover from a system failure. Decreasing this parameter causes more frequent writing of database pages. To help a DBA set the MTTR parameter, Oracle provides the MTTR Advisor to choose parameter values under various transaction workloads. The MTTR Advisor also determines the log file size that is considered optimal based on the current setting of MTTR parameter. To monitor the recovery process, Oracle provides a dynamic dictionary view that contains details about the state of the recovery process.

15.4 Transaction Design Issues

With recovery and concurrency services, it may be surprising that the transaction designer still has important design decisions. The transaction designer can be a database administrator, a programmer, or a programmer in consultation with a database administrator. The design decisions can have a significant impact on transaction processing performance. Knowledge of the details of concurrency control and recovery can make you a better transaction designer. This section describes design decisions available to transaction designers to improve performance.

15.4.1 Transaction Boundary and Hot Spots

A transaction designer develops an application to accomplish some database processing. For example, a designer may develop an application to enable a user to withdraw cash from an ATM, order a product, or register for classes. To build the application, the designer uses the transaction defining statements of SQL and the concurrency control and recovery services of the DBMS. The designer has at least several alternatives about where to use the transaction defining statements of SQL. This decision is called the transaction boundary.

> **Transaction Boundary**: an important decision of transaction design in which an application consisting of a collection of SQL statements is divided into one or more transactions.

The transaction designer typically has the option of making one large transaction containing all SQL statements or dividing the SQL statements into multiple, smaller transactions. For example, the SQL statements in the ATM transaction can be considered one transaction, as shown in Figure 15.1. Another option is to make each SQL statement a separate transaction. When transaction boundary statements (START TRANSACTION and COMMIT) are not used, each SQL statement defaults to a separate transaction.

Trade-offs in Choosing Transaction Boundaries

When choosing a transaction's boundary, the objective is to minimize the duration of the transaction while ensuring that critical constraints are satisfied. DBMSs are designed for transactions of short duration because locking can force other transactions to wait. The duration includes not only the number of reads and writes to the database but the time spent waiting for user responses. Generally, the transaction boundary should not involve user interaction. In the ATM, airline reservation, and online shopping transactions (Figure 15.1, 15.2, and 15.3, respectively), the START TRANSACTION and COMMIT statements could be moved to surround just the SQL part of the pseudocode.

Duration should not compromise constraint checking. Because constraint checking must occur by the end of a transaction, it may be difficult to check some constraints if a transaction is decomposed into smaller transactions. For example, an important constraint in accounting transactions is that debits equal credits. If the SQL statements to post a debit and a credit are placed in the same transaction, then the DBMS can enforce the accounting constraint at the end of the transaction. If they are placed in separate transactions, constraint checking cannot occur until after both transactions are committed.

Hot Spots

To understand the effects of transaction boundary choices, hot spots should be identified. Recall that hot spots are common data that multiple users try to change simultaneously. If a selected transaction boundary eliminates (creates) a hot spot, it may be a good (poor) design.

Hot spots can be classified as either system independent or system dependent. System-independent hot spots are parts of a table that many users simultaneously may want to change. Rows, columns, and entire tables can be system-independent hot spots. For example, in the airline reservation transaction (Figure 15.2), the seats-remaining column of popular flight rows is a system-independent hot spot. The seats-remaining column is a hot spot on any DBMS.

System-dependent hot spots depend on the DBMS. Usually, system-dependent hot spots involve parts of the database hidden to normal users. Pages (physical records) containing database rows or index records can often be system-dependent hot spots. For example, some DBMSs lock the next available page when inserting a row into a table. When inserting a new history row in the ATM transaction (Figure 15.1), the next available page of the history table is a system-dependent hot spot. On DBMSs that lock at the row level, there is no hot spot. There are also typically hot spots with commonly accessed index pages.

Example Transaction Boundary Design

To depict the transaction boundary choice, hierarchical forms provide a convenient context. A hierarchical form represents an application that reads and writes to a database. For example, the registration form of the university database (Figure 15.12) manipulates the *Registration* table in the main form and the *Enrollment* and *Offering* tables in the subform. When using the registration form to enroll in courses, a record is inserted in the *Registration* table after completing the main form. After completing each line in the subform, a row is inserted into the *Enrollment* table and the *OffSeatsRemain* column of the associated *Offering* row is updated. Although the *OffSeatsRemain* field does not appear in the subform, it must be updated after inserting each subform line.

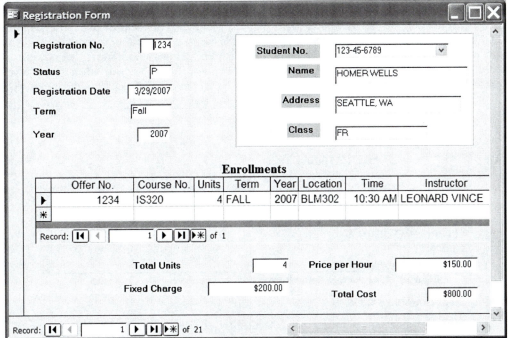

Figure 15.12: Example Registration Form

When designing a hierarchical form, the database programmer has three reasonable choices for the transaction boundary:

- The entire form
- The main form as one transaction and <u>all</u> subform lines as a second transaction
- The main form as one transaction and <u>each</u> subform line as separate transactions.

The third choice is usually preferred because it provides transactions with the shortest duration. However, constraint checking may force the choice to (1) or (2). In the registration form, there are constraints that involve an entire registration such as a minimum number of hours for financial aid and prerequisites for a course. However, these constraints are not critical to check at the end of a transaction. Most universities check these constraints at a later point before the next academic period begins. Thus, choice (3) is the best choice for the transaction boundary.

There are several hot spots common to each transaction boundary choice. The *OffSeatsRemain* column in popular *Offering* rows is a system-independent hot spot in any transaction involving the subform lines. The *OffSeatsRemain* column must be updated after each enrollment. The next page in the *Enrollment* table is a system-dependent hot spot in some DBMSs. After each subform line, a row is inserted in the *Enrollment* table. If the DBMS locks the next available page rather than just the new row, all subform line transactions must obtain an exclusive lock on the next available physical record. However, if the DBMS can lock at the row level, there is no hot spot because each transaction will insert a different row.

Choice (3) provides another advantage due to reduced deadlock possibilities. In choices (1) and (2), deadlocks are possible because the transactions involve multiple course enrollments.

For example, one transaction could obtain a lock on a data communications offering (IS470) and another transaction on a database offering (IS480). The first transaction may then wait for a lock on the IS480 offering, and the second transaction may wait for a lock on the IS470 offering. Choice (3) will be deadlock free if the hot spots are always obtained in the same order by every transaction. For example, if every transaction first obtains a lock on the next available page of *Enrollment* and then obtains a lock on an *Offering* row, then deadlock will not occur.

Avoiding User Interaction Time

Another issue of transaction boundary is user interaction. Normally user interaction should be placed outside of a transaction. Figure 15.13 shows the airline reservation transaction redesigned to place user interaction outside of the transaction. The redesigned transaction will reduce waiting times of concurrent users because locks will be held for less time. However, side effects may occur as a result of removing user interaction. With the user interaction outside of the transaction, a seat on the flight may not be available even though the user was just informed about the flight's availability. A database analyst should monitor the occurrence of this side effect. If the side effect is rare, the interaction code should remain outside of the transaction. If the side effect occurs with a reasonable frequency, it may be preferable to retain the user interaction as part of the transaction.

```
Get reservation preferences
SELECT departure and return flight rows
if reservation is acceptable then
          START TRANSACTION
          UPDATE seats remaining of departure flight row
          UPDATE seats remaining of return flight row
          INSERT reservation row
End If
On Error: ROLLBACK
COMMIT
Send receipt to customer
```

Figure 15.13: Pseudocode for Redesigned Airline Reservation Transaction

Tennis Court Reservation Case

To demonstrate organizational impacts of transaction design choices, the last part of this section presents details about an actual tennis court reservation case. This case depicts the elements of transaction design (hot spots, transaction boundary choices, and user waiting time) and the impact of transaction design on business practices.

The Southside Athletic Club[41] contracts for its online website from Tennis Systems Unlimited, an organization serving many tennis clubs with information services. An important part of the website is an online court reservation system. Although the tennis club is relatively small with about 500 members, members have been experiencing difficulty with making court reservations during peak reservation times. Reservations can be made six days in advance beginning at 7AM. During winter months, indoor tennis courts experience high demand especially during the period from 2:30PM until closing (normally 10PM).

Making a reservation involves choosing a date and time (Figure 15-14), selecting a duration (Figure 15-15), and choosing one to three partners (Figure 15-16). In Figure 15-13, a member can choose only an unreserved (white) time slot. After choosing an available time slot and duration, the reservation is subject to partner availability. Members can only appear on one reservation in each day. A small delay typically occurs in the choice of a duration. Longer delays typically occur when choosing partners as a partner must be selected from a list and the system must check partner availability.

---

[41] The names of the tennis club and external software provider have been changed.

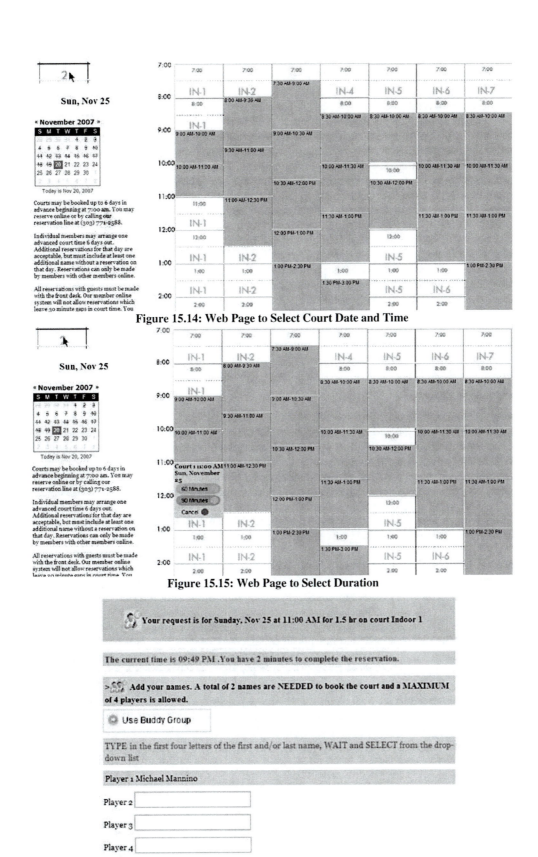

Figure 15.14: Web Page to Select Court Date and Time

Figure 15.15: Web Page to Select Duration

Your request is for Sunday, Nov 25 at 11:00 AM for 1.5 hr on court Indoor 1

The current time is 09:49 PM .You have 2 minutes to complete the reservation.

> Add your names. A total of 2 names are NEEDED to book the court and a MAXIMUM of 4 players is allowed.

◉ Use Buddy Group

TYPE in the first four letters of the first and/or last name, WAIT and SELECT from the drop-down list

Player 1 Michael Mannino

Player 2

Player 3

Player 4

Book Court

Figure 15.16: Web Page to Select Partners

The tennis reservation database has a predictable system independent hot spot. Popular reservation times create contention for locks on the corresponding rows in the reservation table. The reservation table contains columns for the unique reservation number, date, start time, duration, court, player1, player2, optional player3, and optional player4.

In the transaction boundary decision, two options were considered. The minimal duration choice involves no waiting time as it begins after selection of all reservation details (date, time, duration, and partners). However, the minimal duration choice has a side effect that a reservation may not be available after selecting all reservation parts. The alternative choice is to begin the transaction after selection of the date, time, and duration. The alternative choice involves wait time for partner selection, but the member will obtain the court after selection of the date, time, and duration. In actual system deployment, the alternative choice was selected due to the importance of stability of court selection. With high contention for court reservations at initial reservation times, member dissatisfaction became high when selected courts were not available after partner selection. To limit transaction duration, a four minute limit was imposed on partner selection time.

Despite careful design, the online reservation system had substantial problems after deployment. Members had difficulty obtaining desired reservations during peak reservation times. The system was unstable and slow with web pages sometimes taking minutes to load. After consultations among club members, club management, and vendor management, it was decided to divide the reservation period into two periods (6AM to 2:30PM starting at 7AM and 2:30PM to 10PM starting at 8AM). In addition, the current day's reservation calendar was preloaded prior to the beginning of a reservation period. System performance has improved as a result of these changes with stable operation and much faster page loading.

15.4.2 Isolation Levels

Two-phase locking prevents the three concurrency control problems described in Section 15.2.2 if all locks are held until the end of the transaction. However, some transactions may not need this level of concurrency control. The lost update problem is the most serious problem and should always be prevented. Some transactions may be able to tolerate conflicts caused by the uncommitted dependency and the inconsistent retrieval problems. Transactions that do not need protection from these problems can release locks sooner and achieve faster execution speed.

The isolation level specifies the degree to which a transaction is separated from the actions of other transactions. A transaction designer can balance concurrency control overhead with potential interference problems by specifying the appropriate isolation level.

Isolation Level: defines the degree to which a transaction is separated from actions of other transactions. A transaction designer can balance concurrency control overhead with interference problems prevented by specifying the appropriate isolation level.

Table 15-12 summarizes the SQL:2006 isolation levels according to the duration and type of locks held. The serializable level prevents all concurrency control problems but involves the most overhead and waiting. To prevent concurrency control problems, predicate locks are used and all locks are long term (held until commit time). Predicate locks that reserve rows specified by conditions in the WHERE clause are essential to prevent phantom read problems. The repeatable read level uses short-term predicate locks to prevent the incorrect summary and the nonrepeatable read problems. The read committed level uses short-term shared locks to enable more concurrent access. However, it only prevents the uncommitted dependency problem and the traditional lost update problem. Because the read uncommitted level does not use locks, it is only appropriate for read-only access to a database.

Table 15-12: Summary of Isolation Levels

Level	Exclusive Locks	Shared Locks	Predicate Locks	Problems Permitted
Read Uncommitted	None since read-only	None	None	Only uncommitted dependencies because transactions must be read-only
Read Committed	Long-term	Short-term	None	Scholar's lost updates, incorrect summary, non repeatable reads
Repeatable Read	Long-term	Long-term	Short-term read, Long-term write	Phantom reads
Serializable	Long-term	Long-term	Long-term	None

A transaction designer can specify the isolation level using the SQL SET TRANSACTION statement, as shown in Example 15.1. The SET TRANSACTION statement is usually placed just before a START TRANSACTION statement to alter the default settings for transactions. In Example 15.1, the isolation level is set to READ COMMITTED. The other keywords are SERIALIZABLE, REPEATABLE READ, and READ UNCOMMITTED. Some DBMS vendors do not support all of these levels while other vendors support additional levels.

Example 15.1 (SQL:2006): SET TRANSACTION Statement to Set the Isolation Level of a Transaction.

```
SET TRANSACTION ISOLATION LEVEL READ COMMITTED
START TRANSACTION
...
COMMIT
```

In SQL:2006, SERIALIZABLE is the default isolation level. For most transactions, this level is recommended because the REPEATABLE READ level provides only a small performance improvement. The READ UNCOMMITTED level is recommended for read-only transactions that can tolerate retrieval inconsistency.

Although SQL:2006 provides SERIALIZABLE as the default level, some DBMS vendors such as Oracle and Microsoft SQL Server use READ COMMITTED as the default level. READ COMMITTED can be a dangerous default level as it permits a variation of the lost update problem known as the scholar's lost update. The word *scholar* is ironic in that the scholar's lost update problem differs only slightly from the traditional lost update problem. Figure 15.17 depicts the scholar's lost update problem. The only essential difference between the scholar's lost update problem and the traditional lost update problem is that transaction A commits before transaction B changes the common data. Thus, the scholar's lost update is a serious potential problem that should not be permitted for most transactions.

Transaction A	Time	Transaction B
Obtain S lock on SR	T_1	
Read SR (10)	T_2	
Release S lock on SR	T_3	
If SR > 0 then SR = SR – 1	T_4	
	T_5	Obtain S lock on SR
	T_6	Read SR (10)
	T_7	Release S lock on SR
	T_8	If SR > 0 then SR = SR – 1
Obtain X lock on SR	T_9	
Write SR (9)	T_{10}	
Commit	T_{11}	
	T_{12}	Obtain X lock on SR
	T_{13}	Write SR (9)

Figure 15.17: Example Scholar's Lost Update Problem

15.4.3 Timing of Integrity Constraint Enforcement

Besides setting the isolation level, SQL allows control of the timing of integrity constraint enforcement. By default, constraints are enforced immediately after each INSERT, UPDATE, and DELETE statement. For most constraints such as primary and foreign keys, immediate enforcement is appropriate. If a constraint is violated, the DBMS issues a rollback operation on the transaction. The rollback restores the database to a consistent state as the ACID properties ensure consistency at the end of a transaction.

For complex constraints, immediate enforcement may not be appropriate. For example, a faculty workload constraint ensures that each faculty member teaches between three and nine units each semester. If a transaction assigns an entire workload, checking the constraint should be deferred until the end of the transaction. For these kinds of complex constraints, constraint timing should be specified.

Deferred Constraint Checking: enforcing integrity constraints at the end of a transaction rather than immediately after each manipulation statement. Complex constraints may benefit from deferred checking.

Constraint timing involves both constraint definition and transaction definition. SQL provides an optional constraint timing clause that applies to primary key constraints, foreign key constraints, uniqueness constraints, check constraints, and assertions. A database administrator typically uses the constraint timing clause for constraints that may need deferred checking. Constraints that never need deferred checking do not need the timing clause as the default is NOT DEFERRABLE. The timing clause defines the deferability of a constraint along with its default enforcement (deferred or immediate), as shown in Examples 15.2 and 15.3.

Example 15.2 (SQL:2006): Timing Clause for the FacultyWorkLoad Assertion
The constraint is deferrable and the default enforcement is deferred.

```
CREATE ASSERTION FacultyWorkLoad
 CHECK (NOT EXISTS
  ( SELECT Faculty.FacNo, OffTerm, OffYear
    FROM Faculty, Offering, Course
    WHERE Faculty.FacNo = Offering.FacNo
      AND Offering.CourseNo = Course.CourseNo
    GROUP BY Faculty.FacNo, OffTerm, OffYear
    HAVING SUM(CrsUnits) < 3 OR SUM(CrsUnits) > 9 ) )
 DEFERRABLE INITIALLY DEFERRED
```

Example 15.3 (SQL:2006): Timing Clause for the OfferingConflict Assertion
The constraint is deferrable and the default enforcement is immediate.

```
CREATE ASSERTION OfferingConflict
 CHECK (NOT EXISTS
  ( SELECT O1.OfferNo
    FROM Offering O1, Offering O2
    WHERE O1.OfferNo <> O2.OfferNo
      AND O1.OffTerm = O2.OffTerm
      AND O1.OffYear = O2.OffYear
      AND O1.OffDays = O2.OffDays
      AND O1.OffTime = O2.OffTime
      AND O1.OffLocation = O2.OffLocation  ) )
 DEFERRABLE INITIALLY IMMEDIATE
```

For each transaction, the transaction designer may specify whether deferrable constraints are deferred or immediately enforced using the SET CONSTRAINTS statement. Normally the SET CONSTRAINTS statement is placed just after the START TRANSACTION statement as shown in Example 15.4. The SET CONSTRAINTS statement is not necessary for deferrable constraints with deferred default enforcement. For example, if the *FacultyWorkLoad* assertion is deferred, no SET CONSTRAINTS statement is necessary because its default enforcement is deferred.

Example 15.4 (SQL:2006): SET CONSTRANTS Statements for Several Transactions

```
START TRANSACTION
SET CONSTRAINTS FacultyWorkLoad IMMEDIATE
...
COMMIT

START TRANSACTION
SET CONSTRAINTS OfferingConflict DEFERRED
...
COMMIT
```

Implementation of the constraint timing part of SQL is highly variable. Most DBMSs do not support the constraint timing part exactly as specified in the standard. Many DBMSs have different syntax and proprietary language extensions for constraint timing.

15.4.4 Save Points

Some transactions have tentative actions that can be canceled by user actions or other events. For example, a user may cancel an item on an order after discovering that the item is out of stock. Because the ROLLBACK statement removes all transaction changes, it cannot be used to remove just the canceled item if the transaction involves the entire order. The transaction designer can code statements to explicitly delete the tentative parts of a transaction, but this coding can be tedious and involve excessive overhead.

SQL:2006 provides the SAVEPOINT statement to allow partial rollback of a transaction. A transaction designer uses the SAVEPOINT keyword followed by the save point name to establish an intermediate point in a transaction. To undo work since a particular save point, the ROLLBACK TO SAVEPOINT keywords can be used followed by the save point name. Figure 15.18 depicts the usage of a save point. Typically, partial rollback is used conditionally depending on a user action or an external event.

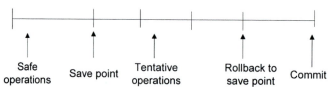

Figure 15.18: Transaction Flow with a Save Point

Save points are also used internally by some enterprise DBMSs to resolve deadlocks. Instead of rolling back an entire transaction, the DBMS rolls back a transaction to its last save point. Implicit save points can be used by a DBMS after each SQL statement to reduce the amount of lost work.

15.5 Workflow Management

Transaction management is part of a much larger area known as workflow management. Workflow management supports business processes, both automated and human performed. In contrast, transaction management supports properties of automated database processing. This section presents workflow management to provide a broader perspective for transaction management. This section first describes workflows, a broader notion than database transactions. This section then discusses enabling technologies for workflow management showing how transaction management is an important component.

15.5.1 Characterizing Workflows

Workflows support business processes such as providing phone service, obtaining a loan, and ordering a product. Workflows consist of tasks that can be performed by computers (software and hardware), humans, or a combination. For example, in providing phone service, software determines the time of a service appointment and updates a scheduling database, while a technician inspects the phone box to determine whether a problem exists. A workflow defines the order of performing the tasks, the conditions for tasks to be performed, and the results of performing tasks. For example, providing phone service involves an initial customer contact, an optional service visit, billing, and payment collection. Each of these tasks can have conditions under which they are performed and may result in actions such as database updates and invocation of other tasks.

> Workflow: A collection of related tasks structured to accomplish a business process.

Many different kinds of workflows exist. Sheth, Georgakopoulos, and Hornrick (1995) classify workflows as human-oriented versus computer-oriented, as depicted in Figure 15.19. In human-oriented workflows, humans provide most of the judgment to accomplish work. The computer has a passive role to supply data to facilitate human judgment. For example, in processing a loan, loan officers often determine the status of loans when the customer does not meet standard criteria about income and debt. Consultation with underwriters and credit personnel may be necessary. To support human-oriented workflows, electronic communication software such as email, chat, and document annotation may be useful. In computer-oriented tasks, software determines the processing of work. For example, software for an ATM transaction determines whether a customer receives cash or is denied the request. To support computer-oriented workflows, transaction management is a key technology.

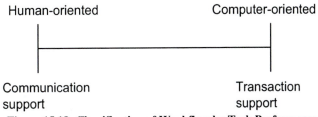

Figure 15.19: Classification of Workflow by Task Performance
(Adapted from Sheth, Georgakopoulos, and Hornrick (1995)

Another way to classify workflows is by task complexity versus task structure as depicted in Figure 15.20. Task complexity involves the difficulty of performing individual tasks. For example, the decision to grant a loan may involve complex reasoning using many variables. In contrast, processing a product order may involve requesting the product data from the customer. Task structure involves the relationships among tasks. Workflows with complex conditions have high structure. For example, processing an insurance claim may have conditions about denying the claim, litigating the claim, and investigating the claim.

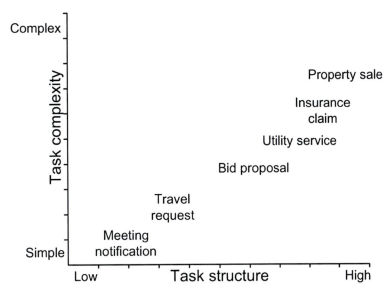

Figure 15.20: Classification of Workflow by Task Structure and Complexity
(Adapted from Sheth, Georgakopoulos, and Hornrick (1995)

15.5.2 Enabling Technologies

To support the concept of a workflow discussed in the previous section, three enabling technologies are important: (1) distributed object management, (2) workflow specification, and (3) customized transaction management. Transaction management as described in previous sections fits as part of the third technology. The remainder of this section elaborates on each technology.

Distributed Object Management

Workflows can involve many types of data in remote locations. For example, data can include photos of an insurance claim, x-rays supporting a diagnosis, and an appraisal documenting a property for a loan application. These types of data are not traditionally managed by DBMSs. A new class of DBMSs known as object DBMSs has been developed to manage diverse types of data. Chapter 18 describes this new class of DBMSs.

In addition to new types of data, the data are typically not stored at one location and may be controlled by different DBMSs. For example, to support a loan application, a loan officer uses a credit report from a credit bureau, an appraisal from a certified appraiser, and loan processing guidelines from government agencies. Accessing and controlling distributed data can be difficult.

Chapter 17 describes important principles of managing distributed data. Difficulties also can arise because the data may be controlled by different systems, some of which may not support SQL.

Workflow Specification and Implementation

To support workflows, the structure of tasks must be properly represented and implemented. Representing a workflow involves identifying the tasks and specifying the relationships among tasks. A complex task can involve a hierarchy of subtasks. A complex workflow can involve many tasks with numerous relationships. Constraints, rules, and graphical notation can be used to depict the task order and completion. One use of task relationships is to define constraints among transactions. For example, workflow specification can indicate that a student should be denied financial aid unless enrolling for a minimum number of hours by a specified date.

After a workflow is specified, it must be efficiently implemented. The implementation may involve diverse hardware, software, and people. A major challenge is to make diverse components communicate efficiently. Optimizing workflows through reengineering has become an important concern in many organizations. Optimization may involve removing duplicate tasks and increasing the amount of parallel work.

A number of software systems have been developed to support workflow specification. The main function of software under the name <u>workflow management</u> is to support workflow specification and implementation.

Customized Transaction Management

The earlier sections of this chapter described how DBMSs support ACID transactions. The ACID properties are indeed important and widely supported by DBMSs. However, to support workflows, the ACID properties may not be sufficient. The following list identifies shortcomings of traditional ACID transactions for workflow management:

- Some workflows involve tasks with a long duration because of user interaction. Traditional transaction management may not work well for these conversational transactions.
- Some tasks may involve subtasks, changing the notion of atomicity. The idea of nested transactions (transactions inside transactions) has been proposed for tasks with complex structures.
- Some tasks may be performed by legacy systems that do not support the ACID properties.
- Some workflows may require tasks to be undone after they are complete. In accounting systems, it is common for compensating transactions to correct mistakes. For example, returning a defective product removes the effect of the original product order.

Some DBMSs support some of these extensions now. For example, Microsoft SQL Server provides nested transactions to support transactions that reside in procedures. Oracle provides autonomous transactions to allow interruption of a transaction by another transaction. In addition, SQL:2006 provides save points so that a ROLLBACK statement can undo only part of a transaction. This extension can reduce the amount of work lost when a long transaction fails.

To more fully support workflow management, transaction management should be customized according to workflow requirements. The transaction properties supported for a workflow should be part of the workflow specification, not hardwired into the software supporting workflow management. DBMSs supporting workflow management may need to be more flexible. DBMSs might support different kinds of transactions or even allow transaction properties to be specified. Event processing in DBMSs can be used to support some features such as compensating transactions. Most DBMSs would need a major extension to support customized transaction management.

Closing Thoughts

This chapter has described concept underlying database transactions, the services provided by a DBMS to support transactions, and design skills for transaction designers. A transaction is a user-defined unit of work with any number of reads and writes to a database. To define a transaction, several new SQL statements were introduced including START TRANSACTION, COMMIT, and ROLLBACK. DBMSs ensure that transactions are atomic (all or nothing), consistent (satisfy integrity constraints after completion), isolated (no interference from concurrent users), and durable (survive failures). To ensure these properties of transactions, DBMSs provide services for concurrency control (making a database seem like a single-user system) and recovery management (automatically restoring a database after a failure). These powerful services are not free as they can consume large amounts of computing resources and add to the cost of a DBMS.

Although the concurrency and recovery services provided by a DBMS are transparent, you should understand some details of these services. Knowledge of these services can help you allocate computing resources, select a DBMS that provides the appropriate level of transaction support, and design efficient transactions. For concurrency control, you should understand the objective, interference problems, and the two-phase locking protocol. For recovery management, you should understand the kinds of failures, the redundant storage needed for recovery, and the amount of work to restore a database after a failure.

To apply your knowledge of transaction management, this chapter demonstrated principles of transaction design. The most important choice in transaction design is the selection of a transaction boundary. The objective of choosing a transaction boundary is to minimize duration subject to the need for constraint checking. Critical constraints such as debit-credit in accounting systems may dictate that an application remains as one transaction rather than be split into smaller transactions. A transaction boundary can also be shortened by removing user interaction. Other important decisions involve the isolation level, the timing of constraint enforcement, and save points for partial rollback. SQL syntax for these elements was shown in the chapter.

As a transaction designer, you should remember that transactions are only one kind of support for organizational work. Workflow management addresses issues beyond transaction management such as dependencies among transactions, different kinds of transactions, and annotation of work.

This chapter has described services of DBMSs to support transaction processing, the operating side of databases. Other chapters in Part 7 examine services to support other kinds of database processing such as data warehousing in Chapter 16. You should contrast the requirements to support transaction processing for operational decision making with the requirements to support data warehousing for tactical and strategic decision making.

Review Concepts

- Transactions containing a user-specified collection of database reads and writes
- SQL statements to define transactions: START TRANSACTION, COMMIT, ROLLBACK, and SAVEPOINT
- ACID properties of transactions: atomic, consistent, isolated, durable
- Transparent services to hide inner details of transaction management
- Concurrency control to support simultaneous usage of a database
- Recovery management to restore a database to a consistent state after a failure
- Concurrency control objective: maximizing transaction throughput while preventing interference problems
- Interference on hot spots, common data manipulated by concurrent users
- Kinds of interference problems: lost update, uncommitted dependency, inconsistent retrieval
- Concurrency control manager to grant, release, and analyze locks
- Growing and shrinking phases of two-phase locking (2PL)
- Resolution of deadlocks with either deadlock detection or timeout followed by transaction restart

- Optimistic concurrency control approaches when interference is rare
- Volatile versus nonvolatile storage
- Effect of local, system, and media failures
- Force writing to control the timing of database writes
- Redundant storage for recovery: log, checkpoint, backup
- Types of checkpoints: cache consistent, fuzzy, and incremental
- Tradeoff in frequency of checkpoints: transaction throughput versus restart time
- Amount of restart work in the immediate update and the deferred update recovery approaches
- Selecting a transaction boundary to minimize duration while enforcing critical integrity constraints
- Removing user interaction to reduce transaction duration except when resource stability is important
- Identifying system-independent and system-dependent hot spots in transactions
- Isolation levels for balancing potential interference against the corresponding overhead of concurrency control
- Potential for lost data when using the READ COMMITTED isolation level
- Constraint timing specification to defer enforcement of integrity constraints until end of transaction
- Save points for partial rollback of a transaction
- Workflow management to support collaborative work

Questions

1. What does it mean to say that a transaction is a user-defined concept? Why is it important that transactions are user-defined?
2. List transactions with which you have interacted in the last week.
3. Explain the purpose of the SQL statements START TRANSACTION, COMMIT, and ROLLBACK. How do these statements vary across DBMSs?
4. Briefly explain the meaning of the ACID properties. How do concurrency control and recovery management support the ACID properties?
5. Briefly explain the meaning of transparency as it relates to computer processing. Why is transparency important for concurrency control and recovery management?
6. What costs are associated with concurrency control and recovery management? In what role, database administrator or database programmer, would you assess these costs?
7. What is the objective of concurrency control? How is the measure used in the objective related to waiting time?
8. What is a hot spot? How are hot spots related to interference problems?
9. Discuss the consequences of each kind of interference problem. Which problem seems to be the most serious?
10. What is a lock? Briefly explain the differences between shared (S) and exclusive (X) locks.
11. What operations are performed by the lock manager?
12. What is a deadlock and how are deadlocks handled?
13. What is locking granularity? What are the trade-offs of holding locks at a finer level versus a coarser level of granularity?
14. What is an intent lock? Why are intent locks used on items of coarse granularity?
15. Why is the third condition of 2PL typically simplified so that locks are released at the end of a transaction?
16. What is the appeal of optimistic concurrency control approaches? Why might optimistic concurrency control approaches not be used even if they provide better expected performance?
17. Explain the difference between volatile and nonvolatile storage.
18. Explain the effects of local, system, and device failures on active and past transactions.
19. Why is force writing the most fundamental tool of recovery management?

20. What kind of redundant data is stored in a log? Why is management of the log critical to recovery?
21. What is the checkpoint interval? What is the trade-off in determining the checkpoint interval?
22. What processing occurs when a cache-consistent checkpoint occurs?
23. What is a fuzzy checkpoint? What are the advantages of a fuzzy checkpoint as compared to a cache-consistent checkpoint?
24. What is an incremental checkpoint? How can the amount of restart work be controlled with incremental checkpoints?
25. What restart work is necessary for a media failure?
26. What restart work is necessary for local and system failures under the immediate update approach?
27. What restart work is necessary for local and system failures under the deferred update approach?
28. What is a transaction boundary? Why can an inappropriate choice for transaction boundary lead to poor performance?
29. What criteria should be used in selecting a transaction boundary?
30. Why must constraints such as the debit-credit constraint be enforced as part of a transaction rather than between transactions?
31. Explain the difference between system-independent and system-dependent hot spots. Why is it useful to identify hot spots?
32. Explain the three choices for transaction boundary of a hierarchical form.
33. How can deadlock possibility be influenced by the choice of a transaction boundary?
34. What side effect can occur by moving user interaction outside a transaction boundary?
35. What is the purpose of the SQL isolation levels?
36. How do the isolation levels achieve more concurrent access?
37. What isolation level can be dangerous and why?
38. Provide an example of a constraint for which deferred enforcement may be appropriate.
39. What SQL statements and clauses involve constraint timing specification?
40. What is the role of the DBA in specifying constraint timing?
41. What is the role of the database programmer in specifying of constraint timing?
42. What is the purpose of a save point?
43. How can a save point be used in deadlock resolution?
44. What is a workflow and how is it related to database transactions?
45. What are the differences between human-oriented and computer-oriented workflows?
46. Provide an example of a workflow with high task complexity and another example with high task structure.
47. Discuss the enabling technologies for workflow management. What role does transaction management play in workflow management?
48. What are limitations of transaction management to support workflows?
49. What is the relationship between incremental checkpoints and recovery processes?
50. What level of involvement is necessary to utilize recovery and concurrency control services provided by a DBMS?
51. Should a transaction design always eliminate user interaction? Please explain your answer.

Problems

The problems provide practice using transaction-defining SQL statements, testing your knowledge of concurrency control and recovery management, and analyzing design decisions about transaction boundaries and hot spots.

1. Identify two transactions that you have encountered recently. Define pseudocode for the transactions in the style of Figures 15.1, 15.2, and 15.3.
2. Identify hot spots in your transactions from problem 1.
3. Using a timeline, depict a lost update problem using your transactions from problem 1 if no concurrency control is used.
4. Using a timeline, depict an uncommitted dependency problem using your transactions from problem 1 if no concurrency control is used.
5. Using a timeline, depict a nonrepeatable read problem using your transactions from problem 1 if no concurrency control is used.
6. Explain whether deadlock would be a problem using your transactions from problem 1 if locking is used. If a deadlock is possible, use a timeline to demonstrate a deadlock with your transactions.
7. Use the following Accounting Database tables and the Accounting Register to answer problems 7.1 to 7.7. Comments are listed after the tables and the form.

Account(AcctNo, Name, Address, Balance, LastCheckNo, StartDate)

Entry(EntryNo, *AcctNo*, Date, Amount, Desc)

Category(CatNo, Name, Description)

EntryLine(*EntryNo*, *CatNo*, Amount, Description)

Accounting Register for Wells Fargo Credit Line			
Entry No.	E101	Date:	3/11/2008
Description:	Purchases at OfficeMax	Amount:	$442.00
Invoice No.	I101		
Category	Description		Amount
Office supplies	Envelopes		25.00
Equipment	Fax machine		167.00
Computer software	MS Office upgrade		250.00

- The primary keys in the tables are underlined. The foreign keys are italicized.
- The Accounting Register records activities on an account, such as a line of credit or accounts receivable. The Accounting Register is designed for use by the accounting department of moderate-size businesses. The sample form shows one recorded entry, but a register contains all recorded entries since the opening of the account.
- The main form is used to insert a record into the *Entry* table and update the *Balance* field of the *Account* table. Accounts have a unique name (Wells Fargo Line of Credit) that appears in the title of the register. Accounts have other attributes not shown on the form: a unique number (name is also unique), start date, address, type (Receivable, Investment, Credit, etc.) and current balance.
- In the subform, the user allocates the total amount of the entry to categories. The *Category* field is a combo box. When the user clicks on the category field, the category number and name are displayed. Entering a new subform line inserts a row into the *EntryLine* table.
- The *Description* field in the subform describes a row in the *EntryLine* table rather than the *Category* table.

538

7.1 What are the possible transaction boundaries for the Accounting Register form?

7.2 Select a transaction boundary from your choices in problem 7.1. Justify your choice using the criteria defined in Section 15.4.1.

7.3 Identify system-independent hot spots that result from concurrent usage (say, many clerks in the accounting department) of the Accounting Register. For each hot spot, explain why it is a hot spot.

7.4 Identify system-dependent hot spots that result from concurrent usage (say many clerks in the accounting department) of the Accounting Register. You may assume that the DBMS cannot lock finer than a database page.

7.5 Describe a lost update problem involving one of your hot spots that could occur with concurrent usage of the Accounting Register. Use a timeline to depict your example.

7.6 Describe a dirty read situation involving one of your hot spots that could occur with concurrent usage of the Accounting Register. Use a timeline to depict your example.

7.7 Is deadlock likely to be a problem with concurrent usage of the Accounting Register? Consider the case where locks are held until all subform lines are complete. Why or why not? If deadlock is likely, provide an example as justification. Would there still be a deadlock problem if locks were held only until completion of each line on the subform? Why or why not?

8. Use the following Patient tables and the Patient Billing Form to answer problems 8.1 to 8.4. Comments are listed after the tables and the form.

Patient(PatSSN, PatName, PatCity, PatAge)

Doctor(DocNo, DocName, DocSpecialty)

Bill(BillNo, *PatSSN*, BillDate, AdmitDate, DischargeDate)

Charge(ChgNo, *BillNo*, ItemNo, ChgDate, ChgQty, *DocNo*)

Item(Itemno, ItemDesc, ItemUnit, ItemRate, ItemQOH)

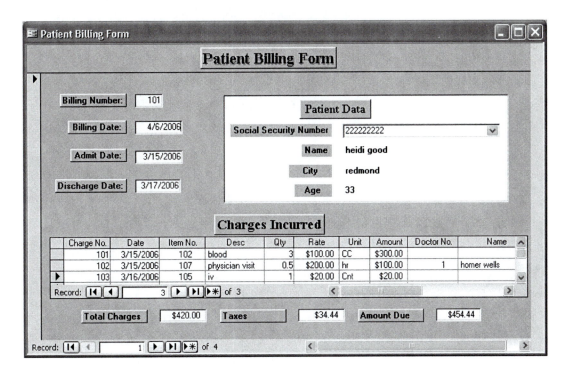

- The main form is used to insert a record into the *Bill* table. Fields from the *Patient* table are read-only in the main form.
- The subform can be used to insert a new row into the *Charge* table. Fields from the *Doctor* and the *Item* tables are read-only.
- When a subform line is entered, the associated item row is updated. The form field *Qty* affects the current value in the field *ItemQOH* (item quantity on hand).

  8.1 What are the possible transaction boundaries for the Patient Billing Form?

  8.2 Select a transaction boundary from your choices in problem 8.1. Justify your choice using the criteria defined in Section 15.4.1.

  8.3 Identify system-independent hot spots that result from concurrent usage (say many health providers) of the Patient Billing Form. For each hot spot, explain why it is a hot spot.

  8.4 Identify system-dependent hot spots that result from concurrent usage of the Patient Billing Form. You may assume that the DBMS cannot lock finer than a database page.

9. Use the following Airline Reservation database tables and the Flight Reservation Form to answer problems 9.1 to 9.4. Comments are listed after the tables and the form.

   Flight(FlightNo, *DepCityCode*, *ArrCityCode*, DepTime, ArrTime, FlgDays)

   FlightDate(*FlightNo*, FlightDate, RemSeats)

   Reservation(ResNo, *CustNo*, ResDate, Amount, CrCardNo)

   ReserveFlight(ResNo, FlightNo, FlightDate)

   Customer(CustNo, CustName, Custstreet, CustCity, CustState, CustZip)

   City(CityCode, CityName, Altitude, AirportConditions)

Flight Reservation Form					
Reservation No.		R101	Today's Date:		8/26/2008
Credit Card No.		CC101	Amount:		$442.00
Customer No.		C101	Customer Name		Jill Horn
		Flight Schedule			
Flight No.	Date	Dep City	Dep Time	Arr City	Arr Time
F101	8/26/2008	DNV	10:30AM	CHG	11:45AM
F201	8/31/2008	CHG	10:00AM	DNV	1:20PM

- The primary keys in the tables are underlined. The foreign keys are italicized. Note that the combination of *ResNo*, *FlightNo*, and *FlightDate* is the primary key of the *ReserveFlight* table. The combination of *FlightNo* and *FlightDate* is a foreign key in the *ReserveFlight* table referring to the *FlightDate* table.
- The Flight Reservation Form is somewhat simplified as it accommodates only a single class of seating, no reserved seats, and no meals. However, commuter and low-cost airlines often have these restrictions.
- The main form is used to insert a record into the *Reservation* table. The fields from the *Customer* table are read-only.
- The subform is used to insert new rows in the *ReserveFlight* table and update the field *RemSeats* in the *FlightDate* table. The fields from the *Flight* table are read-only.

9.1 Select a transaction boundary for the Flight Reservation Form. Justify your choice using the criteria defined in Section 15.4.1.

9.2 Identify system-independent hot spots that result from concurrent usage (say many reservation agents) of the Flight Reservation Form. For each hot spot, explain why it is a hot spot.

9.3 Identify system-dependent hot spots that result from concurrent usage of the Flight Reservation Form. You may assume that the DBMS cannot lock finer than a database page.

9.4 Is deadlock likely to be a problem with concurrent usage of the Flight Reservation Form? If deadlock is likely, provide an example as justification.

10. The following timeline shows the state of transactions with respect to the most recent backup, checkpoint, and failure. Use the timeline when solving the problems in subparts of this problem (10.1 to 10.5).

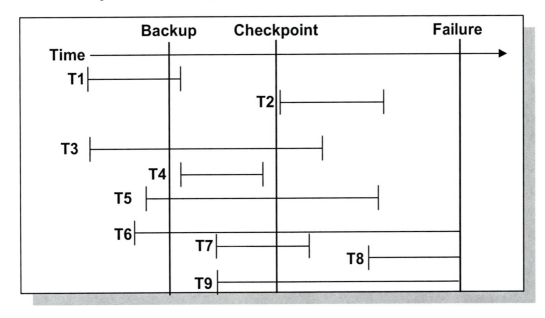

a. Describe the restart work if transaction T3 is aborted (with a ROLLBACK statement) after the checkpoint but prior to the failure. Assume that the recovery manager uses the deferred update approach.

b. Describe the restart work if transaction T3 is aborted (with a ROLLBACK statement) after the checkpoint but prior to the failure. Assume that the recovery manager uses the immediate update approach.

c. Describe the restart work if a system failure occurs. Assume that the recovery manager uses the deferred update approach.

d. Describe the restart work if a system failure occurs. Assume that the recovery manager uses the immediate update approach.

e. Describe the restart work if a device failure occurs.

11. Use the World Wide Web to review transaction processing benchmarks. Why has the debit-credit benchmark been superseded by other benchmarks? How many transactions per minute are reported for various DBMSs? Inspect the code for one or more benchmark transactions. Can you identify hot spots in the transactions?

12. Redesign the ATM transaction (Figure 15.1) to remove user interaction. Please comment on any adverse side effects that may result from removing user interaction.

13. Redesign the online shopping transaction (Figure 15.3) to remove user interaction. Please comment on any adverse side effects that may result from removing user interaction.

14. Why do some enterprise DBMSs use READ COMMITTED as the default isolation level? Try to reason about the advantages and disadvantages about using this level as the default isolation level. In your analysis, you should think carefully about the significance of the scholar's lost update problem.

15. Using the following transaction log, create a table to list the log operations for the immediate update approach. You should use Table 15-10 as the format for your answer.

LSN	TransNo	Action	Time	Table	Row	Column	Old	New
1	1	START	2:09:20					
2	1	INSERT	2:09:21	Resv	1001	*		<101, 400,...>
3	2	START	2:09:22					
4	1	UPDATE	2:09:23	Flight	2521	SeatsRem	10	9
5	2	INSERT	2:09:24	Resv	1107	*		<101, 400,...>
6	2	UPDATE	2:09:25	Flight	3533	SeatsRem	3	2
7	3	START	2:09:26					
8	1	INSERT	2:09:27	Resv	1322	*		<102, 225,...>
9	1	UPDATE	2:09:28	Flight	4544	SeatsRem	15	14
10		CKPT(1,2,3)	2:09:29					
11	2	INSERT	2:09:30	Resv	1255	*		<111, 500,...>
12	2	UPDATE	2:09:31	Flight	3288	SeatsRem	2	1
13	1	COMMIT	2:09:32					
14	3	INSERT	2:09:33	Resv	1506	*		<151, 159,...>
15	3	UPDATE	2:09:34	Flight	3099	SeatsRem	50	49
16	4	START	2:09:36					
17	3	INSERT	2:09:37	Resv	1299	*		<222, 384,...>
18	3	UPDATE	2:09:38	Flight	4522	SeatsRem	25	24
19	4	INSERT	2:09:39	Resv	1022	*		<222, 384,...>
20		CKPT(2,3,4)	2:09:40					
21	2	COMMIT	2:09:41					
22	4	UPDATE	2:09:42	Flight	2785	SeatsRem	1	0
23	3	COMMIT	2:09:43					
24	4	INSERT	2:09:44	Resv	1098	*		<515,99,...>
25	4	UPDATE	2:09:45	Flight	3843	SeatsRem	15	14

16. Using the transaction log from problem 15, create a table to list the log operations for the deferred update approach. You should use Table 15-11 as the format for your answer.

17. Identify the concurrency control problem depicted in the following timeline. Identify the least restrictive isolation level that eliminates the problem. Note that SERIALIZABLE is the most restrictive isolation level. Redraw the timeline showing the locks imposed by the least restrictive isolation level that eliminates the problem.

Transaction A	Time	Transaction B
	T_1	UPDATE $QOH_2 = QOH_2 - 5$ (20)
Read QOH_2 (20)	T_2	
Sum = Sum + QOH_2	T_3	
Read QOH_1 (15)	T_4	
Sum = Sum + QOH_1	T_5	
	T_6	UPDATE $QOH_1 = QOH_1 - 5$ (13)
	T_7	Commit

18. Identify the concurrency control problem depicted in the following timeline. Identify the least restrictive isolation level that eliminates the problem. Note that SERIALIZABLE is the most restrictive isolation level. Redraw the timeline showing the locks imposed by the least restrictive isolation level that eliminates the problem.

Transaction A	Time	Transaction B
	T_1	Read QOH_1 (55)
	T_2	$QOH_1 = QOH_1 - 10$
	T_3	Write QOH_1 (45)
Read QOH_1 (45)	T_4	
Read QOH_2 (15)	T_5	
	T_6	Read QOH_2 (15)
	T_7	$QOH_2 = QOH_2 - 5$
	T_8	Write QOH_2 (10)
	T_9	Rollback

19. Identify the concurrency control problem depicted in the following timeline. Identify the least restrictive isolation level that eliminates the problem. Note that SERIALIZABLE is the most restrictive isolation level. Redraw the timeline showing the locks imposed by the least restrictive isolation level.

Transaction A	Time	Transaction B
	T_1	Read QOH_1 (10)
	T_2	If $QOH_1 > 10$ then $QOH_1 = QOH_1 + 30$
Read QOH_1 (10)	T_3	
$QOH_1 = QOH_1 - 3$	T_4	
	T_5	Write QOH_1 (40)
	T_6	Commit
Write QOH_1 (7)	T_7	

20. Identify the concurrency control problem depicted in the following timeline. Identify the least restrictive isolation level that eliminates the problem. Note that SERIALIZABLE is the most restrictive isolation level. Redraw the timeline showing the locks imposed by the least restrictive isolation level that eliminates the problem.

Transaction A	Time	Transaction B
Read QOH (10)	T_1	
QOH = QOH + 30	T_2	
	T_3	Read QOH (10)
	T_4	QOH = QOH − 10
Write SR (40)	T_5	
	T_6	Write SR (0)
Commit	T_7	
	T_8	Commit

21. Try to create a deadlock among more than two airline reservation transactions. You should assume that locks are granted in the flight time order for a reservation. Thus, a lock on a departing flight is granted before a lock on a return flight for a given transaction. You can add complications such as reservations with multiple legs per departure or return. With multiple legs, a lock on the first leg should be granted before a lock on the second leg, however.

References for Further Study

This chapter, although providing a broad coverage of transaction management, has only covered the basics. Transaction management is a detailed subject for which entire books have been written. Specialized books on transaction management include Bernstein and Newcomer (1997) and Gray and Reuter (1993). Shasha and Bonnet (2003) provide more details about transaction design and recovery tuning. Peinl, Reuter, and Sammer (1988) provide a stock-trading case study on transaction design that elaborates on the ideas presented in Section 15.4. For details about transaction processing performance, consult the home page of the Transaction Processing Performance Council (www.tpc.org).

Appendix 15.A: SQL:2006 Syntax Summary

This appendix summarizes the SQL:2006 syntax for the constraint timing clause, the SET CONSTRAINTS statement, the SET TRANSACTION statement, and the save point statements discussed in the chapter. The conventions used in the syntax notation are identical to those used at the end of Chapter 3.

Constraint Timing Clause

```
CREATE TABLE  TableName
 ( <Column-Definition>*  [ ,  <Table-Constraint>*  ]  )

<Column-Definition>: ColumnName DataType
 [ DEFAULT { DefaultValue | USER | NULL } ]
   [ <Column-Constraint> ]

<Column-Constraint>: [ CONSTRAINT ConstraintName ]
   { NOT NULL    |
      <Foreign-Key-Constraint>   |   -- defined in Chapter 3
      <Uniqueness-Constraint>    |     -- defined in Chapter
3
      <Check-Constraint>   } -- defined in Chapter 14
      [ <Timing-Clause> ]

<Table-Constraint>: [ CONSTRAINT ConstraintName ]
   { <Primary-Key-Constraint>   |   -- defined in Chapter 3
      <Foreign-Key-Constraint>   |   -- defined in Chapter 3
      <Uniqueness-Constraint>    |   -- defined in Chapter 3
      <Check-Constraint> } -- defined in Chapter 14
      [ <Timing-Clause> ]

<Timing-Clause>:
  { NOT  DEFERRABLE  |
    DEFERRABLE { INITIALLY IMMEDIATE |
                 INITIALLY DEFERRED } }

CREATE ASSERTION AssertionName
 CHECK ( <Group-Condition> ) [ <Timing-Clause> ]

<Group-Condition>: -- defined in Chapter 4
```

SET CONSTRAINTS Statement

```
SET CONSTRAINTS  { ALL | ConstraintName* }
 { IMMEDIATE | DEFERRED  }
```

SET TRANSACTION Statement

```
SET [LOCAL] TRANSACTION <Mode>*

<Mode>: { <Isolation-Level> | <Access-Mode> |
           <Diagnostics> }

<Isolation-Level>:  ISOLATION LEVEL
   { SERIALIZABLE      |
     REPEATABLE READ   |
     READ COMMITTED    |
     READ UNCOMMITTED }

<Access-Mode>: { READ WRITE  |  READ ONLY  }

<Diagnostics>: DIAGNOSTICS SIZE Constant
```

Save Point Statements

```
SAVEPOINT <SavePointName>   -- creates a save point

RELEASE <SavePointName>   -- deletes a save point

ROLLBACK TO SAVEPOINT <SavePointName>   -- rollback to a
save point
```

16

Data Warehouse Technology and Management

Learning Objectives

This chapter provides the foundation for an emerging form of databases, called data warehouses, being used increasingly for decision support. After this chapter, the student should have acquired the following knowledge and skills:

- Explain conceptual differences between operational databases and data warehouses
- Understand architectures to apply data warehouse technology in organizations
- Understand the representation and manipulation of data cubes
- Apply relational data modeling and manipulation for multidimensional data
- Explain data quality issues and the role of extraction, transformation, and loading tools when maintaining a data warehouse
- Gain insight about the complex process of refreshing a data warehouse

Overview

Imagine a corporate executive of a national electronics retailer asking the question, "What retail stores were the top producers during the past 12 months in the Rocky Mountain region?" Follow-up questions may include, "What were the most profitable products in the top producing stores?" and "What were the most successful product promotions at the top producing stores?" These questions are typical decision support or business intelligence questions, asked every day by managers all over the world. Answers to these questions often require complex SQL statements that may take hours to code and execute. Furthermore, formulating some of these queries may require data from a diverse set of internal legacy systems and external market sources, involving both relational and nonrelational databases.

Decision-making questions such as those above pose new requirements on DBMSs. This chapter presents the technology and management of data warehouses to satisfy the requirements of decision support. Data warehouse technology complements and extends relational database technology beyond online transaction processing and simple summary capabilities such as the GROUP BY clause in SQL. In this chapter, you will initially learn about the unique requirements for data warehouse processing as opposed to the transaction processing requirements discussed in Chapter 15. Then you will learn about the multidimensional data model and its implementation in relational databases with a special emphasis on the data warehousing features in Oracle 11g. You will learn new data modeling and query formulation skills that complement the data modeling material in Part 3 and the query formulation material in Parts 2 and 5. Finally, you will learn about maintaining a data warehouse, an important process managed by data warehouse administrators.

16.1 Basic Concepts

The type of data used for decision support purposes is conceptually different from that used in transaction processing databases. Consequently, databases that can store such data and computing architectures that can process such data are also different. This section examines these differences to provide a foundation for the detailed study of technology and management issues in later sections.

16.1.1 Transaction Processing versus Decision Support

Transaction processing involves different needs in an organization than decision support. Transaction processing, as presented in Chapter 15, allows organizations to conduct daily business in an efficient manner. Operational or production databases used in transaction processing assist with decisions such as tracking orders, resolving customer complaints, and staffing requirements. These decisions involve detailed data about business processes. In contrast, decision support processing helps management provide medium-term and long-term direction for an organization. Management needs support for decisions about capacity planning, product development, store location, product promotion, and other needs.

Historically, most organizations assumed that operational databases along with relational database technology could provide adequate support for management decision making. As organizations developed operational databases for various functions, an information gap developed. Gradually, organizations and database vendors realized the limitations of operational databases and relational database technology for decision support.

Since the early 1990s, a consensus has developed that operational databases must be transformed for decision support. Operational databases can contain inconsistencies in areas such as formats, entity identification, and units of measure that hamper usage in decision support. In addition, decision support needs a broad view that integrates business processes. Because of the different requirements, operational databases are usually separate from databases for decision support. Using a common database for both kinds of processing can significantly degrade performance and make it difficult to summarize activity across business processes.

Commercial vendors have also performed substantial amounts of research and development to add features for decision support. Initially, a new breed of companies developed storage engines, summary data retrieval, and data transformation tools for decision support. Later relational database vendors added features for storage of summary data, retrieval of summary data, optimization of queries involving summary data, and transformation of operational databases. The technology provided by both decision support companies and relational database vendors has rapidly matured to provide strong commercial solutions for managing data warehouses.

16.1.2 Characteristics of Data Warehouses

Data warehouse, a term coined by William Inmon in 1990, refers to a central data repository where data from operational databases and other sources are integrated, cleaned, and standardized to support decision making. The transformational activities (cleaning, integrating, and standardizing) are essential for achieving benefits. Tangible benefits from a data warehouse can include increased revenue and reduced expenses enabled by business analysis that was not possible before the data warehouse was deployed. For example, a data warehouse may enable reduced losses due to improved fraud detection, improved customer retention through targeted marketing, and reduction in inventory carrying costs through improved demand forecasting.

> **Data Warehouse:** a central repository for summarized and integrated data from operational databases and external data sources.

The processing requirements of decision support applications have led to four distinguishing characteristics for data warehouses, as described in the following:

1. Subject-Oriented: A data warehouse is organized around the major business subjects or entities such as customers, orders, and products. This subject orientation contrasts to the process orientation for transaction processing.
2. Integrated: Operational data from multiple databases and external data sources are integrated in a data warehouse to provide a single, unified database for decision support. Consolidation of data requires consistent naming conventions, uniform data formats, and comparable measurement scales across databases and external data sources.
3. Time-Variant: Data warehouses use time stamps to represent historical data. The time dimension is critical for identifying trends, predicting future operations, and setting operating targets. Data warehouses essentially consist of a long series of snapshots, each of which represents operational data captured at a point in time.
4. Nonvolatile: New data in a data warehouse are appended, rather than replaced, so that historical data are preserved. The act of appending new data is known as refreshing the data warehouse. Lack of update and delete operations ensures that a data warehouse is free of update or deletion anomalies. Transaction data are transferred to a data warehouse only when most updating activity has been completed.

Table 16-1 further depicts the characteristics of data warehouses as opposed to operational databases. Transaction processing relies on operational databases with current data at the individual level, while decision support processing utilizes data warehouses with historical data at both the individual and summarized levels. Individual-level data provides flexibility for responding to a wide range of decision support needs while summarized data provides fast response to repetitive queries. For example, an order-entry transaction requires data about individual customers, orders, and inventory items, while a decision support application may use monthly sales to customers over a period of several years. Operational databases therefore have a process orientation (e.g., all data relevant to a particular business process), compared to a subject orientation for data warehouses (e.g., all customer data or all order data). A transaction typically updates only a few records, whereas a decision support application may query thousands to millions of records.

Table 16-1: Comparison of Operational Databases and Data Warehouses

Characteristic	Operational Database	Data Warehouse
Currency	Current	Historical
Detail level	Individual	Individual and summary
Orientation	Process orientation	Subject orientation
Number of records processed	Few	Thousands
Normalization level	Mostly normalized	Frequent violations of BCNF
Update level	Volatile	Nonvolatile (refreshed)
Data model	Relational	Relational model with star schemas and multidimensional model with data cubes

Data integrity and usage patterns of transaction processing require that operational databases be highly normalized. In contrast, data warehouses are usually denormalized from Boyce-Codd Normal Form to reduce the effort to join large tables. Most data warehouse processing involves retrievals and periodic insertions of new data. These operations do not suffer from anomalies caused by a design that is not fully normalized.

Because of the different processing requirements, different data models have been developed for operational databases and data warehouses. The relational data model dominates for operational databases. In the early years of data warehouse deployment, the multidimensional data model dominated. In recent years, relational databases have been increasingly used for data warehouses with a schema pattern known as a star schema. The multidimensional data model is now typically used as an end user representation of a view of a data warehouse.

16.1.3 Architectures for Data Warehouses

Despite the potential benefits of a data warehouse, many data warehouse projects have failed due to poor planning. Data warehouse projects are large efforts that involve coordination among many parts of an organization. Many organizations have underestimated the time and effort to reconcile different parts of a data warehouse. In addition, the sheer size of a data warehouse can lead to poor performance. An appropriate architecture can help alleviate problems with data warehouse performance and development efforts.

For small organizations, a two-tier data warehouse architecture is appropriate. In a two-tier data warehouse architecture (Figure 16.1), operational data are transformed and then transferred to a data warehouse. A separate layer of servers may be used to support the complex activities of the transformation process. To assist with the transformation process, an enterprise data model (EDM) is created. The EDM describes the structure of the data warehouse and contains the metadata required to access operational databases and external data sources. The EDM may also contain details about cleaning and integrating data sources. Management uses the data warehouse directly to retrieve data for decision support.

Enterprise Data Model: a conceptual data model of the data warehouse defining the structure of the data warehouse and the metadata to access and transform operational databases and external data sources.

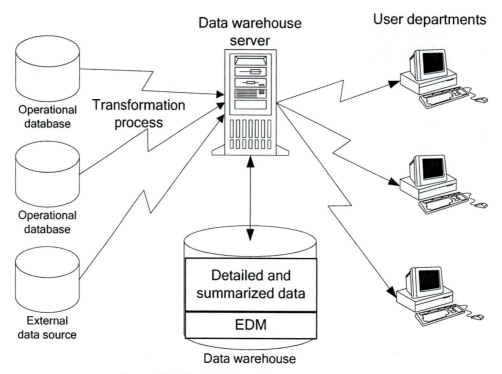

Figure 16.1: Two-Tier Data Warehouse Architecture

The two-tier architecture can have performance problems for large data warehouses with data-intensive applications for decision support. To alleviate these difficulties, many large organizations use a <u>three-tier data warehouse architecture</u> as shown in Figure 16.2. Departmental users generally need access to small portions of the data warehouse, instead of the entire warehouse. To provide them with faster access while isolating them from data needed by other user groups, smaller data warehouses called <u>data marts</u> are often used. Data marts act as the interface between end users and the corporate data warehouse, storing a subset of the warehouse data and refreshing those data on a periodic (e.g., daily or weekly) basis. Generally, the data warehouse and the data marts reside on different servers to improve performance and fault tolerance. Departmental users retain control over their own data marts, while the data warehouse remains under the control of the corporate information systems staff.

> **Data Mart:** a subset or view of a data warehouse, typically at a department or functional level, that contains all data required for decision support tasks of that department.

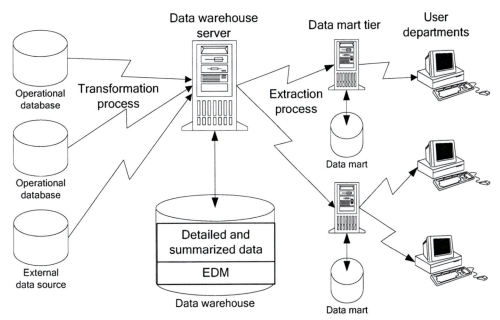

Figure 16.2: Three-Tier Data Warehouse Architecture

Given the enterprisewide context of a data warehouse, some organizations believe building a data warehouse may be unnecessarily delayed with lost business opportunities if too much emphasis is placed on first creating an enterprise data model. Instead, some organizations employ a bottom-up approach to data warehousing, as depicted in Figure 16.3. In a <u>bottom-up data warehouse architecture</u>, data are modeled one entity at a time and stored in separate data marts. Over time, new data are synthesized, cleaned, and merged into existing data marts or built into new data marts. The set of data marts may evolve into a large data warehouse if the organization can justify the expense of building an enterprise data model.

A more recent development is the emergence of <u>oper marts</u> (short for operational mart) as noted by Imhoff (2001). An oper mart is a just-in-time data mart, usually built from one operational database in anticipation or in response to major events such as disasters and new product introductions. An oper mart supports peak demand for reporting and business analysis that accompanies a major event. After the decision support demand subsides, the oper mart may be dismantled or it may be merged into an existing data warehouse.

16.1.4 Data Mining

Data warehouses improve the quality of decision making by consolidating and aggregating transactional data. The value of a data warehouse can be increased if hidden patterns in the data can be discovered. Data mining refers to the process of discovering implicit patterns in data and using these patterns for business advantage. Data mining facilitates the ability to detect, understand, and predict patterns.

> **Data Mining**: the process of discovering implicit patterns in data stored in a data warehouse and using those patterns for business advantage.

The most common application of data mining techniques is target marketing. Mail-order companies can increase revenues and decrease costs if they can identify likely customers and eliminate customers not likely to purchase. Data mining techniques allow decision makers to focus marketing efforts by customer demographic and psychographic data. The retail, banking, travel, and consumer goods industries also have benefited from data mining techniques. For example, the retail industry uses data mining techniques to target promotions and change the mix and the arrangement of store items.

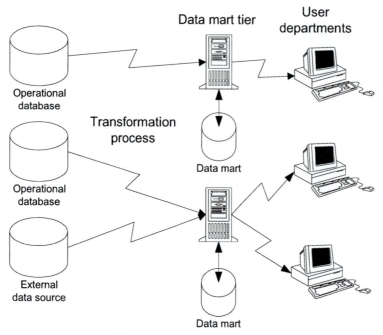

Figure 16.3: Bottom-Up Data Warehouse Architecture

Data mining is best considered as an adjunct to a mature data warehouse. Data mining needs more detailed data than traditional data warehouses provide. The volumes of data and the dimensionality of data can be much greater for data mining techniques than other data warehouse analysis tools. Data mining techniques thrive with clean, high-dimensional, transaction data. To support these data mining requirements, many data warehouses now store detail data at the level of the individual customer, product, and so on.

Data mining requires a collection of tools that extend beyond traditional statistical analysis tools. Traditional statistical analysis tools are not well suited to high dimensional data with a mix of numeric and categorical data. In addition, traditional statistical techniques do not scale well to large amounts of data. Data mining typically includes the following kinds of tools:

- Data access tools to extract and sample transaction data according to complex criteria from large databases,
- Data visualization tools that enable a decision maker to gain a deeper, intuitive understanding of data,
- A rich collection of models to cluster, predict, and determine association rules from large amounts of data. The models involve neural networks, genetic algorithms, decision tree induction, rule discovery algorithms, probability networks, and other expert system technologies.
- An architecture that provides optimization, client-server processing, and parallel queries to scale to large amounts of data.

As a complement to data warehousing, data mining provides insights that may elude traditional techniques. Data mining holds the promise of more effectively leveraging data warehouses by providing the ability to identify hidden relationships in the data stored there. It facilitates a data-driven discovery, using techniques such as building association rules (e.g., between advertising budget and seasonal sales), generating profiles (e.g., buying patterns for a specific customer segment), and so forth. This knowledge can be used to improve business operations in critical areas, enabling target marketing efforts, better customer service, and improved fraud detection.

16.1.5 Applications of Data Warehouses

Data warehousing projects have usually been undertaken for competitive reasons: to achieve strategic advantage or to stay competitive. In many industries, a few organizations have pioneered data warehousing technology to gain competitive advantage. Often a data warehousing project has been undertaken as part of a corporate strategy to shift from a product focus to a customer focus. Successful data warehouses have helped identify new markets, focus resources on profitable customers, improve retention of customers, and reduce inventory costs. After success by the pioneering organizations, other organizations have quickly followed to stay competitive.

Data warehousing projects have been undertaken in a wide range of industries. A few key applications have driven the adoption of data warehousing projects as listed in Table 16-2. Highly competitive industries such as retail, insurance, airlines, and telecommunications (particularly long-distance service) have invested early in data warehouse technology and projects. Less competitive industries such as regulated utilities have been slower to invest although they are increasing investments as data warehouse technology and practice mature.

Table 16-2: Data Warehousing Applications by Industry

Industry	Key Applications
Airline	Yield management, route assessment
Telecommunications	Customer retention, network design
Insurance	Risk assessment, product design, fraud detection
Retail	Target marketing, supply-chain management

The maturity of data warehouse deployment varies among industries and organizations. Early adopters of data warehouses have deployed data warehouses since the early 1990s while late adopters have deployed data warehouses since the late 1990s. With the rapid development of data warehouse technology and best practices, continued investment in data warehouse technology and management practices are necessary to sustain business value. To provide guidance about investment decisions and management practices, organizations are interested in comparisons to peer organizations to gauge the level of data warehouse usage.

The data warehouse maturity model has been proposed to provide guidance for data warehouse investment decisions (Eckerson 2004). The maturity model consists of six stages which are summarized in Table 16-3. The stages provide a framework to view an organization's progress, not an absolute metric as organizations may demonstrate aspects of multiple stages at the same time. As organizations move from lower to more advanced stages, increased business value can occur. However, organizations may have difficulty justifying significant new data warehouse investments in the teenager and adult stages as benefits are sometimes difficult to quantify.

Table 16-3: Stages of the Data Warehouse Maturity Model

Stage	Scope	Architecture	Management Usage
Prenatal	Operational system	Management reports	Cost center
Infant	Individual business analysts	Spreadsheets	Management insight
Child	Departments	Data marts	Support business analysis
Teenager	Divisions	Data warehouses	Track business processes
Adult	Enterprise	Enterprise data warehouse	Drive organization
Sage	Inter-enterprise	Web services and external networks	Drive market and industry

Source: Eckerson 2004

An important insight of the maturity model is the difficulty of moving between certain stages. For small but growing organizations, moving from the infant to the child stages can be difficult because a significant investment in data warehouse technology is necessary. For large organizations, the struggle is to move from the teenager to the adult stage. To make the transition, upper management must perceive the data warehouse as a vital enterprise resource, not just a tool provided by the information technology department.

16.2 Multidimensional Representation of Data

After understanding the unique data requirements for decision support, you are ready to learn about technology to satisfy the requirements. The multidimensional data model supports data representation and operations specifically tailored for decision support processing in data warehouses. The multidimensional data model was originally proposed as a replacement for the relational model for data warehouses. Over time, the multidimensional model has evolved into an end user representation of a data model, complimenting the relational model for data warehouse storage. This section describes the terminology and operations of the multidimensional data model.

16.2.1 Example of a Multidimensional Data Cube

Consider a company that sells electronic products in different parts of the United States. In particular, the company markets four different printer products (mono laser, ink jet, photo, and portable) in five different states (California, Washington, Colorado, Utah, and Arizona). In order to store daily sales data for each product and each location in a relational database, you need Table 16-4 which consists of three columns (*Product*, *Location*, and *Sales*) and 20 rows (four instances of *Product* times five instances of *Location*).

The representation of Table 16-4 can be complex and unwieldy. First, imagine that the company wishes to add a fifth product (say, color laser). In order to track sales by states for this new product, you need to add five rows, one each for each state. Second, note that the data in Table 16-4 represents sales data for a particular day (for example, August 10, 2008). In order to store the same data for all 366 days of 2008, you need to add a fourth column to store the sales date, and duplicate the 20 rows for each date 366 times to yield a total of 7,300 rows. By the same token, if you wish to store historic data for a period of 10 years, you need 73,000 rows. Each new row must contain the product, state, and date values.

Table 16-4: Relational Representation of Sales Data

Product	Location	Sales
Mono Laser	California	80
Mono Laser	Utah	40
Mono Laser	Arizona	70
Mono Laser	Washington	75
Mono Laser	Colorado	65
Ink Jet	California	110
Ink Jet	Utah	90
Ink Jet	Arizona	55
Ink Jet	Washington	85
Ink Jet	Colorado	45
Photo	California	60
Photo	Utah	50
Photo	Arizona	60
Photo	Washington	45
Photo	Colorado	85
Portable	California	25
Portable	Utah	30
Portable	Arizona	35
Portable	Washington	45
Portable	Colorado	60

An examination of the data in Table 16-4 reveals that the data contain two dimensions, *Product* and *Location*, and a numeric value for the unit sales. Table 16-4 therefore can be conceptually simplified by rearranging the data in a multidimensional format (Table 16-5).

Table 16-5: Multidimensional Representation of Sales Data

Location	Product			
	Mono Laser	Ink Jet	Photo	Portable
California	80	110	60	25
Utah	40	90	50	30
Arizona	70	55	60	35
Washington	75	85	45	45
Colorado	65	45	85	60

The multidimensional representation is simple to understand and extend. For example, adding a fifth product category requires an additional column to the right of Table 16-4. Adding dates requires a third dimension called *Time*, resulting in a three-dimensional arrangement as shown in Figure 16.4. You can conceptually think of this three-dimensional table as a book consisting of 365 pages, each page storing sales data by product and state for a specific date of the year. In addition, the multidimensional table is more compact because the row and column labels are not duplicated as in Table 16-3.

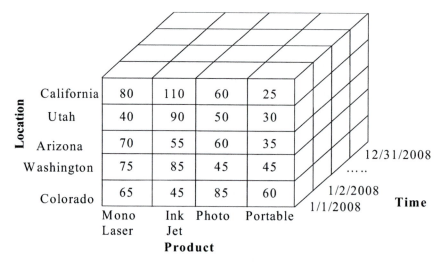

Figure 16.4: A Three-Dimensional Data Cube

The multidimensional representation also provides a convenient representation of summary totals. Each dimension in a cube can accommodate totals (row totals, column totals, depth totals, and overall totals) that a user can identify easily. For example, to add row totals to Table 16-5, a *Totals* column can be added with one value per row as shown in Table 16-6. In the relational representation as depicted in Table 16-4, totals must be added by using null values for column values. For example, to represent the total California sales for all products, the row <–, California, 275> should be added to Table 16-4 where – indicates all products.

Table 16-6: Multidimensional Representation of Sales Data with Row Totals

Location	Product				
	Mono Laser	Ink Jet	Photo	Portable	Totals
California	80	110	60	25	275
Utah	40	90	50	30	210
Arizona	70	55	60	35	220
Washington	75	85	45	45	250
Colorado	65	45	85	60	255

In addition to advantages in usability, the multidimensional representation can provide increased retrieval speed. Direct storage of multidimensional data obviates the need to convert from a table representation to a multidimensional representation. However, the multidimensional representation can suffer from excessive storage because many cells can remain empty. Even with compression techniques, large multidimensional tables can consume considerably more storage space than corresponding relational tables.

In summary, a multidimensional representation provides an intuitive interface for business analysts. As the number of dimensions increase, business analysts find a multidimensional representation easy to understand and visualize as compared to a relational representation. Because the multidimensional representation matches the needs of business analysts, this representation is widely used in business reporting tools even when relational tables provide physical storage.

16.2.2 Multidimensional Terminology

A data cube or hypercube generalizes the two-dimensional (Table 16-5) and three-dimensional (Figure 16.4) representations shown in the previous section. A data cube consists of cells containing measures (numeric values such as the unit sales amounts) and dimensions to label or group numeric data (e.g., *Product*, *Location*, and *Time*). Each dimension contains values known as *members*. For instance, the *Location* dimension has five members (California, Washington,

Utah, Arizona, and Colorado) in Table 16-4. Both dimensions and measures can be stored or derived. For example, purchase date is a stored dimension with purchase year, month, and day as derived dimensions.

> **Data Cube**: a multidimensional format in which cells contain numeric data called measures organized by subjects called dimensions. A data cube is sometimes known as a hypercube because conceptually it can have an unlimited number of dimensions.

Dimension Details

Dimensions can have <u>hierarchies</u> composed of levels. For instance, the *Location* dimension may have a hierarchy composed of the levels country, state, and city. Likewise, the *Time* dimension can have a hierarchy composed of year, quarter, month, and date. Hierarchies can be used to drill down from higher levels of detail (e.g., country) to lower levels (e.g., state and city) and to roll up in the reverse direction. Although hierarchies are not essential, they allow a convenient and efficient representation. Without hierarchies, the *Location* dimension must contain the most detailed level (city). However, this representation can be difficult to compute aggregates across the dimension. Alternatively, the *Location* dimension can be divided into separate dimensions for country, state, and city resulting in a larger data cube.

For flexibility, dimensions can have multiple hierarchies. In a dimension with multiple hierarchies, usually at least one level is shared. For example, the *Location* dimension can have one hierarchy with the levels country, state, and city, and a second hierarchy with the levels country, state, and postal code. The *Time* dimension can have one hierarchy with levels year, quarter, and date and a second hierarchy with levels year, week, and date. Multiple hierarchies allow alternative organizations for a dimension.

Another dimension feature is the ragged hierarchy for a self-referencing relationship among members of the same level. For example, a manager dimension could have a ragged hierarchy to display relationships among managers and subordinates. An analyst manipulating a data cube may want to expand or contract the manager dimension according to the relationships among managers and subordinates.

The selection of dimensions has an influence on the sparsity of a data cube. <u>Sparsity</u> indicates the extent of empty cells in a data cube. Sparsity can be a problem if two or more dimensions are related. For example, if certain products are sold only in selected states, cells may be empty. If a large number of cells are empty, the data cube can waste space and be slow to process. Special compression techniques can be used to reduce the size of sparse data cubes.

Measure Details

Cells in a data cube contain <u>measures</u> such as the sales values in Figure 16.4. Measures support numeric operations such as simple arithmetic, statistical calculations, and simultaneous equations. A cell may contain one or more measures. For example, the number of units can be another measure for the sales data cube. The number of nonempty cells in a multidimensional cube should equal the number of rows in the corresponding relational table (Table 16-5 contains 20 nonempty cells corresponding to 20 rows in Table 16-4).

Derived measures can be stored in a data cube or computed from other measures at run-time. Measures that can be derived from other measures in the same cell typically would not be stored. For example, total dollar sales can be calculated as total unit sales times the unit price measures in a cell. Summary measures derived from a collection of cells may be stored or computed depending on the number of cells and the cost of accessing the cells for the computation.

Other Data Cube Examples

As this section has indicated, data cubes can extend beyond the three-dimensional example shown in Figure 16.4. Table 16-7 lists common data cubes to support human resource management and financial analysis. The dimensions with slashes indicate hierarchical dimensions. The time and location dimensions are also hierarchical, but possible levels are not listed since the levels can be organization specific.

Table 16-7: Data Cubes to Support Human Resource Management and Financial Analysis

Data Cube	Typical Dimensions	Typical Measures
Turnover analysis	Company/line of business/department, location, salary range, position classification, time	Head counts for hires, transfers, terminations, and retirements
Employee utilization	Company/line of business/department, location, salary range, position classification, time	Full time equivalent (FTE) hours, normal FTE hours, overtime FTE hours
Asset analysis	Asset type, years in service band, time, account, company/line of business/department, location	Cost, net book value, market value
Vendor analysis	Vendor, location, account, time, business unit	Total invoice amount

16.2.3 Time-Series Data

Time is one of the most common dimensions in a data warehouse and is useful for capturing trends, making forecasts, and so forth. A time series provides storage of all historic data in one cell, instead of specifying a separate time dimension. The structure of a measure becomes more complex with a time series, but the number of dimensions is reduced. In addition, many statistical functions can operate directly on time-series data.

A time series is an array data type with a number of special properties as listed below. The array supports a collection of values, one for each time period. Examples of time-series measures include weekly sales amounts, daily stock closing prices, and yearly employee salaries. The following list shows typical properties for a time series:

- Data Type: This property denotes the kind of data stored in the data points. The data type is usually numeric such as floating point numbers, fixed decimal numbers, or integers.
- Start Date: This property denotes the starting date of the first data point, for example, 1/1/2008.
- Calendar: This property contains the calendar year appropriate for the time series, for example, 2008 fiscal year. An extensive knowledge of calendar rules, such as determining leap years and holidays embedded in a calendar, reduces effort in data warehouse development.
- Periodicity: This property specifies the interval between data points. Periodicity can be daily, weekly, monthly, quarterly, yearly (calendar or fiscal years), hourly, 15-minute intervals, 4-4-5 accounting periods, custom periodicity, and so forth.
- Conversion: This property specifies conversion of unit data into aggregate data. For instance, aggregating daily sales into weekly sales requires summation, while aggregating daily stock prices into weekly prices requires an averaging operation.

16.2.4 Data Cube Operations

A number of decision support operations have been proposed for data cubes. This section discusses the most commonly used operations. A standard set of data cube operations is still under development, and not all data warehouse tools currently support all operations.

Slice

Because a data cube can contain a large number of dimensions, users often need to focus on a subset of the dimensions to gain insights. The slice operator retrieves a subset of a data cube similar to the restrict operator of relational algebra. In a slice operation, one or more dimensions are set to specific values and the remaining data cube is displayed. For example, Figure 16.5 shows the data cube resulting from the slice operation on the data cube in Figure 16.4 where Time = 1/1/2008 and the other two dimensions (*Location* and *Product*) are shown.

A variation of the slice operator allows a decision maker to summarize across members rather than to focus on just one member. The slice-summarize operator replaces one or more dimensions with summary calculations. The summary calculation often indicates the total value across members or the central tendency of the dimension such as the average or median value. For example, Figure 16.6 shows the result of a slice-summarize operation where the *Product* dimension is replaced by the sum of sales across all products. A new column called *Total Sales* can be added to store overall product sales for the entire year.

Location	Product			
	Mono Laser	Ink Jet	Photo	Portable
California	80	110	60	25
Utah	40	90	50	30
Arizona	70	55	60	35
Washington	75	85	45	45
Colorado	65	45	85	60

(Location × Product Slice for Time = 1/1/2008)
Figure 16.5: Example Slice Operation

Location	Time			
	1/1/2008	1/2/2008	...	Total Sales
California	400	670	...	16,250
Utah	340	190	...	11,107
Arizona	270	255	...	21,500
Washington	175	285	...	20,900
Colorado	165	245	...	21,336

Figure 16.6: Example Slice-Summarize Operation

Dice

Because individual dimensions can contain a large number of members, users need to focus on a subset of members to gain insights. The dice operator replaces a dimension with a subset of values of the dimension. For example, Figure 16.7 shows the result of a dice operation to display sales for the State of Utah for January 1, 2008. A dice operation typically follows a slice operation and returns a subset of the values displayed in the preceding slice. It helps focus attention on one or more rows or columns of numbers from a slice.

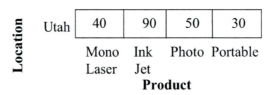

Figure 16.7: Example Dice Operation

Drill-Down

Users often want to navigate among the levels of hierarchical dimensions. The drill-down operator allows users to navigate from a more general level to a more specific level. For example, Figure 16.8 shows a drill-down operation on the State of Utah of the *Location* dimension. The plus sign by Utah indicates a drill-down operation.

Location	Product			
	Mono Laser	Ink Jet	Photo	Portable
California	80	110	60	25
+ Utah				
Salt Lake	20	20	10	15
Park City	5	30	10	5
Ogden	15	40	30	10
Arizona	70	55	60	35
Washington	75	85	45	45
Colorado	65	45	85	60

Figure 16.8: Drill-Down Operation for the State of Utah in Figure 16.5

Roll-Up

Roll-up (also called drill-up) is the opposite of drill-down. Roll-up involves moving from a specific level to a more general level of a hierarchical dimension. For example, a decision maker may roll-up sales data from daily to quarterly level for end-of-quarter reporting needs. In the printer sales example, Figure 16.5 shows a roll-up of the State of Utah from Figure 16.8.

Pivot

The pivot operator supports rearrangement of the dimensions in a data cube. For example, in Figure 16.8, the position of the *Product* and the *Location* dimensions can be reversed so that *Product* appears on the rows and *Location* on the columns. The pivot operator allows a data cube to be presented in the most appealing visual order.

The pivot operator is most typically used on data cubes of more than two dimensions. On data cubes of more than two dimensions, multiple dimensions appear in the row and/or column area because more than two dimensions cannot be displayed in other ways. For example, to display a data cube with *Location*, *Product*, and *Time* dimensions, the *Time* dimension can be displayed in the row area inside the *Location* dimension. A pivot operation could rearrange the data cube so that the *Location* dimension displays inside the *Time* dimension.

Summary of Operators

To help you recall the data cube operators, Table 16-8 summarizes the purpose of each operator.

Table 16-8: Summary of the Data Cube Operators

Operator	Purpose	Description
Slice	Focus attention on a subset of dimensions	Replace a dimension with a single member value or with a summary of its measure values
Dice	Focus attention on a subset of member values	Replace a dimension with a subset of members
Drill-down	Obtain more detail about a dimension	Navigate from a more general level to a more specific level of a hierarchical dimension
Roll-up	Summarize details about a dimension	Navigate from a more specific level to a more general level of a hierarchical dimension
Pivot	Allow a data cube to be presented in a visually appealing order	Rearrange the dimensions in a data cube

16.3 Relational DBMS Support for Data Warehouses

The multidimensional data model described in the previous section was originally implemented by special-purpose storage engines for data cubes. These multidimensional storage engines support the definition, manipulation, and optimization of large data cubes. Because of the commercial dominance of relational database technology, it was only a matter of time before relational DBMSs provided support for multidimensional data. In recent years, the major DBMS vendors have invested heavily in research and development to support multidimensional data. Because of the investment level and the market power of the relational DBMS vendors, most data warehouses now use relational DBMSs, at least in part.

This section presents features of relational DBMSs to support multidimensional data. The features include data modeling approaches, dimension representation, extensions to the GROUP BY clause, materialized views with query rewriting, and specialized storage structures and optimization techniques. To provide a specific context for the features, some examples use Oracle 11g SQL.

16.3.1 Relational Data Modeling for Multidimensional Data

When using a relational database for a data warehouse, a new data modeling technique is needed to represent multidimensional data. A star schema is a data modeling representation of multidimensional data cubes. In a relational database, a star schema diagram looks like a star with one large central table, called the <u>fact table</u>, at the center of the star that is linked to multiple <u>dimension tables</u> in a radial manner. The fact table stores numeric data (facts), such as sales results, while the dimension tables store descriptive data corresponding to individual dimensions of the data cube such as product, location, and time. There is a 1-M relationship from each dimension table to the fact table.

Star Schema: a data modeling representation for multidimensional databases. In a relational database, a star schema has a fact table in the center related to multiple dimension tables in 1-M relationships.

Figure 16.9 shows an ERD star schema for the sales example presented in Section 16.2. This ERD consists of four dimension entity types, *Item*, *Customer*, *Store*, and *TimeDim*, along with one fact entity type called *Sales*. When converted to a table design, the *Sales* table has foreign keys to each dimension table (*Item*, *Customer*, *Store*, and *TimeDim*). The *Item* entity type provides data for the *Product* dimension shown in the Section 16.2 examples, while the *Store* entity type provides data for the *Location* dimension.

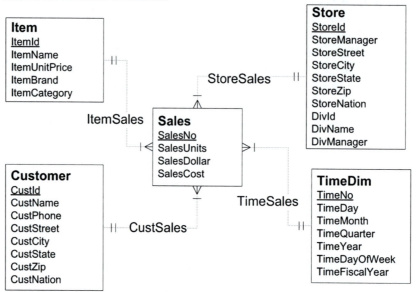

Figure 16.9: ERD Star Schema for the Store Sales Example

The store sales ERD in Figure 16.9 provides fine-grain detail for a data warehouse. The store sales ERD provides detail to the individual customer, store, and item. This level of detail is not necessary to support the sales data cubes presented in Section 16.2. However, a fine-grained level provides flexibility to support unanticipated analysis as well as data mining applications. This fine-grained level may replicate data in operational databases although the data warehouse representation may differ substantially because of the subject orientation of the data warehouse and the cleaning and integration performed on the source data.

Variations to the Star Schema

The star schema in Figure 16.9 represents only a single business process for sales tracking. Additional star schemas may be required for other processes such as shipping and purchasing. For related business processes that share some of the dimension tables, a star schema can be extended into a constellation schema with multiple fact entity types, as shown in Figure 16.10. When converted to a table design, the *Inventory* entity type becomes a fact table and 1-M relationships become foreign keys in the fact table. The *Inventory* entity type adds a number of measures including the quantity on hand of an item, the cost of an item, and the quantity returned. All dimension tables are shared among both fact tables except for the *Supplier* and *Customer* tables.

Constellation Schema: a data modeling representation for multidimensional databases. In a relational database, a constellation schema contains multiple fact tables in the center related to dimension tables. Typically, the fact tables share some dimension tables.

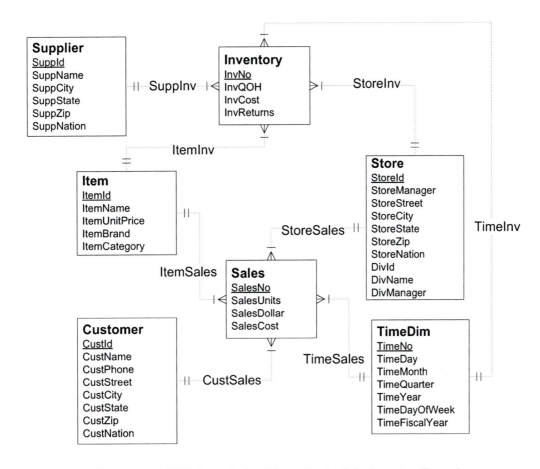

Figure 16.10: ERD Constellation Schema for the Sales-Inventory Example

Fact tables are usually normalized while dimension tables are often not in third normal form. For example, the *Store* entity type in Figures 16.9 and 16.10 is not in 3NF because *DivId* determines *DivName* and *DivManager*. Normalizing dimension tables to avoid storage anomalies is generally not necessary because they are usually stable and small. The nature of a data warehouse indicates that dimension tables should be designed for retrieval, not update. Retrieval performance is improved by eliminating the join operations that would be needed to combine fully normalized dimension tables.

When the dimension tables are small, denormalization provides only a small gain in retrieval performance. Thus, it is common to see small dimension tables normalized as shown in Figure 16.11. This variation is known as the <u>snowflake schema</u> because multiple levels of dimension tables surround the fact table. For the *Customer* and *Item* tables, full normalization may not be a good idea because these tables can contain a large number of rows.

Snowflake Schema: a data modeling representation for multidimensional databases. In a relational database, a snowflake schema has multiple levels of dimension tables related to one or more fact tables. You should consider the snowflake schema instead of the star schema for small dimension tables that are not in 3NF.

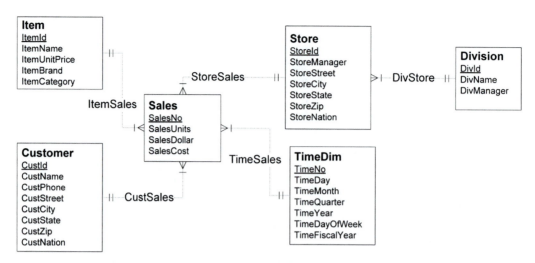

Figure 16.11: ERD Snowflake Schema for the Store Sales Example

The star schema and its variations require 1-M relationships from the dimension tables to the fact table. The usage of 1-M relationships simplifies query formulation and supports optimization techniques discussed in Section 16.3.5. Sometimes the source data has exceptions that involve M-N relationships, not 1-M relationships. For example, if the *Sales* fact table is derived from customer invoices, some invoices may involve multiple customers such as roommates or spouses. Two ways to revise the star schema for M-N relationships are explained below.

- If there are a small, fixed number of possible customers, a simple adjustment can be made to a fact table. Multiple columns can be added to a fact table to allow for more than one customer. For example, the *Sales* table can have an additional foreign key column *CustId2* to identify an optional second customer on an invoice.
- If there can be groups of customers for an invoice, the representation is more difficult. A customer group table can be added with an associative table that connects the customer group, *Sales*, and *Customer* tables via 1-M relationships.

Time Representation in Star Schemas

Time representation is a crucial issue for data warehouses because most queries use time in conditions. The principal usage of time is to record the occurrence of facts. The simplest representation is a timestamp data type for a column in a fact table. In place of a timestamp column, many data warehouses use a foreign key to a time dimension table as shown in Figures 16.9 to 16.11. Using a time dimension table supports convenient representation of organization-specific calendar features such as holidays, fiscal years, and week numbers that are not represented in timestamp data types. The granularity of the time dimension table is usually in days. If time of day is also required for a fact table, it can be added as a column in the fact table to augment the foreign key to the time table.

Most fact tables involve time represented as a foreign key to the time table with augmentation for time of day if required. For fact tables involving international operations, two time representations (time table foreign keys along with optional time of day columns) can be used to record the time at source and destination locations. A variation identified by Kimball (2003) is the accumulating fact table that records the status of multiple events rather than one event. For example, a fact table containing a snapshot of order processing would include order date, shipment date, delivery date, payment date, and so on. Each event occurrence column can be represented by a foreign key to the time table along with a time of day column if needed.

For dimension tables, time representation involves the level of historical integrity, an issue for updates to dimension tables. When a dimension row is updated, related fact table rows are no longer historically accurate. For example, if the city column of a customer row changes, the

566

related sales rows are no longer historically accurate. To preserve historical integrity, the related sales rows should point to an older version of the customer row. Kimball (April 1996) presents three alternatives for historical integrity:

- Type I: overwrite old values with the changed data. This method provides no historical integrity.
- Type II: use a version number to augment the primary key of a dimension table. For each change to a dimension row, insert a row in the dimension table with a larger version number. For example, to handle the change to the city column, there is a new row in the *Customer* table with the same customer number but a larger version number than the previous row. Besides the version number, additional columns are needed to record the beginning effective date and ending effective date for each historical column.
- Type III: use additional columns to maintain a fixed history. For example, to maintain a history of the current city and the two previous city changes, three city columns (*CustCityCurr*, *CustCityPrev*, *CustCityPast*) can be stored in the *Customer* table along with associated six date columns (two date columns per historical value column) to record the effective dates.

Figure 16.12 shows Type II and Type III alternatives for the *CustCity* column. The Type II alternative involves multiple rows for the same customer, but the entire history is represented. The Type III alternative involves just a single row for each customer, but only a limited history can be represented.

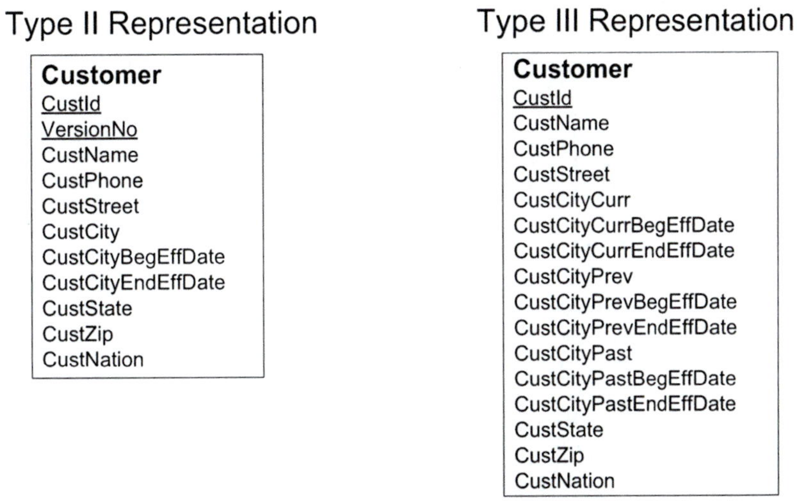

Type II Representation

Customer
CustId
VersionNo
CustName
CustPhone
CustStreet
CustCity
CustCityBegEffDate
CustCityEndEffDate
CustState
CustZip
CustNation

Type III Representation

Customer
CustId
CustName
CustPhone
CustStreet
CustCityCurr
CustCityCurrBegEffDate
CustCityCurrEndEffDate
CustCityPrev
CustCityPrevBegEffDate
CustCityPrevEndEffDate
CustCityPast
CustCityPastBegEffDate
CustCityPastEndEffDate
CustState
CustZip
CustNation

Figure 16.12: Alternatives for Historical Dimensional Integrity of *CustCity*

16.3.2 Dimension Representation

The star schema and its variations do not provide explicit representation of hierarchical dimensions because dimension tables do not define the hierarchical relationships among the levels of a dimension. Because dimension definition is important to support data cube operations as well as optimization techniques for query rewriting (section 16.3.4), many relational DBMS vendors have created proprietary SQL extensions for dimensions. This section reviews the Oracle CREATE DIMENSION statement to indicate the types of extensions that can be found in relational DBMSs.

The Oracle CREATE DIMENSION statement[42] supports the specification of levels, hierarchies, and constraints for a dimension. The first part of a dimension declaration involves the

---

[42] Do not put blank lines in CREATE DIMENSION statements. The Oracle SQL compiler generates error messages when encountering blank lines in CREATE DIMENSION statements.

specification of levels. For flat (nonhierarchical) dimensions, there is only a single level in a dimension. However, most dimensions involve multiple levels as depicted in Example 16.1 for the *StoreDim* dimension. Each level corresponds to one column from the *Store* source table.

Example 16.1: Oracle CREATE DIMENSION Statement for the *StoreDim* Dimension with the Specification of Levels

```
CREATE DIMENSION StoreDim
  LEVEL StoreId    IS Store.StoreId
  LEVEL City       IS Store.StoreCity
  LEVEL State      IS Store.StoreState
  LEVEL Zip        IS Store.StoreZip
  LEVEL Nation     IS Store.StoreNation ;
```

The next part of a CREATE DIMENSION statement involves the specification of hierarchies. The Oracle CREATE DIMENSION statement supports dimensions with multiple hierarchies as shown in Example 16.2. Specification of a hierarchy proceeds from the most detailed level to the most general level. The CHILD OF keywords indicate the direct hierarchical relationships in a dimension.

Example 16.2: Oracle CREATE DIMENSION Statement for the *StoreDim* Dimension with the Specification of Levels and Hierarchies

```
CREATE DIMENSION StoreDim
  LEVEL StoreId    IS Store.StoreId
  LEVEL City       IS Store.StoreCity
  LEVEL State      IS Store.StoreState
  LEVEL Zip        IS Store.StoreZip
  LEVEL Nation     IS Store.StoreNation
  HIERARCHY CityRollup (
    StoreId CHILD OF
    City    CHILD OF
    State   CHILD OF
    Nation )
  HIERARCHY ZipRollup (
    StoreId CHILD OF
    Zip     CHILD OF
    State   CHILD OF
    Nation );
```

The Oracle CREATE DIMENSION statement supports dimensions with levels from multiple source tables. This feature applies to normalized dimension tables in snowflake schemas. Example 16.3 augments Example 16.2 with the inclusion of an additional level (*DivId*) along with an additional hierarchy containing the new level. In the level specification, the *DivId* level references the *Division* table. In the *DivisionRollup* hierarchy, the JOIN KEY clause indicates a join between the *Store* and the *Division* tables. The JOIN KEY clause at the end of the hierarchy specification is required when a hierarchy has levels from more than one source table.

Example 16.3: Oracle CREATE DIMENSION Statement for the _StoreDim_ Dimension with the Usage of Multiple Source Tables

```
CREATE DIMENSION StoreDim
  LEVEL StoreId   IS Store.StoreId
  LEVEL City      IS Store.StoreCity
  LEVEL State     IS Store.StoreState
  LEVEL Zip       IS Store.StoreZip
  LEVEL Nation    IS Store.StoreNation
  LEVEL DivId     IS Division.DivId
  HIERARCHY CityRollup (
   StoreId CHILD OF
   City    CHILD OF
   State   CHILD OF
   Nation )
  HIERARCHY ZipRollup (
   StoreId CHILD OF
   Zip     CHILD OF
   State   CHILD OF
   Nation )
  HIERARCHY DivisionRollup (
   StoreId CHILD OF
   DivId
   JOIN KEY Store.DivId REFERENCES DivId );
```

The final part of a CREATE DIMENSION statement involves the specification of constraints. The ATTRIBUTE clause defines functional dependency relationships involving dimension levels and nonsource columns in dimension tables. Example 16.4 shows ATTRIBUTE clauses for the non source columns in the _Division_ table.

Example 16.4: Oracle CREATE DIMENSION Statement for the _StoreDim_ Dimension with the Usage of ATTRIBUTE Clauses for Constraints

```
CREATE DIMENSION StoreDim
  LEVEL StoreId   IS Store.StoreId
  LEVEL City      IS Store.StoreCity
  LEVEL State     IS Store.StoreState
  LEVEL Zip       IS Store.StoreZip
  LEVEL Nation    IS Store.StoreNation
  LEVEL DivId     IS Division.DivId
  HIERARCHY CityRollup (
   StoreId CHILD OF
   City    CHILD OF
   State   CHILD OF
   Nation )
  HIERARCHY ZipRollup (
   StoreId CHILD OF
   Zip     CHILD OF
   State   CHILD OF
   Nation )
  HIERARCHY DivisionRollup (
   StoreId CHILD OF
   DivId
   JOIN KEY Store.DivId REFERENCES DivId )
  ATTRIBUTE DivId DETERMINES Division.DivName
  ATTRIBUTE DivId DETERMINES Division.DivManager ;
```

In Example 16.4, the DETERMINES clauses are redundant with the primary key constraint for the _Division_ table. The DETERMINES clauses are shown in Example 16.4 to reinforce the constraints supported by the primary key declarations. DETERMINES clauses are required for constraints not corresponding to primary key constraints to enable query optimizations. For example, if each zip code is associated with one state, a DETERMINES clause should be used to enable optimizations involving the zip and state columns.

16.3.3 Extensions to the GROUP BY Clause for Multidimensional Data

Beginning in SQL:1999 and continuing through SQL:2006, new summarization capabilities have been available in the GROUP BY clause. These features are an attempt to unify the proliferation of proprietary data cube extensions, although they do not obviate the need for visual tools that directly support data cube operations. The extensions involve the ability to produce summary totals (CUBE and ROLLUP operators) as well as more precise specification of the grouping columns (GROUPING SETS operator). This section describes these new parts of the GROUP BY clause using Oracle11g as an example DBMS that implements the standard SQL features.

CUBE Operator

The CUBE operator clause produces all possible subtotal combinations in addition to the normal totals shown in a GROUP BY clause. Because all possible subtotals are generated, the CUBE operator is appropriate to summarize columns from independent dimensions rather than columns representing different levels of the same dimension. For example, the CUBE operator would be appropriate to generate subtotals for all combinations of month, store state, and item brand. In contrast, a CUBE operation to show all possible subtotals of year, month, and day would have limited interest because of the hierarchy in the time dimension.

> **CUBE Operator**: an operator that augments the normal GROUP BY result with all combinations of subtotals. The CUBE operator is appropriate to summarize columns from independent dimensions rather than columns representing different levels of a single dimension.

To depict the CUBE operator, Example 16.5 displays a SELECT statement with a GROUP BY clause containing just two columns. Only six rows are shown in the result so that the effect of the CUBE operator can be understood easily. With two values in the *StoreZip* column and three values in the *TimeMonth* column, the number of subtotal combinations is six (two *StoreZip* subtotals, three *TimeMonth* subtotals, and one grand total) as shown in Example 16.6. Blank values in the result represent a summary over all possible values of the column. For example, the row <80111, -, 33000> represents the total sales in the zip code 80111 over all months (- represents a do not care value for the month).

Example 16.5: GROUP BY Clause and Partial Result without Subtotals

```
SELECT StoreZip, TimeMonth, SUM(SalesDollar) AS SumSales
  FROM Sales, Store, TimeDim
  WHERE Sales.StoreId = Store.StoreId AND
        Sales.TimeNo = TimeDim.TimeNo
    AND (StoreNation = 'USA' OR StoreNation = 'Canada')
    AND TimeYear = 2007
  GROUP BY StoreZip, TimeMonth;
```

StoreZip	TimeMonth	SumSales
80111	1	10000
80111	2	12000
80111	3	11000
80112	1	9000
80112	2	11000
80112	3	15000

Example 16.6 (Oracle): GROUP BY Clause and Result with Subtotals Produced by the CUBE Operator

```
SELECT StoreZip, TimeMonth, SUM(SalesDollar) AS SumSales
 FROM Sales, Store, TimeDim
 WHERE Sales.StoreId = Store.StoreId
   AND Sales.TimeNo = TimeDim.TimeNo
   AND (StoreNation = 'USA' OR StoreNation = 'Canada')
   AND TimeYear = 2007
 GROUP BY CUBE(StoreZip, TimeMonth);
```

StoreZip	TimeMonth	SumSales
80111	1	10000
80111	2	12000
80111	3	11000
80112	1	9000
80112	2	11000
80112	3	15000
80111		33000
80112		35000
	1	19000
	2	23000
	3	26000
		68000

With more than two grouping columns, the CUBE operator becomes more difficult to understand. Examples 16.7 and 16.8 extend Examples 16.5 and 16.6 with an additional grouping column (*TimeYear*). The number of rows in the result increases from 12 rows in the result of Example 16.7 without the CUBE operator to 36 rows in the result of Example 16.8 with the CUBE operator. For three grouping columns with M, N, and P unique values, the maximum number of subtotal rows produced by the CUBE operator is $M + N + P + M*N + M*P + N*P + 1$. Since the number of subtotal rows grows substantially with the number of grouped columns and the unique values per column, the CUBE operator should be used sparingly when there are more than three grouped columns.

Example 16.7: GROUP BY Clause with Three Grouping Columns and the Partial Result without Subtotals

```
SELECT StoreZip, TimeYear, TimeMonth, SUM(SalesDollar) AS
SumSales
 FROM Sales, Store, TimeDim
 WHERE Sales.StoreId = Store.StoreId
   AND Sales.TimeNo = TimeDim.TimeNo
   AND (StoreNation = 'USA' OR StoreNation = 'Canada')
   AND TimeYear BETWEEN 2007 AND 2008
 GROUP BY StoreZip, TimeYear, TimeMonth;
```

StoreZip	TimeYear	TimeMonth	SumSales
80111	2007	1	10000
80111	2007	2	12000
80111	2007	3	11000
80112	2007	1	9000
80112	2007	2	11000
80112	2007	3	15000
80111	2008	1	11000
80111	2008	2	13000
80111	2008	3	12000
80112	2008	1	10000
80112	2008	2	12000
80112	2008	3	16000

Example 16.8 (Oracle): GROUP BY Clause with Three Grouping Columns and the Result with Subtotals Produced by the CUBE Operator.

```
SELECT StoreZip, TimeYear, TimeMonth, SUM(SalesDollar) AS
SumSales
 FROM Sales, Store, TimeDim
 WHERE Sales.StoreId = Store.StoreId
   AND Sales.TimeNo = TimeDim.TimeNo
   AND (StoreNation = 'USA' OR StoreNation = 'Canada')
   AND TimeYear BETWEEN 2007 AND 2008
 GROUP BY CUBE(StoreZip, TimeYear, TimeMonth);
```

StoreZip	TimeYear	TimeMonth	SumSales
80111	2007	1	10000
80111	2007	2	12000
80111	2007	3	11000
80112	2007	1	9000
80112	2007	2	11000
80112	2007	3	15000
80111	2008	1	11000
80111	2008	2	13000
80111	2008	3	12000
80112	2008	1	10000
80112	2008	2	12000
80112	2008	3	16000
80111		1	21000
80111		2	25000
80111		3	23000
80112		1	19000
80112		2	22000
80112		3	31000
80111	2007		33000
80111	2008		36000
80112	2007		35000
80112	2008		38000
	2007	1	19000

	2007	2	23000
	2007	3	26000
	2008	1	21000
	2008	2	25000
	2008	3	28000
80111			69000
80112			73000
		1	40000
		2	48000
		3	54000
	2007		68000
	2008		74000
			142000

The CUBE operator is not a primitive operator. The result of a CUBE operation can be produced using a number of SELECT statements connected by the UNION operator, as shown in Example 16.9. The additional SELECT statements generate subtotals for each combination of grouped columns. With two grouped columns, three additional SELECT statements are needed to generate the subtotals. With N grouped columns, $2^N - 1$ additional SELECT statements are needed. Obviously, the CUBE operator is much easier to write than a large number of additional SELECT statements.

Example 16.9: Rewrite Example 16.6 without Using the CUBE Operator

In each additional SELECT statement, a default value (0 for numeric columns and ' ' for text columns) replaces the column in which totals are not generated.

```
SELECT StoreZip, TimeMonth, SUM(SalesDollar) AS SumSales
  FROM Sales, Store, TimeDim
  WHERE Sales.StoreId = Store.StoreId
    AND Sales.TimeNo = TimeDim.TimeNo
    AND (StoreNation = 'USA' OR StoreNation = 'Canada')
    AND TimeYear = 2007
  GROUP BY StoreZip, TimeMonth
  UNION
SELECT StoreZip, 0, SUM(SalesDollar) AS SumSales
  FROM Sales, Store, TimeDim
  WHERE Sales.StoreId = Store.StoreId
    AND Sales.TimeNo = TimeDim.TimeNo
    AND (StoreNation = 'USA' OR StoreNation = 'Canada')
    AND TimeYear = 2007
  GROUP BY StoreZip
UNION
SELECT '', TimeMonth, SUM(SalesDollar) AS SumSales
  FROM Sales, Store, TimeDim
  WHERE Sales.StoreId = Store.StoreId
    AND Sales.TimeNo = TimeDim.TimeNo
    AND (StoreNation = 'USA' OR StoreNation = 'Canada')
    AND TimeYear = 2007
  GROUP BY TimeMonth
UNION
SELECT '', 0, SUM(SalesDollar) AS SumSales
  FROM Sales, Store, TimeDim
  WHERE Sales.StoreId = Store.StoreId
    AND Sales.TimeNo = TimeDim.TimeNo
    AND (StoreNation = 'USA' OR StoreNation = 'Canada')
    AND TimeYear = 2007;
```

ROLLUP Operator

The SQL ROLLUP operator provides a similar capability to the roll-up operator for data cubes. The roll-up operator for data cubes produces totals for more general parts of a dimension hierarchy. The SQL ROLLUP operator produces subtotals for each ordered subset of grouped columns to simulate the effects of the roll-up operator for data cubes. For example, the SQL operation ROLLUP(TimeYear, TimeQuarter, TimeMonth, TimeDay) produces subtotals for the column subsets *<TimeYear, TimeQuarter, TimeMonth>*, *<TimeYear, TimeQuarter>*, *<TimeYear>* as well as the grand total. As this example implies, the order of columns in a ROLLUP operation is significant.

> **ROLLUP Operator:** an operator that augments the normal GROUP BY result with a partial set of subtotals. The ROLLUP operator is appropriate to summarize levels from a dimension hierarchy.

As the previous paragraph indicates, the ROLLUP operator produces only a partial set of subtotals for the columns in a GROUP BY clause. Examples 16.10 and 16.11 demonstrate the ROLLUP operator in order to contrast it with the CUBE operator in Example 16.6. Note that Example 16.10 contains three subtotal rows compared to six subtotal rows in Example 16.6 with the CUBE operator. In Example 16.11, subtotals are produced for the values in the column combinations *<StoreZip, TimeYear>*, *<StoreZip>*, and the grand total. In Example 16.8 with the CUBE operator, subtotals are also produced for the values in the column combinations *<StoreZip, TimeYear>*, *<TimeMonth, TimeYear>*, *<TimeMonth>*, and *<TimeYear>*. Thus, the ROLLUP operator produces far fewer subtotal rows compared to the CUBE operator as the number of grouped columns and unique values per column increases.

Example 16.10 (Oracle): GROUP BY Clause and Result with Subtotals produced by the ROLLUP Operator

This example should be compared with Example 16.6 to understand the difference between the CUBE and ROLLUP operators.

```
SELECT StoreZip, TimeMonth, SUM(SalesDollar) AS SumSales
  FROM Sales, Store, TimeDim
 WHERE Sales.StoreId = Store.StoreId
   AND Sales.TimeNo = TimeDim.TimeNo
   AND (StoreNation = 'USA' OR StoreNation = 'Canada')
   AND TimeYear = 2007
 GROUP BY ROLLUP(StoreZip, TimeMonth);
```

StoreZip	TimeMonth	SumSales
80111	1	10000
80111	2	12000
80111	3	11000
80112	1	9000
80112	2	11000
80112	3	15000
80111		33000
80112		35000
		68000

Example 16.11 (Oracle): GROUP BY Clause with Three Grouping Columns and the Result with Subtotals Produced by the ROLLUP Operator

This example should be compared with Example 16.8 to understand the difference between the CUBE and ROLLUP operators.

```
SELECT StoreZip, TimeYear, TimeMonth, SUM(SalesDollar) AS
SumSales
 FROM Sales, Store, TimeDim
 WHERE Sales.StoreId = Store.StoreId
   AND Sales.TimeNo = TimeDim.TimeNo
   AND (StoreNation = 'USA' OR StoreNation = 'Canada')
   AND TimeYear BETWEEN 2007 AND 2008
 GROUP BY ROLLUP(StoreZip, TimeYear, TimeMonth);
```

StoreZip	TimeYear	TimeMonth	SumSales
80111	2007	1	10000
80111	2007	2	12000
80111	2007	3	11000
80112	2007	1	9000
80112	2007	2	11000
80112	2007	3	15000
80111	2008	1	11000
80111	2008	2	13000
80111	2008	3	12000
80112	2008	1	10000
80112	2008	2	12000
80112	2008	3	16000
80111	2007		33000
80111	2008		36000
80112	2007		35000
80112	2008		38000
80111			69000
80112			73000
			142000

Like the CUBE operator, the ROLLUP operator is not a primitive operator. The result of a ROLLUP operation can be produced using a number of SELECT statements connected by the UNION operator as shown in Example 16.12. The additional SELECT statements generate subtotals for each ordered subset of grouped columns. With three grouped columns, three additional SELECT statements are needed to generate the subtotals. With N grouped columns, N additional SELECT statements are needed. Obviously, the ROLLUP operator is much easier to write than a large number of additional SELECT statements.

Example 16.12: Rewrite of Example 16.11 without Using the ROLLUP Operator

In each additional SELECT statement, a default value (0 for numeric columns and ' ' for text columns) replaces the column in which totals are not generated.

```
SELECT StoreZip, TimeYear, TimeMonth, SUM(SalesDollar) AS
SumSales
 FROM Sales, Store, TimeDim
 WHERE Sales.StoreId = Store.StoreId
   AND Sales.TimeNo = TimeDim.TimeNo
   AND (StoreNation = 'USA' OR StoreNation = 'Canada')
   AND TimeYear BETWEEN 2007 AND 2008
 GROUP BY StoreZip, TimeYear, TimeMonth
```

```
      UNION
      SELECT StoreZip, TimeYear, 0, SUM(SalesDollar) AS
      SumSales
        FROM Sales, Store, TimeDim
        WHERE Sales.StoreId = Store.StoreId
          AND Sales.TimeNo = TimeDim.TimeNo
          AND (StoreNation = 'USA' OR StoreNation = 'Canada')
          AND TimeYear BETWEEN 2007 AND 2008
        GROUP BY StoreZip, TimeYear
      UNION
      SELECT StoreZip, 0, 0, SUM(SalesDollar) AS SumSales
        FROM Sales, Store, TimeDim
        WHERE Sales.StoreId = Store.StoreId
          AND Sales.TimeNo = TimeDim.TimeNo
          AND (StoreNation = 'USA' OR StoreNation = 'Canada')
          AND TimeYear BETWEEN 2007 AND 2008
        GROUP BY StoreZip
      UNION
      SELECT '', 0, 0, SUM(SalesDollar) AS SumSales
        FROM Sales, Store, TimeDim
        WHERE Sales.StoreId = Store.StoreId
          AND Sales.TimeNo = TimeDim.No
          AND (StoreNation = 'USA' OR StoreNation = 'Canada')
          AND TimeYear BETWEEN 2007 AND 2008;
```

GROUPING SETS Operator

For more flexibility than is provided by the CUBE and ROLLUP operators, you can use the GROUPING SETS operator. When you use the GROUPING SETS operator, you explicitly specify the combinations of columns for which you need totals. In contrast, the specification of subtotals is implicit in the CUBE and ROLLUP operators. The GROUPING SETS operator is appropriate when precise control over grouping is needed. If explicit control is not required, the CUBE and ROLLUP operators provide more succinct specification.

> **GROUPING SETS Operator**: an operator in the GROUP BY clause that requires explicit specification of column combinations. The GROUPING SETS operator is appropriate when precise control over grouping and subtotals is required.

To depict the GROUPING SETS operator, the previous examples are recast using the GROUPING SETS operator. In Example 16.13, the GROUPING SETS operator involves subtotals for the *StoreZip* and *TimeMonth* columns along with the grand total denoted by the empty parentheses. The subset (*StoreZip*, *TimeMonth*) also must be specified because all column combinations must be explicitly specified, even the normal grouping without the GROUPING SETS operator. Example 16.14 contains eight column combinations to provide the same result as Example 16.8 with the CUBE of three columns. Example 16.15 contains three column combinations to provide the same result as Example 16.11 with the ROLLUP of three columns.

Example 16.13 (Oracle): GROUP BY Clause Using the GROUPING SETS Operator
This example produces the same result as Example 16.6.

```
      SELECT StoreZip, TimeMonth, SUM(SalesDollar) AS SumSales
        FROM Sales, Store, TimeDim
        WHERE Sales.StoreId = Store.StoreId
          AND Sales.TimeNo = TimeDim.TimeNo
          AND (StoreNation = 'USA' OR StoreNation = 'Canada')
          AND TimeYear = 2007
        GROUP BY GROUPING SETS((StoreZip, TimeMonth), StoreZip,
              TimeMonth, ());
```

Example 16.14 (Oracle): GROUP BY Clause Using the GROUPING SETS Operator
This example produces the same result as Example 16.8.

```
SELECT StoreZip, TimeYear, TimeMonth, SUM(SalesDollar) AS
SumSales
 FROM Sales, Store, TimeDim
 WHERE Sales.StoreId = Store.StoreId
   AND Sales.TimeNo = TimeDim.TimeNo
   AND (StoreNation = 'USA' OR StoreNation = 'Canada')
   AND TimeYear BETWEEN 2007 AND 2008
 GROUP BY GROUPING SETS((StoreZip, TimeYear, TimeMonth),
     (StoreZip, TimeMonth), (StoreZip, TimeYear),
     (TimeMonth, TimeYear), StoreZip, TimeMonth, TimeYear,
() );
```

Example 16.15 (Oracle): GROUP BY Clause Using the GROUPING SETS Operator
This example produces the same result as Example 16.11.

```
SELECT StoreZip, TimeYear, TimeMonth, SUM(SalesDollar) AS
SumSales
 FROM Sales, Store, TimeDim
 WHERE Sales.StoreId = Store.StoreId
   AND Sales.TimeNo = TimeDim.TimeNo
   AND (StoreNation = 'USA' OR StoreNation = 'Canada')
   AND TimeYear BETWEEN 2007 AND 2008
GROUP BY GROUPING SETS((StoreZip, TimeYear, TimeMonth),
     (StoreZip, TimeYear), StoreZip,() );
```

Example 16.16 depicts a situation in which the GROUPING SETS operator is preferred to the CUBE operator. Because the *TimeYear* and *TimeMonth* columns are from the same dimension hierarchy, a full cube usually is not warranted. Instead, the GROUPING SETS operator can be used to specify the column combinations from which subtotals are needed. Subtotals involving *TimeMonth* without *TimeYear* are excluded in Example 16.16 but are included in a full CUBE operation.

Example 16.16 (Oracle): GROUP BY clause using the GROUPING SETS operator.
This example indicates the column combinations from which subtotals are needed.

```
SELECT StoreZip, TimeYear, TimeMonth, SUM(SalesDollar) AS
SumSales
 FROM Sales, Store, TimeDim
 WHERE Sales.StoreId = Store.StoreId
   AND Sales.TimeNo = TimeDim.TimeNo
   AND (StoreNation = 'USA' OR StoreNation = 'Canada')
   AND TimeYear BETWEEN 2007 AND 2008
 GROUP BY GROUPING SETS((StoreZip, TimeYear, TimeMonth),
     (StoreZip, TimeYear), (TimeYear, TimeMonth),
     StoreZip, TimeYear, () );
```

Variations of the CUBE, ROLLUP, and GROUPING SETS Operators

The CUBE, ROLLUP, and GROUPING SETS operators can be combined to provide the appropriate mix of explicit grouping specifications with the GROUPING SETS operator along with subtotals provided by the ROLLUP and the CUBE operators. This list provides some of the possible variations when using these operators.

- A partial CUBE can be done to produce subtotals for a subset of independent dimensions. For example, the clause GROUP BY TimeMonth, CUBE(ItemBrand, StoreState) produces totals on the column subsets *<TimeMonth, ItemBrand, StoreState>*, *<TimeMonth, ItemBrand>*, *<TimeMonth, StoreState>*, and *<TimeMonth>*.
- A partial ROLLUP can be done to produce subtotals for a subset of columns from the same dimension hierarchy. For example the clause GROUP BY ItemBrand, ROLLUP(TimeYear, TimeMonth, TimeDay) produces totals on the column

subsets <ItemBrand, TimeYear, TimeMonth, TimeDay>, <ItemBrand, TimeYear, TimeMonth >, <ItemBrand, TimeYear >, and <ItemBrand>.

- Composite columns can be used with the CUBE or ROLLUP operators to skip some subtotals. For example, the clause GROUP BY ROLLUP(TimeYear, (TimeQuarter, TimeMonth), TimeDay) produces totals on the column subsets < TimeYear, TimeQuarter, TimeMonth, TimeDay>, < TimeYear, TimeQuarter, TimeMonth >, < TimeYear>, and < >. The composite column <TimeQuarter, TimeMonth> is treated as a single column in the ROLLUP operation.
- CUBE and ROLLUP operations can be included in a GROUPING SETS operation. For example the clause GROUP BY GROUPING SETS(ItemBrand, ROLLUP(TimeYear, TimeMonth), StoreState) produces totals on the column subsets < ItemBrand>, <StoreState>, <TimeYear, TimeMonth>, <TimeYear>, and < >. The nested ROLLUP operation creates subtotals on the column subsets <TimeYear, TimeMonth>, <TimeYear>, and < >.

Other Extensions for Decision Support

In addition to the GROUP BY extensions, a number of new aggregate functions can be used in the SELECT statement. Some of the typical extensions are listed below.
Ranking functions support requests for the top or the bottom percentage of results.
Ratio functions simplify the formulation of queries that compare individual values to group totals.
Functions for moving totals and averages allow smoothing of data for time-series analysis. The OLAP extension in SQL:2006 provides the WINDOW clause to specify moving averages.

16.3.4 Materialized Views and Query Rewriting

To support queries involving large fact tables, relational DBMSs provide materialized views. A materialized view is a stored view that must be periodically synchronized with its source data. Materialized views are attractive in data warehouses because the source data is stable except for periodic refreshments that can usually be performed during nonpeak times. In contrast, traditional (nonmaterialized) views dominate operational database processing because the refresh cost can be high. Along with materialized views, most relational DBMSs support automatic substitution of materialized views for source tables in a process known as query rewriting. This section depicts materialized views using the Oracle 11g syntax and provides examples of the query rewriting process.

> **Materialized View**: a stored view that must be periodically synchronized with its source data. Materialized views support storage of summarized data for fast query response.

Materialized Views in Oracle 11g

Specification of a materialized view in Oracle 11g involves elements of base table specification and the mapping specification of traditional views along with the specification of materialization properties. Because materialized views are stored, most of the storage properties for base tables can also be specified for materialized views. Since the storage properties are not the focus here, they will not be depicted. The mapping specification is the same for traditional views as for materialized views. A SELECT statement provides the mapping necessary to populate a materialized view. The materialization properties include

> Method of refresh (incremental or complete): Oracle has a number of restrictions on the types of materialized views that can be incrementally refreshed so incremental refreshment will not be discussed here.
> Refresh timing (on demand or on commit): For the on demand option, Oracle provides the DBMS_MView package with several refresh procedures (Refresh, Refresh_All_MViews, Refresh_Dependent) to specify refresh timing details.
> Build timing (immediate or deferred): For the deferred option, the refresh procedures in the DBMS_MView can be used to specify the details of populating the materialized view.

Examples 16.17 to 16.19 depict the syntax of the CREATE MATERIALIZED VIEW statement. These statements appear similar to CREATE VIEW statements except for the materialization clauses. The build timing is immediate in Examples 16.17 and 16.19, while the build timing is deferred in Example 16.18. The refresh method is complete and the refresh timing is on demand in all three materialized views. The SELECT statement following the AS keyword provides the mapping to populate a materialized view.

Example 16.17 (Oracle): Materialized View Containing Sales for all Countries for Years after 2005 Grouped by State and Year

```
CREATE MATERIALIZED VIEW MV1
BUILD IMMEDIATE
REFRESH COMPLETE ON DEMAND
ENABLE QUERY REWRITE AS
SELECT StoreState, TimeYear, SUM(SalesDollar) AS
        SUMDollar1
 FROM Sales, Store, TimeDim
 WHERE Sales.StoreId = Store.StoreId
   AND Sales.TimeNo = TimeDim.TimeNo
   AND TimeYear > 2005
 GROUP BY StoreState, TimeYear;
```

Example 16.18 (Oracle): Materialized View Containing USA Sales in all Years Grouped by State, Year, and Month

```
CREATE MATERIALIZED VIEW MV2
BUILD DEFERRED
REFRESH COMPLETE ON DEMAND
ENABLE QUERY REWRITE AS
SELECT StoreState, TimeYear, TimeMonth,
        SUM(SalesDollar) AS SUMDollar2
 FROM Sales, Store, TimeDim
 WHERE Sales.StoreId = Store.StoreId
   AND Sales.TimeNo = TimeDim.TimeNo
   AND StoreNation = 'USA'
 GROUP BY StoreState, TimeYear, TimeMonth;
```

Example 16.19 (Oracle): Materialized View Containing Canadian Sales before 2006 Grouped by City, Year, and Month

```
CREATE MATERIALIZED VIEW MV3
BUILD IMMEDIATE
REFRESH COMPLETE ON DEMAND
ENABLE QUERY REWRITE AS
SELECT StoreCity, TimeYear, TimeMonth,
        SUM(SalesDollar) AS SUMDollar3
 FROM Sales, Store, TimeDim
 WHERE Sales.StoreId = Store.StoreId
   AND Sales.TimeNo = TimeDim.TimeNo
   AND StoreNation ='Canada'
   AND TimeYear <= 2005
 GROUP BY StoreCity, TimeYear, TimeMonth;
```

User awareness is another difference between traditional views and materialized views. For queries using operational databases, traditional views are used in place of base tables to simplify query formulation. A user perceives the database as a view shielding the user from the complexities of the base tables. In contrast, for data warehouse queries submitted by users, fact and dimension tables are used. The fact and dimension tables may be hidden through a query tool to simplify query formulation. Data warehouse users are not aware of materialized views as materialized views are solely performance aids managed by the DBMS. The DBMS provides tools to help determine the appropriate materialized views and to use the materialized views to improve performance of queries in a process known as query rewriting.

Query Rewriting Principles

The <u>query rewriting</u> process for materialized views reverses the query modification process for traditional views presented in Chapter 10. Recall that the query modification process (Figure 16.13) substitutes base tables for views so that materialization of the views is not needed. In contrast, the query rewriting process (Figure 16.14) substitutes materialized views for fact and dimension tables to avoid accessing large fact and dimension tables. The substitution process is only performed if performance improvements are expected.

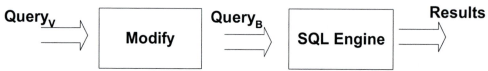

Query$_V$: query that references a view

Query$_B$: modification of Query$_V$ such that references to the view are replaced by references to base tables.

Figure 16.13: Process Flow of View Modification

Query$_{FD}$: query that references fact and dimension tables

Query$_{MV}$: rewrite of Query$_{FD}$ such that materialized views are substituted for fact and dimension tables whenever justified by expected performance improvements.

Figure 16.14: Process Flow of Query Rewriting

Overall, query rewriting is more complex than query modification because query rewriting involves a more complex substitution process and requires the optimizer to evaluate costs. In both processes, the DBMS, not the user, performs the substitution process. In the query rewriting process, the query optimizer must evaluate whether the substitution will improve performance over the original query. In the query modification process, the query optimizer does not compare the cost of the modified query to the original query because modification usually provides substantial cost savings.

Query Rewriting: a substitution process in which a materialized view replaces references to fact and dimension tables in a query. The query optimizer evaluates whether the substitution will improve performance over the original query without the materialized view substitution.

Query Rewriting Details

Query rewriting involves a matching process between a query using fact and dimension tables and a collection of materialized views containing summary data. In brief, a materialized view can provide data for a query if the materialized view matches the row conditions, grouping columns, and aggregate functions as explained below and summarized in Table 16-9.

> Row condition match: rewrite is not possible if a materialized view contains more restrictive conditions than a query. From a query's perspective, the query's conditions must be at least as restrictive as the conditions in the materialized view. For example, if a materialized view has the conditions StoreNation = 'USA' AND TimeYear = 2007, but a

query only has the condition StoreNation = 'USA', the materialized view cannot provide data for the query.

Grouping match for level of detail: rewrite is not possible if the grouping in a materialized view is at a higher level (less detailed) than in a query. From a query's perspective, the grouping columns must be no more detailed than the grouping columns in a materialized view. For example, a query with a grouping on *TimeMonth* cannot use a materialized view with a grouping on *TimeYear*. However, a materialized with grouping on *TimeMonth* can be rolled up to provide data for a query with grouping on *TimeYear*.

Grouping match for functional dependencies: rewrite is not possible if a query contains grouping columns not in a materialized view unless the columns can be derived by functional dependencies. Functional dependencies are derived from primary keys, candidate keys, and dimension dependencies (via the DETERMINES clause). For example, a query with a grouping on *StoreCity* can be derived from a materialized view with a grouping on *StoreId* because *StoreId* → *StoreCity*. Joins can be used to retrieve columns in a query but not in a materialized view as long as there is a functional relationship (usually a 1-M relationship) involving the tables.

Aggregate match: aggregates in the query must match available aggregates in the materialized view or be derivable from aggregates in the materialized view. For example, a query containing average is derivable from a materialized view containing sum and count.

Table 16-9: Summary of Matching Requirements for Query Rewriting

Matching Type	Requirements
Row conditions	Query conditions must be at least as restrictive as materialized view conditions.
Grouping detail	Query grouping columns should be no more detailed than materialized view grouping columns.
Grouping dependencies	Query columns must match or be derivable by functional dependencies from materialized view columns.
Aggregate functions	Query aggregate functions must match or be derivable from materialized view aggregate functions.

Example 16.20 presents an example data warehouse query and the rewritten query to depict the matching process. Table 16-10 depicts matching between *MV1* and the query in Example 16.20. *MV1* and the query match directly on the grouping columns and aggregate computations. The condition on *TimeYear* (> 2005) in *MV1* contains the query condition (2007). In addition, the query contains an extra condition on *StoreNation*. Grouping is not necessary in the rewritten query because identical grouping is already performed in *MV1*.

Example 16.20: Data warehouse Query and Rewritten Query using the *MV1* Materialized View

```
-- Data warehouse query
SELECT StoreState, TimeYear, SUM(SalesDollar)
 FROM Sales, Store, TimeDim
 WHERE Sales.StoreId = Store.StoreId
   AND Sales.TimeNo = TimeDim.TimeNo
   AND StoreNation IN ('USA','Canada')
   AND TimeYear = 2007
 GROUP BY StoreState, TimeYear;

-- Query Rewrite: replace Sales and Time tables with MV1
SELECT DISTINCT MV1.StoreState, TimeYear, SumDollar1
FROM MV1, Store
WHERE MV1.StoreState = Store.StoreState
  AND TimeYear = 2007
  AND StoreNation IN ('USA','Canada');
```

Table 16-10: Matching between Materialized View and Example 16.20

	Materialized View	Query
Grouping	StoreState, TimeYear	StoreState, TimeYear
Conditions	TimeYear > 2005	TimeYear = 2007
		StoreNation = ('USA', 'Canada')
Aggregates	SUM(SalesDollar)	SUM(SalesDollar)

Example 16.21 presents a more complex example of query rewriting involving three SELECT blocks combined using the UNION operator. Table 16-11 depicts matching between the materialized views (*MV1, MV2, MV3*) and the query in Example 16.21. The first query block retrieves the total sales in the United States or Canada from 2005 to 2008. The second query block retrieves the USA store sales in 2005. The third query block retrieves Canadian store sales in 2005. The GROUP BY clauses are necessary in the second and third query blocks to roll-up the finer level of detail in the materialized views. In the third query block, the condition on *StoreNation* is needed because some cities have identical names in both countries.

Example 16.21: Data Warehouse Query and Rewritten Query using the *MV1, MV2,* and *MV3* Materialized Views

```
-- Data warehouse query
SELECT StoreState, TimeYear, SUM(SalesDollar)
 FROM Sales, Store, TimeDim
 WHERE Sales.StoreId = Store.StoreId
   AND Sales.TimeNo = TimeDim.TimeNo
   AND StoreNation IN ('USA','Canada')
   AND TimeYear BETWEEN 2005 and 2008
 GROUP BY StoreState, TimeYear;


-- Query Rewrite
SELECT DISTINCT MV1.StoreState, TimeYear,
        SumDollar1 AS StoreSales
FROM MV1, Store
WHERE MV1.StoreState = Store.StoreState
  AND TimeYear <= 2008
  AND StoreNation IN ('USA','Canada')
UNION
SELECT StoreState, TimeYear,
        SUM(SumDollar2) as StoreSales
FROM MV2
WHERE TimeYear = 2005
GROUP BY StoreState, TimeYear
UNION
SELECT DISTINCT StoreState, TimeYear,
               SUM(SumDollar3) as StoreSales
FROM MV3, Store
WHERE MV3.StoreCity = Store.StoreCity
  AND TimeYear = 2005 AND StoreNation = 'Canada'
GROUP BY StoreState, TimeYear;
```

Table 16-11: Matching between Materialized Views and Example 16.21

	MV1	MV2	MV3	Query
Grouping	StoreState, TimeYear	StoreState, TimeMonth, TimeYear	StoreCity, StoreState, TimeYear	StoreState, TimeYear
Conditions	TimeYear > 2005	StoreNation = 'USA'	TimeYear <= 2005 StoreNation = 'Canada'	TimeYear BETWEEN 2005 AND 2008 StoreNation = ('USA', 'Canada')
Aggregates	SUM(SalesDollar)	SUM(SalesDollar)	SUM(SalesDollar)	SUM(SalesDollar)

Example 16.22 extends Example 16.21 with a CUBE operator. In the rewritten query, the CUBE is performed one time at the end rather than in each SELECT block. To perform the CUBE one time, the FROM clause should contain a nested query. An alternative to the nested query in the FROM clause is to place the nested query in a separate CREATE VIEW statement.

Example 16.22: Data Warehouse Query and Rewritten Query Using the *MV1, MV2,* and *MV3* Materialized Views

```
-- Data warehouse query
SELECT StoreState, TimeYear, SUM(SalesDollar)
 FROM Sales, Store, TimeDim
 WHERE Sales.StoreId = Store.StoreId
   AND Sales.TimeNo = TimeDim.TimeNo
   AND StoreNation IN ('USA','Canada')
   AND TimeYear BETWEEN 2005 and 2008
 GROUP BY CUBE(StoreState, TimeYear);

-- Query Rewrite
SELECT StoreState, TimeYear,
       SUM(StoreSales) as SumStoreSales
 FROM (
  SELECT DISTINCT MV1.StoreState, TimeYear,
         SumDollar1 AS StoreSales
   FROM MV1, Store
   WHERE MV1.StoreState = Store.StoreState
     AND TimeYear <= 2008
     AND StoreNation IN ('USA','Canada')
 UNION
  SELECT StoreState, TimeYear,
         SUM(SumDollar2) as StoreSales
   FROM MV2
   WHERE TimeYear = 2005
   GROUP BY StoreState, TimeYear
 UNION
  SELECT DISTINCT StoreState, TimeYear,
                  SUM(SumDollar3) as StoreSales
   FROM MV3, Store
   WHERE MV3.StoreCity = Store.StoreCity
     AND TimeYear = 2005 AND StoreNation = 'Canada'
   GROUP BY StoreState, TimeYear )
 GROUP BY CUBE(StoreState, TimeYear);
```

These examples indicate the range of query rewriting possibilities rather than capabilities of actual DBMSs. Most enterprise DBMSs support query rewriting, but the range of query rewriting supported varies. Because of the complexity and the proprietary nature of query rewrite algorithms, the details of query rewriting algorithms are beyond the scope of this textbook.

16.3.5 Storage and Optimization Technologies

Several storage technologies have been developed to provide multidimensional data capabilities. The storage technologies support On Line Analytic Processing (OLAP), a generic name applied to decision support capabilities for data cubes. This section describes the features of OLAP storage technologies with an emphasis on current market trends.

MOLAP (Multidimensional OLAP)

Originally, vendors of decision support software developed a storage architecture that directly manipulates data cubes. This storage architecture, known as <u>MOLAP</u> for Multidimensional OLAP, was the only choice as a storage technology for data warehouses until the mid-1990s. At the current time, MOLAP has been eclipsed as the primary storage architecture for data warehouses, but it still is an important technology for summary data cubes and small data warehouses and data marts.

MOLAP storage engines directly manipulate stored data cubes. The storage engines of MOLAP systems are optimized for the unique characteristics of multidimensional data such as sparsity and complex aggregation across thousands of cells. Because data cubes are precomputed, MOLAP query performance is generally better than competing approaches that use relational database storage. Even with techniques to deal with sparsity, MOLAP engines can be overwhelmed by the size of data cubes. A fully calculated data cube may expand many times as compared to the raw input data. This data explosion problem limits the size of data cubes that MOLAP engines can manipulate.

> **MOLAP:** a storage engine that directly stores and manipulates data cubes. MOLAP engines generally offer the best query performance but place limits on the size of data cubes.

ROLAP (Relational OLAP)

Because of the potential market size and growth of data warehouse processing, vendors of relational DBMSs have extended their products with additional features to support operations and storage structures for multidimensional data. These product extensions are collectively known as <u>ROLAP</u> for Relational OLAP. Given the growing size of data warehouses and the intensive research and development by relational DBMS vendors, it was only a matter of time before ROLAP became the dominant storage engine for data warehouses.

In the ROLAP approach, relational databases store multidimensional data using the star schema or its variations, as described in Section 16.3.1. Data cubes are dynamically constructed from fact and dimension tables as well as from materialized views. Typically, only a subset of a data cube must be constructed as specified in a user's query. Extensions to SQL as described in section 16.3.3 allow users to manipulate the dimensions and measures in virtual data cubes.

> **ROLAP:** relational DBMS extensions to support multidimensional data. ROLAP engines support a variety of storage and optimization techniques for summary data retrieval.

ROLAP engines incorporate a variety of storage and optimization techniques for summary data retrieval. This list explains the most prominent techniques:

> <u>Bitmap join indexes</u> (see Chapter 8 for details) are particularly useful for columns in dimension tables with few values such as *CustState*. A bitmap join index provides a precomputed join from the values of a dimension table to the rows of a fact table. To support snowflake schemas, some DBMS vendors support bitmap join indexes for dimension tables related to other dimension tables. For example, a bitmap index for the *Division.DivManager* column has an index record that contains a bitmap for related rows of the *Store* table and a second bitmap for rows of the *Sales* table related to matching rows of the *Store* table.

Star join query optimization uses bitmap join indexes on dimension tables to reduce the number of rows in a fact table to retrieve. A star join involves a fact table joined with one or more dimension tables. Star join optimization involves three phases. In the first phase, the bitmap join indexes on each dimension table are combined using the union operator for conditions connected by the OR operator and the intersection operator for conditions connected by the AND operator. In the second phase, the bitmaps resulting from the first phase are combined using the intersection operator. In the third phase, the rows of the fact table are retrieved using the bitmap resulting from the second phase. Star join optimization can result in substantially reduced execution time as compared to traditional join algorithms that combine two tables at a time.

Query rewriting using materialized views can eliminate the need to access large fact and dimension tables. If materialized views are large, they can be indexed to improve retrieval performance. Query rewriting uses the query optimizer to evaluate the benefit of using materialized views as compared to the fact and dimension tables.

Summary storage advisors determine the best set of materialized views that should be created and maintained for a given query workload. For consistency with other components, the summary advisor is integrated with the query rewriting component and the query optimizer.

Partitioning, striping, and parallel query execution provide opportunities to reduce the execution time of data warehouse queries. The choices must be carefully studied so that the use of partitioning and striping support the desired level of parallel query execution.

Despite the intensive research and development on ROLAP storage and optimization techniques, MOLAP engines still provide faster query response time. However, MOLAP storage suffers from limitations in data cube size so that ROLAP storage is necessary for fine-grained data warehouses. In addition, the difference in response time has narrowed so that ROLAP storage may involve only a slight performance penalty if ROLAP storage and optimization techniques are properly utilized.

HOLAP (Hybrid OLAP)

Because of the tradeoffs between MOLAP and ROLAP, a third technology known as HOLAP for Hybrid OLAP has been developed to combine ROLAP and MOLAP. HOLAP allows a data warehouse to be divided between relational storage of fact and dimension tables and multidimensional storage of summary data cubes. When an OLAP query is submitted, the HOLAP system can combine data from the ROLAP managed data and the MOLAP managed data.

HOLAP: a storage engine for data warehouses that combines ROLAP and MOLAP storage engines. HOLAP involves both relational and multidimensional data storage as well as combining data from both relational and multidimensional sources for data cube operations.

Despite the appeal of HOLAP, it has potential disadvantages that may limit its use. First, HOLAP can be more complex than either ROLAP or MOLAP, especially if a DBMS vendor does not provide full HOLAP support. To fully support HOLAP, a DBMS vendor must provide both MOLAP and ROLAP engines as well as tools to combine both storage engines in the design and operation of a data warehouse. Second, there is considerable overlap in functionality between the storage and optimization techniques in ROLAP and MOLAP engines. It is not clear whether the ROLAP storage and optimization techniques should be discarded or used in addition to the MOLAP techniques. Third, because the difference in response time has narrowed between ROLAP and MOLAP, the combination of MOLAP and ROLAP may not provide significant performance improvement to justify the added complexity.

16.4 Maintaining a Data Warehouse

Although data warehouses largely contain replicated data, maintaining a data warehouse is much more difficult than simply copying from data sources. Maintaining a data warehouse involves initially populating the warehouse with source data and periodically refreshing the warehouse as source data changes. Determining data to load in a warehouse involves matching decision support needs to the realities of available data. To fulfill decision support needs, data warehouses use data from many internal and external sources. Reconciling the differences among data sources is a significant challenge especially considering that source systems typically cannot be changed. As its data sources change, a data warehouse should be refreshed in a timely manner to support decision making. Because data sources change at different rates, the determination of the time and content to refresh can be a significant challenge. Because of these challenges, maintaining a data warehouse can involve significant investments in hardware, software, and personnel to achieve a satisfactory solution.

This section presents several important aspects of maintaining a data warehouse. The first part describes the kinds of data sources available for populating a data warehouse. The second part describes the workflow for maintaining a data warehouse. The final part discusses the problem of determining the frequency of refreshment and the content to refresh.

16.4.1 Sources of Data

Accessing source data presents challenges in dealing with a variety of formats and constraints on source systems. External source systems usually cannot be changed. Internal source systems may or may not be changeable to accommodate the requirements of a data warehouse. Even if a source system can be changed, budget constraints may allow only minor changes. Source data may be stored in legacy format or modern format. Legacy format generally precludes retrieval using nonprocedural languages such as SQL. Modern format means that the source data can be accessed as a relational database or as Web pages. Unless stored as with formal meta data, Web pages can be difficult to parse and will be nonstandard across websites. Formal meta data usually involves XML data along with an XML schema to provide interpretation of the XML data.

Change data from source systems provides the basis to update a data warehouse. Change data comprises new source data (insertions) and modifications to existing source data (updates and deletions). Further, change data can affect fact tables and/or dimension tables. The most common change data involves insertions of new facts. Insertions of new dimensions and modifications of dimensions are less common but are still important to capture.

Depending on the characteristics of the source system, change data can be classified as cooperative, logged, queryable, or snapshot as summarized in Table 16-12. Cooperative change data involves notification from the source system about changes. The notification typically occurs at transaction completion time using a trigger. Cooperative change data can be input immediately into a data warehouse or placed in a queue for later input possibly with other changes. Because cooperative change data involves modifications to both a source system and the data warehouse, it is the least common format for change data.

Logged change data involves files that record changes or other user activity. For example, a transaction log contains every change made by a transaction, and a Web log contains page access histories (called clickstreams) by website visitors. Logged change data usually involves no changes to a source system as logs are readily available for most source systems. However, logs can contain large amounts of irrelevant data. In addition, derivation of the relevant data needed for the data warehouse can require matching related log records, a resource-intensive task. Logged change data is most commonly used for the customer relationship subset of a data warehouse.

As its name implies, queryable change data comes directly from a data source via a query. Queryable change data requires timestamping in the data source. Since few data sources contain timestamps for all data, queryable change data usually is augmented with other kinds of change data. Queryable change data is most applicable for fact tables using columns such as order date, shipment date, and hire date that are stored in operational data sources.

Snapshot change data involves periodic dumps of source data. To derive change data, a difference operation uses the two most recent snapshots. The result of a difference operation is called a delta. Snapshots are the most common form of change data because of applicability. Snapshots are the only form of change data without requirements on a source system. Because computing a snapshot can be resource intensive, there may be constraints about the time and frequency of retrieving a snapshot.

586

Table 16-12: Summary of the Change Data Classification

Change Type	Description	Evaluation
Cooperative	Source system notification using triggers	Requires modifications to source systems
Logged	Source system activity captured in logs	Readily available but significant processing to extract useful data
Queryable	Source system queries using timestamps	Requires timestamps in the source data and non legacy source systems
Snapshot	Periodic dumps of source data augmented with difference operations	Resource intensive to create and significant processing for difference operations; no source system requirements so useful for legacy data

16.4.2 Workflow for Maintaining a Data Warehouse

Maintaining a data warehouse involves a variety of tasks that manipulate change data from source systems. Figure 16.15 presents a generic workflow that organizes the tasks. The preparation phase manipulates change data from individual source systems. Extraction involves the retrieval of data from an individual source system. Transportation involves movement of the extracted data to a staging area. Cleaning involves a variety of tasks to standardize and improve the quality of the extracted data. Auditing involves recording results of the cleaning process, performing completeness and reasonableness checks, and handling exceptions.

The integration phase involves merging the separate, cleaned sources into one source. Merging can involve the removal of inconsistencies among the source data. Auditing involves recording results of the merging process, performing completeness and reasonableness checks, and handling exceptions.

The update phase involves propagating the integrated change data to various parts of the data warehouse including fact and dimension tables, materialized views, stored data cubes, and data marts. After propagation, notification can be sent to user groups and administrators.

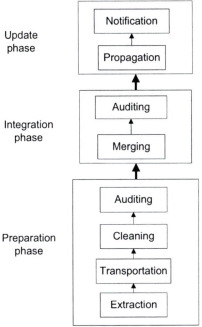

Figure 16.15: Generic Workflow for Data Warehouse Maintenance

The preparation and integration phases should resolve data quality problems as summarized in Table 16-13. Data from legacy systems are typically dirty, meaning that they may not conform to each other or to enterprisewide data quality standards. If directly loaded, dirty data may lead to poor decision making. To resolve data quality problems, the auditing task should include exception handling. Exceptions can be noted in a log file and then manually addressed. Over time, exceptions should decrease as data quality standards are improved on internal data sources.

Table 16-13: Typical Data Quality Problems

Multiple identifiers: some data sources may use different primary keys for the same entity such as different customer numbers
Multiple names: the same field may be represented using different field names
Different units: measures and dimensions may have different units and granularities.
Missing values: data may not exist in some databases; to compensate for missing values, different default values may be used across data sources
Orphaned transactions: some transactions may be missing important parts such as an order without a customer
Multipurpose fields: some databases may combine data into one field such as different components of an address
Conflicting data: some data sources may have conflicting data such as different customer addresses
Different update times: some data sources may perform updates at different intervals

In addition to exception handling, the auditing task should include completeness checks and reasonableness checks. A completeness check counts the number of reporting units to ensure that all have reported during a given period. A reasonableness check determines whether key facts fall in predetermined bounds and are a realistic extrapolation of previous history. Exceptions may require reconciliation by business analysts before propagation to a data warehouse.

The generic workflow in Figure 16.15 applies to both the initial loading and the periodic refreshment of a data warehouse. The initial loading often requires a long period of data cleaning to resolve data quality problems. A goal of initial loading is to discover the data quality problems and resolve them. The refresh process typically varies among data sources. The workflow process should be customized to fit the requirements of each data source. For example, auditing may be minimized for high-quality data sources.

To support the complexity of data warehouse maintenance, software products known as Extraction, Transformation and Loading (ETL) tools have been developed. These tools, available from both third-party vendors and DBMS vendors, eliminate the need to write custom code for many maintenance tasks. Most ETL tools use rule specifications rather than procedural coding to indicate logic and actions. Some ETL tools can generate code that can be customized for more flexibility. ETL tools are essential to reduce the effort to implement the workflow tasks.

ETL Tools: software tools for extraction, transformation, and loading of change data from data sources to a data warehouse. ETL tools eliminate the need to write custom coding for many data warehouse maintenance tasks.

In addition to ETL tools, enterprise DBMS vendors provide data loading programs and proprietary SQL extensions that support some maintenance tasks. The following list summarizes the data loading programs and SQL extensions available in Oracle 11g.

- SQL*Loader is a long standing Oracle utility for loading data from text files into Oracle tables. SQL*Loader provides datatype conversion, conditional loading of data, simple NULL handling, transformation of data before loading using SQL functions, and direct-path loading for improved performance.
- The proprietary Oracle SQL MERGE statement provides the ability to update or insert a row conditionally into a table.
- The proprietary Oracle SQL multiple table INSERT statement provides the ability to segregate data on logical attributes for insertion into different target objects.

- Oracle Change Data Capture supports synchronous (via triggers) or asynchronous capture (via log files) of change data. The Change Data Capture feature uses a Publish and Subscribe model to control change data availability and notify subscribers about change data availability.
- The Oracle Data Pump enables very high-speed movement of data and metadata from one database to another using import and export utilities.

16.4.3 Managing the Refresh Process

Refreshing a data warehouse is a complex process that involves the management of time differences between the updating of data sources and the updating of the related data warehouse objects (tables, materialized views, data cubes, data marts). In Figure 16.16, <u>valid time lag</u> is the difference between the occurrence of an event in the real world (valid time) and the storage of the event in an operational database (transaction time). <u>Load time lag</u> is the difference between transaction time and the storage of the event in a data warehouse (load time). For internal data sources, there may be some control over valid time lag. For external data sources, there is usually no control over valid time lag. Thus, a data warehouse administrator has most control over load time lag.

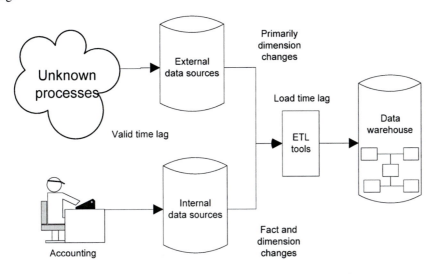

Figure 16.16: Overview of the Data Warehouse Refresh Process

Figure 16.13 implies that data sources can change independently leading to different change rates for fact tables and dimension tables. Fact tables generally record completed events such as orders, shipments, and purchases with links to related dimensions. For example, inserting a row in the *Sales* table requires foreign keys that reference the *Customer*, *Store*, *TimeDim*, and *Item* tables. However, updates and insertions to the related dimension tables may occur at different times than the fact events. For example, a customer may move or an item may change in price at different times than orders, shipments, or inventory purchases. As a result of the different change rates, a data warehouse administrator should manage the load time lag separately for dimension tables and fact tables.

The primary objective in managing the refresh process is to determine the refresh frequency for each data source. The optimal refresh frequency maximizes the net refresh benefit defined as the value of data timeliness minus the cost of refresh. The value of data timeliness depends on the sensitivity of decision making to the currency of the data. Some decisions are very time sensitive such as inventory decisions. Organizations along a supply chain attempt to minimize inventory carrying costs by stocking goods as close as possible to the time needed. Other decisions are not so time sensitive. For example, the decision to close a poor performing store would typically be done using data over a long period of time.

Fisher and Berndt (2001) have proposed a method to measure the value of data timeliness. They defined a measure of the error rate of a data warehouse with respect to a given workload of queries. To determine the error rate, the data volatility of queries and dimensions is estimated. Even if a data warehouse stores individual-level data, most queries will involve aggregations, not retrieval of the individual-level data. For example, most queries on the store sales schema would involve the item brand or category, not the individual items. Given an assessment of the error rate, the value of data timeliness can be assessed using the frequency or other weighting for data warehouse queries.

The cost to refresh a data warehouse includes both computer and human resources. Computer resources are necessary for all tasks in the maintenance workflow. Human resources may be necessary in the auditing tasks during the preparation and integration phases. The level of data quality in source data also affects the level of human resources required. The development effort to use ETL tools and write custom software is not part of the refresh cost unless there is ongoing development cost with each refresh. An important distinction involves the fixed cost and the variable cost of refreshment. Large fixed cost encourages less frequent refresh because the fixed cost occurs with each refresh. Fixed cost may include startup and shutdown effort as well as resource rental.

Along with balancing the value of timeliness against the cost of refresh, the data warehouse administrator must satisfy constraints on the refresh process as summarized in Table 16-14. Constraints on either the data warehouse or a source system may restrict frequent refresh. Source access constraints can be due to legacy technology with restricted scalability for internal data sources or coordination problems for external data sources. Integration constraints often involve identification of common entities such as customers and transactions across data sources. Completeness/consistency constraints can involve maintenance of the same time period in change data or inclusion of change data from each data source for completeness. Data warehouse availability often involves conflicts between online availability and warehouse loading.

Table 16-14: Summary of Refresh Constraints

Constraint Type	Description
Source access	Restrictions on the time and frequency of extracting change data
Integration	Restrictions that require concurrent reconciliation of change data
Completeness/consistency	Restrictions that require loading of change data in the same refresh period
Availability	Load scheduling restrictions due to resource issues including storage capacity, online availability, and server usage

Closing Thoughts

This chapter provided a detailed introduction to the concepts and practice of data warehousing. The chapter began by examining conceptual differences between relational databases, traditionally used for transaction processing, and multidimensional databases, suggested for the new generation of decision support applications. The unique characteristics of decision support data were outlined, followed by a discussion of data warehouse architectures, data mining, and data warehouse usage in organizations.

Data warehouses can be implemented using the multidimensional data model, the relational model, or a combination of both models. For the multidimensional data model, this chapter presented the terminology associated with data cubes and the operators to manipulate data cubes. For the relational data model, the chapter presented data modeling techniques (the star schema and its variations), SQL extensions in the GROUP BY clause for querying dimensional data, materialized views, and storage technologies. The storage technologies support data warehouses using both relational and data cube storage engines.

Irrespective of the data model and storage architecture, maintaining a data warehouse is a difficult process that must be carefully managed. The chapter presented the kinds of data sources used in maintaining a data warehouse, a generic workflow describing the tasks involved in maintaining a data warehouse, and design issues to consider in the refresh process. The chapter advocated the usage of ETL tools to reduce the amount of custom code to implement procedures that populate a data warehouse.

Review Concepts

- Data needs for transaction processing versus decision support applications
- Characteristics of a data warehouse: subject-oriented, integrated, time-variant, and nonvolatile
- Architectures for deploying a data warehouse: two-tier, three-tier, bottom-up
- Stages of data warehouse development (prenatal, infant, child, teenager, adult, and sage) and difficulty of moving between some stages (infant to child and teenager to adult)
- Multidimensional data cube: dimensions, measures, hierarchies, time-series data type
- Multidimensional operators: slice, dice, drill-down, roll-up, pivot
- Star schema: fact table and related dimension tables
- Variations of the star schema: snowflake schema (multiple dimension levels) and constellation schema (multiple fact tables)
- Maintaining historical dimensional integrity using a Type II representation for unlimited history and a Type III representation for limited history
- Dimension representation to support data cube operations and query rewriting techniques
- Extensions of the GROUP BY clause for subtotal calculation: CUBE, ROLLUP, and GROUPING SETS operators
- Materialized views for storage of precomputed summary data
- Query rewriting involving substituting materialized views for fact and dimension tables to improve performance of data warehouse queries
- Multidimensional storage architectures: ROLAP, MOLAP, and HOLAP
- Kinds of change data used to populate a data warehouse: cooperative, logged, queryable, and snapshot
- Phases in the workflow for maintaining a data warehouse: preparation, integration, and propagation
- Importance of ETL (extraction, transformation, loading) tools to reduce the coding in procedures to populate a data warehouse
- Determining the refresh frequency for a data warehouse: balancing the frequency of refresh against the cost of refresh while satisfying refresh constraints
- Types of refresh constraints: source access, integration, completeness/consistency, availability

Questions

1. Why are operational databases not particularly suited for decision support applications?
2. How is a data warehouse different from a data mart?
3. When is the three-tier data warehouse architecture more appropriate than the two-tier data warehouse architecture?
4. What are the components of an enterprise data model?
5. What are some causes for failures in data warehouse projects?
6. Does a bottom-up data warehouse architecture use an enterprise data model?
7. What is an oper mart?
8. What is the purpose of the data warehouse maturity model?
9. What is an important insight provided by the data warehouse maturity model?
10. What are the advantages of multidimensional representation over relational representation for business analysts?
11. Explain why a dimension may have multiple hierarchies.
12. What are the advantages of using time-series data in a cell instead of time as a dimension?
13. How is slicing a data cube different from dicing?
14. What are the differences between drilling-down and rolling-up a data cube dimension?
15. How is a pivot operation useful for multidimensional databases?
16. Explain the significance of sparsity in a data cube.
17. What is a star schema?
18. What are the differences between fact tables and dimension tables?
19. How does a snowflake schema differ from a star schema?

20. What is a constellation schema?
21. How is time represented for a fact table?
22. What is an accumulating fact table?
23. What is the difference between Type II and Type III representations for historical dimension integrity?
24. What is the purpose of the Oracle CREATE DIMENSION statement?
25. What is the purpose of the SQL CUBE operator?
26. What is the purpose of the SQL ROLLUP operator?
27. What is the purpose of the SQL GROUPING SETS operator?
28. Briefly list some of the variations of the CUBE, ROLLUP, and GROUPING SETS operators.
29. Why are materialized views important for data warehouses but not important for operational databases?
30. What materialization properties does Oracle 11g provide for materialized views?
31. Compare and contrast query rewriting for materialized views to query modification for traditional (nonmaterialized) views.
32. Briefly explain the matching processes to enable query rewriting.
33. Explain the significance of indexing fact and dimension tables in a data warehouse.
34. What are the pros and cons of a MOLAP storage engine?
35. What are the pros and cons of a ROLAP storage engine?
36. What are the pros and cons of a HOLAP storage engine?
37. List some storage and optimization techniques in ROLAP engines.
38. What is cooperative change data?
39. What is logged change data?
40. What is queryable change data?
41. What is snapshot change data?
42. Briefly describe the phases of data warehouse maintenance.
43. List common data quality problems that should be resolved by the preparation and integration phases.
44. What is the benefit of using ETL tools in data warehouse maintenance?
45. What is valid time lag?
46. What is load time lag?
47. What is the primary objective in managing the refresh process for a data warehouse?
48. What types of constraints affect the refresh process?

Problems

Part 1: Automobile Insurance Problems

Part 1 provides practice with data cube definition and operations as well as star schemas. The questions in Part 1 involve the database shown below used by an automobile insurance provider to support policy transactions (create and maintain customer policies) and claims transactions (claims made by other parties). The policy transactions utilize the tables *Item*, *Agent*, *InsuredParty*, *Policy*, *InsuredAuto*, and *PolicyItem*, while the claims transactions use the tables *InsuredParty*, *Claimant*, *ThirdParty*, *InsuredAuto*, *Policy*, and *Claim*. The nine tables in this database are shown, along with the primary keys (shown in bold font) and the foreign keys (shown in italics). For each table, assume the field formats of your own choice.

Table: Item

ItemNo	ItemDesc	ItemMinCoverage	ItemMaxCoverage

Primary key: ItemNo
Foreign keys: None

Table: Agent

AgentNo	AgentName	AgentPhone	AgentDept	AgentType	AgentRegion

Primary key: AgentNo
Foreign keys: None

Table: InsuredParty

IPSSN	IPDrivLicNo	IPState	IPName	IPPhone	IPAddr	IPDOB	IPCity	IPZip	IPRiskCat

Primary key: IPSSN
Foreign keys: none
IPDOB is the insured party's date of birth

Table: Claimant

ClmtNo	ClmtName	ClmtPhone	ClmtInsComp	ClmtPolNo	ClmtAddr	ClmtCity	ClmtState	ClmtZip

Primary key: ClmtNo
Foreign keys: None

Table: ThirdParty

TPSSN	TPName	TPPhone	TPDesc	TPAddr	TPCity	TPState	TPZip

Primary key: TPSSN
Foreign keys: None

Table: Policy

PolNo	PolBegDate	PolEndDate	IPSSN	AgentNo	PolPremium	PolEffDate

Primary key: PolNo
Foreign keys: IPSSN, AgentNo

Table: InsuredAuto

IAVIN	IALicPlateNo	IAState	IAMake	IAModel	IAYear	IAAirBags

IADriverSSN	*PolNo*

Primary key: IPVIN
Foreign keys: IADriverSSN (refers to InsuredParty), PolNo

Table: PolicyItem

IAVIN	**ItemNo**	PICoverage	PIPremium	PIComments

Primary key: IAVIN, ItemNo
Foreign keys: IAVIN, ItemNo

Table: Claim

ClaimNo	ClaimAmount	ClaimEstimate	ClaimDesc	ClaimDate	*IAVIN*

ClmtNo	*TPSSN*

Primary key: ClaimNo
Foreign keys: IAVIN, ClmtNo, TPSSN

1. Identify dimensions and measures in a data cube for automobile policy analysis.
2. Draw a star or snowflake schema to support the dimensions and measures in the data cube from problem 1. You may want to use denormalization to reduce the number of dimension tables and the relationships among dimension tables.
3. Identify dimensions and measures in a data cube for claims analysis.
4. Draw a star or snowflake schema to support the dimensions and measures in the data cube from problem 3. You may want to use denormalization to reduce the number of dimension tables and the relationships among dimension tables.
5. In the policy schema, what level of detail should be stored? What should be the finest-level grain in a data cube?
6. Identify hierarchies in the dimensions in the data cube for the policy transaction.
7. In the claims schema, what level of detail should be stored? What should be the finest-level grain in a data cube?
8. Identify hierarchies in the dimensions in the data cube for the claims analysis.
9. Describe the data cube resulting from the operation to slice the policy data cube by a certain agent.
10. Describe the data cube resulting from the operation to dice the data cube result of the slice operation in problem 9 by insured parties having zip codes in a specified state.
11. Begin with a data cube with four dimensions (*InsuredParty*, *InsuredAuto*, *Item*, and *Agent*) and one measure (policy amount) in the cells. From this data cube, describe the operation to generate a new data cube with three dimensions (*InsuredParty*, *Item*, and *Agent*) and one measure (average auto policy amount).
12. Identify dimension levels and hierarchies within the *Agent* table. You do not need to use the Oracle CREATE DIMENSION statement.
13. Identify dimension levels and hierarchies within the *InsuredParty* table. You do not need to use the Oracle CREATE DIMENSION statement.
14. Identify dimension levels and hierarchies within the *InsuredAuto* table. You do not need to use the Oracle CREATE DIMENSION statement.
15. Is it necessary to have a time dimension table for the automobile insurance data warehouse? Please justify your answer and explain how time is represented if not in a separate dimension table.
16. For the *InsuredParty* dimension table, discuss the stability of the columns in the table. What columns would typically change together? What columns would history be desirable?
17. For the *InsuredAuto* dimension table, discuss the stability of the columns in the table. What columns would typically change together? What columns would history be desirable?
18. Modify the *InsuredParty* dimension table for a history of the *IPRisk* column. Provide a type II representation and a type III representation with current and previous risk values.
19. Modify the *InsuredParty* dimension table for a limited history of the *IPCity*, *IPState*, and *IPZip* columns. The limited history should record the current and previous values and change dates for the combination of columns.
20. Modify the *InsuredParty* dimension table for an unlimited history of the *IPCity*, *IPState*, and *IPZip* columns. The unlimited history should record the change dates for the combination of columns, not the individual columns.

Part 2: Store Sales Problems

Part 2 provides practice with relational database manipulation of multidimensional data. The questions in Part 2 involve the store sales snowflake schema used in section 16.3. For your reference, Figure 16.P1 displays the ERD for the store sales snowflake schema. To support the usage of Oracle 11g with these problems, the student section of the textbook's website contains Oracle CREATE TABLE statements and sample data for the tables of the store sales schema.

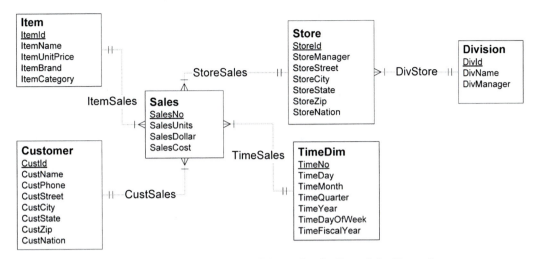

Figure 16.P1: ERD Snowflake Schema for the Store Sales Example

1. Write a SELECT statement to summarize sales by store state, year, and item brand. The result should compute the SUM of the dollar sales for the years 2007 and 2008. The result should include full totals for every combination of grouped fields.

2. Write a SELECT statement to summarize sales by year, quarter, and month. The result should compute the SUM of the dollar sales for the years 2007 and 2008. The result should include partial totals in order of the grouped fields (year, quarter, and month).

3. Write a SELECT statement to summarize sales by store state, month, and year. The result should compute the SUM of the dollar sales for the years 2007 and 2008. The result should include partial totals in order of the hierarchical dimension (year and month). Do not use the GROUPING SETS operator in your SQL statement.

4. Write a SELECT statement to summarize sales by customer state, customer zip, year, and quarter. The result should compute the SUM of the dollar sales for the years 2007 and 2008. The result should include partial totals for hierarchical dimensions (year/quarter and state/zip). Do not use the GROUPING SETS operator in your SQL statement.

5. Rewrite the SQL statement solution for problem 1 without using the CUBE, ROLLUP, or GROUPING SETS operators. To reduce your time, you can write the first few query blocks and then indicate the pattern to rewrite the remaining query blocks. In rewriting the queries, you may use two single quotes (with nothing inside) as the default text value and 0 as the default numeric value.

6. Rewrite the SQL statement solution for problem 2 without using the CUBE, ROLLUP, or GROUPING SETS operators. In rewriting the queries, you may use two single quotes (with nothing inside) as the default text value and 0 as the default numeric value.

7. Rewrite the SQL statement solution for problem 3 without using the CUBE, ROLLUP, or GROUPING SETS operators. In rewriting the queries, you can use two single quotes (with nothing inside) as the default text value and 0 as the default numeric value.

8. Rewrite the SQL statement solution for problem 3 using the GROUPING SETS operator instead of the ROLLUP operator.

9. Rewrite the SQL statement solution for problem 4 using the GROUPING SETS operator instead of the ROLLUP operator.

10. Perform the indicated calculation and show the underlying formula for the following problems. The number of unique values in each dimension is shown in parentheses.
    - Calculate the maximum number of rows for a query with a rollup of year (2), quarter (4), and month (12). Separate the calculation to show the number of rows appearing in the normal GROUP BY result and the number of subtotal rows generated by the ROLLUP operator.
    - Calculate the maximum number of rows in a query with a rollup of year (2), quarter (4), month (12), and weeks per month (4). Separate the calculation to show the maximum number of rows appearing in the normal GROUP BY result and the maximum number of subtotal rows generated by the rollup operator.

- Calculate the maximum number of rows in a query with a cube of state (5), brands (10), and year (2). Separate the calculation to show the maximum number of rows appearing in the normal GROUP BY result and the maximum number of subtotal rows generated by the cube operator.
- Calculate the number of subtotal groups in a query with a cube of state (5), division (4), brand (10), and year (2). A subtotal group is equivalent to a SELECT statement when formulating the query without any GROUP BY operators.

11. Write an Oracle CREATE DIMENSION statement for a customer dimension consisting of the customer identifier, the city, the state, the zip, and the country. Define two hierarchies grouping the customer identifier with the city, the state, and the nation and the customer identifier with the zip, the state, and the nation.

12. Write an Oracle CREATE DIMENSION statement for a time dimension consisting of the time identifier, the day, the month, the quarter, the year, the fiscal year, and the day of the week. Define three hierarchies grouping the time identifier, the day, the month, the quarter, and the year, the time identifier and the fiscal year, and the time identifier and the day of the week.

13. Write an Oracle CREATE MATERIALIZED VIEW statement to support the store sales schema. The materialized view should include the sum of the dollar sales and the sum of the cost of sales. The materialized view should summarize the measures by the store identifier, the item identifier, and the time number. The materialized view should include sales in the year 2005.

14. Write an Oracle CREATE MATERIALIZED VIEW statement to support the store sales schema. The materialized view should include the sum of the dollar sales and the sum of the cost of sales. The materialized view should summarize the measures by the store identifier, the item identifier, and the time number. The materialized view should include sales in the year 2006.

15. Rewrite the SQL statement solution for problem 1 using the materialized views in problems 13 and 14. You should ignore the CUBE operator in the solution for problem 1. Your SELECT statement should reference the materialized views as well as base tables if needed.

16. Rewrite the SQL statement solution for problem 1 using the materialized views in problems 13 and 14. Your SELECT statement should reference the materialized views as well as base tables if needed. You should think carefully about how to handle the CUBE operator in your rewritten query.

17. Rewrite the SQL statement solution for problem 3 using the materialized views in problems 13 and 14. You should ignore the ROLLUP operator in the solution for problem 3. Your SELECT statement should reference the materialized views as well as base tables if needed.

18. Rewrite the SQL statement solution for problem 3 using the materialized views in problems 13 and 14. Your SELECT statement should reference the materialized views as well as base tables if needed. You should think carefully about how to handle the ROLLUP operator in your rewritten query.

19. Write an Oracle CREATE MATERIALIZED VIEW statement to support the store sales schema. The materialized view should include the sum of sales units and the sum of the cost of sales. The materialized view should summarize the measures by the customer zip code and year of sales. The materialized view should include sales in 2007 and before.

20. Write an Oracle CREATE MATERIALIZED VIEW statement to support the store sales schema. The materialized view should include the sum of sales units and the sum of the cost of sales. The materialized view should summarize the measures by the customer zip code, sales year, and sales quarter. The materialized view should include USA sales only.

21. Write an Oracle CREATE MATERIALIZED VIEW statement to support the store sales schema. The materialized view should include the sum of the sales units and sum of the cost of sales. The materialized view should summarize the measures by the customer zip code, sales year, and sales quarter. The materialized view should include Canadian sales for 2007 and 2008.

22. Write a SELECT statement using the base data warehouse tables to retrieve the sum of the sales cost divided by the sum of the unit sales in the USA and Canada in 2007. The result should include customer zip code, year, and sum of the sales cost per unit. Rewrite the SELECT statement using one or more materialized views defined in problems 19 to 21.
23. Write a SELECT statement using the base data warehouse tables to retrieve the sum of the sales cost divided by the sum of the unit sales in the USA and Canada from 2006 to 2008. The result should include customer zip code, year, and sum of the sales cost per unit. Rewrite the SELECT statement using one or more materialized views defined in problems 19 to 21.

References for Further Study

Although this chapter provided a detailed introduction about data warehouses, you may want to augment this chapter with specialized material due to the importance and the scope of the subject. Kimball (2002) and Inmon (2002), the father of data warehousing, have written widely read books on data warehouses. To elaborate on specific details in the chapter, you should consult Bouzeghoub et al. (1999) and Fisher and Berndt (2001) about the refresh process. For details about Oracle 11g data warehousing features, you should consult the online documentation in the Oracle Technology Network (http://www.oracle.com/technology). You can find additional information in websites under the topics "Data Warehouses" and "Data Mining" in the Web Resources section of the textbook's website.

17

Client-Server Processing, Parallel Database Processing, and Distributed Databases

Learning Objectives

This chapter describes the ways that database management systems utilize computer networks and remote computers to support client-server processing, parallel database processing, and distributed databases. After this chapter, the student should have acquired the following knowledge and skills:

- List reasons for client-server processing, parallel database processing, and distributed data
- Describe two-tier, three-tier, and multiple-tier client-server database architectures
- Describe common architectures for parallel database processing
- Describe differences between technology for tightly integrated and loosely integrated distributed databases
- Compare the different kinds of distributed database transparency
- Understand the nature of query processing and transaction processing for distributed databases

Overview

Chapters 15 and 16 described database processing for transactions and decision support. As both chapters explained, transaction and decision support processing are vital to modern organizations. In this chapter, you will learn how computer networks, remote computers, and remote data storage can improve reliability and performance for both kinds of processing.

This chapter explains the ways that DBMSs utilize computer networks, remote computers, and remote data storage. Before understanding the details, you should understand the motivation for utilizing these resources. This chapter discusses the business reasons for client-server processing, parallel database processing, and distributed data. After grasping the motivation, you are ready to learn architectures for distributing different tasks in a client-server organization and dividing large amounts of work among resources using parallel database technology. Description of parallel database processing in Oracle and IBM DB2 complement the conceptual presentation. Distributing data in addition to distributing processing allows more flexibility but also involves more complexity. To depict the trade-off between flexibility and complexity, this chapter explains distributed database architectures, levels of transparency for distributed data, and distributed database processing for queries and transactions. Examples of transparency for Oracle distributed databases complement the conceptual material.

17.1 Overview of Distributed Processing and Distributed Data

To understand the issues, it is easier to separate distributed processing from distributed data. Both areas have distinct architectures, design problems, and processing technologies. After learning them separately, you can understand how to combine them. This section begins your study by discussing the motivations behind two different kinds of distributed processing (client-server and parallel database processing) and distributed databases.

17.1.1 Motivation for Client-Server Processing

The client-server approach supports usage of remote computing resources for performing complex business processes consisting of a variety of subtasks. For example, electronic shopping is a complex process consisting of product selection, ordering, inventory management, payment processing, shipping, and product returns. A <u>client</u> is a program that makes requests to a server. The <u>server</u> performs requests and communicates results to the clients. Clients and servers can be arranged across networked computers to divide complex work into more manageable units. The simplest arrangement is to divide the work between clients processing on personal computers and a server processing on a separate computer as shown in Figure 17.1. Section 17.2 presents more powerful architectures for client-server processing along with typical divisions of work among computers.

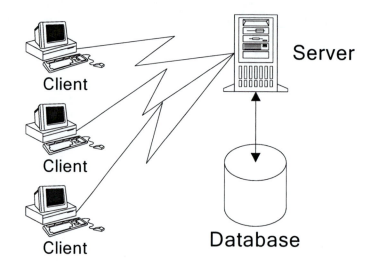

Figure 17.1: Simple Client-Server Architecture for Distributed Processing

Distributed processing with the client-server approach offers a number of advantages related to flexibility, scalability, and interoperability. <u>Flexibility</u> refers to the ease of maintaining and adapting a system. Maintenance costs often dominate the cost of initially developing an information system because of long life and system revisions. The client-server approach promotes flexibility because volatile sections of code can be isolated from more stable sections. For example, user interface code can be separated from the business rules and the data access code. If a new interface is deployed, other parts of the code remain unchanged. In addition, the client-server approach is ideally suited for object-oriented programming to support reusability. Chapter 18 describes object-oriented databases and programming.

The client-server approach supports scalable growth of hardware and software capacity. <u>Scalability</u> refers to the ability to add and remove capacity in small units. Vertical scalability refers to the ability to add capacity on the server side. For example, work from an overloaded server may be moved to a new server to alleviate a bottleneck or handle new demand from additional workstations. The new server can have just the level of additional computing capacity necessary. Horizontal scalability refers to the ability to add capacity on the client side through additional workstations and movement of work between clients and servers. For example, work can be moved from clients to a server to allow the use of inexpensive client hardware (thin clients). Work also can move in the opposite direction (from server to client) to alleviate server processing loads and take advantage of client computing capabilities.

Scalable growth also can lead to improved performance. For example, adding middleware can reduce contention problems caused by many users accessing a database. The next section describes middleware that can efficiently manage many simultaneous users accessing a database. In addition, specialized servers can be employed to handle work that would otherwise slow all users. For example, multimedia servers can handle requests for images, thus freeing other servers from this time-consuming task.

Client-server systems based on open standards support interoperability. <u>Interoperability</u> refers to the ability of two or more systems to exchange and use software and data. Open standards promote a marketplace of suppliers, leading to lower costs and higher quality. Software components in the marketplace are interoperable if they conform to the standards. The most heavily standardized area is the Internet, where client-server databases are becoming increasingly important.

Despite the advantages of client-server processing, some significant pitfalls may occur. Developing client-server software may be more complex because of architectural choices. A client-server architecture specifies an arrangement of components and a division of processing among the components. Section 17.2 presents several possible architectures for client-server database processing. The choice of an inappropriate architecture can lead to poor performance and maintenance problems. In addition to architectural issues, the designer may face a difficult decision about building a client-server database on proprietary methods versus open standards. Proprietary methods allow easier resolution of problems because one vendor is responsible for all problems. Proprietary methods may also have better performance because they are not as general as open standards. In the long run, proprietary methods can be expensive and inflexible, however. If a vendor does not grow with the industry, a client-server database may become outdated and expensive to upgrade.

17.1.2 Motivation for Parallel Database Processing

In contrast to the usage of client-server processing to distribute complex work among networked computers, parallel database processing divides large tasks into many smaller tasks and distributes the smaller tasks among interconnected computers. For example, parallel database processing may be used to perform a join operation on large tables. The usage of RAID architectures described in Chapter 8 is a simple form of parallel database processing. Section 17.3 presents more powerful architectures for parallel database processing.

Parallel database processing can improve performance through scaleup and speedup. Scaleup involves the amount of work that can be accomplished by increasing computing capacity. Scaleup measures the increased size of a job, which can be done while holding the time constant. The ideal scaleup is linear in which increasing computing capacity n times allows completion of n times the amount of work in the same time. Due to coordination overhead, linear scaleup is not possible in most situations. Scaleup is measured as the ratio of the amount of work completed with the larger configuration to the amount of work completed with the original configuration. For example, if 100 transactions per minute can be processed in the original configuration and 175 transactions per minute can be processed when the computing capacity is doubled, the scaleup is 1.75.

Speedup involves the decrease in time to complete a task rather than the amount of work performed. With added computing capacity, speedup measures time reduction while holding the task constant. For example, organizations typically need to complete daily refresh processing in a timely manner to ensure availability for the next business day. Organizations need to determine the amount of additional computing capacity that will ensure completion of the work within the allowable time. Speedup is measured by the ratio of the completion time with the original configuration to the completion time with the additional capacity. For example, if doubling capacity decreases the refresh processing time from 6 hours to 4 hours, the speedup is 1.5.

Availability is the accessibility of a system often measured as the system's uptime. For highly available or fault-resilient computing, a system experiences little downtime and recovers quickly from failures. Fault-tolerant computing takes resiliency to the limit in that processing must be continuous without cessation. The cost of downtime determines the degree of availability desired. Downtime cost can include loss of sales, lost labor, and idle equipment. For a large organization, the cost of downtime can be hundreds of thousands of dollars per hour. Parallel database processing can increase availability because a DBMS can dynamically adjust to the level of available resources. Failure of an individual computer will not stop processing on other available computers.

The major drawback to parallel database processing is cost. Parallel database processing involves high costs for DBMS software and specialized coordination software. There are possible interoperability problems because coordination is required among DBMS software, operating system, and storage systems. DBMS vendors provide powerful tools to deploy and manage the high complexity of parallel database processing. Performance improvements if not predictable would be a significant drawback. Predictable performance improvements enable organizations to plan for additional capacity and dynamically adjust capacity depending on anticipated processing volumes and response time constraints.

17.1.3 Motivation for Distributed Data

Distributed data offer a number of advantages related to data control, communication costs, and performance. Distributing a database allows the location of data to match an organization's structure. For example, parts of a customer table can be located close to customer processing centers. Decisions about sharing and maintaining data can be set locally to provide control closer to the data usage. Often, local employees and management understand issues related to data better than management at remote locations.

Distributed data can lead to lower communication costs and improved performance. Data should be located so that 80 percent of the requests are local. Local requests incur little or no communication costs and delays compared to remote requests. Increased data availability also can lead to improved performance. Data are more available because there is no single computer responsible for controlling access. In addition, data can be replicated so that they are available at more than one site.

Despite the advantages of distributed data, some significant pitfalls may occur. Distributed database design issues are very difficult. A poor design can lead to higher communication costs and poor performance. Distributed database design is difficult because of the lack of tools, the number of choices, and the relationships among choices. Distributed transaction processing can add considerable overhead, especially for replicated data. Distributed data involve more security concerns because many sites can manage data. Each site must be properly protected from unauthorized access.

17.1.4 Summary of Advantages and Disadvantages

Before moving forward, you should take a moment to compare distributed processing and distributed data. Table 17-1 summarizes the advantages and the disadvantages of client-server processing, parallel database processing, and distributed data as separate technologies. To gain maximum leverage, the technologies can be combined. At this time, distributed processing with the client-server approach is the more mature and widely deployed technology although parallel database processing is gaining rapid acceptance. As distributed database technology matures and gains acceptance, organizations will deploy all three technologies.

Table 17-1: Summary of Distributed Processing and Data

Technology	Advantages	Disadvantages
Client-server processing	Flexibility, interoperability, scalability	High complexity, high development cost, possible interoperability problems
Parallel database processing	Speedup, scaleup, availability, scalability for predictive performance improvements	Possible interoperability problems, high cost
Distributed databases	Local control of data, improved performance, reduced communication costs, increased reliability	High complexity, additional security concerns

17.2 Client-Server Database Architectures

The design of a client-server database affects the advantages and the disadvantages cited in the previous section. A good design tends to magnify advantages and reduce disadvantages relative to an organization's requirements. A poor design may exacerbate disadvantages and diminish advantages. Proper design of a client-server database may make the difference between success and failure of an information system project. To help you achieve good designs, this section discusses design issues of client-server databases and describes how these issues are addressed in various architectures.

> **Client-Server Architecture:** an arrangement of components (clients and servers) among computers connected by a network. A client-server architecture supports efficient processing of messages (requests for service) between clients and servers.

17.2.1 Design Issues

Two design issues, division of processing and process management, affect the design of a client-server database. Division of processing refers to the allocation of tasks to clients and servers. Process management involves interoperability among clients and servers and efficient processing of messages between clients and servers. Software for process management is known as "middleware" because of its mediating role. This section describes these issues so that you will understand how various architectures address them in the next section.

Division of Processing

In a typical client-server database, there are a number of tasks that can be performed locally on a client or remotely on a server. The following list briefly describes these tasks.

<u>Presentation</u>: code to maintain the graphical user interface. The presentation code displays objects, monitors events, and responds to events. Events include user-initiated actions with the mouse and the keyboard as well as external events initiated by timers and other users.

<u>Validation</u>: code to ensure the consistency of the database and user inputs. Validation logic often is expressed as integrity rules that are stored in a database.

<u>Business logic</u>: code to perform business functions such as payroll calculations, eligibility requirements, and interest calculations. Business logic may change as the regulatory and the competitive environments change.

<u>Workflow</u>: code to ensure completion of business processes. Workflow code may route forms, send messages about a deadline, and notify users when a business process is completed.

<u>Data access</u>: code to extract data to answer queries and modify a database. Data access code consists of SQL statements and translation code that is usually part of the DBMS. If multiple databases are involved, some translation code may reside in software separate from a DBMS.

Parts of these tasks can be divided between clients and servers. For example, some validation can be performed on a PC client and some can be performed on a database server. Thus, there is a lot of flexibility about the division of processing tasks. Section 17.2.2 describes several popular ways to divide processing tasks.

Middleware

Interoperability is an important function of middleware. Clients and servers can exist on platforms with different hardware, operating systems, DBMSs, and programming languages. Figure 17.2 depicts middleware allowing clients and servers to communicate without regard to the underlying platforms of the clients and the servers. The middleware enables a client and a server to communicate without knowledge of each other's platform.

> **Middleware**: a software component in a client-server architecture that performs process management. Middleware allows servers to efficiently process messages from a large number of clients. In addition, middleware can allow clients and servers to communicate across heterogeneous platforms. To handle large processing loads, middleware often is located on a dedicated computer.

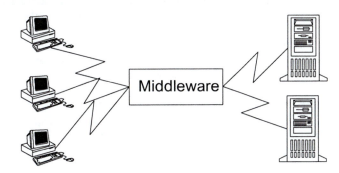

Figure 17.2: Client-Server Computing with Middleware

Efficient message control is another important function of middleware. In a typical client-server environment, there are many clients communicating with a few servers. A server can become overloaded just managing the messages that it receives rather than completing the requests. Middleware allows servers to concentrate on completing requests rather than managing requests. Middleware can perform queuing, scheduling, and routing of messages allowing clients and servers to perform work at different speeds and times.

Based on the functions of interoperability and message control, several kinds of middleware are commercially available, as described in the following list:

Transaction-processing monitors are the oldest kind of middleware. Traditionally, transaction-processing monitors relieve the operating system of managing database processes. A transaction-processing monitor can switch control among processes much faster than an operating system. In this role, a transaction-processing monitor receives transactions, schedules them, and manages them to completion. Recently, transaction-processing monitors have taken additional tasks such as updating multiple databases in a single transaction.

Message-oriented middleware maintains a queue of messages. A client process can place a message on a queue and a server process can remove a message from a queue. Message-oriented middleware differs from transaction processing monitors primarily in the intelligence of the messages. Transaction-processing monitors provide built-in intelligence but use simple messages. In contrast, message-oriented middleware provides much less built-in intelligence but supports more complex messages.

Object-request brokers provide a high level of interoperability and message intelligence. To use an object-request broker, messages must be encoded in a standard interface description language. An object-request broker resolves platform differences between a client and a server. In addition, a client can communicate with a server without knowing the location of the server.

Data access middleware provide a uniform interface to relational and nonrelational data using SQL. Requests to access data from a DBMS are sent to a data access driver rather than directly to the DBMS. The data access driver converts the SQL statement into the SQL supported by the DBMS and then routes the request to the DBMS. The data access driver adds another layer of overhead between an application and a DBMS. However, the data access driver supports independence between an application and the proprietary SQL supported by a DBMS vendor. The two leading data access middleware are the Open Database Connectivity (ODBC) supported by Microsoft and the Java Database Connectivity (JDBC) supported by Oracle.

17.2.2 Description of Architectures

The design issues are addressed in a number of architectures. For each architecture, this section describes typical division of processing, message management approaches, and trade-offs among architectures.

Two-Tier Architecture

The two-tier architecture features a PC client and a database server as shown in Figure 17.3. The PC client contains the presentation code and SQL statements for data access. The database server processes the SQL statements and sends query results back to the PC client. In addition, the database server performs process management functions. The validation and business logic code can be split between the PC client and the database server. The PC client can invoke stored procedures on the database server for business logic and validation. Typically, much of the business logic code resides on the client. PC clients in a two-tier architecture are sometimes called "fat clients" because of the large amount of business logic they contain.

> **Two-Tier Architecture**: a client-server architecture in which a PC client and a database server interact directly to request and transfer data. The PC client contains the user interface code, the server contains the data access logic, and the PC client and the server share the validation and business logic.

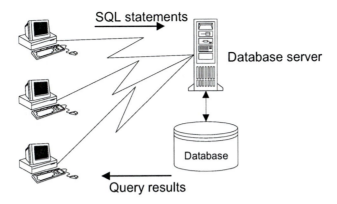

SQL statements

Database server

Database

Query results

Figure 17.3: Two-Tier Architecture

The two-tier architecture is a good approach for systems with stable requirements and a moderate number of clients. On the positive side, the two-tier architecture is the simplest to implement due to the number of good commercial development environments. On the negative side, software maintenance can be difficult because PC clients contain a mix of presentation, validation, and business logic code. To make a significant change in business logic, code must be modified on many PC clients. In addition, utilizing new technology may be difficult because two-tier architectures often rely on proprietary software rather than open standards. To lessen reliance on a particular database server, the PC client can connect to intermediate database drivers such as the Open Database Connectivity (ODBC) drivers instead of directly to a database server. The intermediate database drivers then communicate with the database server.

Performance can be poor when a large number of clients submit requests because the database server may be overwhelmed with managing messages. Several sources report that two-tier architectures are limited to about 100 simultaneous clients. With a larger number of simultaneous clients, a three-tier architecture may be necessary. In addition, connecting to intermediate drivers rather than directly to a database server can slow performance.

Three-Tier Architecture

To improve performance, the <u>three-tier architecture</u> adds another server layer as depicted in Figure 17.4. One way to improve performance is to add a middleware server (Figure 17.4(a) to handle process management. The middleware usually consists of a transaction-processing monitor or message-oriented middleware. A transaction-processing monitor may support more simultaneous connections than message-oriented middleware. However, message-oriented middleware provides more flexibility in the kinds of messages supported. A second way to improve performance is to add an application server for specific kinds of processing such as report writing. In either approach, the additional server software can reside on a separate computer, as depicted in Figure 17.4. Alternatively, the additional server software can be distributed between the database server and PC clients.

Although the three-tier architecture addresses performance limitations of the two-tier architecture, it does not address division-of-processing concerns. The PC clients and the database server still contain the same division of code although the tasks of the database server are reduced. Multiple-tier architectures provide more flexibility on division of processing.

Three-Tier Architecture: A client-server architecture with three layers: a PC client, a backend database server, and either a middleware or an application server.

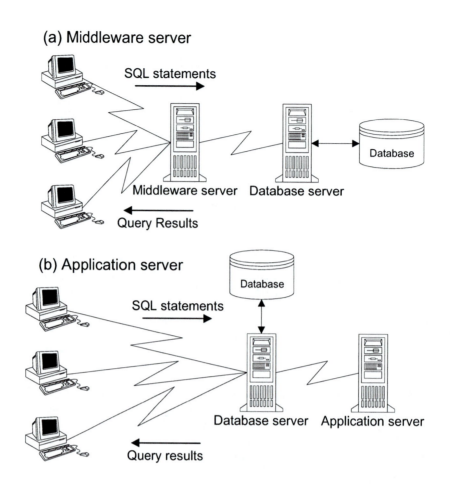

(a) Middleware server

SQL statements

Middleware server   Database server

Database

Query Results

(b) Application server

Database

SQL statements

Query results

Database server   Application server

Figure 17.4: Three-Tier Architecture

Multiple-Tier Architecture

To improve performance and provide flexible division of processing, <u>multiple-tier architectures</u> support additional layers of servers, as depicted in Figure 17.5. The application servers can be invoked from PC clients, middleware, and database servers. The additional server layers provide a finer division of processing than a two- or a three-tier architecture. In addition, the additional server layers can also improve performance because both middleware and application servers can be deployed.

Multiple-Tier Architecture: a client-server architecture with more than three layers: a PC client, a backend database server, an intervening middleware server, and application servers. The application servers perform business logic and manage specialized kinds of data such as images.

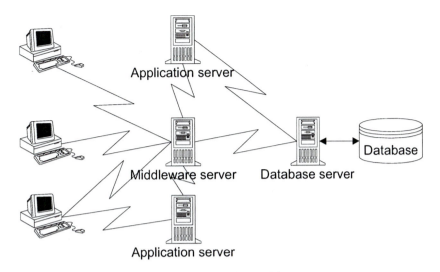

Figure 17.5: Multiple-Tier Architecture

Multiple-tier architectures for electronic commerce involve a Web server to process requests from Web browsers. The browser and the server work together to send and receive Web pages written in the Hypertext Markup Language (HTML). A browser displays pages by interpreting HTML code in the file sent by a server. The Web server can interact with a middleware and database server as depicted in Figure 17.6. Requests for database access are sent to a middleware server and then routed to a database server. Application servers can be added to provide additional levels of client-server processing.

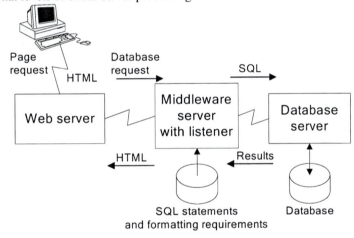

Figure 17.6: Web Server interacting with Middleware Server and Database Server

Web Services Architecture

Web services generalize multiple-tier architectures for electronic business commerce using Internet standards to achieve high interoperability. Electronic business commerce involves services provided by automated agents among organizations. Web services allow organizations to reduce the cost of electronic business by deploying services faster, communicating new services in standard formats, and finding existing services from other organizations. Web services operate in the Internet, a network of networks built with standard languages and protocols for high interoperability. Web services use general Internet standards and new standards for electronic business commerce.

The Web Services Architecture supports interaction between a service provider, service requestor, and service registry as depicted in Figure 17.7. The service provider owns the service and provides the computing platform offering the service. The service requestor application searches for a service and uses the service after it is discovered. The service registry is the repository where the service provider publishes its service description and the service requestor searches for available services. After a service requestor finds a service, the service requestor uses the service description to bind with the service provider and invoke the service implementation maintained by the service provider.

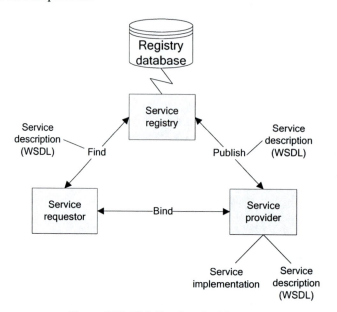

Figure 17.7: Web Services Architecture

Web Service Architecture: an architecture that supports electronic commerce among organizations. A set of related Internet standards supports high interoperability among service requestors, service providers, and service registries. The most important standard is the Web Service Description Language used by service requestors, service providers, and service registries.

To support interoperability, the Web Services Architecture uses a collection of interrelated Internet standards. Table 17-2 summarizes the core web service standards. XML (eXtensible Markup Language) is the underlying foundation for most of the standards. XML is a meta language that supports the specification of other languages. In the Web Services Architecture, the WSFL, UDDI, WSDL, and SOAP standards are XML-compliant languages. For a service requestor and provider, the WSDL is the standard directly used to request and bind a Web service. A WSDL document provides an interface to a service enabling the service provider to hide the details of providing the service. The core standards are augmented by a wide array of additional standards for security, reliable messaging, transactions, meta data, and messaging.

Table 17-2: Summary of Core Standards for Web Services

Standard	Usage
Web Services Flow Language (WSFL)	Specification of workflow rules for services
Universal Description, Discovery Integration (UDDI)	Specification of a directory of Web services including terminology and usage restrictions
Web Services Description Language (WSDL)	Specification of Web services
Simple Object Access Protocol (SOAP)	Sending and receiving XML messages
HTTP, FTP, TCP-IP	Network and connections

To fulfill a Web service, a service provider may utilize client-server processing, parallel database processing, and distributed databases. The details of the processing are hidden from the service requestor. The Web Services Architecture provides another layer of middleware in which to publish, find, and execute services among electronic businesses.

17.3 Parallel Database Processing

In the last five years, parallel database technology has gained commercial acceptance for large organizations. Most enterprise DBMS vendors and some open source DBMSs support parallel database technology to meet market demand. Organizations are utilizing these products to realize the benefits of parallel database technology (scaleup, speedup, and availability) while managing possible interoperability problems. This section describes parallel database architectures to provide a framework to understand commercial offerings by enterprise DBMS vendors.

> **Parallel DBMS**: a DBMS capable of utilizing tightly-coupled computing resources (processors, disks, and memory). Tight coupling is achieved by networks with data exchange time comparable to the time of the data exchange with a disk. Parallel database technology promises performance improvements and high availability although interoperability problems may occur if not properly managed.

17.3.1 Architectures and Design Issues

A parallel DBMS uses a collection of resources (processors, disks, and memory) to perform work in parallel. Given a fixed resource budget, work is divided among resources to achieve desired levels of performance (scaleup and speedup) and availability. A parallel DBMS uses the services of a high-speed network, operating system, and storage system to coordinate division of work among resources. Thus, purchasing a parallel DBMS involves a decision about all of these components not just the DBMS.

  The degree of resource sharing determines <u>architectures for parallel database processing</u>. The standard classification of architectures are known as shared everything (SE), shared disks (SD), and shared nothing (SN) as depicted in Figure 17.8. In the SE approach, memory and disks are shared among a collection of processors. The SE approach is usually regarded as a single multiprocessing computer rather than a parallel database architecture. In the SD architecture, each processor has its private memory, but disks are shared among all processors. In the SN architecture, each processor has its own memory and disks. Data must be partitioned among the processors in the SN architecture. Partitioning is not necessary in the SD and SE architectures because each processor has access to all data.

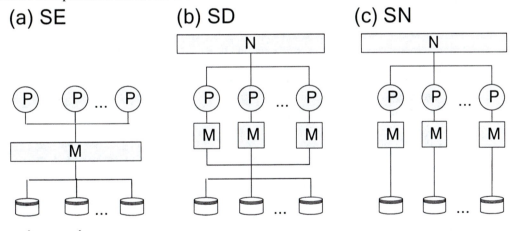

Legend
P: processor
M: memory
N: high-speed network
SE: shared everything
SD: shared disk
SN: shared nothing

Figure 17.8: Basic Parallel Database Architectures

For additional flexibility, the basic architectures are extended with clustering. A cluster is a tight coupling of two or more computers so that they behave as a single computer. Figure 17.9 extends Figure 17.8 with clustering to depict the clustered disk (CD) and clustered nothing (CN) architectures. In the CD architecture, the processors in each cluster share all disks, but nothing is shared across clusters. In the CN architecture, the processors in each cluster share no resources, but each cluster can be manipulated to work in parallel to perform a task. Figure 17.9 shows only two clusters, but the clustering approach is not limited to two clusters. For additional flexibility, the number of clusters and cluster membership can be dynamically configured. In addition, each processor node in a cluster can be a multiprocessing computer or an individual processor.

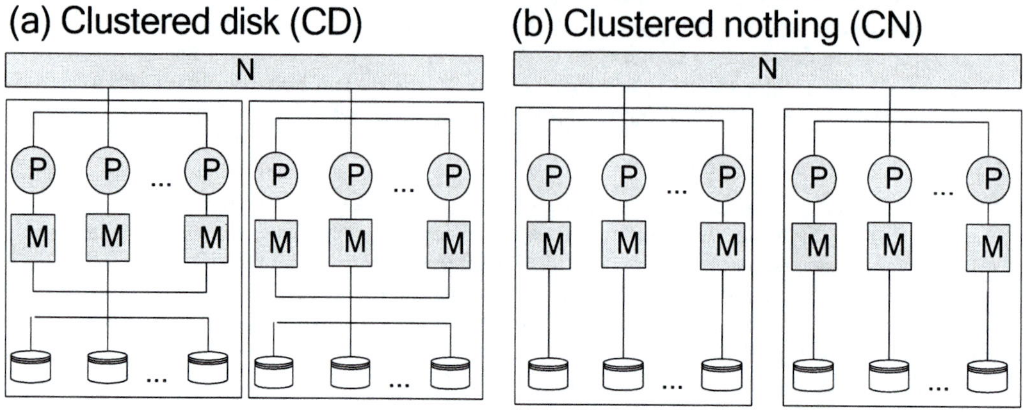

(a) Clustered disk (CD)   (b) Clustered nothing (CN)

Figure 17.9: Parallel Database Architectures with Clustering

In all parallel database architectures, resource sharing is transparent to applications. Application code (SQL and programming language statements) does not need to be changed to take advantage of parallel database processing. In contrast, distributed database architectures presented in Section 17.4 usually do not provide transparent processing because of different goals for distributed databases.

> **Architectures for Parallel Database Processing**: the clustered disk (CD) and clustered nothing architectures dominate in commercial DBMSs. A cluster is a tight coupling of two or more computers that behave as a single computer. In the CD architecture, the processors in each cluster share all disks, but nothing is shared across clusters. In the CN architecture, the processors in each cluster share no resources, but each cluster can be manipulated to work in parallel to perform a task.

The primary design issues that influence the performance of the parallel database architectures are load balancing, cache coherence, and interprocessor communication. Load balancing involves the amount of work allocated to different processors in a cluster. Ideally, each processor has the same amount of work to fully utilize the cluster. The CN architecture is most sensitive to load balancing because of the need for data partitioning. It can be difficult to partition a subset of a database to achieve equal division of work because data skew is common among database columns.

Cache coherence involves synchronization among local memories and common disk storage. After a processor addresses a disk page, the image of this page remains in the cache associated with the given processor. An inconsistency occurs if another processor has changed the page in its own buffer. To avoid inconsistencies, when a disk page is accessed, a check of other local caches should be made to coordinate changes produced in the caches of these processors. By definition, the cache coherence problem is limited to shared disk architectures (SD and CD).

Interprocessor communication involves messages generated to synchronize actions of independent processors. Partitioned parallelism as used for the shared nothing architectures can create large amounts of interprocessor communication. In particular, partitioned join operations may generate a large amount of communication overhead to combine partial results executed on different processors.

Research and development on parallel database technology has found reasonable solutions to the problems of load balancing, cache coherence, and interprocessor communication. Commercial DBMS vendors have incorporated solutions into parallel DBMS offerings. Commercially, the CD and CN architectures are dominating. The next subsection depicts enterprise DBMSs using the CD and CN architectures.

17.3.2 Commercial Parallel Database Technology

This section presents details of enterprise DBMSs that offer parallel DBMSs. Since the classification discussed in section 17.3.1 is not sufficient to understand the differences among actual products, this section provides details about two prominent parallel DBMSs. Although both DBMSs promise high levels of performance, scalability, and availability, trade-offs among the levels are inevitable given the contrasting approaches of the two parallel DBMS approaches.

Oracle Real Application Clusters

Oracle Real Application Clusters (RAC) requires an underlying hardware cluster, a group of independent servers that cooperate as a single system. The primary cluster components are processor nodes, a cluster interconnect, and a shared storage subsystem as depicted in Figure 17.10. Each server node has its own database instance with a log writing process, a database writing process, and a shared global area containing database blocks, redo log buffers, dictionary information, and shared SQL statements. All database writing processes in a cluster use the same shared storage system. Each database instance maintains its own recovery logs.

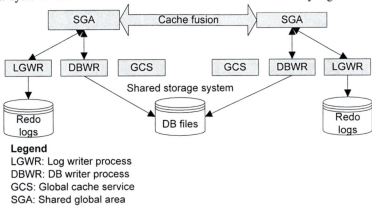

Legend
LGWR: Log writer process
DBWR: DB writer process
GCS: Global cache service
SGA: Shared global area

Figure 17.10: Example Two-Node Oracle Cluster

Cache Fusion technology in RAC enables synchronized access to the cache across all the nodes in a cluster, without incurring expensive disk I/O operations. The Global Cache Service (GCS) is a RAC component that implements the Cache Fusion technology. The GCS maintains a distributed directory of resources such as data blocks and queues access to the resources. To optimize performance, a resource is assigned to the node with the most frequent accesses to the resource. Access to a resource by other nodes is controlled by its master node.

Oracle RAC supports a number of features as listed below. All of these features are available without database or application partitioning.

- The query optimizer considers the number of processors, degree of parallelism of the query, and CPU workload to distribute the workload across the nodes in the cluster and to optimally utilize the hardware resources.
- Load balancing automatically distributes connections among active nodes in a cluster based on node workload. Connection requests are sent to the least congested node in a cluster.
- Automatic failover enables fast switching from a failing node to a surviving node. Switching among nodes can be planned to allow for periodic maintenance.
- The high availability framework maintains components in a running state at all times. High availability involves monitoring critical components and restarting them if they stop. The framework enables clients to immediately react to changes, enabling application developers to hide outages and reconfigurations from end users.

- Oracle Clusterware provides a complete, integrated cluster management solution on all Oracle platforms. Oracle Clusterware features include node membership, group services, global resource management, session information for nodes in a cluster, SQL statement tracing, and high availability functions.
- Service management supports the enterprise grid vision. Services are entities that you can be defined in Oracle RAC databases. Service management enables grouping of database workloads and routing the work to the most appropriate instance. In addition, resources can be assigned to services to process and monitor workloads. Applications assigned to services acquire the workload characteristics, including high availability and load balancing rules.

IBM DB2 Enterprise Server Edition with the DPF Option

The Database Partitioning Feature (DPF) option provides CN style parallel processing for DB2 databases. DB2 without the DPF option supports transparent parallel database processing for multiprocessor machines. DB2 access plans can exploit all CPUs and physical disks on a multiprocessor server. The DPF option adds the ability to partition a database across a group of machines. A single image of a database can span multiple machines and still appear to be a single database image to users and applications. Partitioned parallelism available with the DPF option provides much higher scalability than multiprocessor parallelism alone.

Partitioning with the DPF option is transparent to users and applications. User interaction occurs through one database partition, known as the coordinator node for that user. Figure 17.11 depicts coordination in a partitioned database for multiprocessor server nodes. The database partition to which a client or application connects becomes the coordinator node. Users should be distributed across servers to distribute the coordinator function.

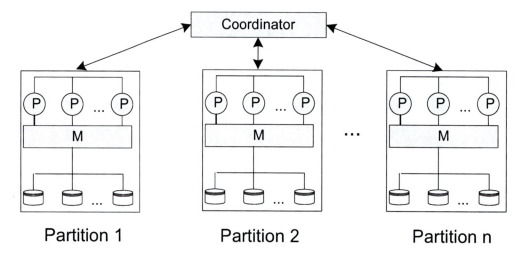

Figure 17.11: Coordination for Partitioned Parallelism in DPF

The DPF option supports automatic partitioning or DBA determined partitioning. With automatic partitioning, data is distributed among partitions using an updatable partitioning map and a hashing algorithm, which determine the placement and retrieval of each row of data. For DBA determined partitioning, a column can be selected as a partitioning key. With either approach, the physical placement of data is transparent to users and applications.
The DPF option of DB2 supports a number of features as listed below. All of these features require database partitioning.

- The query optimizer uses information about data partitioning to search for access plans. While comparing different access plans, the optimizer accounts for parallelism of different operations and costs associated with messaging among database partitions.
- DPF provides a high degree of scalability through its support of thousands of partitions. Near linear performance improvements have been reported for the DPF option.

- Partitioned parallelism provides improved logging performance because each partition maintains its own log files.

17.4 Architectures for Distributed Database Management Systems

Distributed DBMSs involve different technology than client-server processing and parallel database processing. Client-server processing emphasizes distribution of functions among networked computers using middleware for process management. A fundamental difference between parallel database processing and distributed database processing is autonomy. Distributed databases provide site autonomy while parallel databases do not. Thus, distributed databases require a different set of features and technology.

To support distributed database processing, fundamental extensions to a DBMS are necessary. Underlying the extensions are a different component architecture that manages distributed database requests and a different schema architecture that provides additional layers of data description. This section describes the component architecture and schema architecture to provide a foundation for more details about distributed database processing in following sections.

17.4.1 Component Architecture

Distributed DBMSs support global requests that use data stored at more than one autonomous site. A site is any locally controlled computer with a unique network address. Sites are often geographically distributed, although the definition supports sites located in close proximity. Global requests are queries that combine data from more than one site and transactions that update data at more than one site. A global request can involve a collection of statements accessing local data in some statements and remote data in other statements. Local data is controlled by the site in which a user normally connects. Remote data involves a different site in which a user may not even have an account to access. If all requests require only data from one site, distributed database processing capabilities are not required.

To depict global requests, you need to begin with a distributed database. Distributed databases are potentially useful for organizations operating in multiple locations with local control of computing resources. Figure 17.12 depicts a distributed database for an electronic retail business. The company performs customer processing at Boise and Tulsa and manages warehouses at Seattle and Denver. The distribution of the database follows the geographical locations of the business. The *Customer*, *Order*, and *OrderLine* tables (customer-order data) are split between Boise and Tulsa, while the *Product* and *Inventory* tables (product data) are split between Seattle and Denver. An example of a global query is to check both warehouse sites for sufficient quantity of a product to satisfy a shipment invoice. An example of a global transaction is an order-entry form that inserts records into the *Order* and *OrderLine* tables at one location and updates the *Product* table at the closest warehouse site.

To support global queries and transactions, distributed DBMSs contain additional components as compared to traditional, nondistributed DBMSs. Figure 17.13 depicts a possible arrangement of the components of a distributed DBMS. Each server with access to the distributed database is known as a *site*. If a site contains a database, a local data manager (LDM) controls it. The local data managers provide complete features of a DBMS as described in other chapters. The distributed data manager (DDM) optimizes query execution across sites, coordinates concurrency control and recovery across sites, and controls access to remote data. In performing these tasks, the DDM uses the global dictionary (GD) to locate parts of the database. The GD can be distributed to various sites similar to the way that data are distributed. Because of the complexity of the distributed database manager, section 17.6 presents more details about distributed query processing and transaction processing.

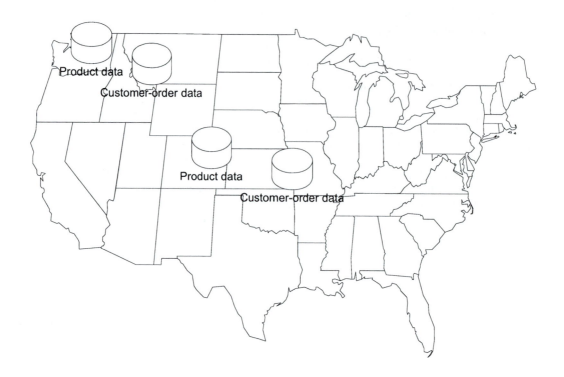

Figure 17.12: Distribution of Order-Entry Data

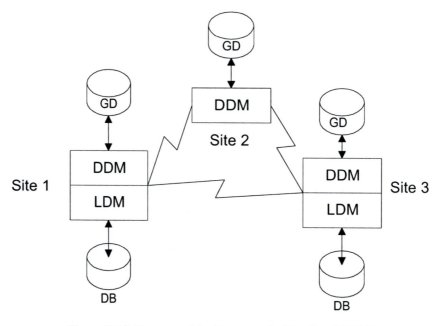

Figure 17.13: Component Architecture of a Distributed DBMS

In the component architecture, the local database managers can be homogeneous or heterogeneous. A distributed DBMS with homogeneous local DBMSs is *tightly integrated*. The distributed database manager can call internal components and access the internal state of local data managers. The tight integration allows the distributed DBMS to efficiently support both distributed queries and transactions. However, the homogeneity requirement precludes integration of existing databases.

A distributed DBMS with heterogeneous local data managers is *loosely integrated*. The distributed database manager acts as middleware to coordinate local data managers. SQL often provides the interface between the distributed data manager and the local data managers. The loose integration supports data sharing among legacy systems and independent organizations. However, the loosely integrated approach may not be able to support transaction processing in a reliable and efficient manner.

17.4.2 Schema Architectures

To accommodate distribution of data, additional layers of data description are necessary. However, there is no widely accepted schema architecture for distributed databases like the widely accepted Three Schema Architecture for traditional DBMSs. This section depicts possible schema architectures for tightly integrated distributed DBMSs and loosely integrated distributed DBMSs. The architectures provide a reference about the kinds of data description necessary and the compartmentalization of the data description.

The schema architecture for a tightly integrated distributed DBMS contains additional layers for fragmentation and allocation as depicted in Figure 17.14. The fragmentation schema contains the definition of each fragment while the allocation schema contains the location of each fragment. A fragment can be defined as a vertical subset (project operation), a horizontal subset (restrict operation), or a mixed fragment (combination of project and restrict operations). A fragment is typically allocated to one site. If the distributed DBMS supports replication, a fragment can be allocated to multiple sites. Typically, one copy of a fragment is considered the primary copy and the other copies are secondary. Only the primary copy is guaranteed to be current.

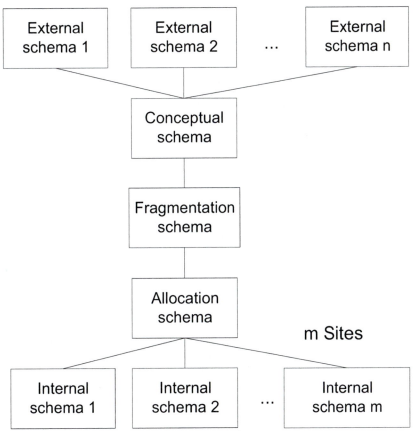

Figure 17.14: Schema Architecture for a Tightly Integrated Distributed DBMS

The schema architecture for a loosely integrated distributed DBMS supports more autonomy of local database sites in addition to data sharing. Each site contains the traditional three schema levels, as depicted in Figure 17.15. To support data sharing, the distributed DBMS provides a local mapping schema for each site. The local mapping schemas describe the exportable data at a site and provide conversion rules to translate data from a local format into a global format. The global conceptual schema depicts all of the kinds of data and relationships that can be used in global requests. Some distributed DBMSs do not have a global conceptual schema. Instead, global external schemas provide views of shared data in a common format.

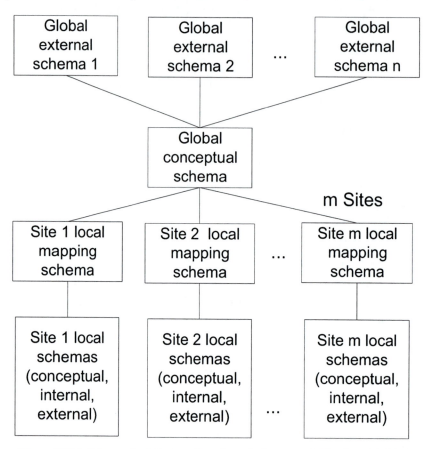

Figure 17.15: Schema Architecture for a Loosely Integrated Distributed DBMS

There can be many differences among the local data formats. Local sites may use different DBMSs, each with a different set of data types. The data models of the local DBMSs can be different, especially if legacy systems are being integrated. Legacy systems might use file interfaces and navigational data models (network and hierarchical) that do not support SQL. Even if local sites support a common SQL standard, there can be many differences such as different data types, scales, units of measure, and codes. The local mapping schemas resolve these differences by providing conversion rules that transform data from a local format into a global format.

The commercial realization of loosely integrated distributed databases has been partially eclipsed by XML document standards and information aggregators. XML schemas provide a set of rules governing document types to facilitate data interchange among independent organizations. An organization publishes XML documents conforming to a particular schema to provide access to a wide range of organizations. Information aggregators use web pages, XML documents and schemas, and other data gathering methods to provide access to a wide range of heterogeneous data including public records, home sales, credit scores, and comparison shopping. In a sense, XML schemas play the role of global conceptual schemas. Cooperating organizations provide the local mapping to convert local data stored in various formats into XML documents conforming to the schema rules.

17.5 Transparency for Distributed Database Processing

Recall from Chapter 15 that transparency refers to the visibility (visible or hidden) of internal details of a service. In transaction processing, concurrency and recovery services are transparent, or hidden from database users. Parallel database processing emphasizes transparency. In distributed database processing, transparency is related to data independence. If database distribution is transparent, users can write queries with no knowledge of the distribution. In addition, distribution changes will not cause changes to existing queries and transactions. If the database distribution is not transparent, users must reference some distribution details in queries and distribution changes can lead to changes in existing queries.

This section describes common levels of transparency and provides examples of query formulation with each level. Before discussing transparency levels, a motivating example is presented.

17.5.1 Motivating Example

To depict the levels of transparency, more details about the order-entry database are provided. The order-entry database contains five tables, as shown in the relationship diagram of Figure 17.16. You may assume that customers are located in two regions (East and West) and products are stored in two warehouses (1: Denver, 2: Seattle).

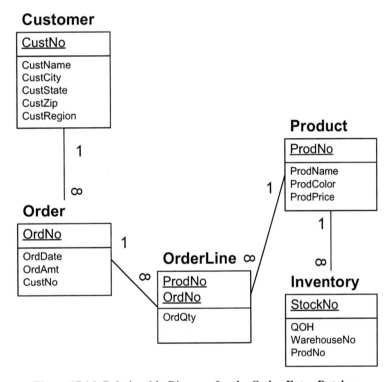

Figure 17.16: Relationship Diagram for the Order-Entry Database

One collection of fragments can be defined using the customer region column as shown in Table 17-3. The *Western-Customers* fragment consists of customers with a region equal to "West." There are two related fragments: the *Western-Orders* fragment, consisting of orders for western customers and the *Western-OrderLines* fragment, consisting of order lines matching western orders. Similar fragments are defined for rows involving eastern customers.

The order and order line fragments are derived from a customer fragment using the semi-join operator. A <u>semi-join</u> is half of a join: the rows of one table that match the rows of another table. For example, a semi-join operation defines the *Western-Orders* fragment as the rows of the *Order* table matching customer rows with a region of "West." A fragment defined with a semi-join operation is sometimes called a derived horizontal fragment. Because some fragments should have rows related to other fragments, the semi-join operator is important for defining fragments.

Semi-Join: an operator of relational algebra that is especially useful for distributed database processing. A semi-join is half of a join: the rows of one table that match with at least one row of another table. Only the rows of the first table appear in the result.

Table 17-3: Fragments Based on the *CustRegion* Field[43]

CREATE FRAGMENT Western-Customers AS SELECT * FROM Customer WHERE CustRegion = 'West'
CREATE FRAGMENT Western-Orders AS SELECT Order.* FROM Order, Customer WHERE Order.CustNo = Customer.CustNo AND CustRegion = 'West'
CREATE FRAGMENT Western-OrderLines AS SELECT OrderLine.* FROM Customer, OrderLine, Order WHERE OrderLine.OrdNo = Order.OrdNo AND Order.CustNo = Customer.CustNo AND CustRegion = 'West'
CREATE FRAGMENT Eastern-Customers AS SELECT * FROM Customer WHERE CustRegion = 'East'
CREATE FRAGMENT Eastern-Orders AS SELECT Order.* FROM Order, Customer WHERE Order.CustNo = Customer.CustNo AND CustRegion = 'East'
CREATE FRAGMENT Eastern-OrderLines AS SELECT OrderLine.* FROM Customer, OrderLine, Order WHERE OrderLine.OrdNo = Order.OrdNo AND Order.CustNo = Customer.CustNo AND CustRegion = 'East'

Warehouse fragments are defined using the *WareHouseNo* column as shown in Table 17-4. In the fragment definitions, warehouse number 1 is assumed to be located in Denver and warehouse number 2 in Seattle. The *Product* table is not fragmented because the entire table is replicated at multiple sites.

Table 17-4: Fragments Based on the *WareHouseNo* Field

CREATE FRAGMENT Denver-Inventory AS SELECT * FROM Inventory WHERE WareHouseNo = 1
CREATE FRAGMENT Seattle-Inventory AS SELECT * FROM Inventory WHERE WareHouseNo = 2

Fragmentation can be more complex than described in the order-entry database. There can be many additional fragments to accommodate a business structure. For example, if there are additional customer processing centers and warehouses, additional fragments can be defined. In addition, vertical fragments can be defined as projection operations in addition to the horizontal fragments using restriction and semi-join operations. A fragment can even be defined as a combination of projection, restriction, and semi-join operations. The only limitation is that the fragments must be disjoint. Disjointness means that horizontal fragments do not contain common rows and vertical fragments do not contain common columns except for the primary key.

After fragments are defined, they are allocated to sites. Fragments are sometimes defined based on where they should be allocated. The allocation of order-entry fragments follows this approach as shown in Table 17-5. The Boise site contains the western customer fragments, while the Tulsa site contains the eastern customer fragments. Similarly, the inventory fragments are split between the Denver and the Seattle sites. The *Product* table is replicated at the Denver and the Seattle sites because each warehouse stocks every product.

---

[43] The syntax in Table 17-3 is not official SQL syntax.

Table 17-5: Allocation of Fragments of the Order Entry Database

Fragments	Site
Western-Customers, Western-Orders, Western-OrderLines	Boise
Eastern-Customers, Eastern -Orders, Eastern-OrderLines	Tulsa
Denver-Inventory, Product	Denver
Seattle-Inventory, Product	Seattle

In practice, the design and the allocation of fragments is much more difficult than depicted here. Designing and allocating fragments is similar to index selection. Data about the frequency of queries, the frequency of parameter values in queries, and the behavior of the global query optimizer are needed. In addition, data about the frequency of originating sites for each query are needed. The originating site for a query is the site in which the query is stored or submitted from. Just as for index selection, optimization models and tools can aid decision making about fragment design and allocation. The details of the optimization models and the tools are beyond the scope of this book. The references at the end of the chapter provide details about fragment design and allocation.

17.5.2 Fragmentation Transparency

<u>Fragmentation transparency</u> provides the highest level of data independence. Users formulate queries and transactions without knowledge of fragments, locations, or local formats. If fragments, locations, or local formats change, queries and transactions are not affected. In essence, users perceive the distributed database as a centralized database. Fragmentation transparency involves the least work for users but the most work for distributed DBMSs. Parallel database processing in shared nothing architectures involves fragmentation transparency.

> **Fragmentation Transparency**: a level of independence in distributed DBMSs in which queries can be formulated without knowledge of fragments.

To contrast the transparency levels, Table 17-6 lists some representative queries and transactions that use the order entry database. In these queries, the parameters $X and $Y are used rather than individual values. With fragmentation transparency, queries and transactions can be submitted without change regardless of the fragmentation of the database.

Table 17-6: Representative Requests Using the Order-Entry Database

Find Order
SELECT * FROM Order, Customer 　WHERE Order.Custno = $X 　　AND Order.CustNo = Customer.CustNo
Find Product Availability 　SELECT * FROM Inventory 　WHERE ProdNo = $X
Update Inventory 　UPDATE Inventory SET QOH = QOH - 1 　WHERE ProdNo = $X AND WareHouseNo = $Y
Customer Move 　UPDATE Customer SET CustRegion = $X 　WHERE CustNo = $Y

17.5.3 Location Transparency

<u>Location transparency</u> provides a lesser level of data independence than fragmentation transparency. Users need to reference fragments in formulating queries and transactions. However, knowledge of locations and local formats is not necessary. Even though site knowledge is not necessary, users are indirectly aware of a database's distribution because many fragments are allocated to a single site. Users may make an association between fragments and sites.

Location Transparency: a level of independence in distributed DBMSs in which queries can be formulated without knowledge of locations. However, knowledge of fragments is necessary.

Location transparency involves more work in formulating requests as shown in Table 17-7. In the "find" queries, the union operator collects rows from all fragments. The Update Inventory query involves about the same amount of coding. The user substitutes a fragment name in place of the condition on *WareHouseNo* because this condition defines the fragment.

In the Customer Move request, much more coding is necessary. An update operation cannot be used because the column to update defines the fragment. Instead, rows must be inserted in the new fragments and deleted from the old fragments. For the customer fragment, the SELECT ... INTO statement stores field values in variables that are used in the subsequent INSERT statement. The deletions are performed in the stated order if referenced rows must be deleted last. If deletions cascade, only one DELETE statement on the *Western-Customers* fragment is necessary.

Table 17-7: Requests Written with Location Transparency

Find Order
SELECT * FROM Western-Orders, Western-Customers
WHERE Western-Orders.CustNo = $X
AND Western-Orders.CustNo = Western-Customers.CustNo
UNION
SELECT * FROM Eastern-Orders, Eastern-Customers
WHERE Eastern-Orders.CustNo = $X
AND Eastern-Orders.Custno = Eastern-Customers.CustNo
Find Product Availability
SELECT * FROM Denver-Inventory
WHERE ProdNo = $X
UNION
SELECT * FROM Seattle-Inventory
WHERE ProdNo = $X
Update Inventory (Denver)
UPDATE Denver-Inventory SET QOH = QOH - 1
WHERE ProdNo = $X
Customer Move (West to East)
SELECT CustName, CustCity, CustState, CustZip
INTO $CustName, $CustCity, $CustState, $CustZip
FROM Western-Customers WHERE CustNo = $Y
INSERT INTO Eastern-Customers
(CustNo, CustName, CustCity, CustState, CustZip, CustRegion)
VALUES ($Y, $CustName, $CustCity, $CustState, $CustZip, 'East')
INSERT INTO Eastern-Orders
SELECT * FROM Western-Orders WHERE CustNo = $Y
INSERT INTO Eastern-OrderLines
SELECT * FROM Western-OrderLines
WHERE OrdNo IN
(SELECT OrdNo FROM Western-Orders WHERE CustNo = $Y)
DELETE FROM Western-OrderLines
WHERE OrdNo IN
(SELECT OrdNo FROM Western-Orders WHERE CustNo = $Y)
DELETE Western-Orders WHERE CustNo = $Y
DELETE Western-Customers WHERE CustNo = $Y

The SQL statements for the first two requests do not reveal the number of union operations that may be required. With two fragments, only one union operation is necessary. With *n* fragments, *n-1* union operations are necessary, however.

To some extent, views can shield users from some of the fragment details. For example, using a view defined with union operations would obviate the need to write the union operations in the query. However, views may not simplify manipulation statements. If the DBMS does not support fragmentation transparency, it seems unlikely that updatable views could span sites. Thus, the user would still have to write the SQL statements for the Customer Move request.

17.5.4 Local Mapping Transparency

Local mapping transparency provides a lesser level of data independence than location transparency. Users need to reference fragments at sites in formulating queries and transactions. However, knowledge of local formats is not necessary. If sites differ in formats as in loosely integrated distributed databases, local mapping transparency still relieves the user of considerable work.

> **Local Mapping Transparency**: a level of independence in distributed DBMSs in which queries can be formulated without knowledge of local formats. However, knowledge of fragments and fragment allocations (locations) is necessary.

Location transparency may not involve much additional coding effort from that shown in Table 17-8. The only changes between Tables 17-7 and 17-8 are the addition of the site names in Table 17-8. If fragments are replicated, additional coding is necessary in transactions. For example, if a new product is added, two INSERT statements (one for each site) are necessary with local mapping transparency. With location transparency, only one INSERT statement is necessary. The amount of additional coding depends on the amount of replication.

From the discussion in this section, you may falsely assume that fragmentation transparency is preferred to the other levels of transparency. Fragmentation transparency provides the highest level of data independence but is the most complex to implement. For parallel database processing in shared nothing architectures, fragmentation transparency is a key feature. For distributed databases, fragmentation transparency conflicts with the goal of site autonomy. Data ownership implies user awareness when combining local and remote data. In addition, fragmentation transparency may encourage excessive resource consumption because users do not perceive the underlying distributed database processing. With location and local mapping transparency, users perceive the underlying distributed database processing at least to some extent. The amount and complexity of distributed database processing can be considerable, as described in section 17.6.

Table 17-8: Requests Written with Local Mapping Transparency

Find Order

SELECT *
 FROM Western-Orders@Boise, Western-Customers@Boise
  WHERE Western-Orders@Boise.CustNo = $X
   AND Western-Orders@Boise.CustNo =
    Western-Customers@Boise.CustNo
UNION
SELECT *
 FROM Eastern-Orders@Tulsa, Eastern-Customers@Tulsa
  WHERE Eastern-Orders@Tulsa.CustNo = $X
   AND Eastern-Orders@Tulsa.CustNo =
    Eastern-Customers@Tulsa.CustNo

Find Product Availability

SELECT * FROM Denver-Inventory@Denver
  WHERE ProdNo = $X
UNION
SELECT * FROM Seattle-Inventory@Seattle
  WHERE ProdNo = $X

Update Inventory (Denver)
UPDATE Denver-Inventory@Denver SET QOH = QOH - 1   WHERE ProdNo = $X

Customer Move (West to East)

SELECT CustName, CustCity, CustState, CustZip
  INTO $CustName, $Custcity, $CustState, $CustZip
  FROM Western-Customers@Boise WHERE CustNo = $Y
 	
INSERT INTO Eastern-Customers@Tulsa
 (CustNo, CustName, CustCity, CustState, CustZip, CustRegion)
 VALUES ($Y, $CustName, $CustCity, $CustState,
    $CustZip, 'East')
 	
INSERT INTO Eastern-Orders@Tulsa
 SELECT * FROM Western-Orders@Boise WHERE CustNo = $Y
 	
INSERT INTO Eastern-OrderLines@Tulsa
 SELECT * FROM Western-OrderLines@Boise
  WHERE OrdNo IN
   (SELECT OrdNo FROM Western-Orders@Boise
    WHERE CustNo = $Y)
 	
DELETE FROM Western-OrderLines@Boise
  WHERE OrdNo IN
   (SELECT OrdNo FROM Western-Orders@Boise
    WHERE CustNo = $Y)
 	
DELETE Western-Orders@Boise WHERE CustNo = $Y
 	
DELETE Western-Customers@Boise WHERE CustNo = $Y

17.5.5 Transparency in Oracle Distributed Databases

Oracle 11g supports homogeneous and heterogeneous distributed databases. In the homogenous case, each site contains a separately managed Oracle database. The requirement for separate management provides autonomy for each participating site. Individual databases may utilize any supported Oracle version although functionality in global requests is limited to the lowest version database. Oracle supports replication in distributed databases through designated master sites and asynchronous processing at secondary sites. Non-Oracle databases can also participate in global requests using Heterogeneous Services and Gateway Agents. This section provides details about transparency in pure (nonreplicated) homogeneous distributed databases.

Database links are a key concept for Oracle distributed databases. A database link provides a one-way connection from a local database to a remote database. A local database is the database in which a user connects. A remote database is another database in which a user wants to access in a global request. Database links allow a user to access another user's objects in a remote database without having an account on the remote site. When using a database link, a remote user is limited by the privilege set of the object's owner.

Table 17-9 demonstrates Oracle statements for creating links and synonyms as well as using the links and synonyms in a global query. The first statement creates a fixed link to the database "boise.acme.com" through the remote user "clerk1." The next statement uses the link to access the remote *Order* table. It is assumed that the current user is connected to the Tulsa database and uses the link to access the Boise database. In the FROM clause, the unqualified table names on both sites are the same (*Order* and *Customer*). The CREATE SYNONYM statements create aliases for remote tables using the remote table names and link names. The SELECT statements can use the synonyms in place of the table and link names.

Table 17-9: Oracle Statements for a Global Request using a Link

Create Link
CREATE DATABASE LINK boise.acme.com CONNECT TO clerk1 IDENTIFED BY clerk1
Find Order (using the link name)

SELECT *
 FROM Order@boise.acme.com WO, Customer@boise.acme.com WC
  WHERE WO.CustNo = 1111111
   AND WO.CustNo = WC.CustNo
    UNION
 SELECT *
 FROM Order, Customer
  WHERE Order.CustNo = 1111111
   AND Order.CustNo = Customer.CustNo

Create Synonyms
CREATE PUBLIC SYNONYM BoiseOrder FOR order@boise.acme.com; CREATE PUBLIC SYNONYM BoiseCustomer FOR customer@boise.acme.com;
Find Order (using the link name)

SELECT *
 FROM BoiseOrder WO, BoiseCustomer WC
  WHERE WO.CustNo = 1111111
   AND WO.CustNo = WC.CustNo
    UNION
 SELECT *
 FROM Order, Customer
  WHERE Order.CustNo = 1111111
   AND Order.CustNo = Customer.CustNo

As Table 17-9 demonstrates, database links provide local mapping transparency to remote data. To create a link, a user must know the global database name. A global database name usually contains information about an organization's structure and business locations. To use a link, a user must know the remote object names and details. Local mapping transparency is consistent with an emphasis on site autonomy. Oracle allows more transparency (location transparency) in remote data access through the usage of synonyms and views.

Oracle provides more features for links than depicted in Table 17-9. The details include link scopes (public, private, and global), link users, and administration of roles and privileges for remote database access. The link scopes differ according to which user groups are allowed to use the link to access to remote data. Table 17-10 provides a summary of the link scopes. The link owner should determine who can use the link to access remote data. Fixed users are the simplest to understand but connected users and current users provide more flexibility as summarized in Table 17-11. The Oracle 11g Database Administrators Guide provides more details about managing database links including security administration.

Table 17-10: Summary of Database Link Scopes

Scope	Details
Private	A more secure than a public or global link, because only the owner of the private link, or subprograms within the same schema, can use the link to access the remote database
Public	A database-wide link in which all users and PL/SQL subprograms in the database can use the link to access database objects in the corresponding remote database
Global	A network-wide link in which users and PL/SQL subprograms in any database can use the link to access objects in the corresponding remote database; Simplifies link management

Table 17-11: Summary of Link User Types

User Type	Details
Connected User	A local user accessing a database link in which no fixed username and password have been specified; A user referencing the link connects to the remote database as the same user. Credentials do not have to be stored in the data dictionary.
Current User	Utilizes a global user who must be authenticated and be a user on both databases involved in the link. However, the user invoking the current user link does not have to be a global user if accessing a remote database through a stored procedure.
Fixed User	A user whose username/password is part of the link definition; Connects a user in a primary database to a remote database with the security context of the user specified in the connect string.

17.6 Distributed Database Processing

Just as distributed data can add complexity for query formulation, it adds considerable complexity to query processing and transaction processing. Distributed database processing involves movement of data, remote processing, and site coordination that are absent from centralized database processing. Although the details of distributed database processing can be hidden from programmers and users, performance implications sometimes cannot be hidden. This section presents details about distributed query processing and distributed transaction processing to make you aware of complexities that can affect performance.

17.6.1 Distributed Query Processing

Distributed query processing is more complex than centralized query processing for several reasons. Distributed query processing involves both local (intrasite) and global (intersite) optimization. Global optimization involves data movement and site selection decisions that are absent in centralized query processing. For example, to perform a join of distributed fragments, one fragment can be moved, both fragments can be moved to a third site, or just the join values of one fragment can be moved. If the fragments are replicated, then a site for each fragment must be chosen.

Many of the complexities of distributed query processing also exist for parallel databases with shared nothing architectures. The major difference is the much faster and more reliable communication networks used in parallel database processing.

Distributed query processing is also more complex because multiple optimization objectives exist. In a centralized environment, minimizing resource (input-output and processing) usage is consistent with minimizing response time. In a distributed environment, minimizing resources may conflict with minimizing response time because of parallel processing opportunities. Parallel processing can reduce response time but increase the overall amount of resources consumed (input-output, processing, and communication). In addition, the weighting of communication costs versus local costs (input-output and processing) depends on network characteristics. For public networks such as the Internet, communication costs can dominate local costs. For local area networks and private networks, communication costs are more equally weighted with local costs.

The increased complexity makes optimization of distributed queries even more important than optimization of centralized queries. Because distributed query processing involves both local and global optimization, there are many more possible access plans for a distributed query than a corresponding centralized query. Variance in performance among distributed access plans can be quite large. The choice of a bad access plan can lead to extremely poor performance. In addition, distributed access plans sometimes need to adjust for site conditions. If a site is unavailable or overloaded, a distributed access plan should dynamically choose another site. Thus, some of the optimization process may need to be performed dynamically (during run-time) rather than statically (during compile time).

To depict the importance of distributed query optimization, access plans for a sample query are presented. To simplify the presentation, a public network with relatively slow communication times is used. Only communication times (*CT*) are shown for each access plan. Communication time consists of a fixed message delay (*MD*) and a variable transmission time (*TT*). Each record is transmitted as a separate message.

$$CT = MD + TT$$
MD = Number of messages * Delay per message
TT = Number of bits / Data rate

Global Query: List the order number, order date, product number, product name, product price, and order quantity for eastern orders with a specified customer number, date range, and product color. Table 17-10 lists statistics for the query and the network.

```
SELECT * EO.OrdNo, OrdDate, P.ProdNo, QtyOrd, ProdName, ProdPrice
   FROM Eastern-Orders EO, Eastern-Orderlines EOL, Product P
  WHERE EO.CustNo = $X AND EO.OrdNo = EOL.OrdNo
                    AND P.Color = 'Red'
   AND EOL.ProdNo = P.ProdNo and OrdDate BETWEEN $Y AND $Z
```

Table 17-11: Statistics for the Query and the Network

Record length is 1,000 bits for each table.
The customer has 5 orders in the specified date range.
Each order contains on the average 5 products.
The customer has 3 orders in the specified date range and color.
There are 200 red products.
There are 10,000 orders, 50,000 order lines, and 1,000 products in the fragments.
Fragment allocation is given in Table 17-6.
Delay per Message is 0.1 second.
Data Rate is 1,000,000 bits per second.

1. Move the *Product* table to the Tulsa site where the query is processed.
   $CT = 1,000 * 0.1 + (1,000 * 1,000) / 1,000,000 = 101$ seconds

2. Restrict the *Product* table at the Denver site. Then move the result to Tulsa where the remainder of the query is processed.
$CT = 200 * 0.1 + (200 * 1,000) / 1,000,000 = 20.2$ seconds

3. Perform join and restrictions of *Eastern-Orders* and *Eastern-OrderLines* fragments at the Tulsa site. Move the result to the Denver site to join with the *Product* table.
$CT = 25 * 0.1 + (25 * 2,000) / 1,000,000 = 2.55$ seconds

4. Restrict the *Product* table at the Denver site. Move only the resulting product numbers (32 bits) to Tulsa. Perform joins and restrictions at Tulsa. Move the results back to Denver to combine with the *Product* table.
CT (Denver to Tulsa) $= 200 * 0.1 + (200 * 32) / 1,000,000 = 20.0064$ seconds
CT (Tulsa to Denver) $= 15 * 0.1 + (15 * 2,000) / 1,000,000 = 1.53$ seconds
$CT = CT$ (Denver to Tulsa) $+ CT$ (Tulsa to Denver) $= 21.5364$ seconds

These access plans show a wide variance in communication times. Even more variance would be shown if the order fragments were moved from Tulsa to Denver. The third access plan dominates the others because of its low message delay. Additional analysis of the local processing costs would be necessary to determine the best access plan.

17.6.2 Distributed Transaction Processing

Distributed transaction processing follows the principles described in Chapter 15. Transactions obey the ACID properties and the distributed DBMS provides concurrency and recovery transparency. However, a distributed environment makes the implementation of the principles more difficult. Independently operating sites must be coordinated. In addition, new kinds of failures exist because of the communication network. To deal with these complexities, new protocols are necessary. This section presents an introduction to the problems and solutions of distributed concurrency control and commit processing.

Distributed Concurrency Control

Distributed concurrency control can involve more overhead than centralized concurrency control because local sites must be coordinated through messages over a communication network. The simplest scheme involves centralized coordination, as depicted in Figure 17.17. At the beginning of a transaction, the coordinating site is chosen and the transaction is divided into subtransactions performed at other sites. Each site hosting a subtransaction submits lock and release requests to the coordinating site using the normal two-phase locking rules.

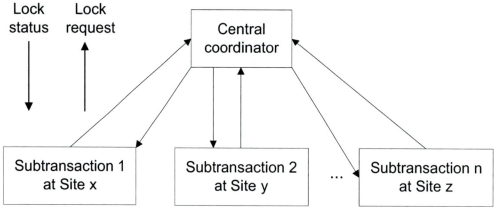

Figure 17.17: Centralized Concurrency Control

Centralized coordination involves the fewest messages and the simplest deadlock detection. However, reliance on a centralized coordinator may make transaction processing less reliable. To alleviate reliance on a centralized site, lock management can be distributed among sites. The price for higher reliability is more message overhead and more complex deadlock detection. The number of messages can be twice as much in the distributed coordination scheme as compared to the centralized coordination scheme.

With both centralized and distributed coordination, replicated data are a problem. Updating replicated data involves extra overhead because a write lock must be obtained on all copies before any copy is updated. Obtaining write locks on multiple copies can cause delays and even rollbacks if a copy is not available.

To reduce overhead with locking multiple copies, the primary copy protocol can be used. In the primary copy protocol, one copy of each replicated fragment is designated as the primary copy, while the other copies are secondary. Write locks are necessary only for the primary copy. After a transaction updates the primary copy, updates are propagated to the secondary copies. However, secondary copies may not be updated until after the transaction commits. The primary copy protocol provides improved performance but at the cost of noncurrent secondary copies. Because reduced overhead is often more important than current secondary copies, many distributed DBMSs use the primary copy protocol.

> **Primary Copy Protocol**: a protocol for concurrency control of distributed transactions. Each replicated fragment is designated as either the primary copy or a secondary copy. During distributed transaction processing, only the primary copy is guaranteed to be current at the end of a transaction. Updates may be propagated to secondary copies after end of transaction.

Distributed Commit Processing

Distributed DBMSs must contend with failures of communication links and sites, failures that do not affect centralized DBMSs. Detecting failures involves coordination among sites. If a link or site fails, any transaction involving the site must be aborted. In addition, the site should be avoided in future transactions until the failure is resolved.

Failures can be more complex than just a single site or communication link. A number of sites and links can fail simultaneously leaving a network partitioned. In a partitioned network, different partitions (collections of sites) cannot communicate although sites in the same partition can communicate. The transaction manager must ensure that different parts of a partitioned network act in unison. It should not be possible for sites in one partition to decide to commit a transaction but sites in another partition to decide not to commit a transaction. All sites must either commit or abort.

The most widely known protocol for distributed commit processing is the two-phase commit protocol[44]. For each transaction, one site is chosen as the coordinator and the transaction is divided into subtransactions performed at other participant sites. The coordinator and the participant sites interact in a voting phase and a decision phase. At the end of both phases, each participant site has acted in unison to either commit or abort its subtransaction.

> **Two-Phase Commit Protocol (2PC)**: a rule to ensure that distributed transactions are atomic. 2PC uses a voting and a decision phase to coordinate commits of local transactions.

The voting and decision phases require actions on both the coordinator and the participant sites as depicted in Figure 17.18. In the decision phase, the coordinator sends a message to each participant asking if it is ready to commit. Before responding, each participant forces all updates to disk when the local transaction work finishes. If no failure occurs, a

---

[44] Do not confuse two-phase commit with two-phase locking. The two-phase commit protocol is used only for distributed transaction processing. Two-phase locking can be used for centralized and distributed concurrency control.

participant writes a ready-commit record and sends a ready vote to the coordinator. At this point, a participant has an uncertain status because the coordinator may later request the participant to abort.

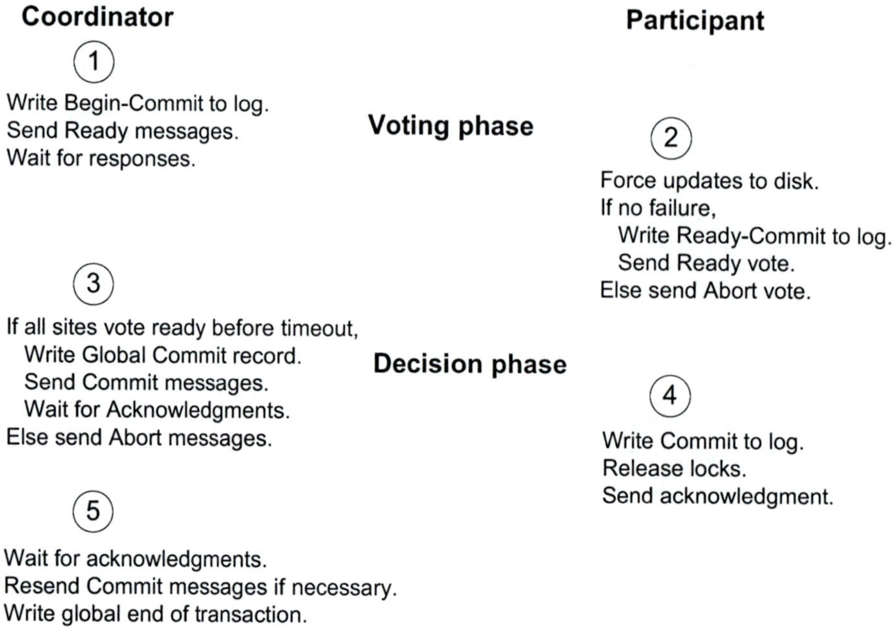

Coordinator   **Participant**

①

Write Begin-Commit to log.   **Voting phase**
Send Ready messages.   ②
Wait for responses.
                                                Force updates to disk.
                                                If no failure,
                                                    Write Ready-Commit to log.
                                                    Send Ready vote.
③   Else send Abort vote.

If all sites vote ready before timeout,
    Write Global Commit record.   **Decision phase**
    Send Commit messages.   ④
    Wait for Acknowledgments.
Else send Abort messages.
                                                Write Commit to log.
                                                Release locks.
⑤   Send acknowledgment.

Wait for acknowledgments.
Resend Commit messages if necessary.
Write global end of transaction.

Figure 17.18: Two-Phase Commit Processing for Coordinator and Participants

The decision phase begins when the coordinator either receives votes from each participant or a timeout occurs. If a timeout occurs or at least one participant sends an abort vote, the coordinator aborts the entire transaction by sending abort messages to each participant. Each participant then performs a rollback of its changes.

If all participants vote ready, the coordinator writes the global commit record and asks each participant to commit its subtransaction. Each participant writes a commit record, releases locks, and sends an acknowledgment to the coordinator. When the coordinator receives acknowledgment from all participants, the coordinator writes the global end-of-transaction record. If a failure occurs in either the voting or the decision phase, the coordinator sends an abort message to all participating sites.

In practice, the two-phase commit protocol presented in Figure 17.18 is just the basic protocol. Other complications such as a failure during recovery and timeouts complicate the protocol. In addition, modifications to the basic protocol can reduce the number of messages needed to enforce the protocol. Because these extensions are beyond the scope of this book, you should consult the references at the end of the chapter for more details.

The two-phase commit protocol can use a centralized or a distributed coordinator. The trade-offs are similar to centralized versus distributed coordination for concurrency control. Centralized coordination is simpler than distributed coordination but can be less reliable.

The two-phase commit protocol does not handle any conceivable kind of failure. For example, the two-phase commit protocol may not work correctly if log records are lost. There is no known protocol guaranteeing that all sites act in unison to commit or abort in the presence of arbitrary failures. Because the two-phase commit protocol efficiently handles common kinds of failures, it is widely used in distributed transaction processing.

Closing Thoughts

This chapter has described the motivation, architectures, and services of DBMSs that support distributed processing and distributed data. Utilizing distributed processing and data can significantly improve DBMS services but at the cost of new design challenges. Distributed processing can improve scalability, interoperability, flexibility, availability, and performance while distributed data can improve data control, communication costs, and system performance.

To realize these benefits, significant challenges caused by the complexity of distributed processing and data must be overcome.

Choosing an appropriate architecture is one way to manage additional complexity. This chapter described client-server architectures and parallel database architectures to utilize distributed processing. The two-tier, three-tier, and multiple-tier architectures provide alternatives among cost, complexity, and flexibility for dividing tasks among clients and servers. Parallel database processing distributes a large task among available resources. Parallel database technology of Oracle and IBM was described to indicate the implementation of the clustered disk and clustered nothing architectures.

The last part of the chapter described architectures and processing for distributed DBMSs. Architectures for distributed DBMSs differ in the integration of the local databases. Tightly integrated systems provide both query and transaction services but require uniformity in the local DBMSs. Loosely integrated systems support data sharing among a mix of modern and legacy DBMSs. An important part of the data architecture is the level of data independence. This chapter described several levels of data independence that differ by the level of data distribution knowledge required to formulate global requests. Examples of transparency in Oracle distributed databases complemented the conceptual presentation. To provide an introductory understanding to the complexity of distributed database processing, this chapter described distributed query processing and transaction processing. Both services involve complex issues not present in centralized DBMSs.

Review Concepts

- Motivations for client-server processing: scalability, interoperability, and flexibility
- Motivations for parallel database processing: scaleup, speedup, high availability, predictable scalability
- Motivations for distributed data: increased local control, reduced communication costs, and improved performance
- Design issues in distributed processing: division of processing and process management
- Kinds of code to distribute between a client and a server
- Process management tasks performed by database middleware
- Differences between transaction-processing monitors, message-oriented middleware, data access middleware, and object request brokers
- Characteristics of two-tier, three-tier, multiple-tier, and Web services architectures
- Characteristics of parallel database architectures: clustered disk and clustered nothing
- Problems of parallel database processing: load balancing, cache coherence, and interprocessor communication
- Global queries and transactions
- Role of the local database manager, the distributed database manager, and the global dictionary in the component architecture of a distributed DBMS
- Schema architectures for tightly integrated and loosely integrated distributed DBMSs
- Relationship of distributed database transparency levels and data independence
- Kinds of fragmentation: horizontal, vertical, and derived horizontal
- Complexity of fragment design and allocation
- Query formulation for fragmentation transparency, location transparency, and local mapping transparency
- Usage of database links in Oracle for providing remote data access with site autonomy
- Usage of synonyms in Oracle to hide location details
- Performance measures and objectives for distributed query processing
- Use of two-phase locking for distributed concurrency control
- Use of the primary copy protocol to reduce update overhead with replicated data
- Additional kinds of failures in a distributed database environment
- Two-phase commit protocol for ensuring atomic commit of participant sites in a distributed transaction

- Trade-offs between centralized and distributed coordination for distributed concurrency control and recovery

Questions

1. What is the role of clients and servers in distributed processing?
2. Briefly define the terms flexibility, interoperability, and scalability. How does client-server processing support interoperability, flexibility, and scalability?
3. Discuss some of the pitfalls of developing client-server systems.
4. Briefly define the terms scaleup and speedup and the measurement of these terms.
5. Define high availability and indicate how parallel database processing supports high availability.
6. How can a distributed database improve data control?
7. How can a distributed database reduce communication costs and improve performance?
8. Discuss some of the pitfalls when developing distributed databases.
9. Discuss why distributed processing is more mature and more widely implemented than distributed databases.
10. Why are division of processing and process management important in client-server architectures?
11. Explain how two-tier architectures address division of processing and process management.
12. Explain how three-tier architectures address division of processing and process management.
13. Explain how multiple-tier architectures address division of processing and process management.
14. What is a thin client? How does a thin client relate to division of processing in client-server architectures?
15. List some reasons for choosing a two-tier architecture.
16. List some reasons for choosing a three-tier architecture.
17. List some reasons for choosing a multiple-tier architecture.
18. What is the Web Services Architecture?
19. How does the Web Services Architecture support interoperability?
20. Briefly describe the basic architectures for parallel database processing.
21. Briefly describe the clustering extensions to the basic distributed database architectures.
22. What are the primary design issues for parallel database processing? Identify the architecture most affected by the design issues.
23. What is the cache coherence problem?
24. What is load balancing?
25. What parallel database architecture is supported by Oracle Real Application Clusters? What is a key technology in Oracle Real Application Clusters?
26. What parallel database architecture is supported by IBM DB2 DPF option? What is a key technology in the DPF?
27. What is a global request?
28. How does the integration level of the distributed DBMS affect the component architecture?
29. When is a tightly integrated distributed DBMS appropriate? When is a loosely integrated distributed DBMS appropriate?
30. Discuss the differences in the schema architecture for tightly and loosely integrated distributed DBMSs.
31. How is distributed database transparency related to data independence?
32. Is a higher level of distribution transparency always preferred? Briefly explain why or why not.
33. What is a derived horizontal fragment and why is it useful? What is the relationship of the semi-join operator and derived horizontal fragmentation?
34. What is the larger difference in query formulation: (1) fragmentation transparency to location transparency or (2) location transparency to local mapping transparency? Justify your answer.
35. Why is fragment design and allocation a complex task?

36. Why is global query optimization important?
37. What are differences between global and local optimization in distributed query processing?
38. Why are there multiple objectives in distributed query processing? Which objective seems to be more important?
39. What are the components of performance measures for distributed query processing? What factors influence how these components can be combined into a performance measure?
40. How does two phase-locking for distributed databases differ from two-phase locking for centralized databases?
41. Why is the primary copy protocol widely used?
42. What kinds of additional failures occur in a distributed database environment? How can these failures be detected?
43. What is the difference between the voting and the decision phases of the two-phase commit protocol?
44. Discuss the trade-offs between centralized and distributed coordination in distributed concurrency control and recovery.
45. What level of transparency is provided by Oracle distributed databases?
46. What are database links in Oracle distributed database processing?
47. What is the difference between a current user and connected user when using an Oracle link?

Problems

The problems provide practice with defining fragments, formulating queries at various transparency levels, and defining strategies for distributed query processing. The questions use the revised university database tables that follow. This database is similar to the database used in Chapter 4 except for the additional campus columns in the *Student*, *Offering*, and *Faculty* tables.

Student(StdNo, StdName, StdCampus, StdCity, StdState, StdZip, StdMajor, StdYear)

Course(CourseNo, CrsDesc, CrsCredits)

Offering(OfferNo, CourseNo, OffCampus, OffTerm, OffYear, OffLocation, OffTime, OffDays, FacNo)
        FOREIGN KEY CourseNo REFERENCES Course
        FOREIGN KEY FacNo REFERENCES Faculty
Enrollment(OfferNo, StdNo, EnrGrade)
        FOREIGN KEY OfferNo REFERENCES Offering
        FOREIGN KEY StdNo REFERENCES Student
Faculty(FacNo, FacName, FacCampus, FacDept, FacPhone, FacSalary, FacRank)

1. Write SQL SELECT statements to define two horizontal fragments as students who attend (1) the Boulder campus and (2) the Denver campus.
2. Write SQL SELECT statements to define two horizontal fragments as faculty who teach at (1) the Boulder campus and (2) the Denver campus.
3. Write SQL SELECT statements to define two horizontal fragments as offerings given at (1) the Boulder campus and (2) the Denver campus.
4. Write SQL SELECT statements to define two derived horizontal fragments as enrollments associated with offerings given at (1) the Boulder campus and (2) the Denver campus.
5. Write a SELECT statement to list the information systems courses offered in spring quarter 2006. Information systems courses contain the string "IS" in the course description. Include the course number, the description, the offer number, and the time in the result. Assume fragmentation transparency in your formulation.
6. Write a SELECT statement to list the information systems courses offered in spring quarter 2006. Information systems courses contain the string "IS" in the course

description. Include the course number, the description, the offer number, and the time in the result. Assume location transparency in your formulation.

7. Write a SELECT statement to list the information systems courses offered in spring quarter 2006. Information systems courses contain the string "IS" in the course description. Include the course number, the description, the offer number, and the time in the result. Assume local mapping transparency in your formulation. The *Offering* fragments are allocated to the Boulder and the Denver sites. The *Course* table is replicated at both sites.

8. Move offering number O1 from the Boulder to the Denver campus. In addition to moving the offering between campuses, change its location to Plaza 112. Assume fragmentation transparency in your formulation.

9. Move offering number O1 from the Boulder to the Denver campus. In addition to moving the offering between campuses, change its location to Plaza 112. Assume location transparency in your formulation.

10. Move offering number O1 from the Boulder to the Denver campus. In addition to moving the offering between campuses, change its location to Plaza 112. Assume local mapping transparency in your formulation.

11. For the following query, compute communication time (*CT*) for the distributed access plans listed below. Use the formulas in section 17.6.1 and the query and network statistics (Table 17-A1) in your calculations.

```
SELECT Course.CourseNo, CrsDesc, OfferNo, OffTime,
FacName
  FROM BoulderOfferings BOF, Course, DenverFaculty DF
  WHERE Course.CourseNo = BOF.Course
  AND    OffTerm = 'Spring'
    AND OffYear = 2008 AND DF.FacNo = BF.FacNo
    AND FacDept = 'Information Systems'
```

Table 17-A1: Statistics for Problem 11

Record length is 1,000 bits for each table.
32 bits for *FacNo*.
20 information systems faculty.
5,000 spring 2008 offerings
10 spring 2006 Boulder offerings taught by Denver faculty.
4,000 courses, 20,000 offerings, and 2,000 faculty in the fragments.
Course table is replicated at both the Denver and the Boulder sites.
BoulderOfferings fragment is located at the Boulder site.
DenverFaculty fragment is located at the Denver site.
Delay per message is 0.1 second.
Data rate is 100,000 bits per second.

12. Move the entire *DenverFaculty* fragment to the Boulder site and perform the query.
13. Move the entire *BoulderOfferings* fragment to the Denver site and perform the query.
14. Move the restricted *BoulderOfferings* fragment to the Denver site and perform the query.
15. Move the restricted *DenverFaculty* fragment to the Boulder site and perform the query.
16. Restrict the *DenverFaculty* fragment and move the join values (*FacNo*) to the Boulder site. Join the *FacNo* values with the *Course* table and the *BoulderOfferings* fragment at the Boulder site. Move the result back to the Denver site to join with the *DenverFaculty* fragment.
17. Investigate the client-server, parallel database, and distributed database features of a major DBMS. Identify the architectures used and important product features.

References for Further Study

This chapter, although providing a broad coverage of distributed processing and data, has only covered the basics. Specialized books on distributed database management include the classic by Ceri and Pelagatti (1984) and the more recent book by Ozsu and Valduriez (1991). The book by Ceri and Pelagatti has a well-written chapter on distributed database design. Date (1990) presents 12 objectives for distributed systems with the most emphasis on distributed DBMSs. Bernstein (1996) provides a detailed presentation of the role of middleware in client-server architectures.

18

Object Database Management Systems

Learning Objectives

This chapter describes extensions to DBMSs to support complex data and operations. After this chapter, the student should have acquired the following knowledge and skills:

- List business reasons for using object database technology
- Define the principles of object-oriented computing
- Compare and contrast architectures for object database management
- Understand features in SQL:2006 for defining and manipulating user-defined types, typed tables, and subtable families
- Understand features in Oracle 11g for defining and manipulating user-defined types and typed tables

Overview

Chapter 17 described ways to utilize remote processing capabilities and computer networks for client-server processing, parallel database processing, and distributed databases. An increasing amount of distributed database processing involves complex data and operations that DBMSs have not traditionally supported. In many cases, database processing can be improved if new kinds of data and operations are more closely integrated with traditional data. In this chapter, you will learn about extensions to DBMSs for objects, combinations of complex data and operations.

This chapter provides a broad introduction to object DBMSs. You will first learn about the business reasons to extend database technology. This chapter discusses the increasing use of complex data and the mismatch between DBMSs and programming languages as the driving forces behind object database technology. After grasping the motivation, you are ready to learn about object technology and its impact on DBMSs. You will learn about the principles of object-oriented computing and DBMS architectures to support these principles. This chapter presents inheritance, encapsulation, and polymorphism as the underlying principles of object technology. To support these principles, this chapter presents architectures for object DBMSs. The last part of this chapter presents object support in SQL:2006, the emerging standard for object-relational DBMSs and Oracle 11g, a significant implementation of the SQL:2006 standard. You will learn about data definition and data manipulation features for object-relational databases.

18.1 Motivation for Object Database Management

This section discusses two forces driving the demand for object database management. After a discussion of these forces, example applications are presented to depict the need for object database management.

18.1.1 Complex Data

Most relational DBMSs support only a few data types. Built-in data types supported in SQL include whole numbers, real numbers, fixed-precision numbers (currency), dates, times, logical (true/false), and text. These data types are sufficient for many business applications, or at least significant parts of many applications. Many business databases contain columns for names, prices, addresses, and transaction dates that readily conform to the standard data types.

Advances in hardware and software capability have enabled complex data to be captured and manipulated in a digital format. Almost any kind of complex data including images, audio, video, maps, and three-dimensional graphics can be digitally stored. For example, an image can be represented as a two-dimensional array of pixels (picture elements) in which each pixel contains a numeric property representing its color or shade of gray. Digital storage is usually cheaper and more reliable than traditional means such as paper, film, or slides. In addition, digital storage allows easier retrieval and manipulation. For example, you can retrieve digital images by content and similarity to other images. Digital images can be manipulated in an image editor with operations such as cropping, texturing, and color tuning.

The ability to store and manipulate complex data does not by itself drive the demand for object database technology. Rather, the need to store large amounts of complex data and integrate complex data with simple data drives the demand for object database technology. Many business applications require large amounts of complex data. For example, insurance claims processing and medical records can involve large amounts of image data. Storing images in separate files becomes tedious for a large collection of images.

The ability to jointly use standard and complex data is increasingly important in many business applications. For example, to review a patient's condition, a physician may request X-rays along with vital statistics. Without integration, two separate programs are required to display the data: an image editor to display the X-rays and a DBMS to retrieve the vital statistics. The ability to retrieve both images and vital statistics in a single query is a large improvement. Besides retrieving complex data, new operations also may be necessary. For example, a physician may want to compare the similarity of a patient's X-rays with X-rays that show abnormalities.

18.1.2 Type System Mismatch

Increasingly, software written in a procedural language needs to access a database. Procedural languages support customized interfaces for data entry forms and reports, operations beyond the capability of SQL, and batch processing. For example, writing a computer program is often necessary to operate on self-referencing data such as a parts hierarchy. Embedded SQL is often used to access a database from within a computer program. After executing an embedded SQL statement, database columns are stored in program variables that can be manipulated further.

A mismatch between the data types in a relational DBMS and the data types of a programming language makes software more complex and difficult to develop. For example, payroll processing can involve many kinds of benefits, deductions, and compensation arrangements. A relational database may have one representation for benefits, deductions, and compensation arrangements while a programming language may have a rather different representation. Before coding the complex calculations, the data must be transformed from the relational database representation (tables) into the programming language representation (records, objects, and arrays). After the calculations, the data must be transformed back into the relational database representation.

Data type mismatch is even more pronounced for complex data. Programming languages usually have richer type systems than DBMSs. For example, relational databases provide a tedious representation of geometric shapes in a building's floor plan. Objects such as points, lines, and polygons may be represented as one text column or as several numeric columns such as X and Y coordinates for points. In contrast, a programming language may have custom data types for points, lines, and polygons. There may be considerable coding to transform between the relational database representation and the programming language representation.

In addition, a relational DBMS cannot perform elementary operations on complex data. Thus, a computer program must be written instead of using a query language. For example, a complex program must be written to compute the similarity between two images. The program will probably contain 10 to 100 times the amount of code found in a query. In addition, the program must transform between the database and the programming language representations.

18.1.3 Application Examples

This section depicts several applications that involve a mix of simple and complex data as well as ad hoc queries. These applications have features increasingly found in many business applications. As you will see, object DBMSs support the requirements of these kinds of applications.

Mapping Websites and GPS Devices

Mapping websites and Global Positioning System (GPS) devices are the most prominent applications involving a mix of simple and complex data. Millions of individuals use mapping websites and GPS devices everyday. Mapping websites provide several different kinds of maps (street, aerial, and hybrid), complex data types involving coordinates, graphics, and text. The major services provided by a mapping website are maps and directions, queries combining complex data (maps) and simple data (addresses, locations, and directions). Directions involve the fundamental operation of shortest distance calculation between two points on a map. Mapping websites and GPS devices provide additional services including points of interest, gas price locators, and traffic conditions. These additional services involve queries combining maps along with simple data. GPS devices use voice, another complex data type, to guide individuals to specified locations.

Dental Office Support

Dental offices use a mix of simple and complex data to make appointments, conduct examinations, and generate bills. Setting appointments requires a calendar with time blocks for service providers (dentists and hygienists). In conducting examinations, service providers use dental charts (graphic of mouth with each tooth identified), X-rays, patient facts, and dental histories. After an examination, bill preparation uses the list of services in the examination and patient insurance data. Queries involving both simple and complex data are showing a dental chart with recent dental problems highlighted and comparing X-rays for symptoms of gum loss.

Real Estate Listing Service

Real estate listing services increasingly use complex data to facilitate customer searches. A real estate listing includes a mix of simple and complex data. The simple data include numerous facts about homes such as the number of bedrooms, the square feet, and the listing price. Complex data include photographs of homes, floor plans, video tours, and area maps. Queries can involve a mix of simple and complex data. Customers want to see homes in a specified neighborhood with selected features. Some customers may want to see homes with the closest match to a set of ideal features in which a customer assigns a weight to each feature. After selecting a set of homes, a customer wants to explore the appearance, floor plan, and facts about the homes.

Auto Insurance Claims

Auto insurance companies use complex data to settle claims. Analyzing claims involves complex data such as photographs, accident reports, and witness statements as well as simple data such as driver and vehicle descriptions. Settling claims involves a map showing service providers as well as service provider rates and service history. Queries for accident data and a list of service providers in close proximity to a customer involve both simple and complex data.

18.2 Object-Oriented Principles

To provide a foundation to understand the architectures and features of object DBMSs, this section presents three fundamental principles of object-oriented computing. After presenting the principles, this section discusses their impact on object DBMSs and object-oriented programming languages.

18.2.1 Encapsulation

An <u>object</u> is a combination of data and procedures. The data are sometimes referred to as variables and the procedures as methods. Each object has a unique identifier that never changes unless the object is destroyed. Object identifiers are not visible to users. In contrast, primary keys in relational databases are visible.

> <u>Classes</u> contain collections of objects. A class definition consists of a collection of variables and methods. The variables are sometimes called instance variables to distinguish them from variables that apply to the entire class (called class variables). Example[45] 18.1 shows the class *Point* with two variables (*X* and *Y* denoting the Cartesian coordinates) and two methods (*Distance* and *Equals*). Each variable has an associated data type. Each method has an interface and an implementation. The interface shows the inputs and the outputs of the method. The implementation shows the detailed coding. For brevity, implementations are not shown in the examples. Example 18.2 depicts a more business-oriented example.

---

[45] The examples in this section conform to the Object Definition Language (ODL) standard defined by the Object Database Management Group.

Example 18.1: Partial *Point* Class
```
CLASS Point {
// VARIABLES:
 ATTRIBUTE Real X;    // X coordinate
 ATTRIBUTE Real Y;    // Y coordinate
// METHODS:
 Float Distance(IN Point aPoint);
  // Computes the Distance between 2 points
 Boolean Equals (IN Point aPoint);
  // Determines if two Points have the same coordinates
 };
```

Example 18.2: Partial *Bond* Class
```
CLASS Bond {
// VARIABLES:
 ATTRIBUTE Float IntRate; // Interest Rate
 ATTRIBUTE Date Maturity; // Maturity Date
// METHODS:
 Float Yield();
// Computes the Bond's Yield
 };
```

Encapsulation means that objects can be accessed only through their interfaces. The internal details (variable definitions and method implementations) are not accessible. For example, you can use the *Distance* and the *Equals* methods only to manipulate *Point* objects. To use the *Distance* method, you supply two *Point* objects. The first *Point* object is implicit in the interface because *Distance* is a method of *Point*. To make *Point* objects more usable, there should be additional methods for creating points, deleting points, and moving points.

Encapsulation: objects can be accessed only through their interfaces.

Encapsulation provides two benefits for managing software complexity. First, a class is a larger unit of reusability than a procedure. In many cases, classes can be reused rather than just individual procedures. More complex classes can be defined using simpler classes. Examples 18.3 and 18.4 depict classes that use the *Point* and the *Bond* classes defined in Examples 18.1 and 18.2. The new classes (*Rectangle* and *Portfolio*) do not need to recode the variables and methods of the *Point* and the *Bond* classes, respectively.

Example 18.3: *Rectangle* Class Using the *Point* Class
```
CLASS Rectangle {
// VARIABLES:
 ATTRIBUTE Point UpperLeftCorner;   // Upper Left Point
 ATTRIBUTE Point LowerRightCorner;  // Lower Right Point
// METHODS:
 Float Area();
  // Computes the Area of the Rectangle
 Float Length ();
  // Computes the Length
 Float Height ();
  // Computes the Height
 };
```

Example 18.4: *Portfolio* **Class Using the** *Bond* **Class**

```
CLASS Portfolio {
// VARIABLES:
 ATTRIBUTE Set<Bond> BondHoldings; // Set of Bonds
 ATTRIBUTE Set<Stock> StockHoldings; // Set of Stocks
// METHODS:
 Float PortfolioReturn();
// Computes the portfolio's Return
};
```

As a second benefit, encapsulation provides a form of data independence. Because internal details of objects are hidden, changes to the internal details can be made without changing the code that uses the objects. Recall from Chapter 1 that data independence promotes reduced software maintenance costs.

18.2.2 Inheritance

Chapter 5 presented classification and inheritance for the Entity Relationship Model. These concepts are similar in object-oriented models except that inheritance applies to both data and procedures. Chapter 5 described inheritance only for attributes of an entity type. Examples 18.5 and 18.6 present classes that inherit from the *Point* and the *Bond* classes. Figure 18.1 depicts a graphical representation of the inheritance relationships. A color point is a point with color. Likewise a corporate bond is a bond with an issuing company and an investment rating. In the subclasses (a child class that inherits from a parent class), the variables and the methods of the parent classes are not repeated. When using the subclasses, the methods in the parent classes can be used.

Inheritance: sharing of data and code among similar classes (classes and subclasses).

Example 18.5: *ColorPoint* **Example (Subclass of** *Point***)**

```
CLASS ColorPoint EXTENDS Point {
// VARIABLES:
 ATTRIBUTE Integer Color;  // Integer value denoting a
color
// METHODS:
 Integer Brighten(IN Real Intensity);
  // Computes a new color that is brighter
};
```

Example 18.6: *Corporate* **Bond Example (Subclass of** *Bond***)**

```
CLASS Corporate EXTENDS Bond {
// VARIABLES:
 RELATIONSHIP Company TheCompany ; // Company issuing the
Bond
 ATTRIBUTE String Rating; // Moody's Rating
// METHODS:
 Boolean Junk();
// TRUE if the bond's rating means low quality
};
```

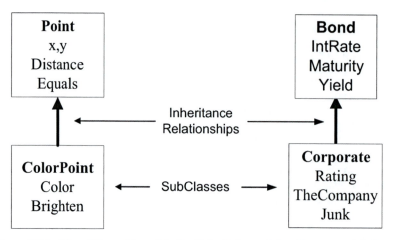

Figure 18.1: Class Hierarchies with the *ColorPoint* and the *Corporate* Subclasses

As discussed in Chapter 5, inheritance can extend to multiple levels. For example, if *Investment* is the parent class of *Bond*, the *Corporate* class inherits from both *Investment* and *Bond*. Inheritance also can extend to multiple parents. Figure 18.2 depicts an investment class hierarchy with multiple inheritance. A convertible security is a bond that becomes a stock if the bondholder chooses. The conversion price and the conversion ratio determine whether a bondholder should convert. The *Convertible* class inherits directly from the *Stock* and the *Bond* classes. Multiple inheritance can be problematic because of conflicts. In Figure 18.2, the *Yield* method can be inherited from either *Stock* or *Bond*. There are various schemes for resolving inheritance conflicts. Ultimately, the database designer must decide on the class from which to inherit.

Inheritance provides an improved organization of software and incremental reusability. The graphical class organization depicts similarity among classes. Programmers can reduce their time to search for similar code by using the graphical class organization. After finding a similar class, database designers and programmers can incrementally add more features (variables and methods). The only new coding is only for the new features, not the existing features.

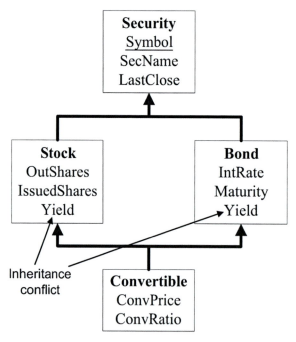

Figure 18.2: Investment Class Hierarchy

18.2.3 Polymorphism

<u>Polymorphism</u> literally means "of many forms." In object-oriented computing, polymorphism permits a method to have multiple implementations. A method implementation in a subclass can override the method implementation in a parent class. Some methods must be overridden because the meaning of the method changes for a subclass. For example, the *Equals* method in class *ColorPoint* compares the coordinates and the color whereas the method implementation in the *Point* class only compares the coordinates. In contrast, the *Area* method has a more efficient implementation for the *Rectangle* class than for the parent *Polygon* class. As another example, the *Yield* method (Figure 18.2) must be overridden in the *Convertible* subclass to combine the calculations in the parent *Stock* and *Bond* classes.

> **Polymorphism:** ability of a computing system to choose among multiple implementations of a method.

Requesting a method execution involves sending a message to an object. A <u>message</u> contains a method name and parameters, similar to a procedure call. One of the parameters is the object that receives the message. The receiver object decides the action to take. If the object's class contains the method, it is executed. Otherwise, the object forwards the message to its parent class for execution. In Figure 18.3, a *ColorPoint* object receives a message requesting a distance calculation. Since the *ColorPoint* class does not contain an implementation of the *Distance* method, the message is sent to the parent class, *Point*. The *Point* class executes the method because it contains an implementation of the *Distance* method.

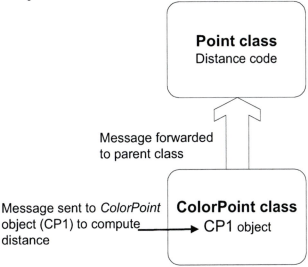

Figure 18.3: Processing a Message

Because object-oriented computing involves messages, client-server processing and object-oriented computing are closely related. Clients and servers are often objects communicating through messages. Client-server processing allows objects to be located on different computers.

In processing a message, the object DBMS assumes responsibility for choosing the appropriate implementation of a method. Associating or <u>binding</u> a message to a method implementation can be done statically when code is compiled or dynamically when code is executed. Static binding is more efficient, but dynamic binding can be more flexible. Dynamic binding is sometimes called "late binding" because it happens just before code execution.

Along with binding, a DBMS ensures that objects and methods are compatible. This function is known as type checking. <u>Strong type checking</u> ensures that there are no incompatibility errors in code. For example, strong type checking prevents computing an area for a point object because the *Area* method applies to polygons not points. Because complex expressions can involve many methods and objects, strong type checking is an important kind of consistency check in object-oriented computing.

> **Strong Type Checking**: the ability to ensure that programming code contains no incompatibility errors. Strong type checking is an important kind of error check for object-oriented coding.

Polymorphism supports fewer, more reusable methods. Because a method can have multiple implementations, the number of method names is reduced. A user needs to know only the method name and the interface, not the appropriate implementation to use. For example, a user only needs to know that the *Area* method applies to polygons, not the appropriate implementation for a rectangle. The DBMS assumes responsibility for finding the appropriate implementation.

Polymorphism also supports incremental modification of code. In coding another implementation of a method for a subclass, much of the code for the method's implementation in the parent class often can be used. For example, to code the redefinition of the *Equals* method in the *ColorPoint* class, another equality condition (for the color of a point) should be added to the conditions to test the *X* and *Y* coordinates.

18.2.4 Programming Languages versus DBMSs

These principles apply to both object-oriented programming languages and object DBMSs. However, the application of the principles varies somewhat between programming languages and DBMSs.

Programming languages have used object-oriented principles for many years. Simula, a language developed in the 1960s, is the first reported object-oriented programming language. As its name implies, Simula was originally developed as a simulation language. Objects and messages are natural in modeling simulations. Smalltalk, a language developed during the 1970s at the Xerox Palo Alto Research Center, was the first popular object-oriented programming language. Smalltalk originally emphasized objects for graphical user interfaces. Inheritance among classes for windows and controls is a natural fit. Since the development of Smalltalk, there have been many other object-oriented programming languages. Java, C++, Visual Basic, and C# are some of the most widely used object-oriented programming languages today.

Object-oriented programming languages emphasize software maintenance and code reusability. To support software maintenance, encapsulation is strictly enforced. The internal details (variables and method implementations) cannot be referenced. In addition, some languages support restrictions on accessing methods. To support reusability, some languages support additional kinds of inheritance to share code. Reuse of code can extend to collections of classes, classes with data type parameters, and redefined code in a subclass.

Object DBMSs are more recent than object-oriented programming languages. Research and development of object DBMSs began in the 1980s. By the early 1990s, several commercial object DBMSs were available. In addition, there was considerable work on extending relational DBMSs with new object features. The next section describes a number of architectures for object DBMSs.

Because early object DBMSs began as extensions of object-oriented programming languages, query language support did not exist. Instead, early object DBMSs provided support for persistent data that last longer than the execution of a program. Large amounts of persistent data could be accessed although in a procedural manner. The early object DBMSs were designed to support applications such as computer-aided design with large amounts of complex data.

Most object DBMSs now support nonprocedural data access. Some of the object-oriented principles are relaxed to accommodate this emphasis. Encapsulation usually is relaxed so that an object's data can be referenced in a query. Database security features provide access to object features rather than public/private distinctions employed in object-oriented programming languages. Inheritance mechanisms usually are simpler because it is assumed that most coding is through a query language, not a procedural language. Multiple inheritance is usually not supported. In addition, most object DBMSs now provide query optimization and transaction processing capabilities.

18.3 Architectures for Object Database Management

The marketplace provides a variety of approaches for object-oriented databases. Part of the variety is historical due to the slow initial development of the technology. Early approaches provided small extensions that left most of the object-oriented processing outside of a DBMS. As user interest increased and research and development matured, more complete approaches for object-oriented databases have emerged. Recent approaches have involved significant rewrites of DBMSs to accommodate objects. The marketplace probably will support a variety of approaches because of the different requirements among customers. This section describes several object database management architectures along with their strengths and weaknesses.

18.3.1 Large Objects and External Software

The earliest approach to add objects to relational databases was to use large objects with external software. Complex data are stored in a column as a binary or text large object. For example, an image uses the <u>BLOB (binary large object)</u> data type while a large text document uses the <u>CLOB (character large object)</u> data type. As depicted in Figure 18.4, large objects usually are stored separately from other data in a table. A query can retrieve but not display large objects. Software external to the DBMS displays and manipulates large objects. External software includes ActiveX controls, Java applets, and Web browser plug-ins.

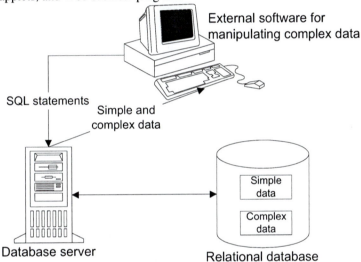

Figure 18.4: Large Object Architecture

Large Object Architecture: storage of large objects (binary or text) in a database along with external software to manipulate large objects. The BLOB (binary large object) and CLOB (character large object) data types are used to store columns with large objects.

The large object approach is simple to implement and is universal. Only small changes to a DBMS are required. All kinds of complex data can be stored. In addition, a large market for third-party software may be available for prominent kinds of complex data. For example, many third-party tools have been implemented for popular image formats.

Despite some advantages, the large object approach suffers from serious performance drawbacks. Because the DBMS does not understand the structure and the operations of complex data, no optimization is possible. Data cannot be filtered using characteristics of large objects. No indexes can be used to select records using characteristics of large objects. Because large objects are stored separately from other data, additional disk accesses may be necessary. The order of the large objects may not coincide with the order of other table data.

18.3.2 Specialized Media Servers

In the specialized media server architecture, complex data reside outside of a DBMS as depicted in Figure 18.5. A separate server may be dedicated to manipulating a single kind of complex data such as video or images. Programmers use an application programming interface (API) to access complex data through a media server. The API provides a set of procedures to retrieve, update, and transform a specific kind of complex data. To simultaneously manipulate simple data and complex data, program code contains a mix of embedded SQL and API calls to the media server.

Specialized Media Server Architecture: the use of a dedicated server to manage complex data outside of a database. Programmers use an application programming interface to access complex data.

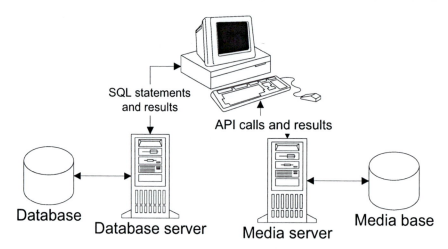

Figure 18.5: Specialized Media Server Architecture

Specialized media servers provide better performance than the large object approach but sacrifice some flexibility. Dedicated servers and highly specialized APIs provide good performance for specific kinds of complex data. Because an API is provided rather than a query language, the range of operations may be limited. For example, a video server may support fast streaming of video but not searching by content.

When combining simple and complex data, the specialized server approach may perform poorly. A query optimizer cannot jointly optimize retrieval of simple and complex data because the DBMS is not aware of complex data. In addition, a media server may not provide indexing techniques for search conditions. Transaction processing is limited to simple data because specialized media servers do not typically support transaction processing.

18.3.3 Object Database Middleware

Object database middleware circumvents problems with media servers by simulating object features. Clients no longer directly access media servers as shown in Figure 18.6. Instead, clients send SQL statements to middleware, which makes API calls to media servers and sends SQL statements to database servers. The SQL statements can combine traditional operations on simple data with specialized operations on complex data. Object database middleware relieves the user of knowing a separate API for each media server. In addition, object database middleware provides location independence because users do not need to know where complex data reside.

Object Database Middleware: the use of middleware to manage complex data possibly stored outside of a database along with traditional data stored in a database.

Object middleware provides a way to integrate complex data stored on PCs and remote servers with relational databases. Without object middleware, some of the complex data could not be combined easily with simple data. Even if an architecture that integrates more tightly with the DBMS is desired, the object middleware approach can be used for complex data that users do not want to store in a database.

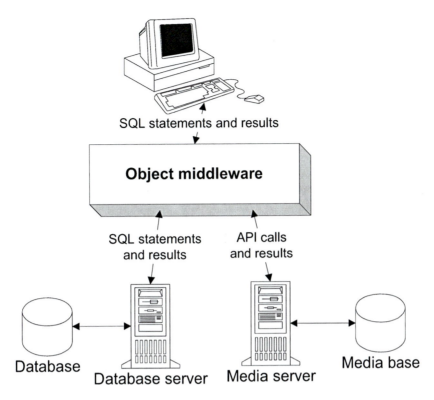

SQL statements and results

Object middleware

SQL statements
and results

API calls
and results

Database   Database server   Media server   Media base

Figure 18.6: Object Middleware Approach

Object middleware can suffer performance problems because of a lack of integration with a DBMS. Combining complex and simple data suffers the same performance problems as with specialized media servers. The DBMS cannot optimize requests that simultaneously combine simple and complex data. Middleware can provide transaction processing that combines simple and complex data. However, transaction performance can be slow because two-phase commit and distributed concurrency control techniques must be used.

18.3.4 Object-Relational Database Management Systems for User-Defined Types

The first three approaches involve little or no change to a DBMS but provide only limited query and optimization capabilities. With larger changes to a DBMS, more query and optimization capabilities are possible.

To provide additional query capabilities, object-relational DBMSs support user-defined types. Almost any kind of complex data can be added as a user-defined type. Image data, spatial data, time series, and video are just a few of the possible data types. Major DBMS vendors provide a collection of prebuilt user-defined types and the ability to extend the prebuilt types as well as to create new user-defined types. Table 18-1 lists pre-built data types supported by major enterprise DBMSs. For each user-defined type, a collection of methods can be defined. These method functions can be used in SQL statements, not just in programming language code. Inheritance and polymorphism apply to user-defined data types. For prebuilt types, specialized storage structures have been created to improve performance. For example, multidimensional Btrees can be provided for accessing spatial data.

Table 18-1: Pre-Built User-Defined Data Types in Object-Relational DBMSs

Product	User-Defined Types
IBM DB2 Extenders	Audio, Image, Video, XML, Spatial, Geodetic, Text, Net Search
Oracle Data Cartridges	Text, Video, Image, Spatial, XML, Medical Images, RFID
Informix Data Blades	Text, Image, Spatial, Geodetic, Web, Time Series, Video

Although user-defined types are the most salient feature of object-relational databases, there are a number of other prominent object features including subtable families (generalization hierarchies for tables), arrays, and the reference and row data types. Section 18.4 presents examples of user-defined types and these other object features in SQL:2006, the standard for object-relational DBMSs. Section 18.5 presents the object features in Oracle 11g, a significant implementation of the SQL:2006 standard.

> **Object-Relational DBMS:** a relational DBMS extended with an object query processor for user-defined data types. SQL:2006 provides the standard for object-relational DBMSs.

User-defined types involve a table-driven architecture as depicted in Figure 18.7. The object query processor uses table-driven code for user-defined types. The parser decomposes references to expressions involving user-defined types and functions. The display manager controls the presentation of simple and complex data. The optimizer searches for storage structures that can be used to optimize expressions containing user-defined types and functions. The relational kernel comprises transaction processing, storage management, and buffer management. It provides the engine used by the object query processor. Little or no changes are necessary to the relational kernel.

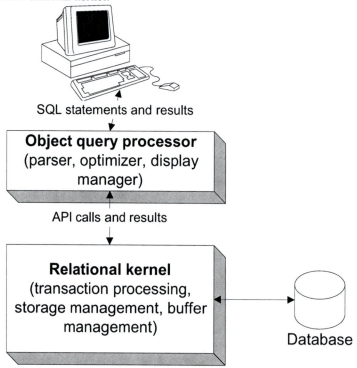

Figure 18.7: Component Architecture for Object-Relational DBMSs

Object-relational DBMSs provide good integration of complex data, but reliability may be a concern. The integration of simple and complex data involves considerable changes to the parser, display manager, and optimizer. However, the base of code in the kernel remains relatively stable. Reliability can be compromised in the implementations of user-defined functions and storage structures. DBMS vendors, third-party vendors, and in-house developers can provide user-defined types, which can be complex and difficult to implement. Implementation errors can affect the integrity of both simple and complex data. In addition, third-party data types can be subject to viruses. Since most user defined types are provided by the DBMS vendor, reliability concerns have not been demonstrated.

18.3.5 Object-Oriented Database Management Systems

Some experts have argued that more fundamental changes to a DBMS are needed to support objects. Both the data model and the kernel must be changed to accommodate objects. This conviction has driven a number of start-up software companies to implement a new class of object DBMSs, as depicted in Figure 18.8. The software companies have banded together to form the Object Database Management Group (ODMG). The ODMG has proposed an object definition language (ODL) and an object query language (OQL). These languages are the counterpart of SQL for object-oriented DBMSs.

> **Object-Oriented DBMS**: a new kind of DBMS designed especially for objects. Object-oriented DBMSs have an object query processor and an object kernel. The Object Data Management Group provides the standard for object-oriented DBMSs.

Object-oriented DBMSs preceded object-relational technology offerings by 10 years. The early products were used in applications where ad hoc query, query optimization, and transaction processing were not important. Instead, the early products emphasized support for complex data in large software systems. Most of the object-oriented DBMSs began as extended programming languages with support for persistent objects (i.e., objects that exist after a program terminates). Gradually, the object-oriented DBMSs have provided ad hoc query, query optimization, and efficient transaction support. Still, questions remained about the ability of object-oriented DBMSs to provide high performance for traditional business applications and to effectively compete in the marketplace.

Commercially, the ODMG effort has been eclipsed by the object-relational standards in SQL:2006. The ODMG group disbanded in 2001 and development of ODMG-compliant DBMSs has faltered also. Only a few commercial or open source products are available. The ODMG standard was a significant development that has been unable to find a significant commercial niche. The market power of the relational DBMS vendors, the open source DBMS movement, and development of object-relational standards have suppressed additional development of ODMG-compliant DBMSs. The added benefit of object-oriented database technology over object-relational technology has not been persuasive enough to generate commercial or open source success.

Despite the disbanding of the ODMG group and the demise of commercially compliant products, the Object Management Group committed to a new object database standard in 2006. The new "4th generation" standard will facilitate broader adoption of standards-based object database technology. The emphasis will be on the emerging market for open database software products. As of the completion date of this chapter (March 2008), no new object database standard had been produced.

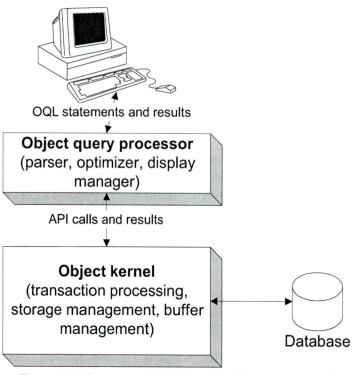

OQL statements and results

Object query processor
(parser, optimizer, display manager)

API calls and results

Object kernel
(transaction processing, storage management, buffer management)

Database

Figure 18.8: Component Architecture for Object-Oriented DBMSs

18.3.6 Summary of Object Database Architectures

To help you remember the architectures for object DBMSs, Table 18-2 provides a convenient summary. All of the architectures fulfill a certain market niche. The simpler architectures (large objects and media servers) should become less popular over time. The struggle for dominance among the other three architectures has tilted strongly towards the object-relational approach as evidenced by significant commercial and open source offerings. The other two architectures (object database middleware and object-oriented) are just occupying niches in the commercial and open source market.

Table 18-2: Summary of Architectures

Architecture	Example Products	Comments
Large objects	Most SQL-92 DBMSs	Storage of any kind of data; uncertain performance; limited query language support
Media servers	Oracle interMedia	Limited query language support; uncertain performance when combining simple and complex data; Good performance on complex data
Object database middleware	Microsoft Universal Data Access and OLE DB	Ability to combine distributed and diverse data sources; flexible service levels for data sources; uncertain performance when combining and updating simple and complex data
Object-relational (SQL:2006)	Significant implementations of SQL:2006 object-relational features in Oracle 11g, IBM DB2, PostgreSQL, and Virtuoso	Good performance with specialized storage structures; good query language support; some type mismatch with programming languages; reasonable conformance with SQL:2006 object features
Object-oriented (ODMG)	ObjectStore, UniSQL, Versant	Good query language support; uncertain performance for traditional applications; good type match with programming languages; few commercial or open source offerings

18.4 Object Database Features in SQL:2006

To clarify object database concepts, this section provides examples using SQL:2006, the object-relational database language. The SQL:2006 standard includes nine parts and seven packages, as summarized in Table 18-3. Core SQL:2006 consists of parts 1, 2, and 11. Each noncore part contains mandatory and optional features. A package is a collection of optional features for some application area or implementation environment.

The SQL:2006 standard provides several levels of conformance. Minimal conformance includes all features in Core SQL:2006 (parts 1, 2, and 11). Enhanced conformance can be claimed for the mandatory features in a part, the optional features in a part, and the features in a package. Because of the lack of testing suites and independent certification, the conformance level of a specific DBMS is difficult to determine. Most vendors provide checklists of supported features, unsupported features, and features supported with proprietary extensions.

This section presents examples from the Basic Object Support and Enhanced Object Support packages. The examples demonstrate SQL:2006 features for user-defined data types, table definitions with typed tables, subtable families, and usage of typed tables.

Table 18-3: Overview of the SQL:2006 Parts and Packages

SQL:2006 Component	Scope
Part 1: Framework	Syntax notation, terminology, results of statement processing, conformance levels (Core SQL:2006)
Part 2: Foundation	Data structures and basic operations on SQL data (Core SQL:2006)
Part 3: Call-Level Interface	Data structures and functions to use SQL in a computer program
Part 4: Persistent Stored Modules	Programming language statements, procedures, functions, exception handling
Part 9: Management of External Data	Foreign data wrappers and data links for external data
Part 10: Object Language Bindings	Statements to embed SQL in Java programs
Part 11: Information and Definition Schemas	Dictionary tables for tables, integrity, and security (Core SQL:2006)
Part 13: SQL Routines and Types Using the Java TM Programming Language	Usage of Java classes and methods in SQL statements
Part 14: XML Related Specifications	Manipulation of XML documents in SQL statements, publishing both XML and conventional SQL-data in XML form, support for XQuery (XML query language)
Package 1: Enhanced Datetime Facilities	Time zone specification, interval data type
Package 2: Enhanced Integrity Management	Check constraints, assertions, and constraint management
Package 4: Persistent Stored Modules	Programming language statements, procedures, functions, exception handling
Package 6: Basic Object Support	User-defined data types, single inheritance, reference types, arrays
Package 7: Enhanced Object Support	Path expressions, subtable definition, subtable search, subtypes
Package 8: Active Databases	Support for triggers
Package 10: OLAP Facilities	Cube and roll-up operators, row and table constructors, FULL JOIN and INTERSECT operators

18.4.1 User-Defined Types

One of the most fundamental extensions in SQL:2006 is the user-defined type for bundling data and procedures together. User-defined types support the definition of new structured data types as well as the refinement of the standard data types. A structured data type has a collection of attributes and methods. In SQL-92, the CREATE DOMAIN statement supports refinements to standard data types but not the definition of new structured types.

Example 18.7 shows the *Point* type to depict the basic syntax of user-defined types. The first part of a user-defined type contains the attribute definitions. The double hyphen denotes a comment. For methods, the first parameter is implicit meaning that its specification is not needed. For example, the *Distance* method lists only one *Point* parameter (P2) because the other *Point* parameter is implicit. In SQL:2006, methods only use input parameters and should return values. The body of methods is not shown in the CREATE TYPE statement but rather in the CREATE METHOD statement. The keywords NOT FINAL mean that subtypes can be defined. The keyword INSTANTIABLE[46] means that instances of the type can be created.

Example 18.7: *Point* Type in SQL:2006

```
CREATE TYPE Point AS
( X FLOAT,    -- X coordinate
  Y FLOAT )   -- Y coordinate
 METHOD Distance(P2 Point) RETURNS FLOAT,
      -- Computes the distance between 2 points
 METHOD Equals (P2 Point) RETURNS BOOLEAN
   -- Determines if 2 points are equivalent
NOT FINAL
INSTANTIABLE;
```

As stated in the previous paragraph, SQL:2006 methods are somewhat limited in that they must return single values and only use input parameters. In addition, the first parameter of a method is implicitly an instance of the type in which it is associated. SQL:2006 provides functions and procedures that do not have the restrictions of methods. Because functions and procedures are not associated with a specific type, SQL:2006 provides separate definition statements (CREATE FUNCTION and CREATE PROCEDURE). Procedures can use input, output, and input-output parameters whereas functions only use input parameters.

Example 18.8 shows the *ColorPoint* type, a subtype of *Point*. The UNDER keyword indicates the parent type. Because SQL:2006 does not support multiple inheritance, only a single type name can follow the UNDER keyword. In the method definitions, the OVERRIDING keyword indicates that the method overrides the definition in a parent type.

Example 18.8: *ColorPoint* Type

```
CREATE TYPE ColorPoint UNDER Point AS
(Color INTEGER )
 METHOD Brighten (Intensity INTEGER) RETURNS INTEGER,
   -- Increases color intensity
 OVERRIDING METHOD Equals (CP2 ColorPoint)
    RETURNS BOOLEAN
   -- Determines if 2 ColorPoints are equivalent
 FINAL;
```

---

[46] The keywords NOT INSTANTIABLE mean that the type is abstract without instances. Abstract types contain data and code but no instances. Abstract types have been found to enhance code sharing in object-oriented programming.

Besides the explicit methods listed in the CREATE TYPE statement, user-defined types have implicit methods that can be used in SQL statements and stored procedures, as listed below:

- Constructor method: creates an empty instance of the type. The constructor method has the same name as the data type. For example, `Point()` is the constructor method for the *Point* type.
- Observer methods: retrieve values from attributes. Each observer method uses the same name as its associated attribute. For example, `X()` is the observer method for the *X* attribute of the *Point* type.
- Mutator methods: change values stored in attributes. Each mutator method uses the same name as its associated attribute with one parameter for the value. For example, `X(45.0)` changes the value of the *X* attribute.

SQL:2006 features the ARRAY and MULTISET collection types to support types with more than one value such as time-series and geometric shapes. Arrays support bounded ordered collections, while multisets support unbounded, unordered collections. Example 18.9a defines a triangle type with an array of three points. The number following the ARRAY keyword indicates the maximum size of the array. Example 18.9b defines a polygon with a multiset of points. You should observe that maximum length cannot be specified for MULTISET attributes.

Example 18.9a: *Triangle* **Type Using an ARRAY Type**

```
CREATE TYPE Triangle AS
  (Corners Point ARRAY[3], -- Array of Corner Points
   Color INTEGER )
  METHOD Area() RETURNS FLOAT,
   -- Computes the area
  METHOD Scale (Factor FLOAT) RETURNS Triangle
   -- Computes a new triangle scaled by factor
  NOT FINAL;
```

Example 18.9b: *Polygon* **Type Using a MULTISET Type**

```
CREATE TYPE Polygon AS
  (Corners Point MULTISET, -- Multiset of Corner Points
   Color INTEGER )
  METHOD Area() RETURNS FLOAT,
   -- Computes the area
  METHOD Scale (Factor FLOAT) RETURNS Polygon
   -- Computes a new polygon scaled by factor
  NOT FINAL;
```

User-defined types are integrated into the heart of SQL:2006. User-defined types can be used as data types for columns in tables, passed as parameters, and returned as values. User-defined methods can be used in expressions in the SELECT, WHERE, and HAVING clauses.

18.4.2 Table Definitions

The examples in the remainder of Chapter 18 are based on a simple property database with properties and agents as depicted by the ERD in Figure 18.9. For the presentation here, the most important aspect of the ERD is the generalization hierarchy for properties. SQL:2006 provides direct support of generalization hierarchies rather than indirect support as indicated by the generalization hierarchy conversion rule presented in Chapter 6.

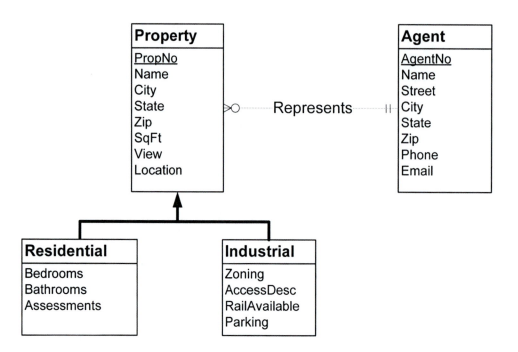

Figure 18.9: ERD for the Property Database

SQL:2006 supports two styles of table definitions. The traditional SQL-92 style uses foreign keys to link two tables. Example 18.10 depicts the *Property* table using a foreign key to reference the agent representing the property. The *View* column uses the binary large object (BLOB) type. If a prebuilt user-defined type for a specific image format is provided, it would be a better choice than the BLOB type.

Example 18.10: *Agent* **and** *Property* **Tables Using the Traditional SQL-92 Definition Style**

```
CREATE TABLE Agent
(AgentNo INTEGER,
 Name    VARCHAR(30),
 Street  VARCHAR(50),
 City    VARCHAR(30),
 State   CHAR(2),
 Zip     CHAR(9),
 Phone   CHAR(13),
 Email   VARCHAR(50),
 CONSTRAINT AgentPK PRIMARY KEY(AgentNo) );

CREATE TABLE Property
(PropNo   INTEGER,
 Street   VARCHAR(50),
 City     VARCHAR(30),
 State    CHAR(2),
 Zip      CHAR(9),
 SqFt     INTEGER,
 View     BLOB,
 AgentNo INTEGER,
 Location Point,
 CONSTRAINT PropertyPK PRIMARY KEY(PropNo),
 CONSTRAINT AgentFK FOREIGN KEY(AgentNo) REFERENCES Agent
 );
```

SQL:2006 supports the row type constructor to allow rows of a table to be stored as variables, used as parameters, and returned by functions. A row type is a sequence of name/value pairs. One use of a row type is to collect related columns together so that they can be stored as a variable or passed as a parameter. Example 18.11 depicts the *Property* table using a row type for the address columns (*Street*, *City*, *State*, and *Zip*).

Example 18.11: Revised Property Table Definition with a Row Type

```
CREATE TABLE Property
(PropNo   INTEGER,
 Address ROW (Street   VARCHAR(50),
             City     VARCHAR(30),
             State    CHAR(2),
             Zip      CHAR(9) ),
 SqFt     INTEGER,
 View     BLOB,
 AgentNo INTEGER,
 Location Point,
 CONSTRAINT PropertyPK PRIMARY KEY(PropNo),
 CONSTRAINT AgentFK FOREIGN KEY(AgentNo) REFERENCES Agent
 );
```

SQL:2006 provides an alternative style of table definition known as typed tables to support object identifiers and object references. With typed tables, a table definition references a user-defined type rather than providing its own list of columns. Example 18.12 depicts the *AgentType* user-defined type and the *Agent* table referring to *AgentType*. In addition, the *AddressType* (a named structured type) is used in place of the unnamed ROW type in Example 18.11. The REF clause defines an object identifier for the table. The SYSTEM GENERATED keywords indicate that the object identifiers are generated by the DBMS, not the user application (USER GENERATED keywords).

Example 18.12: Definition of *AddressType* and *AgentType* followed by the Typed *Agent* Table Based on *AgentType*

```
CREATE TYPE AddressType AS
  (Street   VARCHAR(50),
   City     VARCHAR(30),
   State    CHAR(2),
   Zip      CHAR(9) )
NOT FINAL;

CREATE TYPE AgentType AS
(AgentNo INTEGER,
 Name     VARCHAR(30),
 Address AddressType,
 Phone    CHAR(13),
 Email    VARCHAR(50) )
 NOT FINAL;

CREATE TABLE Agent OF AgentType
(REF IS AgentOId SYSTEM GENERATED,
 CONSTRAINT AgentPK PRIMARY KEY(AgentNo) );
```

Other tables can reference tables based on user-defined types. Object references provide an alternative to value references of foreign keys. Example 18.13 depicts a definition of the *PropertyType* type with a reference to the *AgentType*. The SCOPE clause limits a reference to the rows of a table rather than objects of the type.

Example 18.13: Definition of *PropertyType* and the Typed *Property* Table

```
CREATE TYPE PropertyType AS
(PropNo    INTEGER,
 Address   AddressType,
 SqFt      INTEGER,
 View      BLOB,
 Location  Point,
 AgentRef  REF(AgentType) SCOPE Agent )
 NOT FINAL;

CREATE TABLE Property OF PropertyType
(REF IS PropertyOId SYSTEM GENERATED,
 CONSTRAINT PropertyPK PRIMARY KEY(PropNo) ) ;
```

As these examples demonstrate, SQL:2006 provides a variety of ways to define tables (typed versus untyped tables, references versus traditional foreign keys, ROW types versus columns versus named structured types). For training of application programmers, consistent usage of table definition styles is important. A reasonable rule of thumb is to use either the traditional table definitions (untyped tables with unstructured columns and foreign keys) or typed tables with named structured types and reference types. Mixing table definition styles can burden application programmers because the definition style influences the coding used in retrieval and manipulation statements.

SQL:2006 supports nested tables using the MULTISET type with the ROW type for elements of a multiset. Nested tables are useful at the application level especially for complex business rules involving stored procedures. In addition, nested tables can be useful to reduce the type system mismatch between a DBMS and a programming language as discussed in section 18.1.2. At the table design level, the usage of nested tables is not clear for business databases. Although some design theory exists for nested tables, the theory is not widely known or practiced. Because of the immaturity of nested table practice, no examples of nested tables are presented for table design.

18.4.3 Subtable Families

Inheritance applies to tables in a similar way as it applies to user-defined types. A table can be declared as a subtable of another table. A subtable inherits the columns of its parent tables. SQL:2006 limits inheritance for tables to single inheritance. A potentially confusing part of table inheritance involves type inheritance. Tables involved in subtable relationships must be typed tables with the associated types also participating in subtype relationships as demonstrated in Example 18.14. Note that the REF clauses and primary key constraints are inherited from the *Property* table so they are not specified for the *Residential* and the *Industrial* tables.

Example 18.14: Subtypes and Subtables for Residential and Industrial Properties

```
CREATE TYPE ResidentialType UNDER PropertyType
(BedRooms  INTEGER,
 BathRooms INTEGER,
 Assessments DECIMAL(9,2) ARRAY[6] )
   NOT FINAL
   INSTANTIABLE;

CREATE TABLE Residential OF ResidentialType UNDER
Property;

CREATE TYPE IndustrialType UNDER PropertyType
(Zoning   VARCHAR(20),
 AccessDesc VARCHAR(20),
 RailAvailable BOOLEAN,
 Parking VARCHAR(10) )
   NOT FINAL
   INSTANTIABLE;

CREATE TABLE Industrial OF IndustrialType UNDER Property;
```

Set inclusion determines the relationship of rows of a parent table to rows in its subtables. Every row in a subtable is also a row in each of its ancestor (direct parents and indirect parents) tables. Each row of a parent table corresponds to at most one row in direct subtables. This set inclusion relationship extends to an entire subtable family, including the root table and all subtables directly or indirectly under the root table. For example, a subtable family includes security as the root, bond and stock under investment, and corporate, municipal, and federal under bond. The root of a subtable family is known as the maximal table. Security is the maximal table in this example.

Data manipulation operations on a row in a subtable family affect related rows in parent tables and subtables. The following is a brief description of side effects when manipulating rows in subtable families.

- If a row is inserted into a subtable, then a corresponding row (with the same values for inherited columns) is inserted into each parent table. The insert cascades upward in the subtable family until it reaches the maximal table.
- If a column is updated in a parent table, then the column is also updated in all direct and indirect subtables that inherit the column.
- If an inherited column is updated in a subtable, then the column is changed in the corresponding rows of direct and indirect parent tables. The update cascade stops in the parent table in which the column is defined, not inherited.
- If a row in a subtable family is deleted, then every corresponding row in both parent and subtables is also deleted.

18.4.4 Manipulating Complex Objects and Subtable Families

The richer data definition capabilities of SQL:2006 lead to new features when using row type columns and reference type columns in data manipulation and data retrieval statements. When inserting data into a table with a row type column, the keyword ROW must be used as demonstrated in Example 18.15. If a column uses a user-defined type instead of the ROW type, the type name must be used as depicted in Example 18.16.

Example 18.15: Using the ROW Keyword When Inserting a Row in a Table with a Row Type Column

This example assumes that the *Address* column of the *AgentType* type was defined with the ROW type.

```
INSERT INTO Agent
(AgentNo, Name, Address, Email, Phone)
VALUES (999999, 'Sue Smith',
        ROW('123 Any Street', 'Denver', 'CO', '80217'),
        'sue.smith@anyisp.com', '13031234567')
```

Example 18.16: Using the Type Name When Inserting Two Rows in a Table with a Structured Type Column

This example corresponds to the *AgentType* type defined in Example 18.12.

```
INSERT INTO Agent
(AgentNo, Name, Address, Email, Phone)
VALUES (999999, 'Sue Smith',
  AddressType('123 Any Street', 'Denver', 'CO', '80217'),
  'sue.smith@anyisp.com', '13031234567');

INSERT INTO Agent
(AgentNo, Name, Address, Email, Phone)
VALUES (999998, 'John Smith',
  AddressType('123 Big Street', 'Boulder', 'CO', '80217'),
    'john.smith@anyisp.com', '13034567123');
```

When inserting data into a table with a reference type column, the object identifier can be obtained with a SELECT statement. If object identifiers for a referenced table are user-generated (such as primary key values), a SELECT statement may not be necessary. Even with user-generated object identifiers, a SELECT statement may be necessary if the object identifier is not known when the row is inserted. Example 18.17 demonstrates a SELECT statement to retrieve the object identifier (*AgentOID*) from the related row of the *Agent* table. In the SELECT statement, the other values to insert are constant values. For the *Assessments* column, the constant value is an array of values denoted by the ARRAY keyword along with the square brackets that surround the array element values.

Example 18.17: Using a SELECT Statement to Retrieve the Object Identifier of the Related *Agent* Row

```
INSERT INTO Residential
(PropNo, Address, SqFt, AgentRef, BedRooms, BathRooms,
Assessments)
SELECT 999999, AddressType('123 Any Street', 'Denver', 'CO',
    '80217'), 2000, AgentOID, 3, 2, ARRAY[190000, 200000]
FROM Agent
WHERE AgentNo = 999999;
```

Example 18.17 also demonstrates several aspects about subtypes and subtables. First, the INSERT statement can reference the columns in both types because of the subtype relationship involving *ResidentialType* and *PropertyType*. Second, inserting a row into the *Residential* table automatically inserts a row into the *Property* table because of the subtable relationship between the *Residential* and *Property* tables.

Reference columns can be updated using a SELECT statement in a manner similar to that used in Example 18.17. Example 18.18 demonstrates an UPDATE statement using a SELECT statement to retrieve the object identifier of the related agent.

Example 18.18: Using a SELECT Statement to Retrieve the Object Identifier of the Related *Agent* Row

```
UPDATE Residential
  SET AgentRef =
    ( SELECT AgentOID FROM Agent WHERE AgentNo = 999998 )
  WHERE PropNo = 999999;
```

Path expressions using the dot operator and the dereference operator provide an alternative to the traditional value-based joins in SQL-92. Example 18.19 depicts the use of the dot and the dereference operators in path expressions. For columns with a row or user-defined type, you should use the dot operator in path expressions. The expression `Address.City` references the city component of the *Address* row column. For columns with a reference type, you should use the dereference operator (->) in path expressions. The expression `AgentRef->Name` retrieves the *Name* column of the related *Agent* row. The dereference operator (->) must be used instead of the dot operator because the column *AgentRef* has the type `REF(AgentType)`. The distinction between dot and dereference operators is one of the more confusing aspects of SQL:2006. Other object-oriented languages such as the ODMG query language and Java do not have this distinction.

Example 18.19: SELECT Statement with Path Expressions and the Dereference Operator

```
SELECT PropNo, P.Address.City, P.AgentRef->Address.City
  FROM Property P
  WHERE AgentRef->Name = 'John Smith'
```

Sometimes there is a need to test membership in a specific table without being a member of other subtables. Example 18.20 retrieves industrial properties where the square feet column is greater than 3,000. The FROM clause restricts the scope to rows whose most specific type is the *IndustrialType*. Thus, Example 18.20 does not retrieve any rows of the *Residential* table, a subtable of the *Property* table.

Example 18.20: Using ONLY to Restrict the Range of a Table in a Subtable Family

```
SELECT PropNo, Address, Location
 FROM ONLY (Residential)
 WHERE Sqft > 1500
```

18.5 Object Database Features in Oracle 11g

The most widely implemented part of the SQL:2006 object packages is the user-defined type. The major relational DBMS vendors including IBM and Oracle have implemented user-defined types that provide similar features as the SQL:2006 standard. User-defined types are important for storage and manipulation of complex data in business databases.

Beyond user-defined types, the object features in the SQL:2006 standard are now gaining commercial acceptance. As an example of commercial implementation of the object features in SQL:2006, this section presents the most important object features of Oracle 11g using the examples from the previous section. Although Oracle 11g does not claim complete conformance with the object features, it supports most of the features of the SQL:2006 object packages as well as some additional object features. Even if you do not use Oracle 11g, you can gain insight about the complexity of the SQL:2006 object features and the difficulty of ensuring enhanced conformance with the SQL:2006 standard.

18.5.1 Defining User-Defined Types and Typed Tables in Oracle 11g

Oracle 11g supports user-defined types with a syntax close to the SQL:2006 syntax. As depicted in Example 18.21, most of the differences are cosmetic such as the different placement of the parentheses, the reserved word RETURN instead of RETURNS in SQL:2006, and the reserved word OBJECT for root-level types. Differences in methods are more significant. Oracle 11g supports functions and procedures as methods compared to only method functions in SQL:2006. Thus, the *Print* procedure in Example 18.21 is not used in Example 18.7 because SQL:2006 does not support method procedures. In addition, Oracle 11g supports order methods for direct object to object comparisons, map methods for indirect object comparisons, and static methods for global operations that do not need to reference the data of an object instance.

Example 18.21: *Point* Type in Oracle 11g

This example corresponds to Example 18.7 for SQL:2006.

```
CREATE TYPE Point AS OBJECT
( x FLOAT(15),
  y FLOAT(15),
 MEMBER FUNCTION Distance(P2 Point) RETURN NUMBER,
      -- Distance between implicit point and P2 point
parameters
 MEMBER FUNCTION Equals (P2 Point) RETURN BOOLEAN,
   -- Determines if P2 and implicit parameter are
   -- equivalent
 MEMBER PROCEDURE Print )
NOT FINAL
INSTANTIABLE;
```

Before methods can be used, a body for each method must be created in a CREATE TYPE BODY statement. Example 18.22 contains an implementation for each method in the *Point* type definition. Oracle uses the keyword SELF to refer to the implicit parameter for a method. However, the usage of SELF is optional as shown in each of the method bodies. Example 18.23 demonstrates usage of the methods of the *Point* type. Before demonstrating method usage, a table of points is created and points are inserted into the table.

Example 18.22: CREATE TYPE BODY Statement for *Point* Type in Oracle 11g

```
CREATE TYPE BODY Point AS
  MEMBER FUNCTION Distance(P2 Point) RETURN NUMBER IS
  BEGIN
    RETURN sqrt(power(x - P2.x,2) + power(y - P2.y,2));
-- Equivalent to previous line using SELF
-- RETURN sqrt(power(SELF.x - P2.x,2)
-- + power(SELF.y - P2.y,2));
  END;
  MEMBER FUNCTION Equals(P2 Point) RETURN BOOLEAN IS
  BEGIN
    IF x = P2.x AND y = P2.y THEN
      RETURN TRUE;
    ELSE
      RETURN FALSE;
    END IF;
  END;
  MEMBER PROCEDURE Print IS
  BEGIN
    DBMS_OUTPUT.PUT_LINE('x: ' || to_char(x) || ' - ' ||
                         'y: ' ||
      to_char(y));
  END;
END;
```

Example 18.23: Script to Create Points and Use Methods

```
CREATE TABLE PointTbl of Point;

INSERT INTO PointTbl VALUES(10, 10);
INSERT INTO PointTbl VALUES(3, 4);
SELECT * FROM PointTbl;

SET SERVER OUTPUT ON;
-- Anonymous block to use point methods
DECLARE
  P1 Point;
  P2 Point;
BEGIN
  SELECT VALUE(p) INTO P1 FROM PointTbl p WHERE p.x = 10;
  P1.Print();
  SELECT VALUE(p) INTO P2 FROM PointTbl p WHERE p.x = 3;
  P2.Print();
  DBMS_OUTPUT.PUT_LINE('Distance: ' ||
                       to_char(P1.Distance(P2)));
  IF P1.Equals(P2) THEN
     DBMS_OUTPUT.PUT_LINE('Same Point');
  ELSE
     DBMS_OUTPUT.PUT_LINE('Different Point');
  END IF;
END;
-- PointTbl is not used in the remainder of the examples.
DROP TABLE PointTbl;
```

Oracle 11g supports inheritance for user-defined types similarly to SQL:2006. An important difference involves the overriding of methods. In Oracle 11g, overriding methods have the same name and signature in the parent type and subtype. A signature consists of the method's name and the number, data types, and order of the parameters. If two methods have different signatures, there is no overriding as both methods exist in the subtype. As in SQL:2006, the OVERRIDING keyword should be used when overriding a method. In Example 18.24, there is no overriding as the *Equals* method in *ColorPoint* has a different signature than the *Equals* method in *Point*. The *Equals* method in *ColorPoint* uses a *ColorPoint* argument whereas the *Equals* method in *Point* uses a *Point* argument. However, the *Print* method in *ColorPoint* overrides the *Print* method in *Point* as both methods have the same signature.

Example 18.24: *ColorPoint* Type in Oracle 11g
This example corresponds to Example 18.8 for SQL:2006.

```
CREATE TYPE ColorPoint UNDER Point
(Color INTEGER,
 MEMBER FUNCTION Brighten (Intensity INTEGER) RETURN
INTEGER,
   -- Increases color intensity
 MEMBER FUNCTION Equals (CP2 ColorPoint) RETURN BOOLEAN,
   -- Determines if 2 ColorPoints are equivalent
   -- No overriding: two Equals methods have
   -- different signatures.
OVERRIDING MEMBER PROCEDURE Print )
NOT FINAL
INSTANTIABLE;
```

Oracle 11g supports row types and typed tables similarly to SQL:2006, as depicted in Example 18.25. Like SQL:2006, Oracle 11g supports the ROW type and user-defined types for structuring subsets of columns. For example, in *AgentType*, the address attribute could use the ROW type instead of the user-defined *AddressType*. For the CREATE TABLE statement, Oracle 11g specifies object identifiers differently than SQL:2006. In Oracle 11g, the OBJECT IDENTIFIER clause defines an object identifier as system-generated or user-generated. System-generated object identifiers do not have a name as SQL:2006 requires. However, Oracle provides functions to manipulate system-generated object identifiers so a column name is not necessary.

Example 18.25: Oracle 11g Definition of *AddressType* and *AgentType* followed by the Typed *Agent* Table Based on *AgentType*
This example corresponds to Example 18.12 for SQL:2006.

```
CREATE TYPE AddressType AS OBJECT
( Street  VARCHAR(50),
  City    VARCHAR(30),
  State   CHAR(2),
  Zip     CHAR(9) )
NOT FINAL;

CREATE TYPE AgentType AS OBJECT
(AgentNo INTEGER,
 Name    VARCHAR(30),
 Address AddressType,
 Phone   CHAR(13),
 Email   VARCHAR(50) )
 NOT FINAL;

CREATE TABLE Agent OF AgentType
( CONSTRAINT AgentPK PRIMARY KEY(AgentNo) )
  OBJECT IDENTIFIER IS SYSTEM GENERATED ;
```

Oracle 11g supports reference types for columns similarly to SQL:2006 as depicted in Example 18.26. The usage of the SCOPE clause is somewhat different in Oracle 11g, however. In Oracle 11g, the SCOPE clause cannot be used in a user-defined type as it can in SQL:2006[47]. To compensate, you can define a referential integrity constraint to limit the scope of a reference as shown for the *Property* table in Example 18.26.

Example 18.26: Oracle 11g Definition of *PropertyType* with a Reference to *AgentType* and the Typed *Property* Table

This example corresponds to Example 18.13 for SQL:2006.

```
CREATE TYPE PropertyType AS OBJECT
(PropNo   INTEGER,
 Address AddressType,
 SqFt     INTEGER,
 AgentRef REF AgentType,
 Location Point )
   NOT FINAL
   INSTANTIABLE;

CREATE TABLE Property OF PropertyType
  ( CONSTRAINT PropertyPK PRIMARY KEY(PropNo),
    CONSTRAINT AgentRefFK FOREIGN KEY(AgentRef)
             REFERENCES Agent )
   OBJECT IDENTIFIER IS SYSTEM GENERATED ;
```

Example 18.27 shows the user-defined types for residential and industrial properties along with the table definitions. The constraint and object identifier clauses are repeated in the *Residential* and *Industrial* tables because Oracle 11g does not support subtables.

Example 18.27: CREATE TYPE and CREATE TABLE statements for residential and industrial properties

This example corresponds to Example 18.14 for SQL:2006.

```
CREATE TYPE AssessType AS VARRAY(6) OF DECIMAL(9,2);

CREATE TYPE ResidentialType UNDER PropertyType
(BedRooms   INTEGER,
 BathRooms INTEGER,
 Assessments AssessType )
   NOT FINAL
   INSTANTIABLE;

CREATE TABLE Residential OF ResidentialType
  (CONSTRAINT ResidentialPK PRIMARY KEY(PropNo),
   CONSTRAINT AgentRefFK1 FOREIGN KEY(AgentRef)
             REFERENCES Agent )
   OBJECT IDENTIFIER IS SYSTEM GENERATED ;

CREATE TYPE IndustrialType UNDER PropertyType
(Zoning   VARCHAR(20),
 AccessDesc VARCHAR(20),
 RailAvailable CHAR(1),
 Parking VARCHAR(10) )
   NOT FINAL
```

---

[47] The SCOPE clause can be used in a column definition of a CREATE TABLE statement. However, the table is no longer a typed table when using the SCOPE clause as part of a column definition.

```
        INSTANTIABLE;

        CREATE TABLE Industrial OF IndustrialType
        (CONSTRAINT IndustrialPK PRIMARY KEY(PropNo),
         CONSTRAINT AgentRefFK2 FOREIGN KEY(AgentRef)
                    REFERENCES Agent )
        OBJECT IDENTIFIER IS SYSTEM GENERATED ;
```

Example 18.27 also shows differences between the declaration of array columns in Oracle 11g and SQL:2006. In Oracle 11g, the VARRAY constructor cannot be used directly with columns of a table or attributes of a user-defined type. Instead, the VARRAY constructor must be used in a separate user-defined type as shown in the *AssessType* type in Example 18.27. In addition, Oracle 11g uses parentheses for the array size instead of the square brackets used in SQL:2006.

18.5.2 Using Typed Tables in Oracle 11g

We begin this section with manipulation statements to insert and modify objects in the typed tables. Example 18.28 demonstrates an INSERT statement using a type name for the structured *Address* column. If the *Address* column was defined with the ROW type constructor, the Oracle 11g syntax would be identical to Example 18.15 with the ROW keyword replacing *AddressType*.

Example 18.28: Inserting Two Rows into the typed Agent Table
This example corresponds to Example 18.16 for SQL:2006.

```
        INSERT INTO Agent
        (AgentNo, Name, Address, Email, Phone)
        VALUES (999999, 'Sue Smith',
          AddressType('123 Any Street', 'Denver', 'CO', '80217'),
          'sue.smith@anyisp.com', '13031234567');

        INSERT INTO Agent
        (AgentNo, Name, Address, Email, Phone)
        VALUES (999998, 'John Smith',
          AddressType('123 Big Street', 'Boulder', 'CO',
        '80217'),
          'john.smith@anyisp.com', '13034567123');
```

Because Oracle 11g does not support subtables, additional manipulation statements are used to simulate set inclusion among subtables. In Example 18.29, INSERT statements are used for both the parent table and subtable. Ideally, triggers could be defined to hide the additional manipulation statements.

Example 18.29: INSERT Statements to Add an Object into the *Property* and *Residential* Tables
This example corresponds to Example 18.17 for SQL:2006.

```
        INSERT INTO Residential
        (PropNo, Address, SqFt, AgentRef, BedRooms, BathRooms,
        Assessments)
        SELECT 999999, AddressType('123 Any Street', 'Denver', 'CO',
            '80217'), 2000, REF(A), 3, 2, AssessType(190000, 200000)
        FROM Agent A
        WHERE AgentNo = 999999;

        -- This INSERT statement maintains set inclusion between the
        Property
        -- and the Residential tables.
        INSERT INTO Property
        (PropNo, Address, SqFt, AgentRef)
        SELECT 999999, AddressType('123 Any Street', 'Denver', 'CO',
                '80217'), 2000, REF(A)
        FROM Agent A
        WHERE AgentNo = 999999;
```

Example 18.29 also demonstrates the REF function to obtain a system-generated object identifier. When using the REF function, you must use a correlation variable (table alias) as the parameter. You cannot use the table name instead of the correlation variable. The REF statement can also be used in UPDATE statements, as demonstrated in Example 18.30.

Example 18.30: Using a SELECT statement with the REF Function to Retrieve the Object Identifier of the Related *Agent* Row

This example corresponds to Example 18.18 for SQL:2006.

```
UPDATE Residential
  SET AgentRef =
    ( SELECT REF(A) FROM Agent A WHERE AgentNo = 999998 )
  WHERE PropNo = 999999;

-- Maintain consistency between the Property and
Residential tables.
UPDATE Property
  SET AgentRef =
    ( SELECT REF(A) FROM Agent A WHERE AgentNo = 999998 )
  WHERE PropNo = 999999;
```

Oracle 11g supports path expressions containing the dot operator and the DEREF function. The DEREF function can also be used in SQL:2006 in place of the -> operator. The DEREF function uses an object identifier as a parameter as shown in Example 18.31. When using columns that have an object type such as *Address*, a correlation variable must be used.

Example 18.31: Oracle 11g SELECT Statement with Path Expressions Containing the Dot Operator and the DEREF Function

This example corresponds to Example 18.19 for SQL:2006.

```
SELECT PropNo, P.Address.City,
DEREF(AgentRef).Address.City
  FROM Property P
  WHERE DEREF(AgentRef).Name = 'John Smith';
```

Although Oracle 11g supports the DEREF function, it does not seem necessary to use it. The dot operator can be used in path expressions even when a column has a reference type as shown in Example 18.32. Note that a correlation variable is necessary when using REF columns in a path expression with the dot operator.

Example 18.32: Oracle 11g SELECT Statement with Path Expressions Containing the Dot Operator Instead of the DEREF Function

This example corresponds to Example 18.19 for SQL:2006.

```
SELECT PropNo, P.Address.City, P.AgentRef.Address.City
  FROM Property P
  WHERE P.AgentRef.Name = 'John Smith';
```

Like SQL:2006, Oracle 11g supports the ONLY keyword in the FROM clause. However, the ONLY keyword applies to views not tables in Oracle 11g. Thus, Example 18.20 will not work in Oracle 11g unless object views are used instead of tables.

In place of testing subtable membership, Oracle supports testing the associated type using the IS OF operator. In some situations, the IS OF operator can provide a capability similar to subtable membership testing in SQL:2006. Example 18.33 demonstrates the IS OF operator to test membership in a subtype. The REF operator converts the object type into a reference and the DEREF operator converts a reference into a value so that its type can be tested using the IS OF operator. Example 18.33 does not produce the same result as Example 18.20 because the *Property* rows were not inserted using the *ResidentialType* type. The Oracle syntax for using subtypes does not cover INSERT statements such as Example 18.29 involving reference types.

Example 18.33: Using IS OF to Test Type Membership of a Reference Type.
This example does not produce the same result as Example 18.20 for SQL:2006.

```
SELECT PropNo, Address, Location
 FROM Property P
 WHERE Sqft > 1500 AND DEREF(REF(P)) IS OF
(ResidentialType)
```

The VALUE function takes a correlation variable as a parameter and returns instances of the object table associated with the correlation variable. Thus, the VALUE function can be used to retrieve all columns from typed tables instead of using the * for untyped tables, as shown in Example 18.34[48].

Example 18.34: Using the VALUE Function to Retrieve all Columns from a Typed Table
```
SELECT VALUE(A) FROM Agent A;
```

18.5.3 Dependencies among Types and Typed Tables

Object relational representations involve additional dependencies beyond traditional table designs. User defined types can be referenced in typed tables, columns, and other user defined types. A typed table references its associated type. An attribute or column definition references its associated user-defined type. A subtype references its associated parent type. Figure 18.10 depicts a dependency diagram with subtype references, column usage of types, typed table references, and foreign key references for the objects in the property database.

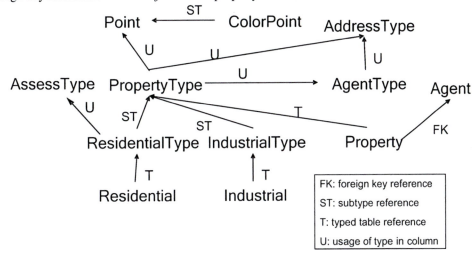

Figure 18.10: Dependency Diagram for the Property Database Objects

The usage of user defined types and typed tables introduce dependencies that must be respected when creating and dropping database objects. When creating objects, referenced objects should be created before referencing objects. Thus, a parent type should be created before its related subtypes, a type should be created before columns that reference it, and a type should be created before it is referenced in table definitions. When dropping objects, referencing objects should be dropped before the referenced object. Thus, a subtype should be dropped before its

---

[48] In early versions of Oracle 10g, the statement in Example 18.33 caused an error message because the VALUE function did not work on tables based on nonfinal types. This error has been corrected in the latest versions of 10g and 11g.

related parent type, a column should be dropped before its related type, and a typed table should be dropped before its related type.

Object orders (list of object names) that respect dependencies are known as topological orders. A topology is a structure with relationships such as a dependency diagram. There are usually many possible orderings that preserve object dependencies. Table 18-3 lists orders consistent with the dependency diagram in Figure 18.10 for CREATE and DROP statements. For CREATE statements, a topological order moves from the top of the diagram to the bottom. For DROP statements, a topological order moves from the bottom of the diagram to the top.

Table 18-3: Topological Orders for the Property Database Objects

SQL Statement Type	Sample Object Ordering
CREATE	Point, ColorPoint, AddressType, AgentType, PropertyType, AssessType, IndustrialType, ResidentialType, Agent, Property, Residential, Industrial
DROP	Residential, Industrial, Property, Agent, ResidentialType, IndustrialType, PropertyType, AssessType, AgentType, AddressType, ColorPoint, Point

18.5.4 Other Object Features in Oracle 11g

Oracle 11g provides additional object features, some of which extend object features in SQL:2006. Type substitutability and object views provide limited alternatives for subtables. The TABLE collection type corresponding to the multiset type of SQL:2006 supports nested tables. Oracle XML DB provides efficient storage and manipulation of large repositories of XML documents. This section provides an overview of these object features. For more details about these object features, you should consult the Oracle 11g online documentation.

Type Substitution and Object Views

The Oracle 11g documentation suggests the use of type substitutability to manage extents of parent tables and related subtables. Type substitutability means that a column or row defined to be of type X can contain instances of X and any of its subtypes. When using type substitutability to support subtables, user-defined types are defined with subtype relationships, but only one typed table (the root table) is defined. All manipulation operations are performed on the root table using type substitution for set inclusion relationships. However, the syntax for using reference types and subtype columns in manipulation statements is not clear. Certain INSERT and UPDATE statements do not work with substituted types. For managing set inclusion relationships, type substitution does not support overlapping subtypes. Thus, type substitutability does not provide a satisfactory solution for subtable families due to limited syntax and incomplete support for set inclusion relationships.

The Oracle 11g documentation also suggests the use of object view hierarchies to manage extents of parent tables and related subtables. An object view is a virtual object table in which each row in the view is an object rather than a table row. An object view hierarchy is a set of object views each of which is based on a different type in a type hierarchy. Unlike subtable families, several storage models are possible to store object view hierarchies. The database administrator must choose the best storage model and ensure that users understand usage of object views in retrieval and manipulation statements. Although object view hierarchies may be useful, they do not provide a satisfactory substitute for subtable families because the DBMS does not manage extents of related tables.

Nested Tables

Oracle 11g provides extensive support for multiple levels of nested tables corresponding to the multiset feature of SQL:2006. As previously stated, the usage of nested tables is not clear for business databases. Until theory and practice provide more insight, nested table usage will be for specialized situations. To indicate the features for nested tables, the following list summarizes Oracle support for nested tables:

- The TABLE and NESTED TABLE type constructors support CREATE TABLE statements with nested tables. A user-defined type can be specified with the TABLE constructor and then used in a CREATE TABLE statement using the NESTED TABLE constructor.
- Columns with nested table types can appear in query results. The TABLE operator flattens nested tables if a user wants to see flat rather than nested results.
- Comparison operators support equality, subset, and membership comparisons among nested tables.
- Set operators support union, intersection, and difference operations on nested tables as well as duplicate removal and nested table cardinality.
- Object views support multiple levels of nested tables.

The strongest case for nested tables is support for XML documents. XML documents have a hierarchical structure, fitting with the representation of nested tables. However, the SQL:2006 standard and most enterprise DBMS products provide a separate collection of tools for XML document support as presented in the last part of this section.

XML Document Support

The eXtensible Markup Language (XML) has emerged as a foundation for electronic business for consumers and organizations. XML is a meta language that supports the specification of other languages. To restrict XML documents, XML schemas can be defined. An XML schema specifies the structure, content, and meaning of a set of XML documents. XML schemas support improved data interchange, Internet searching, and data quality. Many application domains have developed XML schemas as an essential element of electronic commerce.

As a result of the growing importance of XML, support for storage and manipulation of XML documents has become a priority for DBMSs. Part 14 of SQL:2006 is devoted to XML document storage and manipulation. Oracle and other commercial DBMS vendors have devoted large amounts of research and development to supporting the Part 14 specification and additional features. The most prominent feature is a new XML data type that most major DBMS vendors support as a prebuilt data type. To provide insight about the extensive XML support available in commercial DBMSs, the following list summarizes features in Oracle XML DB.

- The XMLType data type allows XML documents to be stored as tables and columns of a table.
- Variables in PL/SQL procedures and functions can use the XMLType data type. An application programming interface for XMLType supports a full range of operations on XML documents.
- XML documents can be stored in a structured format using the XMLType data type or in an unstructured format using the CLOB type. Storage as XMLType data allows indexing and specialized query optimization.
- XML schema support applies to both XML documents and relational tables. Oracle can enforce constraints in an XML schema on both tables and XML documents stored in a database.
- XML/SQL duality allows the same data to be manipulated as tables and XML documents. Relational data can be converted into XML and displayed as HTML. XML documents can be converted into relational data.
- Oracle supports the majority of XML operators in the SQL:2006 standard. In particular, Oracle supports the XML traversal operators existsNode(), extract(), extractValue(), updateXML(), and XMLSequence() operators in the SQL/XML standard.
- Query rewrite transforms operations that traverse XML documents into standard SQL statements. The Oracle query optimizer processes the rewritten SQL statement in the same manner as other SQL statements.

The remainder of this section depicts the basic syntax of the XMLType data type to demonstrate integration of relational databases with hierarchical XML documents. Examples 18.35 and 18.36 demonstrate usage of XMLType for XMLType columns as well as XMLType tables. Examples 18.37 and 18.38 demonstrate insertion of a row into the *AccountXML1* and

AccountXML2 tables. XMLType values are internally stored using the CLOB (Character Large Object) data type.

Example 18.35: Creating a Table with an XMLType Column
```
CREATE TABLE AccountXML1 (
AcctId       INTEGER   PRIMARY KEY,
AcctDetails  XMLType,
AcctBal      NUMBER(9,2) );
```

Example 18.36: Creating a Table of XMLType
```
CREATE TABLE AccountXML2 OF XMLType;
```

Example 18.37: Inserting a Row into a Table with an XMLType Column
```
INSERT INTO AccountXML1 VALUES (1,
    '<Account>
     <AcctFName>John</AcctFName>
     <AcctLName>Smith</AcctLName>
     <AcctStreet>1234567 Quebec St.</AcctStreet>
     <AcctCity>Denver</AcctCity>
     <AcctState>CO</AcctState>
     <AcctZip>80237</AcctZip>
    </Account>',
   1000);
```

Example 18.38: Inserting a Row into a Table of XMLType
```
INSERT INTO AccountXML2 VALUES (
    '<Account>
     <AcctFName>John</AcctFName>
     <AcctLName>Smith</AcctLName>
     <AcctStreet>1234567 Quebec St.</AcctStreet>
     <AcctCity>Denver</AcctCity>
     <AcctState>CO</AcctState>
     <AcctZip>80237</AcctZip>
    </Account>' );
```

Oracle implements the standard XQuery language using XPath expressions to retrieve data from an XML document. XPath represents an XML document as a tree of nodes. An XPath expression is evaluated to yield an object, which is either a node-set (an unordered collection of nodes without duplicates) or a leaf node value (Boolean, number, or string). The existsNode(), extract(), and extractValue() functions use an XPath expression to retrieve data in an XML document. The existsNode() function is used in a WHERE clause to test the existence of a node in an XML document. The extract() function returns nodes that match its XPath expression. The extractValue() function takes an XPath expression and returns the corresponding leaf node value. Examples 18.39 to 18.41 demonstrate usage of the existsNode(), extract(), and extractValue() functions as applied to XMLType columns. Example 18.42 depicts retrieval of the CLOB rows from an XMLType table.

Example 18.39: Selecting the number of rows with a WHERE condition
This example uses the existsNode() function that returns 1 if the node is found in the XPath expression.

```
SELECT  COUNT(*)
 FROM  AccountXML1
 WHERE existsNode(AcctDetails, '/Account/AcctFName') = 1;
```

Example 18.40: Selecting a row using the extractValue() function
```
SELECT  extractValue(AcctDetails, '/Account/AcctStreet')
"Street"
 FROM  AccountXML1
 WHERE extractValue(AcctDetails, '/Account/AcctStreet')
       LIKE '%St%';
```

Example 18.41: Selecting a row using the existsNode() and extractValue() functions
The existsNode() function uses a condition as part of the XPath expression.
```
SELECT  extractValue(AcctDetails, '/Account/AcctCity')
 FROM  AccountXML1
 WHERE existsNode(AcctDetails,
       '/Account[AcctZip="80237"]') = 1;
```

Example 18.42: Retrieving rows from an XMLType table
The result is identical to retrieving all columns using the * in place of the getClobVal() function.
```
SELECT a.getClobVal() FROM AccountXML2 a;
```

Oracle also supports an alternative XQuery notation for retrieval known as FLWOR (pronounced flower; acronym incorporates the five main clauses of For, Let, Where, Order By, and Return). The FLWOR notation is somewhat similar to the SQL SELECT statement with the FLWOR for clause corresponding to the SQL FROM clause, the FLWOR where clause corresponding to the SQL WHERE clause, the FLWOR order by clause corresponding to the SQL ORDER BY clause, and the FLWOR return clause corresponding to the SQL SELECT clause. Example 18.43 demonstrates a simple example to retrieve first names of Denver accounts.

Example 18.43: Retrieving Rows Using the FLWOR Notation
```
SELECT AcctId, XMLQuery(
'for $i in /Account
 where $i /AcctCity = "Denver"
 order by $i/AcctFName
 return $i/AcctFName'
passing by value AcctDetails
RETURNING CONTENT) XMLData
FROM AccountXML1;
```

Closing Thoughts

This chapter has described the motivation, principles, and architectures of object DBMSs. Object database technology is driven by demands to integrate complex and simple data and software productivity problems due to type mismatches between DBMSs and programming languages. Three principles of object-oriented computing, encapsulation, inheritance, and polymorphism were explained and related to object DBMS development. Encapsulation, the hiding of implementation details, supports data independence. Encapsulation is often relaxed for DBMSs to allow ad hoc queries. Inheritance, the sharing of code and data, supports software reusability. Polymorphism, the allowance of multiple implementations for procedures, permits incremental modification and a smaller vocabulary of procedures.

Because of the variety of ways to implement the object-oriented principles and the difficulty of implementation, a number of object DBMS architectures are commercially available. This chapter described five architectures and discussed their advantages and disadvantages. The first two architectures do not fully support the object-oriented principles as they involve simple schemes to store large objects and invoke specialized servers outside of a DBMS. The last three architectures provide different paths to implement the object-oriented principles. The architectures differ primarily on the level of integration with a DBMS. Object database middleware involves the least integration with a DBMS but provides the widest scope of complex data. Object-relational DBMSs contain an object query processor on top of a relational kernel. Object-oriented DBMSs contain both an object query processor and an object kernel. With the growing acceptance of the object-relational features in SQL:2006, the marketplace is strongly favoring the object-relational approach.

To provide a more concrete view of object databases, this chapter presented the object database definition and manipulation features of SQL:2006. Uuser-defined types support new kinds of complex data. Expressions in queries can reference columns based on user-defined types and use methods of user-defined types. SQL:2006 supports inheritance and polymorphism for user-defined types as well as set inclusion relationships for subtable families. Due to the complexity of SQL:2006, there are few DBMSs that support enhanced conformance of the standard. Object-relational features of Oracle 11g were presented to demonstrate the implementation of many SQL:2006 object features.

Review Concepts

- Examples of complex data that can be stored in digital format
- Use of complex data as a motivation for object database technology
- Type mismatches as a motivation for object database technology
- Encapsulation as a kind of data independence
- Relaxing encapsulation to support ad hoc queries
- Inheritance as a way to share code and data
- Polymorphism to reduce the vocabulary of procedures and allow incremental sharing of code
- Difference between static and dynamic binding
- Strong type checking to eliminate incompatibility errors in expressions
- Reasons for a variety of object database management architectures
- Level of integration with a DBMS for each object database management architecture
- Characteristics of each object database management architecture
- Reasons for lack of success of ODMG-compliant DBMSs
- User-defined types in SQL:2006 for defining complex data and operations
- Subtable families in SQL:2006: inheritance and set inclusion
- Relationship of subtable families and user-defined types
- Use of the SQL:2006 row type and reference type in object tables
- Use of path expressions and the dereference operator ($\rightarrow$) in SQL:2006 SELECT statements
- Referencing subtables in SELECT statements
- Defining and using user-defined types and typed tables in Oracle 11g
- Differences in object features between Oracle 11g and SQL:2006
- XMLType data type to store XML documents in columns and rows
- XQuery functions and notation for manipulating XML documents in a SELECT statement

Questions

1. How does the use of complex data drive the need for object database technology?
2. What problems are caused by mismatches between the types provided by a DBMS and a programming language?
3. Present an example application that uses both simple and complex data. Use a different application than discussed in Section 18.1.3.
4. Define encapsulation. How does encapsulation support the goal of data independence?
5. How do object DBMSs relax encapsulation? Why is encapsulation relaxed? What is the role of database security control as a substitute for encapsulation?
6. Define inheritance. What are the benefits of inheritance?
7. Define polymorphism. What are the benefits of polymorphism?
8. What is strong type checking? Why is strong type checking important?
9. What is the difference between static and dynamic binding?
10. Which implementation of object-oriented principles occurred first: object-oriented programming languages or object DBMSs?

11. Compare the emphasis in object-oriented programming languages to object DBMSs.
12. Discuss the reasons that multiple object DBMS architectures have been developed.
13. Discuss the benefits and limitations of storing large objects in the database. Why is external software needed when large objects are stored in a database?
14. Discuss the benefits and the limitations of using specialized media servers.
15. Discuss the benefits and the limitations of using object database middleware. Why does object database middleware support the broadest range of complex data?
16. Discuss the benefits and the limitations of using an object-relational DBMS. What changes are made to the query processor of a relational DBMS to convert it into an object-relational DBMS?
17. Discuss the benefits and the limitations of using an object-oriented DBMS. How does an object-oriented DBMS differ from an object-relational DBMS?
18. What is the status of the ODMG standard and ODMG compliant DBMSs?
19. Which object DBMS architecture do you think will dominate in five years?
20. What is a persistent object? What is the difference between a persistent object and a temporary object?
21. Why are there two standard languages for object DBMSs?
22. What are the components of a user-defined type in SQL:2006?
23. What are the differences between SQL:2006 methods, functions, and procedures?
24. How are SQL:2006 user-defined types used in table definitions and expressions?
25. What is a row type? How are row types used in SQL:2006 table definitions?
26. Explain the differences in encapsulation for user-defined types versus typed tables in SQL:2006.
27. What is a typed table?
28. How do you define a subtable?
29. Discuss the relationship of subtable families and set inclusion.
30. What side effects occur when a row is inserted in a subtable?
31. What side effects occur when a subtable row is updated?
32. What side effects occur when a subtable row is deleted?
33. What is the difference between a foreign key and a reference?
34. When should you use a SELECT statement as part of an INSERT statement when adding objects to a typed table?
35. What is the difference in notation between combining tables that are linked by a foreign key versus a column with a reference type?
36. What is a path expression? When do you use a path expression?
37. When do you need to use the dereference operator ($\rightarrow$) in a path expression?
38. What is the purpose of the ONLY keyword in a SQL:2006 SELECT statement?
39. Compare and contrast methods in SQL:2006 with methods in Oracle 11g.
40. What are criteria for overriding a method in Oracle 11g?
41. What is the most significant limitation for object databases in Oracle 11g as compared to SQL:2006?
42. Briefly discuss the importance of object features in Oracle 11g that are not part of SQL:2006.
43. What is minimal conformance for SQL:2006?
44. What is enhanced conformance for SQL:2006?
45. Briefly discuss the state of conformance testing for SQL:2006.
46. In SQL:2006, what is the difference between the ARRAY and MULTISET collection types?
47. What are the Oracle 11g counterparts of the SQL:2006 collection types?
48. What is the role of nested tables in table design and database application development?
49. What are common prebuilt user-defined data types that are commercially available in enterprise DBMSs?
50. What is a package in the SQL:2006 standard?

51. Evaluate the usage of type substitution as a means of supporting subtable families in Oracle.
52. Evaluate the usage of object view hierarchies as a means of supporting subtable families in Oracle.
53. Evaluate the business case for nested tables.

Problems

The problems provide practice with using SQL:2006 and Oracle 11g to define user-defined types and typed tables as well as to use typed tables. Problems 1 to 26 involve SQL:2006 while problems 27 to 52 involve Oracle 11g. The problems involve the financial database as depicted in Figure 18.P1.

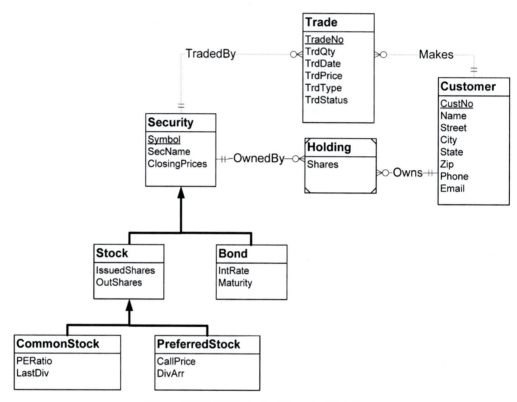

Figure 18.P1: ERD for the Financial Database

1. Using SQL:2006, define a user-defined type for a time series. The variables of a time series include an array of floating point values (maximum of 365), the begin date, the duration (maximum number of data points in the time series), the calendar type (personal or business), and the period (day, week, month, or year). Define methods as listed in Table 18-P1. You need to define the parameters for the methods, not the code to implement the methods. The *TimeSeries* parameter refers to the implicit *TimeSeries* object.

Table 18-P1: List of Methods for the TimeSeries Type

Name	Parameters	Result
WeeklyAvg	TimeSeries	TimeSeries
MonthlyAvg	TimeSeries	TimeSeries
YearlyAvg	TimeSeries	TimeSeries
MovingAvg	TimeSeries, Start Date, Number of Values	Float
RetrieveRange	TimeSeries, Start Date, Number of Values	TimeSeries

670

2. Using SQL:2006, define a security type and a typed security table. A security has fields for the unique symbol, the security name, and a time series of closing prices. Both the security type and table have no parent.

3. Using SQL:2006, define a stock type and a typed stock table. A stock has fields for the number of issued shares, the number of outstanding shares, and the time series of closing prices. The stock table inherits from the security table, and the stock type inherits from the security type.

4. Using SQL:2006, define a bond type and a typed bond table. A bond has fields for the interest rate and the maturity date. The bond table inherits from the security table, and the bond type inherits from the security type.

5. Using SQL:2006, define a common stock type and a typed common stock table. A common stock has fields for the price earnings ratio and the last dividend amount. The common stock table inherits from the stock table, and the common stock type inherits from the stock type.

6. Using SQL:2006, define a preferred stock type and a typed preferred stock table. A preferred stock has fields for the call price and dividend in arrears. The preferred stock table inherits from the stock table, and the preferred stock type inherits from the stock type.

7. Using SQL:2006, define a customer type and a typed customer table. A customer has fields for the unique customer number, the name, the address, the phone, and the e-mail address. The address field is a row type with fields for street, city, state, and zip. The phone field is a row type with fields for country code, area code, and local number. You should define types for the address and phone so that the types can be reused. Both the customer type and table have no parent.

8. Using SQL:2006, define a portfolio holding type and a typed portfolio holding table. A holding has fields for the customer (reference data type), the security (reference data type), and the shares held. The primary key of the Holding table is a combination of the CustNo field of the related customer and the Symbol field of the related security. Define referential integrity or SCOPE constraints to limit the range of the customer reference and the security reference. Both the holding type and table have no parent.

9. Using SQL:2006, define a trade type and a typed trade table. A trade has fields for the unique trade number, customer (reference data type), security (reference data type), trade date, quantity, unit price, type (buy or sell), and status (pending or complete). The primary key of the Trade table is the trade number. Define referential integrity or SCOPE constraints to limit the range of the customer reference and the security reference. Both the trade type and table have no parent.

10. Using SQL:2006, insert an object into the typed CommonStock table for Microsoft common stock.

11. Using SQL:2006, insert an object into the typed CommonStock table for Dell Corporation common stock.

12. Using SQL:2006, insert an object into the typed CommonStock table for IBM common stock. Enter a value in the closing prices (time series type) column by specifying the array of values, the period, the calendar type, the begin date, and the duration.

13. Using SQL:2006, insert an object into the typed Bond table for an IBM corporate bond.

14. Using SQL:2006, insert an object into the typed Customer table. Use 999999 as the customer number, John Smith as the customer name, and Denver as the city.

15. Using SQL:2006, insert an object into the typed Customer table. Use 999998 as the customer number and Sue Smith and Boulder as the city.

16. Using SQL:2006, insert an object into the typed Holding table. Connect the holding object to the Microsoft Security object and the Sue Smith Customer object. Use 200 as the number of shares held.

17. Using SQL:2006, insert an object into the typed Holding table. Connect the holding object to the IBM Security object and the Sue Smith Customer object. Use 100 as the number of shares held.

18. Using SQL:2006, insert an object into the typed Trade table. Connect the trade object to the IBM common stock object and the Sue Smith Customer object. Use 100 as the quantity of shares traded, "buy" as the trade type, and other values of your choice for the other columns.

19. Using SQL:2006, insert an object into the typed Trade table. Connect the trade object to the Microsoft common stock object and the Sue Smith Customer object. Use 200 as the quantity of shares traded, "buy" as the trade type, and other values of your choice for the other columns.

20. Using SQL:2006, insert an object into the typed Trade table. Connect the trade object to the IBM corporate bond object and the John Smith Customer object. Use 150 as the quantity of shares traded, "buy" as the trade type, and other values of your choice for the other columns.

21. Using SQL:2006, update the customer reference column of the Holding object from problem 17 to the John Smith Customer object.

22. Using SQL:2006, update the customer reference column of the Trade object from problem 19 to the John Smith Customer object.

23. Using SQL:2006, write a SELECT statement to list the securities held by Denver customers. Only list the securities with more than 100 shares held. Include the customer name, symbol, and shares held in the result.

24. Using SQL:2006, write a SELECT statement to list securities purchased by Boulder customers. Include the customer name, security symbol, trade number, trade date, trade quantity, and unit price in the result.

25. Using SQL:2006, write a SELECT statement to list the customer name, security symbol, and the closing prices for each stock held by Denver customers.

26. Using SQL:2006, write a SELECT statement to list the customer name, security symbol, trade number, trade date, trade quantity, and unit price for common stock purchases by Boulder customers.

27. Using Oracle 11g, define a user-defined type for a time series. The variables of a time series include an array of floating point values (maximum of 365), the begin date, the duration (maximum number of data points in the time series), the calendar type (personal or business), and the period (day, week, month, or year). Define methods as previously listed in Table 18-P1. You need to define the parameters for the methods, not the code to implement the methods. The TimeSeries parameter refers to the implicit TimeSeries object.

28. Using Oracle 11g, define a security type and a typed security table. A security has fields for the unique symbol, the security name, and a time series of closing prices. Both the Security type and table have no parent.

29. Using Oracle 11g, define a stock type and a typed stock table. A stock has fields for the number of issued shares and the number of outstanding shares. The Stock table inherits from the Security table, and the Stock type inherits from the Security type.

30. Using Oracle 11g, define a bond type and a typed bond table. A bond has fields for the interest rate and the maturity date. The Bond table inherits from the Security table, and the Bond type inherits from the Security type.

31. Using Oracle 11g, define a common stock type and a typed common stock table. A common stock has fields for the price earnings ratio and the last dividend amount. The common stock table inherits from the stock table, and the common stock type inherits from the stock type.

32. Using Oracle 11g, define a preferred stock type and a typed preferred stock table. A preferred stock has fields for the call price and dividend in arrears. The preferred stock table inherits from the stock table, and the preferred stock type inherits from the stock type.

33. Using Oracle 11g, define a customer type and a typed customer table. A customer has fields for the unique customer number, the name, the address, the phone, and the e-mail address. The address field is a row type with fields for street, city, state, and zip. The phone field is a row type with fields for country code, area code, and local number. You can define types for the address and phone so that the types can be reused. Both the Customer type and table have no parent.

34. Using Oracle 11g, define a portfolio holding type and a typed portfolio holding table. A holding has fields for the customer (reference data type), the security (reference data type), and the shares held. The primary key of the Holding table is a combination of the CustNo field of the related customer and the Symbol field of the related security. Define

referential integrity or SCOPE constraints to limit the range of the customer reference and the security reference. Both the Holding type and table have no parent.

35. Using Oracle 11g, define a trade type and a typed trade table. A trade has fields for the unique trade number, customer (reference data type), security (reference data type), trade date, quantity, unit price, type (buy or sell), and status (pending or complete). The primary key of the Trade table is the trade number. Define referential integrity or SCOPE constraints to limit the range of the customer reference and the security reference. Define CHECK constraints for the type and status columns. Both the trade type and table have no parent.

36. Using Oracle 11g, insert an object into the typed CommonStock table for Microsoft common stock. To manage subtables, you should also insert the same object into the typed Stock and Security tables.

37. Using Oracle 11g, insert an object into the typed CommonStock table for Dell Corporation common stock. To manage subtables, you should also insert the same object into the typed Stock and Security tables.

38. Using Oracle 11g, insert an object into the typed CommonStock table for IBM common stock. To manage subtables, you should also insert the same object into the typed Stock and Security tables. Enter a value in the closing prices (time-series type) column by specifying the array of values, the period, the calendar type, the begin date, and the duration.

39. Using Oracle 11g, insert an object into the typed Bond table for an IBM corporate bond.

40. Using Oracle 11g, insert an object into the typed Customer table. Use 999999 as the customer number, John Smith as the customer name, and Denver as the city.

41. Using Oracle 11g, insert an object into the typed Customer table. Use 999998 as the customer number, Sue Smith as the customer name, and Boulder as the city.

42. Using Oracle 11g, insert an object into the typed Holding table. Connect the holding object to the Microsoft Security object and the Sue Smith Customer object. Use 200 as the number of shares held.

43. Using Oracle 11g, insert an object into the typed Holding table. Connect the holding object to the IBM Security object and the Sue Smith Customer object. Use 100 as the number of shares held.

44. Using Oracle 11g, insert an object into the typed Trade table. Connect the trade object to the IBM common stock object and the Sue Smith Customer object. Use 100 as the quantity of shares traded, "buy" as the trade type, and other values of your choice for the other columns

45. Using Oracle 11g, insert an object into the typed Trade table. Connect the trade object to the Microsoft common stock object and the Sue Smith Customer object. Use 200 as the quantity of shares traded, "buy" as the trade type, and other values of your choice for the other columns.

46. Using Oracle 11g, insert an object into the typed Trade table. Connect the trade object to the IBM corporate bond object and the John Smith Customer object. Use 150 as the quantity of shares traded, "buy" as the trade type, and other values of your choice for the other columns.

47. Using Oracle 11g, update the customer reference column of the Holding object from problem 41 to the John Smith Customer object.

48. Using Oracle 11g, update the customer reference column of the Trade object from problem 44 to the John Smith Customer object.

49. Using Oracle 11g, write a SELECT statement to list the securities held by Denver customers. Only list the securities with more than 100 shares held. Include the customer name, the symbol, and the shares held in the result.

50. Using Oracle 11g, write a SELECT statement to list securities purchased by Boulder customers. Include the customer name, security symbol, trade number, trade date, trade quantity, and unit price in the result.

51. Using Oracle 11g, write a SELECT statement to list the customer name, security symbol, and the number of shares held for each stock held by Denver customers.

52. Using Oracle 11g, write a SELECT statement to list the customer name, security symbol, trade number, trade date, trade quantity, and unit price for common stock purchases by Boulder customers.

53. Write DROP statements in a topological order to delete the types and tables created in problems 27 to 52. You might want to create a dependency diagram to help you determine a topological ordering for object removal.
54. Change the order of the DROP statements in problem 53 to another topological order for object removal.

References for Further Study

This chapter has provided a detailed introduction to a broad and deep subject. For more details, you are encouraged to consult specialized books, articles, and websites. The most definitive sources about SQL:2006 are the standards documents available from the InterNational Committee for Information Technology Standards (www.incits.org). The Whitemarsh Information Systems Corporation (www.wiscorp.com) maintains key information about SQL standards. Because the standards documents are rather difficult to read, you may prefer the books about SQL:1999 by Gulutzan and Pelzer (1999) and Melton and Simon (2001). No books about SQL:2006 have appeared as of the completion date of this chapter (March 2008). For more details about object-relational features in Oracle 11g, you should consult the online database documentation in the Oracle technology network (www.oracle.com/technology).

Glossary

Access Plan: a tree that encodes decisions about file structures to access individual tables, the order of joining tables, and the algorithm to join tables. Access plans are generated by the optimization component to implement queries submitted by users.

Accumulating Fact Table: a fact table that records the status of multiple events rather than one event. Each event occurrence column can be represented by a foreign key to the time table along with a time of day column if needed.

ACID Properties: transaction properties supported by DBMSs. ACID is an acronym for atomic, consistent, isolated, and durable. Atomic means all or nothing. Consistent means that a database does not violate integrity constraints before or after a transaction commits. Isolated means that other transactions cannot see the updates made by a transaction until after the transaction terminates. Durable means that the effects of a transaction are permanent after committing even if a failure occurs.

Actions on Referenced Rows: possible actions in response to the deletion of a referenced row or the update of the primary key of a referenced row. The possible actions are restrict (do not permit the action on the referenced row), cascade (perform the same action on the related rows), nullify (set the foreign key of related rows to null), and default (set the foreign key of related rows to a default value). See also referenced rows.

Aggregate Function: a summary or statistical function. The standard aggregate functions in SQL are MIN, MAX, COUNT, SUM, and AVG.

Analyst/Programmer: an information system professional who is responsible for collecting requirements, designing applications, and implementing information systems. An analyst/programmer may create and use external views to develop forms, reports, and other parts of an information system.

Analytic Hierarchy Process: a decision theory technique to evaluate problems with multiple objectives. The Analytic Hierarchy Process supports the selection and evaluation process by allowing a systematic assignment of weights to requirements and scores to features of candidate DBMSs.

ANSI: American National Standards Institute, one of the groups responsible for SQL standards.

Application Profile: a statistical summary of the forms, reports, and queries that access a database. Application profiles are an important input of the physical database design phase because they are used to predict demand for the database.

Assertion: the most general kind of integrity constraint supported in SQL:2006. An assertion can involve a SELECT statement of arbitrary complexity. The CREATE ASSERTION statement defines assertions in SQL:2006.

Associative Entity Type: a weak entity that depends on two or more entity types for its primary key. An associative entity type with more than two identifying relationships is known as an M-way associative entity type. See also M-way relationship, identifying relationship, and weak entity.

Attribute: a property of an entity type or relationship. Each attribute has a data type defining allowable values and operations. Attribute is synonymous with field and column.

Authorization Rules: define authorized users, allowable operations, and accessible parts of a database. The database security system stores authorization rules and enforces them for each database access. Also known as security constraints.

Benchmark: a workload to evaluate the performance of a system or product. A good benchmark should be relevant, portable, scalable, and understandable.

BETWEEN-AND Operator: a shortcut operator to test a numeric or date column against a range of values. The BETWEEN-AND operator returns true if the column is greater than or equal to the first value and less than or equal to the second value.

Binary Large Object (BLOB): a data type for fields containing large binary data such as images. BLOB data can be retrieved but not displayed. The BLOB data type provides a simple way to extend a DBMS with object features. See also the Large Object Architecture.

Binding: in query optimization, binding refers to associating an access plan with an SQL statement. In object-oriented computing, binding refers to associating a method name with its implementation. Binding can be static (decided at compile-time) or dynamic (decided at run-time). Static binding is more efficient but sometimes less flexible than dynamic binding. See also access plan and message.

Bitmap Index: a secondary file structure consisting of a column value and a bitmap. A bitmap contains one bit position for each row of a referenced table. A bitmap column index references the rows containing the column value. A bitmap join index references the rows of a child table that join with rows of the parent table containing the column. Bitmap indices work well for stable columns with few values typical of tables in a data warehouse. See also star join.

Bottom-Up Data Warehouse Architecture: an architecture for a data warehouse in which data marts are built for user departments. If a need for an enterprise data model emerges, the data marts will evolve to a data warehouse. See also two-tier data warehouse architecture and three-tier data warehouse architecture.

Boyce-Codd Normal Form (BCNF): a table is in BCNF if every determinant is a candidate key. BCNF is a revised definition for 3NF.

Btree File: a popular file structure supported by most DBMSs because it provides good performance on both key search as well as sequential search. A Btree file is a balanced, multiway tree. The most popular variation of the Btree is the B+tree, in which all keys are redundantly stored in the leaf nodes. The B+tree provides improved performance on sequential and range searches. A Btree can be used as a primary or secondary file structure.

Buffer: an area in main memory containing physical database records transferred from disk.

Cache Coherence: a problem of parallel database processing using shared disk architectures. Cache coherence involves synchronization among local memories and common disk storage. After a processor addresses a disk page, the image of this page remains in the cache associated with the given processor. An inconsistency occurs if another processor has changed the page in its own buffer. See also shared disk architecture and clustered disk architecture.

Call-Level Interface (CLI): a language style for integrating a programming language with a nonprocedural language such as SQL. A CLI includes a set of procedures and a set of type definitions for manipulating the results of SQL statements in computer programs. The most widely used CLIs, the Open Database Connectivity (ODBC) supported by Microsoft and the Java Database Connectivity (JDBC) supported by Oracle, are compatible with the SQL:2006 CLI.

Candidate Key: a minimal superkey. A superkey is minimal if removing any columns makes it no longer unique.

Cardinality: a constraint on the number of entities participating in a relationship. In an entity relationship diagram, the minimum and the maximum number of entities are specified for both directions of a relationship.

CASE Tool: a tool to facilitate database and information systems development. CASE tools support features for drawing, analysis, prototyping, and data dictionary. CASE is an acronym for computer-aided software engineering.

Change Data: data from a source system that provides the basis to update a data warehouse. Change data comprises new source data (insertions) and modifications to existing source data (updates and deletions). Further, change data can affect fact tables and/or dimension tables. See also cooperative change data, logged change data, snapshot change data, and queryable change data.

Character Large Object (CLOB): a data type for columns containing large text data such as documents and Web pages. The CLOB data type provides a simple way to extend a DBMS with object features. See also the Large Object Architecture.

Checkpoint: the act of writing a checkpoint record to the log and force writing log and database buffers to disk. All transaction activity must cease while a checkpoint occurs. The checkpoint interval should be chosen to balance restart time with checkpoint overhead. A traditional checkpoint is known as a cache-consistent checkpoint. See also fuzzy checkpoint and incremental checkpoint.

Class: a collection of objects. A class definition includes variables for object data and methods for object procedures.

Client: a program that submits requests to a server such as accessing or updating a database.

Client-Server Architecture: an arrangement of components (clients and servers) among computers connected by a network. The client-server architecture supports efficient processing of messages (requests for service) between clients and servers.

Cluster: a tight coupling of two or more computers so that they behave as a single computer. Clusters provide additional flexibility for parallel database processing. See also clustered disk architecture and clustered nothing architecture.

Clustered Disk (CD) Architecture: an architecture for parallel database processing in which the processors in each cluster share all disks, but nothing is shared across clusters.

Clustered Nothing (CN) Architecture: an architecture for parallel database processing in which the processors in each cluster share no resources, but each cluster can be manipulated to work in parallel to perform a task.

Clustering Index: an index in which the order of the data records is close to the index order. A clustering index can be organized as a primary index or a secondary file structure. See also index selection, nonclustering index, primary file structure, and secondary file structure.

Collision: a condition involving insertions to a hash file. A collision occurs when two or more records hash to the same location. For each record, a hash function transforms the key value into an address. See also hash file.

Column: a field or attribute in a table. Each column has a data type defining allowable values and operations. Column is synonymous with field and attribute.

Combined Primary Key: a combination of columns (more than one) designated as the primary key. Also known as a composite primary key.

Completeness Constraint: a constraint about generalization hierarchies. A completeness constraint means that every entity in a supertype has a related entity in one of the subtypes. In other words, the union of the set of entities in the subtypes equals the set of entities in the supertype.

Conceptual Evaluation Process: the sequence of operations and intermediate tables used to derive the result of a SELECT statement. The evaluation process is conceptual because most SQL compilers will take many shortcuts to produce the result. The conceptual evaluation process may help you gain an initial understanding of the SELECT statement as well as help you to understand more difficult problems.

Conceptual Schema: a data description that covers all entities and relationships in a database. The conceptual schema is concerned with the meaning of the database, not its physical implementation. See also Schema, Internal Schema, External View, and Three Schema Architecture.

Concurrency Transparency: a service provided by a DBMS so that users perceive a database as a single-user system even though there may be many simultaneous users. The concurrency control manager is the component of a DBMS responsible for concurrency transparency.

Constellation Schema: a data modeling representation for multidimensional databases. In a relational database, a constellation schema contains multiple fact tables in the center related to dimension tables. Typically the fact tables share some dimension tables. See also snowflake schema, star schema, fact table, and dimension table.

Cooperative Change Data: data obtained from a source system for refreshing a data warehouse. Cooperative change data involves notification from a source system typically at transaction completion time using a trigger. See also logged change data, snapshot change data, and queryable change data.

Cross Product Style: a way to formulate joins in a SELECT statement. The cross product style lists the tables in the FROM clause and the join conditions in the WHERE clause.

CUBE Operator: an operator that augments the normal GROUP BY result with all combinations of subtotals. The SQL:2006 standard provides the CUBE operator as an extension of the GROUP BY clause to support multidimensional data. The CUBE operator is appropriate to summarize columns from multiple dimensions rather than columns representing different levels of a single dimension.

Cursor: a construct in a database programming language that allows storage and iteration through a set of records returned by a SELECT statement. A cursor is similar to a dynamic array in which the array size is determined by the size of the query result. A database programming language provides statements or procedures to declare cursors, open and close cursors, position cursors, and retrieve values from cursors.

Data Access Middleware: provide a uniform interface to relational and nonrelational data using SQL. Requests to access data from a DBMS are sent to a data access driver rather than directly to the DBMS. The data access driver converts the SQL statement into the SQL supported by the DBMS and then routes the request to the DBMS. The two leading data access middleware are the

Open Database Connectivity (ODBC) supported by Microsoft and the Java Database Connectivity (JDBC) supported by Oracle.

Data Administrator (DA): a management position that performs planning and policy setting for the information resources of an entire organization.

Data Cube: a multidimensional format in which cells contain numeric data called measures organized by subjects called dimensions. A data cube is sometimes known as a hypercube because conceptually it can have an unlimited number of dimensions.

Data Dictionary: a special database that describes individual databases and the database environment. The data dictionary contains data descriptors called metadata that define the source, the use, the value, and the meaning of data. See also metadata.

Data Independence: a database should have an identity separate from the applications (computer programs, forms, and reports) that use it. The separate identity allows the database definition to be changed without affecting related applications.

Data Mart: a subset or view of a data warehouse, typically at a department or functional level, that contains all the data required for decision support tasks of that department. In addition, a data mart insulates departmental users from data used by other departments. In some organizations, a data mart is a small data warehouse rather than a view of a larger data warehouse.

Data Mining: the process of discovering implicit patterns in data stored in a data warehouse and using those patterns for business advantage such as predicting future trends.

Data Model: a graphical model depicting the structure of a database. A data model contains entity types and relationships among entity types. See also environment interaction model and process model.

Data Type: defines a set of values and permissible operations on the values. Each column of a table is associated with a data type.

Data Warehouse: a central repository for summarized and integrated data from operational databases and external data sources.

Data Warehouse Maturity Model: a framework that provides guidance about investment decisions in data warehouse technology. The model consists of six stages (prenatal, infant, child, teenager, adult, and sage) in which business value increases as organizations progress to higher stages.

Database: a collection of persistent data that can be shared and interrelated.

Database Administrator (DBA): a support position that specializes in managing individual databases and DBMSs.

Database Management System (DBMS): a collection of components that support data acquisition, dissemination, maintenance, retrieval, and formatting. An enterprise DBMS supports databases that are critical to an organization. A desktop DBMS supports databases for small workgroups and small businesses. An embedded DBMS is part of a larger system such as a device or application. Embedded DBMSs provide limited features but have low memory, processing, and storage requirements.

Database Link: a key concept for Oracle distributed databases. A database link provides a one-way connection from a local database to a remote database. Database links allow a user to access another user's objects in a remote database without having an account on the remote site. When using a database link, a remote user is limited by the privilege set of the object owner.

Database Partitioning Feature (DPF): an IBM technology for parallel database processing. The DPF option of IBM's DB2 Enterprise Server Edition uses the clustered nothing architecture.

Database Programming Language: a procedural language with an interface to one or more DBMSs. The interface allows a program to combine procedural statements with nonprocedural database access. See also call-level interface and statement-level interface.

Database Security: protecting databases from unauthorized access and malicious destruction.

Datasheet: a way to display a table in which the column names appear in the first row and the body in the other rows. Datasheet is a Microsoft Access term.

Deadlock: a problem of mutual waiting that can occur when using locks. If a deadlock is not resolved, the involved transactions will wait forever.

Deferred Constraint Checking: enforcing integrity constraints at the end of a transaction rather than immediately after each manipulation statement. Complex constraints may benefit from deferred checking.

Deferred Update Approach: an approach used by a recovery manager to record database changes on disk. In this approach, database updates are written only after a transaction commits. To restore a database, only redo operations are used.

Denormalization: combining tables so that they are easier to query. Denormalization is the opposite of normalization. Denormalization can be useful to improve query performance or to ignore a dependency that does not cause significant storage anomalies.

Desktop DBMS: support databases used by work teams and small businesses. Desktop DBMSs are designed to run on personal computers and small servers. See also enterprise DBMS and embedded DBMS.

Detail Line: the innermost (most nested) line on a hierarchical report

Determinant: the column(s) appearing on the left-hand side of a functional dependency. Alternatively known as a LHS for left hand side.

Dice: a data cube operator in which a dimension is replaced by a subset of its values. See also slice.

Difference: an operator of relational algebra that combines rows from two tables. The difference operator extracts rows that belong to the first table only. Both tables must be union compatible to use the difference operator.

Dimension: a label or subject that organizes numeric data in a data cube. A dimension contains values known as members such as a location dimension having members for countries. Dimensions may be organized in hierarchies composed of levels to support the data cube operations of drill-down and roll-up. A dimension hierarchy may be ragged showing relationships among members of the same dimension level.

Dimension Table: a table in a star schema or snowflake schema that stores dimensions or subjects used to aggregate facts.

Discretionary Access Control: users are assigned access rights or privileges to specified parts of a database. Discretionary access control is the most common kind of security control supported by commercial DBMSs.

Disjointness Constraint: a constraint about generalization hierarchies. A disjointness constraint means that the subtypes do not share any common entities. In other words, the intersection of the sets of entities in the subtypes is empty.

Distributed Database: a database in which parts are located at different network sites. Distributed database technology supports local control of data, data sharing for requests involving data from more than one site, and reduced communication overhead. A distributed database is managed by a distributed DBMS.

Distributed DBMS: a collection of components that supports requests for data residing on multiple sites. A distributed DBMS finds remote data, optimizes global requests, and coordinates transactions at multiple sites. Also known as a distributed database management system (DDBMS).

Distributed Processing: allows geographically dispersed computers to cooperate when providing data access and other services. See also client-server architecture.

Divide: an operator of relational algebra that combines rows from two tables. The divide operator produces a table in which the values of a column from one input table are associated with all the values from a column of the second table.

Drill-Down: a data cube operator that supports navigation from a more general level of a dimension to a more specific level of a dimension. See also roll-up.

Embedded DBMS: resides in a larger system, either an application or a device such as a Personal Digital Assistant or smart card. Embedded DBMSs provide limited transaction processing features but have low memory, processing, and storage requirements. See also desktop DBMS and enterprise DBMS.

Embedded SQL: using SQL inside a host programming language such as COBOL or Visual Basic. Additional SQL statements that can be used only in a programming language cause other SQL statements to be executed and use database results inside the program. See also Standalone SQL.

Encapsulation: a principle of object-oriented computing in which an object can be accessed only through its interface. The internal details (variables and method implementations) cannot be accessed. Encapsulation supports lower software maintenance costs.

Encryption: involves the encoding of data to obscure their meaning. An encryption algorithm changes the original data (known as the plaintext). To decipher the data, the user supplies an encryption key to restore the encrypted data (known as the ciphertext) to its original (plaintext) format.

Enterprise Data Model (EDM): a conceptual data model of an organization. An enterprise data model can be used for data planning (what databases to develop) and decision support (how to integrate and transform operational databases and external data sources).

Enterprise DBMS: supports databases that are often critical to the functioning of an organization. Enterprise DBMSs usually run on powerful servers and have a high cost. See also desktop DBMS and embedded DBMS.

Entity: a cluster of data usually about a single topic that can be accessed together. An entity can denote a person, place, event, or thing.

Entity Integrity: a constraint involving primary keys. No two rows of a table can contain the same value for the primary key. In addition, no row can contain a null value for any columns of a primary key.

Entity Type: a collection of entities (persons, places, events, or things) of interest in an application, represented by a rectangle in an entity relationship diagram.

Environment Interaction Model: a graphical model showing the relationships between events and processes. An event such as the passage of time or an action from the environment can trigger a process to start or stop. See also data model and process model.

Equi-join: a join operator where the join condition involves equality. See also join and natural join.

ETL Tools: software tools for extraction, transformation, and loading of change data from data sources to a data warehouse. ETL tools eliminate the need to write custom coding for many data warehouse maintenance tasks.

Exact String Matching: searching for one string value using the equality comparison operator. See also Inexact String Matching.

Exclusive Lock: a lock that prevents other users from accessing a database item. Exclusive locks conflict with all other kinds of locks (shared, other exclusive locks, and intent). An exclusive lock indicates that a user will change the value of a database item. Also known as an X lock.

Existence Dependency: an entity that cannot exist unless another related entity exists. A mandatory relationship produces an existence dependency. See also mandatory relationship.

Explicit PL/SQL Cursor: a cursor that can be used in procedures written in PL/SQL, the database programming language of Oracle. An explicit cursor is declared with the CURSOR statement in the DECLARE section. Explicit cursors are usually manipulated by the OPEN, CLOSE, and FETCH statements. Explicit cursors can be referenced anyplace inside the BEGIN section. See also cursor and implicit PL/SQL cursors.

Expression: a combination of constants, column names, functions, and operators that produces a value. In conditions and result columns, expressions can be used in any place that column names appear.

Extended Cross Product: an operator of relational algebra that combines two tables. The extended cross product (product for short) operator builds a table from two tables consisting of all possible combinations of rows, one from each of the two input tables

Extent: an Oracle storage term. An extent is a collection of contiguous blocks in a file.

External View: a description of derived data appropriate for a given user group. Also known as external schema and view. See also Schema and Three Schema Architecture.

Fact Table: A table in a star schema or snowflake schema that stores numeric values of relevance to a decision maker. See also star schema and snowflake schema.

File: a collection of data on a permanent storage device such as a hard disk. The data or physical records on the file are organized to support efficient processing. Files are part of the internal schema of a database.

First Generation Database Technology: proprietary file structures and program interfaces that supported sequential and random searching. However, the user was required to write a computer program to access data. First generation database technology was largely developed during the 1960s.

FLWOR: an alternative notation in XQuery for manipulating XML documents. The FLWOR acronym (pronounced flower) incorporates five main clauses For, Let, Where, Order By, and Return. The FLWOR notation is somewhat similar to the SQL SELECT statement with the FLWOR for clause corresponding to the SQL FROM clause, the FLWOR where clause corresponding to the SQL WHERE clause, the FLWOR order by clause corresponding to the SQL

ORDER BY clause, and the FLWOR return clause corresponding to the SQL SELECT clause. See also XQuery and XPath.

Force Writing: the ability to control when data are transferred to nonvolatile storage. This ability is fundamental to recovery management. Force writing typically occurs at the end of transaction and checkpoint time.

Foreign Key: a column or combination of columns in which the values must match those of a candidate key. A foreign key must have the same data type as its associated candidate key. In the CREATE TABLE statement of SQL:2006, a foreign key must be associated with a primary key rather than merely a candidate key.

Form: a document used in a business process, formatted to provide a convenient way to enter and edit data. A form is designed to support a business task such as processing an order, registering for classes, or making an airline reservation.

Form Entity Type: in the form analysis process, the form entity type is derived from the primary key of the form. The form entity type should be placed in the center of the ERD.

Form Structure: a hierarchy depicting the relationship among form fields. A group of form fields is known as a node. Most forms have a simple structure with a parent node (main form) and a child node (subform).

Forward Engineering: the ability to generate definitions for a target database management system from an ERD and data dictionary properties. See also CASE tool and reverse engineering.

Fourth Generation Database Technology: extend the boundaries of database technology to unconventional data and the Internet. Fourth generation systems can store and manipulate unconventional data types such as images, videos, maps, sounds, and animations as well as provide Web access to databases. Fourth generation database technology was largely commercialized during the 1990s.

Fourth Normal Form (4NF): a table is in 4NF if it does not contain any nontrivial MVDs. A nontrivial MVD is an MVD that is not also an FD.

Fragment: a subset of a table that is allocated to sites. Fragments can be horizontal subsets (restrict operator), vertical subsets (project operator), derived horizontal subsets (semi-join operator), and combinations of these kinds of fragments. See also semi-join operator, fragmentation transparency, location transparency, and local mapping transparency.

Fragmentation Transparency: a level of data independence in distributed DBMSs in which queries can be formulated without knowledge of fragments. See location transparency and local mapping transparency.

Full Outer Join: an outer join that produces the matching rows of the join part as well as the non-matching rows from both tables.

Functional Dependency (FD): a constraint about two or more columns of a table. X determines Y $(X \rightarrow Y)$ if there exists at most one value of Y for every value of X. A functional dependency is similar to a candidate key constraint because if X and Y are placed in a separate table, X is a candidate key.

Fuzzy Checkpoint: an alternative to traditional cache-consistent checkpoints involving less overhead but may require more restart work. In a fuzzy checkpoint, the recovery manager only writes the buffer pages since the previous checkpoint. Most of these pages should have already been written to disk before the checkpoint. At restart time, the recovery manager uses the two most recent fuzzy checkpoint records in the log. See also checkpoint.

Generalization Hierarchy: a collection of entity types arranged in a hierarchical structure to show similarity in attributes. Each subtype or child entity represents a subset of its supertype or parent entity. See also supertype and subtype.

Group Condition: a comparison involving an aggregate function such as SUM or COUNT. Group conditions cannot be evaluated until after the GROUP BY clause is evaluated.

GROUPING SETS Operator: an operator in the GROUP BY clause that requires explicit specification of column combinations. The GROUPING SETS operator is appropriate when precise control over grouping is required. The SQL:2006 standard provides the GROUPING SETS operator as an extension of the GROUP BY clause to support multidimensional data.

Hash File: a specialized file structure that supports search by key. Hash files transform a key value into an address to provide fast access. Hash files may have poor performance for sequential access. A hash file may be static (requires periodic reorganization) or dynamic (does not require periodic reorganization). A hash structure may be used as a primary or a secondary file structure.

Hash Join: a join algorithm that uses an internal hash file for each table. The hash join algorithm can be used only for equi-joins. The hash join performs better than sort merge when the tables are not sorted or indexes do not exist. See also sort merge.

Hierarchical Form: a formatted window for data entry and display using a fixed (main form) and variable (subform) part. One record is shown in the main form and multiple, related records are shown in the subform.

Hierarchical Report: a formatted display of a query using indentation to show grouping and sorting. Also known as a control break report.

Histogram: a two-dimensional graph where the x-axis represents column ranges and the y-axis represents the number of rows containing the range of values. Histograms support more detailed distribution data than the uniform value assumption. Histograms are part of a table profile. A traditional or equal-width histogram has equal column value widths but a varying number of rows in each bar. An equal-height histogram has variable-size column ranges but approximately equal number of rows in each bar. Most DBMSs use equal-height histograms because the maximum and expected estimation error can be easily controlled by increasing the number of ranges.

HOLAP: an acronym for Hybrid On-Line Analytical Processing. HOLAP is an implementation approach that combines the MOLAP and the ROLAP storage engines. HOLAP involves both relational and multidimensional data storage as well as combining data from both relational and multidimensional sources for data cube operations. See also MOLAP and ROLAP.

Homonym: in view integration, a group of words that have the same sound and often the same spelling but have different meanings. Homonyms arise because of context of usage. See also synonym.

Hot Spot: common data that multiple users try to change simultaneously. Without adequate concurrency control, users may interfere with each other on hot spots. A system-independent hot spot does not depend on the details of a particular concurrency control manager. Typically, system-independent hot spots involve fields or rows in a database. A system-dependent hot spot depends on the details of the concurrency control manager, especially the locking granularity.

Hybrid Join: a join algorithm that combines the sort merge and nested loops algorithms. The outer table must be sorted or have a join column index. The inner table must have an index on the join column. This algorithm can only be used for equi-joins. The hybrid join performs better than the sort merge when the inner table has a nonclustering index on the join column. See also nested loops and sort merge.

HyperText Markup Language (HTML): the language in which most Web documents are written. HTML combines the structure, the content, and the layout of a document. See also XML and XSL.

Identification Dependency: involves a weak entity and one or more identifying relationships. See also weak entity and identifying relationship.

Identifying Relationship: a relationship that provides a component of the primary key to a weak entity. See also weak entity and identification dependency.

Immediate Update Approach: an approach used by a recovery manager to record database changes on disk. In this approach, database updates are written to the disk when they occur but after the corresponding log updates. To restore a database, both undo and redo operations may be needed. See also deferred update approach and write ahead log protocol.

Implicit PL/SQL Cursor: a cursor that can be used in procedures written in PL/SQL, the database programming language of Oracle. An implicit cursor is neither explicitly declared nor explicitly opened. Instead a special version of the FOR statement declares, opens, iterates, and closes a locally named SELECT statement. An implicit cursor cannot be referenced outside of the FOR statement in which it is declared. See also cursor and explicit PL/SQL cursors.

Incorrect Summary: a concurrency control problem in which a transaction reads several values, but another transaction updates some of the values while the first transaction is still executing. Also known as an inconsistent analysis.

Incremental Checkpoint: an alternative to traditional cache-consistent checkpoints involving less overhead but may require more restart work. In an incremental checkpoint, no database pages are written to disk. Instead, dirty database pages are periodically written to disk in ascending age order. At checkpoint time, the log position of the oldest dirty data page is recorded to provide a starting point for recovery. The amount of restart work can be controlled by the frequency of writing dirty data pages. See also checkpoint.

Incremental Integration: an approach to view integration where a partially integrated ERD is merged with the next view. To integrate *n* views, there are *n - 1* integration steps.

Index: a secondary file structure that provides an alternative path to the data. Indexes typically contain only key values, not the other fields in a logical record. Indexes may be organized as Btrees, hash structures, or bitmap structures. See also Btree file, hash file, bitmap index.

Index-Organized File: an Oracle file structure. An index-organized file is a BTree in which index nodes contain complete rows (key values and non key values). To ensure that an index-organized file is sufficiently bushy, Oracle uses overflow areas to store long rows separate associated index nodes.

Index Selection: for each table, select at most one clustering index and zero or more nonclustering indexes. In a clustering index, the order of the data records is close to the index order. In a nonclustering index, the order of the data records is unrelated to the index order. Index selection is an important subproblem of physical database design. Index selection usually chooses Btree indexes. Other kinds of indexes (hash and bitmap) also can be considered.

Indirect User: users who access a database through reports or data extracts rather than through their own initiative. See also parametric user and power user.

Inexact String Matching: searching for a pattern of strings rather than just one string. In SQL, inexact matching uses the LIKE operator and pattern-matching characters.

Information Life Cycle: the stages of information transformation in an organization. Typical stages of an information life cycle include acquisition, storage, protection, processing, formatting, dissemination, and usage.

Information Resource Dictionary (IRD): a database of metadata that describes the entire information systems life cycle. The information resource dictionary system manages access to an IRD. Also known as the repository.

Information Resource Management: a broad management philosophy that seeks to use information technology as a tool for processing, distributing, and integrating information throughout an organization.

Information System: a system that accepts data from its environment, processes the data, and produces output data for decision making. An information system consists of people, procedures, input data, output data, databases, software, and hardware.

Information Systems Planning: the process of developing enterprise models of data, processes, and organizational roles. Information systems planning evaluates existing systems, identifies opportunities to apply information technology for competitive advantage, and plans new systems. Also known as business systems planning, information systems engineering, and information systems architecture.

Inheritance: a data modeling feature that supports sharing of attributes between a supertype and a subtype. Subtypes inherit attributes from their supertypes. In SQL:2006, inheritance applies to both user-defined types and subtable families. Inheritance supports sharing of code and data among similar objects.

Integration Strategy: a mix of incremental and parallel approaches to integrate a set of views. The views are divided into subsets. For each subset of views, incremental integration is used. Parallel integration is usually applied to the ERDs resulting from integrating the view subsets.

Intent Lock: a lock on a large database item (such as a table) indicating intention to lock smaller items contained in the larger item. Intent locks alleviate blocking when locking coarse items and allow efficient detection of conflicts among locks on items of varying granularity.

Internal Schema: a description of the physical implementation of a database. See also schema, conceptual schema, external view, and Three Schema Architecture.

Internet: a global "network of networks" that is built from standard protocols.

Interrelated: a fundamental characteristic of databases. Interrelated means that data stored as separate units can be connected to provide a whole picture. To support the interrelated characteristic, databases contain clusters of data known as entities and relationships connecting entities.

Intersection: an operator of relational algebra that combines rows from two tables. The intersection operator finds rows that are common to both tables. Both tables must be union compatible to use the intersection operator.

Intranet: a collection of computers and communication devices using the TCP/IP protocol. For security reasons, computers in an intranet are usually not accessible from computers on the Internet.

ISO: International Standards Organization, one of the groups responsible for SQL standards.

Isolation Level: defines the degree to which a transaction is separated from actions of other transactions. A transaction designer can balance concurrency control overhead with interference problems prevented by specifying the appropriate isolation level.

Join: an operator of relational algebra used to combine rows from two tables. The join operator produces a table containing rows that match on a condition involving a column from each input table. See also equi-join and natural join.

Join Algorithm: an algorithm to implement the join operator. A query optimization component selects the least cost join algorithm for each join operation in a query. The common join algorithms are nested loops, sort-merge, hybrid join, hash join, and star join.

Join Operator Style: a way to formulate joins in a SELECT statement. The join operator style lists join operations in the FROM clause using the INNER JOIN and ON keywords.

Key Preserving Table: an Oracle term for the updatable table in a join view. A join view preserves a table if every candidate key of the table can be a candidate key of the join result table. This means that the rows of an updatable join view can be mapped in a 1-1 manner with each key preserved table. In a join involving a 1-M relationship, the child table could be key preserved because each child row is associated with at most one parent row.

Knowledge Management: applying information technology with human information processing capabilities and organization processes to support rapid adaptation to change.

Large Object Architecture: an architecture for object databases in which large objects (binary or text) are stored in a database along with external software to manipulate large objects.

Law of Transitivity: a rule that states if an object A is related to an object B and B is related to C, then one can conclude that A is related to C. Functional dependencies obey the law of transitivity. See also functional dependency and transitive dependency.

Load Balancing: a problem of parallel database processing. Load balancing involves the amount of work allocated to different processors in a cluster. Ideally, each processor has the same amount of work to fully utilize the cluster. The shared nothing architecture is most sensitive to load balancing because of the need for data partitioning. See also shared nothing architecture and clustered nothing architecture.

Load Time: the time when a data warehouse is updated.

Load Time Lag: the difference between transaction time and load time. Determining the load time lag is an important part of managing the refresh of a data warehouse. See also valid time lag.

Local Mapping Transparency: a level of data independence in distributed DBMSs in which queries can be formulated without knowledge of local formats. However, knowledge of fragments and fragment allocations is necessary. See also fragment, fragmentation transparency, and location transparency.

Location Transparency: a level of data independence in distributed DBMSs in which queries can be formulated without knowledge of locations. However, knowledge of fragments is necessary. See also fragments, fragmentation transparency, and local mapping transparency.

Lock: a fundamental tool of concurrency control. A lock on a database item prevents other transactions from performing conflicting actions on the same item. See also exclusive lock, intent lock, and shared lock.

Locking Granularity: the size of the database item locked. Locking granularity is a trade-off between waiting time (amount of concurrency permitted) and overhead (number of locks held).

Logged Change Data: data obtained from a source system for refreshing a data warehouse. Logged change data involves files that record changes or other user activity such as Web logs or transaction logs. See also cooperative change data, snapshot change data, and queryable change data.

Logical Expression: an expression resulting in a true or false (Boolean) value. Logical expressions can involve comparisons and the logical operators (AND, OR, NOT, etc.).

Lost Update: a concurrency control problem in which one user's update overwrites another user's update. See also scholar's lost update.

Main Form: the fixed part of a hierarchical form. The main form shows one record at a time.

Mandatory Access Control: a database security approach for highly sensitive and static databases. In mandatory control approaches, each object is assigned a classification level and each user is given a clearance level. A user can access a database element if the user's clearance level provides access to the classification level of the element.

Mandatory Relationship: a relationship with a minimum cardinality of one or more. A mandatory relationship produces an existence dependency on the entity type associated with the minimum cardinality of one. See also Optional Relationship and Existence Dependency.

Many-to-Many (M-N) Relationship: in the Entity Relationship Model, a relationship in which objects of each entity type can be related to many objects of the other entity type. M-N relationships have maximum cardinalities of more than one in each direction. In the Relational Model, two 1-M relationships and a linking or associative table represent an M-N relationship. See also one-to-many relationship and relationship.

Materialized View: a stored view that must be periodically synchronized with its source data. Relational DBMSs provide materialized views with summarized data for fast query response. See also query rewriting and view.

Message: a request to invoke a method on an object. When an object receives a message, it looks for an implementation in its own class. If an implementation cannot be found, the message is sent to the object's parent class. See also binding.

Message-Oriented Middleware: maintain a queue of messages. A client process can place a message on a queue and a server can remove a message from a queue. Message-oriented middleware support complex messages among clients and servers.

Metadata: data that describe other data including the source, use, value, and meaning of the data. See also data dictionary.

Middleware: a software component in a client-server architecture that performs process management. Middleware allows servers to process messages efficiently from a large number of clients. In addition, middleware can allow clients and servers to communicate across heterogeneous platforms. Prominent kinds of database middleware include transaction-processing monitors, message-oriented middleware, and object-request brokers.

Model Driven Architecture (MDA): an alternative to the information resource dictionary developed by the Object Management Group (OMG) in the early 2000s. The MDA provides an open specification that supports the formal modeling of all aspects of the software life cycle including business processes, software architectures, data warehousing, metadata repositories, tool integration and even the software development process itself. The MDA has not gained enough commercial acceptance to be considered an important standard.

Modification Anomaly: an unexpected side effect that occurs when changing the data in a table with excessive redundancies.

MOLAP: an acronym for Multidimensional On-Line Analytical Processing. MOLAP is a storage engine that directly stores and manipulates data cubes. MOLAP engines generally offer the best query performance but suffer from limitations in the size of data cubes supported.

Multiple-Tier Architecture: a client-server architecture with more than three layers: a PC client, a backend database server, an intervening middleware server, and application servers. The application servers perform business logic and manage specialized kinds of data such as images. See also two-tier architecture and three-tier architecture.

Multivalued Dependency (MVD): a constraint involving three columns. The MVD $A \rightarrow\rightarrow B \mid C$ (read A multi-determines B or C) means that (1) a given A value is associated with a collection of B and C values; and (2) B and C are independent given the relationships between A and B and A and C. All FDs are also MVDs, but not all MVDs are FDs. An MVD is nontrivial if it is also not an FD. See also relationship independence and functional dependency.

M-way (Multiway) Relationship: a relationship involving more than two entity types. In some ERD notations such as the Crow's Foot, an M-way relationship is represented as an M-way associative entity type. An M-way associative entity type has more than two identifying relationships.

Name Qualification: preceding a column name with its table name. The column name alone is an abbreviation. If the same column name occurs in two tables in an SQL statement, the column name must be qualified with its table name. The combination of the table name and column name must be unique across all tables in a database.

Natural Join: a variation of the join operator of relational algebra. In a natural join, the matching condition is equality (equi-join), one of the matching columns is discarded in the result table, and the join columns have the same unqualified names. See also equi-join and join.

Nested Loops: a join algorithm that uses an outer table and an inner table. The nested loops algorithm is the most general join algorithm as it can be used to evaluate all join operations, not just equi-joins. The nested loops algorithm performs well when there are few rows in the outer table or when all pages of the inner table fit into memory. An index on a foreign key join column allows efficient usage of the nested loops algorithm when there are restrictive conditions on the parent table. See also hash join and sort merge.

Nested Query: a query inside a query. In an SQL SELECT statement, a SELECT statement can be part of conditions in the HAVING and WHERE clauses. See Type I and Type II nested query for two variations. Also known as a subquery and an inner query.

Nested Table: a table inside another table. In object-relational databases, a column may have a table type to support definition of nested tables. Nested tables are useful at the application level especially for complex business rules involving stored procedures. At the table design level, the usage of nested tables is not clear for business databases. SQL:2006 supports nested tables using the MULTISET type with the ROW type for elements of a multiset. Oracle uses the TABLE and NESTED TABLE type constructors to support nested tables.

Node Key: a field(s) in a node of a form structure with unique values. The key of the root node is unique among all form instances. The key of a child node is unique within its parent node.

Nonclustering Index: an index in which the order of the data records is not related to the index order. A nonclustering index is always a secondary file structure. See also index selection, clustering index, and secondary file structure.

Nonmatching Row: a row that does not combine with a row from a second table to satisfy a join condition. The row will not be in the result of the join operation, but it will be in the result of an outer join operation.

Nonprocedural Database Language: a language such as SQL that allows you to specify what part of a database to access rather than to code a complex procedure. Nonprocedural languages do not include looping statements.

Nonrepeatable Read: a concurrency control problem in which a transaction reads the same value more than one time. In between reading the data item, another transaction modifies the data item.

Nontrivial MVD: an MVD that is not also an FD. By definition, every FD is an MVD. However, not all MVDs are FDs. MVDs in which a column is associated with more than one value of two columns, is a nontrivial MVD.

Normal Form: a rule about allowable dependencies.

Normalization: the process of removing redundancies from tables so that the tables are easier to change. To normalize a table, list the functional dependencies and make tables that satisfy a normal form, usually third normal form (3NF) or Boyce-Codd normal form (BCNF).

Null Value: a special value that represents the absence of an actual value. A null value can mean that the actual value is unknown or does not apply to the given row.

Object: an instance of a class in object-oriented computing. An object has a unique identifier that is invisible and nonchangeable.

Object Database Middleware: an architecture for object databases in which middleware manages complex data possibly stored outside of a database along with traditional data stored in a database.

Object-Oriented DBMS: a new kind of DBMS designed especially for objects. Object-oriented DBMSs have an object query processor and an object kernel. The Object Data Management Group (ODMG) provides the standard for object-oriented DBMSs. Commercially, the ODMG effort has been eclipsed by the object-relational standards in SQL:2006. Although the ODMG has been disbanded, the Object Management Group committed to a new object database standard in 2006 although no new standard has yet been produced.

Object-Relational DBMS: a relational DBMS extended with an object query processor for user-defined data types. SQL:2006 provides the standard for object relational DBMSs.

Object View Hierarchy: an Oracle feature to support subtable families. An object view is a virtual object table in which each row in the view is an object rather than a table row. An object view hierarchy is a set of object views each of which is based on a different type in a type hierarchy. Although object view hierarchies may be useful, they do not provide a satisfactory substitute for

686

subtable families because the DBMS does not manage extents of related tables. See also subtable family.

OLAP (Online Analytical Processing): general name of technology to support multidimensional databases. OLAP technology encompasses the multidimensional data model and implementation approaches.

One-Sided Outer Join: an outer join that produces the matching rows (the join part) as well as the nonmatching rows from only one of the tables, the designated input table.

One-to-Many (1-M) Relationship: in the Entity Relationship Model, a relationship in which the maximum cardinality is 1 in one direction and M in the other direction. In the Relational Data Model, a referential integrity constraint usually indicates a 1-M relationship. See also relationship and many to many relationship.

One-to-Many (1-M) Updatable Query: a type of updatable view in Microsoft Access involving one or more 1-M relationships.

Operational Database: a database to support the daily functions of an organization. Operational databases directly support major functions such as order processing, manufacturing, accounts payable, and product distribution.

Oper (Operational) Mart: a just-in-time data mart usually built from one operational database in anticipation or in response to major events such as disasters and new product introductions. An oper mart supports peak demand for reporting and business analysis that accompanies a major event. See also data mart.

Optimistic Concurrency Control: a concurrency control approach in which transactions are permitted to access a database without acquiring locks. Instead, the concurrency control manager checks whether a conflict has occurred. The check can be performed either just before a transaction commits or after each read and write. By reviewing the relative time of reads and writes, the concurrency control manager can determine whether a conflict has occurred. If a conflict occurs, the concurrency control manager issues a rollback and restarts the offending transaction.

Optional Relationship: a relationship with a minimum cardinality of zero. An optional relationship means that entities can be stored without participation in the relationship. See also Mandatory Relationship.

Oracle Real Application Cluster (RAC): an Oracle technology for parallel database processing. Oracle RAC uses the clustered disk architecture.

Outer Join: an operator of relational algebra that combines two tables. In an outer join, the matching and nonmatching rows are retained in the result. See one-sided and full outer join for two variations of this operator.

Overlapping Triggers: two or more triggers with the same timing, granularity, and applicable table. The triggers overlap if an SQL statement causes both triggers to fire. You should not depend on a particular firing order for overlapping triggers. See also trigger and trigger execution procedure.

Package: a PL/SQL unit of modularity. Packages support a larger unit of modularity than procedures or functions. A package may contain procedures, functions, exceptions, variables, constants, types, and cursors. By grouping related objects together, a package provides easier reuse than individual procedures and functions.

Parallel Database Management System (DBMS): a DBMS capable of utilizing tightly-coupled computing resources (processors, disks, and memory). Tight coupling is achieved by networks with data exchange time comparable to the time of the data exchange with a disk. Parallel database technology promises performance improvements and high availability but interoperability problems if not properly managed. See also speedup and scaleup.

Parallel Integration: an approach to view integration where all views are integrated in one step. To integrate *n* views, there are *n* view design steps and one integration step. The view design steps may be performed in parallel by separate design teams.

Parametric User: someone who uses a database by requesting existing forms or reports using parameters, input values that change from usage to usage. See also indirect user and power user.

PCTFREE: an Oracle storage parameter. The PCTFREE parameter indicates the minimum percentage of a data block preserved as free space for updates to rows. The PCTFREE parameter provides a high water mark as a block is marked as full for insertions when the PCTFREE limit is reached.

PCTUSED: an Oracle storage parameter. After reaching the PCTFREE limit, the PCTUSED parameter indicates the minimum percentage of a block that must be available before new rows are added to the block. Thus, the PCTUSED parameter acts as a low water mark in that a block is marked full until it falls to its PCTUSED limit.

Persistent: a fundamental characteristic of databases. Persistent means that data has a lifetime longer than the execution of a computer program. To be persistent, data must reside on stable storage such as magnetic disk.

Phantom Read Problem: a concurrency control problem in which a transaction executes a query with record conditions but another transaction inserts new rows or modifies existing rows while the first transaction is still executing. The first transaction then re-executes the original query again, but the results are different than the results for the first execution. The new rows are phantom because they did not exist for the first execution of the query.

Physical Record: collection of bytes that are transferred between volatile storage in main memory and stable storage on a disk. The number of physical record accesses is an important measure of database performance. Also known as a page or block.

Pivot: a data cube operator in which the dimensions in a data cube are rearranged. See also data cube.

Polymorphism: a principle of object-oriented computing in which a computing system has the ability to choose among multiple implementations of a method. The appropriate implementation is chosen by the system (object DBMS or object-oriented programming language). Polymorphism permits a smaller vocabulary of procedures and incremental sharing of code.

Power User: someone who uses a database by submitting unplanned or ad hoc requests for data. Power users should have a good understanding of nonprocedural access. See also indirect user and parametric user.

Primary Copy Protocol: a protocol for concurrency control of distributed transactions. Each replicated fragment is designated as either the primary copy or a secondary copy. During distributed transaction processing, only the primary copy is guaranteed to be current at the end of a transaction. Updates may be propagated to secondary copies after the end of a transaction.

Primary File Structure: a file structure storing both key data and nonkey data. Sequential files only can be file structures. Hash structures and Btrees can be primary or secondary file structures. See also secondary file structure.

Primary Key: a specially designated candidate key. The primary key for a table cannot contain null values.

Procedural Language Interface: a method to combine a nonprocedural language such as SQL with a programming language such as COBOL or Visual Basic. Embedded SQL is an example of a procedural language interface.

Process Model: a graphical model showing the relationships between processes. A process can provide input data used by other processes or use output data of other processes. The well-known data flow diagram is an example of a process model. See also data model and environment interaction model.

Project: an operator of relational algebra. A project operation retrieves a subset of specified columns of the input table. Duplicate rows are eliminated in the result if present.

Prototype: a fast implementation of an application in an information system. Prototypes can demonstrate forms, reports, and menus to enable feedback from users.

Query: request to extract useful data. Query formulation involves translating a problem into a language (such as an SQL SELECT statement) understood by a DBMS.

Query Binding: the process of associating a query with an access plan. Some DBMSs rebind automatically if a query changes or the database changes (file structures, table profiles, data types, etc.).

Query Rewriting: a substitution process in which a materialized view replaces references to fact and dimension tables in a query. In addition to performing the substitution, the query optimizer evaluates whether the substitution will improve performance over the original query. See also materialized view.

Queryable Change Data: data obtained from a source system for refreshing a data warehouse. Since queryable change data comes directly from a data source via a query, the data source must have timestamps. See also cooperative change data, logged change data, and snapshot change data.

RAID (Redundant Arrays of Independent Disks): a collection of disks (a disk array) that operates as a single disk. RAID storage supports parallel read and write operations with high reliability.

RAID-1: an architecture for RAID storage in which redundant arrays of disks provide high reliability and performance but with large storage overhead. RAID-1 uses disk mirroring to achieve high performance and reliability.

RAID-5: an architecture for RAID storage in which randomly located error-correcting pages provide high reliability without excessive storage overhead. RAID-5 uses striping to achieve good performance and reliability without excessive storage overhead.

Read-Only View: a view that can be used in SELECT statements but not in UPDATE, INSERT, and DELETE statements. All views are at least read-only.

Recovery Transparency: a service provided by a DBMS to automatically restore a database to a consistent state after a failure. The recovery manager is the component of a DBMS responsible for recovery transparency.

Referenced Row: a row of a parent table having a primary key value that is identical to the foreign key values of rows in a child table. See also actions on referenced rows.

Referential Integrity: an integrity constraint involving a candidate key in one table with the related foreign key of another table. Only two kinds of values can be stored in a foreign key: (1) a value matching a candidate key value in some row of the table containing the associated candidate key or (2) a null value. See also primary key, candidate key, and foreign key.

Refresh Constraint: a constraint on a data warehouse or a source system that limits the details of a refresh process. Refresh constraints can be classified as source access, integration, data warehouse availability, completeness/consistency.

Relation: synonymous with table. A term typically used in academic research about databases.

Relational Algebra: a set of operators to manipulate relational databases. Each operator uses one or two tables as input and produces a new table as output.

Relational Data Model: using tables, matching values for connections among tables, and table operators to represent a collection of data.

Relational DBMS: a system that uses the Relational Data Model to manage collections of data.

Relationship: in the Entity Relationship Model, a relationship is a named association among entity types. In the Relational Model, a relationship is a connection among tables shown by column values in one table that match column values in another table. Referential integrity constraints and foreign keys indicate relationships in the Relational Model. See also one-to-many relationship, many-to-many relationship, and referential integrity.

Relationship Cycle: a collection of relationships arranged in a loop starting and ending with the same entity type. You should examine relationship cycles to determine whether a relationship can be derived from other relationships.

Relationship Equivalence: a rule about the equivalence between 1-M and M-N relationships. An M-N relationship can be replaced by an associative entity type and two identifying 1-M relationships. See also associative entity type and identifying relationship.

Relationship Independence: a relationship that can be derived from two independent relationships.

Report: a stylized presentation of data appropriate to a selected audience. Reports enhance the appearance of data that are displayed or printed. See also hierarchical report.

Restrict: an operator of relational algebra. A restrict operation retrieves a subset of rows that satisfy a given condition.

Reverse Engineering: the ability to extract definitions from a target database management system and use the definitions to create an ERD and data dictionary properties. See also CASE tool and forward engineering.

ROLAP: an acronym for Relational On-Line Analytical Processing. ROLAP involves relational DBMS extensions to support multidimensional data. ROLAP engines support a variety of storage and optimization techniques for summary data retrieval.

Roll-Up: a data cube operator that supports navigation from a more specific level of a dimension to a more general level of a dimension. The roll-up operator requires a hierarchical dimension. See also drill-down.

ROLLUP Operator: an operator in the GROUP BY clause that augments the normal GROUP BY result with a partial set of subtotals. The SQL:2006 standard provides the CUBE operator as an extension of the GROUP BY clause to support multidimensional data. The ROLLUP operator is appropriate to summarize columns from the same dimension hierarchy.

Row Condition: a comparison not involving an aggregate function. Row conditions are evaluated in the WHERE clause.

Rules about Referenced Rows: rules that describe actions on related rows when a row in a primary key table (the referenced row) is deleted or its primary key is updated.

Save Point: an intermediate point in a transaction in which a rollback may occur. Save points are supported by proprietary SQL extensions and by the SQL:2006 standard.

Scaleup: in distributed database processing, scaleup involves the amount of work that can be accomplished by increasing computing capacity. Scaleup measures the increased size of the job which can be done while holding time constant. Scaleup is measured as the ratio of the amount of work completed with the original configuration to the amount of work completed with the larger configuration.

Schema: a definition of the conceptual, external, or internal parts of a database. At the conceptual level, a schema is a diagram depicting the entities and relationships in a database. See also the Three Schema Architecture, external view, conceptual schema, and internal schema.

Schema Mapping: describes how a schema at a higher level is derived from a schema at a lower level. A mapping provides the knowledge to convert a request from a higher schema representation to a lower schema representation. See also Three Schema Architecture and schema.

Scholar's Lost Update: a variation of the lost update problem. The word *scholar* is ironic in that the scholar's lost update problem differs only slightly from the traditional lost update problem. The only essential difference between the scholar's lost update problem and the traditional lost update problem is that transaction A commits before transaction B changes the common data. See also lost update.

Second Generation Database Technology: the first true DBMSs that managed multiple entity types and relationships. However, to obtain access to data, a computer program still had to be written. Second generation database technology was largely developed during the 1970s.

Second Normal Form (2NF): a table is in 2NF if every nonkey column is dependent on the whole key, not part of the key.

Secondary File Structure: a file structure storing key data along with pointers to the nonkey data. Bitmap indexes can be secondary file structures only. Hash structures and Btrees may be primary or secondary file structures. See also primary file structure.

Self-Join: a join between a table and itself (two copies of the same table). Typically, a self-join is used to query self-referencing relationships.

Self-Referencing Relationship: a relationship involving the same table or entity type. Self-referencing relationships represent associations among members of the same set. Also known as a unary, reflexive, or recursive relationship.

Semi-Join Operator: an operator of relational algebra that is especially useful for distributed database processing. A semi-join is half of a join: the rows of one table that match with at least one row of another table.

Sequential File: a simple file organization in which records are stored in insertion order by key value. Sequential files are simple to maintain and provide good performance for processing large numbers of records.

Server: a program that processes requests on behalf of a client. A database server may interpret SQL statements, locate data, update tables, check integrity rules, and return data back to clients.

Shared: a fundamental characteristic of databases. Shared means that a database can have multiple uses and users. A large database can have hundreds of functions that use it as well as thousands of users simultaneously accessing it.

Shared Disk (SD) Architecture: an architecture for parallel database processing in which each processor has its private memory, but disks are shared among all processors.

Shared Everything (SE) Architecture: an architecture for parallel database processing in which memory and disks are shared among a collection of processors. The SE approach is usually regarded as a symmetric multiprocessing computer rather than a parallel database architecture.

Shared Lock: a lock that allows some users to read a database item but prevents these users from changing the value of a database item. Shared locks conflict with exclusive locks but not other shared locks. A shared lock indicates that a user will read but not change the value of a database item. Also known as an S lock.

Shared Nothing (SN) Architecture: an architecture for parallel database processing in which each processor has its own memory and disks. Data must be partitioned among the processors in the SN architecture

Simple Synthesis Procedure: a set of steps to produce tables in BCNF using a collection of functional dependencies. The simple synthesis procedure is limited to simple dependency structures.

Slice: a data cube operator in which a dimension is replaced by a single member value or a summary of its member values. See also dice.

Snapshot Change Data: data obtained from a source system for refreshing a data warehouse. Snapshot change data involves periodic dumps of source data. To derive change data, a difference operation uses the two most recent snapshots. See also cooperative change data, logged change data, and queryable change data.

Snowflake Schema: a data modeling representation for multidimensional databases. In a relational database, a snowflake schema has multiple levels of dimension tables related to one or more fact tables. You should use the snowflake schema instead of the star schema for small dimension tables that are not in third normal form. See also star schema, constellation schema, fact table, and dimension table.

Sort Merge: a join algorithm that requires both tables to be sorted on the join column. The sort merge algorithm can be used only for equi-joins. The sort merge algorithm performs well if the sort cost is small or if a clustered join index exists. See also hash join and nested loops.

Sparsity: the extent of empty cells in a data cube. If a large number of cells are empty, the data cube can waste space and be slow to process. Special compression techniques can be used to reduce the size of sparse data cubes. Sparsity can be a problem if two or more dimensions are related such as products and regions where products are sold. See also data cube.

Specialized Media Server Architecture: an architecture for object databases in which a dedicated server manages complex data outside of a database. Programmers use an application programming interface to access complex data.

Speedup: in distributed database processing, speedup involves the decrease in time to complete a task with additional computing capacity. Speedup measures time savings while holding the task constant. Speedup is measured by the ratio of the completion time with the original configuration to the completion time with the additional capacity. See also distributed database management system and scaleup.

SQL: an acronym for the Structured Query Language. SQL is an industry-standard database language that includes statements for database definition (such as the CREATE TABLE statement), database manipulation (such as the SELECT statement), and database control (such as the GRANT statement). SQL began as a proprietary language developed by IBM. SQL is now a widely supported international standard for databases.

SQL:2006: the most recent standard of the Structured Query Language. SQL:2006 supports numerous extensions beyond SQL-92 and updates features first specified in the previous standard (SQL:1999). The SQL:2006 standard includes nine parts and seven packages. Core SQL:2006 consists of parts 1, 2, and 11. Each non-core part contains mandatory and optional features. A package is a collection of optional features for some application area or implementation environment.

Standalone SQL: using a specialized editor that submits SQL statements directly to the DBMS and displays the results returned from the DBMS. See also embedded SQL.

Star Join: a join algorithm that combines two or more tables in which there is one child table related to multiple parent tables in 1-M relationships. Each parent table must have a bitmap join index. The star join is the best join algorithm when there are highly selective conditions on the parent tables. The star join algorithm is widely used to optimize data warehouse queries. See also bitmap index.

Star Schema: a data modeling representation for multidimensional databases. In a relational database, a star schema has a fact table in the center related to dimension tables. See also snowflake schema, constellation schema, fact table, and dimension table.

Statement-Level Interface: a language style for integrating a programming language with a nonprocedural language such as SQL. A statement-level interface involves changes to the syntax of a host programming language to accommodate embedded SQL statements. SQL:2006 specifies statements to establish database connections, execute SQL statements, use the results of an SQL statement, associate programming variables with database columns, handle exceptions in SQL statements, and manipulate database descriptors.

Storage Area Network (SAN): a specialized high-speed network that connects storage devices and servers. The goal of SAN technology is to integrate different types of storage subsystems into a single system and to eliminate the potential bottleneck of a single server controlling storage devices. A SAN is complementary to RAID disk storage.

Stored Procedure: a collection of statements that are managed by a DBMS. Stored procedures extend the capabilities of SQL. Most DBMSs provide a proprietary language in which to write stored procedures.

Stripe: the set of physical records that can be read or written in parallel in RAID storage. Normally, a stripe contains a set of adjacent physical records.

Striping: a technique for allocating physical records in RAID storage so that parallel read and write operations are possible.

Strong Type Checking: the ability to ensure that expressions contain no incompatibility errors. Strong type checking is an important kind of error checking for object-oriented coding.

Subform: the variable or repeating part of a hierarchical form. The subform can show multiple records at a time.

Subquery: see nested query.

Subtype: a child entity type in a generalization hierarchy. A subtype represents a more specialized entity type than its supertype.

Subtable Family: a SQL:2006 feature for table inheritance. SQL:2006. A subtable inherits the columns of its parent tables. Tables involved in subtable relationships must be typed tables with the associated types also participating in subtype relationships.

Summarize: an operator of relational algebra that compresses the rows of a table. A summarize operation produces a table with rows that summarize the rows of the input table. Aggregate functions are used to summarize the rows of the input table.

Superkey: a column or combination of columns containing unique values for each row. The combination of every column in a table is always a superkey because rows in a table must be unique.

Supertype: a parent entity type in a generalization hierarchy. A supertype represents a more general entity type than its subtypes.

System: a set of related components that work together to accomplish some objectives.

Synonym: in view integration, a group of words that are spelled differently but have the same meaning. Synonyms often occur because different parts of an organization may use different vocabulary to describe the same things. See also homonym.

Table: a named, two-dimensional arrangement of data. A table consists of a heading part and a body part.

Tablespace: an Oracle storage term. An Oracle database consists of a collection of tablespaces. Each tablespace is stored on one or more files. Tablespaces contain database objects such as tables and indexes.

Table Body: synonymous with the rows of a table.

Table Heading: consists of the table name, the column names, and a data type for each column.

Table Profile: a statistical summary of the rows, columns, and participating relationships of a table. Table profiles are an important input of the physical database design phase because they are used to predict the fraction of a table accessed in a query.

Ternary Relationship: a relationship involving three entity types. In some ERD notations such as the Crow's Foot notation, a ternary relationship is represented as an associative entity type with three 1-M relationships.

Third Generation Database Technology: relational DBMSs incorporating nonprocedural access, optimization technology, and transaction processing capabilities. Third generation database technology was largely commercialized during the 1980s.

Third Normal Form (3NF): a table is in 3NF if it is in 2NF and every nonkey column is dependent only on the key.

Three Schema Architecture: an architecture for compartmentalizing database descriptions. The Three Schema Architecture contains the external or user level, the conceptual level, and the internal or physical level. The Three Schema Architecture was proposed as a way to achieve data independence.

Three-Tier Architecture: a client-server architecture with three layers: a PC client, a backend database server, and either a middleware or an application server. See also two-tier architecture and multiple-tier architecture.

Three-Tier Data Warehouse Architecture: an architecture for a data warehouse in which user departments access data marts rather than the data warehouse. An extraction process involving the data warehouses periodically refreshes the data marts. See also two-tier data warehouse architecture and bottom-up data warehouse architecture.

Topological Order: an order consistent with relationships in a diagram. There are usually many possible orders consistent with a diagram. For CREATE statements, a topological order moves from the top of the diagram to the bottom. For DROP statements, a topological order moves from the bottom of the diagram to the top.

Traditional Set Operators: the union, intersection, and difference operators of relational algebra.

Transaction: a unit of work that should be processed reliably. DBMSs provide recovery and concurrency control services to process transactions efficiently and reliably.

Transaction Boundary: an important decision of transaction design in which an application consisting of a collection of SQL statements is divided into one or more transactions. Transaction boundary decisions can affect (positively or negatively) transaction throughput.

Transaction Log: a table that contains a history of database changes. The recovery manager uses the log to recover from failures.

Transaction Processing: reliable and efficient processing of large volumes of repetitive work. DBMSs ensure that simultaneous users do not interfere with each other and that failures do not cause lost work. See also transaction.

Transaction Processing Council (TPC): an organization that develops standard, domain-specific benchmarks and publishes the results. The TPC has developed benchmarks for order entry transaction processing, ad hoc decision support queries, business reporting decision support, and Web ecommerce transaction processing. See also benchmark.

Transaction-Processing Monitor: an early and still important kind of database middleware. A transaction-processing monitor receives transactions, schedules them, and manages them to completion. Transaction-processing monitors also may support updating multiple databases in a single transaction.

Transaction Throughput: the number of transactions processed per time interval. It is a measure of transaction processing performance. Typically, transaction throughput is reported in transactions per minute.

Transaction Time: the time when an operational data source is updated.

Transitive Dependency: a functional dependency derived by the law of transitivity. Transitive FDs should not be recorded as input to the normalization process. See also functional dependency and law of transitivity.

Trigger: a rule that is stored and executed by a DBMS. Because a trigger involves an event, a condition, and a sequence of actions, it also is known as an event-condition-action rule. Triggers were not part of SQL-92, although many vendors provided extensions for them. Triggers are part of SQL:2006. See also overlapping triggers.

Trigger Execution Procedure: specifies the order of execution among various kinds of triggers, integrity constraints, and database manipulation statements. Trigger execution procedures can be complex because the actions of a trigger may fire other triggers. See also overlapping triggers.

Two-Phase Commit Protocol (2PC): a rule to ensure that distributed transactions are atomic. 2PC uses a voting and a decision phase to coordinate commits of local transactions.

Two-Phase Locking Protocol (2PL): a rule to ensure that concurrent transactions do not interfere with each other. 2PL requires that locks are used before reading or writing a database item, a transaction waits if a conflicting lock is held on a data item, and locks are not released until new locks are no longer needed. To simplify implementation, most DBMSs hold at least exclusive locks until a transaction commits.

Two-Tier Architecture: a client-server architecture in which a PC client and a database server interact directly to request and transfer data. The PC client contains the user interface code, the server contains the data access logic, and the PC client and the server share the validation and business logic. See also three-tier architecture and multiple-tier architecture.

Two-Tier Data Warehouse Architecture: an architecture for a data warehouse in which user departments directly use the data warehouse rather than smaller data marts. See also three-tier data warehouse architecture and bottom-up data warehouse architecture.

Type I Nested Query: a nested query in which the inner query does not reference any tables used in the outer query. Type I nested queries can be used for some join problems and some difference problems.

Type II Nested Query: a nested query in which the inner query references a table used in the outer query. Type II nested queries can be used for difference problems but should be avoided for join problems.

Type Substitution: type substitutability means that a column or row defined to be of type X can contain instances of X and any of its subtypes. When using type substitutability to support subtables, user-defined types are defined with subtype relationships, but only one typed table (the root table) is defined. All manipulation operations are performed on the root table using type substitution for set inclusion relationships.

Uncommitted Dependency: a concurrency control problem in which one transaction reads data written by another transaction before the other transaction commits. If the second transaction aborts, the first transaction has read phantom data that will no longer exist. Also known as a dirty read.

Uniform Value Assumption: assuming that each column value is equally likely (has the same number of rows). The uniform value assumption allows compact representation of a distribution, but it can lead to large estimation errors that lead to poor choices in query optimization and index selection.

Union: an operator of relational algebra that combines rows from two tables. The result of a union operation has all the rows from either table. Both tables must be union compatible to use the union operator.

Union Compatibility: a requirement for the union, intersection, and difference operators of relational algebra. Union compatibility requires that both tables have the same number of columns and each corresponding column must have a compatible data type.

Updatable View: a view that can be used in SELECT statements as well as UPDATE, INSERT, and DELETE statements. When modifying the rows of an updatable view, the DBMS translates the view modifications into modifications to rows of the base tables.

Valid Time: the time when an event occurs.

Valid Time Lag: the difference between the occurrence of an event in the real world (valid time) and the storage of the event in an operational database (transaction time). See also valid time, load time lag, and transaction time.

View: virtual or derived table. A view is derived from base or physical tables using a query. See also materialized view.

View Materialization: a method to process a query on a view by executing the query directly on the stored view. The stored view can be materialized on demand (when the view query is submitted) or periodically rebuilt from the base tables. For data warehouses, materialization is the preferred strategy for processing view queries.

View Modification: a method to process a query on a view involving the execution of only one query. A query using a view is translated into a query using base tables by replacing references to the view with its definition. For transaction databases, view modification is the preferred strategy for processing most view queries.

Volatile Storage: storage that loses its state when the power is disconnected. Main memory is typically volatile. Nonvolatile storage does not lose its state when power is disconnected. A hard disk is an example of nonvolatile storage.

Waterfall Model: a reference framework for information systems development. The waterfall model consists of iteration among analysis, design, and implementation.

Weak Entity: an entity type that borrows part or all of its primary key from another entity type. A weak entity is also existent dependent. See also identification dependency and identifying relationship.

WITH CHECK OPTION: a clause in the CREATE VIEW statement that can be used to prevent updates with side effects. If the WITH CHECK OPTION is specified, INSERT or UPDATE statements that violate a view's WHERE clause are rejected.

Workflow: a collection of related tasks structured to accomplish a business process.

Web Services Architecture: an architecture that supports electronic commerce among organizations. A set of related Internet standards supports high interoperability among service requestors, service providers, and service registries. The most important standard is the Web Service Description Language used by service requestors, service providers, and service registries.

World Wide Web (WWW): a collection of pages that can be viewed over the Internet. In the WWW, a browser displays pages sent by a Web server. The WWW is the most popular application on the Internet.

Write Ahead Log Protocol: in the immediate update recovery process, log records must be written to stable storage before corresponding database records.

XML (eXtensible Markup Language): a simple language that supports the specification of other languages. XML has evolved into a collection of languages that separate the content, structure, and formatting of documents on the World Wide Web. The XML Schema Language, an important member of the XML language family, supports standardization of the structure of XML documents.

XPath: a notation for manipulating XML documents in an XQuery language statement. An XPath expression represents an XML document as a tree of nodes. An XPath expression is evaluated to yield an object, which is either a node-set (an unordered collection of nodes without duplicates) or a leaf node value (Boolean, number, or string).

XQuery: a query language designed by the W3C for XML documents. XQuery uses XPath expressions and various functions for extracting and change XML documents. XQuery also uses an alternative notation known as FLWOR for manipulating XML documents. See also XPath and FLWOR.